SCUNTHORPE UNITED FOOTBALL CLUB

THE OFFICIAL CENTENARY HISTORY
1899 -1999

By: John Staff

Published by:
Yore Publications
12 The Furrows, Harefield,
Middx. UB9 6AT

British Library Cataloguing-in-Publication Data
A catalogue record for this book
is available from the British Library

ISBN 1 874427 13 5

YORE PUBLICATIONS (established in 1991) specialise in football books, normally of an historic nature.
Titles include Football League club histories, Who's Who books, non-League, and those of general interest.
Three free Newsletters are issued per year; for your first copy, please send a S.A.E. to:
Yore Publications, 12 The Furrows, Harefield, Middlesex. UB9 6AT.

Printed and bound by
Bookcraft, Midsomer Norton, Bath.

❧ INTRODUCTION ❧

Scunthorpe United can by no means be considered one of the country's most glamourous clubs. However, they have survived one hundred years, and they are one of the important pieces of the jigsaw which makes up the competitive family of the Football League. The supporters rate among the best in the land, even though this army is not as large as many others. For some of this devoted group, Scunthorpe United is a major part of their lives. It is hoped that "Scunthorpe United, The Official Centenary History, 1899-1999" will do justice to the club and anyone who has shown an interest in it progress.

This Centenary History of Scunthorpe United is the first complete work on the Glanford Park based side. It tackles the life story of Scunthorpe United from conception to the present time in every aspect, both statistically, pictorially and in text. The record is set straight on how the club was actually formed, after a number of previous inaccurate versions have been logged, and pays attention to forerunners and amalgamations.

From 1912 Scunthorpe and Lindsey United, as the club had been known since 1910, embarked in the Midland League. This was an ambitious venture and had both its high moments, and its disasters which almost brought the downfall of the 'Knuts' in the mid-twenties. However, the generosity of the directors eased the club through the stormy waters to lift the Midland League Championship on two occasions. This history has blown the dust off the archives, to bring to light moments which have slipped into the clouds of time. Every major moment is plotted, including F.A.Cup exploits, even as non-Leaguers, and all the struggles noted.

After the Second World War, Scunthorpe United's directors took the difficult steps to elevate the club into becoming a force in the Football League. All this stemmed from the increasing demands for an expanded town population, enjoying prosperity thanks to the local steelworks. This book follows the tale of how their goal was achieved. It follows the 'Iron', as the team had been re-christened, from the first historical match against Shrewsbury Town on 19th August 1950, and through the relative prosperity of the fifties. The pinnacle of achievement was the Third Division Championship and it was also an era when the F.A.Cup runs produced much excitement. For six thrilling years, United ruled the district from the comfort of the Second Division, and almost reached the First Division in 1962 . From then the Club's slide from grace began, which culminated with a fall into the Fourth Division.

There had been two promotions to savour, but the book also relates the despair of the two re-election applications, and the two terms spent one division higher again. The personalities are included of those who have guided or played for them over the years. Managers such as Bill Corkhill, Ron Suart, Ron Ashman and the current incumbent, Brian Laws, all have their record reproduced. Key players, such as Kevin Keegan and Ray Clemence, are to be found playing in the infancy of their careers at Scunthorpe. This history goes further than these stars, and reminds us of other men who played for their country including Fred Tunstall, Jack Bowers and Joe Johnson.

This book should appeal to all genuine football supporters, whether they follow Scunthorpe United or not. No stone has been unturned during the research into all aspects of the club. Hopefully this will not be the last historical document on this humble football club, which means so much to its loyal supporters. In years to come let us believe that Scunthorpe United will be alive and kicking and the story will be worthy of updating.

GENERAL ACKNOWLEDGEMENTS

First and foremost a big thankyou must be extended to Leigh Edwards, a notable football historian and statistician, who is a Scunthorpe United matchday programme contributor. It was Leigh who first contacted the me in September 1998 and suggested I write this book on United's one hundred year history. If it had not been for his telephone call the seed of the idea would not have been sown. Leigh has made his mark by overseeing the work in the Who's Who section of the book. He has also made a number of suggestions as to how the information could be best presented, and hence provide valuable input.

Many thanks go to Dave Twydell of Yore Publications in Harefield, Middlesex . His assistance and encouragement have made the writing of this volume a great joy for me. Working for Dave, his daughter, has transcribed over one hundred and twenty thousand words of my handwriting; this in itself is an extraordinary feat of endurance! I would like to thank Tony Brown, who through his liaison with Dave, both members of the Association of Football Statisticians, have evolved the easily readable, yet comprehensive statistics.

During the past number of years the backbone of the research has been carried out in Grimsby Library, Scunthorpe Library, and at the Scunthorpe Evening Telegraph. At all times the staff at those establishments have been first class in allowing access to their various records.

(General Acknowledgements continued)

It must be acknowledged, that some of the notes and photographs were given to me by Len Jacklin. Len had already made a start in the research and origins of Scunthorpe United, particularly for the Midland League period. The information he passed on to me was invaluable. Many thanks Len. A quantity of the information had come from an earlier work by James Stott, a local pre-War sportswriter.

I would like to thank my friend Don Rowing, United's Chief Executive, for co-operating with the marketing side of the book, which has been done to coincide with the precise date of the centenary at the end of August 1999. He will, no doubt, have been assisted by the ladies who work in the club offices and souvenir shop, who do a marvellous job throughout the year.

Finally, I would like to say a big thank you to my family, particularly my wife Christine. She has spent many hours with the television barely audible while I have beavered away writing at the back of the room. Without her support the production of the text would have been impossible. Christine contributed a New English Dictionary for the writing of the book, which is now a well thumbed volume, and played its part in reducing the spelling mistakes.

PICTORIAL ACKNOWLEDGEMENTS

Every effort has been made to trace the origins of the photographs within this book. Unfortunately, in many cases the copyright holder is unknown, particularly those from before the Football League days, and therefore an unreserved apology is offered should copyright have inadvertently been broken. The known photographers for various years are: Gerard Studios, H.Lenton, Singleton, Joseph Wilmore all of Scunthorpe, A.Robinson of Sheffield, and Harold Caine. To these, the unknown pioneers and the later day photographers, the Author would like to pay tribute and hope their work has been given suitable respect by its inclusion within.

The Author would like to thank the "Scunthorpe Evening Telegraph" for allowing the reproduction of many of their photographs, generally action shots and team studies, which although not credited individually, form the bulk of the more modern illustrations. The Evening Telegraph continues to have the best coverage of Scunthorpe United F.C., both in the sports and photographic departments. Their assistance is greatly appreciated, and thanks also are extended to Bob Steels for locating other work.

A vote of thanks is also given to the current club photographer, Ian Hewitt, who has kindly given permission for publishing his most recent team line-ups. Ian produced a quantity of quality photographs at short notice and greatly helped the Author in this direction. Andy Brown also deserves a mention for pinpointing some of the team groups, which were missing from the original lists. The Midland League photographs principally came from a collection of photographs given to the Author by Len Jacklin. This has been invaluable in reflecting an era of the Football club in pictorial form. The remainder of the photographs are the Authors own work. This started in the late 1970's and has continued through to the present time, thanks to the kind permission of Scunthorpe United's Chief Executive, Don Rowing, for access.

Finally the Author would like to acknowledge the many others who have supported him in any small way, not least those who assisted in identifying the players on the photographs, and who have not been included above.

THE STATISTICAL ELEMENTS OF THE BOOK

Great attention to detail has been given to the statistics contained within this book in an attempt to ensure their accuracy. It has to be conceded that different sources for information can sometimes reveal alternatives for what should be a single fact. An example is a goalscorer who claims a goal from a colleague, or, when it may later be given as an own goal. Gates are another area where figures may vary. Where such discrepancies occur, recognised sources of information (the major references are detailed below) have been used. The facts contained within the book have been independently researched by the Author, and therefore can be considered to supersede any previously published statistical studies on the Club which are in variance. The majority of the statistics are based on notes from local newspaper sources, researched in Grimsby and Scunthorpe libraries, by the author, in the late 1970's and early 1980's. The North Lincolnshire Star, The Saturday Telegraph, the Scunthorpe Evening Telegraph, and the various football handbooks issued by the Evening Telegraph have all been key sources for discovering United's results, goalscorers and attendances. The Football League period has been updated with information from the Rothmans Football Yearbooks (Football's 'Bible'), the Scunthorpe United Football programme, various national newspapers and of course the Scunthorpe Evening Telegraph. The Scunthorpe Evening Telegraph must be considered the premier contributor to all facts relating to Scunthorpe United.

Finally, notice must be attributed to the help given by Len Jacklin, who many years ago gave the Author a great deal of material involving the club. This included the works and statistics of James Stott, who was a local sports correspondence for the local newspapers. Stott's efforts covered much of the results sequences throughout Scunthorpe and Lindsey United's Midland League days which started before the First World War.

John A. Staff

~ **1998-99 (Promotion) Season** ~

Front: Lee Marshall, Chris Hope, Tim Clarke, Richard Logan, Tom Evans, Ashley Fickling, Sean McAuley
Middle: Nigel Adkins (Physio), John Eyre, Russell Wilcox, Jimmy Neil, John Gayle, James Featherstone,
Darryn Stamp, Gary Bull, Paul Wilson (Youth Devt. Officer)
Front: Steve Housham, Alex Calvo-Garcia, Mark Lillis (Asst. Manager), Brian Laws (Manager),
Jamie Forrester, Paul Harsley, Steve Nottingham.

~ CONTENTS ~

## CHAPTER ONE

IN THE BEGINNING

The County of Lincolnshire has always made a significant contribution to football, particularly in the formative years of the sport during the last Century. Grimsby Town and Lincoln City were original members of the Second Division in 1892, and have histories dating back a number of years before that time. Within a margin of four seasons Gainsborough Trinity had made it a trio of Football League representatives from the area and even the humble Brigg Town Football Club had been a pioneer for North Lincolnshire in the F.A. Cup, appearing in the first round of the 1879-80 season, losing 7-0 away to Turton of Lancashire.

From the point of view of Scunthorpe and District, the formative years of football were a time of industrial revolution, when the five villages of Crosby, Frodingham, Scunthorpe, Brumby and Ashby still had their individual identity. The expansion of the iron and steel industry saw the population explode and those people looked to football as their recreation. The earliest known senior football club was known as Scunthorpe Town, whose seed was sewn around 1880. This club had its results reported in the local newspaper from around 1883, at which time an article noted that its captain had enjoyed three years of service carrying out the duties with the celebrated arm band.

Scunthorpe Town played their games on what was known as the Kempe Fields on Crosby Road, but later moved to a pitch off Frodingham Road around 1894. Generally speaking its matches were in local cup competitions or friendlies. Opponents from Gainsborough, Grimsby and Doncaster, usually the second elevens of those more established clubs, were common place, as well as others from the local district. The town side met with moderate success but often flattered to deceive. More often than not it had to rely on the depth of talent in, as yet, a fairly small population. Perhaps its greatest triumph occurred on 7th September 1895, when a team from nearby Winterton were beaten 16-0, under rules which would be hardly distinguishable today.

Sadly for Scunthorpe Town a lack of a proper enclosure where they could charge patrons a fee for attending their games led in part to the ultimate demise of the club. They were soon overtaken by financial pressures and forced to fold. The date of their decline appears to be around 1897, after which no mention can be found in the local archive.

In the meantime another champion had stepped forward. This football club was Brumby Hall, a side whose results can first be traced from September 1895, when they crashed 7-1 to the reserve team of Scunthorpe Town. Undeterred by this early set back, the ambitious Brumby Hall soon took advantage of the failings of the Town club, not only by taking over their ground once they had become defunct, but also by taking over the mantle as one of the best teams in the area. Brumby Hall's best contribution to this claim came when they pulled down the colours of the visiting Second Volunteer Battalion, Doncaster, by a score of 11-0, in the February of 1899.

It was in the summer of 1899 that players and officials put forward plans to form an elite football club for the district. The local newspaper, the Lindsey and Lincolnshire Star, made an announcement in the sports column, in the Journal of Saturday 2nd September 1899, under the banner of a *"Football Amalgamation"*. The article went on to state that Brumby Hall, the premier club in the Scunthorpe District over the last year, had resolved to amalgamate with other clubs in Scunthorpe under the title of *"Scunthorpe United"*. Presiding over the meeting of over one hundred guests, at the annual meeting of the Brumby Hall Club, was Mr R.A.C. Symes, a local solicitor. The special date of the meeting, and hence the birth of Scunthorpe United, was given as Tuesday 29th August, 1899.

on behalf of the defendant who was fined £1 15s including costs or 28 days.

FOOTBALL AMALGAMATION.—The Brumby Hall Football Club which was the premier one in the Scunthorpe district last year, at their annual meeting on Tuesday night, Mr R C A Symes presiding resolved to amalgamate with the other clubs in Scunthorpe, under the title of the Scunthorpe United Club. There were over 100 persons present at the meeting. During last season, Brumby Hall played 23 matches, won 17, lost 4, and drew 1 ; the goals being 82 against 21 : the cash balance being £1 16s 6d. The following officials were re-elected :—President, the Rev H R Ashdown : joint hon. secretaries, Messrs W Sandwith and J R Downie : treasurer Mr J Robinson : captain, Mr Fred Dodds : and a large representative committee.—It was decided to a junior section in connection with the

...RSHIPPERS OF BACCHUS. At the Scunthorpe ... Court before Messrs J Fletcher and G

At the meeting, the Brumby Hall club's statistics of; played twenty-two games, seventeen of which were won, four lost and one drawn, were given for the previous campaign. During those matches a total of eighty-two goals had been scored, whilst the custodian had conceded the respectful sum of just twenty-one. The paper further reported that the new Scunthorpe United club would enter the world with the secure inheritance of £1-16s-6d, or about £1.82 by today's equivalent. All officials had been re-elected, and so the President was the Reverend H. Ashdown, joint Honorary Secretaries Messrs J.R.Downie and W.Sandwith, Treasurer Mr J.Robinson and Captain Mr Fred Dodds, plus a large representative committee. Finally a decision was taken to form a junior section in connection with the club.

The new Scunthorpe United Football Club was to take over the facilities of Brumby Hall on a ground up the Doncaster Road which had previously been used for the Scunthorpe Show. Thus the ground adopted the name 'The Old Showground', which had been utilized for soccer during the previous couple of years since Brumby Hall had vacated the Frodingham Road premises. Reporting during the early days of Scunthorpe United's first season of existence was certainly sketchy, particularly in the inaugural 1899-1900 season.

Their first historic match appears to have taken place at the Old Showgound on Saturday 16th September 1899, when they overcame the resistance of the villagers of Crowle by 4-1, but no other details are available. However, one of the more important activities reported was an appearance in the Lincolnshire Shield, where Frodingham United were beaten 3-2 after a replay, in what was one of the first ever local derbies.

However, as the seasons rolled on, the editor of the Lindsay and Lincolnshire Star must have realized the interest being generated by the sport, and greater details of Scunthorpe United's early adventures were heralded from the sports pages. By the 1900-01 season the Club were seasoned campaigners in the North Lindsay League, and a minor degree of success was gleaned in reaching the semi-final of the Hull Charity Cup in the March of 1901. They lost, unfortunately, to Grimsby All Saints by a margin of 3-1. Then, in the November of that same year the Scunthorpe club set a record score of 18-0, at home to Broughton in a one sided North Lindsey League match. Finally, in the 1901-02 season, another semi-final was reached in the Grimsby Charity Cup, but the Grimsby Tradesmen side proved far superior, as United were comprehensively beaten 5-1.

Meanwhile another football club had been brought to life with the emergence of North Lindsey United. Little is given of the exact details of this embryo club, but Mr R.A.C. Symes is thought to have encouraged its prosperity. Reports of the scores of North Lindsey United first appear from 1902. Indeed, the first known game of this new side was against Scunthorpe United, from which they came out triumphant, in a closely fought contest, by a score of 2-1, for what was billed as a North Lindsey League match.

Never-the-less Scunthorpe gained a 4-1 victory revenge later in the season at the at the Old Showground in the same competition. But in cup matches honours went the way of North Lindsey United, when they made progress at Scunthorpe's expense in both the Lincolnshire Shield and the Hull Charity Cup. It was in the latter competition that North Lindsay United became runners-up, when they lost at that stage to Grimsby St. John's, in a game played at Frodingham.

In general both the North Lindsey and Scunthorpe United clubs remained the best of enemies. Each took on extra responsibilities in 1903 when they entered the Gainsborough and District League, in addition to duties in the various cup competitions and the North Lindsey League. It was in the September of the 1903-04 season that the North Lindsey team became the centre of controversy, when their match at Ashby Rising Star had to be abandoned because of crowd trouble. Apparently the natives in that neck of the woods became restless at some of the hard tactics on the field of play, as the "Star" were losing 5-1.

During the mid-term of this Edwardian era, Scunthorpe United became the focal point of success. Although results from the newspaper had once again dried up, sources reveal that United had swept most before them and had the silverware of the North Lindsey League, the Winterton Charity Cup and the Frodingham Charity Cup to show for the players honest toil. The occasion is captured forever in a frozen moment of the time, as stern faces stare proudly at the camera, for the photograph of players, officials and their spoils, taken in 1905.

This was to set the scene for a more ambitious approach to the sport, for the Scunthorpe Club wished to remove themselves from the shackles of what was no more than local league football. Sights were set on gaining a foothold into the broader national scene, and they could do so by entering into the Midland League competition. Unfortunately, applications in 1907, and again twelve months later, fell on deaf ears.

Their only consolation was a major success in the Lincolnshire Junior Cup, when Cleethorpes Town lost to them 2-0 in the 1908 final, and the United took runners-up spot in the Moreing Cup Final during the same year.

Scunthorpe United, outside the Oswald Hotel, about to leave to play Ashby Rising Stars in the 1sr round of the Lincolnshire Junior Cup. September 1907.

Not to be thwarted, Scunthorpe United entered into another new venture in the 1909-10 season, for this was to be their first ever historical step into the F.A. Cup competition and the draw paired them at home to Withersea. The very first F.A.Cup line-up was announced as Wogin, Parrot, Barrick, Garrett, Fewster, Foster, Hollin, Clapham, Carr, Cox and Harrison. This eleven stepped out confidently and won a very one-sided affair by an 8-0 scoreline. Cox, Hollin and Chapman were each given credit for bagging a brace of goals, while Harrison and Carr added the others. Scunthorpe United's victory earned them a trip to York City, a forerunner of the present club, but very much a local league club, similar in nature to the lads from the Old Showground. The visit proved too much, and before anyone began to dream of a journey to Crystal Palace for the final, York City had celebrated a 4-0 success. United would have to think about the following year's possibilities.

Time was running out for the Edwardian age, and while Scunthorpe United had a desire for broader horizons, the North Lindsey United camp were feeling the cold draught of financial winds on their diminishing bank account. Neither would have benefitted from a local steel situation, and officials of the two clubs decided to hold a meeting to explore the possibility of an amalgamation in a bid to expand everyone's interest with the strongest team in the whole of the district. This gathering was held on 1st June 1910, chaired by a Mr F.Mason, and despite a poorly attended function all principles were upheld.

Those present agreed that the Old Showground would be the new unit's headquarters, and that tenders would be taken in order to erect a pavilion and dressing room for spectators and players alike. The new club would strive for membership of the Midland League, but in the meantime would have entry into the F.A.Cup, (then known as the English Cup), the North Lindsey League, as well as entering the Lincolnshire Junior Cup, the Scunthorpe Nursing Cup, The North Lindsey Ironstone Cup, The Frodingham Charity Cup and The Hull Times Cup. Before the meeting closed Mr Paul Coombes was elected Secretary, Mr R.A.C. Symes became President, and each member who made a five shilling contribution to the club's funds became a Vice-President. Club affairs were to be the concern of a thirteen man committee, and Mr Frank Hollin, formerly of the Scunthorpe United team, was selected to take over as the newly formed club's captain.

At a later meeting a list of rules and amendments were drawn up, and Mr Symes was instructed to pay the rent at the Old Showground which amounted to £10 for the coming season. Mr W.T.Lockwold was given the honour of officially being the very first chairman, while Mr W.Blenkin was elected as Vice-Chairman. Matches on a friendly basis were to be sought with Hull City to entertain a junior side and also a fixture with Grimsby Rovers. Both matches would be scheduled in early September and were fixed to be played at the Old Showground.

The final part of the jigsaw was put into place on 16th August 1910, when another get together of officials at the Institute building on Winterton Road named the Club *"Scunthorpe and Lindsey United Football Club"*. The name would survive for about forty-five years, until the mid 1950's, when it was

thought it more appropriate to drop the *"and Lindsey"* from the title. Thus, on 3rd September 1910, Scunthorpe and Lindsey United sallied forth in their first duty of combat. Hull City became their first opponents under this new guise and the team given the task of representing the Club on this occasion was: Bailey, Parrot, Long, Barrick, Holland, Wardell, Leaning, Hollin, Fenwick, Cox and Brown. The few hundred spectators who showed an interest were treated to an even battle, which finally tilted towards Scunthorpe's corner, thanks to a hat-trick from star man Cox. At the death, Scunthorpe and Lindsey United were declared winners by three goals to two.

The 1910-11 season was to prove a success for the architects of the amalgamation. Not only did the United side find themselves highly placed throughout their League season, but there were victories which ensured the taking of the Scunthorpe Nursing Cup and the Frodingham Charity Cup. They also performed admirably in reaching the Lincolnshire Junior Cup Final, but lost 2-1 at Blundell Park, Grimsby, to Grimsby Rovers. If there was a disappointment it must have been on 17th September 1910, in the new club's first competitive match. This was in the F.A. Cup, where lady luck had matched them with the experienced no nonsense team of Denaby United on foreign soil. Scunthorpe had no answer to the surefooted Colliery men, who slipped six goals passed the hapless visiting keeper, all without reply.

If their first encounters were anything of a yardstick, then the following 1911-12 season must have left everyone connected with the Club totally ecstatic. There was no holding the side who dominated almost everything before them, certainly in local competitions. The team won the North Lindsey League, the Grimsby Charity Cup, Frodingham Charity Cup, the North Lindsey Ironstone Cup and the Scunthorpe Nursing Cup. In addition they reached the Bellamy Cup Final, but when the referee jumped up and down to applaud one of the Cleethorpe goals, the players had a suspicion it was not going to be their day!

In the F.A.Cup of 1911-12, York City became the United team's opponents, and once again the tie was destined to be played in the Cathedral City. This time it was Scunthorpe who got to grips with the Yorkshiremen first. Blanchard scored twice for the team, whilst at the back the defenders were far more confident and great celebrations followed a 2-1 triumph. This led to a further away visit in the next round, this time to the same county to engage Mexborough Town. Another fiercely fought contest ensued, but despite Ibbotson scoring twice United narrowly lost 3-2.

A footnote to the playing season came when Scunthorpe beat Frodingham and Brumby United in the Frodingham Charity Cup final. At the presentation of the Cup, the reverend Cryspin T. Rust, vicar of Frodingham, said in his presentation speech that Scunthorpe and Lindsey were, indeed, a tough nut to crack. From this statement, the nickname of the "Nuts" or "Knuts" is thought to have evolved. Future team photographs even sported a coconut with a face on it, and the official programme between the two World Wars was called the "Knut". To confirm the clubs standing the 1911-12 season gave returns of: played 38 games, won 27, drawn 7, lost 4. 116 goals were converted and just 38 conceded, a proud record to boast of.

The first Scunthorpe United Programme (14 September 1912). United lost 1-0.

sent a telegram to United's Chairman, Mr Lockwood, who was attending a cricket match at Frodingham. The message contained just one word; "*In*".

Immediately Symes rushed back to the town to break the news to the populace at large. His colleague, Paul Coombes, stayed in Nottingham to arrange for the new fixtures to be drawn up. Then on the Monday of 17th June, Symes addressed a packed gathering of enthusiastic supporters to discuss the financial implications of running this extremely costly Midland League venture. It was his opinion that it was in the club's best interests to form a Limited

It was with these figures that Scunthorpe and Lindsey United sent Mr Reginald Symes and Paul Coombes to Nottingham for the annual general meeting of the Midland League to plead the Lincolnshire club's case for entry into this more competitive level of the game. The meeting took place on 12th June 1912, and the state of play was that Barnsley Reserves, Leicester Fosse Reserves and Huddersfield Town Reserves had all resigned, while Worksop and Denaby United, who had occupied the bottom two positions in the 1911-12 season, were anxious to be re-elected. Applying to take the vacant places were York City, Goole Town, Halifax Town, Mirfield Town and Scunthorpe and Lindsey United. After deliberation with the member clubs, the chairman announced that the bottom clubs would be accepted back into the fold, and the strength of the Midland League was to be brought up to twenty, with four of the five applicants being taken into the family.

Company. Symes proposed that there should be a nominal capital of £500 in ten shilling (fifty pence) shares. Symes himself agreed to conduct the legal matters for the Club free of charge. The meeting, as a whole, supported all of his suggestions, and by the end of the proceedings £50 had been pledged with a total of £66 being raised by the next public gathering.

It was at this next meeting that a draft copy of the articles of association relating to the formation of the new company was presented by the Club secretary. Within a short while the members had accepted the papers and Scunthorpe and Lindsey United had become a Limited Company. Mr Symes also reported that a new stand, capable of seating 340 patrons, had been ordered from the local firm of Pallisters at a cost of £100. It was Pallisters who had been involved in the original work in 1910. This new structure is alleged to have been carried out on the West of the ground, parallel with Henderson Avenue. However, Pallisters' initial work, which included the construction of dressing rooms, appears also to have been on this side of the ground. Accounts of the construction are not totally conclusive, but it is thought that the wooden structure on the eastern side of the pitch did not start until around the time of the First World War, with sections being added as time went on. Thus, with all the legal 'I's' dotted and the 'T's' crossed, Scunthorpe and Linsey United were ready to enter a whole new sphere of football.

Each of the clubs was given two minutes to state their case before a vote was taken. Scunthorpe's evidence was in the hands of the silver tongued solicitor Reginald Symes. It was said that he gave a convincing account of the credentials at the Old Showground and so it proved when the slips were returned. York City and Goole Town registered seventeen votes, Scunthorpe sixteen, Halifax Town fifteen, whilst Mirfield Town found themselves out in the cold. Symes immediately

CHAPTER 2

EARLY MIDLAND LEAGUE BATTLES

~ 1912-13 ~

Saturday 7th September 1912 was to prove to be a watershed in the history of Scunthorpe and Lindsey United. It was on this day that the team and officials travelled to Elland Road, Leeds, to play the now defunct Leeds City Reserve team in their first Midland League match. The United players were clad in a claret and blue strip, with white shorts, adapted from the colours of Aston Villa, one of the country's top sides. On the terraces several hundred enthusiastic Scunthorpe supporters had made their way to one of Yorkshire's top wool towns. United's team consisted: Wogin, Parrot, Burkhill, Drury, Henderson, Brown, Hollin, Hill, Walden, Cox and Bell. Although this eleven gave good account of themselves a 1-0 defeat meant that they returned home empty handed.

One week later Scunthorpe played their first home engagement, when Notts County Reserves were United's visitors. The team selecting committee opted to choose the same defence and half-back line, but elected to change Hall for Hollin and Pearce for Cox in the attack. However, the crowd of around 2,000 spectators noted that United started the game with only ten men. The problem was that Pearce's registration papers had not turned up, and when the Great Central train arrived without the required credentials stamped and signed, the match was twenty minutes old. Therefore, there was no alternative but to send on local man Rusling to make up the strength. Unfortunately, it was to no avail and a second 1-0 reverse was suffered.

Early results in the Midland League continued to go against Scunthorpe. On the third Saturday of the season Lincoln City Reserves hammered the team, putting seven goals past them, but at least Bell scored a consolation to become the club's first goalscorer in that competition. Relief came by way of progress in the F.A. Cup when they travelled to Brodsworth Colliery. Victory was assisted by two goals from Pearce, one a penalty, who by now had received official clearance to play, and another by Walden to give a handsome 3-2 scoreline. Meanwhile League returns continued to be poor and only the defeat of Goole Town in the next round of the Cup kept the supporters happy. But a 9-1 loss at Notts County meant that folks could not contain themselves anymore, and for the first time ever there were calls for a new management.

The Scunthorpe and Lindsey United board took the hint and made team changes. This included the introduction of Harry Burton from Sheffield Wednesday, an experienced defender for either full-back berth. Burton's great claim to fame was in wearing Wednesday's colour when they took the coverted F.A.Cup trophy in 1907 at the Crystal Palace. The effect was immediate and at home to Mexborough the Knuts gathered their first points in an eventful game. Although Walden put them in front the Mexborough men not only equalized, but went ahead. The persistent Scunthorpe forwards stuck to their task and left-winger Bell, formerly of Grimsby Town,

levelled the score. The advantage was re-established when Walden dribbled round the 'keeper to side foot home, and despite the loss of Hargreaves through injury late in the first-half, Walden completed his hat-trick to put his name in the Club record book, for the first to achieve such a feat. The tension mounted as Mexborough raised the stakes by scrambling home the ball from a goalmouth melee. Heartbeats returned to normal, however, ten minutes from time when Bell scored his second with probably the game's best goal. Skilfully he rounded two defenders, then slotted the ball into the bottom corner of the net tantalisingly out of the reach of the opposing goalkeeper.

At last the ice had been broken and although the team was still at the foot of the Midland League, they had broken the psychological barrier. It set the team in an excellent frame of mind for the visit of Gainsborough Trinity, fresh out of the old Second Division after eighteen years of Football League experience. The takings of £53 also put a smile on the faces of the Directors, and based on an entrance fee of 4d, it meant that over 2,000 persons were there to witness the proceedings, thereby setting a new record attendance. A score of two goals each on the afternoon was another acceptable feature of the game.

November was to bring a trio of matches against fellow newcomers in York City, each team having a share of the fortunes. The initial match was billed as an F.A.Cup encounter and despite repeated strikes by top scorer Walden, and another by Bell an impasse at 2-2 remained. It was then back to 'City's' camp four days later to resume battle. This time it was Rusling, Hill and Walden who supplied the goals, the latter scoring a pair, that looked as if 4-3 would be enough with ten minutes remaining on the referee's watch. Alas, it was not to be, and a rushing of the York forwards stole the victory in the dying moments, with a 5-4 result, for what had proved to be a highly entertaining game. Scunthorpe regained the initiative on the following Saturday when it was they who took the Midland League points with a 4-3 result, mainly thanks to Walden's second hat-trick.

As the winter progressed, United's position at the basement of the League was critical but not terminal. Gradually those local players, blended with more experienced signings such as Walden, who had been with former League club, Rotherham Town, and Harry Burton, saw the results begin to change in their favour. Once the flowers of spring began to arrive the whole aspect of Scunthorpe's play had changed for the good. From 1st March 1913, when they were at home to Goole Town, until the end of the campaign, only champions-elect Rotherham County and highly placed Sheffield Wednesday managed to get the better of them, both on the United's travels. Probably the best result was at Gainsborough, where, on the Northolme Ground, Scunthorpe notched the only goals of the hour and a half through Cox, who had assumed the mantle of centre-forward for the afternoon, in a shuffled front line that overcame the absence of Walden through injury. This was in the middle of a sequence of three consecutive away wins in as many games. Hull City's second string had previously been beaten, and it was followed up a week after the Gainsborough match when a third success came on the ground of the eventual wooden-spoonists, Denaby. This time it was Bell's turn to try the number nine shirt and he duly supplied all three goals in the 3-1 result.

The final League table revealed that the Knuts had risen to fifteenth place, with a record of played 38, won 13, lost 17 and 8 draws. Their goals tally had reached 55, while 78 had been conceded. It was considered quite a reasonable set of returns, and generally everyone was happy at the outcome. Special praise was attributed to the local players who had raised their games to meet the extra demands of the higher standard of Midland League soccer. In particular the names of Johnny Wogin, a man to serve for many years as Club 'keeper, and Shem Hill at inside-forward, later to become an established half-back until well after the First War. Billy Long, Danny Sylester, Fred Smith, of Winterton origin, "Buck" Parrot in defence, and Frank Hollin all came in for congratulations on how they had acquitted themselves. It was also noted that wages for these local based players was far less that the likes of Burton, Watkins, Wagstaffe, Henderson, Spelvins, Bell and Drury who had been attracted from more established sources, and whose pay would be nearer £2 per week. The Directors were still happy that the total bill was only around £25 over each seven day period.

It was not long before the well earned rest of summer, accompanied by the sound of cork on willow on the village cricket green ended, only for the time to march on towards the start of another football season. During the closed season United's directors had been busy sifting through the list of available players, and had acted immediately to bring new faces to the Old Showground in an effort to strengthen the team. In this respect four men came from the Leeds City club, including brothers Hugh and Arthur Roberts, Tommy Morris and Tommy Mulholland. Arthur Roberts and Tommy Morris were to play their part in propping up the defence, while Hugh Roberts and Tommy Mulholland made their presence felt in attack.

In addition Root came by way of Derby County, and was considered to be one of the Midland League's fast-est wingers, whilst at the same time pos-sessing a lethal shot. The Club also took on the services of centre-forward Bradbury, a free-scoring former Oldham

Athletic player. Armed with this combination Scunthorpe set out their stall to do battle in their second Midland League season.

~ 1913-14 ~

The 1913-14 season started brightly enough, when an estimated six hundred supporters travelled to watch the Knuts play at Sincil Bank, Lincoln, against the Imps second squad. Excitement must have been at a premium, because each set of defenders blotted out the efforts of the corresponding forwards and no goals were registered. The following week all former Leeds City players rose to the occasion to help secure a 2-1 win over their former club. Both Bradbury and Root took the opportunity to notch their first goals for the claret and blues, and the two points were most welcome.

However, the shortcomings of this improved Scunthorpe side were brutally exposed in the third match of the season, when Rotherham County paid hosts to the Lincolnshire men. County were, frankly, a cut above the rest and would retain the title of the Midland League, and the trophy would remain in their cabinet. They paid little heed to the inadequate efforts of Scunthorpe's defence and were four goals up in ten minutes. United's cause was not assisted by the injury to Bradbury, who had to be carried from the field. Outclassed in all departments, the demoralized Scunthorpe club returned home, defeated by a 7-0 score. One of the goals came from Rotherham's Herbert Lloyd, later to become a player at the Old Showground, and later a well respected trainer for many years.

Fortunately Scunthorpe and Lindsey United had recovered sufficiently seven days later to entertain Chesterfield. Bradbury had overcome his injury problems and was amongst the scorers in a 4-0 drubbing of the Derbyshire set. This, no doubt, held them in good stead to take on Mexborough Town in the F.A.Cup. Mexborough were not having the best of seasons, but put up enough fight to earn a replay. However, goals from Morris, Bradbury and Walden crushed them in the second game, as Scunthorpe ran out worthy 3-0 winners. By coincidence it was back to Mexborough for a League fixture on the following Saturday, and to yet another squared result, this time by 1-1.

The Cup draw was again to send them out to York, and eventually City took the tie 2-1, this ending the Knuts' interest for another twelve months. The time rolled on, and the November of 1913 was to prove a most fruitful time, when Scun-thorpe would have received

The players are put through their places in a training session - 1913/14 season.
Players L.to R.: Millington, Hill, Burkhill, Thompson, Bradbury; Trainer Marsden standing on left.

'The Manager of the Month' if such an award had existed. They took maximum points from all of their games, including wins at home to Rotherham Town, Worksop, Mexborough and Castleford. On their travels they won at Leeds City and Castleford. Once Christmas had arrived they were in a healthy position in the top half of the League, although in no position to challenge for honours. Even the record attendance had been broken, when around 3,000 spectators watched Sheffield Wednesday's Reserves do battle at the Old Showground.

Throughout the winter months the side continued to hold its own, although two players were recruited from what the archive records describe as 'South Bank'. These two men were Jack Thompson and Ernest Wood. Wood gained the reputation of being one of the best centre-forwards to play in the Midland League for Scunthorpe in his short career in the town, and was regrettably killed in France during the First World War. On his debut Wood scored against Rotherham Town, then notched a hat-trick in the next two games when Sheffield United Reserves were beaten 3-2 at Bramall Lane, this game being followed by a 4-1 victory over York City on the Doncaster Road.

Scunthorpe and Lindsey United's final position of seventh out of eighteen teams would surely have been greatly elevated if it had not been for a late disaster of six consecutive defeats towards the end of the season. This was probably as a result of a number of team changes in an effort to breed fresh talent for the coming season. On the important financial front, gates had averaged takings of £61 per game, slightly up on the 1912-13 round of matches. Although the number of matches had been four down in 1913-14, the directors were still optimistic about the future.

~ 1914-15 ~

The 1914-15 season at Scunthorpe, like everywhere, began as the ominous clouds of War hung over Europe. It was a threat not only to peace which eventually was to be lost as the year progressed, but it was also to alter the whole fabric of life. Football, likewise, would suffer. However, a new face by now was to become familiar at Scunthorpe, not as a player but as a secretary. Mr Harry Allcock had taken over the post after the resignation of Paul Coombe late in 1913, and this would prove to be his first complete season in charge of office affairs.

The season also saw a number of new players assemble to bolster the squad. United's directors had realized that no matter how good local talent might be, there was no substitute for experienced men from the Football League. At the same time local talent had to be nurtured and given a chance at the right time. It was with this in mind that Charlie Pinch came by way of Preston North End. Pinch was considered a fine tenor and often would entertain his colleagues going to and from away games. He was supplemented by Jimmy Monaghan of Sheffield Wednesday.

Monaghan was a right-winger, whose accurate crosses could cause chaos in many defences. Later he left to fight for his country in France and lost his sight at the battle of the Somme. Remarkably, it was restored during an operation in Sunderland. Not so lucky was Fred Smith, a tricky left-half

once on Southampton's books. Fred was an Army Reservist and he lost his life in War without kicking a ball for Scunthorpe. Finally, on the left-forward flank, United signed Clarke from Sheffield Wednesday and winger Platts from Lincoln City. These two were reputed to be an extremely fast duo, capable of outpacing most full-backs.

The class of 1914-15 began by taking both points at home to the second eleven of local derby rivals, Grimsby Town. Reports of the game suggest that Scunthorpe just about deserved to win this closely fought contest, as Wood, Clarke and Platts put their names on the score sheet of a 3-2 win. Two days later a trip to Elland Road caused major concern when the Knuts were crushed by 5-0 to a side who had been the bottom club of the previous season. At least those fears were elevated when Rotherham County, by now heading for a hat-trick of Midland League titles, were held 1-1 at the Old Showground as local man Shem Hill came in from the right-half position to convert the United goal. This result was to set the ball rolling on a six game unbeaten run in the League, to which could be added further advances in the F.A.Cup. Only a disastrous 6-2 humiliation at Castleford caused any real disappointment, especially when noting the lowly position of the Yorkshire side in the table.

In the meantime Scunthorpe and Lindsey United had steadily made their way through the chaff in the early rounds of the F.A.Cup qualifying stages. Hull Old Boys were no match, and bowed out with a 5-1 scoreline. Pre-Midland League opponents Grimsby Rovers could no longer bother United and lost 4-0, but Doncaster Rovers, who had once enjoyed a short spell in League circles, proved stern opposition, giving the Knuts more like the expected problems of the Cup. As it came to pass, Robinson scored for Scunthorpe in what became the only goal of an eventful match. Robinson to date had netted in each of the previous ties, making him a prized asset since joining the Club from Rawmarsh Athletic. It was at this stage, when the F.A.Cup was becoming more interesting, that United met their match against Goole Town, who had opted out of the Midland League. Robinson scored his usual goal, but it was only sufficient to earn a replay. In the second pairing at the Victoria Pleasure Ground, Goole ran riot, comfortably winning 5-1.

Finally, as a footnote to the F.A.Cup, United had been drawn away to Hull Old Boys, but on the guarantee of a set gate receipt agreed to play the tie at the Old Showground.

Back on League duty United proved to be a run of the mill team, winning some, but losing as many. When the Club entered the Christmas period they enjoyed one of the most satisfying moments of the year, for an above average crowd saw them methodically beat Gainsborough Trinity 2-0 at the Showground. Unfortunately, that was as far as the season's greetings were extended in their direction. Within the space of four weeks, after beating Trinity, they mustered only one Midland League point in six games, that coming on Christmas Day when neighbours Goole Town dropped in. The match was nothing much of a spectacle, as no team managed a score.

It was at this time that talk of the clubs finances came to light, now feeling a definite squeeze as men left the district to join the War Front in Belgium and France. Gates were understandably low, and the Chairman of the day, Mr A.J.Raynor, took it upon himself to write a letter to the Grimsby Daily telegraph, in reply to criticism in the press and among the public. His response was to underline the work carried out by the Directors in reducing the financial burdens on the club. This included lowering the players wages, making a saving of £10 per week down to a total of £25. He added that unless more support was forthcoming to at least meet an income of £40 per game, the Club could not afford to run in the Midland League.

At a later meeting, called on 5th January 1915 to discuss the Club's circumstances, Mr W.T.Lockwood announced that the overdraft at the bank had gone into the red and it was anticipated to rise to as much as £400 by the end of the season. At that moment in time the coffers contained just £1 to pay the way for the next game at Gainsborough. Despite the stark reality of the situation United somehow found the resources to continue.

On the field of play little was seen to improve United's prosperity. Once into January a slight improvement was noted, particularly when Hull City Reserves were beaten on the other side of the Humber 4-1, and newcomers Heckmondwike lost 6-0 in Scunthorpe. At the end of the season United settled for a point in a remarkable 5-5 draw against Rotherham Town. Then as football took its final curtain before the war closed proceedings down, Scunthorpe bowed out with a fine 4-0 victory over Castleford.

Everyone then sighed with relief as the Club had managed to complete a season where gates dropped at times to around eight hundred spectators, and the directors had put their hands in their pockets to pay some bills. When the final returns came in on the 1914-15 playing season, United had slipped back slightly on the last year and could only manage thirteenth place. Wood was the leading goalscorer in Midland League terms, finding the net fifteen times, followed by Ibbotson on ten and Platts with nine. Football and footballers were allowed to disperse to carry out the more important duties required for the war effort. The Old Showground was to see little soccer until the end of hostilities in 1918, although there was the occasional game between service teams and representative sides from Scunthorpe and Lindsey United. Some footballers found limited activity in the sport at a local level but nothing more to speak of.

At the Old Showground headquarters, the directors main priority was to stop local officials turning the ground into allotments for the people of the immediate area. Concerned at the damage that would be done, and with an eye on Midland League football when the War finished, they successfully repelled all efforts. Mr Harry Allcock agreed to look after the books in his capacity as Secretary 'for a short while', and in 1917 the grazing rights on the field were sold to Messrs Hornsby and Son. Between 4th September 1917 and 16th April 1919 no official business was transacted.

A representative team group taken at the Old Showground during the First World War. Believed to be the Appleby Frodingham Works team, but it included several Scunthorpe players, including Shem Hill - Standing fifth from left, and on the far left, with towel, is 'Lal' White, who later became the Club trainer and an Olympic cycling medallist.

## CHAPTER 3

STRUGGLERS OF THE TWENTIES

After the hostilities of the first world war, interest in the national winter game was, as to be expected, high. The public had suffered extremes of austerity on an already mean existence for most working people. Men returning from the horrors of war needed to turn their attentions, and for football the dawning of the 1919-20 season was as though the sport was coming out of hibernation.

Scunthorpe and Lindsey United awoke to a new situation by appointing Harry Allock as Secretary once again, but this time in a full-time salaried position, from 21st May 1919. From that point events moved quickly in readiness for the field activities in the late summer of that year. Initially Mr Allock was instructed to use the *'Athletic News'*, probably the most widely used sporting paper of the time, as a vehicle to advertize for playing and training staff. It was not long before results from the newspaper produced their first signing, when Mr Tommy Moran was offered the post of trainer in the May of 1919.

~ 1919-20 ~

Very soon a squad of players began to assemble in preparation for the first game, scheduled to be at home to Rotherham County, whose first eleven had now been elected to the Football League. Probably the most outstanding player to be attracted to the Club was former Nottingham Forest and Ireland International goalkeeper Jack Hanna. Jack was quite a character, but at 5'-10" and only 11 stones in weight had the reputation of being one of the best goalkeepers ever to represent Scunthorpe. His positional play and uncanny knack of anticipation was second to none and it was not long before he had endeared himself to the local crowd. Whenever he was unavailable to play United could still rely upon the safe hands of the evergreen Johnny Wogin, whose enthusiasm for the game was as keen as ever. Wogin had witnessed the Club rise from North Lindsey and would still be at the Club twenty years later.

In the full-back positions, Scunthorpe had recruited Bullivant and Robinson. The former was one of the influx of players from Lincoln, whereas Robinson hailed from Barrow. The pair were supplemented by the vastly experienced Matthew Robson, who before the cessation of football activities, had been the defensive pivot at Sincil Bank for Lincoln City. On either side of Robson was Shem Hill, another long-serving local man, who took the right-half spot, and on the other side was former Lincoln End

player Hobson. Later this position was taken by Tommy Wield, who came from Lincoln City. Wield's speciality was a tremendously long throw, which often caused confusion amongst defenders when it was launched into the penalty box.

Scunthorpe's forward line began with the slightly built, but notably fast Ernest Butler on the right-wing, who came from Stillington. His sportsmanship was second to none and he was remembered as a person with an exemplarily conduct both on and off the pitch. Butler's inside man was Jack Spavin who had been on the books of Goole Town. This was a young player with an excellent eye for goal and certainly had plenty of potential for the future. On the far flank Lemon arrived shortly into the season from Sheffield Amateurs, at inside-forward, and was partnered on the far side by Booth, a consistent performer from Sheffield United. Lemon received some unfair criticism from some sections of the crowd when he was continuously barracked towards the end of the season. The picture was completed by the inclusion of John Mahon a centre-forward and useful goalscorer from Shirebrook, but whose refined style may not have always suited the team.

Before the season began Scunthorpe received a request from the Grimsby Telegraph for permission to install a telephone in the main grandstand in anticipation of the huge public interest in the game. This was given United's blessing ready for the 1919-20 season.

The team that trotted out for the first match in five years against Rotherham County on 30th August 1919 consisted of Hanna, Bullivant, Pattison, Hill, Robson, Hobson, Butler, Spavin, Mahon, Lea and Charlesworth. Perhaps the crowd of about 2,000 supporters might have been greater, had it not been for the considerable increase in admission charges. Gentlemen would now be charged one shilling (5p), ladies sixpence (2½p) and boys three pence (1p). This might have been in lieu of the greater running costs, especially as in the June of 1919 the prospect of buying the ground for £7,000 had arisen. This was turned down, being considered to high a price, and the ground was, again leased but at an increased price.

Jack Spavin played in 25 League and Cup games during the 1919-20 season, before being sold to Nottingham Forest for £340.

In the event the Rotherham game proved to be an exciting encounter, and this new side soon blended together in the most positive way. Inside man Jack Spavin helped himself to two goals, and the others were scored by Butler and Hobson, which sent local supporters away happy with a 4-1 win.

Although the next couple of games at Rotherham in the return fixture, and at Halifax, ended in unsatisfactory defeats, the team were soon to head in the right direction up the League ladder. It was particularly encouraging to earn a draw at eventual runners-up Sheffield United Reserves, and a visit to Gainsborough Trinity saw them return home 4-1 winners from the Northolme.

The F.A.Cup, in the meantime, only gave the Knuts limited success. Goole Town did not cause their usual difficulties as the 7-0 drubbing suggests, when Spavin smacked a well taken hat-trick. Broadsworth Colliery took more effort out of the team but were beaten 2-1. Finally a surprise 1-0 loss at the Old Showground to Cleethorpes ended the club's aspirations for the season.

At Christmas, United entered into a pair of games against Lincoln City's second string. On Christmas Day Jack Spavin enhanced his reputation by scoring four of the goals in the 6-0 thrashing. This considerable feat prompted over one thousand Scunthonians to make the Boxing Day journey to the County capital for the return fixture. In the bright winter sunshine the congregation of visiting supporters sat on the grass, some smoking their yuletide cigars. Charlie Lemon opened the scoring in the first-half to excite the visiting hoards, and as the Imps rallied for the equalizer, local player Cox made the game safe in the second period to complete an excellent double for the Knuts. However, on the return back to Scunthorpe the weather changed for the worst, and many folks were caught in a violent snow storm, not arriving home until the early hours.

The turn of 1920 saw a couple of important events before the season was much older. From 6th January 1920 the Share capital was increased to £6,000, again at the price of ten shillings (50p) per Share. This was an effort to raise much needed cash for the purchase of the Old Showground which had finally been agreed in principle on 6th December 1919 for the sum of £2,980. It required an extraordinary general meeting of the Club on 6th March 1920 to agree to the Share transactions.

Another important decision taken by the board involved free-scoring Jack Spavin, who had attracted the attentions of other clubs with his dynamic displays. On 24th February Spavin was offered a wage increase to £6 a week, backdated to August, in an effort to keep him at the club. Two days later Scunthorpe received a firm bid of £340 for his services, from Nottingham Forest. Within the week this had been accepted and Spavin was wearing the red shirt at the City Ground, and any remote chance United had of Midland League honours had evaporated.

Once Spavin had departed the forward line was not able to function with the same fluidity. John Mahon moved to the number eight position as the replacement, and a number of centre-forwards were used in his old slot. Goals became rarer to find, and if anything Charlie Lemon tended to administer most of the final blows, despite his standing with a minority of the support. A flourish at the end of the season, which brought an undefeated run of five games of which three were won, enabled the Club to proudly sit in the third placing within the League table, their best effort to date.

Two meetings paired them at home and away with the newly constructed Leeds United Reserves, born out of the embers of the disgraced Leeds City club, who had been forced by the authorities to disband after financial irregularities.

During the close season of 1920 a lot a activity up and down the country centred around the possibility of forming a Northern Section of the Third Division, which would be admitted on an Associate Membership basis to the Football League. A number of meetings were attended throughout 1920 and the following year, but although this led to a tangible situation for other clubs, Scunthorpe remained on the fringe.

The job of taking on fresh talent for the new campaign took up a considerable amount of time, and despite a successful campaign in the previous twelve months, only Hanna, Wogin, Lemon and Broadhead, a centre-forward used later in the year, were offered new terms. The problems the board were finding was that as a result of the ever increasing popularity of the sport players wages had doubled to a norm of £6 per week, and some more experienced Football League men wanted a signing on fee for dropping down into the Midland League.

To supplement the squad United secured the signature on 11th May 1920 of outside-left Fred Tunstall. Such was the impact of this skilled flank man that his reputation spread so quickly, that Sheffield United paid the unprecedented fee of £1,000 for his services, thought to be the first four figure sum received by a non-League club, after just nineteen matches. Tunstall was shear magic, and went on to play for England and scored the Blades only goal in the 1925 Cup Final against Cardiff City. When he signed, some secrecy surrounded the transfer. On the following Saturday, Scunthorpe received a visit from Peter McWilliam, the Manager of Tottenham Hotspur, who had taken the train from Kings Cross to check on Tunstall's progress. He was amazed to learn that the lad was in London playing for Sheffield United against his own team at White Hart Lane!

Another very important signing was that of Herbert Lloyd, the vastly experienced left-half of Rotherham County, also credited with using his guile to bring Tunstall's career along. In addition Scunthorpe added brothers Robert and John Duffus to their numbers. Robert was to play a major part as the defence's anchorman, while his brother assumed the role of centre-forward. When John Duffus was not available either Lemon or Simpson took his place, but it was a position that caused concern during the ensuing months. Incidently the Duffus brothers arrived at the Club with Scottish origins and styles. Changes were also made in the full-back positions. Ackroyd joined from Rotherham County, being well acquainted with Lloyd, and Arthur "Chaff" Betts made his way via such teams as Newcastle, Derby and Hull. Ackroyd was a great favourite of the supporters, and often cries of *"Good Old Acky"* would be heard shouted from the terraces. On the other hand, for Betts this was his swan song and he was signed very much as a steadying 'Old Head' influence. Finally the return of Matt Robson completed the recognized first team network when he became available shortly into the commencement of the fixtures.

The strength of the 1920-21 side appeared very much on a par with that of twelve months earlier, although their start, a 1-3 home reverse to a moderate Notts County Reserve side did not set the ball rolling as well as Scunthorpe followers would have hoped. Goalscoring also came under scrutiny, with only eight goals coming from the first seven matches. Fortunately, after the failure against Notts County, only two goals were conceded by the admirable defenders and points began to be gathered from the low scoring games. The team opened up against the newly elected Nottingham Forest Reserves, when goals by Lemon, Tunstall and Simpson (two) secured an impressive 4-0 win. Christmas was given plenty of cheer as Hull City Reserves were crushed 3-1 on Christmas Day, and two days later on the Boxing Day Monday, by 4-1 at the Old Showground. It left the team in a strong position towards the top of the League, although Lincoln and Notts County Reserves were ahead of the pack at this time.

In the F.A.Cup, Scunthorpe had stayed in the competition until the end of November, indeed this was their best season to date. Goals had not been a problem against the weaker teams of the standard below Midland League level and they had been expected to make progress against Hull Brunswick (beaten 6-0), Bentley Colliery 3-0 and Grimsby Charlton 4-1 away from home. The stumbling block was Brodsworth Colliery, an old adversary, who took three games to beat. The decider came at Brammall Lane, Sheffield, on neutral territory. Scunthorpe's hero was a young man, Alex Moore, who had been studying at teachers training college in the same city. He supplied United's first goal, and later became not only a well respected headmaster, but chairman of the football club and also mayor of Scunthorpe. Another of the strikes came from Jack Harvey, son of the local Harvey's Transport People family, he too, would serve in later life on the board of Directors. A third goal by Simpson allowed Scunthorpe a Safe passage into the next round with a final score of 3-1.

The F.A.Cup run came to an end on 20th November 1920, when Mansfield Town arrived, but dense fog ruined the game as a contest and really it should never have been played in the first place. It was virtually impossible to follow the course of the proceedings and only those immediately behind the goal at the Crosby End of the ground knew what had happened, when the Nottinghamshire side scored the only goal in front of a larger then average crowd.

If the F.A.Cup had not produced the highlights of the year so far, then perhaps the local match meetings with Gainsborough Trinity and Lincoln were a fair substitute. On New Year's Day Scunthorpe won 4-1 at the Northolme. Roebuck, wearing Scunthorpe's number eight shirt, was the talking point after notching a trio. Then came the games late in the season against Lincoln, who had lost their Football League status for a year and therefore were presenting their first eleven to the Midland League public. Already the City stars had beaten the Knuts in the Lincolnshire Cup 1-0, and at Sincil Bank they had pleased their own supporters again, increasing this score difference to 2-0. When they turned up at the Old Showground just after Easter they were greeted by the season's record crowd. United dominated the early

stages and when outside-left Jenkins, utilized in the team from December, broke through from the halfway line, he was able to create the opportunity to score the only goal of the tussle. Unfortunately, in doing so he collided with the upright and broke his collar bone, an injury that ended his season. For the rest of the game it was a "backs to the wall" job, as Scunthorpe's overworked ten men performed miracles. Jack Hanna played the game of his lifetime, using a liberal amount of sawdust to help grip the greasey ball. Ackroyd and Betts also played out of their skins, and at the final whistle the crowd rushed onto the pitch and carried them from the field in triumph. The result did not stop City from winning the Championship and returning to the League in the 1921-22 season, but it was one of only eight defeats they suffered in thirty-eight Midland League games. As for Jack Hanna, strangely he was not retained at the end of the season, but allowed to move on to Workington.

Scunthorpe's final placing in the table was an excellent fourth position, tucked in behind Chesterfield and runners-up Notts County Reserves. Most folks considered the venture most satisfactory from all aspects.

A footnote to the 1920-21 season came when two announcements were made by the Board of Directors. The first, and most important one, came on 8th March 1921 when, after the December meeting, they agreed to buy the Old Showground. All the legal details were tied up and a final agreement was reached. Then in the April, in view of the tight economic situation both at the Club and in the Town at large, all unemployed persons would be allowed to watch home matches at half price.

Despite a first class season in 1920-21, five of the playing staff were given their cards in the May of 1921 in an effort to create opportunities for more skilful players. Gone were Lemon, Duffus, Butler, Hanna and Robson, while now players would be offered up to £10 as a signing on fee, plus £4 or £5 per week, depending on how highly they were rated. However, before too many signings had been obtained, the Chairmanship of the Club changed as Mr Paul Coombe succeeded Mr Lockwood.

~ 1921-22 ~

When the season was ready to start United had a new 'keeper when Bates linked up following service at Crystal Palace, but after making a poor impression the dependable Johnny Wogin once again stepped up for duty. United also looked to the Broadsworth Colliery centre-half, who had proved very effective against them in the F.A.Cup, but he too found the pace of the Midland League too exacting and was replaced by Duke, a hard hitting stopper from Grimsby Town. More successful signings came in the form of Vic Witham and Harry Maycock, while young Meredith improved as the season progressed, under the watchful eye of Herbert Lloyd. The other addition to the team was in the half-back line, where Herbert Crooks was said to be more dangerous heading the ball than shooting with his feet.

Although United started well enough, drawing with Rotherham County Reserves 2-2 in the first game, and completing three wins over Wath, Forest Reserves and Hull City Reserves by the fourth match, the first part of the season did not go according to plan and the side had slipped to below halfway in the championship race due to a run of eleven games which saw only one League victory. This may have coincided with Moran leaving the Club after three years to take up a similar post in Rotherham as County's trainer. His replacement, at the princely wage of three pounds and ten shillings per week, was Chas White, the local racing cyclist. Nevertheless the Directors were prompted to advertize for an experienced centre-forward or inside man in the *Athletic News*. The answer came in the response by former Chelsea International Robert Whittingham, who was of the highest skill class, and possessed a deadly shot. He certainly proved to be just what was required as he scored on his debut and Scunthorpe managed a Christmas Eve win over Barnsley.

Fred Tunstall of the 1920-21 squad, was transferred to Sheffield United for £1,000.

The improvement in the team's performances continued throughout Christmas and into the New Year. During the next four games United thrilled the crowd with doubles over local rivals Lincoln City Reserves and Doncaster Rovers, whose first team were carrying out Midland League duties two seasons before they were re-admitted to the Football League. Certainly there was a change of fortunes in general and much of it was down to Whittingham who often would act as goal provider. There was a match of note towards the end of the fixtures when Rotherham Town called in at the Old Showground. The Yorkshire lads were totally mesmerized by Witham who was unstoppable that afternoon. His hat-trick was the talk of the public houses in the town as they toasted his name.

It was quite remarkable that the Knuts should have made the fourth table position again behind champions Worksop, then the second teams of Grimsby Town and Sheffield Wednesday. This gave the directors much satisfaction, but a meeting had been called midway through January because of the threatening financial position. Thankfully this storm was weathered thanks to a slight improvement in gate returns when the team picked itself up.

Before leaving the 1921-22 season the efforts of the F.A.Cup must not be forgotten. Following the defeat of Retford, United set a goalscoring record in the competition when they humbled Hull Holderness by ten goals without reply. Among the marksmen, Calthorpe scored four times in the encounter and Witham netted a hat-trick. This led to another tie against Broadworth Colliery, whom they duly disposed of 4-1 at home, before the sterner test against Gainsborough Trinity.

The Gainsborough match attracted a great deal of interest and Scunthorpe soon found themselves trailing before the interval by a goal to nil, despite having the lion's share of the play. The pattern continued into the second-half, when Scunthorpe were awarded a penalty following a foul by the Trinity goalkeeper Elijah Scott, a very well known personality of the day. Scott protested vehemently at the decision, so much so that the usually accurate Ackroyd missed his kick and the ball took all its time to reach the goal-line. Scott attempted a spectacular save but had to dive forward to reach the ball. To add insult to injury he turned the ball round the post before strutting across the penalty area in triumph, much to the delight of the Trinity supporters. Scunthorpe had missed their chance and the home side scored a later second goal to send the Knuts reeling out of the cup for another year.

A final word on the 1921-22 season must be said about work on the Old Showground. Tenders had been taken for the cost of erecting a new West Stand, and again the name of Mr Pallister had been accepted to carry out the work. This time the costs would be substantial and it was decided to request a loan of £4,000 from the bank. To offset the cost, eight mortgage debenture shares of £50 were put up for offer, at an interest rate of £5 per annum, later this was reduced to £10. Running a football club at this level was proving expensive, but somehow Scunthorpe and Lindsey United Football Club was coping, but only just!

~ 1922-23 ~

The 1922-23 season began with United trying out a number of players to satisfactorily accommodate various positions. In goal Johnny Wogin continued to hold his own, but after thirteen League and Cup games he stepped back into the second team, being succeeded by Norman Reynolds, another local 'keeper from the Normanby Park Works team.

There were to be changes in the defensive roles. Gone were the popular Ackroyd and Broadhead, for the pair were replaced with Oscar Hargreaves off Rotherham County's books, and Reg Smith, a partner for "Chaff" Betts. Positional changes later confirmed Hargreaves as a full-back and the drafting of Herbert Crooks across the half-back line to the pivot duty. On either side of Crooks, Shem Hill and Herbert Lloyd continued to supply the team with vast amounts of experience, although Alex Moore was later brought into the frame.

Up in the goalscoring department Robert Whittingham could no longer be afforded, and sadly he was to meet a premature death at the age of thirty-six. Meredith, Witham and Maycock had been retained and Rushby eventually was called in to provide cover at inside-right. The centre-forward slot still remained the immediate problem however. At first James Retford, from Barnsley, was tried without success, as were Talbot and Butterfly, both former Gainsborough Trinity players. The ticket was finally given to Gittos from Staveley Town, and he seemed to have more of what was required. Thus with these credentials at Scunthorpe, the ship set sail into the 1922-23 season.

The sun rose brightly above the Old Showground on 26th August 1922 to herald the beginning of a new set of fixtures, and the team responded confidently enough by beating Notts

County Reserves on a hard pitch. Witham scored the first goal and Hardgreaves came up field to fire the ball home for the second, proving the worth of the defending men when given a chance to roam up front. The 2-0 victory was just what was required, but another home pairing seven days later, this time with Hull City Reserves, frustrated Scunthorpe supporters when chances were spurned by the inadequate front-runners. This resulted in the team going down 2-1, but the double gains in the next two games against Rotherham County Reserves put the Knuts train steaming back on the rail.

It was midway through September when Scunthorpe came unstuck. Three games, all away from home, failed to produce a goal, and yielded only one point from the stalemate at Castleford. Even more alarming was the 6-0 thrashing handed out by Denaby, despite the fact that they were in a more elevated Midland League position in this campaign. The only solution was to introduce team changes and at this time Gittos was given the reins and the tide changed within a short time.

Gittos' first goal came in the F.A.Cup at home to Grimsby Charlton, a team United had been expected to beat, but which put up a splendid fight before failing 3-0 at the Old Showground. Scunthorpe's previous cup exploits gave them exemption from the earliest round of the competition, and their first encounter did not take place until the first week of October.

Safe passage through the first stage gave them consecutive away visits to Gainsborough in both the League and the Cup. In the Midland League Gittos scored twice in a 2-2 draw, thus setting the scene for more excitement in the knockout game. Scunthorpe rose to the occasion in excellent style and the defence was breached only once. In the attack goals came from Rushby and Moore, but the final stages saw a nail-biting finish to a game that was always in doubt. This effort was rewarded by another Lincolnshire rival being drawn, Boston United. For Scunthorpe it meant the journey into the South of the County, but Harry Maycocks single strike from an inside-left position won the visitors the tie. Finally, the F.A.Cup was bowed out of when a tricky visit to Worksop, flying high in the Midland League table, caused the Knuts demise. This time the continual pressure of the home forwards was too much to bear, and United's defenders finally cracked. The 4-2 result in Worksop's favour shows good testimony to this fact.

Much hard work had to be shouldered to turn the corner of the poorer than average start. It was Worksop who, again, figured in one of the roads to recovery. On the Saturday before the Christmas Holiday it was the Nottinghamshire lads who had to do the journeying. Although they arrived in confident mood following the Cup match, it was Scunthorpe who stepped up the pace in the early part of the game. Gittos ran the show, and he was unlucky when an enterprising shot grazed the post. Undeterred, the man made amends, scoring with a driving header, then increased the lead with a terrific low drive. Unfortunately lapses in defence allowed Worksop to come back and equalize. Then, as the game see-sawed backwards and forward, Gittos again became the hero, completing his hat-trick when he beat the defenders once

more and fired home the winning goal. There was no wonder Coventry City stepped in at the end of the season to sign him.

The second-half of the season continued to be an up and down event, although the Worksop match started an undefeated run of nine games through Christmas and January, and putting the Club in touch with the leading pack. This, unfortunately, could not be maintained, and goalscoring remained sporadic. In March and April seven encounters saw the team fail to score, but a 5-0 victory against Rotherham Town did give the Old Showground supporters some encouragement.

Then on Friday 13th April 1923 a disaster of an unparalleled nature hit the club. It was on that date that fire swept through the West Stand completely gutting the structure. Not only was the shelter lost, but also the dressing rooms and the entire playing kit. Immediately an appeal was launched and a sub-committee was formed, headed by Paul Coombe and Mr Talbot Cliff. It was just another distraction to the Club who were by now the sum of £2,158 in debt. The fighting spirit of the Board was demonstrated in the following day's game against Sheffield Wednesday Reserves went ahead as planned.

The sorry season was curtailed from the playing point of view when Chesterfield Reserves were subdued by a 3-0 result at the Old Showground. However, the concern over the tragic fire was compounded with the reduced average size of the turnstile takings. Gates of under 2,000 spectators were now a fact of life, and these were not sufficient for the Club to prosper in view of the extra responsibility the directors had taken on. This was in spite of the fact that Scunthorpe had finished in sixth position out of twenty-two teams. Scunthorpe and Lindsey Football Club's financial problems were by no means unique. Other teams in their league were in the same boat, and life had to go on.

~ 1923-24 ~

The 1923-24 season opened with a new brush sweeping clean, and few of the old guard were retained. Reynolds and Wogin would look after the custodian spot, but the younger man only allowed Wogin a single appearance, and that was when he sustained an injury. In the outfield positions Arthur Betts departed to coach the local Lysaghts Sports Steel Works team, while Herbert Lloyd exchanged the players shirt for the team trainer's towel. Shem Hill was to bade 'farewell' when an old knee injury failed to respond to treatment. He was to become sorely missed. However, Oscar Hargreaves was back in harness, as was Meridith. Meridith was not to stay around his natural right-wing berth for much longer, because along with Jimmy Forbes, from Lincoln City's register, they had attracted the eye of Second Division Blackpool. At the end of September both players packed their bags in a combined deal worth £650 to Scunthorpe, and headed to Bloomfield Road. The cash was a welcome injection into United's coffers and eased the mounting financial problems for a short while.

The most notable new signing was that of former Sheffield United stalwart, Joe Kitchen. Kitchen was fleet of foot, possessed exceptional ball skills, and was a master of the lob shot, something a number of straying goalkeepers had found to their costs. It would not be too long before he made an impact. To support Joe on the right-flank, Meridith's departure after September caused the team selections some concern, but eventually Broksom fitted the bill, having joined from Rotherham County. The inside position was of less a problem, for Burkinshaw from Denaby was considered suitable. On the left side of the forward line Raby came from Lincoln and was partnered by ex-Rotherham Amateur, Foster. Young Foster was so nippy that he earned the nickname of Mumtax, after a racehorse of the day.

The half-back position proved to be an all changing situation, although in the early days of the season a number of players jockeyed for positions. However, once the opportunity occurred, Richard Ashmore, a strongly built young player formerly with Doncaster, seized the chance with both hands. On either side of Ashmore, Frank Skull made the most of his trial from Middlesbrough and began a long association with the Old Showground, whilst on the left hand side Millson, a local player, stepped up from the Ashby Mill team. This left just the full-back position, where the star of the show would be George Bradbury, a tremendously strong man with a good tackle, from Londoners Clapton Orient. His partner for the first-half of the year would be the versatile Hargreaves, but in the New Year he was succeeded by Franklin from the second eleven.

The season started at the Old Fulford ground of York City with a disappointing match void of goals, and in a worsening situation the Knuts failed to win any of their first four games. It was not until home matches against Sutton and York City were won that a ray of sunshine appeared. In between those two games United also progressed in the F.A.Cup. Ironically, what with the luck of the Cup draws, and an extraordinary sequence in the Midland League fixture card, United only played one away game from 15th September until 15th December. Once the team selections had settled down the results began to improve, but consecutive home matches, no doubt, was a contributing factor to the decline in gates. Probably the pick of the Midland League results came at home in the derby against Grimsby Town Reserves. The team that was to be runners-up to Mansfield Town suffered a 3-0 defeat thanks to two strikes by Kitchen and another by occasional player White.

The Autumn run in the F.A.Cup was accelerated by a hat-trick from Kitchen in the 5-0 drubbing against Cleethorpes Town. Gainsborough Trinity followed in the next round, but despite being of a stronger metal than other opponents they could not match Kitchen and Skull's goals, and a 2-0 result in United's favour resulted. Boston were next for Cup action at the Showground, and then Rotherham Town. Usually teams were killed off at the replay stage following an away draw, but in this case Town had held their own in a 0-0 draw at Scunthorpe, during a game remembered for honest endeavour, rather than thrills.

Five days later it was over to the other side of the River Rother for the return, but the home side fell to the deadly boot of Joe Kitchen. A 1-0 scoreline won the tie against the other Rotherham side, the County, but instead of the Yorkshire side's Reserves, this was for real against the first

eleven. Soon afterwards Town and County amalgamated to form Rotherham United.

The Rotherham County Cup-tie saw a record crowd squeeze tightly into the Old Showground to see the Knuts keen to impress. It was they who took the initiative and took a first-half lead when Kitchen conjured a shooting position to fire home the opening goal. The second period continued in the same mould and the advantage could have been increased on at least one other occasion. It was towards the end of the game that United suffered at the hands of a strange refereeing decision. One of the Rotherham players punted the ball aimlessly up field to release the pressure. Reynolds, in goal stood in line to collect the missile, but fumbled it first before launching it back toward the general melee of players. The referee standing on the half-way mark curiously judged the ball to have crossed the line, and despite Reynolds' protests, the goal remained on the sheet, costing United a result. The midweek replay was to be as equally fruitless as Reynolds' efforts to make the official change his mind, and County went through on the strength of a 2-0 win.

Back on Midland League duty Scunthorpe enjoyed an excellent spell during December, January and into the first part of February. This included the double over Lincoln City Reserves, and another two victories against Rotherham Town. At Rotherham, just into the New Year, Raby scored United's first Midland League hat-trick of the season. He repeated the same feat at home to Gainsborough at the beginning of March. In the winter's run of form only Mexborough could beat the Scunthorpe team.

The unfortunate part of the 1923-24 season was that from mid-March the goals dried up, as did the points. Only four goals came in a spell of nine games, which yielded the miserable sum of only one win, at home to Boston. It was something of a relief to see the final two games of this particular season close on a high note as Worksop and Doncaster Rovers Reserves were both beaten 4-0, to raise the spirits. This left the Club finally placed in sixth position in the table, but what was of more concern was the meagre total of fifty-nine goals scored, the lowest number since before the war.

~ 1924-25 ~
The 1924-25 football season was to provide Scunthorpe United with one of the most anxious periods in their entire history. Problems began in 1924 when Chesterfield became the catalyst to form a new League, namely The Midland Combination, for all the Reserve teams of the relatively new clubs of the Third Division North of the Football League. Only Lincoln City opted to remain loyal, and the loss of so many competitors threatened not only the fabric of the Midland League, but also the individual clubs that remained. None of the clubs were able to survive on the twenty-eight fixtures apiece, so from 12th March 1925 a subsidiary competition of a further dozen games was introduced.

Of the playing staff of the 1924-25 season, a number of the faces from the previous year's work were in evidence. Norman Reynold continued to play as the regular 'keeper, and his enthusiasm and ability were never to be questioned. Once again his form only allowed deputy Wogin one game in the calender.

In front of him Bradbury was still in evidence at right full-back, but there was little seen of Oscar Hargreaves and the left side was entrusted to George Greaves. When Bradbury received a long term injury Greaves moved across the park, and Shearsmith from Grimsby took over.

In the midfield engine room Skull and Millson were still to perform sterling service, but they were to stand either side of a new central pivot in Burnham. Once Burnham had overcome an early season injury, he took the honours for some courageous work.

In the forward line the combination of Clarkson, on the left-wing, and Shaw at centre-forward were the only players worthy of mention. Shaw, in particular, was the star of the side, helping to keep everyone's head above water in the trying season to come. He always played with a single aim in mind, and that was to pepper the opposition target with shots. Invariably he was rewarded with at least one goal in most games. Before football started in earnest, local football supporters were greeted by the news that Mr Paul Coombe had resigned as Chairman and Mr Talbot Cliff had taken over the reins in the most difficult of circumstances.

When football did kick-off in August 1924, it began a period of what was to be the worst ever on record for Scunthorpe United. Injuries to key players, difficulties in goalscoring, and the resultant lack of support through bad results were just part of the catalogue of problems. Only two of the first seven games ended in success, and three of the games saw the Knuts defeated without scoring even a consolation goal. It was not until an away fixture at lowly Sutton that Scunthorpe supporters had anything to write home about, when Shaw scored a trio of goals in a 5-0 win.

Usually at this time in the season the F.A.Cup would bring a little light relief, but not particularly so in this year. Barton Town were not quite a pushover in the first qualifying round, but United eased through after struggling to win 2-1. Early in October Boston came to the Old Showground in the next round. Thanks once again to the forwards failing the initiative was lost in a 0-0 disappointment, and worse was to follow, when Boston coasted to a 3-0 result in the replay.

The financial situation was so critical by now that a board meeting was called for 25th November 1924 to discuss the economics of the club. Already the directors had looked after the weekly wages on occasions, and the players had cheerfully accepted a 25% drop in pay. Days before the meeting the game at home to Worksop had seen only 1,272 spectators pass through the turnstile, paying just £65 in receipts. In three short months £300 had been lost on the season, the bank overdraft was £987, with a further £2,700 committed for the purchase of the ground. Added to this was £760 owing for the purchase of two stands on the ground.

A great deal of the money had been loaned from the bank, for which the directors had acted as guarantors. Now the debts had reached the point of no return, and the Club had to say enough was enough. The conclusion of the meeting was regrettably that a letter should be sent to the Midland League by Mr Harry Allcock, informing them that Scunthorpe and Lindsey United would not be competing during the following season. At the same time wheels were put into motion for a sub-committee to effect the sale of all assets including the ground. The Club had gone beyond the brink.

It had already been agreed to sell part of the ground on the east side when at the eleventh hour United's directors had a rethink. Another effort to raise revenue was made with an approach to the Barnsley Brewery Company. They committed themselves to take over the £400 loan the bank held on the ground mortgage. This meant the directors could take out further guarantees on loans to keep the Club afloat. Another letter was hurriedly sent to the Midland League Headquarters withdrawing the resignation. Scunthorpe and Lindsey United had just survived their darkest hour, but they were not out of the woods yet.

It was a pity that the resolve of the directors could not be matched by the claret and blues on the field of play. Shaw was the lone beacon, from 6th December he scored at least one goal in all but one of the next 13 fixtures, and at Frickley his contribution was a hat-trick in the 4-1 win. The only glimmer given by the team started at Christmas when they began a six match unbeaten run. Shaw's four goals at Wath in a 5-4 thriller was the only memorable event in this unforgettable period of the club's history. The main competition ended in March, and Scunthorpe were rated seventh out of 15 teams. This was followed by a total disaster in the secondary competition. United could only squeeze a single 1-0 win out of fellow strugglers Worksop Town. The Club had to suffer the ignominity of taking the wooden spoon for the first time ever. All concerned breathed a huge sign of relief at the passing of the 1924-25 season. The main part of the storm may have moved over, but it was still raining.

~ 1925-26 ~

By the start of the 1925-26 campaign, fortunes had changed for the Midland League and a further six strong non-League sides from the North and Midlands had joined the fold, bringing up the strength to twenty-one teams in the competition. It meant a far more competitive structure from which United would benefit, and gone was the worthless subsidiary games.

Little remained of the 1924-25 staff, and even Shaw moved to pastures new. However, Clarkson was retained and Vic Witham returned after a two year absence. Cawley joined the forwards from Worksop, while Charles Vowles, an old sharpshooter at Exeter was to become an immediate success in the middle. Initially Dawson started at outside-right, but he lost his place to Tommy Laurie after a couple of outings.

In the midfield Wilson eventually became the regular centre-half, Skull continued to impress in the number four shirt, while Evans made the left-half position his own. At right full-back former Oldham Athletic man Glennie answered the vacancy, accompanying Liversege on the left side. The role of Reynolds in goal, with John Wogin as cover still gave the most positive result. Even injury problems to the defence did not expose the Scunthorpe target to opposition forwards, since Reynolds could be relied upon to cover any mistakes. Soon a number of Football League scouts were checking his progress.

At last the team was to provide the town with a level of entertainment that was expected of them. After an uncertain start, before a regular selection of team personnel, the side soon found the right gear. The first seven Midland League matches only saw one defeat. Vowles in particular was an absolute boon, quickly establishing himself as a crowd favourite when he cracked three goals during the visit of Frickley Colliery, the result of which not only gained a 'double' but pleased the Old Showground followers after a 5-0 thrashing. Although there had been a couple of games that could not produce a score, the combination of Whitham, Vowles and Cawley were generally to see a steady stream of shots converted into goals.

In the F.A.Cup, Scunthorpe started well enough, when Cleethorpes lost on their own territory 4-0, Vowles scoring three, then Grimsby Haycroft Rovers were thwarted 5-1, Cawley this time notching four times. It was at the third hurdle that the Knuts were to fail. The opponents were arch-rivals Gainsborough Trinity. Trinity weathered the storm at the Old Showground, 2-2, despite Vowles and Cawley registering for the home side. It was most disappointing to see the Claret and Blues eliminated from the competition when former player Alex Moore scored the game's only goal, with the Northolm defenders holding firm. Some sort of revenge was taken in the R.A.F. Shield match when Scunthorpe won 6-0, quite remarkable as both League games finished void of a score.

At the turn of the New Year Scunthorpe's League position was higher than it had been for a couple of years. They were in the top half a dozen for most of the campaign, and with more consistency, might have challenged for honours. Over Christmas they had a couple of rare results against newly elected Long Eaton. Both sides scored five times against the other, each winning at home, Scunthorpe by 5-3 and Long Eaton by 5-1. The New Year fixture caught a cold through bad weather, but into January Loughborough Corinthians were easily beaten 3-0. This was somewhat spoiled by the seasons biggest defeat, 9-2, away to the Lincoln second team. Extraordinarily the team had shared a couple of goals earlier in Scunthorpe, but there again, three weeks down the road, Loughborough snuffed out the Knuts in a 6-1 disappointment.

The inconsistency continued throughout the season. Who would have expected the team to bounce back after the Loughborough game to win 5-1 away at Castleford? Perhaps that was not such a mystery as the Yorkshire side did occupy the foot of the table. Nevertheless they did have to work hard and Vowles was the talk of the town when he hit the back of the net four times. He was to perform equally well a fortnight later when he fired home a hat-trick against Shirebrook and added another such feat in the beating of Newark, both occasions at Scunthorpe, the latter coming in the final match of the 1925-26 season.

The contrast in this team to twelve months previously did not bear comparison, for apart from the three 0-0 scorelines, in only two other League games did the team fail to register. In the forty outings they performed like a breath of fresh air, and although games were not a sell out, at least this team did stimulate the public for the first time in quite a while.

The statistics for the season showed the team finish in seventh position, ten points off the championship pace set by Mexborough Town, but only six points adrift of runners-up Mansfield Town, who like Scunthorpe were still operating their first team squad in non-League football.

The total of eighty-six goals in forty matches was a tremendous achievement, being eight more than they had conceded. Vowles total of thirty-four in the Midland League created a record for the Club in a season, beating Shaw's total by a couple of strikes. His tally was complimented by five in the F.A.Cup. Whitham was credited with the next highest number of goals on seventeen, while Cawley notched fourteen, to which should be added a further six in the F.A.Cup. These returns gave the Club plenty of heart and at least progress had been made from the desperate times of twelve months earlier.

~ 1926-27 ~
The 1926-27 season would see a couple of changes to the clubs to be played. In the months ahead the team coach was not required to call at Castleford, who failed to regain election as the last term's bottom club, while Mansfield Town sought a different competition to try to gain notice in their attempt to open the key to entry within the Football League. Instead United would have to travel in the same general direction towards Nottinghamshire as they did to meet the Stags, but this time the opponents would be Heanor.

On the playing front the changes to the staff were even more ruthless than usual, something that caused a surprise in view of how well some of the men had represented themselves, particularly up front. Only Reynolds and Skull were required for further duty, but John Wogin, now considered no more than a back-up, was there for emergencies.

During the summer months rumours had spread through the town that United's Directors had been seeking the signature of a former England International. When the season broke, it proved that the speculations were in fact true. Scunthorpe would have the services of Ernie Simms, the ex-Luton, South Shields and Stockport County man who won his cap against Northern Ireland in 1922 while spearheading the attack at Kenilworth Road. Certainly the board considered the extra wages were well worth the investment. Ernie Simms recommended that the Club might do well to sign his Stockport team mate Joey Johnson, a prolific goalscorer, at inside-right. The suggestion was taken up and paid dividends once the season had kicked off. To complete the forward line, the right side of the flank was made up of Thompson on the right-wing. Tommy Allen at inside-left and Fred Alford on the far side. Thompson had seen experience at a number of clubs including Sheffield Wednesday and Portsmouth, but was lately from Castleford. Allen showed a lot of skill and accuracy as the season started, and joined from the previous season's champions Mexborough. His left-wing partner Alford, was at 5'-6" a speed merchant, whose career had taken him to Lincoln City, Barrow and Everton.

The half-back line colleagues of Frank Skull were to be Charles Smith and George Hunter. Skull was no midget, but Smith was almost three inches taller. His high frame was ideal for the rigours of the Midland League, and across the park from the ex-Doncaster man, Hunter was even taller, at a little more than six feet. Hunter had played with clubs at the far corners of the country, being able to boast of times at Sunderland, Southend United and Exeter City. These men would be supported at the back row by the vastly experienced McKenzie and a younger player, Holland, late of Bolsover Colliery. McKenzie gave his team-mate much encouragement as the season went on and the former colliery man improved tremendously as a result of the support. Finally Alex Moore returned from down the road at the Northolme, Gainsborough, to fill in as a utility man, but had little chance to show his skills in anything but second team soccer.

Once the season began and the team had stretched its legs it was obvious that this crew was dangerous. Frickley Colliery were beaten in the opening game 3-1, as Allen Hunter and Smith supplied the killer punches. In the third game former champions Mexborough caused a hold-up and put four goals passed the side without reply, but it was only to be a minor upset. Two days later the lads were back on song, winning 4-1 at home to Lincoln Reserves. Ernie Simms scored his first goals for the Club in the form of a hat-trick. This was to begin a twenty match unbeaten run in the Midland League.

On the 18th of September 1926, United launched another F.A.Cup campaign, and they did it in style. There was no mercy for the visiting Hull Holderness, who became the whipping boys again, as Scunthorpe equalled their record score. The North Humberside men were no match for the rampant claret and blues. Only Thompson of the forwards failed to score, but he had been too busy providing chances. Johnson and Simms had to fight to see who would keep the match ball, as both scored three time. Tommy Allen netted a couple, while Skull and Alford supplied one each. This theme continued in the next round against Grimsby Haycroft Rovers, but those who attended the Old Showground expected little else other than the 7-2 thrashing handed out. Johnson, Simms and Allen all scored two each, as well as another from Smith, roaming from his defensive duties.

Former England International Ernie Simms. His goalscoring was a big factor in the Club's first Championship win.

On the third Saturday of October there was more Cup action, this time in Yorkshire against a much more resilient opposition in Selby Olympia. It made a change to see the defenders coming out on top, and no goal was scored. The replay proved just as intriguing and Tommy Ellen's strike in front of goal was the only difference separating the two teams.

The distraction of the F.A. Cup was of more consequence to Midland League matters. Supporters found the competition a welcome diversion, especially as progress continued to be made on all fronts. The next obstacle was to be old rivals Gainsborough Trinity. Over at the Northolme an abundant crowd packed the terraces, as the blues of Trinity stretched the Knuts defence on numerous occasions, breaching it three times. At the other end United's forwards were equally strong and made up the difference, thanks to scores by Alford and a pair from Johnson. Thrilled by the first tie, the Old Showground swelled to close on five thousand people for the replay. This was not to be as incident packed, but Simms' trusty boot gave United safe passage with a 1-0 result.

Scunthorpe found themselves drawn in the final qualifier against completely new opponents. Never before had they met Kettering Town, but every one was full of confidence when given home advantage. On the day of the game, in miserable Autumn weather, a near record crowd assembled to witness the encounter against the Southern League club. The game was to be one where not a lot went right for the Iron, and several chances went begging. Then the tide turned with a dubious goal for the visitors. Although Johnson put the home side back on terms, another goal from the Kettering men in the second-half won the day. Reports suggested that this was a fitting shot to win the tie and a brave rally by United gave them plenty of credit.

The exit from the Cup was nothing but a minor irritation, and soon it was back to business as usual. November ended with five goals against Ilkeston, and consecutive wins of 6-1 over Alfreton, away, and Long Eaton, at home, which finally took them into the Christmas month. January was equally fruitful, as fifteen goals were scored in the January space of two games. Shirebrook were blitzed 8-1, as Simms and Allen scored hat-tricks, while Johnson was on target with the other two. Simms extended his tally even further by four more scores on the following Saturday when Grantham's visit cost them a 7-1 defeat. Tommy Allen did his reputation no harm with another three in the tussle.

The list of successes went on and on, but a final mention to this momentous season must be made of the one-sided encounter against Sutton Town. Scunthorpe repeated their 10-0 scoring feat, but the hero of the hour was Ernie Simms, who wrote his name in the history books as the first Scunthorpe player to score a double hat-trick at this senior level.

Scunthorpe romped home to their first championship, eleven points clear of nearest rivals Boston. The final record showed: played 38, won 28, drawn 4 and lost 6. Remarkably the team scored 121 goals and only conceded 44. No team in the League could match them.

It was no surprise that Ernie Simms was the leading goalscorer, with 58 League and Cup goals, closely followed by Tommy Allen with 35 and Joey Johnson on 31. This tremendous team that had made history for the Town virtually picked itself, and all the regular eleven played over thirty games each, only being disturbed by the occasional injury.

After years of struggle this side had put United on the map. The supporters and the town at large had every reason to be proud of them. Every department of the team had worked hard to the limit, and success was not only earned but also deserved. If these players had performed together in the Football League Northern section they would surly have been among the leaders. They had created a milestone in the football club's history, but not only that, they had given those persons who had made a personal sacrifice to keep the ship afloat, in the dark old days, a just reward. At last Scunthorpe and Lindsey Football Club had something to shout about!

## CHAPTER 4

STRIVING FOR MORE PERFECTION

~ 1927-28 ~

The situation at the Old Showground was much healthier going into the 1927-28 season, but the financial burden carried by the Club was still a worrying factor. Thanks to the class of 1926-27, interests in the team was greater, and as would be expected with a winning side, the gates over the previous twelve months had steadily increased. The directors were mindful that this extra support would wane if standards could not be maintained. They were also pleased to see that the scar on the west side of the ground, caused by the fire, was now healed, thanks to continued work since 1924 by Mr Pallister's company, but it came at a cost.

On the playing front supporters thought it would be treason to split up the championship squad, but some of the players chose to seek new challenges, and so the directors' hands were tied. There would be no more of Reynolds, McKenzie, Smith, Thompson, Johnson and Alford. Fortunately the man who did most of the past year's damage, Ernie Simms, had agreed to remain, but seasoned ex-International goalscorers only came at a price. He would be part of the remaining skeleton around which the new men were to be blended.

In goal, to replace Reynolds, came Watts, a likely lad from Bradford Park Avenue, but after November he was not to appear again. His place was generally given to local product Unwin, but John Wogin made a final five games in the green jumper, at home to Loughborough, before hanging up his boots on 31st March 1928, to end a worthy twenty year association with Scunthorpe and Lindsey United. Further up the field, in the full-back position, Holland had a new partner in ex-Worksop and Portsmouth man Len Severn, a towering figure at 6ft-1in tall and weighing 12½ stone, as his accomplice. This former Norwich City and Southend player gave the engine room a formidable look.

There were a lot of changes up front. Harry Wainwright on the right-wing had been at Sheffield United and his inside man Brooks was a local man, developed in the works team at Normanby Park. Later, his place was lost to another excellent Scunthorpe player, Arthur "Digger" Maw.

Maw was a student who made an impact at the top of the professional game. The same would be so for another youngster, from Santon, Jack Bowers. This huge young man, like his counterpart, Maw, would go on to International honours with his country, but for now their careers were very much in their infancy.

The remaining position in the forward line went to a consistent left-winger, Foster, who signed from Worksop Town. To complete the picture, Alex Moore came more into the team in the second-half of a very demanding season which extended to fifty games.

At the start of the 1927-28 season there was the welcome news that the strength of the Midland League had been increased by the additions of the reserve teams of Grimsby Town, Notts County and Nottingham Forest, plus the strong non-Leaguers of Scarborough. The fixture card gave the Knuts an easy opening game at Newark Town, and they comfortably won by a score of 5-2. Two of the goals were scored by Brooks on his debut. Days later the team was to know just how tough it was going to be to retain their title. Scarborough arrived to open United's home programme, and in a close game, during which the Scunthorpe rear guard was guilty of a number of costly errors, Scarborough returned to North East Yorkshire with both points after a triumphant 3-2 result.

The ship was steadied somewhat as the Summer turned to Autumn. Although Scarborough repeated the same score on the Seamer Road Ground, Scunthorpe still remained in touch with the League leaders. Twice seven goals were scored to emphasize that the claret and blues were no mugs. The first time was at Heanor, when Ernie Simms credited himself by scored four goals, and it was repeated just into October when Staveley Town called by.

Unfortunately, there was not to be a repeat of the bold F.A.Cup run of 1926-27 season. A home tie against Cleethorpes Town caused little bother, when Simms, again, scored four goals, in a 5-2 victory in Scunthorpe's favour.

The earliest known action photograph of Scunthorpe & Lindsey United, taken around 1928, looking towards the Henderson Avenue/Fox Street corner

It was the away trip to Gainsborough that turned out to be the stumbling block. The dark blues team contained three ex-Knuts, including Laurie McKenzie and not least the effervescent Shaw, who had already converted six of eight goals against Boston that season. At kick-off, close on five thousand spectators greeted the players with a barrier of noise, but it was the Trinity supporters who were still shouting at the end. Trinity won the day at a canter, 3-0, thus making amends for the loss of three out of four Midland League points United had already stolen in September.

Ernie Simms continued to show he was good value for his larger than average pay packet. However, the team he was playing alongside was not the dynamic all conquering one of a year ago and results began to go against them. Gradually the thoughts of another championship diminished as the Knuts slid down the table to just about the half-way mark. Certainly the finger was being pointed at the back quarters which frequently leaked simple goals. When Christmas brought the challenge of stiffer opponents in the shape of Grimsby Town, United could not rise to the bait, and four points were lost in two days. Worse was to follow when Staveley exacted their revenge on the first Monday of the New Year, causing Scunthorpe a 3-0 embarrassment.

At the end of January all remote chances of being among the Midland League leaders had disappeared. Talk was that they were about to lose the services of Ernie Simms. Already he had scored thirty League and Cup goals, and his most recent treat for the fans was a trio of strikes in the beating of Newark in mid-February. This time the whispers were to be true, and Ernie Simms played his last game in the Scunthorpe colours in the home defeat by Wath on 21st February 1928. Coincidentally his next game for his new club, York City, was when they entertained Scunthorpe in Yorkshire.

Scunthorpe and Lindsey United were not to miss the absence of Simms as much as they thought. It was true that this man had scored eighty-eight goals in just over a season and a half, but his departure allowed Maw and Bowers to be given a chance. Both men impressed with their every opportunity. On a purely percentage basis, Jack Bowers total of fourteen goals in nine games was even better than that of Simms. This strike rate enabled the Club to regain its appetite, and only one of the last nine games was not won. Although this sort of form came far too late, it did leave the Club optimistic for the future.

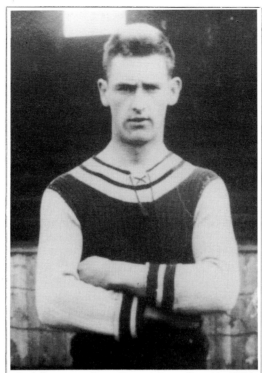

Jack Bowers-a three times International in 1934

The final analysis of the 1927-28 season showed that Scunthorpe had finished eighth out of twenty-three clubs, way off the pace set by Gainsborough Trinity. A least the statistics revealed that the twenty-three wins were six more than the results in the defeats column, but this should have been expected from former champions. Perhaps it was the time to reflect on the reasons for not offering the championship team more money to stay. Nevertheless, the goals scored, one hundred and eighteen, was a respectable total, while those conceded, eighty-five, was on a par with all but the top sides. Now the Club had the yardstick to aim for future improvement.

~ 1928-29 ~

When the fixture lists arrived on Harry Allcock's desk for the 1928-29 season it was obvious the players would be in for a veritable marathon. No less than twenty six teams were in competition for the covered Midland League trophy, and simple arithmetics meant that each team would be expected to complete fifty league games. Any side with strength in depth should be better suited for the long haul ahead.

The coming season at the Old Showground was to see many changes. Only Unwin, Severn, Skull, Maw and Allen were given the green light for more service. Jack Bowers had been too good a bargain for Derby County to miss out on and they had stepped in with a fee for his signature. This tall centre-forward went on to play three times for his country in 1934. He gained a First Division runners-up medal whilst with the Rams, and also set a goalscoring record of thirty-seven strikes in the 1930-31 season, a total still standing in the books at the Midlands club today. Later Bowers assisted Leicester City to the Second Division title.

The great number of games played by Scunthorpe during the 1928-29 season meant that the vast number of men used for a handful of matches makes the role call too long a list to detail. However, Hill was generally partner to Severn, whilst Skull played at right-half alongside the cheerful George Mooney from Newcastle at centre-half, and Bailey appeared on the left side. The forwards were usually compensated by Wadsworth on the right-wing, who appeared in the team from October alongside Arthur Maw, but the centre-forward post was not filled until the second-half of the season when Smith took over regular duty. Before then seven men had tried the number nine shirt, all without success. On the left side Allen had no problem in retaining his inside position, and by now was a firm favourite of the crowd.

Allen was to link up with Webb, who was also considered to be an excellent signing. The last point of discussion had to be the occupation of the goalkeeper's jersey. Unwin filled the spot in the first four games, before being succeeded by Watson for the rest of the season until February. From that time, until the end of the campaign, the gloves were handed to Walker, who had been with Sheffield Wednesday.

The unsettled nature and the number of changes to the team were an obvious consequence to the worse start to a Midland League season since the initial entry of 1912-13. After eight games and only a victory against moderate Doncaster Rovers Reserves, the Knuts were at the wrong end of the table. The greatest of embarrassments in this pathetic run came in the form of a 7-0 thrashing at the hands of a rampant Shirebrook side. United's bunch of players trudged off as a thoroughly humiliated troop on a totally forgettable afternoon.

The inevitable changes enabled the Club to turn the corner and head in the right direction, back up the Midland League. Unfortunately, those early season ditherings were to cost the Knuts dearly, and any chances of making a real impact upon the leadership had already evaporated. The only compensation to the poor Midland League form for supporters was an excellent run in the F.A.Cup. This time the luck of the draw gave them, all but one, away ties. Generally speaking the cup-ties were closely fought games, but Barton Town, Spalding, and Cleethorpes did not provide the sort of obstacles that Midland League opposition might expect to cause. Those victories earned the Club a visit to Boston, where Wadsworth supplied the only goal of the game, coming in to shoot home from the right-wing position.

Disappointment came in the final qualifying round when they lost 2-1 at Grantham. Arthur Maw scored Scunthorpe's goal, and they were unlucky not to share the spoils when a late 'goal' was disallowed. Grantham went on to reach the second round proper by beating Rhyl Athletic 1-0, but then lost at Wigan 1-2

Thankfully, by New Years Day, Scunthorpe and Lindsey United had improved so dramatically that they were back in the top half of the League. The team had certainly been a Jeckle and Hyde combination, and thirteen games on the trot saw them beaten on just one occasion. Probably the best part of this period came in the two Christmas games against the Mariners' Reserve team when narrow 2-1 victories over Grimsby were squeezed out of each tussle.

United were finally checked by the steamroller effect of Mansfield Town, still trying to prise open the door into the Football League. They still had a couple of years to wait, but were happy to win the Midland League championship, streets ahead of everyone else. Scunthorpe could provide no answer to the Nottinghamshire men, and were thankful that the away game on 5th January only ended 5-0. A month later at the Old Showground the Stags were equally dominant and a 3-0 scoreline wrapped up the double.

Scunthorpe and Lindsey United had to wait until the final match of the fixtures for their best result. Admittedly the opposition of Wath was not the strongest to call by the Old Showground, but United failed to show any signs of tired legs after the gruelling season and a 7-2 score thrilled the Scunthorpe public. At this time Smith, from local Sheffield football, was leading the line and Calladine, making a single appearance, each scored a hat-trick. Tommy Allen weighed in with the seventh goal. The match set the seal on a less than illustrious season, when the team finished eleventh of twenty-six runners. At least the goal difference was positive, although only just. The team also won twenty games against sixteen lost. It was by no means a complete disaster, but it was hardly 'Boys Own Annual' stuff. There surely needed to be an improvement from the new players in the coming year, but at least young Calladine would be amongst those starters, who was given the opportunity, thanks to his Wath game efforts.

For a footnote on the 1928-29 season, United played Doncaster Rovers in a freshly contrived "Grimsby Evening Telegraph, War Memorial Hospital Cup" competition, locally referred to as the "Hospital Cup". Rovers, very sportingly sent a strong side to support the charitable event, and a reasonable crowd assembled to witness the proceedings. At the end of ninety minutes neither side had the advantage, and a further half an hour still failed to separate them. However, Scunthorpe called correctly on the toss of a coin to become the first holders of what would become an extremely popular event up until the next hostility period, bringing a number of Football League clubs to the Old Showground on an invitation basis.

~ 1929-30 ~

The 1929-30 season started with the knowledge that young protégé Arthur Maw was to depart for what would be a distinguished career in the football League, starting at Notts County. He left with the full blessing from all concerned at his old club, and for Scunthorpe's troubles a cheque was sent in the post for Harry Allcock to deal with. Of the remainder of the team only Severn, Skull, Bailey, Smalley and Calladine would carry on.

The influx of new blood included a goalkeeper from Frickley Colliery in the form of Bromage. He came after playing well against Scunthorpe previously, and would offer a solution to a situation where a number of players had not resolved the problem in a satisfactory manner during the last season. Bromage was to prove to be the complete answer, and his name would be printed in the programme for a number of years to come. In his initial spell only injury on a single occasion prevented him playing in every Cup and League fixture. To support Bromage, Len Severn was accompanied at left full-back by John Baynham, who hailed from Yeo. Skull and Bailey continued to patrol the midfield, and their centre pivot was to be Cooke of Royston.

The new look forwards included a number of players who supporters were to become accustomed to; Smalley initially was to lead the line. However, following some stirring performances in the Midland League and the F.A.Cup, Smalley was transformed for a fee to Blackpool in November 1929, and his place was generally taken by Baldwin of

Oldham Athletic fame. The inside men to flank this position were destined to be the very useful former Portsmouth man Stringfellow, and the ever improving Calladine. On the right-wing Simmons was to cause plenty of concern amongst opposition defences, while Beynon of Halifax Town and Swansea Town experience completed the picture on a team that would blend together in first class order as the months progressed.

The season began on the last day of August. Hull City Reserves provided a good opposition, and both teams lost plenty of sweat in the summer heat, but it was Scunthorpe who came out on top, 3-1, without totally dominating the game. In the early part of the championship run this was to be the pattern. Scunthorpe and Lindsey United's name was always going to be towards the higher League placings, but they lacked the ability to dominate their opponents. Lincoln City Reserves gave them their first real test, and United lost 2-0 at Sincil Bank against a team they should have beaten if aspirations of Midland League honours were to materialize in May. It was further emphasized in October, and into November, when a consecutive run of three matches, all away from the Showground, were lost against Gainsborough Trinity, Rotherham United Reserves (the recent result of Rotherham County and Rotherham Town amalgamating), and Chesterfield Reserves. The biggest shock was at Trinity, where the 4-1 reverse was a great disappointment considering that the dark blues had already succumbed to the Knuts by a 5-0 scoreline only weeks earlier. The scapegoat was their inconsistency.

On a far brighter front the headline of the 1929-30 season was to be the F.A.Cup. This was to be the year the team embarked on a record breaking run, and at last they broke through the psychological barrier of reaching the first round proper of the prestigious competition. The game against Selby Town, played on foreign soil, started the ball rolling. This was, albeit, a fairly humble beginning, but United were good value with a 3-1 result. In the next round another team from the same town, Selby Olympia, was paired against the Knuts and they made the team work hard for the 1-0 advantage at the end of the game. Simmons on the right flank notched the only goal with an accurate shot. Into the Autumn, Goole Town were the next to feel the fighting force of United's ever developing team. Simmons again was on target, this time supplying two strikes in the 2-1 victory.

The F.A. Cup was certainly bringing out the best in Scunthorpe and Lindsey United. The supporters saw it as a welcome diversion from the run of the mill Midland League fare, particularly as the team was now winning. Next in line for the chop was Broughton from Yorkshire, who found themselves way out of their depth and lost 7-0. Kennedy, making a rare appearance in place of the injured Calladine, scored four goals. Scunthorpe found themselves in the last qualifier once again, and this time there would be no mistake. Their task was to overcome South Kirby on the other side of Doncaster. The United supporters needed to have no fears, for the 6-1 victory was emphatic. Smalley, Simmons and Stringfellow each registered a pair of goals to earn a passage to the advanced stage of the Cup.

The luck of the draw brought Scunthorpe and Lindsey United together with Hartlepool at the Old Showground. 5,305 supporters were in attendance, making as much noise as possible to encourage the gallant claret and blues. Scunthorpe lined-up with the following eleven players: Bromage; Severn; Baynham; Skull; Cooke; Bailey; Simmons; Stringfellow; Smalley, Calladine and Beynon. The match kicked off in typical cup-tie style. Both teams tested each other, and Bromage was into early action in the Scunthorpe goal. Gradually it was the home side that began to gain the upper hand, and not long before the interval the game reached its climax. Stringfellow fed a perfect ball through to Smalley, who controlled it and then let fly into the top corner of the net.

It was a just reward for the team's diligence. In the second-half the pace was as keen as ever, and United were lucky to survive when Hartlepool scrambled the ball in from a goalmouth scrum. Fortunately the referee had blown his whistle and an enormous sigh of relief came from the terraces. Finally, after a last ten minutes of wishing time away, it was the Scunthorpe supporters that roared their heroes off the pitch. There was more than a little interest in the sports report broadcasted into Scunthorpe and Lindsey United's followers homes over the radio on the next Monday. It was then that great excitement gripped the town when it was learned that Scunthorpe would receive Rotherham United at the Old Showground. The match was to break the previous attendance record out of sight, as 8,030 patrons passed through the turnstiles.

Scunthorpe retained the same team that had done sterling service in the Hartlepool game. Everything was on target for a shock Scunthorpe win as they produced a brand of soccer way beyond their station. Goals by Smalley and another two from Smalley helped to put the Knuts 3-1 up as the time ticked away. Then naive defending, mixed with a little stage fright, allowed Rotherham to rather fortunately sneak back into the game and draw level. The disappointment was obvious for all to see.

During mid-week it was back to Millmoor for the same actors to set the stage for another breathtaking scrap. Once again the non-Leaguers were to take all the accolades for their fighting qualities. Rotherham went two up, but a Beynon penalty reduced the arrears by the interval. In the second-half Smalley set the visiting supporters alight with an equalizer as he volleyed home an unstoppable shot. Rotherham restored the lead, but in an end-to-end game Caladine headed the Knuts level for a second time.

Only ten minutes remained when Rotherham made their full time professional fitness tell over United's tiring squad. Two more goals looked to have made the tie safe, but to give the visitors credit they came again and scored in the last minute through Beynon. It had been an incredible tie and the 5-4 score reflected the tremendous effort and entertainment served by both sides. The reward for Rotherham United was a home game against Nottingham Forest. Although this was lost 5-0, it provided much cash for their coffers at a critical financial time.

Returning to Midland League duty may have seemed a little mundane, but this team gained a reputation for playing attractive football, and although the Cup-ties had left games in hand there was little chance of challenging for the top spots in the table. Even the loss of Smalley, after the Cup run had finished, did not upset the team's balance. These men also overcame the usual complaint of lack of goalscoring and could almost guarantee a couple of goals, even in defeat. Calladine, Baldwin and Beynon all netted over twenty goals each, while Stringfellow came next, also in double figures.

Among the highlights of the 1929-30 season, the draw against Scarborough, the runaway champions, must have rated as polished a performance as any. United showed plenty of composure against a team who went on to score one hundred and forty-three goals, particularly in view of the 1-1 result. The home game against Lincoln City Reserves was another closely fought encounter, this time the reward was a 2-1 victory against opponents very highly placed up the table. These matches gave a far better yardstick as to how good United were, rather then when they beat Stavely Town 9-0 on 10th April 1930. In contrast with this high win against inferior opposition, within eleven days United had not only conceded the double to third placed Bradford Park Avenue Reserves, but had been embarrassed 2-5 at home and 9-0 away. Perhaps this was down to the loss of their reliable defender Cooke, who had been sold to Hull City. It certainly left an otherwise excellent season just a little flat.

The final league table showed that Scunthorpe United had finished in seventh place. They scored one hundred and twenty-four goals, more than any other team to that time, however there had been fifty games during the campaign. Honour for the top goalscorer went to Calladine who notched thirty two League and Cup goals. Financially the Club was not out of the woods by any means, but the position had not been impeded by the revenue forthcoming from the extended F.A.Cup exploits. More money was raised as an indirect consequence of the Cup, for Rotherham United had been so impressed by Frank Skull that they came back with a small fee, which took the former Middlesbrough man to Millmoor.

~ 1930-31 ~

The 1930-31 season came at the start of a decade when the attitudes of people were changing. Football was still the king, but money was scarce and for a product to be bought it had to be attractive. This was a point that Scunthorpe and Lindsey Football Club had to bare in mind in an ever changing world.

Frank Skull - the first player to exceed 300 appearances for the Club.

To go along with the change, in an effort to achieve perfection, Bromage, Baynon, Bailey, Stringfellow and Beynon were retained as the backbone of the structure for the coming season..

Scunthorpe chose a number of useful men as replacements for the departing old guard. In defence Webster came as Baynham's full-back companion, having had experience at Sheffield United, Lincoln City and Walsall. Frank Skull was replaced by Pattison, who swapped clubs with his predecessor, and was to become very popular with the home supporters. Later, 'Pat' was to take up the centre-forward position, and he proved a very dangerous character in front of goal. Between Pattison and Bailey, the tall figure of Hilton from Notts County was not totally suited, and Ross, the Scotsman, of equal size, stood in with far greater success. His inclusion coincided with that of Grimsby-born Joey Johnson, who took Pattison's place when the switch to the forward line was made. Johnson was not the same Joey who figured in the 1926-27 championship side. This player was to develop into a cultured half-back before being transferred to Bristol City. Later he was to appear for England whilst with Stoke City, and playing alongside a youthful Stanley Matthews.

The forward line eventually settled and was made up of Oakton, Stringfellow, Rawling, Green and Beynon; Oakton came in from Grimsby Town, Rawling from Boston and Green from Denaby. Of the other players on the peripheral, Wainwright was to figure most, being a left-sided utility man who was once at Sheffield United.

Once the season got underway, it was obvious that this team was going to take some time to settle. An away defeat at Wombwell did not auger well. Wombwell had finished in a lowly table slot in the last season of confrontation, and were destined to be next but one from the bottom in this current round. It was not until the 7-2 thrashing of Rotherham's 'stiffs', that the tide seemed to have turned. This was not made so obvious at Oakwell when the Knuts came in a poor second to the strong Barnsley team, losing 6-2.

Drastic action was required, and one solution was drafting Pattison into the goalscoring role at the end of October, where he duly supplied two goals in beating Loughborough Corinthians 4-2 at the Old Showground. Within one week 'Pat' repeated the act, this time at Scarborough, with the same score. His performances continued with consecutive hat-tricks in the Midland League against Notts County Reserves and Chesterfield Reserves.

November saw United pitched into battle against Worcester City in the F.A.Cup. The success in the competition of 1929-30 gave the Club exemption from the early qualifiers, and thus cut down some of the annual fixture congestion. Worcester were an unknown quantity, but something like the opposition strength of Kettering in 1926-27 was to be expected. The game attracted over three thousand spectators, and although Scunthorpe did not have everything their own way, the 3-0 result was a demonstration that generally they were in charge. The prize for victory meant yet another short tour down the road to Lincolnshire rivals Gainsborough Trinity in the first round, but this time it was Gainsborough's turn to be favoured by lady luck in a close 1-0 match. Gainsborough eventually lost out in the second round to Southport at home 4-0. Their conquerors from the Third Division North League went on to make all the headlines as amazingly they reached the sixth round, before crashing out 9-1 to Everton.

Back in the harness of their Midland League chores, Scunthorpe found that it was Pattison who was still firing all the bullets for their goals. He had scored twice against Worcester in the Cup, but went two better when netting four times on the Saturday before Christmas at Frickley, where Scunthorpe's superiority was illustrated by the emphatic 6-0 result.

The winter months saw Scunthorpe and Lindsey United's League position as something akin to a cork bobbing up and down on the water. Down one minute, then up the next. This was typified by six consecutive matches at the end of January and the start of February. The first three were all lost and the next three won. The arrival of windswept March further demonstrated United's inconsistency in a pair of games against the highly placed Nottingham Forest Reserves. When the Scunthorpe players arrived at the City Ground they knew they would be in for a busy afternoon, especially against the Robin Hood team that finally finished the season on one hundred and fifty-two goals. However, they did not bargain for a 9-0 scoreline which was the final outcome. Forty-eight hours and three Scunthorpe team changes later the roles were reversed, as this time the Knuts played hosts. Only a very brave man would have put money on a home victory, but Pattison's goal gave Scunthorpe a 1-0 present few expected.

The football season was ebbing away when the first flowers of Spring appeared. It was at this time the Club enjoyed a couple of worthy wins. At Mansfield it was Scunthorpe who took advantage of some defensive errors to ease in front and be victorious by 4-3. Two games later they bagged a couple more League points, this time by beating Bradford City (eventual runners-up), at the Old Showground. The 3-1 success came thanks to two goals by Pattison and another from Stringfellow and it helped to avenge an earlier defeat at Valley Parade, Bradford.

If that level of form had been maintained the Club would have fared better than eleventh place on the League ladder, but despite two remaining home fixtures at the very end of the season, the team managed to conjure up two inept performances and lose them both, to Chesterfield and Mansfield respectively. The close season gave the Board time to reflect on the pluses and minuses of the year's work, and to make the inevitable changes that occurred at this time of the season when contracts had run out.

When the long shadows of the failing Summer's evenings fell across the Old Showground grass, much spadework had been completed in assembling what was hoped would be a stronger squad of players with the right blend youth and experience. Indeed, throughout the forthcoming 1931-32 season plenty of local talent would be given the opportunity to shine.

~ 1931-32 ~

The goalkeeper's jersey was still very much the property of the reliable Bromage and only the occasional injury kept him away from active service. In the back quarters Charlie Cross became the right side partner to Baynham, having gained valuable experience in the odd outing during the last campaign. Cross was to become one of the successes of the year, retaining his place throughout all the proceedings to come. The pair were joined by Staniland and Stimpson on a regular basis, who stood either side of either Grainger or Wilson. Staniland at right-half had been spotted in local circles like Cross, and boasted of Broughton Rangers as his previous club. Stimpson on the other side came from further afield, having been noted representing the colours of Mansfield Town and Notts County. The central pivot position was more of a problem. First ex-Hull City man Grainger was given an opportunity, and then he was succeeded by Sheffield Junior Wilson, but even the latter was not to retain his position to the satisfaction of the board, and at least five other faces took up the number five shirt.

The forward line was much changed as well. Gone was the popular Pattison to be replaced by Adams, but after half a dozen appearances he was judged not to be up to standard and the directors replaced him with an extremely useful goalscorer in Methven, who had been with Derby County and then Sheffield United. His inside men would be Hubbard on the right side and Dawson on the left. Hubbard, like Methven, did not start the season, being signed for duty in September from Manton Colliery. Despite limited credentials he was to fit better in the jigsaw than the failures that went before. Dawson, who came from Louth, saw the season out in its entirety, but the right-wing berth was yet another problem. Local man Daws filled the spot to some satisfaction, but it was decided that Tucker from Rotherham area football should be given a chance in the second-half of the season.

Finally, for the outside-left slot Walter "Ginner" Reed, a local man, took preference over Isaac from Louth Town. Reed was so skilful on the far side of the pitch, continuously sending over a stream of accurate crosses, that he attracted the attention of the London aristocrats of Arsenal. In March 1932 his expenses were paid to the capital and Herbert Chapman, the famous Gunners manager of the day, invited Reed to sign. Scunthorpe were happy to receive a modest cheque and move Stimpson into the vacancy. In turn the hole left by Stimpson was filled by another local lad, Sharman.

Scunthorpe and Lindsey United began the season in good enough form, winning the first two fixtures, both at home, to Mansfield Town Reserves and Boston. The next game, also at the Old Showground, saw them go down to Scarborough and start a run of four matches in which only one point was picked up. Even at this tender stage of the season the directors knew they would have to step in to make team alterations, especially when the natives became restless as a result of a loss at neighbours Gainsborough. The necessary changes were made with instant success, and Mexborough were the first victims, losing 4-1 up the Doncaster Road.

Within a week of beating Mexborough, Methven was in the United team making his debut for Gainsborough Trinity's visit in the second fixture. This was only the eighth game since the start of the proceedings, but already six team members from the first day were no longer in the side. Trinity completed the double in their afternoon's work, but Methven scored and the corner was about to be turned.

United entered the October of 1931 in a mid-table position. Their cause was helped by an interesting run of form which had Scunthorpe followers in good heart, as four goals were registered in each of three consecutive games. Methven had his name on the score sheet on all occasions. Then, either side of the F.A.Cup qualifying game against Sutton Junction, two Midland League away fixtures were completed with 6-1 results. The problem was that only one ended in the Knuts favour. At Mexborough, the positive score brought a home and away double, but at Barnsley the smiles turned to gloom. This game was a full turn around of fortune, for the Oakwell Reserves had been beaten 4-2 in Scunthorpe.

Scunthorpe and Lindsey United were once again allowed to opt out of the early qualifying rounds of the Cup. It was not until the second week in November when they put the league scene on hold in order to play in the Nation's favourite competition. Sutton Junction were not in the same class as United in the first of the series, a fact reflected in the comfortable 7-1 score. The Scunthorpe goals came by way of Hubbard, a hat-trick, Methven, a pair, Grainger and Dawson.

The victory brought great jubilation to the town, and the Club waited with baited breath for the announcement of the Cup draw. It was soon learned that their numbered ball was first out of the hat and followed by that of Third Division North Rochdale, a strong side, but one that was by no means invincible, particularly with the United's advantage of home soil. On the day of the game, the question of Rochdale's resilience was put to the test, and roared on by a crowd declared at 4,800, United rolled up their sleeves in true Cup-tie fashion. The match was a see-saw affair, but it was Scunthorpe who triumphed 2-1, thanks to goals by Methven and Hubbard.

The reward for United's labours was another home tie in the Second Round. Their opponents this time were Queen's Park Rangers, not only Scunthorpe's first opponents from the Third Division South, but also the first encounter against a team from London.

The gate of 7,993 was the second highest to that date, and had the Old Showground bulging at the seams; the figure was only a handful short of the top attendance which had been set in the game against Rotherham. If Rangers had brought the same number of supporters as the Millers, then the record would surely have fallen. Even so at least one football special was run out of Kings Cross by the Great Northern Railway, and considering the long distance involved, the visitors in blue hoops were very well represented.

The game against Queen's Park Rangers was one not to be to remembered by local supporters. Reports of the game suggest that United were never allowed to get into their stride. Rangers comfortably sewed up the proceedings from early on, and overstretched the home defenders throughout. At the end of the ninety minutes the 'R's' were celebrating a 4-1 passage into the hat with the big boys of the First and Second Division. The Scunthorpe goal came by way of a consolation penalty spot conversion by Baynham. Queen's Park Rangers beat Leeds United 3-1 at Loftus Road in the Third Round, but another trek up the country to Huddersfield saw their dreams vanquished when they crashed 5-0.

Meanwhile, the Midland League programme was still going in fit and starts. Christmas, in particular, was a cheerless time. Grimsby Town had become the usual Yuletide opponents, and backed by a first team that was in or on the fringe of the First Division, the Mariners Reserves were on the verge of a period that would bring three Championships and a second place. It meant that the pair of games between the two always provided the claret and blues with the sternest of tests. This season was no exception, and a home result of 2-4 was followed the next day at Blundell Park by a score of 0-3, confirmed what was expected. On New Year's Day, the tale of woe continued at Wombwell when United lost 5-3, and the next day at Bradford Park Avenue Reserves the shell-shocked troops capitulated 6-0.

The dismal run of form found the Club well down the Midland League. There was also the inevitable knock-on effect through the turnstiles as gates tumbled and interest waned. However, the rest of January was not quite as severe as the chilled weather. A recovery was staged as the team pulled themselves up by the bootlaces to beat Frickley, Grantham and Chesterfield Reserves, but it was too little too late. Form suffered into the last phase of the activities as too many team changes took place. Only Bromage, Cross, Baynham, Staniland, Stimpson and Dawson lasted the pace throughout the full length of the season.

Scunthorpe and Lindsey United's campaign petered out as April and May brought the Spring. Those two months saw the team settle for only two wins in ten games, although another four League points were extracted from draws. Towards the twilight end of the fixture card a lack of goalscoring came to the forefront as one of the side's problems. The ghost was finally given up when Newark proved too strong for them in the last game, and United went down 2-1.

It left the Knuts in a disappointing ninth League place, twenty six points off Bradford Park Avenue Reserves on seventy-five. Bradford had finished joint top with Grimsby Town Reserves, and the competition rules required them to win the League outright by means of a play-off.

Scunthorpe's directors could look back on the 1931-32 season and at least glean a little satisfaction. The main reason was that the team had provided a keen fight, even when under mounting pressure. A number of locally produced men had appeared when the opportunity presented itself. It suggested that the immediate area was worth investigating to try to unearth useful talent, and Walter Reed was a prime example. Also, the League table revealed that Scarborough above them, was the only non-League club playing a first team in the Midland League. The rest of the sides were Reserve elevens of Football League outfits who were usually tough opposition containing experienced players.

~1932-33 ~

The competitive nature of the Midland League meant that the Club had looked far and wide to be prepared for the 1932-33 season in an effort to provide a meaningful challenge for the championship trophy. At the same time local talent was still on the menu. Bromage's reign in goal was to come to an end after a dozen matches, and he had to surrender his place to the agile Gordon Young from Sheffield Wednesday. Young came to the Club with excellent credentials and he would wear the green jumper of Scunthorpe for a number of terms to come.

In front of Young, the directors decided to give their blessing to the previous combination of Cross and Baynham. This was a rare exception to the rule, where at least one of the full-backs had always been crossmatched. Staniland at half-back was another player thought worthy of a second contract. He was to operate solely at right-half, but his partners Milson, Barke and Sharman would swap and change. Depending on availability and favour, these four men shared the middle order. Milson was making his second set of appearances for Scunthorpe having gained valuable experience at Charlton Athletic following his move South in 1928.

The forward line for the 1932-33 season had only two survivors from the old guard. Hubbard had already impressed with his skill and keen sense in front of goal. He was given the green light to either lead the new attack or guide his new centre-forward, Price. The rest of the line was to consist of Tucker from the old school, and Murfin for the wings, with Chapman as the other inside player.

Harry Allcock - a devout Methodist, and United's prudent Secretary for 40 years from 1915

To a great extent this team was to have the advantage of keeping together as a compact unit, and, apart from the inevitable alterations for injury, it was not disrupted by the constant number of changes that had harassed the class of 1931-32.

Scunthorpe's team started with an easy pair of games against the Club that would finish a mile adrift at the bottom of the table, in Wombwell. The double gained might have seemed encouraging enough at the time but in the true light of day the 3-2 away win, followed by 3-0 at home was not as near the target as would have been hoped, considering the humble Yorkshire triers who conceded one hundred and ninety-five goals in forty-four games, and could muster just two wins and a paltry six league points.

The following pair of fixtures was to be far more meaningful. Scarborough were next to make their way to the players entrance on Henderson Avenue. The outcome was dramatic, and Scunthorpe were convincingly rattled by four goals without reply. Victory for the seaside outfit was no fluke, for within seven days the proof of the pudding was in Scunthorpe again eating humble pie, this time the result was even worse. Scarborough won 6-0 and in two games had made a complete mess of United's goal average. It was at this stage the players previously mentioned were assembled and the chaff taken from the wheat. The settled side selected for the future would soon turn the corner, but not without some hiccups along the way.

The road to recovery began with the visit of Gainsborough Trinity, always a team to add a few extra to the gate numbers. At last the home crowd were to have something to sing about. Hubbard opened the scoring with a thunderous drive for his first goal of the season, and supremacy was established with further conversions by Baynham, overlapping from full-back, and Murfin making his strike from the left of the goal. It was a welcome 3-0 victory and set the team on a cheerful unbeaten five match run.

The best in this episode was another score of 3-0, but it was the previous year's champions, Bradford Park Avenue, that were put to the sword. A week later, however, Bradford restored parity, breaking the unbeaten sequence with a crushing 7-0 defeat. There was no wonder Scunthorpe supporters were left perplexed by their team.

November saw Scunthorpe United with their heads above water, but in their usual position for this time of the season, based on past records. The aim continued to be to play as attractive football as possible and to hope to keep as near in touch with the leaders as they could. At the box office the situation was always tight and many people voted with their feet when the going became tough. Fortunately, enough loyal supporters drifted to each game up to Doncaster Road.

As usual, this time of the year brought the final qualifying round of the F.A.Cup just after firework night, and Scunthorpe hoped that the run would go with a bang. Burton Town were drawn to be played at the Old Showground, and they would not be a barrier to the Knuts' ambitions. The star of the show turned out to be Murfin who plundered three goals. Hubbard added another and Scunthorpe eased through into the first round proper with the 4-1 advantage.

Lady luck was not on Scunthorpe and Lindsey United's side when the teams were pulled out of the bag for the next set of ties. The long journey into Cumberland to play non-League Workington was scant compensation for beating Burton Town. Workington were at least as strong as Scunthorpe but few in local football circles would have predicted a sound 5-1 dispensing of United from the competition. Certainly the tiring trek to the North-West could not veil the competency of the quick moving Workington spearhead; Workington then lost at Halifax in round two.

Once the F.A. competition had been bade farewell, Scunthorpe settled into a couple of first class scores back in the Midland League. Rotherham United Reserves were the first victims, losing 5-0 to a Scunthorpe side on one of their better days. The Millers second string fell for a sucker punch delivered in the form of a hat-trick from Chapman. In the next game a visit to York gained a plausible revenge for the indignity inflected by the City men earlier in the year's proceedings. The 4-2 score in Scunthorpe's favour was a handsome reflection of the efforts put up by all the eleven on display. Then in the next game, eight days before Christmas Day, United fell back down to earth losing 7-1 at Sincil Bank, Lincoln.

This setback did not hinder moral, even though it did little to enhance United's record in the League table, and Christmas was met with a mixed bag of results. A great deal of satisfaction was gained out of beating Bradford City Reserves, a handily placed team, by 4-2 on Christmas Eve Saturday. There was no Christmas Day fixture because of the Sabbath, and bad weather ruined the Boxing Day game at home to the Mariners' Reserves. The conditions were not as bad on the coast, and the Tuesday holiday game went ahead at Blundell Park. Although this was lost by a single goal from the Black and White stripes, Scunthorpe came away with a lot of credit. It would put them in good heart for the rest of the month and into the chill of January. Five matches followed, three on their travels at Mexborough, Grantham and Frickley, all of which saw the team in a victorious light.

During the remaining bite of winter Scunthorpe United continued with their programme of events, winning a few and losing about the same amount. Only Boston, Denaby and Loughborough were able to inflict any real damage on the team. Each of these clubs scored five against the Knuts, but wins in most games at the Old Showground neutralized the effect.

Late into April, Scunthorpe were able to come back with the right answer, for twice in consecutive games they blasted their way through six goal thrillers. The most rewarding was against Hull City Reserves at Doncaster Road, where sharpshooter Hubbard registered the season's best individual tally, with four goals in the game. United won the encounter 6-0. At Newark the 6-3 scoreline provided possibly their best spectacle of all the year's work. There now only remained a fortnight of the campaign, and three games, all at home, to finish the activities before another close season. The rearranged Grimsby Town match saw another close call, but the superior men from the coast edged it by a repeat of the 1-0 score. All that remained was a disappointing 5-2 loss against Chesterfield Reserves and for the conclusion, the beating of Newark 4-2. Scunthorpe had given a chance to Oates, from local sources, over the previous few matches, and he rewarded the faith put in him by the directors by scoring a trio of goals in his best performance to that date.

The record in the final League table showed a slight improvement over the last twenty-four months. In comparison with the 1931-32 results, this side had accumulated five more League points for two outings less. The goal difference had improved dramatically. For the first time in three years, more than a century of goals had hit the oppositions net, and although exactly a ton had been conceded, this represented four goals 'in the black', the first time since the 1929-30 season that a positive figure had been put on the slate.

Another aspect under scrutiny was the gate figures that were constantly on a roller coaster ride. There had been no significant improvement or deterioration on the year's trading, but the F.A.Cup had not produced the excellent extra revenue of more recent Cup exploits. The Barnsley Brewery continued to smile favourably on the Club, and what with their help and personal loans from the pockets of the Board, the Knuts continued to function to the satisfaction of most. Despite this situation prudence was still the key word.

~ 1933-34 ~

Scunthorpe and Lindsey United entered the phase offered by the 1933-34 season with an optimistic view. Boosted by the return of errant players in Ernie 'Pat' Pattison and Arthur Smalley from their travels, United had every reason to be so. At least with these two old warriors in attack, goals should not have been a problem in the immediate future. The situation was greatly improved when 'Paddy' Mills from Hull City joined, with his vast experience of goalscoring.. Barry and Allen made up the other forward positions, plus Walter Reed who had not been retained by the mighty Arsenal. Occasionally Bill Sumpter, late to be Editor of the Scunthorpe Star Newspaper, was used on the right-wing.

In the half-back division only Staniland was given another run, but in the 1933-34 season activities it would be his job to work from the left side of the pitch, while Davidson took his old post and Nicholson found himself favoured in the middle of the park. Charlie Cross resumed at right full-back and was to find a new partner in Hill. Bromage was not offered another contract, but Young was to be very much in evidence, demonstrating in particular his athleticism.

The economic situation faced by Scunthorpe was no different to that endured by other Midland League clubs, only some had not weathered the storm in the same fashion. In meant that on the starting grid there was six teams less competing in the season ahead. To compensate for the meagre total of thirty-two games Scunthorpe United was one of a handful of local sides from the County to become founder members of the Lincolnshire Senior League. The competition would consist of the Midland League sides of the district, including Gainsborough Trinity, Boston, Grantham and of course Scunthorpe, plus the Reserve teams of Lincolnshire's three Football League clubs.

The opening of the 1933-34 season could not have been bettered from United's point of view. Pattison led the way firing on all cylinders and the tremendous start had supporters whispering the word 'Championship'. They should have known better because it was only early days as yet. Barnsley were the first victims, offering little resistance to Pattison and company, as the player rose majestically to the challenge to score three beauties. In mid-week the outcome at Scarborough was far more encouraging than in recent times, and a draw was earned. Away wins at Boston and Gainsborough were topped up by a 6-0 hammering of Chesterfield Reserves, a team strong enough to finally settle just above Scunthorpe in the final analysis at the end of term. Even the absence of Pattison through injury failed to halt the side's excellent progress. Only the loss at Rotherham put the brakes on the Scunthorpe express, at the end of September.

The last Saturday in September saw Scunthorpe back in the hurly-burly of the F.A.Cup. This time they were expected to slug out the qualifying rounds with the other lesser non-League clubs. This was another welcome addition to the fixture card to supplement their income. They were again to have good fortune to be drawn at home in all their ties. Selby Town, 4-1, Humber United, 5-0 and Louth United, 4-1, were all easy passages.

Former Midland League members Heanor were next in line at the final qualifying hurdle stage. Even then Scunthorpe were seldom stretched for their victory. Pattison scored twice and others came from Sumpter and a rare strike from Cross, on an up field sortie, to earn a 4-2 result.

The interest in the first round of the Cup was as keen as ever. Another excited crowd bore witness to the events of the first November day, the size of which numbered over four thousand. Scunthorpe were the initial team to make an impact as Reed and Sumpter carved out chances from the wing for Smalley and Allen. Pattison, too went close on at least one occasion, testing the visiting custodian. At the back Mills and Nicholson won the honours for dominating the middle of the park. Finally Sumpter broke the deadlock, cutting in from the wing and sending a fierce shot past the groping hands of the Accrington Stanley number one.

At half-time, Scunthorpe's dressing room was by far the happiest. The mud-splattered troops trudged out for the second period, hoping to extend their one goal advantage. Reports suggested that they had enough opportunities, but they were all spurned by the over eager front line. Gradually Accrington came back into the game and the full-time players from the heart of hot-pot country made the last ten minutes the telling period of the game. It was at this stage when they pounced for the equalizer.

The 1-1 result meant another outing in the mid-week for the team bus. United's players had no fears as it made its winding way over the narrow roads across the Pennines. The prediction of a tough game did bear fruit, and Stanley were a far more formidable unit on their own Peel Park mud heap. Scunthorpe were by no means humiliated, but it was the home players who took the edge, punishing every mistake. Their 3-0 victory was a fair reflection of how far the Northern section side was in front of their non-League counterparts. If Scunthorpe had made progress they might had got as far as meeting Bristol Rovers, and possibly Millwall, as Accrington Stanley's future was dictated.

October Midland League assignments announced the team as being in first class condition. All four games were won, including an astonishing turn around against Rotherham United Reserves, which ended almost in cricket score fashion at 8-1. Sumpter took the match ball home for his prize after scoring a trio from his right wing berth.

After eleven games the Knuts stood proudly at the top of the table, but now at their zenith it did not take long to reach their nadir. Apart from a win at the start of December, the rest of the month was a total failure.

A Packed Sincil Bank ground watch Lincoln City Reserves in action against United. (Probably in 1934) Scunthorpe players include 'keeper - Young, Allen and Cross.

It was not until mid-January before two more points would be levered from an opponents grasp, at a time of disruption through the annoyance of winter snows. Visits to Notts County Reserves and Doncaster Rovers Reserves saw the team return home after 4-2 maulings. On Christmas Day Grimsby Town, the goliath of the Division, whipped them soundly 5-1. On Boxing Day the Mariners were in town for the tussle at the Old Showground. Their play was as sharp as the knife that cut the Christmas Turkey. The 9-3 scoreline was devastating to all those connected with the Knuts and remains to this day the biggest defeat experienced on home soil. Scunthorpe and Linsdey United's players were left as breathless as the cold December air. Christmas was certainly off the menu in 1933 as far as football was concerned in this quarter of Lincolnshire.

It was probably as well that inclement weather put off the New Year games, because it gave the team time to reflect and regroup. The man made scapegoat for the nine goal hammering was young Lamming, making his one and only appearance that season as the Scunthorpe 'keeper. Just one other team change was thought necessary, and then it was back to business as usual. The unfortunate part of the run was that, rather unceremoniously, United had been dumped by the top teams in the League, and now they found themselves well off the pace, just over half way up the table. Although they did resurrect their aspirations briefly, when York City Reserves were crushed 6-1, it was now all too late.

The remainder of the season was to be something of an anti-climax. In the last section of the 1933-34 saga the team experienced a slowing down of goalscoring, with the exception of two matches. The failure of the forwards to convert in front of goal brought a number of caustic comments from the crowd, comparing them with the opposite gender. Certainly, four games without a worthy strike to their names did little to endear themselves to the hard-working steel workers of the town and Scunthorpe slipped further into the abyss of mid-table mediocrity. There was a brief moment of respite in the final chapter of events. Bradford Park Avenue Reserves were caught on a bad day late in March, and lost 5-3, while the last rites of the season were administered in an emphatic murder of Mexborough, by 6-0. Earlier in the year, Mexborough's eager forwards had stitched up Scunthorpe with a 6-2 scoreline, and so revenge was seen to be sweet. The ever-smiling Bill Sumpter made it another memorable afternoon from his point of view, scoring his second hat-trick of the season.

Mention should be given to the Lincolnshire Senior League which produced some memorable moments in its inaugural campaign. Grimsby Town not only took the Midland League title but also this new trophy. In so doing they won all four meetings with the Knuts. Gordon Young, in between the posts, would not forget the Senior League game at Blundell Park, because, for his bravery, he gained the distinction of being the first Scunthorpe player to be knocked out twice in one match. On the reverse side of the coin it was Gainsborough who felt the same degree of force, against Scunthorpe, for they too lost all four games between the pair in the competitions.

One piece of silverware that did land on the table was the Doncaster Invitation Cup. The semi-final game against Gainsborough was probably the best of the rounds, where Gainsborough suffered yet another defeat at the hands of United, losing a thrilling encounter 5-4. In the final Selby Town were overcome 3-1 in a more comfortable but less memorable affair.

The 1933-34 season closed in May with the showcase game created by the Hospital Cup, which Sheffield Wednesday won 3-1. The labours of the Midland League earned the players a sixth place in the reduced table. This was a disappointment, after so much promise at the initial stages of events. If there was a consolation it was that United had settled in the highest place of the non-League competitors, but a goal difference of plus three and only one more win than loss said it all.

It would have been a treat for Scunthorpe and Lindsey United supporters if the contracts offered to new men in the Summer had set the scene on some better results, but it was to be much of the same in 1934-35. Performances in some cases were to be as grey as the depressed state of the country, which was pessimistic that events in Europe might lead to another major conflict. At least there was to be better news on the football front.

~ 1934-35 ~

The meeting at Nottingham of the Midland League announced that it had accepted into the fold four new teams against the resignation of one. York City would not be competing, but Frickley Colliery and Grantham would return, along with Peterborough United and Norwich City Reserves filling the Division with welcome new blood.

To meet the new challenge a higher number of players than usual were retained. The back quarters were to find the left defensive spot troublesome to sort out. Roberts and Harrison had spells in occupation of the number three shirt, but the best solution was when Skull returned from his sojourn at Rotherham United to take the centre-half position, and Nicholson moved across to left back. Also in the half-back line was Davidson, who took over when Paddy Mills pushed up into the forward line on the right, and the slightly built Barkley to the left. In attack Pattison, Mills, Allen and Noble would be very much in evidence, sometimes supported by Fenwick, but there were two new men on the wings in Barley and Lax.

The pendulum of time soon swung round indicating the end of the trips to Cleethorpes for children to enjoy holidays playing on the beach, as it was time for football and an opportunity to let off steam on the terraces of the Old Showground.

Scunthorpe once again flattered to deceive. Pattison, Allen and Lax combined to beat Mexborough in South Yorkshire, and new boys, Peterborough, proved obstinate opposition at the Showground. No side was able to break the deadlock as the defenders took the biscuit in the honour stakes. The early season did not suffer from the congestion of extra

F.A.Cup matches in the qualifying rounds, with the team's exemption ticket won the previous term. It was not until Scunthorpe's fourth test on the calendar that the doubts began to creep back in. Gainsborough Trinity rolled up with their wicker basket full of kit and promptly showed the Knuts a trick or two since their own re-organisation of the Summer clearout. They demonstrated a far more direct form of football, brisk in attack and less vulnerable at the back than the side that lost to their old adversaries five times during the previous twelve month period. There was little between the teams on the afternoon, but it was Trinity's supporters who were the ones to celebrate the 3-2 final score. One month later they would enjoy another victory at the Northolme.

Throughout the Autumn months, Scunthorpe trundled along in the Midland League in their own sweet way. The lack of inspired games was reflected in the cash bags sent to the bank after each game - they were never completely full! To be fair to the players, they all worked hard enough but there were no flashes of great excitement, or sterling battles upsetting leading teams in the league, nor were there any major disasters. The 4-2 beating of Chesterfield Reserves did set the Claret and Blues in good spirit for the trials of the F.A. Cup on the first Saturday of November 1934.

Scunthorpe and Lindsey United had been given the good fortune of home advantage in the second visit of Kettering Town in the Cup. It was known that the Northamptonshire team was at least on level standing in the Southern League as the Knuts in their own competition. There would be no complacency if the team was to progress, and the side had to work hard. In the event one thousand spectators more than usual swarmed up the Doncaster Road and through the turnstiles. They were pleased to see an open game played in Cup-tie fashion, with no quarter asked and none given. Both sides scored twice to gain no overall supremacy.

Once again United were on their travels, knowing that the Thursday game would be no pushover and that the team in Red would be favourites on their own turf. Only on one occasion had Scunthorpe won away from home in the Cup after a draw at the Old Showground. The game was played on a heavy pitch and Gordon Young was frequently called into action, pushing the leather sphere around the posts to avoid conceding any goals. Despite constant pressure from the Robins, it was Scunthorpe who made the most of their chances. It would not be until late in the game that their tireless efforts were confirmed as a victory at the sounding of the referee's shrill whistle. Scunthorpe took the game by 3-1 on a day when it was the wingers who nailed their colours to the marksmen's list. Lax had converted two shots from the left, while youngster Barley drilled home the third from the other flank.

United found themselves in the draw for the first round proper with the Football League teams, and it was hoped to be paired at home to one of them. Instead it was the will of the Gods to send them South down to the Midlands to play Coventry City. The Sky Blues were domiciled in the Third Division at the time, jockeying for a place amongst the leading positions. A crowd of 12,939 packed into the tidy Highfield Road ground, the greatest number at that time to watch a game featuring Scunthorpe. From the Knut's point of view the extra revenue this brought was as much of the proceedings they would wish to remember. Coventry City completely overwhelmed them, and the bewildered Scunthorpe team had no answer to City's quick thrust in attack. Each of the home forwards scored in the 7-0 crushing. Coventry went on to beat Hartlepool in the North-East, then failed the more demanding test when they lost 5-1 to Birmingham City at St. Andrews.

The doldrums of that F.A.Cup defeat followed Scunthorpe United around for a number of weeks and their returns for the next games was as depressing as the drizzly weather. It was not long before they discovered how testing Norwich City Reserves could be. The trek down to East Anglia was made to seem even longer on the return journey following a sound smacking by the bright yellow Canaries. Norwich City's second side won a comfortable 5-0 victory, to add two points to a tally that was to make them the League's Runners-up. Incidently, the game was one in the last season on their old ground, The Nest, before they moved to Carrow Road. Fortunately there was only one more setback, a blistering 1-7 dive at Hull City, the worst ever score recorded against the Anlaby Road crew, before some good news could be announced from the Old Showground.

Only twelve months had passed since the debacle on Boxing Day 1934, when Grimsby Town caused the greatest humiliation that has ever occurred at the Old Showground. Clearly the wounds of frustration were still wide open in the minds of Scunthorpe and Lindsey United's supporters. Any revenge would extract some compensation against their local rivals. On Christmas Day swords were crossed again. The Mariners young squad was not as powerful as their predecessors, but on the other hand no Scunthorpe side sent to do battle at the Old Showground would capitulate in the same fashion. Bent on laying the black memory, United kicked off in a more determined fashion. The defence was far tighter, marshalled by Frank Skull, in a way that closed opponents down by not allowing them the space to create chances. There again, no opportunities were offered to the Knuts forwards. None, that is, until Sid Allen seized the one vital chance that won the game with an unstoppable shot. At least the ghost of Grimsby Town had been exorcized for the moment.

The next day Grimsby showed their power on the East Coast, and won 3-0, but this was followed by some better form by Scunthorpe. Norwich City Reserves made their first visit up to this part of Lincolnshire and gave a full contribution to a highly entertaining 3-2 result in the favour of United. The see-saw game was always in doubt until the final whistle. New Year was void of activity, but the party continued on the following two Saturdays as Rotherham United and Mexborough both left the Old Showground with only the sweat on their brow to show for their toil.

The onset of Winter gave little cheer for Scunthorpe supporters. Heads dropped in this cold period of time, and the goals dried up like running water turning to ice. It was certainly a barren section in the programme. At one stage in February no goals were scored, but ten conceded, in a three match run. Hopes of lifting themselves up the table evaporated as the poor results continued until the daffodils began to wilt in the lengthening days offered by April. Just as the winter results were depressing, the little flurry of form at the end of the campaign extended the frail hand of hope.

It was on April 19th that Scunthorpe began to turn the corner and restored some respectability to their lowly League position. At Scarborough, Paddy Mills scored the Club's first hat-trick of the season, and, with ammunition fired by Allen and Lax, United enterprisingly won 5-3, a rare victory in the land of candy floss. This Good Friday fixture was immediately backed the next day by an admirable 4-2 revenge against Hull's Reserves. On the following Tuesday this success was added to, as six goals were traded for the loss of two in the second leg of the affairs against Scarborough. All that remained were two away trips, to Bradford Park Avenue and Frickley Colliery. Scunthorpe settled for a share of the spoils, losing the first game, but going out on a high note, following the 5-1 beating of the miners' side.

Details of the final League table made uninteresting reading. United had to compromise for a lower than usual position of eleventh out of twenty teams. There would be no mention in dispatches for that conclusion, but at least the F.A.Cup had provided the local public houses with a topic of conversation for a couple of weeks. The rest of the statistics were best dispatched in the rubbish bin. Three months of cricket provided the well earned rest required for even the most optimistic of local football followers. At the same time the tremendous efforts under the most severe of financial restraints could not in any way be belittled. Scunthorpe United and its board were as ambitious as the next club, but patience was an important factor in the equation.

~1935-36~

The sands of time brought forth fresh opportunities and different fortune in the shape of the brand new 1935-36 season. The major change for this twelve months umbrella of club activities was that, to keep up the modern trend, United would appoint a player-manager for the first time, and he would be in charge of team selection. It came to pass that the man to be accepted from the shortlist of interested candidates was the former Derby County full-back Tom Crilly, signed from the South London club Crystal Palace. Crilly would oversee operations from the left-back position, alongside Charlie Cross on the right side of defence, while Gordon Young remained in between the sticks.

In the middle of the park Frank Skull would figure very little, instead he would use his experience, more often than not, casing a keen eye over the junior players in the reserve team who were now playing in the Yorkshire League. The half-back line would be chiefly made up of Davies, Millington and Barker. Mal Millington, in the centre of this trio, was to become something of a local legend. He came, with Yorkshire origins, from Torquay United. Mal was a strapping great lad bearing the type of grin which made Barnsley Bitter go sour. More than one of his teeth was to be sacrificed for the benefit of the team. Meanwhile on the left Geoff Barker would give many years service to the Club in two spells for the Knuts. Barker was a far more subtle player than Millington and went on to play football at a higher level.

The forward line was to see more of Noble and Allen particularly, and on lesser occasions Pattison, Chapman, Oates and Sumpter. A new man in Snaith would lead the line, supported by Kilsey, Noble or Lewis on the right, and Roberts and Lewis on the left. When the season came to pass this team was to prove to be no better, nor any worse than the Scunthorpe teams that had gone before them.

United's goalkeeper catches safely in the 3-1 replay victory at Kettering in November 1934. Another F.A.Cup (first) replay would not be won on foreign soil until 1997, at Ilkeston!

It was an eleven that only rarely conceded large scores, although at Burton a 6-1 reverse was reported. There were a number of 'highs' in the 1935-36 season that make interesting fables when plucked off the shelves of history. Perhaps the most outstanding example came in mid-September when the 'Silver Dawn' players coach trundled into Sincil Bank to allow the side to stretch their legs against the Imps second team. The supporters present were advised not to blink, at the risk of missing any of the incidents in a match so packed with memorable moments that they would have needed an abacus, to keep the score. At the risk of missing a goal the referee declared the result at the incredible sum of 8-5 in favour of the visitors. Snaith, above all, took the headline for his three successful efforts in front of goal.

A footnote of the Lincoln City against Scunthorpe tussles must be taken to its conclusion. On the first Saturday of the New Year, Lincoln rolled up at the Old Showground determined to seek revenge. In the event it was they who won the day when they outfoxed United by four goals to one. This meant that both sides had scored an aggregate of nine goals, and each was happy to gain two of the four League points at stake.

The F.A.Cup was another part of the 1935-36 campaign that would make the excitement of Scunthorpe supporters reach a high, although everything started in a fairly low key. Denaby had to be faced at home, and on paper did not pose too much of a threat. The United forwards soon got to grips with the game and twin strikes by Snaith and Lewis put the edge on Scunthorpe's play. Their 4-1 triumph was a true reflection of how much better they were on the day than their opposite numbers.

News of the draw for the first round proper brought a great deal of dismay to the town, for once again Scunthorpe had been paired away to Coventry City. At first some supporters thought it was a wind-up, and suggested that the numbered balls needed a further shake-up. When the realisation of the truth sank in those near to the Club wondered if it was worth turning up, in view of the previous season's seven goal thrashing. There was even more bad news from Coventry City, for instead of being just a leading Third Division South side, this season they actually sat on the pinnacle of the table, and would be declared champions in May.

Scunthorpe rolled up at Highfield Road hoping for the best, and with a much changed team from twelve months before. Player-manager Tom Grilly had made the team go through its paces and was well prepared by extra Cup training. This time the side was far more determined, and lined up; Cross, Crilly, Davies, Millington, Barker, Kilsby, Lewis, Snaith, Roberts and Allen. The notable moments for the Scunthorpe men was a tremendous fighting action by the defenders, and some quality goalkeeping by Gordon Young, who made full length saves on more than one occasion. Honours in attack went to Snaith, who not only survived a bruising afternoon at the hands of the no-nonsense Sky Blues defence, but rounded off a marvellous performance with Scunthorpe's goal. It was with great delight that the town received notification of the outstanding one each draw.

Scunthorpe and Lindsey United had to wait just under a fortnight before the replay could be staged. A partisan crowd of 7084 spectators gathered around the perimeter of the Old Showground pitch, breaths held in anticipation of a new Cup shock. However, first on ten minutes then after half an hour they were rocked back on their boots as Coventry City's swift moving forwards eased into a two goal lead.

The second goal brought silence that shouted. Then from the terraces came the call 'Play up the Knuts'. The next few moments were pure 'Boys Own Paper' material. Lifting their game, Scunthorpe surged down the field. Kilsby won a free kick in front of goal allowing Davies to shoot through the wall to reduce the arrears. Moments later Kilsby was involved again, pushing the ball to Roberts for his opportunity to slam home. Then, as if the crowd was not delirious enough, Kilsby made them more so by supplying another accurate pass, this time giving Lewis space to fire Scunthorpe into a 3-2 lead by half time.

The crowd was buzzing with emotion and the interval whistle was doubtless an unwanted distraction. No supporter would have gambled on Scunthorpe's turn around after they were two goals adrift. In the second-half there was no stopping them, although for those persons watching the tension was electric. The Knuts needed another goal to settle the tie, and it was 'King for a Day' Kilsby who was up for it, sealing a display worthy of a much greater theatre. Certainly Kilsby and the 4-2 result was on the lips of every furnace hand throughout all the steelworks in each corner of the town.

The reward for Scunthorpe for this phenomenal performance was the rather sticky away tour to the Wirral for a game against Tranmere Rovers. It was obvious that the Northern Section team had sent their scouts to spy on the Lincolnshire side, and never did they allow the enthusiasm of the non-Leaguers to surface. Their forwards were in excellent form and had no problems in winning the day by 6-2. Scunthorpe received all the pats on the back for a courageous effort. At least the bank manager would have a smile on his face when he was met by Harry Allcock on the following Monday morning.

Returning to the Midland League, Scunthorpe for once could gloat over the way that Grimsby Town Reserves were turned over. Never could anyone remember such a feast on Christmas Day. The Mariners were certainly made to do the turkey trot as they were comprehensively roasted 5-0. Only Allen in the forward line failed to register while Snaith's present to the supporters was a pair.

On Boxing Day Crilly was forced to withdraw himself, but the huge presence of Frank Skull made sure the strength of the team was not diminished. The reversal of home advantage made the young Mariners a far more difficult proposition, and the Blundell Park game was probably a better one to watch, being a much closer contest than hours before. Not to be outdone, the Scunthorpe lads again showed their mastery and won the honours 3-2.

Late in the year's round of events the pick of what remained was the visit to Mexborough. The Yorkshire men had earned a draw on the opening day of the season at Scunthorpe. Much to everyone's surprise this was the occasion the Knuts would fire all guns in the second meeting. It was a case of grasping every opportunity as the sharpshooters in claret and blue came up trumps with each trick they tried. They equalled the Lincoln total, but played tighter in all the back quarters to record an inspiring 8-3 result. This time all of the forward line did score and Snaith managed the golden three.

When the final Midland League table was published, in the first week of May, United were in mid-table, having forty points from forty games. There were four other candidates with similar credentials, but Scunthorpe's goals scored column showed a deficit of four compared with the goals against. Snaith finished the year as the leading goalscorer on twenty-three in League and Cup action, while Roberts and Kilsby made double figures. Financial losses continued to accrue, but at least the situation was well under control, and there was plenty to build on for the future.

The Directors for the present time were happy to allow Tom Crilly to continue in his capacity as manager, but his role as a player would now become ever diminishing as he concentrated on orchestrating team affairs. Instead Cross would be chiefly partnered by Jones, late of Blackhall Colliery. They would have another new man behind them wearing the goalkeeper's gloves. Gordon Young was off to pastures in other parts and gave way to a huge young lad, Earnshaw, whose previous employment had been keeping out shots at Denaby.

In the half-back line Millington could not be denied the central pivot's job and had won the overwhelming support of the crowd for his strength and character. For a time Jeff Barker was his left sided support, but the talent of this slightly built 'will 'o the wisp' was too obvious to be ignored. After only a dozen games Aston Villa brought out the cheque book, and paid around £400 for his signature. It meant that Harry Stocks, a Grimsby Junior, and Sid Allen, dropping down from the forward line, eventually became the regular midfielders.

The forward line was to suffer from continuous changes throughout the calendar. Only Stan Norris, a Leeds United junior player, was to make use of all his opportunities. The other positions went to Gill, Porter, Smithson, Beckett, Mosses and Horton. The pick of these man was probably Arthur Smithson, who was a canny goalscorer, having played at Aldershot and Scarborough. His name, along with that of Porter, would be a feature of United's marksmen list for the foreseeable future.

~ 1936-37 ~

The 1936-37 season saw Scunthorpe and Lindsey United in a position where goals would be a problem. At the end of the season they only had seventy-six to their name, a relatively low tally by Midland League standards of the day. A contrast to this was illustrated in the fact that seven other clubs scored over the ton, and immediately below

Scunthorpe, Notts County Reserves had amassed ninety-two goals. Fortunately the defence was far more resilient or there could have been a disaster on their hands. It also meant that there would not be the tremendously high scoring games experienced on some other grounds.

Getting to grips with the fixtures Scunthorpe set off on the wrong foot, losing at Newark 3-1. The situation did not improve throughout the early part of the Autumn, thanks to a poor run which saw only two points from one win in nine dismal performances. This was minimally relieved by a 5-1 beating of bottom club Frickley, whose record was by far and away the worst in the Midland League.

The win against the Colliery men was just before the start of the Club's journey into the fantasy world of the F.A. Cup, where disappointments of league failures could be put to one side. Having lost 3-0 already at Gainsborough Trinity in the season, Scunthorpe supporters knew that anything could be possible in this next encounter. Trinity started the game as favourites, but an excellent closing down job carried out by Millington, Cross and Jones restricted the advances of the blue-shirted home forwards. Little separated the teams, in the Cup-tie, where chances were at a premium. The deadlock was finally broken when Norris in the number eight shirt scored the only goal of the match. Stan had an outstanding game that afternoon, and took the eye as one of United's shrewder signings that year.

The draw for the first round proper of the F.A.Cup competition gave Scunthorpe no picnic for beating Gainsborough. Their lot was a journey of around one hundred miles to play against Walsall, who were still crowing about beating the mighty Arsenal only four years earlier. Although Scunthorpe put up a spirited fight, it was the Saddlers who mastered the conditions, and had to be respected for their 3-0 advantage. Walsall eventually reached the fourth round, when they went out at Blundell Park, 5-1 to First Division Grimsby.

Scunthorpe kick-started the Midland League season by travelling to Peterborough, and in taking the initiative presented by some slack defending, came back two points the richer and with a charming 5-3 result. Smithson scored four of the Knuts goals. Bad weather disrupted part of the holiday programme in December, but the rum sauce on the Christmas Pudding went down much better when Burton, from the Midlands, were beaten on Christmas morning, 2-0.

It was into the New Year that Scunthorpe and Lindsey United suffered their heaviest defeats in consecutive matches, both on opponents' turf. At Grantham, on the first Saturday of 1937, the home team cruised to a 7-0 score, and seven days later a similar performance at Bradford Park Avenue saw a 6-1 reverse. Manager Crilly could not have been happy with his warriors inept displays. At least in the next game, two weeks later, the team had a chance of revenge against the Park Avenue second team. Only two team changes were made, and surprisingly the side made good with Moses scoring the only goal of the game for the Claret and Blues.

Scunthorpe and Lindsey United probably reached the zenith of the season when they had two games to face against high-riding Barnsley Reserves. The men from Oakwell were head and shoulders above everyone else in the Division. All season they were destined to only lose eight of their games. The cold blast of the February climate cooled the Yorkshiremen's fire, as they were given the Barnsley chop by a vibrant Scunthorpe side. Both at home and away, on the first two Saturday's of February, it was the Knuts that eased in front by two goals to one. It was astonishing that such an average side like Scunthorpe could be top of their trade one moment but in the doldrums the next.

Scunthorpe finished the 1936-37 season in better form than they started it. One reason was that Porter had recovered from an injury that caused his omission for a couple of months, and was promoted to centre-forward. When he combined with Smalley, United were at their most effective. Against Denaby, Porter scored four times in the 7-2 victory, while at well-fancied Bradford City Reserves, Smithson hit his second score of four goals, as United delighted their hard-pressed following with a 4-1 result. In the same month his hat-trick at Meadow Lane in conflict against Notts County Reserves underlined his excellent vein of form.

Before the season was wrapped up, Scunthorpe finished off with an horrendous disaster at Frickley. Frickley had won only two games, but in their fortieth game Scunthorpe surrendered all logic and lost 2-0 to the basement side. The Knuts had the Lion's share of the play, but falling to two sucker punches was no excuse for a pathetic showing. Little interest was left now of what was left of the season, and this result must have contributed considerably to the poor turnstile figures of the final two fixtures. At least the Knuts went part of the way to making amends by beating the Reserve teams of Notts County and Rotherham United.

The end of the 1936-37 campaign saw Scunthorpe fourteenth in the table. Tommy Crilly, not surprisingly, packed his bags and departed from the Old Showground. His days in charge had not endeared the idea of having a manager to either the Club or its supporters. It seemed that the heads together approach in the boardroom, and Harry Allcock being asked to pin the results up on the back of the dressing room door, had been far more successful. Never-the-less, managers at football clubs was an innovation not to be ignored, and later United were to give it a another test.

Tom Crilly's time in charge was not a total waste of time. He left behind the nucleus of a fine young side. As a parting shot, one of them, Emptage, was signed up for £250 by Manchester City. The rest would soon start to emulsify and with a shrewd intake of experienced players the 1937-38 season would see some positive movement for United.

~ 1937-38 ~

The Board of Directors kept faith in the whole of the back two divisions for the 1937-38 season, and this settled part of the team required little or no pruning at all, except for the odd alteration for injury. It was never a surprise to pick up the telegraph and find that Earnshaw, Cross, Jones, Stocks,

Millington and Allen were all selected in that order. Late in the season an injury to Cross brought in Clark, and Earnshaw lost his place in the last few games to Wilf Poxton, of Pilkingtons Works team in Doncaster.

The big news in the forward line was the signing of former Oldham Athletic and Southend United centre-forward Harry Johnson. Johnson was a well built man, who could handle himself in the area of the park where it really hurt. He adapted so well to the rigours of the Midland League that his goalscoring feats were a revelation, and each Saturday it was his name that was on everyone's lips in the pubs and clubs of the town.

Around Johnson the main strike force consisted of Norris, Lewis and Bett from the 1936-37 team plus a supplement of Whittaker, Wilkinson and Baldry. Whittaker was not required after October, and young Bett, a debutant of the last March, left the Club after an unwelcomed approach from Sunderland lured him away into the Football League.

Once the team was given the green light it was obvious for a change that at last this was a team that could come up with the goods. All of the side pulled in one direction and the lean times of not knowing where the next goal was coming from were at an end. Johnson led the line like a cavalry officer in the Crimea. He opened his account on the opening day at home to Denaby, scoring twice in the 5-0 pasting of Denaby. Odd defeats at home to Scarborough, and a double conceded to Gainsborough, suggested that this was not quite the finished article, but a number of diamonds that had been uncovered were at last starting to shine.

Even when defeats did come United put up an outstanding showing, and were never outclassed. One of the unluckiest displays was in their sojourn to Lincoln, where the balance of play just tipped against them. It was still a memorable game and Scunthorpe supporters cheered themselves hoarse at the sight of Harry Johnson's first hat-trick in the Club's colours.

The F.A.Cup brought the supporters of 1937 mixed fortunes. Grantham were drawn in the first game, the fourth qualifying round. Scunthorpe's players knew they were in for a tough old time because they had been held to a goalless draw already, in the Midland League meeting in South Lincolnshire. Home advantage tipped the scales and Wilkinson on the left-wing was the hero for a day by setting the seal on the 4-2 result with his maiden hat-trick. Harry Johnson could not be outdone and added the other.

The reward for the win meant a trip across the Humber estuary via Goole to play Hull City, but the first team at Anlaby Road was a different proposition, from their Midland League side. On the day this was to be the case. A crowd of only 6,000 supporters gathered for the game, less than a normal average fixture at their old ground. The home side gave Scunthorpe the run around and even Johnson could not manage a goal. In the event the 4-0 score meant it was curtains again for another year, but a valuable lesson had been learned by Scunthorpe's ever improving young team. Hull went on to beat Exeter but then lost to Huddersfield.

Scunthorpe relieved their frustration for their F.A.Cup shortcomings by taking Mansfield Town Reserves to task by 4-1. This was to be United's last win for three games, but once the Yuletide holiday was over they set off on an unbeaten run of nine matches, which sent them towards the top of the table. The pick of this run was a toss up between the 2-1 beating of champions-elect Shrewsbury at home, and the highly entertaining thrill a minute 6-4 victory away at Bradford City Reserves. Each game had its merits but perhaps the Shrewsbury result, against a cultured team of all round strength, had more meaning to the team's progress. At Newark, Johnson made his mark during the productive period scoring another three goal burst, in a fine 5-2 away victory.

The brakes were not put on the Scunthorpe wheels until early March, when the long journey West into Shropshire to play Shrewsbury a second time put Scunthorpe`s Championship challenge into true perspective. The Shrews won 5-1 at a canter, and emphasized that they were leaps and bounds in front of the Claret and Blues. If any game had the effect of ending United's trophy ambitions then this was it. At least spirits were not totally dampened and the brand of soccer the lads were able to produce was having the desired effect on the size of the Old Showground gates.

The fixture card gave the Scunthorpe team four consecutive games for them to reacquaint themselves with the home crowd. Thoughts of any inhibitions as a consequence of the Shrewsbury setback were soon dismissed when Notts County Reserves took a 4-0 hammering in the next game. Hat-tricks followed for the inevitable Johnson and another for inside-left Lewis in consecutive matches with Bradford Park Avenue Reserves and Lincoln City Reserves. The team may not have been top but the supporters of Scunthorpe loved the entertainment value of the eleven.

In the final phase of the 1937-38 season there was time for the players to earn some late glory. There was still a matter of two fixtures at Easter against Hull City's second team, and at least they were more up to the Knuts size. The fifty odd mile trip by road around the water was made all the better when Scunthorpe edged ahead in the stakes, 2-1. Wilkinson was, again, in a scoring mood and supplied both of the Scunthorpe strikes.

On the following Tuesday afternoon, the lighter nights allowed all but the two to ten o'clock shift workers time to see the return fixture. Those unfortunate to still be scheduled at work did swaps with their mates or double shifts at other times to be present at the Showground. The inconvenience was well worth it for those involved in the change of work rota. Scunthorpe soon tore into Hull with all guns blazing. Norris, Lewis, Clavis and Wilkinson were all on target, but none could outdo Johnson with the other three. The final tally was 7-1 in favour of the dominant Knuts.

Scunthorpe and Lindsey sang their swan song of success when they bade farewell to their supporters, for the time being, at home to Grantham. Grantham had sneaked up on the rails and were a team to finish in a very honourable

second spot in the table, that for once was not over run by the usual procession of Reserve Teams. It was a glowing tribute to United that they should be able to beat this accomplished Grantham side a second time, although the 4-3 result was a reflection of a much closer affair.

The curtain fell on this much more productive year of events with a single goal defeat at Nottingham Forest Reserves. At least this team had given the town a degree of respectability in its football team. The Scunthorpe goals total of one hundred and nine was only marginally bettered by two extra strikes by Shrewsbury Town on top of the pyramid. A little more homework was still needed in the defence, of which Mal Millington took much credit for organising his colleagues. However, the Knuts position of sixth was a highly satisfactory return on the season, and only ten points away from the championship trophy.

It was with these interesting figures that Scunthorpe and Lindsey United met with the lengthening queue to join the Football League. They had missed the boat in 1921 when the Third Division Northern Section was born, but it was quite obvious that they were not prepared for the upgrading at that time, either financially or in the strength of the playing staff. This was to be the first application ever made, and although the fine detail of their standing was set out by the Board of Directors, few member clubs gave any real support to Scunthorpe's plea. They would have to make a more meaningful challenge to secure the Midland League if they were to succeed in obtaining a higher sphere of football. Shrewsbury had already accomplished this, and they too had been rebuffed.

The wheel of fortune had now turned full circle. United were slowly emerging as one of the most progressive non-League clubs. Gates were on the increase. Steel had given a new dimension to the area and the population was spiralling towards the fifty thousand mark. For once the finances of the Club were under control and all was rosy in the garden. Scunthorpe United's supporters looked optimistically towards the future, knowing success was only just over the horizon.

United's experiment in appointing a player-manager was still abandoned, for the time being, but the Board did look out for a top name to sign. This came in the form of ex-Manchester United and Welsh International full-back, Tom Jones now at the end of his Football League career but still fast enough to catch out any number of Midland League players, including the younger element. At least this player was to play a leading part in driving the team, and all that Jones would need to do was to fine tune an engine that was running into a rich seam of form.

~ 1938-39 ~
During the close season of 1938, few other players were signed for first team consideration. The first man to deserve a mention was a huge goalkeeper by the name of Clunie, recommended from Old Trafford by Tom Jones. At six feet and one inch tall, and weighing thirteen stone, he was a mountain of a man that could rub shoulders against the

burliest of rushing forwards. Poxton held his place in the first-half of the season, but an unfortunate injury gave Clunie a chance.

At full-back Thorpe supplemented Tom Jones, and Bill Jones. Thorpe was quite a nomadic player and Scunthorpe was his fifth club, in a line which included Norwich City and Wolverhampton Wanderers. Thorpe was given the harness in the initial stages, but the two Jones' took over as a partnership into the Autumn. Ironically Thorpe turned up with his boots for a game against Burton Town, and donned the number nine shirt in Johnson's absence.

There was to be no change in the half-back line-up, which generally remained as Stock, Millington and Allen, backed up by the up and coming Staniland. However, there were two significant additions to the forward line. First, Eddie Fleetwood came with vast experience, chiefly gained at Barnsley and Blackburn Rovers. He may have been of advancing years in football terms, but at this level he was lethal. Eddie was signed as the right inside-man for Harry Johnson, while on the left came the youthful Sammy Nightingale from Lincoln City. Nightingale was fleet of foot and accurate in his shot. Stan Norris and John Wilkinson made ideal wing partners and with Harry Johnson at the arrow head, this was to be the best attack of the League. If supporters thought Johnson had dazzled them with his thirty-eight goals up to 1938, then they had not seen anything yet.

Scunthorpe and Lindsey United played so well in the 1938-39 season that some results belittled their efforts. The rocket was launched at Mansfield when Johnson, back by Fleetwood, scored the first of a sackful of goals, as United won 2-0. They stepped up the gas in their first home game, when Newark were dispatched by an incredible 10-3 scoreline. Johnson fired the warning shot that he was the man in form, registering five goals. At the end of September he had already scored fifteen goals and United were ahead of the pack, undefeated, having won six of nine league games. Defeat would not be tasted until the visit of a Nottingham Forest Reserve team, boosted for the occasion by some faces that had worn the Club's red shirt in the Football League. Even then the game as a whole was an entertaining affair, but the 2-3 result spoiled the record at the tenth attempt.

The F.A.Cup was to see United in the same devastating form as in the Midland League. Four of the qualifiers were against fairly local teams, and luck dictated that all would be played up the Doncaster Road in town. The first victims turned out to be Barton Town, and the 9-1 scoreline was a mere formality. Harry Johnson scored five times. In the second qualifying round the works team Appleby-Frodingham put up more of a fight using some ex-United stars, but lost 4-1. Harry Johnson scored three times. The third hurdle brought the other works team, Lysaghts Sports, from over Foxhills way and they were totally annihilated by an 11-3 score which made all other Scunthorpe United records fade into insignificance. Harry Johnson scored five times. Not to be outdone Sammy Nightingale scored four others, and the rest of Scunthorpe's total was met by Stan Norris and Eddie Fleetwood.

These fine performances set November up to be potentially a very fruitful month. In the League another Johnson hat-trick was small beer in the beating of Grimsby Town Reserves, but getting one over the neighbours thrilled Scunthorpe supporters, particularly as the 5-0 score was decisive. Back on F.A. Cup duty Scunthorpe had another Lincolnshire opponent to deal with. Boston were just above halfway in the Midland League table, and the incentive of a Football League club in the first round proper if they could surmount the challenge of the Knuts had them all fired up. Their enthusiasm was apparent for all to see, and they were not overawed by Scunthorpe's rampant attack. Sammy Nightingale gave Scunthorpe the advantage, but it needed another from Harry Johnson to make sure of progress through a 2-1 result in a tense encounter.

There was a certain amount of disappointment in the draw for the first round proper. Although home soil would give them the edge, the fact that Lanchester City were non-League did not stir the imagination in the same way that other pairings had. The routine would be exactly the same when the referee indicated that play could start. From the very off, United's forwards took the match to the visitors. The City defence stuck to their job stoutly, but it was only a matter of time before Wilkinson and deputy winger Oxley, in for injured Norris, would carve a way down the flanks for the eagerly awaiting trio of Fleetwood, Johnson and Nightingale. At the end of ninety minutes all three had registered in the 4-2 safe voyage to the Second Round, and of those men, Eddie Fleetwood scored a couple.

Preparations for the Watford Cup-tie.
The players train under the watchful eye of Trainer Herbert Lloyd.

United were rewarded for the labours against Lancaster with a plum tie at the Old Showground against Watford of the Third Division South section. The game took on a very high profile in the calendar of the town's events. Everyone in the district wanted to see this one, and on 10th December 1938 a record crowd of 11,800 spectators made the Old Showground gasp with the pressure of bodies. For this historic game United lined up; Poxton, Jones(T.), Staniland, Stocks, Millington, Allen, Norris, Fleetwood, Johnson, Nightingale and Oxley.

The game kicked off and moved at a quick tempo. Both defences were called into action and a Johnson header almost brought the first blow. In the Watford forward line the burly Dunderdale was the man to watch, and the Knuts needed a timely tackle from Tom Jones to halt his flow.

But it was Dunderdale that was to change the whole course of the game. On one of his charges he collided full-on with Wilf Poxton in the Scunthorpe goal. A loud crack made a sickening echo around the ground and the crowd fell silent at the horrific sight of the prostrate custodian on the cold turf. Poxton's leg had folded under the crushing impact and his season was now at an end. Scunthorpe rapidly regrouped. Staniland volunteered for the green jersey, while his place was taken by Millington alongside Jones, and Stocks filled in, in the middle. Despite the severe restraints the team was under at the loss of Poxton, they surged forward to try and make a battle of it. To give them credit they matched Watford in every department, and defied the odds to take the lead. Oxley jinxed his way down the left side of the field, but was up-ended as he entered the box. Penalty! Was the roar from the ground, as though of one voice. The man in black pointed to the spot and Tom Jones took the responsibility upon himself of converting the kick.

Although Scunthorpe had been carried along on a tide of patriotic emotion, It was Dunderdale who was of a more positive nature as he diverted a through ball past the bemused Staniland unused to his present occupation between the posts. Scunthorpe continued to give a good account of themselves but eventually the fateful moments began to tell as they inevitably tired. Dunderdale was to make one more impact on this epic cup-tie, as he dramatically fired the winner within ten minutes of the last whistle and Scunthorpe's ship was scuttled.

The cost of the defeat in the Cup against Watford was that they missed out on their first ever trip to London, to play at White Hart Lane against the pride of the capital, Tottenham Hotspur. Watford would make no further impression, as the North Londoners thrashed the Hertfordshire side 7-1.

December also brought to the Old Showground a very famous face when Notts County Reserves paid a call. Dixie Dean of Everton fame, whose record of sixty goals in a Football League season still stands to date, had been transferred to the Meadow Lane club, and was in the team making up the numbers. He may have only been there for his appearance money, because his contribution to the ninety minutes of football was minimal. Scunthorpe saw the game in a different light, and took the opportunity to enter into some useful target practice. Each forward registered in the 8-0 success.

At the mid-point of the season Scunthorpe received a slight set-back when they lost by five goals without reply at Valley Parade, against Bradford City, but this could be attributed to the loss of Stocks and Nightingale through injury and the utilisation of a very inexperienced 'keeper before Clunie settled into the team following Poxton's serious breakage. The response of the players was to regroup, scoring five times against Bradford Park Avenue, and recording nine when Denaby called by. The 9-1 defeat of Denaby was remarkable for Johnson's six goals equalling Ernie Simms individual match scoring record. Denaby were, frankly, not at the races, and less than a week later Scunthorpe messed up the New Year celebrations in the colliery district by beating them 10-0. This was Scunthorpe and Lindsey United's biggest away win, and made a record aggregate score, incredibly, of 19-1. At Denaby all the forwards celebrated by scoring a couple apiece.

Harry Johnson, Scunthorpe's number 9 heads the ball between two Peterborough defenders in the home Midland League match in 1939.

The 1939 fixtures continued to see the Scunthorpe train steam on without hindrance. Their trouncing of Denaby began the start of a twelve match unbeaten period, and only three more losses would be added to the Knuts statistics until the end of their commitments. Generally speaking it was a case of how many Scunthorpe would win by. In attack they purred like a Rolls Royce, while in defence they were corked as tight as a bottle of Guinness. Johnson was undoubtedly the star of the show. Another hat-trick arrived with the visit of Barnsley Reserves and a barrage of four came in the Doncaster Rovers Reserve game. It was only a pity that this side had not been allowed membership of the Football League because it would have been among the front runners.

Scunthorpe and Lindsey United sealed their runaway Midland League Championship on a winning note at Frickley Colliery. In many respects this had been a more prestigious title to win than that of the 1926-27 season. More games had been played and against a stronger set of opposition. Scunthorpe finished comfortably in front of Barnsley Reserves in second place with a record of; played 42, won 28, drawn 8, lost 6, for 133, against 57 and points 64.

Two players deserved special praise. Harry Johnson had blasted his way to a staggering sixty-nine goals, of which fifteen came in the F.A.Cup and another five in the Lincolnshire Senior League. Mal Millington, at centre-half, was the lynch-pin of a defence that had conceded the least number of goals in the Club's history, bar the previous championship, who on goals per game were marginally in front. In total Millington wore a Scunthorpe shirt on sixty-one occasions, including twice for the Yorkshire League side because they were short.

The termination of Football came with three exhibition matches. First the champions took on a select eleven chosen from the remaining Midland League teams, and United came out with an honourable draw. Then came the annual visit of Sheffield Wednesday, for the 'Hospital Cup'. Wednesday displayed plenty of class but they struggled to keep hold of the trophy, scraping home by the only goal. Finally, a visit of Barnsley was arranged, and invitations sent to the representatives of the Football League clubs who would be eligible to vote, when Scunthorpe made another bid to join the Football League. All those present must have been impressed at both the size of the support, standard of the team, and state of the ground. Indeed since the Autumn of 1938 a half shelter had been erected to cover the back of the Fox Street terracing. Not too many non-League side could boast of a protection from the elements for supporters on three sides of their enclosures.

Once football was finished for the year Scunthorpe's band of Directors, headed by Mr Talbot Cliff, headed South, via Doncaster, along L.N.E.R. metals to Kings Cross in order to attend the Annual General Meeting of the Football League. This time they were far better prepared, and even had a brochure with them, highlighting the forward planning of Scunthorpe and Lindsey United Football Club in a six point programme to get into the national competition offered by the Third Division Northern Section.

The points made clear included:

1. To improve on the already impressive non-League average gate of 5,200.
2. To develop part of the ground for a shopping area to secure extra revenue.
3. To seek the support of the influential business community of the area.
4. To impress on existing members that Scunthorpe United would be worthy of a League position.
5. To pursue a ground enlargement programme to raise the capacity of 15,000 up to as many as 50,000.
6. To develop a nursery club to supply a constant stream of youngsters for first team duty.

Scunthorpe United's group toured the hotels and gathering places of their influential representatives of the voting members. Many of them expressed their interest, especially when it was the Scunthorpe party that was paying for the whisky. Some, such as Grimsby Town and Sheffield Wednesday gave personal assurances. When it came to the count only four votes were cast in Scunthorpe United's favour. It was a great disappointment, but there again it must have been to some degree expected.

The Midland League Winners Medal won by United forward Stan Norris.

The Directors made their weary way back home at least a little wiser for the experience. If they were to succeed in future another Midland League Championship must be secured in 1940.

Scunthorpe United's supporters were horrified to see that in the name of progress the championship side was being changed and possibly not for the better in order to retain the trophy during the 1939-40 season. Poxton was still incapacitated and Clunie had been discharged. Instead Jenkinson arrived full of promise from Boston United. The backs and half-backs remained the same, but Campbell was signed to try and emulate the feats of Harry Johnson, being late of Leicester City and Lincoln. Fleetwood was preferred at inside-right and Arthur Maw returned after ten years at Leicester and Notts County. On either wing Rickards and J.Millington came from Notts County and Swansea Town respectively. Other old favourites such as Norris, Johnson, Nightingale and Staniland would have to wait their turns for first team action.

Scunthorpe supporters' grumbles over team selection seemed justified. Although the first two games of the season resulted in victories, and Campbell had managed to score in each game, the third fixture of the season, at home to Grimsby Town Reserves was lost. Hardly the type of result to win a championship. While the debate on whether Johnson and company should be recalled the situation altered when a one time Austrian painter with a strange haircut and funny moustache took a stroll in Poland. The person in question was, of course, Hitler, and when the German High Command invaded their neighbours the brewing clouds of War produced the storm that would throw the World into chaos.

The whole football programme was terminated within the week, including the Midland League fixtures. Contracts were suspended as the Country prepared for the conflict. Jenkinson, T.Jones, Rickards, Campbell and winger Millington all packed their brown suitcases and took up with the War effort. Local based players remained within the town until their time to be called up was imminent. Harry Allcock was instructed to arrange a number of friendly fixtures to keep the Club ticking over until further instructions had been issued as to what was happening with the Midland League. Invitations were extended to, and met by Gainsborough Trinity, Grimsby Town, Lincoln City and Bradford Park Avenue to provide some form of sport throughout the Autumn. At least the War settled some of the problems of who should be included in the team.

The players pool that was now available allowed a flexing of the muscles in the first team for either Mayberry or Middleton as custodian. Bill Jones, Staniland and Pickering, a former Southampton stalwart, teamed up for the full-back positions, and fortunately the entire half-back line remained intact. Norris was recalled to the right-wing until he joined up, and then Greaves stood in for him. Fleetwood and Maw took the inside berths and Sammy Nightingale roamed the middle of the park. Harry Johnson did come back to the fold as time went on, but ex-Mariner, Swain, completed the picture on the left-wing.

The friendly fixtures running into October served their purpose but football was not the same. A sigh of relief did come when an unofficial Midland League was inaugurated on a recognized basis involving eight clubs. To stretch the fixtures the league would be doubled and a 'part one' and 'part two' would be played for. Scunthorpe found that their nearest rivals in terms of strength was Peterborough United, and they would be the team to watch.

In the first part of the competition only Frickley Colliery was able to beat the Knuts over the first ten games. Sammy Nightingale was in cracking form, taking over the mantle of Johnson as marksman. At home to Boston, Sammy scored five times and at Gainsborough he destroyed the opposition with six explosive strikes.

At Peterborough a 1-1 draw looked as though Scunthorpe had weathered the storm, but the Posh came to the Old Showground a week later and won an extraordinary match 6-3. This made no difference to the final table which put Scunthorpe two points ahead of their challenger.

The second-half of the season did not see all the fixtures completed as the Second World War was intensifying. Peterborough and Scunthorpe were unable to complete one game each, but in the two matches against each other, home advantage gave a share of the spoils. Other matches in the round robin always finished with high scoring results. Scunthorpe managed to beat Boston 8-2 and Grantham 8-0, but marginally they did not quite fare as well as in the first part of the competition. Peterborough headed the second series of games by one point from Scunthorpe. In its wisdom the Midland League awarded the trophy to the Knuts, but it was never put on the statute book as part of the records. All that remained was for the journey to Peterborough in mid-May of 1940 for the champions to play the runners-up. The Posh gained a little consolation out of the fact that on the day they triumphed by a 3-2 scoreline.

Football for Scunthorpe and Lindsey United was now concluded until after the dramas of war had been settled throughout Europe and the rest of the World. Harry Allcock was still 'looking after the books for a short while', and Barnsley Brewery were generous over their terms on the Club's loan. Scunthorpe football followers might have been condemned to park soccer if it had not been for an approach by Grimsby Town's Directors. Falling crowds at Blundell Park, and restriction on crowds gathering in coastal areas forced them to seek help for an unlimited time until they could set up home again in Cleethorpes. United happily agreed to meet their request.

Grimsby Town filled in at the Old Showground until 1943. Several local players guested for them, including Harry Johnson, Bill Jones, Mal Millington and Harry Stocks. Occasionally star players would play an odd game for the Mariners and the likes of Peter Doherty and Len Shackleton shimmied their way round defenders on the Old Showground pitch. The highlight of Grimsby Town's stay came in 1942 when a record crowd of 11,896 squeezed inside the ground to see Town play Sunderland in the second leg of the League War Cup. Everything was up for grabs, as no goals had been converted in the first leg. Local supporters at that time had a leaning towards the Town, but a 3-2 reverse shattered their dreams.

When the Mariners bade United and the quaint surroundings of the Old Showground a grateful farewell, it meant local football followers would be almost completely void of sport. There was only the odd representative match to starve off the boredom, although for most of the youngest element conscription required their presence elsewhere. It was not until the resonant drone of the enemy aircraft had been chased away over the Lincolnshire Wolds that football, and peace in general, would return to normal. Until then the shutters were put up at the Old Showground and Harry Allcock would keep the key.

CHAPTER 5

THE AFTERMATH OF THE WAR

hurch Bells rang around the country at the end of the Second World War. V.E. Day signalled a nationwide party at the relief that the bombing and slaughter was over. Europe might have been in tatters but the spirit of the British people remained intact. Soon the boys would be returning home from the front and life would get back to something like normal. The demand for recreation would bring football to the forethought of everyone's minds and the sport was to experience a boom the likes of which had never been seen before.

Many football clubs had to pick up the pieces after six years of disruption which had witnessed the players losing a major part of their careers. When they had reached a peak, some men, sadly, would not return, being killed in action for the cause. Scunthorpe was no exception, but some of the younger element of the 1939 period was still available and turned up to enthusiastically wear the claret and blue. These faces were mixed with a blend of new talent. Players were signed who had pre-war experience at other grounds, and together they formed a Scunthorpe team eager to do duty for the 1945-46 season. In terms of the Midland League, the nineteen clubs who lined-up to do battle constituted an official competition, but the Football League would not be recognized for another twelve months. For them the F.A.Cup was their sole major official competition.

~ 1945-46 ~

The programme notes for Scunthorpe and Lindsey United's first game for six long seasons, against Mansfield Town Reserves, started with the team listings declaring Wilf Poxton in goal. Wilf had not played for the Club since the unfortunate incident against Watford. His safe hands would defend Scunthorpe's goal in virtually all games of that coming year.

Directly in front of Poxton the full-back positions would be shared principally by Charles Betts and the much more mature John Staniland, who had been growing in stature before the hostilities. Midway through the activities, the back quarters were joined by the formidable talents of George Lax, an ex-Wolverhampton Wanderers man. Lax was not only recruited for his defending skills, but to lend a hand coaching the junior ranks. Unfortunately, his services were lost at the end of the events of the 1945-46 season, when he accepted a similar role at Hull City.

In the middle of the park the irrepressible Mal Millington, a one time pugilist, was back playing as if he had never left his post. Sid Allen would accompany him on the left hand side, although later a left-wing berth became his preference, and a strapping local lad, Alan Leeman, moved from inside-left to left-half. On Millington's other side James Burnip played well enough to take the nod throughout the fixture card. Burnip was another local lad to make good.

The star of the forward line was another local son, Jack Marriott, a winger versatile for duty on either wing. This was the first part of his learning curve that would take the dark-haired speed merchant on to greater fields of achievement. The rest of the forward line consisted of Readhead from the Lysaghts Sports works team on the other wing, and Fleetwood, Carver, Leeman and occasionally Harry Johnson. Fleetwood may have been at the end of his career but his exceptional fitness level allowed him to appear in most games. Harry Johnson struggled throughout with injury and was restricted to less than a dozen games. His position spearheading the attack went to Carver from Mexborough, who was to be a gemstone in goalscoring. When March came they were to be joined by a softly spoken Scotsman, George Wallace, an Aberdeen junior player. George would enhance the team with delicate ball skills that delighted United's followers for quite a time to come. He was also no slouch when it came to poking the ball into the net.

The shrill note of the referee's whistle on the 25th August 1945 was greeted with a huge wave of noise and emotion. At last the black moments of the war were behind them and football recommenced with a visit of Mansfield Town Reserves. Scunthorpe made it a real carnival day out for local supporters in the gentle sunshine. Despite a limited time together the Knuts blended very well with each other, and Marriott came into the reckoning, scoring the goal that the crowd was all waiting for. Leman at number ten obtained two more goals, while the impressive Carver scoring a hat-trick. It was a wonderful result at 6-1 to welcome everyone back to the fold.

Although the situation would never be the same, it was still apparent that the team assembled, under the still difficult conditions, was going to be in the forefront of Midland League events. They put up a worthy effort in their next game, despite losing by three goals without reply, at Notts County. The team was announced as being the County reserve eleven, but in truth United had gone down to the Meadow Lane senior squad. A more realistic balance of the opposition was able to be judged at Lincoln. Here the same score was recorded as at Nottingham, but this time it was in the Knut's favour. Eddie Fleetwood demonstrated he had not lost any of his aggression in front of goal and scored twice; the following week a second post-war hat-trick went to the Lincolnshire born Leeman. Scunthorpe supporters were encouraged at the lively performance which had the visiting Gainsborough Trinity team back-peddling. They wrapped up the win at 4-1, thanks to another goal from the deadly Carver.

It was now quite obvious that the high scoring games of the pre-war era were gone. Only on rare occasions would a total blitz of a Midland League opponent be witnessed.

The strength of the teams had risen to a high plateau. This meant that any achievements would have to be fought hard for. Nevertheless, United were already showing how much of an industrious side they were, and although not everything was going their way, the team was well in touch with the top half of the table.

During this early section of the campaign Scunthorpe supporters warmed to the re-emergence of old favourite Harry Johnson. He was a little battle-scarred by now, and like most footballers, he did not benefit from the lay-off from competitive sport during the conflict. It was pleasing to see him have a three match burst in the senior squad, but injury left him unable to sustain a regular shirt peg in the dressing room. Given this opportunity, Johnson showed he had lost none of his zest for the game with a goal in each of his three appearances, and the old-timer was able to match the young upstarts.

The qualifying rounds of the F.A.Cup were no different to the usual format in the 1945-46 season, but from the proper round, ties would be two-legged. Scunthorpe were not given the usual exemptions, and had to take on Lysaughts Sports at an early stage. The match promoted a lot of local interest because of the ex-Scunthorpe players in the works team again, but they could never rekindle their old form to threaten the present squad. Harry Johnson, not quite on crutches, was back in the line-up and scored twice in the 4-1 victory.

In the next game, home advantage gave Scunthorpe every opportunity to make progress with the draw against Yorkshire Amateurs. Events on the field were not to be so clear cut, and whether it was complacency or lack of motivation is not certain, but Scunthorpe had an off day. They struggled to find their form that afternoon and crashed out of the competition after losing by a score of 2-1.

As the Autumn mists appeared on the hedgerows, Scunthorpe experienced one of their best results of the season. Ollerton Colliery may have been of less a difficult opponent, but Scunthorpe still had to work hard for their bonus pay. Only Fleetwood failed to score of the forwards, but Carver made up the deficit by notching a pair. There was encouraging news on the left-wing as one of the goals came from the slightly built Swain making his debut. The job was wrapped up at 5-1.

Not all of Scunthorpe's entertaining games resulted in positive scores. The two games at Christmas were excellent value for money, but only yielded one Midland League point. At Blundell Park the 4-3 defeat left the Mariners supporters in total admiration of the way the visitors had played. Perhaps the first Saturday of 1946 saw the best performance of the whole season, at Frickley Colliery. Both sides were virtually neck and neck in the table, and each team rolled up their sleeves to do battle in the bitter conditions. It must be said that neither of the defences had a field day, and Millington must have thought he had run his legs off. Despite scoring four away goals, this team returned empty handed, losing by the odd goal in nine. The only consolation was the applause of the crowd ringing in their ears as they left the field of play.

A number of team changes at the end of the list of fixtures did not assist Scunthorpe United's League form towards the latter part of their Midland League journey, and the Club's position among the leaders slipped as results went against them. Not all the players tried were a failure. Although not regular performers, Burton, Sheen and Priestley all scored hat-tricks when given the chance, but none of them were capable of matching Carver when he was fit. This man made himself responsible for the best individual scoring feat of the season, when he scored all four goals to home to Denaby, in the 4-1 victory.

The season tended to fizzle out somewhat, and this was epitomized by the 2-3 set-back at Ollerton in the final conflict of the season. It meant that Scunthorpe had finished sixth, 18 points behind Shrewsbury who were champions for the second time. Carver was the leading goalscorer, having put the ball in the net twenty times. This was an outstanding effort considering that little was seen of him after February. Harry Johnson, again in limited circumstances, weighed in with a dozen strikes in far fewer appearances. Although the supporters would liked to have seen the Knuts attain a position of higher status, they would not argue too much with the level of entertainment that the players provided, and this was a period of consolidation after the War.

~ 1946-47 ~

The 1946-47 season dawned, and one of the outstanding signings of the close season was that of former Sheffield Wednesday stalwart, Ted Catlin. Catlin had won top honours with the Owls and was a nationally known figure. Scunthorpe may have thought they were getting a bargain in signing this old soldier, but when only eight appearances were made by the ex-Wednesdayite it was something of a let-down.

A more reliable prospect was Harry Reed from Yeovil, whose West Country accent caused a stir, and along with Stan Cooke from Rotherham, they formed a tight curtain in front of Poxton. Mal Millington refused to relinquish his post and with Staniland and Harper, the half-backs were only disturbed through injury.

The mainstay of the forward line was Bowers, Wynn and Wallace, with Hydes from Newport County playing a role in the second part of the year. There was no doubt that the discovery of the close season was the unstoppable Timmy Bowers. The former Middlesbrough man was to be so dynamic in the marksmen department that he would rival the likes of Ernie Simms and Harry Johnson. James Wynn was also a noted goalscorer, and with Wallace's ball craft the forward line was honed to a sharp edge.

The picture was finally developed with the inclusion of Jack Marriott on the right-wing and Arthur 'Curly' Robertshaw on the left. Marriott eventually became such a hot property that Sheffield Wednesday offered a record transfer fee for Scunthorpe of what was widely reported as £2,000. The Directors could not refuse this type of money, nor was it fair to stand in Marriott's way. It was just as well that this transfer coincided with the return of the brave Stan Norris.

Norris had survived the prison camps in the jungles of the Far East in the War and had suffered unspeakable conditions at the hands of the Japanese tyrants. After a rehabilitation period he regained his fitness and resumed where he left off in 1940.

By a strange quirk of fate the secretary of the Midland League chose to draw up the same opening fixture against Mansfield Town Reserves as twelve months earlier. Again the match was one to savour, with a high goal count. The difference was that the Stags had far sharper antlers and gave a good account of themselves. In all, nine goals were scored, and United took the League points by netting five. James Wynn marked his card with three of the shots that thumped the back of the net. Timmy Bowers and George Wallace were on target with the other two.

It was soon apparent that this team was to become a very well oiled goal-scoring machine, particularly as the Winter approached. Timmy Bowers formed an excellent partnership with Wynn, but after injury to the latter, Bowers took it upon himself to become 'Mr. Perpetual Motion' personified, and hat-tricks became commonplace. The compatibility of the two front men was well illustrated when each man supplied trios against Notts County Reserves late in November, then followed this up by scoring seven between them in the next Midland League match at home to Frickley Colliery. Bowers scored four of that total in the year's biggest win of 9-0. Results of this size were an exception to the rule and it should not go unnoticed that the likes of Jack Marriott, George Wallace and Arthur Robertshaw were supplying the ammunition for others to fire the trigger.

The story of the 1946-47 season was mainly concerned with another memorable epic in the F.A.Cup. Lack of progress one year earlier required extra lessons in the qualifiers, and the initial rounds brought opponents of nuisance value only. The silver lining for the Club was that the likes of Bowers and company received some welcome target practice. Norton Woodseats, Haworth Colliery and Wombwell all were sacrificial lambs to the slaughter, each losing 5-2. Rawmarsh lost, after the Haworth Colliery game by a similar margin, but to a different score, of 3-0. The Norton Woodseats match was of particular interest because it marked the farewell performance of Eddie Fleetwood, a man who had never given the Club short change in the times he had represented them. His parting shot was to have the crowd cheering by scoring his swan-song effort.

The F.A.Cup brewed up greater excitement as the team progressed towards the first round proper, which started midway through November. Before their name was included in the black balls used for the draw, there was a little matter of Boston to clear as the last obstacle. Home advantage favoured the Knuts, as well as a higher position in the table than their Midland League opponents. The bookies would have offered no realistic odds on anything but a Scunthorpe win. All predications turned out to be built on solid foundations and a 4-1 win signalled celebration time amongst the army of Scunthorpe fans that packed the Old Showground.

Scunthorpe and Lindsey United found themselves in what was by now a familiar position of competing in the first round proper. The tie handed to them was an extremely difficult one, for home advantage had not been forthcoming. Their task would be to rub shoulders with York City, a well placed Third Division North team, at Bootham Crescent.

Atrocious weather swept across the North of England on the allotted day, and when the referee noticed his own reflection in the vast expanse of puddles on the sinking pitch he had no option but to postpone the game until the following Wednesday. The afternoon kick-off to beat the fading light of the shorter days did not stop a large crowd, including more than a thousand from Scunthorpe, to be in place for the first whistle. Scunthorpe United knew that this was the real standard they would have to maintain on a weekly basis, if they ever made the Football League. Early signs were that they were able to give a good account of themselves. Indeed, after four minutes the skills conjured up by the educated feet of Wallace put Robertshaw through, who crossed to Marriott. Young Jack controlled the leather, then drove it hard and low. The ball found its way to the back of the net, diverted off the side of the body of the despairing goalkeeper.

The rest of the game was balanced on a knife edge in which the defence played a key role. More than once the United custodian, Wilf Poxton, was called upon to make a number of cat-like pounces to retrieve the situation at the last gasp. It was his agility two minutes from time that saved the day for Scunthorpe when he survived a one-on-one with an oncoming forward. The 1-0 away win was the shock of the round and earned the team numerous accolades in the national Press. It was the first win against a League club that Scunthorpe had achieved on foreign soil, and a moment for all connected at the Old Showground to drink in the occasion.

The second round of the F.A.Cup drew Scunthorpe and Lindsey United out of the silk bag with Rotherham United, an old adversary. Rotherham were even more formidable than the Minstermen, and for United's following it was another journey into the depths of Yorkshire. This time Rotherham stopped the Knuts gallop and the match was less of a contest. The 4-1 score showed that Scunthorpe were second best, but did have a Timmy Bowers goal as a consolation for the travelling hoards to applaud. At least the F.A.Cup exploits gave them another line to scribble on their C.V. when they applied for a place in the Third Division at the end of the season.

The month of December brought some of the best action out of the team when they returned to the Midland League fare, although they did not have things all their own way. Three local derby games saw them in superior mood at Lincoln, winning 3-0, but two games against Grimsby Town failed to produce a clear advantage. Perhaps the most exhilarating of these two matches was at home, where six goals were divided, and the hot Vimto tasted much better when Bowers had his fourth hat-trick to celebrate.

Denaby spoiled New Year's Day on tour, but a goal in the game from Stan Norris was a great tonic in his come-back attempt. A full recovery was signalled within nearly a fortnight as the mercurial Norris smacked home a welcome hat-trick when Denaby were made to pay at the Old Showground, losing 7-1. The same month saw two encouraging 5-1 victories against Notts County Reserves and Bradford Park Avenue Reserves, sandwiched in between the matches against the colliery district outfit.

The weather was to take charge of football during early 1947, and the country suffered intolerable hardships. Late snow fell in thick layers throughout the land, then a rapid thaw set a deluge of water loose, causing vast areas to be flooded. Much of the sports programme, including football, was lost to the weather, and for the first time in the Club's history they would later experience an almost non-existent close season, as weary soccer players plodded around football fields until well into June.

A large percentage of the season was crammed into April and May, while the final termination of events did not occur until 14th June when Scunthorpe went to play Ollerton Colliery. Throughout the season United kept in touch with the League leaders Grimsby Town, and it was not until the last handful of games that they fell away. However, they maintained their tradition for smooth effective football, and attracted larger than average crowds whenever they played. A resting place of fourth in the table gave justification for the conscientious application the team had provided. Timmy Bowers took full credit for his performance which yielded sixty League and Cup goals. It might have been a different story had Cooke at full-back and Wallace, the inside man, not been injured late on.

The first post-War visit to London preoccupied United's minds in the early part of the Summer of 1947, for the re-election meeting of the Football League. Little headway was made for yet again, despite the tide of feeling throughout the sport that it was time for a change, and that a club with the facilities, support and strength in the playing staff as Scunthorpe should be given a chance. The pedestrian attitude of the gentlemen of mature years representing those sides in that exclusive club would not be altered. For Scunthorpe United it was like knocking their heads on a brick wall.

All they could do was make sure the Lincolnshire club was at the forefront of non-League football and make a good run in the F.A.Cup as a vehicle for the national newspapers to press their case.

~ 1947-48 ~

Strenuous efforts were continued in the middle of 1947 to make sure of the promotion of the Club to an even higher Midland League status. Bernard Harper made himself available as player-manager in the same left-half position, and Millington would not be denied for another full term. Less was seen of Staniland, and eventually Alan Leeman was given the remit to succeed in that department.

Behind these men there would be seen a crumbling of the empire of Poxton, Cook and Reed. George Rymer was handed the green woolly jumper, while Albert Watford settled in at right-back. The new face for the number three shirt was the lean Jack Brownsword, a name that was to become synonymous with Scunthorpe United. He had the speed of a greyhound and a tackle as deadly as a viper. Hull City had astonishingly discarded his services after a handful of games, possibly thinking him on the smallish side, but he had continued to pursue the game at Frickley Colliery. Scunthorpe unearthed this gem and put him into their first team almost immediately, and he remained there for many a year. Liverpool's legendary manager Bill Shankly once described dear old Jack as the best uncapped full-back in the country. For the moment his debut against Scarborough at the Old Showground, in United's second fixture of the season was just a kickstart to his illustrious career.

Further up the field Timmy Bowers, whose first name was in fact Percy, was re-employed to lead the battle forces. Wallace, Robertshaw and Norris would again take up the fight in the forward positions, but Rowney was a new addition to their ranks. Little was to be viewed of Harry Johnson, but to his great credit and determination this ageing warrior put on his armour for another ten appearances after the colder weather had eased at the back end of the campaign.

The last, very influential signing, came too late to make a significant impact on affairs, for he played only three games; Dick Taylor was regularly down as R.E.Taylor on the team list.

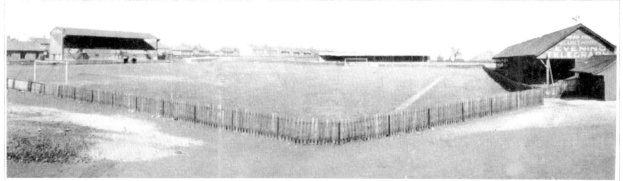
The Old Showground c.1948. Taken pre-League, and after the Fox Street stand was built behind the goal in 1938.

This man was a real snip, having had First Division experience at Grimsby Town, who astonishingly discarded his services. To step down into the Midland League was a brave decision for this tank-like centre-half, but it was one which would pay dividends. Mal Millington had the heart of a lion but all footballers have to look the day in the face when their legs do not respond to what their minds want them to do. Taylor was the ideal replacement, being intelligent, well balanced and strong.

Scunthorpe United soon demonstrated a resilience that was the envy of other clubs. The side they had assembled was a candidate for honours, although a lot of team changes took place before a rhythm could be found in their play. It was also plain to see that this side was not going to be able to match the titanic goalscoring record of one hundred and twenty-one goals attained during the 1946-47 season. This was to be inconsequential, since the regular trio of Watford, Brownsword and Millington would offer a watertight solution to the rearguard. Supporters would have to reflect on the team's workmanlike performances which did enough to swing the balance their way, and more importantly steal the points, generally without a large goal difference.

The opening months of the season saw Scunthorpe shoot to the top quarter of the Division. This was assisted by an express start at Bradford City Reserves where an entertaining 4-3 result saw Bowers in fine early form scoring twice. Brownsword was introduced into the fray at home to Scarborough and won the game, scoring from the penalty spot, a job for which he would win national fame for Scunthorpe in the years to come.

An area where goals did flow was in the annual trek down the path that was plotted by the F.A.Cup. It was uncanny why a club of the standing of Scunthorpe and Lindsey United should still have to tip-toe past the minnows of the lesser standing leagues when they had already given a smart reckoning of themselves in seasons past. Harry Allcock might have welcomed the cash flow but there was still an administrative headache for him organising the games and injury problems were an inevitable risk.

The first encounter in the F.A.Cup matched Scunthorpe against the oldest club in the country. Known as The Sheffield Club, the visitors had a history as ancient as the game itself. It came to pass that ninety minutes was all that was needed in the formality of going through to the next round, courtesy of a 5-1 win. In the following game, Rawmarsh were more of a pushover, and Timmy Bowers must have been in his element, scoring five of the eight goals without reply.

The third qualifier was not such a foregone conclusion and Denaby had to be paid far more respect. They had already inflicted damage on the Knuts in the League, but now the pendulum was swinging towards Scunthorpe as the venue selected was to be the Old Showground. Scunthorpe were shackled for much of the game by a fast moving opposition defence.

Fortunately their own back line was just as firm. Chances were at a premium but when Scunthorpe's opportunity arose Rowney was on hand to score. It might have been a single goal victory, but it made everyone happy.

In parallel, the Midland League programme was going particularly well at this time, especially at home, where the Old Showground had become a fortress. Interest amongst the home fans was intense and there were always large crowds flocking along Doncaster Road and Henderson Avenue whenever they were at home. Even the second team would enjoy gates approaching four figures. However, the tremendous response for the game against Gainsborough Trinity was unprecedented in terms of the Midland League. A grand total of 9,100 fans pushed, squeezed and shoved their way into every conceivable corner of the Old Showground. The vast majority were quite contented with what they saw. Bowers, Rowney and Norris were all on target and United marched on with a 3-1 win. Up to that point Trinity had yet to surrender their unbeaten record.

Back on F.A.Cup duty Norton Woodseats knocked on the door a second time in consecutive seasons. They arrived as a much stiffer opposition, but although United had to toil hard and long for a 2-1 passage, a string of missed opportunities brought much of this extra work on themselves. Both of Scunthorpe United's goals came from young Pinchbeck who was to make only a handful of appearances, but possessed obvious raw talent.

The last qualifier was to put pressure on Scunthorpe and Lindsey's record crowd, because great local excitement was created with the calling of Gainsborough Trinity into the arena once again. This time the third highest attendance to that date crushed into the Showground, and when the dials on the turnstiles were checked it was declared that 9,905 spectators had taken time out to watch, and extra help was needed to struggle to the bank with the bulging money bags. If anything the Cup game against the Northolme Blues was a fraction less demanding than the League match. Certainly the forwards agitated the visiting defenders to a greater degree, and the 4-2 result in favour of Scunthorpe was a mirror of how well they played and victory was deserved.

Luck was to desert the Knuts in the first round proper as they lost the right to defend their Cup tradition at home. The journey to be undertaken was to the Wirral to play an unknown quantity in Runcorn. It was unfortunate that they never came off the blocks on the appointed afternoon, and the home forwards pinned them back for long periods. United's defence finally crumbled under the extremes of pressure, and eventually they were humbled in a 4-2 scoreline.

The stunned reaction left by the F.A.Cup exit did not leave a hangover in the Midland League, and soon the Scunthorpe train was whistling back along the track. Another consolation came by way of a cheque for £2,000, the sum paid for Pinchbeck by Everton, who were happy to develop his abilities in their Central League team in the hope of turning him into a top grade player.

To prove United could bounce back they decided to let rip against the unfashionable Ollerton Colliery side. Timmy Bowers was left to conduct the orchestra, and he obliged by scoring six goals in a 7-1 win. At that stage of the season Scunthorpe were still undefeated at home and the beginning of the festive season saw this run continue under difficult circumstances.

The Club's traditional fixtures with Grimsby Town Reserves included men who would soon experience First Division football, and they brought the best out of the Knuts. In the pair of fixtures both sides traded blows with each other, and both times the home side was victorious. Days later United produced arguably the most exhilarating performance of the year. The visitors were a very useful Peterborough United, a team rapidly evolving into one of the stronger non-League clubs in the country. A large holiday crowd was in place for kick-off, some of whom were no doubt happy with a hint of alcoholic cheer. It was not long before their tongues were loose with the high spirits of the Scunthorpe play. Whatever, United ran riot repeating the 7-1 scoreline as achieved against Ollerton. Bowers scored a hat-trick and Rowney a pair. The other goals came from Norris and Wallace.

The cold dark winter month of January found Scunthorpe and Lindsey United flirting with the leadership. Shrewsbury Town were their chief rivals for the Championship trophy, but despite a draw at Gay Meadow in the early part of their season, it was the Shrews who were in the driving seat. Chances of closing that gap increased as the Knuts remained undefeated throughout the beginning of 1948, but then the run ended when Peterborough exacted revenge at their huge open London Road ground early in February. This was only a minor setback and the next six games reverted to the same undefeated manner.

Scunthorpe and Lindsey United's season went from strength to strength, unlike in most other years which saw a rapid trailing off at the end of the campaign. Hopes were raised that they might just sneak the trophy for the third time when a huge gathering saw Scunthorpe lower Shrewsbury Town's colours by 2-0. It was not until right at the death that the Salop team won the Midland League title. Ironically, United bowed out at home to Lincoln City Reserves, one of the top contenders. It was not until this game that Scunthorpe gave up their home record. The 4-2 defeat suggested tiredness rather than a lack of commitment. Sadly this home loss confirmed that Scunthorpe would be runners-up, but it was a fact already known before the match with the Imps had kicked off. Never-the-less, this team had made a great achievement worth celebrating. Unfortunately it would cut no ice with the voting members at the Football League A.G.M. The door was to be slammed tightly shut in the faces of the non-League applicants, including Champions Shrewsbury and themselves. United would have to prepare for another season on the same plain, but at least they knew that for the immediate future everything in the garden was in full bloom.

With that knowledge Scunthorpe and Lindsey United prepared for a new term. This time team building only required the recruitment of a handful of men since most of the spadework had already been done.

~ 1948-49 ~

The great news at the back end of Summer 1948 was the return of their former young son, Jeff Barker, now a battle hardened veteran following his days as a left half-back at Aston Villa and later Huddersfield Town. His task was to replace Bernard Harper in that position, and immediately this bronzed figure, who had enjoyed an invigorating Summer, was given the Captain's armband. Dick Taylor took the centre-half position, but the last was not seen of Mal Millington, for he could not keep his nose out, and supporters were delighted to see him deputize. This was particularly so when injuries befell the luck of either half-back and Taylor moved across to fill the hole. The right-half slot was more of a problem. Lee took up the shirt originally, but then Dai Davies, and at a later date Eddy Lindley, tried it out for size.

In the back quarters no fault could be found with the combination of Rymer, Watford, and Brownsword. When it came to team selection they had been disturbed infrequently in the 1947-48 season, and the trio remained intact for every League and Cup game in the following campaign, with one exception, when Jack Brownsword was unable to appear through injury against Doncaster Rovers Reserves at home. It meant a continuous run of fifty-one selections.

The forward line would still see the utilisation of Bowers, although not until the second half of the year. Wallace continued at inside-left and supplemented his considerable ball skills with another supply of goals. Stan Norris had decided to hang up his boots which gave the opportunity for Little to come in on the right-wing. Rowney had to share his position as inside man with John Taylor and Robertshaw gave way to Whitehead. Two outstanding other signings strengthened the forward line, first in the form of former West Bromwich Albion and Hull City man Spud Murphy. Spud was actually a Welsh International and had a number of weird and wonderful days of planting the hard leather ball into the back of the net. He was always something of a character and it is alleged that on a number of occasions he would ask Harry Allcock for a sub on his wages to have a bet on the old Gee-gees! He was, never-the-less one very good artist at goalscoring, and proved his worth in that capacity for the Knuts. It came as something of a surprise that he was not invited to wear the Scunthorpe shirt after March, for reasons widely rumoured to be 'misdemeanours'.

The absence of Murphy at this time was cancelled out by another very astute signing, when Jimmy Whitfield became one of Grimsby Town's cast-offs. Whitfield was a very fast inside-forward, with a mastery of the dribble and a demon shot. He was to become a regular feature of Scunthorpe line-ups for years to come, and Grimsby surely were made to regret his departure from Blundell Park.

The team changes were something of a surprise to supporters, especially in the front runners, although some were forced upon the Club.

After such an efficient run in the 1947-48 season, most followers would have settled for more of the same. In the event the search for perfection brought new men into the limelight, and the result would not alter the flow of entertaining football once everything settled down. This team immediately went towards the top of the Midland League and was to be in contention throughout.

Scunthorpe and Lindsey United began with three straight wins, two away, the first at Lincoln City - thus eking out some revenge for the last game of the previous season - and the second at Scarborough. The margin of three goals in each case demonstrated that a strong challenge would be made in all competitions. Their first setback did not come until they lost narrowly at home 1-0, when Shrewsbury Town enforced their own determination to retain their championship. Another hiccup came when the side was embarrassed in front of their neighbours at Gainsborough by a 5-2 scoreline. Scunthorpe just had an off day. The absence of Jeff Barker and John Taylor from the regular team was not a plausible excuse.

To make up the leeway the team went on a five match run without dropping a point. At Nottingham, the beating of the Forest Reserves was an astonishing accomplishment, but none of United's travelling supporters would have guessed that they would manage a 5-0 result. This was followed by a close 4-3 win at York, then 7-0 at home to Gainsborough in the return fixture. How Scunthorpe could sink to the depths, then rise up to top form against Trinity left everyone speechless.

Scunthorpe had been left to get on with the Midland League programme, because for once their progress in the previous F.A.Cup campaign was recognized. It was not until the second week of November that Selby Town were picked up in the last qualifying round. A crowd of over six thousand spectators watched with interest the chess-like struggle to gain supremacy. Spud Murphy edged the Knuts through into the next round, but the 2-1 score was only achieved after a lot of sweat and toil.

The first round proper saw them in the ring with the gloves on against Halifax Town in a difficult tie at the Shay. On the afternoon of the kick-off the weather was hardly kind, for the natural shape of the bowl that made up the Yorkshire team's ground was shrouded in a grey murky fog, and the mist closed in and engulfed the playing area. There was no other sane decision but to abandon the procedures until a few days later.

When the battle was able to recommence the game developed into very much a cat and mouse affair, as both teams probed for an opening. Defences were very much in control and a disappointing blank was drawn all round, although it was the non-Leaguers who were the happiest.

The replay was rapidly arranged for two days on, so that there would be less possibility of a holdup to the second round should a second replay be required. Secretary Allcock had no problems in selling seating for the replay; he could probably have sold double the allocation if there had been room in the stand. The takings on the balance sheet showed that the record crowd was lifted by almost a thousand to 12,775.

If anything, the replayed Cup-tie was clear evidence that Scunthorpe could hold their own in the Football League, Third Division. They matched Halifax in every department, although chances still came few and far between. The was no doubt in everyone's mind that the highlight of the adventure came when United won a direct free kick in front of goal for an infringement. It was obvious that something special was afoot when Murphy cheekily stepped in to become part of the Halifax wall. Jeff Barker took a pace back, then ran to the ball, blasting it straight at Spud. At that moment Murphy dropped like a stone to the deck, and the ball sped through the gap into the net. In the blink of an eye the Shaymen had been eclipsed, and it was Scunthorpe that marched on.

Once again Scunthorpe had reached the second round, and the state of affairs, because of postponed matches and replays, meant that only five days was the period before a coach containing the Stockport County team rolled up outside Henderson Avenue. Harry Allcock was having trouble keeping up with events, because he had yet another record gate to deal with. Much to everyone's delight 13,775 found room in every corner of the ground. The match was described as containing much 'scientific' football. In reality, Scunthorpe tried to play the same type of soccer as their superior visitors instead of keeping to their own game. A single goal, again, robbed Scunthorpe of the chance to great glories in the third round, which was still a bridge too far. The reward would have been a trip to Portsmouth, who were of First Division status at that time, and another big pay day.

The F.A.Cup form had been transferred into their Midland League games. When Mansfield ended the unbeaten run in October, Scunthorpe soon forgot the reverse of fortune and simply slipped into top gear and could not be suppressed again until Christmas Day when the Mariners second team, of all opposition, sneaked in with a 1-0 success. Like all games with Town, this was a tight contest, and on Christmas Monday a draw proved how close the competitive edge between these two old foes had become.

The New Year saw Gainsborough Trinity move a step ahead of the pack, closely attended by the Reserve sides of Nottingham Forest and Bradford Park Avenue. Grimsby and Scunthorpe were also in with a shout, and it was obvious that the honours would be decided among these leading clubs. Scunthorpe had played most of the difficult games against these sides and generally saw the better of the conflict. No other team had been so decisive in beating Trinity, while the double was taken over Forest. In the second half of the season a bitter cold Saturday in February saw the fall of the Park Avenue Reserves. Murphy spun his web of intrigue with three goals in the 5-1 win, but two weeks later the Yorkshire supporters in the Avenue's 'Doll's House' cheered their lad's on to revenge.

Towards the end of the season a number of team changes took place, and combined with a long hard season some mistakes began to creep in, particularly in defence. One or two vital games, that really ought to have yielded points, saw the team slip. A prime example was at home to Grantham, and away at Peterborough. A visit to Shrewsbury might have expected a share of the spoils, but the size of the defeat, at 5-1, suggested they were out of salts after a long day's travelling. It was not all doom and gloom, and the re-emergence of Timmy Bowers in place of the now departed Murphy made sure that when they were on song, United would cause plenty of mayhem in front of goal. Bowers' most impressive form was in scoring twice in the 5-0 victory at Frickley Colliery, then going one better with a hat-trick in the Bradford City game at the Old Showground. This produced a similar result in what was the penultimate match of the season, and the second goal made the one hundredth scored by the team. Unfortunately, at the end of the Bradford City match, it was all over, for United knew mathematically it was impossible to win the League. Honour for that department settled on Gainsborough Trinity.

Scunthorpe should have taken the runners-up spot but on the run-in there was another banana skin waiting. Boston, just below mid-table caused a surprise, and stole the points by winning 2-1. It meant that the Knuts had eased into fourth place, but would still be the Midland League's highest placed team stating their case for League Football status.

The attitudes at the Football League A.G.M. remained steadfast. None of them wanted to put an existing League club to the sword just because it had fallen on bad times. The door that faced Scunthorpe United's directors looked to be shut tight, and so Ernest Plowright, father of the popular actress Joan Plowright leading the Scunthorpe group, decided a switch of tactics might be the best course of action. If there were too many pigeons for the pigeon holes then surely they needed more pigeon holes? In other words, why not canvass instead for an extension to the number of League places? After all it had been done before.

When the proposition of an increase to the clubs of the two Third Divisions was suggested by Scunthorpe's delegation, the only decisive reaction was one of indecisiveness! No Football League clubs wished to get involved in the proposed change of legislation. A number of them said that they would support the action if it was put forward. The problem in hand was to find two delegates able to propose and second the motion. Fortunately, with a little burning of the midnight oil such support came, when warmed by the mellowing effect of a double whisky or two, voting members from Sheffield Wednesday and Everton agreed to put forward a proposal for the increase of the League from eighty-eight to ninety-two clubs.

The next day the Scunthorpe party were delighted with the course of events. Those four places, two for the North and two for the South, would not be available until 1950, but at last a narrow shaft of light was now shinning through the door. It was just as well because the usual impasse blocked the aspirations of the other non-League clubs, and everyone agreed United had done them a great service. Scunthorpe went back to their Old Showground headquarters to regroup and set out their strategy for the coming saga ahead.

~ 1949-50 ~

The news that greeted Scunthorpe supporters was that some of the hard earned cash from their F.A.Cup exploits had been spent to actually buy a player of real substance. United's board had agreed the then considerable sum of £250 for George Thompson, the talented Chesterfield goalkeeper. As soon as supporters witnessed him in action they all agreed he was in line with the best custodians to represent United, and as time passed so he developed as a cultured expert at this specialized and dangerous art.

Thompson was to have regular support in his full-backs, but Barker took over from Watford, whilst Brownsword was immovable at left-back. Once again this section of the side picked itself, and injury to Barker on three occasions was its only disturbance.

The central defence pivot was to be solely the employ of Dick Taylor, whose bald pate became a regular feature. He too, would not surrender his shirt at any time in the coming season. However, Maurice Conroy, late of Accrington, and Joe McCormick, ex-Oldham and Rochdale, became Taylor's operatives on each side of the park.

Up front Heseltine was preferred, having a good pedigree from Tottenham Hotspur, but the Southerner lost his place to the ever determined Timmy Bowers for a time. When Bowers became unavailable, inside man Whitfield led the line with distinction, until Heseltine reappeared at the trailing edge of the fixture card. Wallace took the inside-left spot, while Wilson and Malcolm from Rotherham and Barnsley respectively, operated down the wings.

This team performed with few team changes, except for major injuries altering the situation. A settled team was the key to consistency when the right men were able to line up, and this group saw six men make forty or more appearances, with three others topping the thirty or more mark.

The serious business of trying to get hold of Midland League silver was started with a nine match unbeaten run from the start of the season. Up to that time their fluent brand of direct football suggested that this team's chance of taking the top honour was not beyond the realms of possibility. What was more, in the early escapades, United had taken a maximum of twelve points from their six home matches, scoring eighteen goals and yet to concede one. It would seem that the money for George Thompson had been wisely spent.

Crowds, too, were up and edged towards the eight thousand point whenever United had a fixture on Doncaster Road. Even the reserves could expect a four figure crowd, although the warmer weather in the early part of events probably had a baring on these factors. However, the 11,573 spectators for the first team match with Gainsborough broke all Midland League records.

This excellent run was certainly punctuated by the exuberant form of Timmy Bowers, now in the final phase of his Scunthorpe career. In three consecutive games he scored two goals, then three and finally four against Gainsborough, Grantham and Goole, respectively. The latter two matches recorded emphatic 5-0 advances by the slick Knuts.

The pattern of United's play was put out of joint slightly at Bootham Crescent, for York City Reserves ended the unbeaten scheme of things, when they narrowly took a 1-0 victory. It may have looked as though the bubble had burst when Goole unexpectedly weighed-in with another defeat for Scunthorpe, this time by 2-1. Perhaps it was the kick in the pants the Claret and Blues needed. These losses allowed other contenders to play catch up with them, and it made any complacent team members realise that trophies had to be earned; the silverware was not heaven sent.

Scunthorpe soon went up a gear and found the run through into early November much more productive. They reasserted themselves and only York City Reserves upset the apple cart by completing the double with a deserved 3-1 win. On the reverse side of the coin it was Scunthorpe's chance to shatter dreams and they did so at the highly rated Nottingham Forest Reserves. It may have been the closest of results, but shading this one against a top contender, by a 3-2 result, was priceless. It was far more rewarding than when they claimed seven goals without replay, on Guy Faulkes night, against the floundering bottom club Doncaster Rovers. The enjoyment experienced by supporters, especially at Jimmy Whitfield's first hat-trick for the Club, was none-the-less a tremendous boost at the time.

Unfortunately the first team squad was dealt two extreme blows to key members. Between October and December, three regulars suffered broken bones; Albert Wilson and Joe McCormick were sidelined for some length of time when they each broke a collar bone. Jeff Barker was just as unlucky with a painful break to a small bone in a toe, but at least this did not keep him from playing for quite so long.

It might have been these injuries that caused United to fail at the first hurdle of the F.A.Cup. The fourth qualifier saw them up against Goole Town, a team of which they were well acquainted. Despite the loss of McCormick they were still expected to make progress. Goole Town had other ideas and put a stranglehold on the free-scoring Scunthorpe forwards. A stalemate void of a single score was a disappointing outcome. The midweek replay saw dozens of coaches commandeered for the army of Knuts supporters, waving rattles and wearing claret and blue rosettes, making the short journey to the Victoria Pleasure Grounds. It was probable that the biggest cheer of the afternoon they made went up as the referee blue his whistle to abandon the game due to the dense fog, for United were faltering at 3-1 down. This was a grave injustice for Goole who, frankly, were a million miles in front of the inept Scunthorpe team. A second attempt to settle matters followed days later, but a United team further ravaged by more injury worries eventually lost by the same 3-1 score. The result meant that they would forfeit a trip to Chester in the first round proper.

One of the consequences of the long injury list was that it gave some of the second teamers their debuts in the senior squad for which would not have otherwise been given the opportunity. Len Sharpe was a young local lad that had made his way through the Scunthorpe boys team and finally grasped his chance with both hands. His baptism came in the right-wing berth in place of Albert Wilson, against Nottingham Forest Reserves. This game resulted in Forest seeking their revenge, and winning by two clear goals at the Old Showground. Len retained his place until a more mature replacement in the form of Timmy Bowers was available. In his fourth trip out he scored his first goal against Rotherham United Reserves. Ten years later Sharpe would still treasure wearing the claret and blue.

Scunthorpe and Lindsey United would not be hampered by injuries throughout the season and all the indisposed players did make full recoveries. An illustration of this was seen when both Wilson and McCormick scored in the game that saw the arrival of Bradford Park Avenue Reserves at the Old Showground. Jimmy Whitfield stole the limelight with a hat-trick, and Lennon added another to finalize a 6-1 result. What was more, the crowds continued to flock to Scunthorpe's matches, and were greater than a number of teams in the Football League.

The pressure at the top of the League was maintained right into the dying moments of the season. Whereas some other campaigns had see a tailing off at the end, this team went for the title hammer and tongs. They were not without competition, because other teams had taken a lead on them when the playing strength had been reduced. Nottingham Forest Reserves always had a little in hand, and sharing the Christmas points with the Mariners second eleven was of vital consequence to the neck and neck finish in the table. Scunthorpe could hardly be faulted during the last quarter of around a dozen matches. Only Hull City Reserves got the better of them, 1-0, and that oddly enough came four days after United had thrashed them 5-0 at the Old Showground. Only one point was dropped in the last twelve available, and strange to say the last four games all ended in 2-1 victories.

At the final reckoning Scunthorpe curtailed their playing activities as the third strongest team. Nobody could overhaul Nottingham Forest Reserves, who were worthy champions, five points clear of Grimsby. Three more wins would have given the Knuts another title because they had the League's top goal average.

Now that the team was in Summer recess the directors would have to concentrate on the more important job of winning the Club a place in the Football League. In the first week in June 1950, Scunthorpe and Lindsey United's party, headed by Ernest Plowright and M.P. David Quibell, set off South for the business in front of them with far more optimism than usual. There could be no complacency, despite two positions in the League for new clubs to fill in the Northern Section. An early start would allow plenty of time to do that extra canvassing and to put the Scunthorpe story across to those people who mattered.

Once around the hotels and exclusive clubs of the capital they generally met with a favourable response, although by then they knew there was a lot of competition from other non-League teams that might prove to be more worthy of taking those two precious places.

At the A.G.M., the business of re-electing the bottom clubs came as the usual formality. Voting then resulted in Colchester United and Gillingham taking the two Southern places as expected. Tensions mounted as the ballot was made for the reciprocal Northern positions. Scunthorpe eyed up the opposition and considered Shrewsbury Town as their main rivals. However, when the vote was taken the result shook the Scunthorpe Directors to their boots.

Shrewsbury Town had indeed led the way and were in front of the pack on votes, but Workington and Wigan were level just behind, but Scunthorpe's total put them in fourth spot. For a moment the Scunthorpe United group were in despair as the holy grail slipped from their grasp.

Unprepared for the indecisive ballot, the Chairman of the day announced a second ballot involving all but Shrewsbury, who were given the thumbs up for the Third Division North section. The reprieve set the palms sweating and the heart beating faster again. This second vote was so important to the future welfare of the Club. It seemed like an age to reorganize the slips and for the members to make a second choice, but eventually the returns were in. The drama of the announcement of this second attempt was just as astonishing. This time Wigan and Scunthorpe had tied at the top of the poll.

Harry Johnson, the all-time record goalscorer in the Midland League (including 69 in all competitions during the 1938-39 season).

In near chaos a third ballot was hastily agreed upon. The third and final shoot-out would be a direct confrontation between Wigan and Scunthorpe. All that United's band could do was cross their fingers and pray. The last declaration awarded Wigan eighteen votes and Scunthorpe thirty. Plowright and company let out a great cheer of relief, shaking hands and embracing each other. At last after fifty years of struggles the Club had achieved its ambition to join the country's National Football competition.

News of this great achievement was slashed across the front page of the Scunthorpe Evening Telegraph. It was a momentous occasion for Scunthorpe and Lindsey United and was greeted with great enthusiasm around the town and its immediate surroundings. Supporters could not wait until August, which would bring the first match in this wonderful new sphere. The Directors said they would need gates of at least 15,000, and arrangements were straight away put in hand to increase the capacity by banking the Doncaster Road terracing. A new manager was to be advertised for, and money be made available for footballers of strength and character for the conflicts ahead. Sadly, some of the old-timers of the Midland League would not be good enough to participate in the journey ahead. Some of them, like Harry Johnson and Mal Millington would at least be retained to look after junior and reserve teams, or to carry out scouting missions. Supporters had also to become accustomed to far tighter and lower scoring games than in the past, although since the Second World War this was something they had come to expect anyway, as the competition of the Midland League had developed. Suddenly everyone was talking about the Club, and life at the Old Showground had never been better.

## CHAPTER 6

INTO THE LEAGUE

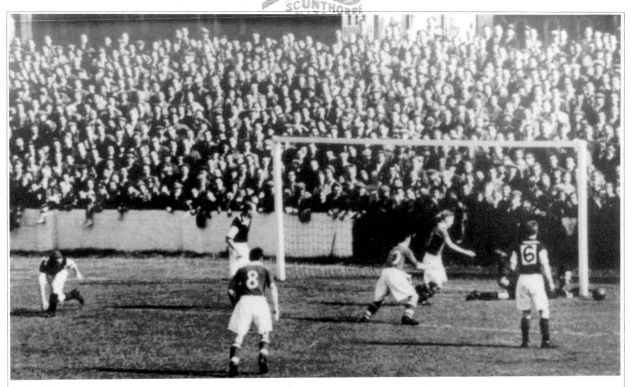

A packed Doncaster Road terrace watch the action in the first Football League match versus Shrewsbury Town. United players repelling an attack, are: Barker (falling), Taylor, McCormick (no.6), and 'keeper Thompson

When the sun rose over the back of the old wooden East Stand on the morning of Saturday 19th August 1950, Mr Allcock had made sure everything was in place for the start of Scunthorpe and Lindsey United's career in the Football League. On the occasion of that morning he arrived early for work to busy himself in the one hundred and one jobs to be completed, although his industry made sure it was a case of dotting the 'I's and crossing the 'T's. Demand to see the first game was high and everyone wanted to be there as a witness.

Much work had been done beforehand to prepare the Club. The first task was in appointing a quality manager. This was fulfilled when former Arsenal and Wales full-back Leslie Jones, now conversant in the ways of coaching and management skills, accepted the position in charge of team affairs. Jones was a shrewd tactician and never made rash promises of promotion or other illusions of grandeur. Instead he went about his job in a quiet and confident way, bringing in talent to improve the team, and schooling everyone in the simple methods he wanted the game played. It was said that with the influx of Welsh players, the Club was to receive lessons in the Welsh language so all and sundry could communicate with each other!

The eye Jones cast over the old team had him satisfied with most of the back division players. Only the strengthening of the right-half position was required and from York City, Scunthorpe offered terms to the solidly built Bill Allen. Bill had been part of the city team to lose to United in the 1946-47 season Cup. Before long Allen was to swap over the left-side in preference to Joe McCormick. Two matches into the season Scunthorpe plucked Jack Hubbard from non-League football at Scarborough for the number four shirt that Allen first wore. Both new signings would pay the Club loyal service, particularly Hubbard who was to remain at the Old Showground for over a decade. He forged a back line partnership with the Peter Pan of Scunthorpe football, Jack Brownsword. On rare occasions Dick White was called from the second team to develop his great potential.

The forward line was not as stable, and only Jimmy Whitfield survived, although George Wallace remained on the books, but his reluctance to give up his steelworks job and train full-time relegated him to second team duties.

To spearhead the new forward line Ted Gorin signed as a bustling centre-forward of the traditional type from Cardiff City. Ted was never afraid to get in amongst the action and make his physical presence felt. His inside men would turn out to be Joe Payne from Newport County and Neath born

Mal Rees from Barry Town. The Welsh flag was firmly flying over Lincolnshire with this trio. To complete the team the popular Harold Mosby and the vastly experienced Wally Boyes were offered terms. Harold, smaller in stature, but nimble in foot, arrived from Rotherham. His left-wing accomplice, Wally Boyes, was already thirty-seven years of age. This did not concern Leslie Jones, who brought the balding ex-West Bromwich Albion and England man for the way he could still jinx down the aisles and cross the ball with pin-point accuracy. Shortly into the season, competition for wingers places was intensified with the arrival of Horace Cumner, yet another player born in the Valleys, who joined the staff from Watford for £900.

~ 1950-51 ~

Before the first game got underway, another small innovation had to be taken on board. The Club decided to adopt a new nickname for this new Football League era, which would reflect the association with the Town's industry. Instead of the affection of 'play up the Knuts' the Club would now respond to being referred to as 'The Iron'.

It was a coincidence that the fixture secretary had come up with the novelty of pitching both the Northern Section's youngest members, Shrewsbury Town and Scunthorpe United into the fray together. Despite home advantage and a lot of encouragement through the local and national press there was hardly a favourite to choose. The expected tight strategic game ensued before a huge 11,847 crowd, a figure that only F.A. Cup-ties had surpassed on two occasions. United's team for that historic occasion lined up; Thompson, Barker, Brownsword, Allen, Taylor, McCormick, Mosby, Payne, Gorin, Rees and Boyes.

At the end of the ninety minutes of honest endeavour no goals had been scored and a fair result was on the board. Everyone was happy with what they had seen, and the general synopsis of opinion was that Scunthorpe would be able to handle themselves in this new competition..

During mid-week, United had to make the short journey to meet a very strong Lincoln City side at Sincil Bank. The Scunthorpe eleven contained one team change, where Jimmy Whitfield replaced Joe Payne. The distinction of scoring the first Football League goal fell in this match to Ted Gorin, making the most of a misunderstanding in the Imps defence. Scunthorpe made a major contribution to the game but went down 2-1. They may have considered themselves very unfortunate when Dick Taylor headed the ball high into the net, but the goal was ruled out for an infringement, much to the disgust of the noisy Scunthorpe element amongst the 16,857 gate.

The inclusion of Whitfield was to bring further goals, this time from the former Mariner himself. On the next Saturday his goal at Mansfield brought another point in the 1-1 draw. A second midweek meeting with Lincoln yielded a similar result with the assistance of the same scorer. The interesting part of this encounter was that with the increased capacity on the Doncaster Road the record attendance ceiling was raised to the handsome figure of 14,840.

Three days later the record almost toppled again, but the excellent goalless draw with eventual champions Rotherham United was a couple of hundred folks short.

Scunthorpe and Lindsey United's supporters were now gagging for the first ever win in their new adventure. Although the statistics were tidy, a digit in the all important 'win' column was imperative. It finally arrived in the sixth game against Oldham Athletic when Whitfield fired in a shot, scoring his third of the season, and allowing United to win 1-0. Another point to note was that, in what was a third consecutive home match, the attendance dropped by a little over six and a half thousand. Oldham Athletic would figure in another part of Scunthorpe United's 'firsts', for eight days later they became the Iron's first away victims and thus the first to be claimed as a double. Those who crossed the Pennines to be present were thrilled by goals from Whitfield, Mosby and a couple from Gorin in the topsy-turvy 4-3 assault.

At the end of September the visit of Accrington Stanley provided another new line in the ledger. It was on this occasion that Ted Gorin set out to make his mark and score the first League hat-trick for Scunthorpe. Supporters went home very happy after watching a commanding 3-0 exhibition from the Iron in the mild conditions.

A feature of the Autumn was that the Football Association still required the four newcomers to enter the cup at the qualifying stage for one more year. It meant a break from the excitement of the Third Division North, and for Harry Allcock to see what quote Lincolnshire Road Car could offer, when the long away trip to Hereford was selected. The journey was to prove to be fruitless for United, and the black and white shirts won the cup-tie with a single shot that George Thompson could not get near. Jeff Barker was a hero for a captain's command performance and a villain for the weak penalty kick that the home 'keeper acrobatically saved.

The arrival of Christmas saw Scunthorpe surviving far better than the other of the Division's babies. Shrewsbury were struggling just above the bottom four places, while United were happily sailing in a position around the half-way mark. The team then traded blows with Wrexham in home and away games. At the Old Showground on Christmas Day, United deserved the 2-0 victory because of tight marking in defence and the taking of opportunities in attack. The Boxing Day feature saw the roles reversed on the Racecourse ground. Wrexham took advantage of slackness in the Scunthorpe ranks to win 3-1.

Ted George had been a prolific goalscorer throughout his time wearing the number nine shirt. Other Third Division North sides had tasted the havoc he could dish out, and of these Shrewsbury Town thought that they could lure the Welshman back nearer home to do the same job in Salop. Scunthorpe were happy to receive an undisclosed fee and release him from his contract. His dozen goals in twenty six appearances would not be beaten all season, but of greater importance the question to answer was would his absence alter the balance of the team? The response was fortunately no, because the huge frame of Dave Clelland was summoned from the second team to admirably fill the void. Clelland's dominating stature was such that when he left the game he joined the Police force.

Towards the end of the first Football League season another milestone was reached. The biggest win was settled at 6-0 over the bottom club, New Brighton. Clelland notched a pair, as did the newly installed Len Comley, while Payne and Horace Cumner - a penalty - scored the rest of the batch.

The season drifted away at Prenton Park, where, despite a 1-0 loss, a highly satisfactory state of affairs prevailed. Scunthorpe had finished twelfth in the table, having defended well to provide the best home record of any team in all four Divisions. Only York City had shot down the flag at the Old Showground and nine goals conceded was the meanest total offered by any club. There was still some latitude in away games to be pursued, but the three wins on opponents soil, at Oldham, Stockport and New Brighton paved the way for three doubles. No team managed to prize away all four points from the grip of the Iron.

The only irritating part of the campaign came at the end of the season. Leslie Jones had received some unwelcome criticism from certain quarters and thought his management had been undermined. His results should have spoken for themselves, but he was aggrieved sufficiently so that he tendered his resignation. The board reluctantly accepted his letter but were in no rush to appoint a successor at the drop of a hat. They decided to bide their time and seek out the appropriate candidate, no matter how long it would take. The situation also led to resignations from the board, and former player and respected headmaster, Alex Moore, took over as Chairman.

Scunthorpe and Lindsey United chose coach Bill Cockhill, a long servicing Notts County man, to step in and sooth the bubbling cauldron. Initially the board would have him to oversee the situation in a caretaker/manager role. His first job was to discharge Payne, Rees and Boyes. Jimmy Whitfield had also found another club and sought to leave for a career at Southport for a small fee.

~ 1951-52 ~

Replacements, to a great degree, were found in the second teams ranks. There was to be greater employment for Len Sharpe and Dick White. In addition Corkhill recognised the enormous benefit of the ball skill wizardry from George Wallace, languishing in the Midland League Reserve team and left to waste by Leslie Jones. Others given a chance would be Peter Platts, George Gray, and South African goalkeeper Norman Malan, who stepping into the spotlight on the rare occasions when George Thompson was unavailable.

Most of the major team developments were to be in the forward positions. Jack Hubbard initially took up a place at inside-right next to Ray Powell, a Welshman from Swansea playing in his home town's team, with Arthur Hall from Goole, then George Wallace, as the left sided inside-men. Eventually Hubbard slipped into the half-back line and in the last days of the season as a full-back in place of ageing Barker. Mosby and Cumner continued to run the wings. Into October the forwards were to be joined by a very canny acquisition in left-winger or inside-man, Jimmy Rudd, A £1,500 investment from Rotherham United. In previous years his pedigree had allowed him to be part of the Manchester City team at Maine Road. Rudd quickly settled down and became a popular member of Scunthorpe's attack.

The rest of the eleven was very much a case of the old guard continuing to give first class service once again, although Corkhill rang the changes when necessary. At right-half, Cecil Stirland was signed from New Brighton with immense experience but was not utilised after a handful of appearances at the start of the season, until a prolonged run at the very end. John Babes, an Arsenal Junior from Lurgan, was given the reins when Barker was injured, but again he was unable to impress enough to make a sustained impact on playing matters. These were the only disturbances to the numbers one to six shirts, who each virtually picked themselves.

Scunthorpe opened their fixtures by excelling in front of just over ten thousand shirt-sleeved supporters at home to Bradford City. There were plenty of beads of perspiration on the brows of all players, but it was Scunthorpe United that took the points with Horace Cumner the single goalscorer. The Club then went on a run that only gained one more win in the next ten games. Lincoln City acted in an unneighbourly fashion, walking all over the Iron to win 3-1 at the Old Showground in the most noteworthy match of this sequence. Fortunately the wolf was kept from the door with points picked up in draws, mainly at home, plus a welcomed pillage of the points on tour to the North-East to the railway town of Darlington. Peter Platts had the honour of scoring Scunthorpe's second goal on his debut at number nine in the 3-2 victory. Cumner and Wallace fired the other battery rounds.

United returned to winning ways with another away day special. This time Wrexham were the foes to lose home advantage and Powell scored twice in the 2-1 result. Although United had not won in four games before the trip into North Wales, drawn matches meant that after the game they had not lost in four. An extension to the sequence was added in front of their own patriots with an execution of Halifax Town the week after.

The major talking point of the 1951-52 season was about to unfold, and started in November. United's annual pilgrimage in the F.A.Cup began when the draw brought them face to face with the quaintly named Billingham Synthonia Recreation, a team of North-East stock. Suddenly the roles were reversed, and it was The Iron that was the giant ready to be killed. Billingham were well represented in the 9,861 crowd, but thoughts of any score that was not par for the course were speedily dispelled when Scunthorpe took immediate command of the game.

Jack Hubbard scored one of his infrequent goals, and both Wallace and Powell hit a pair. It had been an easy workout for the Claret and Blues who were quick to commend the gallant efforts of their adversaries.

The second round draw brought great elation to the Club and its supporters. United had been matched with Millwall, a London side of Third Division South fame. Pundits suggested that United would be bowled over during their first ever trip to the Capital, but urged on by a huge posse of followers that had packed a number of special trains, they gave a good account of themselves.

During the game it was the forwards that were to find the going the toughest, for chances were few and far between. In the Scunthorpe goal George Thompson demonstrated why he had become a top specialist at this level, capably dealing with a couple of shots from the onrushing Lions advanced troops. Brownsword showed how nimble he could be, and Dick Taylor pulled out all his mastery, which had been learned in the heat of the First Division at Grimsby. Jeff Barker was mentioned in dispatches for his captain's role. It certainly was not all back to the wall football, and up front Powell led the Scunthorpe line with plenty of fire. Despite the perseverance of both combatants neither could break down the other defence.

On the following Thursday it was all to be repeated in the Scunthorpe backyard. Steelworks shifts had to be swapped and lieu days put in to make sure supporters were off work. Quite a few supporters had to attend Granny's funeral that day and sickness among school children rose dramatically, as a mystery one day influenza virus swept through the district! The situation was so serious that the Old Showground filled to 13,580, just short of a record level. Scunthorpe United remained unchanged for the second clash and continued to rely on the youthful Len Sharpe at left-half.

The replay turned out to be a different kettle of fish altogether and Scunthorpe and Lindsey United were really on their metal on that fresh December afternoon. Once the teams had finished sparring with each other it was Scunthorpe who made the decisive play ten minutes from the interval. Horace Cumner crossed the ball high into the crowded box, but when the heads went up it was only partially cleared. Jimmy Rudd used his predatory instincts to seize the ball and drill it at top speed into the net.

The crowd erupted and a wave of emotion was let loose around the crowd. Millwall were spurred into action and a number of heart-stopping moments followed in the second period.

With time slipping away, the Londoners left the gate open at the back. Mosby was to make the game safe on eighty minutes, as a low cross found Powell to shoot home for a two goal lead. Again the crowd erupted, but before they had time to settle back in their seats the same combination struck yet once more. On this occasion Mosby's cross allowed Powell a diving header and at last United were home and dry at 3-0.

After the two struggles with Millwall the Board of Directors met to discuss the situation of the managership. The obvious solution was to officially offer Bill Corkhill the position on a permanent basis. Everyone was delighted when he placed his faithful old pipe of St. Bruno on one side and put his signature on the dotted line.

Folks could hardly wait for the third round draw, for it was the first time the Club had progressed that far. Fingers were crossed that they would be pulled out of the hat to meet a top First Division team, and in the event they could not come much bigger than Tottenham Hotspur at the Old Showground. Before the Cup-tie could be played there was the matter of some Third Division North material to sift through.

On the Saturday after the Millwall game United were still on song to beat the newcomers to the League, Workington, freshly elected in the place of the New Brighton team, who had spiralled into a sad decline. Over Christmas came two meetings with Grimsby Town. Never before had there been an encounter where both first teams were involved. It was also surprising how these games had become part of the fixture list, for in 1948 the Mariners had been of noble First Division stock, while Scunthorpe had been of far more humble Midland League status. In the end Grimsby produced the upper hand in both encounters, but at least the Boxing Day attraction at the Old Showground broke all box office records when 15,734 spectators were present. Before the eagerly awaited Cup-tie, United had time to lose at Oldham 2-0, and then thrash Darlington 5-2, in front of less than half the Grimsby game crowd, in the next home match.

Time marched on, and eventually the Tottenham team coach rolled up outside the players entrance. Accompanying the London aristocrats was a whole army of navy and white clad fans, all talking in a strange accent, similar to those of the Millwall supporters.

The teams for the Third Round game were as follows:
Scunthorpe: Thompson, Barker, Brownsword, Hubbard, Taylor, Sharpe, Mosby, Hall, Powell, Rudd and Cumner.
Tottenham: Ditchburn, Ramsey, Withers, Nicholson, Clarke, Burgess, Walters, Bailey, Duquemin, Hamer and Mealey.

At that time Duquemin was the England centre-forward, while Alf Ramsey would manage the England World Cup winning eleven in 1966, and Bill Nicholson, at right-half would win the League at White Hart Lane, as both a manager and a player.

When the game got underway, quite remarkably 22,652 people were in position. Young boys were passed high over the head of adults and down in front of the perimeter fence to see the match, while the St. Johns ambulance crews worked overtime on those folk who fainted in the crush.

The game they were about to witness was something of a letdown from the point of view of the home fans, although they did marvel at the technical skills of the First Division wizards.

Scunthorpe tried to match Tottenham at what the top side did best but it did not pay dividends. Under the eye of primitive T.V. cameras, Duquemin showed why he was the master of all in that position. He weaved his magic twice, and Bailey scored a third for a yawning 3-0 margin.

The remainder of the season had its ups and downs in the battle for points in the Third Division. A trouncing was experienced at Southport when Jimmy Whitfield led the men in gold shirts to a 5-1 victory. Perhaps it was then when a sniff of the air suggested Jim was homesick, and was there an opening for an early return? Whatever may have been said, Jimmy Whitfield was back wearing claret and blue by the end of the same February month. A fortnight later United signed the considerable figure of Sid Ottewell, a man with roots in the mining community of Nottinghamshire. Sid arrived from Mansfield Town and featured in his second match in the undoing of his former club by a 4-1 scoreline. He scored his first goal for the Iron on that winter's day, along with others from Mosby, Cumner and Rudd.

At the death Scunthorpe rallied in the 1951-52 campaign to finish with a six match unbeaten run, four of which ended all square. Statistics revealed that they had dropped two League positions on the previous year, but the total number of League points won was exactly the same at forty-four from forty-six games. Once again the Old Showground had been virtually impregnable, and only first and second placed Lincoln City and Grimsby Town had inflicted defeats there. Powell was the leading marksman on fourteen goals, three in front of Horace Cumner; Powell also had four more F.A.Cup goals to be considered. Sid Ottewell had impressed with eight in just fourteen appearances. Gates were a touch down on the baptism season, but the little extras taken in the Cup more than outweighed this problem.

~ 1952-53 ~

Despite having done some business late in the previous campaign, there were still some changes in the team for the commencement of the 1952-53 season. Sammy Cox had a go at the right full-back position but he spurned his chance, and Jack Hubbard was introduced as a permanent fixture alongside Jack Brownsword. Injury to Brownsword in December caused him to miss his first Football League game after one hundred and thirteen consecutive first team appearances. He also lost the last part of the season for the same reason, and Eddie Lockwood took over.

In the half-back divisions there was to be no more of the reliable Bill Allen, but a more than capable Andy McGill arrived from Bradford City, and was to be a feature of the first team for the next four years. Further runs were given to Dick White and Len Sharpe, but they were not quite ready for permanent duties, especially when their National Service in the forces interrupted the flow. Dick Tyalor, on the other hand, was too good to be ousted by White, but United did persevere with an experiment to put the young local player at centre-forward.

Bill Corkhill was of the opinion that the forward line would be enhanced by some surgery and new blood was called in

to make improvements in this department. The most notable man to make his way to the players entrance was the tall Jack Haigh, whose awkward style caused lots of problems to defenders, who just could not get their feet round his lean frame. Jack was signed from Liverpool, where his chances of a regular first team run had been restricted by the abundance of talent at Anfield. He was to be given a stage at Scunthorpe where his skills could be performed, and the genial Yorkshireman became a crowd favourite for many years. Over on the left-wing another player to secure first team football was Alan 'Digger' Daley, a tricky, wide player, who would later be employed on the right flank.

In the middle of the park, it became a problem to find a settled scorer in the centre-forward position. When the season found itself underway, Les Mynard, from Derby County, was given the run, but with limited success, and Les Broadley tried to fill the spot. In the end Jimmy Whitfield and Horace Cumner also had a shot at the position, but none of the hopefuls left Bill Corkhill entirely satisfied.

Unfortunately, the campaign did not begin in the manner intended. A solitary point was all that was gleaned from the first four games. Two of the losses were at the hands of Grimsby Town, but the local rivalry brought the aggregate number of spectators to over forty thousand, including a record 18,974 for a League match at the Old Showground. Grimsby would be one of the fancied sides in the Division and so the damage was not fatal. It just made Scunthorpe's early season look a little messy.

The tide turned for the Iron when they took Rochdale to task, going nap with their five card trick. The afternoon was jubilant for the five different names on the scoresheet. In order of merit were McGill, Mynard, Whitfield, Mosby and Haigh. This highly entertaining game, from Scunthorpe's viewpoint, was an oasis in a desert. Goals dried up and Corkhill continued to shuffle the pack. His solution was to introduce Alan Bushby, stepping up a grade from the Reserve team squad. Yorkshire-born Bushby quickly adapted himself to the rigours of the extra demands and never lost his place throughout the rest of the season. His fluent stream of passes soon had the forwards back on song, and his debut coincided with an unbeaten run of eight matches.

Unfortunately, supporters would have to come to terms with the loss of their popular 'keeper, George Thompson, who had served them well for four years. His consistent form had brought the scouts flocking to see his performances, and Preston North End were the first of the pack to make their minds up and offer the Iron an acceptable proposition. Thompson was to make the most of the opportunity of First Division football, and enhanced his career with a runners-up medal at Wembley in the F.A.Cup Final at Wembley. He left with all the good wishes of everyone at the Club. There was no panic to sign a replacement, because Norman Milan made a first class deputy.

The highlight of the unbeaten run in October came when Accrington Stanley paid a visit. United were soon on top of their game and won 5-2. One pleasing feature of the afternoon was the two goals scored by Dick White, who was acting as an experimental centre-forward. Two more goals came from Alan Daley, while Jack Brownsword made the total five when he converted a penalty kick. Jack had taken on the mantle of penalty taker when he scored against York City, and from that time his high conversion rate was to make him the man for the job.

In the F.A.Cup the Scunthorpe bandwagon began to roll again when their name was brought out of the black bag with the handily placed Carlisle United from their own Third Division North. A tight game took place, but favoured by home advantage, United won the day with Jimmy Whitfield's strike. The second round brought them a very sticky tie away at non-League Hereford, in a repeat of what had cost United dearly two years ago. Hereford had already beaten Leyton Orient 3-2 following a draw in London and so they could not be underestimated. In the event it was the defenders that won the day, particularly Norman Malan who had played his first Cup-tie at Edgar Street in the absence of George Thompson in the 1950 clash, and the result was 0-0.

The replay took place in Scunthorpe on the Thursday afternoon of that same week in conditions that suited football. A crowd of just in excess of ten thousand was in place to urge the Iron on. It was imperative that they took the upper hand from early on in the game so as not to allow Hereford's enthusiasm to take hold. On the half hour Scunthorpe won the break they had been pressing for. Dick White's shot was only partially cleared by the goalkeeper, and Haigh pounced on the ball, shooting from close range. The crowd roared expectantly, but it was scrambled away only for White to get a second bite of the cherry and fire home.

After this goal Scunthorpe rested on their laurels enabling the Hereford lads to claw their way back. It came as no surprise to see the visitors scramble an equalizer, and so the mountain had to be climbed again. There were only eight minutes left on the watch when Jimmy Whitfield scored the vital goal with an unstoppable angled drive. Hereford United were on their knees, and the game was now beyond them, as once again Scunthorpe United were making their presence felt in the F.A.Cup competition.

The F.A.Cup draw on the following Monday morning was an absolute money-spinner. Sunderland at Roker Park was as good as anything that they had hoped for. The Rokerites had won every honour in the game, and had not played a Football League game outside the First Division. Before the journey up to the cold depths of the North-East, United had a few Third Division North games to get their heads round.

December's League programme started with an excellent 3-2 win at Wrexham, but they had to rely on a Brownsword penalty to complete the scoring. Then came a triple disaster, first when Barrow raided the Old Showground and stole two points, winning their only away game of the season. This was the prelude to a couple of holiday matches against the vanquished Carlisle.

On Christmas Day the Cumberland side hit Scunthorpe with an unforgiving barrage. The 8-0 defeat was unparalleled, and was followed on Boxing Day Monday with a 2-1 victory at the Showground to rub in their revenge over the F.A.Cup defeat. The home game was the final straw for Bill Cockhill, and it cost Dick White and Les Mynard their places. Unruffled, the manager planned trips to Southport and Stockport, which produced three points from results of 3-2 and 1-1 respectively.

Ten days into the New Year and United were due to play the role of giant-killers, if they could. At kick-off time, the huge arena of Roker Park was brimming full with a crowd of 56,507 making a deafening roar. Never before, nor since, has such an enormous crowd gathered to watch a Scunthorpe game. Even before the match started, United's directors could see pound note signs rolling in front of their eyes.

The two teams lined-up as following.
Sunderland: Threadgold, Hedley, Hugell, Aitken, Hall, Wright, Bingham, Kirtley, Ford, Shackleton and McSeveny.
Scunthorpe Utd: Malan, Hubbard, Brownsword, McGill, Taylor, Bushby, Mosby, Haigh, Ottewell, Whitefield and Mynard.

Having experienced the more sophisticated style of football served up in the First Division during the 'Spurs Cup-tie, United knew they would have to raise their game. Once the proceedings were underway Sunderland's artistry was plain to see. In front of goal Shakleton and Ford were obviously the most dangerous of players, and they looked to sniff out goals from the slightest of chances, but were policed very well by the whole Scunthorpe back line, thus the threat was kept to a minimum. Up field, Haigh and Whitefield caused problems, and Threadgold was called into action to hold shots from both of these roaming forwards. The more the game wore on, the more frustrated the home crowd became, as their side failed to produce the vital thrusts.

Sunderland continued to frustrate their biased following until ten minutes from time. Shackleton found space in the penalty box and lobbed the ball to Ford. Despite pressure to close him down, he did enough to put sufficient pace on the ball to beat Malan, who let it slip gently into the corner of the net. It should have signalled the end of the Iron, but if anything they did not lack courage, and the game still had a sting in the tail.

Urged on by the claret and blue army, almost lost in the great swell of the crowd, they won a corner thanks to Sid Ottewell's persistence, with four minutes remaining. Mynard swung over a high looping cross which Threadgold seemed powerless to rise to collect, with Ottewell in front of him. Andy McGill was handily placed to dive headlong at the ball and send it spinning into the back of the net. One explanation for Threadgold's lack of anticipation - allegedly - was that when the corner was taken nobody noticed Ottewell stand on the 'keepers feet, and he was literally rooted to the spot! An old wives tale or not, it was the Scunthorpe supporters who did the celebrating that evening.

The 1-1 draw meant the battle lines were drawn on the following Thursday. Another mammoth crowd of over twenty-one thousand cheered the players on to the park. Les Mynard had suffered a knock, but with Horace Cumner replacing him, this probably strengthened the team. With so many people right up to the perimeter fence the Scunthorpe eleven could feel the breath of the supporters as they urged them on.

The replay soon took a similar shape as the first tie, and it would have taken a good judge to tell which of the pair was the top division side. It soon looked as though Whitfield had given United the lead with a cracking shot, but much to the home supporters dismay, Harold Mosby on the very far side and hardly part of the play, caused a linesman's flag to be raised for offside. To add insult to injury, late in the half, Sunderland produced the one flash of magic to allude the Scunthorpe defence, when Wright was fed the ball to side-foot the first goal.

In the second period, roared on by the crowd, Scunthorpe surged around the Sunderland box looking to equalize. Alan Bushby, playing on his twentieth birthday, was having a storming game. He was involved in the move all Scunthorpe supporters wanted to see, when he punted a free-kick high into the penalty box from near the halfway line. Up rose both attackers and defenders in unison, but it was Alan Daley who stretched an inch more than anyone else, to guide the ball into the net. The crowd went mad as they anticipated a grandstand finish. An injury to Ford gave the advantage to Scunthorpe when the Rokerites were reduced to ten effective men, but they were made to pay for not taking enough notice of him, when, with ten minutes remaining Sunderland struck. After overcoming continuous pressure they broke upfield, the ball ran loose on the edge of the box, and Ford forgot his injury to crash it clean into the goal past the groping Malan. From that moment there was no way back, and Cup dreams had to be shelved for another year.

At least the F.A.Cup took none of the edge off the team's ability to produce some first class form in the Third Division North. Perhaps the next encounter in this competition brought out the most gripping performance of the season, against Bradford City. Unfortunately the crowd was only a third the size that watched the Cup-tie, but those loyal fans were totally entertained. They saw a fast brand of attacking football in which Jack Haigh led the way with the first strike. Whitfield and Daley increased the scoring, and Jack rounded off the afternoon with his second.

One of the most astute pieces of transfer action came towards the beginning of Spring. Bill Corkhill dipped into the coffers to lure nineteen-year-old Gordon Brown from Wolverhampton Wanderers. He was to play the rest of the ten remaining fixtures in the number seven shirt, as a right-wing man, but his predatory instincts would soon see Corkhill push him further into the middle. His four goals at the end of the 1952-53 campaign were just a prelude of what was to come.

The irony of the third season Scunthorpe had enjoyed in the Third Division North was that they had finished in their worst position, on the fifteenth rung of the ladder, but had won forty-six points, two more than the first two sets of figures. The F.A.Cup had been of great financial reward to the Club, and a little money was in hand to spend on players if Bill Corkhill thought it necessary. Caution was still the word the board were focusing on, but everyone agreed that a satisfactory state of affairs prevailed.

~ 1953-54 ~

The Summer of 1953 had barely begun when it seemed it was time for the first public practice matches of 'Probables against Possibles'. During the close season Scunthorpe supporters played the usual game of scanning the sports pages of the Scunthorpe Evening Telegraph to read the 'Poachers' column and speculate on who might be joining the Club. All was revealed in those first public trials, and the answer was that Bill Corkhill had played only a minor role in the transfer market.

There were, however, a couple of 'extras' added to the forward line. The most notable was a pint sized left-winger, Merfyn Jones, a Welshman who had made a limited number of appearances for Liverpool. He would enjoy the chance to link up with his former colleague, Jack Haigh, and a good understanding was soon evident between them. Another top class competitor was the Londoner Jack Gregory, who was released by West Ham United. Jack could not establish himself in the Hammers team, but when he received his chance in the other claret and blue shirt at Scunthorpe he was a revelation. During his stay in Scunthorpe, Jack had a son, John, who went on to represent his country in the game, and finally he became a noted manager with Aston Villa in the Premiership.

Other 'bit' part players were to include Harry Roberts, a versatile winger for either flank, goalkeeper Peter Barley, and the stocky Brian Heward, a young defender making his first tentative steps in the senior grade. Heward would have more opportunities in future years.

Once the whistle had blown to start the first ball rolling, it was quite apparent that this Scunthorpe team was the most superior they had ever assembled. The old adversary Grimsby Town provided the opposition for the first game, and Scunthorpe soon realized they could break their duck against a poorer than usual set of Mariners at Blundell Park. Over eighteen thousand supporters saw Scunthorpe quickly take command, and although only one goal separated the two at the end of the affair, Scunthorpe were worthy winners. Jack Haigh turned provider for the special moment, breaking upfield and just managing to keep the ball in play. He then eluded a black and white defender, before crossing in for Gordon Brown. Brown was left with the easiest of side-foots, for his debut goal.

Scunthorpe continued the run at Gateshead without either side scoring, and kept on buzzing in the first competitive match up the Doncaster Road, against York City. Supporters guessed United had plenty of petrol in the tank when they camped for long periods in the Minstermen's territory. Early in the match they had a goal disallowed for an infringement, and then cracked in three without reply. At this point Norman Malan had hardly mudded his jersey, and was yet to concede a goal in the League that season. This did not happen until he was beaten just once by a Gateshead forward in the fourth game. The goal was neutralized when a penalty was awarded, and Jack Brownsword cooly stepped up to play the ball low, and firmly into the usual right hand side of the net against the stanchion.

It was not until the visit to Southport that Scunthorpe lost a game, and that was an action packed enterprise which saw them lightweight by an odd goal in seven. The secret of success was the few team changes made when Corkhill pinned the team sheet on the back of the dressing room door. Even the disruption of Jack Gregory's loss through an injury for half a dozen matches did nothing to alter the smooth flow. Harry Roberts was called up for duty, and the locomotive steamed on regardless.

Now at last the young upstarts of the League from North Lincolnshire were making an impact on the top spots in the division. Another innovation introduced by Bill Cockhill was an extended run for Dick White in place of Dick Taylor. Taylor had given precious service in his five years at Scunthorpe, but now his age was against him, and White possessed the physical presence to be a natural replacement.

It was with White at the centre of defence that Scunthorpe produced one of the most memorable performances of the calendar. On the weekend before the commencement of the F.A.Cup games, United turned up for a visit to Bradford City's Valley Parade Ground. The recent heavy rain made for a pitch condition which the Scunthorpe players enjoyed, but they were caught on the hop when City took the lead in front of a smaller than usual, but typically biased Yorkshire crowd. This lead was maintained until thirteen minutes from time, when Scunthorpe slipped the noose. Sharpe fed the ball to Jones who comfortably beat the 'keeper from close range.

Instead of hanging on, United went for the kill. Two minutes of play remained when another Jones - Sharpe combination left Whitefield in the clear, to produce a surprise lead. The Bradford City heads were certainly down, and Sharpe was involved in a third goal right on time. This time he was unlucky not to score when a defender punched the ball off the goal line, but Brownsword restored the injustice from the penalty spot. The 3-1 result proved to be a tremendous recovery, and marked the best game to date for Len Sharpe.

The F.A.Cup brought Scunthorpe face to face with an old Midland League adversary, when Boston United were invited to play up the Old Showground. Boston could not match United's quick silver style and soon a cricket score was being notched up. Jack Haigh was on hand for his first club hat-trick and thus was allowed to keep the mudstained ball.

Everyone seemed to be getting on the scoresheet as the goals totted up; every forward that is, except the non-stop Harold Mosby. Mosby had cued up plenty of passes for his colleagues to convert, and late in the game it was thought he should get his chance. They sent a steady stream of balls in his direction so he could net, at least, one shot. It did not come until the last minute of the game, when the biggest cheer of the afternoon was reserved for his goal, which made the score 9-0.

Before Scunthorpe could play their second round tie they had to travel to Carlisle, where their 1-5 reverse hardly put them in the mood for historical Cup exploits, although the result was still marginally better than the debacle a year earlier. When the team returned from the far North-West, Bill Corkhill had to get them in shape for a tough tie at home to Bournemouth.

When Bournemouth arrived in Scunthorpe it was discovered that the referee was not happy with their cherry shirts in the kit basket. In his opinion a colour clash existed and one team would have to change. Bournemouth was a little distant to pop back for a different strip, and so Scunthorpe rang around and found Lysaghts Sports only too willing to oblige by lending their strip. The only problem being that it was a replica of the black and white stripes of local rivals Grimsby Town, and it was hoped that this would not put a hoodoo on the home team.

After the match had started, there was no need to worry, for Scunthorpe had got over their recent inhibitions.

United in an unfamiliar striped kit at home to Bournemouth in the F.A.Cup. Gordon Brown, out of camera shot, scores the only goal, Gregory and Jones watch on.

This hero of the day turned out to be the visiting goalkeeper, who reduced the Iron to a solitary goal. This came on thirty-seven minutes when Sharpe punted a high ball upfield to Whitfield. The centre-forward controlled the awkward bounce, flicked it to Brown, who beat his full-back and glided it home. On paper it may have been a narrow victory, but the lads were full value for their efforts. At the end the twelve thousand crowd stood to applaud both sets of players from the ground.

The progress made in the F.A.Cup was just the lift they needed to face Grimsby Town just before Christmas. A very disappointing attendance of less than ten thousand suggested many local wives had kept their husbands away, insisting rather that they went Christmas shopping. Within the first nineteen minutes ex-Mariner Jimmy Whitfield made his old team pay by scoring one goal and creating another. First he lobbed the 'keeper for a goal of his own, then a pinpoint pass in the penalty area gave Jack Gregory the easiest of chances to make it two. At this stage the points looked beyond the men in stripes, but to give them credit they stuck to their task. In the second half they did pull one back, but Malan was always in control in the home goal.

Once the New Year had been rung-in, Scunthorpe were back on Cup duty. The draw had seen them line up with Wrexham away, a team that was optimistic of progress with their home advantage, and the knowledge that the League match already played had seen them cruise to a 3-1 result. Scunthorpe had another idea and took a 2-0 lead through an Alan Bushby header and a Harold Mosby lobbed shot.

At half-time the tie looked dead and buried, but in the second-half Wrexham swarmed round the Scunthorpe goal and not only pulled back the deficit, but amazingly stole the lead. United needed someone to put their foot on the ball and to dictate the pace. Fortunately Andy McGill was that man, and gradually sanity returned to the flow of Scunthorpe's game. In the dying minutes Alan Bushby restored parity to the contest when he burst through and cracked home the third Scunthorpe goal.

The Thursday replay was not quite as hectic for the Iron, but they still had to work hard to make the fourth round. Gregory's header from a McGill cross nosed United ahead, and Brownsword put them further in front from the penalty spot. Around-half time the tie was made safe as Whitfield shot in from an acute angle. The only misfortune befell the tireless Jack Hubbard, who turned a ball into his own net, but it was of no consequence to United's progress in making the fourth round for the first time.

Scunthorpe United received a plum tie, when it was learned that First Division Portsmouth were to be played. Within the previous few years the team from the naval dockyard city had twice been crowned the League Champions. Supporters soon forgot the team contests in the Third Division, and three draws suggested the players had their minds elsewhere. All talk was on the epic ahead - against Pompey. On the day of the game, Secretary Harry Allcock could hardly keep pace, and the all-ticket battle was a guaranteed record gate.

The numbers on the turnstile dials rolled round to declare a figure of 23,935, a total never to be surpassed. The programme notes showed the team line ups as:

Scunthorpe: Malan, Hubbard, Browsword, McGill, White, Bushby, Mosby, Haigh, Whitfield, Gregory and Jones.
Portsmouth: Platt, Wilson, Mansell, Philips, Rutter, Dickinson, Harris, Gordon, Ried, Barnard and Henderson.

The initial stages of the historic Cup-tie produced a stalemate, and Scunthorpe gave as good as they got. However, on the half hour Portsmouth took the lead with a class move that put Harris clear on the right, and he cut into the box and fired home. Scunthorpe did not allow Portsmouth to take the upper hand, and just after the interval it was a Merfyn Jones shot from a poor piece of defending that raised the Scunthorpe crowd. In the bitterly cold weather it was the Scunthorpe supporters that thought they had stolen the game when Gregory challenged Platt in the Portsmouth goal to force the ball over the line, but the incident did not impress the man in black and a free kick was awarded to the 'keeper instead.

At a score of 1-1 the work was all to do on the following Wednesday. Before play could start an army of snow clearers set to work and brought the pitch up to scratch. Scunthorpe had plenty of vocal support amongst a huge assembly, and the team made sure they would not take second fiddle. Despite playing into a stiff breeze the Lincolnshire side were quite comfortable, but just before the interval a misunderstanding gave Portsmouth the lead. Jack Brownsword kicked the ball away from Norman Malan's grasp during a Portsmouth raid, and Henderson side-footed the ball home for an easy strike.

The goal spurred the Scunthorpe eleven into action, but it was not until after the half-time cup of tea that the arrears were settled. It was McGill's through pass that put Jones clear with only the 'keeper to beat, and he was first to the ball to put enough on it to divert it into the net. Portsmouth were visibly rattled and did not bargain for the extra time deemed necessary. Within a minute of the restart Scunthorpe looked sunk. Harris appeared to be creating no danger until he found Henderson, whose snap shot surprised everyone and crept into the back of the net. Although Pompey seemed to be sailing into the next round they did not reckon for the 'never say die' fighting spirit of little Scunthorpe. Jones was the hero for the second time, and when Bushby found him in the clear his swerving shot went in off the 'keepers arm.

Scunthorpe blazed the headlines of all the National Newspapers. There was even a suggestion that they would eventually overcome Portsmouth and take on Bolton Wanderers in the fifth round. Unfortunately this was not to be, and in the second replay the legs tired and the 4-0 defeat on the famous Highbury pitch, home of the Arsenal, did little to reflect their tremendous achievements. At least the twenty-four thousand spectators in this magnificent stadium had made a splendid platform for them to demonstrate their skills.

In the Third Division, Scunthorpe and Lindsey United continued to scale the heights, although they were never a threat to runaway leaders Port Vale. However, they were one of only seven teams to gain a point in the Potteries. Two more worthy achievements came against second placed Barnsley, only a point in front of the Iron in the final League table. Over Easter, Scunthorpe gained the double over the men from Oakwell in a run which sandwiched an away tour to Halifax. The three encounters produced maximum points, and ten goals for with none conceded. Trouble started for Barnsley when they were thrashed 6-0 at the Old Showground, and they even gave their host the gift of an own goal.

The class of 1953-54 was the best so far. They had competed with the top sides in both the Third Division North and the F.A.Cup and held their own. Cup returns showed that over one hundred and thirty thousand persons in aggregate had viewed their adventures, and League gates had risen by over seven hundred spectators on average per game.

Jack Gregory was the leading goalscorer with sixteen to his name, but what was more encouraging was that five more players had notched eight or over. All that the Club needed was a little more luck and an improvement on their third place in the Division for them to win promotion.

~ 1954-55 ~

The squad for the 1954-55 season was considered strong enough without making any significant changes. Only an injury to Alan Bushby for six weeks brought in Harry Lamb to right full-back, while the utility services of Jack Hubbard were used in place of the incapacitated man from the second week of the campaign.

Norman Malan holds a Grimsby cross, watched by Brownsword, White, and McGill. United were 4-1 victors in August 1954.

A similar situation occurred when Jack Haigh had to drop out. Hubbard moved to inside-forward and Lamb, an ex-Aston Villa squad player, once again took the full-back slot. Perhaps the major disappointment was the gradual disappearance of Jimmy Whitfield who had given sterling

service to the Club. The new season began with one or two changes at Scunthorpe before a ball was rolled. For some time the Club had been referred to as 'Scunthorpe United', whilst the 'and Lindsey' part of the title had been omitted. From now on the Club would be officially known by the shortened name.

At the Old Showground supporters were to be given extra comfort on the terraces on the South side. Doncaster Road had been given a complete overhaul and the steps of the terrace were now of concrete slabs. Over the whole of the structure a proper covering had been erected in the close season, and the contractors made a neat job to secure a capacity for eight thousand spectators on that bank. The money to pay for the fabrication came from the surplus taken from the F.A.Cup activities. The Sunday Pictorial Newspaper had been so impressed by United's Cup achievements, they decided to introduce the "Sunday Pictorial Giant Killers Cup", to be presented to the best David who could slay a Goliath.

The new shelter at Doncaster Road was fairly well packed for the draw against Halifax Town on the opening day. Summer weather provided shade from the warm sun, rather than cover for the rain that would come in the winter period. The roof also produced good acoustics, which were first tested when Jack Haigh scored twice, and players were met with the sound on the rebound. The new sight was in complete contrast to the previous wooden fenced enclosed low terrace which had the town's gasworks as a back drop in former times.

Supporters of the Club were more interested in the second match, to be played at Blundell Park, now a regular highlight of the fixture card. Trains, coaches and cars transported three to four thousand of the locals to see the game, which was played in mid-week on the Tuesday. In all, just short of twenty thousand spectators were present to witness Scunthorpe United in devastating form. The final outcome may not have been apparent after twelve minutes, when the Mariners went a goal up. All this did was to inspire United to lay siege to the Grimsby goal, and McGill's shot was diverted into the net from an awkward lunge by a defender. In the second-half everything United did turned to gold, and goals by Gregory, Brown and Jones emphasized the visiting team's superiority.

United were set up for the home game with Grimsby after Jack Gregory scored his second career hat-trick for the Club at York the following Saturday.

When Town arrived for the second phase at the Old Showground there were hopes among the local supporters that another double could be repeated over the traditional enemy. Unfortunately the Mariners team was not the Rolls Royce of previous years and seemed content to hammer United with rough tactics. Gordon Brown soon became a limping passenger and a confrontation between Gregory of Scunthorpe and Hughes of Grimsby led to the pair being given their marching orders by a strict referee who would have none of it.

Jack Haigh and Len Sharpe, two of United's long-serving players during the 1950's, in training with medicine balls both former players are still regular Iron supporters.

Colliery, and the draw meant that it was the Iron that had to put in the mileage. The 1-0 victory the team earned as a result of a goal scored by Andy McGill did not mirror the tremendous amount of work by Scunthorpe. Chance after chance went begging and the Horden goal lived a charmed life. In the end the Iron were just pleased to make it into round two.

The next stage of the F.A.Cup brought back memories of the 1930's, when for the third time United were selected to visit the Highfield Road Ground of Coventry City. This time there was to be no celebrations. Coventry flattered themselves before a twenty-one thousand crowd, with a lead at half-time, when it had been Scunthorpe that had done the lions share of the attacking. Gregory should have restored the equilibrium, but blasted over when it was easier to score. A measure of how the luck was going was shown in the second goal for the home side. Malan dived full length to apparently make an excellent save, but the ball got away from his fingers and rolled agonisingly over the line. Continued Scunthorpe efforts were thwarted, and at 4-0 the result was somewhat an insult to the team.

Although the play settled down for the remaining hour it was not the spectacle the fifteen thousand crowd had paid to see. Merfyn Jones secured the points for the Iron in the eightieth minute when he ran through to score, and demonstrated that he was the best player on view. However, it should have been more, but Brownsword was a little too casual in taking his spot kick, and the Grimsby number one earned himself some glory with the save.

It was obvious that this Third Division North team would provide as satisfactory a conclusion as they had done twelve months earlier. One of the secrets of their early success was that only thirteen men had been used by the end of October. York City, Barnsley and Accrington were all amongst the pacesetters, and all were beaten by the eager Scunthorpe team by the end of Autumn.

The exit from the F.A.Cup had only the consolation that the Iron would now be able to concentrate on promotion to the Second Division, but it is more likely they would have preferred to have been at Huddersfield on Cup duty, than at Chester, on the day. However, Chester was not such a bad place to be, for Jimmy Whitfield scored a trio of goals in what was only his second appearance of the season.

The most enterprising of all the results was against Accrington, when the club from Peel Park attracted another couple of thousand on the average crowd. Phil Turner scored on his League debut and Gordon Brown added two more. Accrington had no answer and Scunthorpe made them suffer, despite the higher table position of the Reds. Norman Malan showed a clean pair of hands to star in the defence, while Jack Haigh finished off the scoring at 4-0. Not every game went according to plan, and Scunthorpe found themselves on the receiving end at Hartlepool. In a similar vein they conceded four goals, when the understanding between Hubbard, Brownsword and White exposed Malan in goal. Jack Gregory did his best to keep United in the picture but his two strikes still had Scunthorpe playing 'catch up'.

One of the most astonishing matches occurred when Hartlepool travelled to Scunthorpe for the second game of the series. Bill Corkhill had not been happy with the inside-right position since he had lost Jack Haigh through injury. Whitfield had done well, but was then put out of commission himself. Phil Turner and Alan Bushby had been tried, but Bill thought he would give Jack Hubbard, a man of many parts, a shot in the number eight shirt. On the afternoon, Jack was a revelation and toured that part of the park as though it was his own. Incredibly Hubbard belted in four goals in the 5-1 score. Then without any fuss, despite being the first Scunthorpe player to register that many goals in the Football League, he went about his business and did what was requested of him in the next match.

Scunthorpe had the chance to win the newly installed Giant-Killers Cup in November when the team trotted out for the start of their F.A.Cup trials. Their opponents were Horden

The Hartlepool game started the last session of a dozen matches to the end of the season. During that run only a defeat at Chesterfield blunted their steel. A loss at Saltergate came as no surprise, because United had yet to win on the Derbyshire ground, and the Spireites had a team running neck and neck with the Iron.

There had been some very good performances to gladden the heart, no more so than that of beating Oldham 6-1, and up in Gateshead when Gordon Brown's strike sorted out the points.

The marvellous run at the end of the campaign saw United once again take the honour of third place in the Third Division North, with a point more than twelve months previous. Although the F.A.Cup had not provided the revenue that was always a lifeline, Third Division North attendances were up to a figure not far short of an average nine thousand. This number could not compensate for the crowds that swarmed to watch the three Portsmouth Cup-ties, but they did help to balance the books.

On the players front Gordon Brown and Jack Gregory had to be congratulated for their performances as the deadliest partnership in the Division. Gordon Brown had scored one more goal in this forty-five strike total. The duo were amongst a group of eight men that made over forty appearances for the Club in the season, of which Dick White and Gordon Brown had not missed a game.

~ 1955-56 ~

Within a few short weeks the break from football was over. This meant that the last few swings of the cricket bat were being made as the footballers were again flexing their muscles. Scunthorpe United did not invest heavily in the transfer of players, but some changes were made. In fact far too many alterations than Bill Corkhill would have liked.

The goalkeeper's jersey was the first to be designated a new owner. Norman Malan started the season as expected, but Peter Marshall, who arrived in 1954 from Worksop, was given first team experience when Malan was injured, and towards the end of the year Marshall had earned the exclusive rights to the position for himself. Another area to be strengthened was in midfield, when Brian Heward was given the opportunity to eventually step up a grade. This stocky Lincoln-born player had served a useful apprenticeship in the Midland League football played by the reserves.

A well attended pre-season practise match, August 1955. Note the Doncaster Road end had been covered by that time.

Corkhill was happy to make him a regular member of the first team squad, but initially it was still the domain of Dick Taylor. In the half-back positions John Barratt was utilized for about a third of the games as extra support, having been with Harry Lamb at Aston Villa. Barratt was quite versatile and could be thrown in on either the left or right side of the centre of the park.

The forward line was sharpened by the arrival of two men who would operate solely on the wing, and chiefly on the right side, now that Gordon Brown was used as the spearhead of the attack. The preferred candidate was John Davies, a Portsmouth born player signed from his home city club.

Davies was the perfect partner to Jack Haigh, and the pair gave excellent balance to that part of the pitch. When they worked in tandem the new lad would go on to score some valuable goals, particularly in the F.A.Cup. When Davies was not available, team fluency was not effected, because Glasgwegian Bobby Callaghan, signed from Scottish Junior Football, was more than adequate with his tricky footwork.

Scunthorpe United began the season in an uncharacteristic fashion, conceding two defeats in the first two games at Bradford Park Avenue and Mansfield Town. Each of the reverses was attributed to lack of enterprize by the sluggish forwards, where the usual combination of Gregory and Brown was definitely lack lustered. The trip to the Field Mill against the Stags was particularly frustrating because Scunthorpe dictated three-quarters of the play. Only ten minutes remained and the Iron were leading 2-1, but defensive blunders cost two silly goals and a 3-2 scoreline went against them. Fortunately these lapses were just a temporary distraction and the points soon rolled in. One of the results on the comeback trail was the 3-0 win over Mansfield, when the men of amber played on the green at the Old Showground. It was said that the home team used the simple aspects of the game to their advantage, and let the visitors make the mistakes. Perhaps the own goal that came their way spoke volumes on this point.

The big news at the start of November was that the brilliant talent United had developed in Dick White had been recognized, and Liverpool decided to step forward with the cheque book and offer what for Scunthorpe was a record £8,000 fee.

United would not step in front of the young protégé's way, as he strove for a career in a higher sphere of the game. Everyone wished him the best of luck, but for a time the hole he left would take some filling. The immediate effect was that for the rest of November the team was unable to capture any victories in the Football League.

Dick White's absence from the central defensive position may have led to inconsistency in the Third Division North, but it did not halt United being 'Up for the Cup'. They may have been fortunate in the home draw which brought the non-Leaguers of Shildon Colliery down from the North, and on paper the gritty miners team should have been a set of opponents Scunthorpe ought to have been capable of easily beating.

As is often the case, non-League opposition can cause an unpredicted upset. This was all too plain to see once the game kicked off. The Colliery side gave a good account of themselves, receiving appreciative ripples of applause from the Scunthorpe crowd for a number of pressing moves. If it had not been for some determined defending in the Iron's rear guard, they may have had an embarrassment on their hands. In the event Brownsword showed why he was one of the strongest full-backs in the lower divisions, and helped to keep the score sheet clean.

Gradually United's professionalism was beginning to show through, and right on the stroke of half-time, John Davies took control of the ball and his shot squeezed past the helpless goalkeeper. The drama was not yet over for the first-half, because seconds later Brownsword nipped in behind Malan to head the ball off the Scunthorpe goal line. Shildon pressure continued in the second-half, but in leaving the latch off the gate at the back it was the Iron who scored the second goal. Brown poked home a Gregory shot that the Shildon custodian could only fumble. A flattering 3-0 result was finally secured in the dying embers of the match, when Gregory did manage to finish a goalbound effort himself.

The reward for levering Shildon out of the Cup was a visit to the pitmens' neighbours Bishop Auckland. The Bishops were renowned fighters in Cup competitions in the fifties, and at this time were no strangers to Wembley for their own Amateur Cup Final games. To win the tie in the second round they had already beaten Northern League, Durham City. Scunthorpe knew that it would be a stiff test, especially when they had to face a match on the Amateur team's three-sided ground. The battle was a severe struggle for the Iron, but because no goals were scored they survived with no apparent scars.

In the replay Gregory had recovered from injury and replaced Parrott, while Corkhill swapped Davies for Callaghan. These two alterations made all the difference, but it was not until Jack Gregory stretched his neck and guided a header into the back of the net in the seventy fifth-minute that Scunthorpe managed to inch in front. This was to signal an all-out attack by the Bishops tireless men. Their tactics even brought the goalkeeper off his line as an extra defender, but with precious little time left this approach became the visitors downfall. The man in green rushed out too quickly to take a throw in, but in his hurry he was unaware of Jack Hubbard who intercepted the ball and lobbed it into the vacant net.

Scunthorpe United's supporters barely had a moment to draw breath, before it was time for Santa to make his annual visit. Before the turkey was served, the United players had the matter of a trip into North Yorkshire to play Bradford City. It was a visit relished by Andy McGill, who enjoyed the experience of trying to put one over his old club. On this occasion the beer seemed a little flat, for they lost out on a Christmas cracker by 4-3.

On Boxing Day it was United's turn to play Scrooge, and McGill was not only the star player, but capped the chilly day with a goal from an angled shot. Jack Haigh ensured United would pocket the points, notching Scunthorpe's second from close range. The result left United in a comfortable mid-table position, but a yawning gap away from the promotion teams, lead by a resurgent Grimsby Town and a humbled Derby County, suffering their first season in the depths of the Third Division.

In the New Year the only thoughts supporters had was of the jewel that was the F.A.Cup. The luck of the draw was to provide them with a journey to Millmoor, to play the red-breasted Rotherham team, who were causing waves in the higher reaches of the Second Division. The Iron knew it would be no picnic, but they had plenty of guts if nothing else, and in a match like this League status was the last consideration.

On the afternoon of the battle, over two thousand screaming Iron fans were mustered in place. The sudden exposure to the biting cold made the players draw sharp breath as they entered the stadium. Soon the freezing temperature was forgotten as the contest got underway. In the early stages the Scunthorpe back lines impressed as they shut out all attempt the Rotherham forwards made. Any high balls were dealt with competently by Peter Marshall in the Iron goal.

The first blow of significance came in the twenty-fourth minute, and it was Scunthorpe who held the hammer. Rotherham's 'keeper could only punch out a ball punted his way from a corner, and Gordon Brown, lurking menacingly, returned it with a header that found its way high into the net. Half-time was only a minute away when Rotherham made their own strike. Once again it was a corner which evaded a goalkeeper, and had the crowd jubilant and celebrating a goal. In the second-half both teams missed chances to settle the affair, but on a day when defences were generally supreme a replay was ordered from the menu.

Before the replay could be staged both clubs knew that for the winners there would be the prize of a money spinning trip to Liverpool. The mid-week replay attracted a crowd of 13,362 spectators to the Old Showground, but snow and ice put the start in jeopardy. An army of volunteers wielding shovels cleared the pitch, but the surface was slippery and in poor shape.

Despite the conditions, the crowd soon warmed to United's efforts. It was the home supporters who were first to be cheering when Brown powered in a shot, after Merfyn Jones' drive had been blocked by a full-back near the goal line.

Rotherham would not lay down, and for long periods they probed the Scunthorpe rearguard. Five minutes from the break the stout resolution of the Iron's defence was breached. Peter Marshall, playing in only his second Cup game, could not be blamed for missing the hard accurate volley that was well out of his reach.

In the second period of play, instead of the Red and Whites taking control, it was Scunthorpe

The crowd in the Fox Street end are about to erupt as Brown scores one goal of his hat-trick in the F.A.Cup replay versus Rotherham United.

who pressed up the field. Gordon Brown led the charge and not more than ten minutes from the resumption he lifted the ball out of the mire and into the goal for his second strike. United were fired up. The swaying hoards on the terraces bayed for more, and he obliged with his third drive to make the net bulge.

At this moment Scunthorpe went against all principles and rather unwisely relaxed. It was just the spur the Millers needed and within a short while they pulled the score back to 3-2. A few anxious heart-stopping minutes followed before a John Davies header killed the game with the last goal of the ninety minutes. All that was left for the noble Rotherham side was to depart for South Yorkshire and lick their wounds back at Millmoor.

Next, however, Scunthorpe United had one of the top clubs as opposition, when they faced the competent battlers of Derby County, who were looking to regain higher status with an immediate return to Second Division duties. The Rams were the better team on the day, and no one would argue with their 2-0 success. Perhaps United's players had one eye on the Cup.

At the end of January it was all hands to the pumps to try and beat the pride of Merseyside. If Scunthorpe thought that Rotherham were a difficult opponent, then the task of beating Liverpool before over fifty thousand soccer mad supporters was even more daunting. Nevertheless United more than held their own as they raised their play. Then Jack Haigh stunned the Kop into silence when he delicately chipped the ball over the goalkeeper's head for the first goal of the match. Liverpool counter-attacked, producing some quick thrusts, which allowed Payne and Liddle to score and the lead changed hands before the interval.

Supporters who thought the Iron had been worthy candidates in the first forty-five minutes were more impressed with what

was to follow. They took the fight to Liverpool and caused mayhem in their back positions. John Davies then balanced the scales with the strike of the afternoon. He collected the ball on the right, beat as many as three red-shirted opponents as he cut into the box, before shooting home on the run. The battalion of four thousand travelling supporters cheered themselves hoarse, but within a minute there was more. Brownsword swung over a free kick deep in Liverpool territory. A bad clearance broke to Davies, who lifted the heavy leather over the defence with a snap shot, and Scunthorpe were re-established in the lead.

As time slipped away United looked to be on the way to a famous victory, but just as the referee checked his watch towards the end of the game, Liddle raced in and saved the homesters bacon with a headed equaliser.

It all had to be done again back at the Old Showground, and if the Iron should manage to win, a home time against Manchester City was in the offing. Once again winter snows fell and the original date was postponed. Eventually the mess was cleared from the pitch and play allowed to get underway. Liverpool were the first to adapt to the difficult surface conditions, and their pressure paid off as it was they who took the lead. When Scunthorpe settled down they created enough chances to at least equal. Jack Brownsword had the easiest opportunity from the penalty spot, but the usually reliable full-back must have been unnerved in front of the near twenty thousand crowd, and he missed his kick.

After half-time United came out inspired by Bill Corkhill's team talk. At the back Hubbard and Brownsword marked their men tighter, and Brian Heward marshalled his back line with more confidence. The threat of Liddle and A'Court was blunted, and McGill and Bushby pushed the ball up for Scunthorpe's forwards to make more use of it. The break came from a dash down the left by Jones. His cross found the head of John Davies to glance it home, and make it 1-1.

Jack Brownsword was United's penalty-king during the 50's and early '60's. Here, he adds another to his overall total of 49.

Scunthorpe from then on went hammer and tongs for a second success, but it would not come. An extra thirty minutes only went to stress Liverpool's superior fitness and their next strike wrapped up the tie at 2-1. United trudged off the park with their heads bowed, but the ovation from the crowd was left ringing in their ears.

Jack Gregory out jumps an opponent. Gregory forged a tremendous goalscoring partnership with Gordon Brown. Gregory's son, John, became an England player and Premiership Manager.

The rest of the season could not compare with the euphoria of the epic sojourn in the F.A.Cup. Results did not favour the side which had twice finished third in the last two campaigns. They had to be content with a mid-table spot this time, and it was hard for the eager supporters to digest. Not all the games that remained were run of the mill. At Easter the pair of games with Champions-to-be Grimsby Town produced two lively encounters before packed houses. Each team would win 1-0 on the others' ground. For Grimsby the loss at Blundell Park was one of just two League games that went wrong on the Cleethorpes Road enclosure. At the Old Showground the attendance figure of 19,067 has never been surpassed for a League meeting.

Eventually the season ebbed away with a string of disappointing results that put the team into the bottom section of the table. Only two away wins, at Halifax Town and Chester, with respective scores of 3-0 and 5-3, made a small climb possible to finish in ninth place. It put a face of respectability on the bread and butter part of the season, but the fondest memories were of the F.A.Cup.

Before a new term could begin, United would see the end of an era on two counts. Bill Corkhill had decided that now was the time to move on to fresh challenges. The parallel post had been advertised at Bradford Park Avenue, and his application was the one chosen. At the same time Harry Allcock had reached forty years in the secretary's chair, and it was the right moment to enjoy an easier life in Theodore Road, just up from the Old Showground. Both men would be sorely missed on the day to day running of the Club and they departed with all the blessings of the board. Getting rid of Harry Allcock was not quite a foregone conclusion, because he had already chosen his seat at the front of the Directors box for all future home matches. Harry had earned his retirement, and it was pleasing to see him in place at most matches until he was well into his nineties.

CHAPTER 7

THE SUART ERA

~ 1956-57 ~

At the dawn of the 1956-57 season, the Board of Directors had successfully advertized and secured the man they thought most fit to fill the shoes left by Bill Corkhill, and from the short-list Ron Suart was the unanimous choice. Suart was a former Blackburn Rovers and Blackpool full-back but as the season matured it was made plain that his methods were not defensive minded. It might take time for him to settle, but all concerned had every confidence in the new manager. Suart's first recommendation was that they offer Ray Oates a contract to take over the post of Secretary, where he had been operating in the position at Blackpool.

It was not long before Suart was shuffling his cards ready for the opening game at home to Darlington. His first important signing was for the muscular Doug Fletcher from Bury to bolster the forward line, initially at the expense of Jack Gregory, but soon the partnership Gregory had forged with Brown was functioning as usual. Another chance was at the heart of the defense, where Malcolm Hussey was preferred in the number five shirt, but the ex-Rotherham pivot could not hold on to the job when Brian Heward made a claim for the first team. The cheque book was finally put away in September, when George Luke was given space at centre-forward, being a former Blades player from Sheffield. This move necessitated Gordon Brown switching to the right-wing, and it was not until just before Christmas that John Davies re-emerged from the reserves.

The season did not get off to the start Suart would have wished, and a disjointed production surrendered the game to Darlington in the first act. It was only a temporary hitch, for visits to Southport and Barrow won the team three valuable League points. Gordon Brown was in devastating form at this early stage of the fixtures. He scored in each of the initial five matches, including two at Southport. It meant that his name was top of the goalscorers board for a while.

One very interesting encounter was the 1-1 result that attracted a pinch over eleven thousand spectators to see the men in black and amber of Hull City.

The Tigers had been relegated from Division Two at the end of a poor showing in the 1955-56 season, and for a couple of years at least this became another local derby, as long as the New Holland paddle steamers were working.

United managed to secure a run of eight undefeated games, the most bountiful of which was the 6-1 beating of Halifax Town, where George Luke showed his shooting boots, by bagging a pair. Unfortunately, the Iron was incapable of maintaining this sort of consistency, and a period of losses followed.

The 1956-57 campaign was not to see a prolonged assault on the F.A.Cup which supporters had become accustomed to. Although Rochdale had dismissed them by three goals without a Scunthorpe reply at Spotland in the League, a home cup game was a different proposition altogether. This time United marked much tighter and goalscoring chances were kept to a minimum on both sides. It took a little bit of something special

Ron Suart discusses tactics, on camera with Doug Fletcher, Jack Haig and Merlyn Jones.

in front of the Rochdale goal to break the stalemate and Brown's low drive won the glory. It mattered not that only a single goal separated the sides, because the right to entertain Wrexham belonged to the Iron.

Scunthorpe United already knew that the Welshman were a stubborn set of fighters, having played them in the competition at the beginning of 1954 and also encountered them each season in the Third Division North. The two sides had not met in the Football League that season, and home advantage favoured the Iron. Despite Gordon Brown's absence through a knock, the strike force of Haigh, Gregory and Fletcher should have put at least one goal on the board, but a lethargic performance up front saw no side gain the advantage, and both teams missed simple chances.

On the following Tuesday, United knew if they could surmount the task ahead, they would take on Reading from the Third Division South. This may not have been a great inspiration, but by half-time, with Brown restored to the team, Jack Gregory had scored with two shots to apparently put Scunthorpe in an unassailable position. They did not reckon with the tough grit of the home side.

Wrexham stormed the Scunthorpe fortress, and gave themselves hope by reducing the score. It was a signal for the onslaught to continue unabated until five minutes from the end, when a second Welsh goal levelled the tie, and meant a further period of thirty minutes of extra play. What happened then is a matter of folklore in the town of Wrexham. A lightening period saw them smash in four more goals past United's bemused defenders, and the Welsh dragon breathed fire to the scoring tune of 6-2.

Scunthorpe were now reduced to the every day chores of the Third Division, but by the New Year they knew there was to be no heady successes in this direction, and a transitionary period would have to be the order of the day. The difference in the class they would have to achieve was experienced at Christmas, when top of the shop Derby County challenged them to a couple of games. At the Baseball Ground the Rams saw Scunthorpe as inferior and had no trouble in knocking the Yuletide stuffing out of them 4-0. United were left chasing shadows, and on Boxing Day fared little better at the Old Showground. The disappointing factor was that a meagre 4,103 spectators bothered to leave the fireside. Scunthorpe lost 4-1, which was only eased by McGill converting a rare penalty.

Ron Suart knew the situation was critical, and he decided to make the required alterations. Terry Charlesworth was given an extended run in goal. His inclusion, along with Barry Horstead from Brigg demonstrated that local youngsters, if good enough, would be thrown in at the deep end. Neither let the side down. Horstead's inclusion meant Hubbard was moved across to right-half, a job he frequently enjoyed.

It was not long before other changes took place when Jack Gregory opted for a move nearer his family roots; he waved a sad farewell, and signed on the dotted line with Aldershot. Hardly had the ink dried on the contract when Ronnie Waldock was whisked away from Bramall Lane, Sheffield, and arrived with a pair of football boots slung over his shoulder. If folk thought Gregory had an eye for goal, then this new speed merchant showed that they had not seen anything yet. In his second game against Chesterfield he bowled in with a hat-trick, the second goal of which had the crowd buzzing. Waldock controlled the ball, beat a defender, ran fully forty yards, then round the 'keeper and side-footed home. By the end of the afternoon the Derbyshire lads had been dismantled with a 5-1 thumping.

There was a continuation of inconsistency through the rest of what was left on the fixture card, although a total of nine Waldock goals did raise interest. Bright spots occurred in beating Wrexham by the odd goal in seven, which came at the beginning of April, as did the news of the signing of a well respected goalkeeper from Second Division neighbours Doncaster Rovers. Ken Hardwick had already won the Third Division North Championship medal, and for a time he had kept out Harry Gregg, an Irish International 'keeper, at Belle Vue. His experience would blend well at the Old Showground, and gradually the jigsaw was coming to being.

The fourteenth position in the final League table would pale into insignificance as the new squad was assembled ready for the real mountains to be climbed at the end of the summer of 1957.

Ron Suart continued in his search for perfection, and he was always on the telephone asking if the right players were available at the right price. Before he could settle his own plans Derby County approached Scunthorpe for Gordon Brown, in an attempt to strengthen the squad at the Baseball Ground for their new escapades in the Second Division. The £5,000 cheque would go a long way in adding weight to Ron's position in the bidding for players of his choice, although it was acknowledged that the hole Brown was leaving was a deep one to fill.

A large portion of the cash went on the return of the former United player of Midland League days, the local born Jack Marriott. Since he had left the Club his wing play skills had been honed to perfection at the top level. Jack's career took him to Huddersfield Town after he left Sheffield Wednesday and news of his return caused great excitement. The other major first team signing was of the experienced Frank Marshall from Rotherham. Frank would put his foot on the ball and dictate the pace of the game. He was just the old head to make the engine room function with precision.

The inclusion of Marshall meant that Hubbard could resume in front of Hardwick with Brownsword. The half-backs were to assemble as Marshall, Heward or Horstead, and Bushby. Towards the end of the year Len Sharpe appeared more in the picture, usually in the left-half section of the field.

Up front supporters would expect to see the new line-up, at first, of Marriott, Waldock, Fletcher, Haigh and Jones, with John Davies on stand by. Davies' inclusion meant a swapping of Marriott to the opposite wing berth.

The blue touch paper was put to the match at Chesterfield and Marriott marked his return with a goal that earned a point on a very blustery afternoon. However, in mid-week the team really got to grips with matters in hand when the players coach pulled up outside Prenton Park for a scrap with Tranmere. They had to contend with going a goal in arrears, but by half-time, combination play by the forwards gave Waldock the chance to equalize, then Jones made another goal for the same player to score a second. After the cup of tea at the break, a Marriott to Waldock interchange produced a pass for Fletcher to score, and put the game safe. To emphasize their superiority, Waldock sealed the points on the eightieth minute at 4-1, thus completing his hat-trick.

Scunthorpe continued their enterprise in the opening home fixture with the arrival of Darlington. It took only twenty minutes, for Jack Marriott to follow up on the right, and crack the first of three, in a whirlwind four minute spell. Two more were later added, to make a total of five without a response. Perhaps the pick of the bunch was the third, a full length diving header by Dougy Fletcher, off the cross of pocket-sized winger, Merfyn Jones.

Scunthorpe United continued to gather the points throughout the early stages of the season, as the Summer sun weakened, to be replaced with condensation of the Autumn mornings. This team looked to be the likely lads, and two points gained over Mansfield, when leaders Bury slipped, saw the Iron sit proudly on top of the table.

It was only when Workington lowered the Scunthorpe flag for the first time that minor ripples were experienced, but it could not stop the Scunthorpe destroyer steaming on.

In October a new novelty attracted over eleven thousand spectators to the Old Showground against Rochdale. On 3rd October 1957, Scunthorpe United had the pleasure of switching on the new floodlights for the first time. At a cost of £16,000, the green pylons would be a dominant feature on the Scunthorpe horizon for many years to come. The quality of the lights was second to none, with thirty lamps glaring down from each pillar, bathing the ground as a perfect substitute for daylight. To finish the exercise, United rose to the occasion with a 2-0 victory, further staking a claim for the one promotion spot available.

November brought the Iron into Cup conflict, this time at home to Goole Town of the Midland League. Goole would turn out to be a plucky side and it was not always clear to see which of the two teams belonged to the Football League. Even when Doug Fletcher put the Iron ahead they did not look comfortable, and by half-time a number of chances had been squandered. Goole then had the audacity to equalize through a penalty goal, and Scunthorpe were made to play hard to earn their corn.

In the end the game was settled by a training ground perfected move, as Marriott crossed the ball 'onto a sixpence' and new man Eric Davis from Plymouth hit his debut goal. Davis' presence was to be the decisive factor and it was the first of many games he would play. Although he would not be Scunthorpe's leading goalscorer at the end of the season, his ratio of goals per game would not be bettered.

At the start of Winter the second round of the F.A. Cup meant that United would have consecutive games at home to Bury, who were hard on Scunthorpe United's heels, together with Bradford City and Accrington Stanley. Hull City were also up there with aspirations. The two Bury matches put the Lancashire men to the sword, and on each occasion they returned to North Manchester without even the consolation of a goal.

At this level Bury had proved they were a useful opponent, but Scunthorpe could step up a gear without drawing breath. A Waldock goal settled the League points when the Third Division North leadership was in doubt. Only a week further on, in the Cup, Ronnie ruled supreme with another goal from a blistering shot, and Merfyn Jones settled the score, showing he could do as well from picking up the scraps on the left side of the penalty box.

Throughout the shortest days of the year the Scunthorpe machine efficiently rolled along. Most wins may only have been by an odd goal, but they were meticulous at doing it. An unbeaten span of fourteen League matches started when Bury lost at the Old Showground. The secret was a tremendous team spirit, control of midfield, tight cover at the back and a forward line that always could nip a goal at a vital stage in a match.

During the first week in January, United recommenced F.A.Cup football. The team that Scunthorpe were up against was Bradford City, the only side so far that season to take points away from the Old Showground. It gave the Iron a measure of what to expect. Despite temperatures only just hovering above zero, close on twelve thousand supporters wrapped up tight to cheer the Claret and Blues on. Unfortunately the match was not the third round spectacle that was hoped for. Both sides seemed too intent on not giving anything away and a scrappy encounter was served up. On three occasions Scunthorpe found the back of the net, but only Jack Haigh's effort satisfied the official in black, but this was sufficient to tip the scales.

Life at Scunthorpe United could not be rosier. The team was perched on the top of the Third Division North table, and gates for League matches were regularly in the ten thousand or more bracket. United still had an interest in the F.A.Cup, and for the third time they were part of the fourth round brigade. A wave of excitement then swept the town as it was learned that the next step would be away at St. James Park, against Newcastle United. The Magpies had already won the converted trophy three times in the decade and so supporters thought they had been blessed with a plum tie.

British Railways put on five special trains from Scunthorpe and Frodingham station, and an estimated five thousand supporters made the arduous journey, in atrocious winter conditions. The weather was so bad that weekend that about one third of the football programme was postponed. Scunthorpe's Cup-tie was one to survive, despite a pitch that skaters would be more at home on. At kick-off the 39,407 spectators saw the teams line up as follows:
Newcastle Utd: Simpson, McKinney, McMichael, Schouler, Paterson, Franks, Hughes, Hall, White, Eastham and Mitchell.
Scunthorpe Utd: Hardwick, Sharpe, Brownsword, Marshall, Horstead, Bushby, Marriott, Waldock, Davis, Haigh and Jones.

Once the game got underway Scunthorpe showed no consideration for Newcastle United's superior League status. It was they that adapted the better of the two sides on the slippery surface which was liberally sprinkled with puddles. At the back they were firm, and in the middle of the park Marshall played a captain's game keeping his troops flowing. Ronnie Waldock caused a major concern, and the noise of the home supporters was silenced as he burst through to beat Simpson. Unfortunately for the Iron, he was judged to be marginally offside.

It was just on half-time that more drama took place. Jack Haigh rose high to head a Scunthorpe corner, but in so doing collapsed when he received a nasty knock. He was on the floor for several minutes, obviously concussed, the referee suggested that, with not long to go before half-time, he might be better to leave for the dressing room. Haigh would have none of it and as the Iron won another corner-kick, he lifted his body majestically above the defence and headed the opening goal.

Jack Haigh rises majestically above the Newcastle defenders to put Scunthorpe into the lead, in the F.A.Cup 4th round match. Marvyn Jones and Eric Davies look on.

It was just the boost all the travellers wanted, but they knew that Newcastle would come out charged up after a stiff talking-to during the interval. Soon after the restart the Magpies had conjured up an equalizer, but instead of taking command it was Scunthorpe that continued to dictate the pace of the proceedings. Underestimating the Iron was a grave mistake to make, and the lead was restored with another headed goal, this time as Eric Davies outstripped the defence. Cheered on by the strains of Lincolnshire accents, United made Newcastle look second rate. Then the home supporters had to suffer yet again with the clock showing fifteen minutes to play. Davies was the sole architect as he collected a ball deep in enemy territory, advanced to the nearest defender, tricked past him, then balanced himself for a volley high into the back of the net.

The game was effectively beyond Newcastle, but they battled on for pride until the last whistle. For Scunthorpe United's mud splattered crew there was the glory of another honourable page in their history, and a first ever place in round five.

United were to have precious little time before they were up for the Cup again. The gods had favoured them with a home tie against Second Division Liverpool, who would bring back Dick White as their captain and star at the centre of the defence. Plans to keep the Scunthorpe team in peak condition were disrupted by the arctic weather and the only game played between the two Cup-ties was a draw against lowly Workington at the Old Showground.

On the day of the Cup game over twenty-three thousand spectators saw that Ron Suart had selected the same team which beat Newcastle as they ran out onto the pitch. Liverpool would take to the park in the knowledge that they had a real fight on their hands, but if anything it was the visitors that won the accolades for the first-half, although at the half-time interval no team held a lead. In the second period the advantage changed, and it was Scunthorpe who conducted the affairs.

The game looked to be heading towards a goal starved stalemate, when the whole course of the action was to alter with a decisive move from the swift Liverpool forward line. Alan A'Court on the wing fed a telling ball through to Murdock, who slipped it under Hardwick's body with five minutes of time on the watch. United made a valiant effort to pull the tie out of the fire, but it was too late. The wonderful run had hit the buffers. They did not lift the F.A.Cup, but later in the season the *Sunday Pictorial* presented them with the Giant-Killers Cup. Liverpool went on to travel to First Division Blackburn Rovers, where they too were eclipsed with a 2-1 scoreline.

It was at this time when Scunthorpe received their only set-back. One evening, smoke was seen pouring from the back of the wooden stand on the East side of the ground. When Ron Suart went to investigate, the structure was well on fire, and there was little the bemused Scunthorpe official could do. However, every cloud has a silver lining, and for Scunthorpe it was to build a new cantilever stand, the first one of that construction to grace a football stadium.

In the meantime the last half a dozen matches would have to be played with a gallery on only three sides of the Old Showground.

Attention switched to the Third Division North. Bury were losing some ground, but Accrington Stanley and Bradford City still remained a threat. Scunthorpe did have games in hand and had the edge over the chasing pack. The finishing line could almost be seen, but April was to prove an anxious time with all to play for. Wrexham caused a wobble when the Iron lost by a single goal, but supporters did not need to worry, for two home wins followed, including the return against the Welshmen, in which United had to rely on Jack Brownsword's accuracy from the spot to take the points. A second defeat of the month happened at Bury, a team who was not throwing in the towel. Still United's resolve was holding. At this stage fixture congestion was beginning to be a real headache, and two or more games a week was in order.

Suddenly the alarm bell began to ring when United lost a vital home match 2-1 to York City, then repeated the same mishap at Stockport. Suddenly promotion was not a foregone conclusion. The trip to Bradford City would decide a lot regarding whose hard work throughout the year was to be rewarded. Scunthorpe were starting to feel the effect of injuries, and Ronnie Waldock was the man suffering most. To replace him United gave the opportunity of a debut to the strong running Albert Minton, from Suart's previous club, Blackpool.

Ronnie Waldock challenges the Liverpool 'keeper during the fifth round F A Cup match. United's Eric Davies awaits the outcome

The game attracted over eighteen thousand people to view the event. Scunthorpe took a two goal lead through the reluctant hero Minton, plus another from the evergreen Eric Davis. City reduced the arrears as United contrived to give it all away in the second-half. Fortunately the youngsters in defence ran their legs off, particularly Sharpe and Horstead.

The upperhand was retaken with Marriott supplying a through ball for Minton to hammer away. This strike was desperately needed because the Valley Paraders scored a second to finalize the score at 2-3.

Scunthorpe still required more points to guarantee promotion, and a couple arrived in the home game with Chester, but the visitors made United fight hard for them. Chester sent the hearts racing with a shock lead before half-time, but Jack Haigh equalized. Urged on by over ten thousand supporters, United left it late before they went ahead. Eric Davis provided the extra punch, stooping low to head the vital goal. News then filtered through that points dropped around the country by other rivals meant that Scunthorpe had an unassailable lead. Promotion to the Second Division was now definitely theirs.

The remaining two games of the season were a formality, and the maximum was taken from them at Harlepool and in the last fixture, at home to Carlisle. Against Carlisle United a carnival spirit was present amongst the Scunthorpe crowd, and 12,555 turned up for the party. The players responded with a 3-1 result in which Waldock was fit to join in. An interesting facet of the Spring evening entertainment was the two players on the park who had appeared in the first ever Football League encounter United had played eight years before. They were Jack Brownsword, who scored from a penalty, and George Thompson, who appeared for Carlisle United between the posts.

Scunthorpe United had given the town a sense of pride. From non-League football to Second Division in such a short space of time was beyond everyone's wildest dreams. United's record was: played 46, won 29, drawn 8, lost 9, goals scored 88, goals conceded 50, and points 66. The margin of promotion was seven points over their nearest challengers, Accrington Stanley, and the thirteen away wins could not be beaten by anyone in the Football League. The honour of being the Club's leading marksman went to Ronnie Waldock who hit twenty-one goals in thirty-three appearances, whilst Eric Davis scored seventeen in twenty-three outings. Hardwick, Horstead and Marshall received mentions in dispatches for not missing a game, while Brownsword and Haigh were absent a total of just three times. To recognize their high level of achievement the Club were invited to a civic reception.

There was one small piece of regretful news when everything had simmered down. Ron Suart had fulfilled his contract with Scunthorpe and was going to move back to his old club Blackpool. Scunthorpe United were very sorry to see such a determined man walk away from the Old Showground. But they thanked him for his tireless work and sincerely hoped he would be equally successful in the future.

CHAPTER 8

THE HALCYON DAYS OF DIVISION TWO

Before the 1958-59 season could start United had the business of finding a new manager to guide their destiny. The man they chose was the unassuming Tony McShane who had gained some managerial experience at Chesterfield. McShane did not pretend that he was going to turn Scunthorpe into a First Division club overnight, but he did promise to maintain standards.

~ 1958-59 ~

The first decision McShane made was to give the promotion side the opportunity to prove themselves in the higher grade, but the Club did allow the departures of Doug Fletcher and John Davies to Darlington and Walsall, respectively. The only newcomer of note for the beginning of the season was left-winger Billy Ormand from Barrow. The new man was given an immediate selection for the first three games until Merfyn Jones was declared fit for play by the equally new physio, Charlie Strong. Charlie was to be part of the backroom staff patching up injuries for the next twenty years.

On 23rd August 1958, United were well prepared for the visit of Ipswich Town for the first ever Second Division match to be played in the town. The scar on the East side of the ground had been healed and a beautiful 2,500 seater stand built out of the embers of the tragedy that happened months before. In front of the seats, which were divided into three sections, was sheltered standing accommodation for another 1,000 spectators. Not a space was available when the structure was officially opened by local dignitary Commander Wells, and a crowd of 13,317 packed into the ground in open-shirts to see the kick-off.

The first game was fast and open with both teams making a number of half chances, but without finding the finishing touch. Generally it was Scunthorpe that were the more aggressive element, but in the second period Ipswich shot into the lead. United needed all their enthusiasm to equalise, and as Ronnie Waldock broke away Eric Davis hit a rocket that found the back of the net.

A huge roar greeted the goal, and supporters appeared pleased with what they had seen. It looked as if it would be a tough old campaign, but United had the stamina to hold their own.

After the first fixture, Scunthorpe found themselves travelling to parts of the country that were only known as places on the road map. Swansea Town and Bristol Rovers were to be hard lessons on the learning curve. Naive defending cost them two defeats, and it was not until Swansea came to Scunthorpe for the first match in September, that the initial illusive win arrived. Swansea were fully stocked up with Welsh Internationals but they could not compete with the Iron on the evening. The rearguard tightened up, and Jones returned to the forward line.

Two goals from the Davis Waldock combination put the Iron in a strong position by the interval, although the Swans tried matching this in the second session, and pulled one goal back. In the time left it was a struggle for supremacy, but when Eric Davis headed Jack Marriott's corner home with five minutes to play the contest was effectively over.

Points were hard to be gleaned in the first part of the campaign and United were continually near the foot of the table. However, they always had their heads just above water, as most folks had suspected would happen when the season kicked-off. Supporters never knew if the strength of Scunthorpe's opponents could be overpowered, now they were under the extremes of higher level pressure. However, they did know they were guaranteed an entertaining encounter, which would be liberally sprinkled with class, and as a result gates were at bumper levels.

Illustrations of the tough nature of the Autumn period were shown in some interesting results, which did not yield victories, but kept Scunthorpe supporters enthralled. These fixtures started with the visit of Derby County. Gordon Brown looked out of place in the black and white shirt of the Rams, but he was given a warm reception by the Scunthorpe crowd, who remembered his record-breaking goals they had enjoyed earlier. Scunthorpe took the lead in the tussle, but thanks to Brown, had to fight hard to salvage a point late in the proceedings.

Then at Stoke, Scunthorpe were probably worth a point, but went down fighting in an epic 4-3 thriller. Sheffield Wednesday called by for their first official visit since the friendly games in the Hospital Cup, and drew a crowd of over seventeen thousand to the Old Showground. Unfortunately, the difference in class was a yawning divide, and for the gallant Scunthorpe crew it was a case of keeping the score down to 4-1, and only a Brownsword penalty kick was consolation for the Iron fanatics.

At this junction in time Tony McShane moved in to sign a well developed blond haired utility half-back from Oldham Athletic, by the name of Peter Neale. Neale became affectionately known as Noddy Neale once the crowd got to know him. His hallmark was some very strong tackling, which would bring cheers from the home supporters, and shrieks of anger from the opposite camp. Not long into his Scunthorpe career he scored his first goal, at Ayresome Park against Middlesbrough. Unfortunately Brian Clough scored three, and Middlesbrough won 6-1, thus inflicting the heaviest defeat of the season.

At Christmas the situation had not changed, but a series of 1-0 wins, notably at Bristol City and Huddersfield, where Jack Marriott had demonstrated his shooting prowess, and in a rearranged night game with Cardiff City, maintained stability.

Jack Haigh about to take a shot in the home game against Sheffield United, in March 1959

Generally speaking there was never any joy against the leading teams, as they discovered in a rain-soaked game at home to Liverpool, which was lost by two goals to one, when Jimmy Melia controlled the match.

It was during the holiday period when United had a pair of very attractive fixtures against Sunderland. The gate was swelled to fourteen-and-a-half thousand because vouchers were available on the turnstiles for the home F.A.Cup third round tie against F.A.Cup holders, Bolton Wanderers.

When the Sunderland game got underway United knew they were up against the best, for this was the Roker club's first season outside the First Division. Scunthorpe were quickest to the ball and looked better for an own goal from Jack Ashurst. Peter Neale scored a second before Sunderland realised they needed something to stop an avalanche. Before the fight-back could be completed a rather bizarre event affected Jack Haigh. He dived full length to head the ball goalwards, but only succeeded in heading the post. Jack was out cold, and it was some time into Sunderland's revival that the gaunt figure of the brave crusader stood on the touchline with Charlie Strong, asking permission to resume. The game by now was evenly balanced at two goals apiece. Only seven minutes were left when Len Sharpe seized on the ball in midfield. His advance was not halted, and once within firing range he released the unstoppable winner.

The second match against Sunderland, in the North-East was not to see any heroics from the Iron, and a 3-1 result against them was clear cut. Pressure was now mounting on Ken Hardwick, a man amongst men only months ago in the promotion run-in. Supporters were unfairly pointing the finger in his direction, possibly because they wanted a glimpse of Welsh under twenty-three International Ken

Jones, who had been persuaded to join from Cardiff City. McShane decided to make up his own mind and he elected to blood this exciting new talent in the first match of the New Year, against Bristol Rovers at home. Most supporters were left with a favourable impression, and would have liked to see more of the athletic young Welshman. Instead, McShane decided to stick with the steadier old head of Hardwick. Nevertheless the charismatic Jones would still go on to play a major part at the Club.

The F.A.Cup brought the crowds wending their way up the Doncaster Road in a great swell. At kick-off the attendance of 23,706 was only a handful short of the record. A tricky pitch had a coating of snow on the surface, but all was well to make a start. The Cup-holders, led by the Lion of Vienna, Nat Lofthouse, soon demonstrated why they had been able to lift the polished silverware at Wembley. Nat Lofthouse was dominant and gave Barry Horstead the stiffest test of his career thus far. In two moments of magic, the England centre-forward bagged two goals and Bolton eased into round four, for a more demanding contest against the Wanderers of Wolverhampton.

Shortly after the third round Cup game, Scunthorpe decided to do some trading with their own centre-forward. They allowed the free-scoring Eric Davis to leave for Chester, but immediately lined up a replacement in the tall dark haired Peter Harburn, who was struggling for a first team place at Everton. He was to be joined, as the season petered out, by Peter Donnelly from down the road at Doncaster. Donnelly would have more impact the following season, but he hit the newspaper headlines with the caption "Dustbin Donnelly", for practising his shooting between a pair of rubbish containers.

The desired effect from the exchanging of forwards did not arrive instantly, and six consecutive defeats put the Club's status in jeopardy. In the return fixture with Middlesbrough, Brian Clough hit another hat-trick, and it took a single goal win by Harburn at bottom club Barnsley to halt the slide. The men from Oakwell had their own problems, and after an encouraging start to the season, they sank to the depths of despair.

A late scramble for points began to see Scunthorpe United move to safety. At home to Lincoln City the team wore a strange dark blue shirt which had not been seen before. Ken Jones was one of the heroes, but was left unconscious when diving at the feet of an on-rushing forward. Brownsword had no option but to fist the ball away from the goal and a penalty was awarded. Several minutes passed before Jones could rise off the floor and face the kick, which led to the opening goal. In the second-half, United played like a team possessed, and Harburn steered them back into the game with a headed goal from a Merfyn Jones centre. Peter Donnelly then took centre stage and a spectacular diving header tipped the scales towards Scunthorpe, as he scored on his debut. The tension could almost be touched as the floodlights beamed down on the pitch. Lincoln needed the points for their own survival but had to concede when the City 'keeper fumbled the ball and left Donnelly with a simple tap-in.

The win against Lincoln was followed at the end of the week by Scunthorpe United's first success in London. In a confident mood they engaged a Charlton Athletic side who were just outside the promotion fringe. The height of Harburn and the speed of Waldock were the determining factors in a 3-2 victory, which tested the nerve of the travelling support. A point was then eked out from a visit by Bristol City, which was played during a continuous downpour. Scunthorpe needed a thrice taken penalty to arrive at the three a piece draw. Brownsword had two attempts saved, but each time the 'keeper was judged to have moved, before it was suggested the Donnelly have a go on the third shot. Safety was finally confirmed when a first class all round performance plundered a 2-0 win at Cardiff. It was just as well, because the last two games were both lost 3-0, against Liverpool away, and Huddersfield at home. The Huddersfield match saw the Town manager, Bill Shankley, parade seventeen-year-old Dennis Law from Aberdeen. In another rain-soaked match the mini dynamo exploded with two of the goals to further his increasing reputation.

The word satisfactory could not be overstated in the first test of the Second Division grade. Scunthorpe had finished in eighteenth place and avoided the drop by five points from Grimsby Town and Barnsley. Waldock was the leading scorer on fourteen, while Harburn's total of eight in fifteen games played a significant part during the closing stages of the campaign. To conclude the 1958-59 season, Scunthorpe United once again received a letter of resignation, and by mutual agreement, Tony Mcshane decided to leave the Club.

At first United thought they had the solution to the Manager's chair. The matter appeared to have been resolved when Bill Lambton left Grimsby Town, but after three days he decided to return to Blundell Park and resume the coaching role he had vacated. The Scunthorpe board then turned to former Stoke City half-back Frank Soo, who had an English mother and Chinese father, but this didn't stop him representing England during some Wartime Internationals.

~ 1959-60 ~

Two other innovations to get used to included a complete covering for the Fox Street End of the ground, and a new kit. The old claret and blue did not stand up under the floodlights and it was decided to switch to a blue and white kit with old gold facings.

Gradually the season was to see a breaking up of the promotion team that had given supporters such fond memories. Ken Hardwick gradually gave way to Jones, and Jack Hubbard decided his legs were getting no younger and it was time to retire. Hubbard's reward was a job with the Juniors, earned by a career which covered over four hundred appearances. Frank Marshall opted to drop down the Leagues and finished his career at Doncaster Rovers, whilst Merfyn Jones took up with Crewe Alexandra.

In the arrivals lounge, Dennis John was signed as a stocky right-back from Swansea Town. The black-haired man with a crew cut was an ideal replacement for Jack Hubbard. It was also said he had a decent voice, because reports suggested that when his football career was over he became a pop singer in South Africa. He was joined by Martin Bakes, a Bradford born left-winger, who had played in his home city at Valley Parade. Bakes also had another vocation after his football career, for he was to take up teaching for many years in the Scunthorpe district.

The season started, and by chance the pattern of the first eight games was identical to those of the 1958-59 campaign. A draw at home to Bristol City, levelled through a Brownsword penalty, opened the season. Two defeats followed before newly promoted Plymouth Argyle were sunk with torpedoes by Len Sharpe, now firmly established in the first team, and Jack Haigh. Haigh rattled in another for a hard earned away point at Rotherham before the team lost at Liverpool, and at home to Cardiff City. Cardiff became the dark horses of the League and deceived everyone by stealing the runners-up promotion place.

The last game of the sequence was the attractive match at the Old Showground with Liverpool. The one goal each draw was secondary to the fact that the locally based supporters in the eleven thousand crowd, to a man, yelled and shouted every inch of the way for a Scunthorpe victory. The only people in the ground urging a Liverpool win had travelled from the North-West port that day. How loyalty has changed!

It was around this time that the door revolved for more changes in the dressing room. United swooped to sign the former Leicester City forward Barry Thomas for a small fee from Mansfield. In less than ten days Ronnie Waldock packed his kit bag and left for Plymouth Argyle and later Middlesbrough. At the same time a tall centre-forward named Harry Middleton signed from Wolverhampton Wanderers. As if the changes were not helping to sell more copies of the Scunthorpe Evening Telegraph, the door was to open just once more to welcome another face.

Jeff Barker was offered a role on the coaching staff, and it was great to see the old-timer back, and he was to be around in various capacities for many years to come.

It was not long before Thomas and Middleton would be in the first team. Thomas earned his right by scoring five times in three reserve matches. His debut in the Second Division was against Sheffield United in front of his new home crowd. A highly creditable draw was the result, and although Thomas did not score, he showed an awesome turn of speed. Eventually his first goal materialised away at Middlesbrough, but it was when he linked up with Middleton that supporters saw the measure of this new structure.

Ivor Williams and Brian Howard repel an Ipswich Town attack (October 1959). This was the first season in blue, white and gold.

United entertained Ipswich Town, and Middleton had the dream debut of a goal in just two minutes. However, the joy was shortlived when Thomas received a bad knock ten minutes later to leave him a virtual passenger and limping for the rest of the game. The visitors took full advantage of the handicap and eventually stole the lead. United's bench was resigned to seeing the two points slip away to East Anglia, when in the last minute of play the ball fell to Thomas. At the cost of great pain, Thomas thumped the sphere with his injured limb into the goal for an equaliser. Such was the steel of this player.

Thomas was out for five games, but United coped without him, only losing once in the South of the country, against Portsmouth. He was back in the team, fit and well, for an excellent performance when Sunderland visited. The men in the red stripes always pulled a decent crowd, and almost twelve thousand were present. Peter Donnelly hit two goals and Thomas celebrated his comeback with another in the 3-1 victory. This win set United up to travel to Villa Park to entertain the League leaders Aston Villa seven days later.

The team to play Aston Villa included a local goalkeeper, Ivor Williams, who had made it through all the Scunthorpe junior ranks. Unfortunately during the game he damaged his hand at a very early stage, and despite a brave performance by all the Scunthorpe United side, it was a contributing factor for a heavy loss. At half-time the score stood at 3-0 and two more were buried into the net by the end. Ivor stayed on the books for a number of years, but he lost his

place to Ken Jones and never made the first eleven again. To his credit he remained loyal to his Club and has stood on the terraces as a supporter ever since.

Ironically, United dished out the same hardships a week later when their visitors were Lincoln City. At half-time they were three up after a barrage by Middleton, Thomas and Bakes. In the second period Brownsword topped the score up with a penalty. The pick of the goals was the fifth, which was Middleton's second. He burst through to find himself one-on-one with the 'keeper, and shaped to blast the ball, which encouraged his opponent to dive. Harry waited for the 'keeper's commitment then, with contempt, side-footed it into the opposite corner.

It was not long before United were on F.A.Cup duty, and their task was to topple Fourth Division Crystal Palace. The Londoners tactics were quite robust, and Scunthorpe were dragged down to their level. Embarrassment was saved when Harry Middleton scored in the second-half. There was just time to beat Rotherham 2-1 in a local derby before the next round of the Cup. Incidently the game against the Millers, on a snow covered pitch, was spiced up because of the homesters F.A.Cup heroics in beating Arsenal 2-0, after a replay. Eventually Scunthorpe found themselves matched against a lively Port Vale from out of the Third Division. The Potteries team walked straight down the pitch, and put the ball in the net after just one minute. From that moment on all and sundry were camped in the Vale half, and despite the attacking aggression from the Iron, they could not get a foot in the door. At 0-1, there would be no running round Wembley with the Cup!

The results of the Second Division had shown an improvement on the 1958-59 returns. Survival was by no means certain, but they were in a far more comfortable position, just under halfway in the table. United's fire power from Thomas, Middleton and Donnelly was doing the business up the top end of the field. It was that combination which helped to lift the doldrums from the Cup exit, and in a fast flowing game against relegation threatened Hull City, each of these players scored passed Bly, the Tigers' long serving 'keeper. Ken Jones in the Scunthorpe goal won the admiration of the crowd at the other end, when he dived full length to stop a penalty and preserve a clean sheet.

Other games of note included the first visit to Scunthorpe of Aston Villa, by now way out in front of the Division with the Bluebirds of Cardiff City. The result may have gone against the Iron by a narrow 2-1 margin, but it was noteworthy for some educated football and an experimental dark orange ball. This form was continued at Stoke when United won 3-1 and a young Bob Pashley scored on his debut. Pashley was not the only second team man to be given a chance by Frank Soo in the elevated grade. Tom Passmoor, a well structured centre-half from the North-East, and Tony Needham a Scunthorpe born left-half, also received the call when injuries demanded it. There was even a late night final swan song-for Jack Hubbard, in the penultimate game against Lincoln City, before he could continue with his retirement.

Scunthorpe concluded the 1959-60 season safely in fifteenth position on the Second Division ladder. The thirty-six points was an improvement of three on twelve months previous. It should have been more, but a lack of concentration was punished when the last three games all were terminated in defeat. There was yet another letter of resignation on the table for the Scunthorpe board at the conclusion of the fixture list, when Frank Soo decided to opt for coaching abroad. Scunthorpe United's Chairman of the hour, Jack Wharton, was only too happy to write a reference for a Manager who had carried out his duties in an outstanding manner.

When the season closed Scunthorpe United received a sack full of applications for the post of Manager. The successful candidate was to be the rotund, balding, Dick Duckworth. In his playing days, Duckworth had played for a string of Northern clubs, and he had gained management skills at York City and Darlington. Other members of his family had represented England at both football and cricket.

~ 1960-61 ~

Duckworth soon got weaving in the transfer market. One of the first to clear his locker was the much respected Jack Haigh, leaving for Doncaster Rovers after almost four hundred competitive games and seventy goals, which made him joint top scorer with Jack Gregory. Also on the way out was Peter Donnelly, who would try a new career at Cardiff City in an exchange deal with the Welsh club's top goalscorer, Joe Bonson. Bonson was a burly sort of a player who would sometimes become the subject of calls from some of the lesser well versed sections of the crowd. They did not appreciate his off the ball work and the huge number of goals he would unselfishly carve out for his colleagues.

Another Welshman for the forwards was the clever inside-right Brian Godfrey, an Everton Junior signed from Goodison Park. Godfrey's talents were so abundant that he was honoured with an under twenty-three International cap, and after his Scunthorpe days were over, won a full appearance for his country. Duckworth next brought cover for the goalkeeper spot. His signing was Joe Turner from Darlington. Turner was to be kept out of the senior squad by Jones, but after a 4-0 loss to Rotherham United in February, Turner was handed the gloves until the season was out.

The last of Duckworth's array of new men was an exceptional star. He was Archie Gibson, signed from Leeds United. How, such a magnificent half-back could be released by the Elland Road club was beyond comprehension. The quietly spoken scot had a dribble that mesmerized the quickest of opponents. His nerve was as cool as ice and he could distribute the ball onto a sixpence. Only a surplus of players in that position stopped Archie winning a Scottish Cap. Sometimes Gibson would frighten his own supporters by taking on men near his own goal line, such was the confidence of the man. Duckworth was the first to suggest that here United would leave the captain's arm band.

United kicked-off in the capital at Charlton, and a Thomas strike secured a point, where in April they had been busted 5-2. On the following Thursday, Alf Ramsey arrived with the educated skills of his Ipswich Town team. Their rise to fame was only in its infancy, but United could not be

bothered with formalities, and crushed them 4-0. Ipswich would win the Second Division championship this same season, but they were left flat-footed that evening before eleven thousand rejoicing Scunthorpe fans. To be fair to the East Anglian club they did gain revenge at Portman Road. Nevertheless, thanks to the combination of Godfrey, Thomas, and Bonson, United were having a purple patch and the Club had never been so high up the League table. There could be no doubt that the best result was at Derby County. When the BBC Television announcer gave out the 5-2 away win in favour of the Lincolnshire team, he had to pause to check it was the right score.

United embarked on the road to a new competition in the October of 1960. It was Football League Secretary Alan Hardaker's dream, and known as the League Cup. Many clubs boycotted it, others showed indifference.

Jack Marriott avoids a tackle at Swansea, Barry Thomas looks on.

Scunthorpe drew 1-1 at Rochdale and historically Joe Bonson's shot was the Clubs initial contribution to the competition. In the replay the attendance dropped by over three thousand from the previous League game, and United played half-hearted against their Fourth Division opponents. A single goal from the visitors ended any lingering interest the Scunthorpe players might have harboured.

United found the Second Division no such distraction, and until the last whistle, games could always change direction. At half-time against Portsmouth, the away dressing room must have been a cosy place. Pompey were a goal up and playing well within themselves. At the end of the game Jimmy Dickinson's men must have felt like First World War soldiers bombarded in the trenches, for Scunthorpe had stuck five past them. Thomas and Godfrey accounted for two each and Sharpe made it five.

It was this same 'never say die' spirit that levered a point out of the visit of Sunderland when all seemed lost. At half-time United had been over generous in defence and allowed Sunderland a 3-1 advantage. It was not until ten minutes from time that they found the key to unlock the North-

Eastern back line. Joe Bonson collected a ball on the half-way line and ran forty yards. A hesitant defence backed off, giving him the time to sweep home the ball majestically from twenty yards. There was no time to celebrate, and he ran into the net to collect the leather and rushed back to the centre spot, ready for the restart. Several times the rejuvenated Scunthorpe forwards had the ball cleared from the opposition line. Then in the last minute a visiting full-back was judged to have handled in the goal area. Up stepped Jack Brownsword, United's reliable senior figure, and without any fuss he calmly stroked in the penalty kick for a 3-3 score.

Jack was to save the day again in the match against Brighton and Hove Albion at Christmas, but this time he went one better. At 0-2 the presents seemed to have been given out by Santa, but parity was regained when Brownsword twice steadied himself and the usual low and hard side foot had the ball nestling just inside the iron stanchion both times.

A match that was to stand out in Scunthorpe folklore was played in January 1961. Scunthorpe had been paired with First Division Blackpool in the F.A.Cup at the Old Showground. Talk was of the legendary Stanley Matthews, the veteran of English football, whose wing skills could still make the ball talk. On the morning of the match Jack Marriott phoned in sick with a stomach virus, and a slight shuffling of the dominos was required.
At kick-off the two teams line-ups were as follows:-
Scunthorpe Utd: Jones, John, Brownsword, Gibson, Horstead, Sharpe, Middleton, Godfrey, Thomas, Bonson and Bakes.
Blackpool: West, Armfield, Garrett, Kelly, Gatrix, Salt, Matthews, Mudie, Charnley, Parry and Perry.

Once the game got underway the players responded to the atmosphere of 19,303 supporters, hanging on to every vantage point offered by the space within the Old Showground. Brownsword was not giving Matthews an inch of space, and only had a break when Stan briefly left the pitch to change his boots. In the middle Barry Horstead was enjoying a commanding performance. Only ten minutes had been played when Bonson was put clear in front of goal by Thomas, and Scunthorpe had stolen the lead. This prompted Blackpool to demonstrate their skills. Jacky Mudie slipped the Iron back lines for a shot to equalise, then big Ray Charnley drilled home another goal just before it was time for the hot Bovrils.

When Scunthorpe emerged from the tunnel, Dick Duckworth's team talk had an immediate effect. Sixty seconds from the restart another Thomas to Bonson exchange enabled the Welshman to equalise. Minutes later the noise was enough to burst the ear drums. Thomas shot, but as it went wide Bonson lunged out a leg and diverted it into the net. At 3-2 Duckworth was seen at the dugout ringing the changes. He pushed Middleton out to the flank and gave Thomas more freedom to roam the box. Thomas responded with two lightening flashes in three minutes, and the Iron were 5-2 up. The rout was completed virtually on time when another Thomas thunderbolt gave him a fully deserved hat-trick, and probably caused an argument as to which player would keep the match ball as a souvenir.

In the fourth round, United had plenty of scope to make further progress when they were drawn at home to Norwich City. The Canaries still had players that two years earlier had seen them reach the F.A.Cup semi-final as a Third Division unit. One of those players was the captain Ron Ashman, a powerful defender who would play a part in shaping the future of Scunthorpe United. At that time, the Iron had already won a League match against Norwich, and towards the end of the season the double was snatched at Carrow Road.

For the F.A.Cup game more than fifteen thousand patrons were present, in time for the first pass of the ball. On this occasion it was the canary yellow that completely dominated the order of play. The warnings were plain to see and it needed a Martin Bakes equaliser to keep United in the game. Thomas and company could not get a look-in, and defensive slips allowed Norwich an easy day out, winning 4-1. The Norwich prize was a visit from fellow Second Division club, Sunderland, But they too could not rediscover their form and lost 1-0.

Scunthorpe United continued their quest for points in the League, led by the perpetual motion of Barry Thomas. At this stage of the season he was making a cottage industry out of scoring goals, and his twenty-six in the League set a Club record. Thomas was characterised by a barrel chest and short shorts, which were pulled up to expose his muscular thighs. He would never give up on the slimmest of chances. Against Sheffield United the visiting goalkeeper attempted a goal-kick to a player on the edge of the box. Thomas intercepted the ball and put it in the net. The referee did not allow the goal to stand because he could not believe the ball had cleared the area. Ten thousand pairs of eyes thought he was wrong.

At the end of the season, United did not slow down as in previous campaigns. Even when youngsters such as John Kaye, Tony Needham, Arthur Thorpe and Derek Hemstead were coaxed into first team situations the results never suffered. The team remained unbeaten in each of the last five games, although only the tour to Lincolnshire by Plymouth actually saw United enjoy a victory. A comment on the 2-2 game at Elland Road should be made of the crowd. Only 6,975 spectators bothered to turn out to follow the mighty Yorkshire side. The result meant that the Iron had managed to secure ninth place in the table, their highest status to that time.

~ 1961-62 ~
The word in Scunthorpe working mens clubs and public houses was that this team could only get better. During the pre-season run-in, there was not many player movements. Although a small fee was picked up when Harry Middleton departed to Walsall. This and a little more was spent with the arrival of Ron Howells from Portsmouth, where he would appear chiefly in the left-half position, succeeding Len Sharpe whose career had taken a down-turn through injury. Cash also brought Andy Wilson from Sheffield United for the right-wing berth. The policy of giving juniors a bite of the cherry continued. Youngsters blooded late season were given more experience, especially pint-sized local lad Barry Lindsey.

When the season did get underway it was incomprehensible why only eight thousand people bothered to turn out for the visit of Brighton and Hove Albion. Indeed the average attendance had slumped over the previous year as performances had improved. Those who did make the effort were treated to six goals shared in a thriller. There was also the unusual sign of Jack Marriott converting a penalty when Jack Brownsword was unavailable to make the start. However, United needed a last gasp equaliser from Thomas after leading 2-0 at one stage. It was a trick they repeated at Norwich, days later. A two goal lead served up by Barry Thomas was only enough to earn a draw. In the Old Showground return, Thomas again supplied two goals but the defence was watertight that night and the first win was taken on board.

Scunthorpe United at this time entered into an experiment of Friday evening home fixtures, and this was introduced for the visit of Charlton Athletic, when United went rampant. Every forward, except Bonson, scored, not that the player was left out of the thick of the action, and Brownsword added his customary penalty. All the goals came in an incredible first-half, and amazingly at the break the score stood at 6-1. This was the start of a run which saw Scunthorpe nearly invincible at the Old Showground.

In another home fixture, Rotherham United were made to suffer. Scunthorpe scored five times in the seven goal extravaganza. Barry Thomas was always the architect, and this time his contribution was two goals. One of the efforts came from a free kick, some thirty yards from goal. Archie Gibson moved the ball on to Thomas, who fired it like a cannon. For a second it was not apparent where the ball was, but as it bobbled in the space behind the goal-line, the crowd rose to cheer the successful shot.

By the end of September, Thomas had notched eleven goals, and his fame was starting to spread. His strike against Stoke City was the first in a run of seven games in which he registered without fail. For the visit of Southampton he added two more, probably because of the extra room everyone enjoyed when Ron Howells and Terry Paine were sent off for fighting. At least, as they disappeared up the tunnel the heat had been taken from the situation because they shook hands with each other.

It is possible that the best game of the season was viewed when the black and white stripes of Newcastle United ran out onto the Old Showground after a turbulent 1960-61 season had seen them lose their First Division crown. During the day rain had fallen and the top surface of the pitch was of a greasy nature, but the evening was mild, and just short of fourteen thousand spectators paid at the turnstiles.

Once the game got underway it was Scunthorpe who had to defend as the quick moving Geordie forwards swarmed round the home goal. The first strike came when a Brownsword clearance ricocheted off Noddy Neales' back, and presented Ivor Allchurch with the opportunity to flash the ball past Ken Jones. Jones was not one to mince words and a few choice ones were directed poor old Jack's way. United fought in vain to get back into the game, but just

before half-time Suddick was first to a Newcastle corner, and Jones was picking the ball out of the net for a second time.

In the second-half, United came out a different team, ready to attack the Doncaster Road kop. Back came all the old tricks and skills, and play was concentrated around the Newcastle line. Then a penalty awarded to the Iron gave Brownsword the chance to redeem himself and he made no mistake with his placed kick.

Roared on by the crowd, Archie Gibson, United's man of the match, put young John Kaye away down the right side. Kaye sent over a low and hard cross towards Barry Thomas. In a flash, Thomas clipped in a shot beyond Hollins in the visiting goal. At this point seventy minutes had passed and Newcastle were doing all the back-peddling. The crescendo of noise that greeted the goal continued at the same pitch as the home supporters sensed more blood. Five minutes later Ron Howells collected the ball in midfield. Looking up he saw Thomas in space, and pushed through a looping pass. Thomas set off like an antelope, stretching his neck muscles and just succeeded in diverting the flight past the groping Hollins. As Scunthorpe celebrated, Hollins angrily lashed out at the post with his boot.

Scunthorpe were now rubbing shoulders with the teams at the top of the leader board - Sunderland, Leyton Orient and Liverpool. This was an order that was juggled week by week. Thomas continued to supply the goals and dreams of the First Division began to materialise. Plymouth Argyle were another team to conceded five goals, and Thomas scorched in with four to his name in the 5-1 result. Interest on a National scale came when the team played on the South Coast at Brighton. The BBC radio sports programme covered the match live over the airwaves, but the 3-0 advantage at the interval could not be improved upon.

At Christmas, United went to Elland Road for a Boxing Day fixture. The freezing weather did not stop Thomas and company. Aided by Archie Gibson, having a field-day against his old club, Thomas gave big Jack Charlton the run around. At the end of the proceedings, Thomas had added four more goals to his tally, and the 4-1 reverse was the worst Leeds United had the misfortune to suffer all season.

Interest in Thomas had been mounting for some time. Already he had been invited to train with the England squad, but his immediate attention was on two fixtures in London with Charlton Athletic. The first was in the F.A.Cup, which was lost 1-0. Seven days later he scored in the game notable for six goals shared. It was to be Barry Thomas' last Second Division appearance for Scunthorpe United. Newcastle opened the cheque book and paid the monster sum of £35,000, plus Ken Hodgson and John McGuigan. This fee would be the equivalent of several million pounds by the late-1990's. It should also be noted that the men moving in part exchange were top quality players, who were able to slot straight into the first team. Despite this, many supporters thought this cold January day was when the Iron's bubble burst. The legacy of Thomas would never be equalled, and his thirty-one goals in twenty-four appearances is little short of phenomenal.

In the meantime, United had to pick up the thread of where they left off. A draw against the eventual champions, Liverpool, suggested that Scunthorpe could still maintain a challenge at the top. Once McGuigan found the groove, he proved to be nearly as prolific as Thomas, and averaged over a goal in every two games. The loss of Thomas gave Kaye the opportunity to hone his goal scoring skills, and in only his second game in that position he launched a blistering drive towards the Rotherham goal at Millmoor for a 1-0 win. Later the same month United strolled to a comfortable 2-0

Barry Thomas in full flight. Scorer of 96 goals, bettered by only two other players in United's Football League career

success over a lack-lustre Leeds, now being guided by the single minded Don Revie. The fixture had been re-arranged because of Christmas time frost which had hardened the Old Showground pitch like stone. John McGuigan's goal on the evening started a personal run of scoring in each of the next seven consecutive matches.

Scunthorpe United were still in contention for a top place, but as the season ebbed away, Liverpool were striding ahead, with Leyton Orient just a pinch in front of Sunderland, whilst the Iron led the chasing group. United continued to play entertaining football but the crowds at home were declining, and although not all efforts brought success, supporters were able to see them play an excellent brand of football. At Southampton, the ten thousand folks at the Dell warmed to the Lincolnshire visitors as they lost by a mammoth 6-4

scoreline, a record aggregate number of goals in a Football League match involving the Iron. Another visit to Newcastle in front of thirty seventhousand brought applause from those who watched Scunthorpe dish up a flowing brand of soccer, but lose 2-1. However, John McGuigan had some satisfaction scoring against his old club.

In the last month of the campaign the Second Division runners-up place was still within their grasp. Wins at home to Derby and Preston, and away at Leyton Orient and Huddersfield set up a grandstand finish. At Leyton Orient, United scored after nine seconds against the team jostling for the second spot. Orient kicked-off, but John McGuigan intercepted, passed to John Kaye who shot home. The score stood at 1-0 and set a new fastest time record for a Scunthorpe goal from the kick-off.

Unfortunately injuries to key players, particularly in budding John Kaye, probably caused defeats in the last two matches, and promotion was denied. The final League table highlighted Scunthorpe United in fourth position in the Second Division. It was the zenith of the Club's achievement and made supporters proud of their team. There was a concern that the average crowd of 9,657 had not been more, and if United had actually won the right to First Division football this figure would not have been sufficient to maintain costs within the top bracket.

Plenty of action but no ball! the home draw with eventual Champions, Liverpool. Marriott and Hodgson are the two attacking United players.

~ 1962-63 ~

The 1962-63 season started with virtually the old team that finished the last tour of duty in May. Dennis John had moved to the Isle of Dogs to roar with the Lions of Millwall. His right-back position was initially allocated to Mike Gannon, who was signed from Everton. This situation did not work out, but Gannon did come into the reckoning in the final phase of the campaign at left-half. Meanwhile Derek Hemstead was tried at right full-back, before Barry Horstead made it his permanent domain. Another notable absentee was the much admired Len Sharpe, who left for the black and amber of Hull City. In his ten years Sharpe had represented his town team at every level, and was noted as a gentleman player. The next time local residences were to see him was as manager of the local, but now defunct, Ashby Institute, in the Midland League. In this role Len had changed, and his fiery tongue had him in trouble with referees on many occasions. Since those days, Sharpey has mellowed. Currently residing behind the Clugston Stand, he tells today's supporters how the game ought to be played!

The season started for Scunthorpe on a positive 2-1 note, when Ken Hodgson's goal was followed up by a second, after Southampton defender Knapp sliced the ball into his own net. Events took a turn for the worse with consecutive three goals defeats at Chelsea and Grimsby, who were both new arrivals in the division that year. At Chelsea, United were overrun, and at Blundell Park defensive slips cost dearly.

Scunthorpe then had to defend their home status for the first visit of Chelsea, in the return fixture. The warm late summer saw just over eleven thousand folks in place to watch the proceedings. United's team included two youngsters in Derek Hemstead and Barry Lindsey, and Duckworth also gave Andy Wilson a first of the campaign run-out. From the start the Iron showed no sign of a hangover and pressured Chelsea into making mistakes. After nine minutes Ken Hodgson supplied an accurate through ball for John Kaye to latch onto, and the lad from Goole made no error in shooting the opening goal. Soon after United took the lead, Derek Hemstead fell awkwardly and needed prolonged treatment. Charlie Strong looked across to signal that his collar-bone was broken. Despite being patched up, the referee rightly refused to let him continue. Fortunately the reduction of Scunthorpe to ten fighting men did nothing to dampen their resolve. Relishing the challenge, Kaye weaved his way into the box and cracked his second goal just before the interval.

United were pleased for the half-time pause, in order to get their breaths back. They all needed the break, as in the next forty-five minutes the London aristocrats tried to get back on terms. Archie Gibson summonsed all his magic to dictate the game to United's tempo, and the extra running in Barry Lindey's legs were a boon. During the fading moments, Gibson swept a Scunthorpe free kick high into the box. Kaye attacked the ball with Bonetti, the Chelsea man in green. Bonetti could not hold it, and Kaye pushed it home for a 3-0 victory. The victory over Chelsea was the beginning of a run of five wins on the trot. After the fifth game, against Swansea,

United sat briefly on top of the Second Division table for the one and only time. The Swansea affair was of a scrappy nature and played on a Friday evening; other teams caught up hours later after their Saturday afternoon games. United then failed to score in the next four outings and could not win a League match until the visit of Derby County.

Meanwhile the League Cup caused some interest. A marathon three games against Southampton was finally terminated on neutral soil at London Road, Peterborough. Assisted by an own goal, United eventually cruised to a comfortable 3-0 success. The pleasure of victory did not last long, for Sunderland upstaged them at Roker Park in round three.

The unmistakable figure of Stanley Matthews, being shadowed by Jack Brownsword: September versus Stoke City

Back on duty in the Second Division, the team embarked on a more productive tour in which nine games all yielded points. At Newcastle, Scunthorpe earned their first League point. At Christmas, a draw with Grimsby Town brought over twelve thousand supporters to witness a rare strike from the cultured feet of Archie Gibson. This was the last time the Old Showground would be fit to stage a match until the first week in March, for the whole of the country was gripped by the coldest Winter in living memory. There was little in the way of snow, but for days on end the thermometer refused to budge above zero. Halifax Town even had the bright idea of opening their Shay Ground as a skating rink!

Scunthorpe did manage to play two games in the slightly milder edges of the country in the far South. At Portsmouth, their F.A.Cup game featured on the television, and against all the odds they hung on for a draw with a team of walking wounded. At the end Marriott was a total passenger, McGuigan, the goalscorer, was concussed, and both Howells and Wilson were unable to run at full speed as a result of knocks. One month later the weather in Plymouth eased to allow United to steal two points from a 3-2 win.

It was a long time before the arctic finger receded away to the poles. Every club had to deal with the fixture backlog and congestion was inevitable. The first comeback in anything like normal conditions for Scunthorpe was the third round F.A.Cup replay against Portsmouth. Almost ten thousand supporters welcomed the team for the first time in three months, and John McGuigan looked to have supplied them with a golden chance to play Coventry in round four, but the star in the blue Portsmouth shirt was Saunders, who ran the show and won the applause with two solo goals.

A coincidence in the fixture list gave United another throw of the dice two days later, at Fratton Park. This time the side, weakened by injury and flu, unexpectedly returned from the five hundred mile

1962/63 season: John Kaye, John McGuigan and Barry Lindsey in action at the Old Showground.

round trip two points to the good, from a similar 2-1 scoreline.

The most fruitful exercise of the year was to be the re-arranged visit of Preston North End. It was only their second visit since relegation from the First Division and they had not regained any sort of composure since the retirement of the flying 'Preston Plumber', Tom Finney. United treated the Lancashire team with contempt under the glare of the Old Showground floodlights, and registered four goals for the only time that season. McGuigan was the chief slayer, scoring twice in the 4-1 result.

The match at Derby County has to have special mention because of the repercussions that came later. Life at the Baseball Ground had become difficult and points were desperately needed to avoid relegation to the Third Division which had been created in 1958. Rumours abounded before the match of heavy betting on the game. United lost a match that was well within their capabilities of winning, and by the unprecedented score of 6-2. Two own goals and two penalties assisted in guiding the Rams to victory.

Later a court case found Scunthorpe United player Ron Howells guilty of match fixing charges and for the shame he brought upon himself and his sport he was sent to prison.

Scunthorpe United were by now heading towards mid-table safety. At the later stages of the season they signed a utility winger or inside man in Ian Crawford, who gradually took over much of the work of Jacky Marriott. Tom Passmoor was given more chance to shine when Peter Neale was unavailable, and in goal an injury to Ken Jones brought work for ex-Blackburn 'keeper Brian Reeves.

The new balance of the team kept the points flowing in and a good home spirit in the cluttered months of April and May kept everyone happy, although gates did cascade down to six

and a half thousand, a dangerously low figure if the Club was to survive the financial battles of the Second Division. However, the most rewarding match of the campaign as regards to achievement must have been when United called in at the Victoria Ground, Stoke, where the Potters surveyed all below them from their top position in the League.

To record the rise of the City side with the ageing Stanley Matthews, now back with his old club, the BBC had the cameras in place to broadcast the game to the Nation in glorious black and white. United seemed to enjoy the publicity, and inflicted only the third reverse Stoke had to swallow at home all season. Goals from all three front-runners, McGuigan, Kaye and Hodgson, made compelling viewing in North Lincolnshire later that evening, as United stole a cheeky 3-2 win.

At the end of the forty-two games, Stoke took the championship from Chelsea, and Scunthorpe were down the order in ninth place. It was another satisfactory performance but holes on the terraces were thought to be due to the transfer of Thomas, and fewer numbers had passed through the turnstiles. Certainly the fifty-seven goals scored was a massive twenty-nine short of the 1961-62 total. In the end John Kaye emerged as the leading scorer on thirteen, one more than Ken Hodgson.

~ 1963-64 ~

Scunthorpe United were to see more of the established squad leave the Club in the close season. The supporters were not thrilled when West Bromwich Albion enticed John Kaye to the Midlands for a fee reported as £40,000. John McGuigan emptied his locker and moved to the far end of the country at Southampton, and shortly into the activities of 1963-64 Brian Godfrey opted for a career at Preston. At the end of May he was on standby for the Lilywhites team in the Cup Final against West Ham United.

To fill the boots of the players that served the Club with distinction, Duckworth bought a number of replacements, but there was only limited successes. Of the influx of new material the most notable was Ian Lawther an ex-Northern Ireland International from Blackburn Rovers.

In January another invaluable addition to the squad was Irishman David Sloan of Bangor. David learned his apprenticeship well at Scunthorpe, and the popular youngster worked hard enough to be invited to play for his Country's under twenty-three side. After he left the Iron he would go on to gain full honours for Northern Ireland.

Other players picked up by Duckworth also came in for bit parts. Among these were Andy Smillie, Jim Conde, Cliff Mason and Keith Ellis. All offered more than a small amount of hope but little impact could be made in significant quantities by any of them.

The money received in big transfer fees began to dwindle away, and soon the wisdom of the transactions was questioned. There was even an alleged suggestion that the Club had said they could survive without supporters if they could make money in selling their top seeds. This was certainly never established and probably could be put down as just another rumour.

The start of the season in the August of 1963 was nothing short of disaster. In the first dozen games no win was recorded, and only once did the team manage to score more than one goal. This titanic event came at home to Swansea Town, and arrived via an own goal and a Brownsword penalty. The weak functioning of the forward line put continuous pressure on the defence which had been usually reliable. However, even the best backlines cracked when under total siege, and this one was no exception. Jack Brownsword, now in the twilight of his career, had never been so fit because of the extra running he was expected to do. Ken John in goal was getting backache picking the ball from the net, and supporters' remarks from behind his goal were far from sweet.

It was not until the thirteenth game of the season that Andy Wilson scored against Middlesbrough and Scunthorpe hung on to a 1-0 victory to break their duck. At this stage United were flirting at the bottom of the pile with Grimsby Town, Plymouth Argyle, Swansea Town and Bury. A brief respite lifted them off the foot of the table during a more respectable run of form in November, when three consecutive 1-0 victories were enjoyed, at home to Huddersfield and Plymouth, plus the third at the Valley against Charlton Athletic. Hope of a complete recovery was raised with the biggest win thus far, when Swindon Town, a recently promoted club, lost 3-0 at the Old Showground, but it was only a small oasis in the desert.

The true measure of the team's weakness was experienced when the Boxing Day fixture had them travelling to Maine Road to play the illustrious talents of Manchester City. United had signed Alan Kirkman from Newcastle United on the eve of the match, in time to make his debut. At half-time all looked well at 1-1, and Ian Lawther had provided Scunthorpe travellers with a trifle of Christmas Cheer.

At the end of the ninety minutes there was nothing but humiliation and embarrassment. The Iron had folded under the shear weight of the City attack and lost by a massive 8-1 scoreline.

Two days later a swarm of light blue scarves left the railway station to make their way up to the Old Showground to support Manchester City's anticipated second blitz. It was not long in coming and Scunthorpe back-peddled throughout the 4-2 defeat. Alan Kirkman scored on his home debut, but must have wondered why he had ever left the relative comfort of Rotherham United. Jack Brownsword scored the other United goal, as ever from the penalty spot.

January continued the sorry tale of Scunthorpe woe. Barnsley knocked them out of the Cup, after a replay, and the losing 3-2 score at Oakwell was only made respectable by Brownsword, who converted both goals from penalties. In the League they were unable to scrape a win, and sunk to the depths of despair losing 4-1 and 7-2 at Swansea and Southampton respectively. The goals of newly installed David Sloan offered some consolation, but by now Scunthorpe were rock bottom and odds-on for relegation. United supporters needed a brave smile and nerves of steel every time they went to cheer their team on.

It looked as though a second visit to Portsmouth in consecutive away games to Hampshire would end in another heavy defeat. Twenty-five minutes of the match saw the Iron run ragged, and 3-0 down, but then came a remarkable comeback. Ken Hodgson scored a hat-trick and Andy Smillie added a fourth to achieve an unlikely 4-3 win. This was recognised by a national award for the victory of the week, and Scunthorpe won a complete football kit to be donated to a local boys club of their choice.

A similar score was arrived at seven days later, from the visit of Rotherham United. Twice United trailed to the Millers and twice they equalised. Then Rotherham unluckily lost their goalkeeper, who was stretchered off injured and out for the rest of the battle. Scunthorpe next had the fortune of an own goal, and won the game in the last minute when David Sloan drilled the ball hard and low through a crowded goalmouth.

Scunthorpe's hopes hung by a thread as they tried to ward off the persistent fears of going down. Leeds United did not do them any favours on the way to their Championship, when they scored the only goal of the game direct from a corner. Southampton took two more points back to the Dell, but there was the unusual sight of left-back Brownsword scoring his only goal ever from open play. Ironically it was a misdirected cross that looped behind the bemused keeper. This bonus effort made Jack's total of forty-nine career goals. He topped up the fifty, which set a Football League record for strikes from a full-back, with the winner in the cliffhanger against Derby County, which United nicked at the death, in the 3-2 final score. Late into April, United were still in with a slender chance of a reprieve, but the season's last home match, against Newcastle, had seen no fireworks by half-time to suggest they had found the escape route. A stern talk by Duckworth during the break brought the desired response.

A fine view of Scunthorpe's famous Cantilevered Stand, in April 1963. Players in action: Jack Hutton, Peter Neale, Ian Lawther, David Sloan and Keith Ellis.

It was a great advantage to United, that Newcastle had nothing at stake apart from the win bonus, and it was the Iron who showed the most determination, as the second-half got under way. Ian Lawther took hold of the ball just inside the box and rifled Scunthorpe into pole position, and not long remained when Keith Ellis shot through the Magpies defence for number two. It was only a disappointment that when Scunthorpe needed cheering on from the terraces, a meagre crowd of six and a half thousand turned out to see the 2-0 result.

Everything hinged on the last match at Huddersfield. Scunthorpe had to win and hope results at Grimsby and Plymouth went their way. In the event the Scunthorpe eleven gave it their best shot, but it was not enough.

The last days of United's (old) Second Division days at Grimsby. Jack Brownsword and Tony Needham provide cover for Welsh under 23 'keeper, Ken Jones.

They took a two goal deficit in with them at half-time, but to everyone's credit, pulled the score back to an even plateau. The attempt to gain glory and secure the win that was imperative inevitably left gaps at the back.

Five minutes from time Huddersfield Town exploited the situation to gain a fortunate 3-2 result. Sadly Scunthorpe were bottom of the Division and relegated as a consequence. Another phase of the Club's history had reached a conclusion.

CHAPTER 9
A NEW LIFE IN DIVISION THREE

There was a sombre mood about the Scunthorpe United camp when they began to pick up the pieces after the failures of the previous campaign. The issue of a new set of fixtures did lift spirits and the optimism of an attack on promotion with the young players at the Club quickly restored morale.

Duckworth had seen numerous changes in the playing staff and there was virtually a clean sweep in the players he had inherited four years before. The close season of 1964 saw more departures. Already Archie Gibson had been transferred to Barnsley in the last campaign, but now Jack Marriott had decided to retire. The illustrious career of Jack Brownsword was fading fast, and he only had three more appearances left before he too hung up his boots. At least Brownsword was to continue in a coaching role at the Club, and supporters would see him in the future dashing onto the field with a wet sponge to tend to the wounded soldiers. There would be no more of Tom Passmoor, who had thrown in his hat with Carlisle United, and one day would return to the Second Division at the heart of the Cumberland team's defence. There would also be the departure of the players signed on short term contracts to try and shore up the ailing Second Division side.

Those left on the books were first joined by Barry Betts, in defence, from Manchester City, Jack Bannister from West Bromwich Albion for midfield, and Barry Ratcliffe to take the left-wing position, from Blackburn Rovers. These players blended with what remained of the old Second Division warriors but the number of team changes throughout the season made it hard to keep abreast of events. Even by early October, Andy Smillie went on his travels to Southend, and his replacement was the tall blond Dick Scott. Scott was a character in his own right and possessed a similar style to Archie Gibson, being also clever with his feet.

~ 1964-65 ~

Scunthorpe United were reintroduced to Third Division football when Bristol City were faced at the Old Showground. Duckworth paraded all his three new signings and everything appeared rosy. Then the red-breasted Robins took the lead on a quarter of an hour. Ian Lawther redressed the deficit, and then led the charge in the second period which saw the Iron run riot with three goals in four minutes.

The 5-2 outcome had supporters wondering if this team could restore Scunthorpe pride. Within a week they knew the answer, and in all probability it would be no. A bore-draw at Gillingham sent over fourteen thousand spectators to sleep, and the loss at Loftus Road of two points to Queens Park Rangers underlined the stark difference between the supporters dreams and the reality of the new division.

September started brightly enough, and a home win over Shrewsbury was followed by another at Boothferry Park, Hull. The Shrewsbury game had heartbeats put on hold when Neale handled in the box during the last five minutes, but Reeves saved the kick. At Hull, United soaked up some early pressure, and man of the match, Ian Lawther, wrapped up a good evening for over a thousand travelling supporters with a two goal strike for United's 2-1 success. Unfortunately there was little else for Scunthorpe supporters to cheer, and Duckworth was by now becoming alienated by the crowd.

United were soon floundering around mid-table with none of the promise of a promotion drive that the Club envisaged. Attendances had been reduced to five thousand, and the Board thought it was time to take appropriate action. Mr Duckworth was summoned before the Chairman on 9th October and informed that he had been relieved of his duties. Within a short period, the Board advertised the position and accepted the application forwarded by Fred Goodwin, the former Manchester United and Leeds United player. Fred

Brian Reeves punches clear, at Reading, whilst Peter Neale and Barry Horstead cover.

was to become player-manager, but injury restricted him to only a minimum number of appearances.

At first Fred's hands were tied with the number of men on the staff at Scunthorpe. His work from the start revolved round rebuilding confidence and changing the pattern of play. One of his first promotions was that of local born Stuart Bramley to the first team at inside-right. His next piece of business acumen was to negotiate with Newcastle United for the return of Barry Thomas. Thomas had not fitted in at St. James Park as the Geordies had hoped. For long periods his stay had been plagued by injury and a £20,000 deal was set-up. The last throw of the dice was to give an extended run to Scunthorpe boy Ian Harper at left-half.

A rare appearance for player-manager Freddie Goodwin, on right. In aerial combat are Barry Thomas and David Sloan - at Swansea.

Such was the interest in the signing of Barry Thomas that the attendance rose from five thousand for the F.A.Cup defeat at home by Darlington of the Fourth Division, by over fifty percent for the Colchester United game on the following Friday night. All eyes were on Thomas, and although no goals were scored, Barry did sufficient to suggest that once he was familiar with his new colleagues, he would make an impact. United started to pick up now that the whole direction of play had changed course.

Barry Thomas scored his first goals since returning, at Bristol City's Ashton Gate. It turned out to be a personal triumph as he netted both strikes in a highly rated 2-2 draw, in which Scunthorpe finished with nine fit men. The team kept up its excellent form by gaining revenge over the difficult Queens Park Rangers team a week before Father Christmas set forth with Rudolf and company. On Boxing Day, United had another challenge from the fancied Mariners from down the Cleethorpes Road. The Old Showground saw a five figure attendance for the first time in fourteen months. A thin layer of hard snow made conditions crispy underfoot, but not enough to stop the referee approving the start on time.

In the early exchanges the Grimsby team tended to enjoy the better football strategy, but Scunthorpe were more direct. Barry Ratcliffe was first to make the supporters cheer, intercepting a poor back-pass, before side-footing the ball home to convert a simple chance from close in. On the half-hour, Foster restored the balance for Grimsby with a swerving shot that Reeves could not move to. It set up a grandstand finale, which provided Alan Kirkman the perfect platform from which to execute. The winger steered the ball into the net through a congested goal area, when successive drives by Thomas and Bramley had bodies diving all over trying to make blocks. The 2-1 victory could have been spoiled, but hero Foster turned villain, blazing over the top of the bar in the dying moments, when a simple side footed shot would surely have levelled the score.

The period of the 1964-65 season in the New Year was even more of a frustration than the first-half. Form at home, in particular, plummeted and only three further wins were enjoyed, but a couple of worthy performances at Exeter City and Southend United made coach journeys home a great deal more pleasant, thanks to positive scores. Fred Goodwin could only wait until the right players came along before he could improve the situation. Unfortunately United's huge pile of cash had been frittered away to next to nothing, and big money transfers were out of the question, but the Directors did agree to two men joining the staff. The first was goalkeeper Geoff Sidebottom, a custodian of considerable agility, who had represented Aston Villa at the top level. He had also won a League Cup final medal for the Midlands club in its inaugural season. The second player was the talented mid-fielder Bobby Smith. Smith, a bronze haired lad of almost twenty-one years of age had appeared over one hundred times for Manchester United's Central League side but never the Old Trafford first team squad.

It was not until the end of the season, when, after a barren run of five matches with only one goal and one point, the team all clicked together on the same day. The occasion was in the ultimate home fixture, for the visit of Luton Town, who needed to win by a huge margin and hope Oldham Athletic lost, to avoid relegation. The attendance of 2,755 was the lowest to attend a Scunthorpe United Football League match, and probably the meanest since the sombre days of the Midland League when the Club was living hand to mouth before the War. Those who bothered to turn up were in for a treat from the top draw.

Scunthorpe went a goal up on ten minutes, when Luton's slack defence allowed Andy Wilson to score. Barry Mahy, a signing from the Channel Islands, side-stepped his man and made it two, and before half an hour Stuart Bramley whipped in number three. Luton did make an effort to pull one back by the interval, but it was the players in the visiting dressing room that were the warmest after the roasting they must have received.

The second-half belonged to one man only. Barry Thomas took centre stage and put in a record-breaking performance. On fifty minutes he cracked in a square pass from Barry Linsdey. On sixty-eight minutes he followed up Derek Hemstead's shot to take the score to 5-1. Two minutes later he headed his hat-trick goal, and a minute later he fired in his fourth. If this was not enough, Barry scored a fifth goal in the last minute, not only to register an 8-1 record result for the Iron, but also to set an individual personal tally of five in a Third Division game; to date, has been equalled but never overhauled.

Scunthorpe wrapped up the season with a losing performance at Brentford which was about as exhilarating as watching the paint dry on the dressing room wall. It was not a season that would wished to be remembered by supporters. The final table place of eighteenth was a poor one to say the least. Fred Goodwin was not held in anyway responsible for the

Brian Bedford outjumps a Brighton defender, while Frank Burrows (later to move into football management) looks on.

result, and his remit was to continue to seek the right formula for a successful team. Gradually Goodwin was to find a more promising blend in the 1965-66 season, and after making his come-back, he even repaid back the compensation he had received from the Football League, for the injury which caused the premature end to his career.

There was to be a weeding out of the usual crop of players not required by the Club, and Scunthorpe waved farewell to Brian Reeves, Alan Kirkman, Barry Betts, Jack Bannister, Andy Wilson and Tony Needham. Ian Lawther was also missing, but his departure had been well before the end of activities. He became the first player to sign his papers for a new club at the House of Commons, where the Chairman of his new team, Brentford, was an M.P.

On the other side of the coin, United offered terms to a tall thin half-back from Workington, by the name of Keith Burkinshaw. Burkinshaw was a Yorkshireman with an acute football brain, and his long legs made it difficult for opponents to relieve him of the ball. His job would be as a left side partner to Dick Scott and Barry Horstead, and occasionally Peter Neale. Up front John Colquhoun, a Scotsman from Oldham, took up position on the left-wing with great success. Mick Ash arrived from Sheffield United for either the inside-right or right-flank slots, and there would be work for local lads Keith Lindsey - brother of Barry - Monty Brown, and Frank Barton. Before the season was a couple of games old, United made their most prestigious signing in Brian Bedford, a powerful front runner, who had been Queens Park Rangers' top marksman.

Scunthorpe United began the 1965-66 season with an excellent performance, but it unfortunately yielded no points. It came at Boothferry Park against Hull City who had been given the fillip of a cash injection by the ruling Needler family. United twice held the lead but succumbed to a late rally from the Tigers. The goal of the game was undoubtedly the first, scored by young Monty Brown. Brown took on virtually all the defence, before slotting in an amazing goal. There was a pause in the third pairing of the season at home to Reading, when a small piece of history was made.

It was at this stage of time that pressure from football clubs nationwide enabled the much heralded introduction of substitutes to the great game. The rules in those day demanded that players had to be all but dead or dying before a change of personnel could be made, and then it was only one player who sat on the bench. An injury that incapacitated Barry Lindsey during the match with the Berkshire side, allowed Barry Mahy to swap places with him.

Scunthorpe supporters must have wondered if their team would ever get into gear when the first eight matches produced the crumbs of a single win, and momentarily the name of Scunthorpe United appeared in bottom place. Gradually they sorted themselves out, and when John Colquhoun scored the third goal against his old club, Oldham, on a trip into Lancashire, United were on the way up. A feature of the team's rise up the table was their inspired away form, where a Club record of five consecutive League trips ended with victories. At Brentford it was a slender single goal by Smith that won the game.

The trip to Swansea was a swash-buckling 4-3 affair with all guns blazing. Against Workington the story was of a tight defence and patient forward building. Their York trip, a journey of less than fifty miles, was supported by Hull City fans, whose game at Sunderland had been postponed. Finally the Shrewsbury visit was a 4-1 extravaganza thanks to a Brian Bedford hat-trick. The only blip in this record came in the F.A.Cup at Crewe. United had plenty of support in the crowd, but shot themselves in the foot when Keith Lindsey fell foul of the referee for a rash tackle and was sent off. The ten men of Scunthorpe could not cope with the enthusiastic running of the Fourth Division men of Gresty Road, and they were soundly thrashed 3-0.

A visit to Shrewsbury gave the Club a run of six straight League wins and came on the Christmas Monday. It was strange that after they had beaten the Shrews by 4-1, the same opponents would appear the next day to inflict the same defeat on Scunthorpe at the Old Showground. The turning point of the game was when a hand at the end of a dark blue shirt rose up and clearly punched the ball away from the goal line. Over six thousand pairs of eyes saw it, but the all important man in black inexplicably did not. By this time Scunthorpe had no colour clash with teams in blue strips, for Freddy Goodwin changed the colour to white with blue facings, to be more in line with his old Leeds United team.

Scunthorpe United continued to rise up the table and became a team to be feared. In January the visit of Hull City produced the biggest attendance at the Old Showground for almost ten years. Fifteen thousand spectators packed the terraces, many of them wearing the colours of the unstoppable Tigers who were near the top of the League. Hull included players of the calibre of Houghton, Chilton and Wagstaff, and for the one and only time United were left to chase their own tail, losing to the eventual champions 4-2.

There was no such humiliation when Millwall visited the North. Millwall would settle as runners-up to Hull, but their young 'keeper Alex Stepney was asked to pick the ball out of the net four times. Scunthorpe were cruising to victory at 4-2 with ten minutes to go but relaxed to let the Lions in for an undeserved draw. It was, of course, the same Alex Stepney who was to win a European Cup Final medal, as well as other honours, with Manchester United.

Possibly the most rewarding result of the year was at Grimsby. The Town club had a cast iron home record and Scunthorpe had a list of away scalps as long as their arm. The Easter fixture meant that something had to give. At kick-off the twenty-two combatants ran out onto a heavy pitch. They soon got to grips with each other and generally Scunthorpe had by far the better of the exchanges. But as often the case, it was the submissive side which took the lead, when a Foster header got the better of Sidebottom.

After the break, United looked to the speed of black-haired Irish lad David Sloan to fire the ammunition. He mesmerized the Town defence and scored a hat-trick in the forty-five minute period. Only Harry Wainman, the home 'keeper, prevented an avalanche of Scunthorpe goals.

The Sloan hat-trick was not the last trio of goals United supporters would enjoy that season, for Barry Thomas was still in the mood to increase the total he had scored for the Club. A week after sinking Grimsby it was Workington's turn to suffer. Thomas hit three and David Sloan scored another as United's League position was reinforced by the 4-1 result. Scunthorpe curtailed the season with an unbeaten six match run, which saw a win at Oxford United in the last game. It left the Club in the elevated position of fourth in the table, a marvellous achievement under the circumstances. Brian Bedford was the leading scorer on twenty-two goals, while David Sloan and Barry Thomas both reached double figures.

A footnote to the campaign must include a mention of the debut for a young goalkeeping recruit, Ray Clemence, who made four appearances for the Iron that season. It was only a small step at the start of a career, but one that would lead to International fame.

~ 1966-67 ~

The commencement of the 1966-67 fixtures saw the absence of Dick Scott from the key competitors of the previously successful campaign, for he had packed his bags and moved to nearby Lincoln City. In the signing-in register there would be only one new name, that of the rugged Scotsman Frank Borrows. The man with the sideburns was a natural for the centre of Scunthorpe United's defence.

One of the reasons for the prudent transfer market transactions was the lack of cash. The Iron had been steadily losing money over the previous three years, and income at the turnstiles was nowhere near the expenditure of running the Third Division team. It meant that during the season United would have to blood a copious amount of talent from the junior ranks. During the season there would be employment for Ray Clemence, Frank Barton, John Barker, Stuart Taylor and Don Welbourne.

Scunthorpe United began the season in predictable fashion, losing their first three games. Frank Goodwin was exasperated with his senior professionals, and pointed the finger of blame in their direction. His solution was to put in all the youngsters at once, in a very important local derby at Blundell Park, Grimsby. The average age of the team struggled to rise above nineteen, while Barry Thomas and Brian Bedford came into the reckoning as the senior part of the crew. Grimsby Town were bristling for the fight, and produced a devastating performance which left United's inexperienced team numb. The 7-1 victory enjoyed by the Mariners was one of the hardest that Scunthorpe United had the indignation to swallow. To every player's credit who had worn the United colours that dark evening, not one stopped running until the ninety minute nightmare was over. Each one of them went on to make football a full-time career for many years. Ray Clemence in goal never let in as many goals again and was given the vote to carry on in the next match. Brian Bedford scored Scunthorpe's consolation goal, the last of the game, but never played for the Iron again. He chose a career in the South with Brentford.

The aftermath of the debacle at Grimsby was an apology by the manager in the Evening Telegraph. Goodwin was a gentleman and fully appreciative of the feelings of supporters. He took the weight of the defeat on his own shoulders alone. The result was that the players took a long hard look at themselves and bounced back at the end of the week with a heartening victory at Swansea which supplied the first points of the season. Despite the improvement, the first home game after the crash at Blundell Park brought an attendance struggling to reach four thousand spectators, for the attractive visit of Middlesbrough.

Those who did attend were delighted to see United fully recovered. The team excelled in every department and were full value with their 3-2 success. Unfortunately there was a tinge of sadness, for when Peter Neale ran onto the park as a replacement for Barry Horstead it signalled the last game that the long serving player was to make for the Iron. He was to leave in the sunset of his senior career for a couple of years at Chesterfield, before sinking into non-League football.

The team continued to pick up points now that the problems of the initial fixtures had been sorted out, but they could never be thought of as consistent. There was another bone of contention to answer by the board when it was decided to sell the immortal Barry Thomas for a second time. The most ardent fan recognized that he had been in and out of the team through injury. His best days were now behind him, and any cash received would ease the deepening depression at the bank. Barnsley stepped in with a modest fee, and as children watched the fireworks go off on 5th November, Barry Thomas played for Scunthorpe at Darlington for the final time.

November brought the team into the knockout games of the F.A.Cup, with a trip to neighbouring Lincoln City, who were languishing a division below them, and this was a hurdle they had a feeling they could clear. At kick-off the congested roads of the county capital still had cars unable to park near the ground. By the time Lincolnshire Road Car had disembarked its passengers, Smith and Burrows had fired the Iron into a two goal lead in the first ten minutes. By half-time the two goal margin was maintained, but at 3-1. In the second period Lincoln managed to wipe out all of United's advantage, and former Scunthorpe attacker Joe Bonson was at the heart of the action. It was a worrying time for the visiting supporters and visions of another derby match disaster looked to be looming on the horizon. Just as they feared the worst, the ball ran loose to lively Barry Mahy, and the slightly built player scorched in a shot, which was destined for the back of the net.

There was not enough time to fit in the F.A.Cup round two match, allotted to be played at the Field Mill against Mansfield Town, when it was announced that Fred Goodwin was leaving to become manager of the New York Generals in the new American soccer 'circus'. Part of the deal involved negotiations with the Board to take three players with him, namely Mick Ash, Barry Mahy and Geoff Sidebottom. Compensation for these players was rated at £10,000, and the money was a welcome windfall to ease United's cash flow. In the meantime United were content to utilize Keith Burkinshaw in a temporary position to look after team affairs.

The battle to win the F.A.Cup-tie at Mansfield was the next major thought on supporters' minds. Over Christmas the teams had met twice and each had gained points in their respective home matches. A possible money-spinning treat for the winners gave this tie plenty of needle, with players well used to the others' strategies. In the end home soil familiarity told for the Stags, and they ran out narrow 2-1 winners. This was the prelude to beating Middlesbrough, before they lost in the fourth round at Sheffield Wednesday.

Once the Iron were back on Third Division duties they discovered a diamond in local football who was able to stand up to the strain of the Third Division. He was steelworks electrician Graham Rusling, a man used to the physical side of the game in the lowly Lincolnshire League. Rusling stepped up a considerable grade and became a regular performer from then on. He caused a sensation in his debut at home to Swansea Town, looking like a natural born leader. Scunthorpe's second goal was down to his strong running, and a boisterous match, in wet conditions, was won 4-3.

Scunthorpe continued to hold their own, usually bobbing along in a comfortable but uninspired position in mid-table. They could hold their own against the majority of teams, but had no answer against anyone with a little class. This was clearly seen when the exceptional Queen's Park Rangers side completed the double over them at Loftus Road, crushing the Iron 5-1. It was the beginning to the last phase of seasonal events, but a poor run to the tape only produced four points in seven games, thanks to moderate successes at home to Watford and Bristol Rovers. The last three games left the team defeated on all accounts, and that mini-slump was a valid reason for a slightly miserable showing of eighteenth position on the League table. Three or four more points would have improved that position considerably. Perhaps the root of the problem was highlighted when Frank Barton was seen as the Club's only double score goalscorer, on eleven.

There was, however, one team within the Club that hit the headlines. Much hard work had been put in by the Juniors at under-eighteen level. Their labours were rewarded by an astonishing extended run in the F.A.Youth Cup. After a number of games they beat Port Vale in the Quarter-Final, only to lose to a highly rated Sunderland team in the Semi-Final. The Sunderland side contained a number of promising players who would play for the club in the First Division. A crowd of over five thousand turned out for the home leg against the Weirsiders and they saw a very gutsy performance end in defeat against a stronger eleven. The achievement by the Junior Irons was hailed as a success of paramount proportion. Many of them earned a contract as a result and were to later feature in the first team.

~ 1967-68 ~

The changing of the seasons soon had the players assembling for pre-season training, bronzed with the summer sun. Most of the team to finish the 1966-67 campaign were still at the Club, but United, who had been managerless for quite a while, did have a few new faces to supplement the squad. The first problem to solve was that of a new goalkeeper. Ray Clemence had displayed such character and potential at a tender age that Liverpool decided he was worth an investment of £18,000 for an Anfield apprenticeship in the Merseyside club's Central League team. Such an offer could not be rejected by Scunthorpe, and they chose Brian Arblaster, a Londoner, from Chesterfield as the replacement. In front of him, at full-back, John Barker, the son of former stalwart Jeff, was given the vote of confidence, and new signings came when Dave Harney joined from Grimsby and Peter Foley by way of Workington. The Grimsby lad, Harney, was a lithe player who was signed to score goals from the front of the attack. Foley came with a recommendation from Keith Burkinshaw, who knew the left-winger from his days at the Cumberland club. Peter was a Scotsman by birth, with a matching Glaswegian accent to suit, but he also had the honour of being the first black player to distinguish himself in United's colours.

Scunthorpe United began the 1967-68 season in a modest way, gaining two draws, one at Peterborough, and the other at home to Mansfield. Within a month the team had made it quite clear there would be no promotion challenge, and the only bright spot was two points from a see-saw game at Oldham, which although won by 4-3, did expose some glaring gaps in the back quarters.

There was just a little better news from performances in the League Cup. At least Scunthorpe did manage to out-fox their Fourth Division opponents down the road at Belle View, when Doncaster Rovers were subdued by 2-1. It led to a bumper crowd of over thirteen thousand at the Old Showground for First Division Nottingham Forest's visit. At one stage United looked to be in control and capable of a shock win, but ten minutes from time Scunthorpe-born Ian Storey-Moore hit an unlikely winner, which he sent screaming into the net for a Forest victory.

Meanwhile form in the Third Division showed little sign of improving, and United struggled below the mid-way mark in the table. The stress was showing on Keith Burkinshaw, who was doing his best with the demanding split role of both manager and player. In all this time he had never been officially upgraded, and the final straw came when eleven 'headless chickens' lost at home by 5-2 to Walsall at the Old Showground, one week into October. It was then that the Board decided the Club must have a full-time official residing in the manager's office.

The chosen man was a former Norwich City long-serving player, and short-time manager, Ron Ashman. Ron was generally a quietly spoken man, but he would could bark whenever necessary. He was a man with a sharp eye for footballing talent, and did not suffer fools gladly. United's decision to bring this gentleman to the Club was one of the more far-sighted measures they ever made. Ashman did not have a magic wand to wave, but he would keep the Club afloat for some time with his shrewd practices.

Ron Ashman soon made his assessment of the Club, and must have thought that a complete restructuring was necessary. The situation was inflamed by a long term injury to David Harvey, who was not able to report for duty again until the final gasp of the season. Team spirit was not a problem, and despite the team's shortcomings, it rallied for two games against Oxford United, the eventual champions. By now, Ashman had signed Stephen Deere from Norwich City and was to change his original choice of goalkeeper, with Stephen Drake replacing Scotsman Jim Lavery. In midfield Ron had bought Mel Bythe from Great Yarmouth.

The first game against the top side was at the Old Showground, when under four thousand spectators made up the holiday crowd, but they were pleased with David Sloan's contribution of a goal, and Oxford were fortunate to hang on. In the return fixture, four days later, United completely upset the form book to inflict serious damage on Oxford's promotion hopes at the Manor Ground. The 3-2 result would have given punters good odds from the bookies before the game. Stephen Deere, whose ungainly style of running caused comments from the crowd, played brilliantly, scoring twice; David Sloan had always been a maestro and he added the third.

The win over Oxford United signalled the last game at the Club for Frank Barton, who was going to join Second Division Carlisle United. Cash was the prime mover, as gates were at their lowest point for about thirty years, and an F.A.Cup loss at the hands of Halifax Town, a League below them in the second round dried up that source of income.

Weeks later, after scoring for the final time wearing a Scunthorpe shirt against Barrow, David Sloan was also on his way out of the door. Oxford thought him too good a bargain to miss after the run-arounds he had given them, and they came up front with some ready money.

The modest income earned left a surplus to buy three additional men to prop up the ailing team. From Sheffield United Ron Ashman paid a modest sum for his old Norwich team mate Bill Punton. Bill's balding pate gave him the look of a very senior member of the squad, but his wizardry of the dribble, out on the left-wing, belied his age. Supporting Punton on the other wing, or at inside-right, Ashman brought in George Kerr, who would run through a barn door if the manager requested it. George was a Scot with a wicked sense of humour, and was signed from Barnsley. The last of the players to cost a fee was another player with pace and guile, the former Leicester City inside man Terry Heath. Heath was a match-winner in his own right, and soon became a crowd pleaser with the Iron's fans. There was also a promotion from the reserves for promising full-back, Graham Foxton. Harrogate born Foxton had been a member of the successful Junior team of the 1966-67 season. It was early days, but he too was about to develop.

The winter had been extremely difficult for Scunthorpe United, as they went through their transitionary period existing on a shoe string. Gradually the poor showing on the field saw them plunge down the League. Against Colchester at Layer Road, Barry Horstead took his leave of the Club after a magnificent career with Scunthorpe, his only club, which saw over three hundred appearances in ten years.

Two weeks on, at home, Scunthorpe scored their biggest win of the season against the same club, who were fellow strugglers. The game marked the debut strikes from two Scunthorpe men, Bill Punton and Terry Heath. It was a rare oasis, and the 5-1 win was a culmination of the efforts of all of Ashman's new recruits. The only survivors from the start of the season were Hemstead, Barker, Lindsey, Burrows and Colquhoun.

It would need a concerted effort if Scunthorpe were going to survive a second relegation in four years. Unfortunately the Colchester United victory, in early March, was to be followed by a disastrous two months which produced just two more wins. Ironically, during this period goals were not a problem, and only a 4-0 loss at promotion chasing Shrewsbury failed to see Scunthorpe hitting the target.

The final League table revealed the Club's inadequacies, with a leaking defence, and a pathetic travelling record. Only two visits had produced victories, and too much disruption had taken place in team changes. All this pointed to Scunthorpe United dropping to the lowest Division of the League. Perhaps if Ashman had been offered the reins at the start of the season, United's story might have been different. As it was Scunthorpe long suffering supporters were left to rue another period in the decline of the Club's fortunes.

LIFE IN THE BASEMENT

Scunthorpe United had to steal themselves for a more austere brand of football in the 1968-69 season. Gone were the prospects of lucrative matches against some of the country's top clubs, filled with star names and attracting bumper crowds. All the glitter of the life in a faster lane had crumbled in a few short years. As soon as the best players were sold on, the cash received could not replace those men whose dazzling skills made them a name to be respected. The snowballing effect of the economic repercussions was devastating, for once the downward spiral had started, it continued to a new lowly level.

Those supporters who had stayed loyal were less than half in number, and many followers of the Third Division North times steadfastly refused to go to the Old Showground again. They considered that they had been sold down the river.

The Board at the Club must have realized that some mistakes had been made, although often supporters on the fringe did not see the whole picture, and it is the Directors who have to juggle with the finances of the Club on a day-to-day basis. It was now time to move on, and try to restore the former glories. Ironically before this could commence two more players walked away from Henderson Avenue for the last time. Frank Burrows was moving back to the Third Division with Swindon Town, and his short-time colleague Mel Blyth had progressed to the Capital to play for Crystal Palace. Both men would raise their games and be promoted to the next Division up with their respected clubs. Blythe was later bought by Southampton, where he would win an F.A.Cup winners medal in 1976.

~ 1968-69 ~

Among the new players on view, Ron Ashman had secured an extremely reliable goalkeeper from Norwich City, in Geoff Barnard who had excellent positional sense. Over the previous twelve months this had been an area of the field which had caused concern, but Barnard was to be an ever-present in the season ahead, illustrating that the hole had now been plugged. Another new player for the defence was Ray Holt, a tall centre-half who signed from Halifax Town as a direct replacement for Frank Burrows. On either side of him would be two youthful half-backs who would each see over three hundred appearances in a Scunthorpe shirt. From

Keith Burkinshaw, right, later 'Spurs Manager, makes one of his last appearances, at Bristol Rovers in February 1968. 'keeper Tim Lavery gathers the ball safely.

Grimsby Town came the tenacious Angus Davidson, a fiery Scot who was like a terrier dog with a bone when he had the ball. Opposite, in the left half-back slot, Don Welbourne was another of the juniors from local sources to earn his place with consistently strong performances. Certainly the calibre of the men Ron Ashman was moulding gave the side a good blend of youth and experience.

When the season did kick-off, United found themselves in the area of the dark satanic hills of Rochdale. The stark message of the swift Lancashire team was that nobody was going to wait until the Iron got into gear for a return to Division Three. United were run ragged in the first hour and only Barnard stood between the Dale and a score greater than 3-0. A little more urgency saw George Kerr and Steve Deere reduce the deficit, so at least it looked a little more presentable on paper.

The team was to appear for the first time at home that season, in the League Cup, but their usual tradition of an early exit was abandoned when four and a half thousand spectators witnessed a tough local derby with the fellow steelmakers of Rotherham. Steve Deere proved to be the hero of the game topping up his goalscoring with two more strikes. Each time United had to rely on Bill Punton waltzing round his full-back, and pinpointing a ball onto Deere's head. The best part of the 2-1 safe passage was that the whole team played with more zip and purpose.

The story of the League Cup run continued with another derby, against Lincoln City. Interest in the second round was such that the crowd rose to just over eleven thousand, on a warm September evening. There was plenty of backing for the Imps, and it was that section of the ground that were first to greet their side breaching their opponents' defence. United battled hard to restore the redress, and did so when Steve Deere fed George Kerr before half-time. Kerr's shot set up a thrilling second period which was always in doubt. Ten minutes from time George Kerr made it a double with a fierce drive. At 2-1 United could never be sure of victory until the last whistle, and they needed a point blank save from Barnard to preserve the slender advantage.

Progress in the League Cup was then forgotten, to concentrate instead on the bread and butter of the Fourth Division.

A magical performance at Doncaster Rovers left them with empty pockets, when the Champions-to-be pulled back from 2-0 down, both goals scored by United's Terry Heath, to win 4-3 in a grandstand finish. At Colchester the Iron were in a class of their own, against a team that was to be in contention for a promotion spot. The 4-0 success spoke volumes on how Scunthorpe conducted themselves under the Layer Road lights.

During September, United travelled to Peterborough for another midweek clash. The significance of the game was not the innocuous 3-2 defeat, but the inclusion of a young player who had impressed his mentors in the reserves. His name was Kevin Keegan, who had a run-out in the forward line wearing the number seven shirt. Keegan's career has been much documented, but on the green of the London Road pitch it took its first tentative steps. Keegan had been spotted and natured by the likes of Jack Brownsword and Ron Ashman among others. Kevin had tried his luck at Doncaster Rovers, his home town club, but it had not worked out. At Scunthorpe the youngster's progress would blossom.

It was not long before Keegan would get a severe first team test in the League Cup third round against Arsenal. The game was played in un unrelenting downpour. From United's point of view the seventeen thousand crowd was the biggest bonus. They did not realistically believe they could beat the smooth operators from the smoke, but they did not expect Arsenal to score a 6-1 victory. To be perfectly accurate, Arsenal actually put the ball in the net on seven occasions, for it was an own goal by Peter Simpson that supplied United's point!

In the New Year, Scunthorpe had the opportunity to take a good look at themselves, when Ron Ashman would not have been too happy with the situation. Workington had knocked them out of the F.A.Cup at the first round stage, the side was languishing in a mid-table position, home form was patchy, and gates had dipped below three thousand. Part of the solution was by the inclusion of two new players. Nigel Cassidy had been signed just before Christmas to add drive to the forwards, joining from Ron Ashman's old East Anglian haunt at Norwich. The black-haired man with drooping Mexican style moustache would soon be in the middle, mixing it alongside George Kerr and Terry Heath. His supply of goals would make him extremely popular with the crowds, as they cheered his contribution with both feet and head. Also to be given a run was local apprentice Nigel Jackson, who dropped into the full-back position for a spell. It was still early days in Jackson's career, but he would improve enough for inclusion in battles during the seasons to come.

The signing of Cassidy was to be the ace up United's sleeve for a revenge visit to Blundell Park, to confront a Grimsby Town team that had slumped out of all recognition. They had already won a rare away win, at the Old Showground, which in the past the Mariners had treated as a home venue. United sensed they could overturn the reverse and played a very tight defensive strategy at the rear to stifle Grimsby's rushing forwards. Up front, the power of Cassidy's head was not contained on one vital occasion, and Macey was beaten in goal for the only strike, on this fresh January afternoon. At the end of the campaign, Scunthorpe United had an inward smile, when Grimsby were obliged to seek re-election for a second bottom placing.

The winter of 1968-69 saw the harsh climate postpone a number of game and United finished their activities with five home games. It was probably this problem that made the gates drop sharply, and not one was in excess of two and half thousand during this period. At least the advantage of the Old Showground familiarity gave them three wins and a draw, to produce a slight upturn in fortunes. Two of the games, against Aldershot and Southend, were by encouraging 4-1 margins. In the final game, against the side from Essex, the last twenty minutes of meaningless football was played in semi-darkness, when a couple of floodlight pylons failed. Under normal circumstances an abandonment would certainly have taken place.

The conclusion of soccer at the end of the 1968-69 season had the Iron in sixteenth rung on the ladder, a position far lower than supporters would have wished. Eight home defeats was the root cause of the team's difficulties, and spoilt an away record of eight victories. The minimum requirement should have been a concerted push on the promotion positions, which never looked remotely like materialising. In all competitions Heath and Kerr shared the leading marksman spot with fifteen goals each, but in half a season Cassidy looked to be able to hold his own, scoring eight times.

During the close season no new faces appeared at the Old Showground, but to reduce the wage bill a transfer of Derek Hemstead to Carlisle United was sanctioned. Bill Punton slipped off to East Anglia with Great Yarmouth, and another Andy Wilson (A.P.), who like his predecessor of the same name was a right-winger, left for non-League football and Corby Town. It meant a first team pool of Barnard, Foxton, Barker, Jackson, Davidson, Lindsey, Deere, Holt, Welbourne, Rusling, Kerr, Keegan, Heath and Cassidy to start the ball rolling in the 1969-70 season. Another point to note was the highly successful conversion of the tall thin long blond haired Steve Deere to a centre defensive position in which his game would go from strength to strength.

~ 1969-70 ~

The main activity during the summer had been in the kit room, where United had elected to change their colours completely. From now on the team would be seen in an all red strip with white facings. Depending on who manufactured the apparel in future, then so would be the variation of the of red and white in the make up. To introduce the new strip, United played a showpiece friendly against Leicester City. Leicester brought a strong following in the crowd of around five thousand, and a youthful Peter Shilton in the visitors goal was able to keep the Iron at Bay. The Foxes eventually showed their superior class and comfortably won 4-0.

The new campaign saw Scunthorpe United's standing in the League with a slight improvement, but again not one to put any serious pressure on the places at the top of Division Four. The team lost the two opening matches of the season, first against Chester in the League, then to Hartlepool in the League Cup. It was just a taster for what supporters could expect under the continued constraints of the financial

Graham Rusling, of Scunthorpe, now playing in an all red strip, looks on in dismay as Macclesfield clear their lines at Moss Rose in the Cup.

pressures the Club was under. At least the first month of the campaign finished with a run of three consecutive victories, but United had flattered to deceive.

It was not until November when the real story of the 1969-70 season began to unfold. The F.A.Cup took them away to play the non-League silkmen of Macclesfield. Included in the team was a new central-defender Mick Atkin, a schoolteacher with a mop of ginger hair. His weight in the back line was to become a telling factor from then on. Macclesfield were unable to make any early impression and the Iron dictated the pace. Terry Heath shot them ahead when Graham Rusling's shot had only been partially cleared. If other softer options had been dealt with more directly the game would have been won by half-time, but Macclesfield soldiered on with the roar of the crowd, and their enthusiasm rewarded them with an equalizer, plus a midweek continuation of the opera in Lincolnshire.

The replay on the Tuesday saw a larger than normal attendance of over five thousand at kick-off. Macclesfield caused plenty of concern, twice taking the lead. United were in no mood to be mugged, and their superior fitness was the telling factory over the men of Cheshire. A lightening spell of two goals in three minutes saw them sprint ahead, and not to be caught out again. United supporters finished the night in high spirits after the 4-2 victory took them through to round two for a tie against Stockport, who were a division higher.

Before the Stockport encounter, United just had enough time to spoil Port Vale's party in the most entertaining League match of the season. They came back from a goal down, to end a twenty match unbeaten run by Vale, first equalizing through Heath's penalty. Then Sproson, the Potteries team's long-serving defender, put the ball into his own net for the Scunthorpe winner, but without doubt the Iron were full value for money.

Back to the plot of the F.A.Cup. United were to make a return visit to Cheshire, where Stockport County were a jaded outfit, only just clinging on to a place in Division Three. Scunthorpe met them at exactly the right moment. A goalless draw brought them back to the Old Showground for a ritual slaughter. Cassidy, Kerr and Keegan did the damage in front of goal, to supply a classic 4-0 Cup win. Kerr's second goal, to make the score 3-0, was definitely the coup de grace, as he ran thirty yards before launching a quality shot screaming into the back of the quivering net. Each of United's goals were greeted with the customary hail of toilet rolls waving in the night breeze high over the goal posts.

The third round of the F.A.Cup brought a sobering home tie after the New Year's celebrations, against Second Division Millwall, thus reviving memories of the 1951-52 season. United set about the cultured Lions in a workmanlike fashion, by not giving them an inch. At the back Barnard was given more than adequate protection by Foxton and Barker, while Deere commanded the box cutting out the ariel threat of the tall London forwards. Up front Heath was in his element in the brisk winter conditions, and probed the Southerners bylines with a couple of searching runs. The rhythm of Scunthorpe's play was not disrupted when Barry Lindsey limped off with a pulled muscle after twenty minutes play. Mick Atkin filled in like a natural.

Ten minutes after the substitution it was Scunthorpe that struck first. Steve Deere moved up into an advanced position, and when the ball ran loose to him outside the penalty box, he belted it back past the visiting custodian. The goal was just the boost the Iron wanted, for it subdued the Lions back into their defensive cages. Urged on by the decibels from the screaming crowd Scunthorpe struck again on the hour. George Kerr caught Keith Weller in possession, robbed him, and squared for Terry Heath to blast home with a first time shot. At 2-0 United were cruising and could have had more. Only late in the proceedings did Millwall raise their game, and not until two minutes from time did Bolland reduce the arrears, but it was all too late.

The luck of the draw gave Scunthorpe United an absolute beauty, when they were selected to be the guests of First Division Sheffield Wednesday at Hillsborough. Wednesday were having a thin time, but most of the 38,047 crowd, of which around seven thousand were from Scunthorpe, thought them too good for the likes of United. Once the teams had left the warmth of the dressing rooms, reputations meant nothing and the Iron set about stealing the feathers from the Owls. The team line-ups on that frozen January day were as follows:-

Sheffield Wed.: Springett (P.), Pugh, Megson, Ellis, Prophett, Craig, Sinclair, Witham, Warboys, Smith and Coleman. Sub. Burton.

Scunthorpe Utd.: Barnard, Foxton, Barker, Deere, Atkin, Welbourne, Keegan, Cassidy, Kerr, Heath and Davidson. Sub. Rusling.

Conditions underfoot were perfect at the start of play, even though blades of grass were at a premium. Straight away, Wednesday's tall players tried to exert their authority on the game and the Iron were pinned back in their own half. The watch showed only four minutes had been played when Sam Ellis' header was nodded off the line by Graham Foxton, but instead of going over the bar it came into the path of Jack Witham, who had the easiest task to score. The next quarter of an hour was a crucial one for the Scunthorpe defence as it fought tooth and nail to keep out the marauding Owls' forward line. Gradually the team weathered the storm and made progress up the field themselves.

The large contingent of Scunthorpe fans were hardly made welcome, as they outsang and outchanted the Yorkshire masses. Then there was to be drama at the other end on twenty-one minutes play. Heath dashed through the Owls back lines, only to be upended in full flight. George Kerr was given responsibility for the free kick. He squared to Deere who centred the ball to Barker, on a sortie up field. John Barker bravely dived between the swinging boots to head a terrific goal, and beat the grasp of Springett.While the goal was being celebrated, Barker lay motionless, having been accidentally kicked in the head. Trainer Jack Brownsword immediately called for a substitute, and Barker could remember nothing until the next morning. Graham Rusling ran on as a replacement, but the addition of an attacker for a defender made no difference to United's flow once they had re-organized.

Nigel Cassidy, far left, turns to celebrate as he scores the winner against Wednesday......

If anything it charged them up for the conquest ahead, and the Iron more than held their own. The second-half was to belong to Scunthorpe United and the man orchestrating the play, Terry Heath, thrived in the extra space he was allowed. Time and time again he ran at the cowering Owls defence and was unfortunate not to score on at least a couple of occasions. In the seventieth minute United made the decisive move of the match when they won a corner, after Smith cut out a Heath pass intended for Keegan. Kerr swung over a high kick beyond the whole defence towards the far post where Nigel Cassidy was lurking. His looping header, back across the goal, beat all groping attempts by the Owls players to clear. Scunthorpe were 2-1 up and went on to gain the banner headlines.

.... and in the next round, at the County Ground, Swindon, a packed ground see Nigel Cassidy give United the lead.

The Scunthorpe public were now transfixed with the Club's prosperity in the F.A.Cup. For the second time in their history the team had stretched as far as the fifth round of the competition. When the draw was made a cry of disbelief greeted the live radio broadcast - an away trip to Second Division Swindon. On the day the Iron was well supported in the twenty-four thousand crowd, and the home side had the familiar face of Frank Burrows in the line up. But the biggest disappointment for the Scunthorpe players was the state of the pitch, for it was

Back on League duty, Nigel Cassidy - again - scores at home to Lincoln in February

so deep in mud that it resembled the battlefields of the Somme in Winter. Each step made was accompanied by a displacement of slime that came back over the top of the boots. How the match was allowed to start is still a mystery.

Despite the quagmire United gained the lead on ten minutes. Steve Deere cleared the ball to Kerr, then Kerr put a through pass in the path of Cassidy, who beat Burrows to the ball, and hit a low shot past 'keeper Downsborough. It was the last high United enjoyed during the game, as gradually Swindon wore them down. Three goals followed, and Scunthorpe eventually ran out of stamina on the strength-sapping pitch. The last whistle was the end of a courageous run which had seen United at the forefront of the nation's football headlines. For four months the team had lit up the town's interest with their outstanding feats.

The Fourth Division League programme seemed to pale into insignificance in comparison to what had happened in the F.A.Cup. Ron Ashman now had to get the players minds focused on the task in this department. He had not seen them win since December, two months earlier, although points had been gleaned out of four one apiece draws in seven days. However a victory was at last gained towards the end of February at lowly Hartlepool, by a slender 2-1 margin.

The season was quickly ebbing away, as an earlier than usual finish was scheduled, due the World Cup finals taking place that Summer. Thus it was deep into March when Scunthorpe served up their best home win of the season at the cost of Newport County. A goalless first-half gave no hint of the ground to be won in the second period, and United fans were given the joy of goals by George Kerr, Nigel Cassidy (a brace), and Angus Davidson, for a handsome 4-0 result. At this stage United were running to one point average per game, and April only left three matches to play. The first of these was a piece of history in the jigsaw puzzle of the Football League, although it was not appreciated at the time. United travelled to Bradford Park Avenue, who were rooted to the foot of the table for the third season running.

Scunthorpe established a record 5-0 away victory, four goals arriving in another scorching second-half. This was Bradford's last home fixture of the campaign, and when the rest of football rejected their pleas for re-election, it meant that Scunthorpe had witnessed the end of an era. Only one more point was added to the Iron register, thanks to the sharing of two goals at Workington, and so United ended in twelfth position in the table. At least the season had seen them financially break even, but an improvement in the League had to be made a priority in future.

The thrills of the magical Brazilian's winning the World Cup in Mexico masked the work carried out behind the scenes by Ron Ashman during the summer holidays. Once again a little pruning was necessary, with the release of Ray Holt and Stephen Drake. All the remaining players that were out of contract accepted the new terms offered, as did forward Colin McDonald, a lean-bodied forward from Norwich City, and local boy Terry Muldoon who played on the right-wing. Sadly Terry played only one game, and passed away before the season had reached its conclusion.

~ 1970-71 ~
Kevin Keegan opened the scoring for Scunthorpe in the second-half of the first game, a 1-1 draw against Exeter City in glorious Devon. A suggestion of better luck in the Fourth Division came when Southend United were flattened by a first-half bombardment which saw their defence leak goals scored by George Kerr and a very rare shot from back line man Graham Foxton. Terry Heath rounded the display off with United's third. It was good to see the back quarter hold firm in front of Geoff Barnard, and keep a clean sheet.

Hopes of a sustained Fourth Division campaign fizzled out from there on, with a familiar picture of inconsistency which followed the team into the Autumn. At this time Barry Lindsey was seriously injured, and it was effectively to end a very brave and loyal career at the Club which had spanned ten years. His place was to be taken by Chris Kisby who was a United apprentice. Eventually the position was to be occupied by the more experienced Mick Atkin as the season went on.

One of the problems the side was to endure was a frustrating time in front of their own supporters, but with better fortunes on their travels. Home defeats by Oldham Athletic, York City and Grimsby Town only frayed the nerves of exasperated fans on the steps of the Old Showground terraces. Away from those pressures, Aldershot, Bournemouth and Newport County found Scunthorpe United's red demons no joke. Of these performances the trek to Dean Court, Bournemouth, was far and above the best thus far. Steve Deere was the main ingredient of the Scunthorpe formula, for he policed Ted MacDougal throughout the game, allowing him no chance to extend his considerable goalscoring reputation. Captain Deere also offered his services in attack, supplying the first goal, and Cassidy added the second, for a 2-0 lead, and final score, before it was time to undo the flask for the half-time cup of tea.

Scunthorpe United did not completely starve their supporters at the Old Showground. Three days after beating Exeter City at home 3-0, came a splendid performance against Peterborough United, a team who played football on the night and made a full contribution to the ninety minutes. At the break there had been plenty of activity and the score stood at 2-1 to the Iron. In the second period it was even busier and at 5-2 the crowd stood to applaud both teams from the park. Perhaps it was John Barker's goal, away from defensive duties, that pleased them most. He was, after all, only to score twice all season.

The Autumn days were to see a number of changes at the Old Showground, the first of which was the sad event of a broken leg sustained by George Kerr in the Lincolnshire Cup game at Gainsborough. It was to keep George out of action for the rest of the season, as he struggled to regain his strength and fitness. Four weeks later United were offered the considerable sum of £20,000 from Oxford Untied, for the signature of Nigel Cassidy, their free-scoring forward. That amount of money did not become available often, and although the cost to the team on the park would have its repercussions, it had to be taken. This left some finance in hand, after outstanding bills had been paid, to reinvest in the team.

Within a short time Tony Woolmer, a Londoner by birth, joined having played at the declining Bradford Park Avenue. Woolmer was a front-runner but did not possess the same goalscoring attributes as Cassidy. Ashman then switched his attention to a tricky winger, Harry Kirk, from Hartlepool. Not only could Kirk dribble past his man, but he also distributed the ball to his colleagues, unlike some wide men who would insist on going too far and getting caught in possession. Harry's no nonsense style made him very popular with his new supporters.

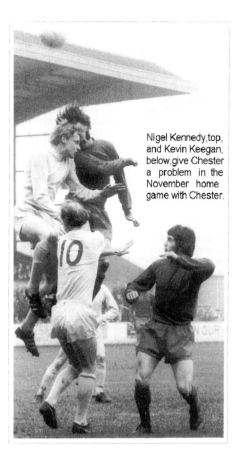

Nigel Kennedy, top, and Kevin Keegan, below, give Chester a problem in the November home game with Chester.

November brought the F.A.Cup into the conversation, and thoughts of the 1969-70 exploits which were now part of local folklore. United were picked out to fight it out against the stubborn opposition of Tranmere Rovers, a division higher in the League. At Prenton Park, Woolmer scored his first Scunthorpe goal, but the sides could not be separated. In mid-week, a goalless game that went the distance of extra-time, still had the two teams neck and neck.

The second replay was down for neutral territory, and Tranmere, who won the toss of a coin, chose the open spaces of Goodison Park. It was not until another period of extra time that Kevin Keegan laid on a simple chance for Graham Rusling, that the Iron went through 1-0. Even then Rusling needed two stabs at the ball before he squeezed it past Lane in the Tranmere goal.

Scunthorpe United's task in round two was possibly even more demanding. They had to deal with Mansfield Town, also in division three, but a team in a high position. Home advantage was on their side, and a healthy crowd of over seven and a half thousand supporters paid to watch Scunthorpe in a determined frame of mind.

At half-time both teams had sparred with each other, but no openings had been exploited. A minute from the restart Foxton crossed into the penalty box, and Tony Woolmer challenged the 'keeper, causing the ball to drop free. Graham Rusling accepted the gift and smacked it home for the precious lead.

United kept up the pressure, and ten minutes later the ball was punched to Harry Kirk out on the left. Kirk swung his foot and placed the ball out of reach, high into the net. The traffic down at the Doncaster Road goal did not stop there. Kirk was again the architect, setting up another Rusling strike for the third goal, effectively blunting any further thrust from the antlers of the bewildered Stages.

Although excellent progress was being persued in Cup matters, United's League form had hit the stop blocks. After beating Peterborough so handsomely the Club saw no more League victories until after the New Year, when ironically it was the completion of the double over the Posh at London Road which stopped the rot.

The nadir of this period had to be the loss at Southport. Their trip to the seaside brought no fun on the roller coaster, and three first-half goals against them suggested a hammering. In the end they did have Kevin Keegan's consolation goal, but were crushed by a 5-1 scoreline.

In the F.A.Cup, United's board were rubbing their hands at the certainty of some much needed cash in prospect from the draw in the third round against West Bromwich Albion, at the Hawthorne's. Albion were a force in the First Division, and contained a number of top International players within their ranks. One player was the England front runner Jeff Astle, fresh from his World Cup experiences in Mexico. It meant a busy afternoon for all the United

Steve Deere, Tony Woolmer and Graham Rusling test the West Brom. Defence in the Cup.

crew, including Steve Deere, who was given the job of man-marking Astle. To the visitors credit, they stuck to the task given to them, and blotted out every chance the Baggies tried to create. In the last minute of the game, the twenty-one thousand spectators were not sure if Tony Woolmer had bundled the ball into the net to put the Iron through. However, the referee judged that a hand had been used, and so a stalemate remained throughout the ninety minutes.

The question being asked by supporters was could Scunthorpe overturn their aristocratic opposition? Over sixteen thousand people were present at kick-off to find out the answer. Certainly the Iron created all the early chances, enough to cause worry in the Albion defence. Then in the thirty-third minute, Harry Kirk pumped across a ball which beat Jim Coombes' in the visiting goal, but Steve Deere rose high, and sent it spinning off his head and over the goal line. Albion needed some very supportive work from former Scunthorpe idle, John Kaye, to steady the nerves, but at the interval it was the Iron fans who were wearing the smiles.

The second-half was a completely different affair. West Bromwich had been given a severe rollicking by their manager Alan Ashman. They were straight off the starting blocks, increasing the pace, and generally went on to give United the run around. Two goals by Scottish International Tony Brown, and another by Jeff Astle, wrapped up the score at 3-1, and won the Midland team the right to entertain Ipswich.

In the League, United's story continued unchanged, and throughout the latter end of the programme they managed to pick up points in dribs and drabs. This allowed them to settle in a position below halfway in the League, but out of the direction of re-election trouble, which was destined to be the fate of Barrow, Hartlepool and Newport County, plus one other. As long as that was not Scunthorpe United it did not matter, and fears were eased in March with two results against Colchester United and Lincoln City.

Colchester had just reached the heights of F.A.Cup glory with a stirring defeat of the all-conquering Leeds United side which won blanket media coverage. The record-breaking run for the Division Four outfit finished against Everton, and their battle weary troops could not find the legs to outrun

Scunthorpe at the Old Showground. A blank sheet on forty-five minutes was altered by two goals in the second-half. Tony Woolmer hit the first, while the other was supplied by Paul O'Riley, on loan from Second Division Hull City until the end of the season. Paul went one better on the following Saturday adding a brace in the derby match with Lincoln City. The Imps were having even more difficulties than the Iron, and a two goal lead at the break had finished the game as a contest. It finally wound up at 3-1 in United's favour.

Scunthorpe ended the 1970-71 season winning three of the last seven games, with no draws. At least they wrapped up their affairs on a high note, beating mid-table Workington 4-0. Nigel Jackson, at full-back, left it late in the crusade to score his first goal of his career. The result left Scunthorpe in seventeenth position, and as one of five teams on forty-three points. A couple more points could have pushed them up the ladder another half a dozen places, and made a much more respectable view of the finishing line up.

The talk of the town was of United's highly rated young forward player Kevin Keegan, and it was patently obvious that this was a busy talent destined for the stars. How high he would climb towards the top was anyone's guess, but United kept on dishing out complimentary tickets to visiting scouts to see which club would be first to put cash on the table. It turned out to be Liverpool, who were already reaping the rewards of the goalkeeping prowess of Ray Clemence.

When a fee of £35,000 was put on the cheque the Club had no alternative but to take the money. It meant that as Keegan was scoring two debut goals, at Anfield, against Nottingham Forest on one side of the land, United were on the other side, at Grimsby, and doing their best without him.

~ 1971-72 ~

Ron Ashman did spend a little of his coin on a strong running forward in Ron Fletcher from Lincoln City. Fletcher was a serious sort of a player, who had other career roots in teaching, but once he found his depth in the team he became a quality goalscorer. Ron Ashman was also to give a limited run to Dave Hutchinson, who had been a prolific goalscorer in non-League circles at Brigg, but he was never able to repeat the same consistency in the League. Eventually the experiment was curtailed.

However, there was to be more encouraging news of George Kerr, for he had resumed light training and was fit enough for a comeback at the end of October. Ashman may have wished to retain Paul Riley, but he returned across the Humber to Hull City, and Graham Rusling went back to his electrical trade, while playing part-time for Goole Town.

It may have been sunny on the first day of the 1971-72 season, but Scunthorpe were feeling the heat of the fire given out by a rejuvenated Grimsby Town. The Mariners, and the eventual champions, bundled the Iron with a stylish 4-1 score.

A debut goal from Rod Fletcher was of little consolation, and days later, in the League Cup, he was unable to repeat this against his old club, Lincoln City. United were out of this competition at the first round stage for the third consecutive time. United's followers feared the worse, but there was no need for panic. This worm was about to turn.

The coincidence of the fixture list had Lincoln City at home as the visitors three days following their League Cup success. United changed Woolmer for Kisby and although the attendance was nearly seven hundred down, those present saw Scunthorpe United in a completely different light against a useful set of opponents. Quite out of the blue, United played intelligent and inspired football and took the first points of the season. The goals in the 2-1 result came from Terry Heath, and Nigel Jackson from the penalty spot. This was the start of a ten match unbeaten run which, for a welcome change, saw the team in the top reaches of the table. During this period the defence helped Geoff Barnard, as reliable as ever, keep five clean sheets.

There was a hiccup to the team's progress in October, when defensive slip-ups at Bury (where 2,733 spectators seemed lost within the spaces of the ground), and they lost the game 3-1. This was at a time when Bury had suggested to their supporters that they change their name to Manchester North End. Another week rolled on and Grimsby Town were knocking on the door at the Old Showground. Eleven thousand people saw the slick fisherman steal the points, winning a close encounter by the odd goal in three. It had to be admitted that they did appear to be the best team that the Iron had confronted all season.

Meanwhile, Scunthorpe had been pitched in with South Shields of the Northern League in the F.A.Cup. It required a long journey for the growing army of Scunthorpe supporters, and they knew it would not be an easy ninety minutes. On the afternoon the usual solid defence was pulled apart by the non-League men. But United matched them, goal for goal, and earned a 3-3 result, thanks to a late disputed effort from George Kerr; this was the first since his long lay-off. The replay should have been a formality, but the hand of fate was pointing the finger of upset at Scunthorpe. South Shields played as if their lives depended on a win, and they overcame United's early superiority to climb to the peak of their ambitions, handing out an embarrassing 3-2 defeat to United.

The wastage of the F.A.Cup opportunity did not filter down into the form Scunthorpe United was enjoying in the Fourth Division. One week before this knock-out competition they embarked on a fifteen match unbeaten run by beating Workington.

Days after the Cup exit, a long haul down to Gillingham saw them rewarded when lone wolf up front, Rod Fletcher, made the running and hit a solo goal to secure the two points. One week later there was a great deal of concern when Don Welbourne was carried from the field in the win at home to Chester. It was another long term injury and a blow to the side's promotion challenge.

The Club's next away visit was on the Saturday before Christmas, but this was the short hop to play Doncaster at Belle Vue. Although the crowd was only four thousand, United had plenty of support on the wide open terraces. The spectators saw Scunthorpe's tight defence put a strangle hold on the Rovers roaming forwards. Up in attack United always had enough to out-fox the Doncaster rear guard. Rod Fletcher scored the first goal, directly from a corner, and received a fist in the face from an apologetic Rovers goalkeeper. Then George Kerr sewed it up at 2-0 with a drive through a crowded penalty box.

On the Monday after Boxing Day, United entertained Hartlepool at the Old Showground. The sharing of the points was to see another serious setback of losing Terry Heath through a groin injury that took time to heal. Unfortunately it was the end of the season for him, and was a blow to the Club, now they were at last jockeying up with the Division's leading group. United's resources were stretched to breaking point, and there was no money to find a replacement. It should also be said that Hartlepool proved to be one of the brightest of teams to visit all season and thoroughly deserved the 2-2 result. They may have gleaned more from the game if Kerr had not crashed in on a defensive mix-up five minutes from the end.

Scunthorpe United kept plugging away during the rest of 1972 and produced their most satisfying performance of the campaign away to second in the table Brentford. An army of coaches set off South to Griffin Park, and another good following was in place at kick-off amongst a crowd of eleven thousand plus. The game was of vital importance to both sides and played in a Cup-tie spirit. Scunthorpe made a tremendous start, relying on the running of Fletcher and Kerr to cause confusion. They were well supported by the distribution of Kirk and Davidson, while at the rear United were solid. It was with this industry that Colin McDonald put Scunthorpe ahead. Fletcher's effort was goal bound, but the home 'keeper was able to punch the shot out only as far as McDonald. McDonald promptly returned the shot, and this time there was to be no stopping it.

The goal spurred Brentford into retaliation, and Barnard did well to keep out a barrage of shots, for the next twenty minutes. Gradually the tempo of the play came down to a level the Iron could dictate, and holes began to appear in the Bees defence. Fletcher was left up field and every time Kerr and Kirk could find the opportunity they pumped up balls for Fletcher to chase. In the sixty-fifth minute one such incident left him clear to run at the wide open defence. As soon as the goalkeeper came off his line, Fletcher let fly with number two. Brentford threw everything up the top end of the field in a vain bid for parity. Fletcher was left to do a repeat performance with two minutes left, and Scunthorpe were home and dry at 3-0.

The Brentford result was one of three similar scores in four games, with United's odd one out being that at Workington. On the return from the North-West, United were ruing the missed chances up front, and the 1-2 reverse closed the account on the fifteen unbeaten outings, which started and finished, ironically, with the same opposition.

The run to the end of the season was to be a tense period as five teams, including Scunthorpe, raced to take up the four promotion spots. Injury problems at the Old Showground had Charlie Strong pulling out his silver hair, and Ashman was virtually down to selecting anyone not bandaged or on crutches. Easter was vital and on Good Friday the team was up at the Feetham's to play Darlington, a side with a good home record. United's defenders did their usual effective work, and Fletcher's shot on the run created the ideal situation. The rest of the game saw the whole team hold its discipline and the points were bagged.

Overnight, Scunthorpe stayed in a hotel for the second away game, which required a short hike to Hartlepool. The 'Pool were about on a par with their neighbours, but with an untidier home record. At kick-off they displayed far more resolve than expected, and Fletcher could not get his usual look in. It was a frustrating time for visiting supporters, especially when former favourite Bobby Smith burst through the Iron's defence with a goal in the last action of the game.

The shattered troops regrouped on the Tuesday night and produced a very uncertain performance against Aldershot. It marked the debut of Scunthorpe youngster Peter Markham, forced into the fray through depleting numbers. He never let the side down, and the 1-0 conclusion was satisfying under the extreme circumstances. The edgy side of United's character was again revealed the next Saturday.

To avoid clashing with the Grand National, United opted for an evening kick-off. Once again the supporters went through agony, as United dithered against basement opposition Stockport County. The visitors had only one away victory all season, but Scunthorpe made them look good. Playing with all the conviction of men about to be shot in the morning, the side conjured up a suicidal performance, which culminated in a 2-0 loss. Fortunately, the nerves and prospects of their competitors were of equal merit and the team remained on course, but only just.

Gradually the finishing line could be seen. Cambridge United were next in Town and posed some awkward questions.

Urged on by the voices of six thousand local believers, Scunthorpe inched a little closer. Rod Fletcher went on one of his searching runs, and with Kerr and McDonald in close order, they found the right combination. At last there was a performance worthy of the team's League position. Supporters wondered if they would falter when Cambridge opened the scoring after half-time, but showing such authority there could be only one winner, and Fletcher paved the way with two headed goals. The first was from Kerr's cross and the second from Harry Kirk's corner kick.

The pressure was now on Lincoln City, particularly away from Sincil Bank, where they often suffered from travel sickness. Scunthorpe may have lost ground at Reading, but news came through on the same day that the Imps unbeaten home record had crumbled.

Promotion was actually clinched during the last week in April. Southend United were the visitors and needed a point themselves to confirm a place the next season in Division Three. Almost nine thousand folk filled the Old Showground with a pleasant atmosphere. The majority of them danced with joy when after just four minutes of play Harry Kirk sent in a teasing corner which beat everyone and landed in the far side of the net. It was a great boost which injected a quiet confidence throughout the team. United continued to play a delicate brand of controlled soccer worthy of a team destined to go up. Then before half-time the defence conceded a soft goal, when indecision at the back left players inviting each other to clear the ball. Instead, it gently trickled between them, and agonisingly into the net. Fortunately there was no more errors and no more goals. Southend United were promoted, and when Lincoln failed the next night, Scunthorpe United were guaranteed to join them. It was just as well because the depleted forces lost the last two games of the season, at Cambridge and Newport.

Nevertheless Scunthorpe United had won promotion, taking the fourth place in the table. Ron Ashman had done a great job, along with his stouthearted players. At last there was something to celebrate and it was hoped the resurgence would continue. The team was a mixture of local youngsters and budget signings, and everyone was proud of them. Great credit went to the defence, where only thirty seven-goals were conceded in the season, which thus created a new Club record. In attack Rod Fletcher headed the list with twenty first team goals. Now the players would have to roll up their sleeves and start again in Division Three.

Harry Kirk's goal direct from a corner against Southend, earns a 1-1 draw, and seals promotion for Scunthorpe.

CHAPTER 11

SEVENTIES STORMS BEFORE EIGHTIES OPTIMISM

The beginning of the 1972-73 season was to herald a new era for Scunthorpe United, and it was not one of success or prosperity. Words like 'disappointment' and 'struggle' would be part of the everyday vocabulary, as they had been in the dark days of the 1920's, long before supporters of the seventies had been born. However, out of adversity there are always people to call upon as heroes, and Scunthorpe United found plenty of champions for their cause, both on the staff and on the terraces.

~ 1972-73 ~

There was little or no money in the kitty for Ron Ashman to spend on players, but he did offer contracts to two men. The first was former Nottingham Forest man Graham Collier, who had enjoyed a handful of games with the senior prof-essionals at the City Ground. Graham was a lean player, with typical long hair which at that time was the vogue. He had plenty of ball skills and soon took a forward role, before later dropping into the centre of the park. The other signing was that of Gary Sargent, a forward from Ashman's old school, Norwich City. There was to be some extra work for Mike Williams, already on the books, but given a run in the first eleven at times as competition to Geoff Barnard. Williams had joined from Hull City and was generally regarded as the reserve 'keeper, but he was a reliable deputy whenever the demand was necessary.

The start of the new Third Division season gave no hint of the turmoil to come, and the lack of investment in top quality replacements had already been noted by supporters. On the first day, Scunthorpe began with a workmanlike performance against a tall Swansea City side, playing in all white to match the mood of the hot sunny day. United kept it very tight and just about deserved the late winner which Steve Deere nodded in from a Harry Kirk corner. Angus Davison followed the ball into the net, causing a debate as to who actually did score. In midweek the visit of a powerful Chesterfield side in the League Cup did not overawe the Iron.

The first game back in Division 3: Rod Fletcher gets a cross in, watched by Terry Heath, and the white-shirted Swansea players.

More Welsh opposition at the end of August. Graham Collier's shot just fails to beat the Wrexham 'keeper, and a 1-1 draw was the final result.

To their credit the defence did what was expected and they earned a replay from a game with no goals to offer. It was only the 5-0 drubbing at Saltergate in the return that suggested caution was required. Nevertheless the toils of August saw the Club in a comfortable mid-table position and all looked to be completely acceptable.

If a few spots of rain had fallen in September, it was bucketing down by the beginning of October. The defence was under so much pressure during most matches that it was difficult for the midfield to get the ball anywhere near Rod Fletcher, George Kerr or Terry Heath. When they did, the pressure of dominant defenders gave them precious little opportunity to score. The result was six straight losses and little prospect of an immediate recovery. United slumped to the bottom reaches of the League.

October was fractionally better with 1-0 victories eked out of shear hard work against fellow promoted sides Brentford and York City, but neither of these teams would be high flyers in the Division. It was probable that the best of all the performances came at Bolton, were the Wanderers took the crown as Champions in May. United were like a punch-drunk boxer at the end of ninety minutes, but somehow the ball had not beaten Barnard in the Scunthorpe goal. At the other end the Bolton 'keeper must have been shivering with inactivity.

The news in November was a little more cheery as the signing of a new player was announced. Neil Warnock came for a modest fee from Hartlepool to boost the midfield. At least there was some respite and briefly there was a mini-revival. In Warnock's debut game at Rochdale, goals by Heath and Kirk, one in each half, provided the Iron with a valuable away win. The only drawback to an uplifting day was that one cowardly hooligan thought it fit and proper to put a brick through the supporters coach window, making for a freezing journey home.

A week later United had to face Fourth Division Hartlepool in the F.A.Cup. At the Victoria Ground the teams acted out an inconclusive goalless draw. The replay was equally fallow after a further period of extra time. It was not until the second replay at Roker Park that a goal was seen. Hartlepool took an early lead and held it for a long period of the game, despite Scunthorpe's valiant efforts to restore the equilibrium, but it did not come until four minutes from the end of normal time. The Hartlepool defender Dawes, a former Aldershot man, was put under pressure by the attentions of Terry Heath, and he had the misfortune of scooping the ball into his own net.

A further thirty minutes of play was ordered and Hartlepool suffered some more cruel luck. Three minutes of the seemingly never ending night remained when Kirk received a quick return from his own corner. He whipped across an accurate lob to the head of Steve Deere, who glanced the ball in for a 2-1 result.

The team eased the burden in the League, beating Shrewsbury Town by a whisker, 1-0, but crashed aimlessly 5-1 at Bristol Rovers, before it was time to do further F.A.Cup battles. This tie was on home soil with Halifax Town. The Shaymen had already plundered the League points, and there was ample opportunity to restore a little respect. It all seemed to be plain sailing when Heath and Kirk put United 2-0 up on twenty-five minutes, but they contrived to make hard work of the game and by the sixtieth minute Town had clawed back the deficit. The decider came ten minutes later as a punched clearance from the visiting 'keeper, White, was returned by a looping header from Scunthorpe's defensive trooper John Barker, who made it 3-2 in United's favour.

On League duty, Scunthorpe made brave efforts to make ends meet and hence keep their heads above water. There was a 'backs to the wall' performance against Notts County, who were caught on an off day. Even then the high flying Magpies of Nottingham should have done better at the Old Showground, but a first-half goal by the busy Angus Davidson helped United take the two points, that on paper were expected to be lost by the Iron. The victory still saw Scunthorpe three places off the bottom of the League. A chance of stepping out of the relegation positions arrived on Boxing Day, but a visit to Blundell Park for the Christmas extravaganza with Grimsby Town was not one for the fainthearted. Town had adapted to the Division far better and were a fringe team for promotion. United held out for a long period of the game, but under siege conditions the sixteen thousand attendance was just waiting for the inevitable. It only took a Lew Catterley shot to keep the two points at Blundell Park, and United had lost out in a derby match again.

Although Scunthorpe had lost at Grimsby, it was generally acknowledged that there had been plenty of effort and a resemblance of a football pattern. This was not so in the next match against Bristol Rovers where a 3-1 defeat in the familiarity of their own Old Showground environment was just not up to scratch. It came as something of a surprise when the team returned from Wrexham on the first Saturday in the New Year richer by two points from a 2-1 win. Wrexham were mid-table at the time and since beating Grimsby they had gone the four previous games without a win. Scunthorpe caught them at the right time, and goals in each of the forty-five minute periods, first by Heath and the other by Fletcher, eased the pain.

This episode led the team up to another F.A.Cup game against Welsh opponents. Second Division Cardiff City were dispatched from the Principality, geared up for the third round. On the day they were always a stride too fast for the Iron, but to give the local lads credit, they did raise their game and make a genuine fight of it. In the end United could count themselves unlucky to go down by the odd goal in five, although on two occasions they fought back to get on terms. The first was a header by local lad Don Welbourne making excellent progress in the first team, and the second a scorching twenty-five yard drive from Harry Kirk. Unfortunately it was insufficient, because with four minutes remaining on the watch, the Cardiff City midfielder, Phillips, blasted the ball through a melee of bodies to stich up the tie for the jubilant Bluebirds.

From that point on the season turned to acid for the Iron. Twelve games without a win, including seven consecutive defeats not only dumped them in the bottom slot, but left them adrift in the mire without a paddle. The continuous disappointment was too much for even the most ardent of supporters, and they drifted away in droves. The home match with Watford attracted the smallest Football League crowd to that time to watch a first class game, when a meagre 1,687 loyal supporters filed into the stadium. The echos of the crowd in the open spaces gave no atmosphere, and the hollow cheer to greet Fletcher scoring the only goal seemed a thin response. However, it was something players would have to get use to.

The season was terminated at Walsall at one goal apiece, made remarkable for the inclusion of a utility man, Nolan Keeley, a twenty-one year old signed from Great Yarmouth. It marked the beginning of a career that would span almost a decade of dedicated service in the club colours. What remained of the season, after twelve months of weary toil, left everybody drained physically and emotionally, but few of the performances were worthy of reflection. The last place in the division meant the team had to pick up the pieces and start again in the Fourth.

~ 1973-74 ~

During the summer the news that made the Evening Telegraph headlines was that on 23rd June Ron Ashman resigned his post as manager, to move across to Grimsby Town as a replacement for Lawrie McMenamy, who had switched to First Division Southampton. United immediately advertized the position, and from the thirty-four candidates, they chose Ron Bradley as the successor. It was his first position as a manager, but he was a shrewd tactician, and had plenty of coaching experience, principally with Ashman as his second in command.

There were to be changes in the playing staff to alter the operation of the team structures. Nigel Jackson was forced to retire from football at this level because of a knee injury. At the end of the 1972-73 season there had been rumours of a possible move for Steve Deere, the vital cog of the overworked defence for the past few years. Hull City was the prime mover, and the popular central defender switched allegiances across the Humber to Boothferry Park. As part of the deal United received two players in exchange. The first was the respected old head of Ken Houghton, a competitor who had see the Tigers through the best of the most recent years. He was to bring with him Stuart Pilling, a utility player, who was strongest on his left side. Stuart had become known as Harry because of the number of 'Stuarts' at his previous club. This young man, once a junior at Preston North End, went on to provide the Iron with much appreciated service. What endeared him to local supporters was that he was genuine in all aspects of his approach to the game.

These players were joined by Grimsby Town back line man Barry Lynch, Bruce Collard, a reserve at West Bromwich Albion for the midfield, and a very youthful Richard Money. Money was another of the crop of East Anglian talent to make their way in the League with Scunthorpe United, signing from his home town club of Lowestoft. This was another raw prospect who would have an extended association at the Old Showground and beyond.

The start of the season of 1973-74 saw the Iron in amongst company they were more familiar with, and able to compete against, although in the early days there was a struggle. After the fifth contest of the season, a best forgotten goalless draw against Crewe, the Club was abysmally placed in twentieth position in the table, having lost 7-2, days before at Gillingham. To be fair everything that the Gills touched did turn to gold, but even then it was still a humiliation. There was better news on the League Cup front, and Peterborough United were knocked out of the contest on aggregate in the first round.

By the end of September Scunthorpe had failed to produce a satisfactory recovery and a fee was offered to Blackpool for former Hull City midfielder Chris Simpkin to shore up the middle of the park. Simpkin was as hard as nails, being the ideal type of man to add bite to the engine room. He took up duty and United showed an improvement over the next few weeks. This included a much improved draw against a strong Second Division Bristol City side at home in the League Cup second round. The team lost the replay at Ashton Gate, but the supporters faith was being restored in the team.

Scunthorpe United's trip to Bristol City was not altogether fruitless, because they brought back with them Eddie Woods for a loan period of four games. One of these, at home to Brentford, produced the first score of four goals in a match since 1971. Indeed United were three nil up in ten minutes. Simpkin was bang on target with the first, after a ball from Houghton cut across the box for an inviting shot. Stuart Pilling engineered the second as Eddie Woods was left with a soft tap in.

A delay of six more minutes had to be endured before a well directed shot from Keeley virtually made the points a guarantee. It might have been the prelude to an avalanche when a Davidson to Lynch combination allowed the latter to cross onto the head of Woods for number four with only seventeen minutes showing on the watch. The Londoners licked their wounds, pulled one back, and the second-half saw no more scoring activity.

In the annual knockout competition of the F.A.Cup, United were up against Darlington, whose plight was even more sorrowful than Scunthorpe United's, having no team below them in the Fourth Division. The game was spoiled as a spectacle by strong winds. Morritt, in the visitors goal, did his best to upset United's party, but a long strike by the reliable Ken Houghton was enough to send most of the three thousand crowd home happy.

United were then requested to meet Mansfield Town in the second round of the action. The Stags had raced off to a great start to their Fourth Division campaign and there was an outside suggestion of promotion. However, the week before the Cup game, they slipped up badly by 5-3, of all places at the Old Showground. For Scunthorpe supporters it was the best Fourth Division game of the year. As a result a cagey match took place at the Field Mill, but another Houghton strike before half-time made sure United shared the spoils, and earned the right of a replay.

Both sides could have won the second Cup encounter but there was not to be a repeat of the bonanza of goals that had been seen in the League. Scunthorpe plugged away until the fifty-second minute, when Neil Warnock sent the ball flying past Brown in the Stag's goal, after indecision by the defenders in front of him.

The mid-point in the campaign showed mixed fortunes. A crowd of less than a thousand watched Scunthorpe outplayed at Hartlepool, but on Boxing Day the season's top Fourth Division assembly enjoyed victory over lowly Doncaster Rovers. Most of those present were so impressed that they

Steve Deere falls backwards as he sends the ball goalwards. Graham Rusling and the Southport defence watch the goalbound shot.

returned for another helping at the end of the week for the visit of the division leaders, Peterborough United. Scunthorpe gave the visitors a run for their money, and held a two goal lead by the interval. The Posh came back with menace, pulling one goal back, but could not find the equalizer. United then threw it all away, crashing by five goals without reply to Barnsley. It was hardly the type of preparation to put them in the right frame of mind for an important F.A.Cup tussle with Second Division Millwall at the Den.

The cold London weather did not stop the Iron raising their play to match their Southern counterparts. United's formula was simple - stifle the home side's capable attackers and get the ball up front for a quick breakaway. It was a brave plan, which was very effective, and the longer the afternoon carried on without a score, the more frustrated the Lions' players became. At the sounding of the referee's whistle to indicate ninety minutes the visitors had done better than expected. Graham Collier's strike late on equalled that of former Manchester City man Alfie Wood.

It meant a replay at the Old Showground which was played in early afternoon. Floodlights for football matches had been banned by the Government, who were in the middle of operating power cuts as a result of a strike by the country's miners. This situation produced five thousand people in attendance at the game, plus many more supporters with one ear to their transistor radios at work. Scunthorpe lined up in a formation never seen before, and enough to form frowns of confusion on the opposition's faces.

All United's forwards stood in a row on one side of the centre circle. Houghton passed the ball to Collier on the first blast from the referee's whistle. Collier turned to ease it back to Simpkin. Simpkin ran forward, moved to the left, and passed to Pilling. Stuart Pilling lobbed the ball high

over the top of the stretching fingers of King in the Millwall goal, as he toppled backwards in despair. Twelve seconds, 1-0, and the game effectively won. It was not quite as simple as that, but the main facts were already being printed for the Evening Telegraph's late night final.

All that remained was to see if Newcastle would beat Hendon in a replay, after an inept display at St. James Park, to discover the identity of their fourth round opponents. In the end the Magpies made amends and United's supporters knew it would be a trip to the North-East. For those old enough it was to revive memories of 1958.

The teams lined up on this memorable day as follows:-
Newcastle Utd: McFaul, Craig, Howard, Clark, Kennedy, Smith, McDermott, Cassidy, Barrowclough, MacDonald and Tudor.
Scunthorpe Utd: Barnard, Collard, Lynch, Simpkin, Welbourne, Money, Houghton, Pilling, Warnock, Kelly and Davidson.

At the start of this fourth round encounter, four thousand or so Scunthorpe followers had filled the corners of St. James Park to produce a total of almost thirty-eight thousand spectators.

The game produced much of the pattern that Newcastle United had experienced against Hendon, and it was the visitors, Scunthorpe, who settled quicker, as the non-Leaguers had done previously. The First Division side seemed to be easily put out of step, and the Iron enjoyed more space than they normally could expect. Within a short period, a bizarre event had a radical effect of the game. It happened when the Magpies' Scottish International Jim Smith collided with the embarrassed referee. When he picked himself up, a bounce up was in order near the centre of the pitch.

The ball was won by the home side, but Alan Kennedy mistimed a pass back to McFaul in goal. Nolan Keeley nipped in between the pair and steered it into the target. The goal charged Scunthorpe United's resolve and the team rose in stature. Richard Money was unlucky when he hit the post and Ken Houghton brought the "Ahh's" from the crowd when he narrowly shot wide with McFaul beaten.

In the second-half it was a different story. Newcastle swept forward in a series of dangerous waves, and Scunthorpe's defence was stretched to breaking point, with opportunities of sorties up field few and far between. A quarter of an hour into the second-half they fell to a thunderous twenty-five yard drive by Terry McDermott. The rest of the match was a case of hanging on for the draw, which the courageous Fourth Division troop just managed.

The replay caused a nightmare for local industry as workers applied for holiday days. Some schools gave in to the request to allow school children time off to attend the Cup replay, and a half-day was granted. It helped to produce one of the Club's top ten home attendances, of just over nineteen thousand. Unfortunately the game that unfolded was not a shadow of the first tie. Scunthorpe were completely overawed and only a third minute strike by Stuart Pilling was worth reporting. Newcastle were totally rampant.

England centre-forward Malcolm MacDonald had a field day, scoring twice and Stewart Barrowclough added another. The 3-0 result was a complete vindication of Newcastle United's superiority. The victory allowed them to go on to play West Bromwich Albion in round five, and subsequently Liverpool in the Final at Wembley. Kevin Keegan helped to remind Newcastle United of his Scunthorpe roots scoring twice in the 3-0 showpiece, which sent the trophy to Merseyside.

Angus Davidson, a utility player who totalled over 350 games for United, from 1969 to the late '70's.

League form for United in Division Four became patchy after their exit from the F.A. Cup comp-etition. The loss at Barnsley was the start of a nine match run in which the only points picked up were from home draws with Lincoln City and Swansea City.

Unfortunately, the goals had dried up, and in an effort to turn the flow back on, Dudley Roberts was signed from Mansfield Town, while Les Andrews was borrowed from Wolverhampton Wanderers for a couple of months. It did have an improved effect on the team which picked up slightly, particularly at home.

The two new men actually both registered their names on the scoresheet at Roberts' old club, in a 2-2 draw. If it had not been for a fadeout at the death of the campaign, where defeats came in the last three games, then there might have been a better final resting place than eighteenth. When it was revealed that Nolan Keeley was the leading goalscorer with nine goals, the overall picture spoke for itself.

~ 1974-75 ~

During the close season United supporters learned of the disappearance of Mike Williams, Ken Houghton and Bruce Collard, but there were replacements. The most notable was Alan Sproates from Darlington, who had worn the Quakers shirt on more than three hundred occasions. Sproates had been on loan at Hartlepool, and a career change at Scunthorpe was a move that it was hoped would benefit everyone. At first the player enjoyed a forward position, but later was seen roaming the midfield regions.

Another new regular was John Peacock to partner Peter Markham. Both were to continue the tradition of players brought through the Junior ranks. Peacock was a Leeds-born man who was generally used on the left side of the bank four. During the first season he would make his contribution in almost half the games. Other players to be utilized were Eddy Taylor, Steve Earl and Derek Charnley. At an early stage Jim Lavery was brought back on the scene, in what was his second spell with the Club since dropping into non-League football.

Scunthorpe United knew they were not considered to be one of the star attractions of the division, when on the starting day of the 1974-75 season only 1,656 supporters at Workington bothered to turn up at Borough Park. At least Angus Davidson did manage to settle a point for Scunthorpe with a goal in the second-half. Perhaps if at that stage in the season the people present had known how the final Fourth Division table was to be resolved, they would have realized that this was not the clash of the Titans.

Scunthorpe United were at home on the following Tuesday to Sheffield Wednesday in the League Cup. Wednesday had lost their way in recent times and were just starting life for the first time in the Third Division. Most gamblers would still have hedged their bets on an Owls victory, but Scunthorpe worked hard on the night. They rode their luck, taking advantage of a penalty award which Angus Davidson converted, to see them safely through into the second round.

It was doubtful that a much more difficult draw could have been imagined for Scunthorpe United, when it was their lot to do battle at Manchester City. The City side was full to overflowing with class, and contained many Internationals, including Dennis Tueart, Mike Summerbee, Colin Bell and Rodney Marsh. At one stage that season they were to lead the First Division table, and the game with humble Scunthorpe was little more than a training exercise for them. Credit had to be given to the Iron in the first-half, and they went in for the break only 1-0 down. The second-half was too much for them and as the legs became leaden, City opened up. Colin Bell completed a hat-trick and Scunthorpe were overwhelmed by a 6-0 scoreline.

In the League, goalscoring was the cause of the problem, and in the second week in September, United slumped to the bottom of the League. This theme was to continue throughout the season, and it was not until the visit of mid-table Barnsley in October before the first game yielded them two points, under the glare of the Old Showground lights. Neil Warnock scored in the first-half, and from then on it was all hands to the pumps to hang on. The cheer at the end was of relief rather than triumph.

The terrible form continued unabated until November, with the club firmly fixed at the foot of the table and showing little sign of an improvement, whilst finances were bleak and bills had become difficult to pay. Ron Bradley accepted full responsibility for the team's failures, and on the 7th November, like the gentleman he was, he took the honourable course of resigning. Jeff Barker looked after affairs on a temporary basis, and the board sought a new man to revive the fortunes for the proud supporters. In the end it was decided to put Dickie Rooks in charge, a former Bristol City player who was taking his first steps into Football League management. He promised to do what he could, but the best would be to avoid the re-election zone if at all possible.

This was not the only activity the board had to deal with, for a bid of £70,000 was made for the Old Showground by the council. After careful consideration this was rejected in the best interests of the Club.

The dust had barely time to settle down when it was discovered that United would be receiving a visit from Altrincham in the F.A.Cup. The way Scunthorpe had been playing, it was Altrincham who had to be considered the favourites for the second round. Indeed, although Scunthorpe did perform marginally better, they soon forgot any chance of a pay packet through this route, as the non-Leaguers beat them after a replay.

At the turn of the year United's grim position was still unchanged. They had only two wins to their name and away from home only four draws had gained them a sparse reward. The Club was even notified that in January they were to become part of a football documentary for television, portraying life at the bottom of the League. They duly obliged by producing their best performance of the year, beating Newport County 4-1. There was the unusual sight of a distinguished hat-trick by hero of the hour Dudley Roberts. This was the first such feat since 1966 when Barry Thomas had delivered the goods. However, this was not sufficient to raise the Club off the bottom of the League.

There was precious little Dickie Rooks could do, but he was brave enough to blood Bob Oates from Leeds Junior club, Ashley Road, for the left side of the defensive block, which was leaking goals. He also gave a run to Mike Norris, a local apprentice goalkeeper, in place of Geoff Barnard, but times were hard and the most optimistic supporters could not see a way out of this mess. They had to wait until March just to see two consecutive victories, following visits of Shrewsbury and Workington, and briefly the team raised themselves above the Cumbrian side.

The rest of the season was shear hard work under the strain of the failures the team continued to endure. It was not through the lack of effort produced by the men on the field, but this squad was not strong enough to compete against the rest of the Division. Throughout the final month of the campaign, two draws produced the only points in the last seven games. At least one of those was against arch derby rivals Lincoln City in front of 6,044 spectators, the biggest Old Showground attendance of the season. Perhaps the penultimate game of the season, away to Champions Mansfield Town, summed up the whole miserable situation. Eleven thousand Nottinghamshire fans revelled in a 7-0 thrashing of a Scunthorpe United team run ragged as they chased their own tails all night.

The final analysis declared that Scunthorpe United were bottom of the whole ninety-two clubs in the Football League. It was the first time the Club had finished as wooden-spoonists in their entire existence.

The total of twenty-nine points was the lowest in their history, and nine away from safety. It meant that during the early part of the Summer, United's Director's would have to report a good case to the Football League's annual meeting as they sought re-election. The boot was now firmly on the other foot as they went cap in hand, hoping a non-League club would not be given Scunthorpe's League status, after they had suffered just one bad season.

No doubt there was a great sigh of relief when Scunthorpe United's explanation was accepted and they comfortably won the required vote of confidence. Nevertheless, the message was quite clear that they must perform far better, or they might end up in the same position in which Bradford Park Avenue and Barrow had recently found themselves.

~ 1975-76 ~

It was with these thoughts fresh in their minds that Scunthorpe United prepared for another chance in the 1975-76 season. The problem was that the poor results of the previous season had left the kitty barren, and getting class replacements to a club in Scunthorpe United's predicament was going to be a task of great magnitude.

During the inactivity of the warmer months, United said goodbye to a number of first team players. In particular it was upsetting to see the end of the career of Geoff Barnard, whose two hundred and sixty-five appearances was a club record for a goalkeeper. He had been a dedicated competitor who gave the team one hundred per cent at all times. Barnard was not the only 'keeper leaving, for it was decided not to renew Jim Lavery's contract. He would drift into local football, along with Mick Atkin, whose priority was to become a schoolteacher.

Chris Simpkin was the next notable player to seek employment elsewhere. He departed for Huddersfield for a small fee, and finally Alan Sproates decided to take his family to the far side of the world and emigrate to Australia.

On the other side of the coin, Alan O'Meara joined as a youthful apprentice 'keeper to shadow Mike Norris. O'Meara soon found himself called up by Dick Rooks and was to see first team duty during the season. In the middle of the field United signed the small blonde Archie Irvine, a Scotsman from Doncaster Rovers. Originally with Sheffield Wednesday, Irvine came to the Old Showground after five years at Belle Vue. The defence was to be injected by the presence of a strong tackling centre pivot in Clive Wiggington. It was United's good fortune that he was in dispute with his club, Grimsby Town, and a transfer to Scunthorpe was a welcome release to a player highly rated at this level.

To support the forwards, United signed two front runners. For the left side of the attack ex-Mansfield Town winger Dougy O'Connor signed from Barnsley. As an out and out striker John Woodward came with lots of experience from Port Vale, having already played at Walsall, Aston Villa and Stoke. Dickie Rooks had now selected his cards for the new 1975-76 season, and it was up to him to play them in the right order and make sure he came up trumps, with enough tricks for a brighter future. Unfortunately the season began just where the old had finished.

The first six games failed to produce a single goal, and within that time United had been knocked out of the League Cup by Mansfield Town. Under the new rule of a home and away leg in the first round, Scunthorpe lost by an aggregate score of six goals to nil. The loss against Huddersfield Town in the last of this series saw the Club once again anchored to the bottom of the Fourth Division table.

Rooks needed to find a solution to the crisis immediately. He found it at Hull City, where he took on loan Jeff Hemmerman. In his debut at Hartlepool, Hemmerman scored Scunthorpe United's first goal in a 2-1 away victory, which lifted them four places off the bottom. It was only a small gesture but it had started the season off for the Iron. Although another favourable result came one week later at home to Torquay, the season was to continue to be a struggle.

Rooks could not rely on the services of Hemmerman, who went back to Boothferry Park, and so instead he turned to a local player on the books of Appleby Frodingham, the tall lean Rick Green. Rick was a steelworker who had won a reputation as a dangerous goalscorer at non-League level. When given the opportunity he was to do his Town's League club proud. His first goal was at home to Rochdale, but Scunthorpe still lost, and as the Winter drew on they continued to have one foot in the re-election zone.

Scunthorpe United did have some respite with a decent three goal win against Workington. This was still nothing to get carried away with, since the visitors were only one of two teams below the Iron in the Fourth Division table at the time. A goalless game at the interval had supporters shuffling about trying to keep warm, wondering if they would see their team score.

They were pleased to observe Nolan Keeley open up the Workington resolve by dancing round a defender and firing home. Rick Green sealed a deserved victory with his first brace for the side to confirm the United's domination.

Rick Green dives full length at an Old Showground match.

Two weeks after the Workington result, the Iron set out for Third Division Preston's old Deepdale Ground for the trail of the F.A.Cup, that would end on the doorstep of Wembley for two lucky sets of supporters. Needless to say neither of these two clubs would get that far. Scunthorpe had Alan O'Meara in goal, and although he looked dwarfed between the posts, he won the praise of the crowd for a brave display containing a number of commendable saves, although it was actually the Iron who took the lead on thirty-three minutes.

Richard Money had a shot punched out by Tunks at the opposite end, whereupon the ball fell to Rick Green who lobbed it straight back into the target. The lead lasted just over twenty minutes, and then the luck went against the visitors. Clive Wigginton's outstretch leg brought down Morley in the box, and the same player tapped home the spot kick. It looked as though United's legions might hold out, but with little left on the watch, Elwiss headed the winner after Scunthorpe's back line failed to clear.

During the middle of the season Dickie Rooks acted on the goalkeeping situation which, clearly, was not satisfactory. Mick Norris was having a tough time, and Alan O'Meara was not quite ready to take over completely. Both did their utmost when called upon, but it needed no statistician to see that the number of defeats required a new approach. Rooks went to Bristol City, where he persuaded Len Bond, an old colleague, to come to Scunthorpe for a month on loan over Christmas. This he did, and the bottom line showed that he kept clean sheets in draws at home to Stockport and away to Bradford City.

Bond's greatest contribution perhaps was enjoyed in the arrival at the Old Showground, on the Saturday after Christmas, of Doncaster Rovers. Local interest pulled in around four thousand extra supporters, to swell the attendance to 5,801. For once it was the Scunthorpe supporters who had something to crow about. The Iron found a level of football not seen for a long time. Shots were taken from all angles by the side that had been usually shy in front of the goalposts.

Angus Davidson opened his account as early as the fourth minute when he fastened onto a Rick Green pass, and hit a bullet strike on the target. Despite Kitchen levelling the difference at half-time, it was United that were the more dangerous. The second period was just as furious, and John Woodward finally settled the dispute, finding room in the box before sending in an explosive drive.

It was easy to recall the successes of the season, but they were like the needles, and the defeats were the proverbial haystack. United once again could not keep up the pace. Dickie Rooks had not found the overall solution despite his efforts under difficult conditions.

Supporters were far from happy, and newspaper reports suggested that if League clubs could not compete they should be succeeded by the stronger teams from the competitions immediately below. In January the inevitable happened. Scunthorpe United's chairman Mr Jack Empson announced the dismissal of Mr Rooks and three days later Ron Ashman, no longer in full-time football, was reinstated.

It was a very popular move to see Ashman once again dictating the destiny of the club, but this time he would have to be a miracle worker if he was to save the team from a second application for re-election, when they were so far away from safety. The Club's whole football League status was on a knife edge, and he knew there was not a moment to lose.

Ashman set about his job in a businessman like way. He needed to make the players believe in themselves and regain their confidence. Football should be a simple game, and he made them play it that way. The back lines had to be tightened up, there was to be no frills in midfield, and every opportunity that presented itself was one to pump the ball up to the front lines. Forwards had the simple message to be direct whenever they received a chance up front. Ron was not even allowed the luxury of any new signings. Indeed, the situation was just the opposite, with Don Welbourne and Dudly Roberts sidelined through long term injuries. At last the troops were focused and a new battle strategy appointed.

Ron Ashman's first game in charge brought the gift of an unexpected point at Cambridge, considering the team's away performances which had generally been feeble. They may have lost at home to high flying Watford, but there was an extra five hundred supporters on the average gate, and soon the points began to roll in. They further improved their away record, winning for the second time when they took two points from fellow strugglers Workington.

At home there was to be a boost in performances, too, for only Graham Taylor's high flying Lincoln would out-gun them at the Old Showground. The record breaking Imps helped to increase the Old Showground attendance to over ten thousand. Scunthorpe United's supporters could also look to the accuracy of Rick Green in front of the goalpost as one of the main sources of the revival. He did his cause no harm, bagging another pair of goals when Hartlepool were trounced 5-1 at home.

The arrival of Easter saw Scunthorpe United fired up ready to continue the fight. They had a series of three games which would make or break them. In the first they beat the Yorkshire visitors of Bradford City 2-0, and eased themselves out of the danger zone for the first time since October. The job was not finished, but the result sounded alarm bells in Darlington and Stockport as they slipped further towards trouble. On Easter Monday two points were plundered from Doncaster, thanks to Rick Green's single effort, and a day later a similar result was greeted with jubilation by most of the 4,770 crowd at home to Barnsley. The cheers that echoed round the stands were of relief, as the two points guaranteed the club's safety.

The season was curtailed on the following Friday night at Exeter. Both teams shed their inhibitions and produced an attacking exhibition which saw nine goals scored. United happened to lose by the odd goal in that total, but won the applause of the Devon supporters for making an open game of this top entertainment. This was to secure the club in a final position of nineteenth, and only the most optimistic of supporters would have hoped for such a conclusion in the dark days of the New Year. The great escape act was unarguably masterminded by Ron Ashman alone, and at that moment in Scunthorpe's history they owed their survival to this shrewd but modest man.

~ 1976-77 ~

During the break between the seasons, Ron Ashman did not lavish cash around on new players, for it was a case of wheeling and dealing. On the outgoing side the cards were given to Mike Norris, Archie Irvine, Ray Charnley, Dudley Roberts, John Woodward, and regretfully Don Welbourne. Don Wellbourne had been injured for some time, and after close on three hundred appearance this one club man was allowed to leave. His epitaph was that his name would always be remembered by all supporters who were lucky enough to see him play.

The new brush that swept clean the dressing room, allowed a modest number of signings, and also a slight reduction in the wage bill. To begin with, supporters had a tongue-twister to get used to, having signed Mike Czuczman from Grimsby as a back four player, although he could also be utilized in other promotions. There were also terms offered to Gainsborough Trinity's front runner Mick Wadsworth. When Mick took on defenders in full flight he was to excite the crowd, and they would often encourage other players to get the ball out wide to him.

This new structure gave plenty of chance for the younger element to develop. Players that were promoted prematurely and found themselves under pressure were now older and more able to cope. Youngsters such as John Peacock, Bob Oates, Richard Money and Peter Markham adapted far better. There was still one hole to be dealt with, and that was for the goalkeeper's green jersey. Ashman needed experience in such a vital position and it was decided that Alan O'Meara needed more time.

To fill in the spot, Ron decided to borrow Glen Letheran, a Welsh under twenty-three International enjoying reserve team football at Elland Road, Leeds. He took the solidly built 'keeper first on one month's loan, before finally handing him back at the start of March.

Although United disappointed by losing their first two League matches of the 1976-77 season, there was better news on the League Cup front. The two legs against Mansfield Town in round one gave them an ample chance to get even after the previous year's thrashing. The pair of teams traded punches and each took a two goal lead at home without the other scoring. Seeing that nobody could find a key to the solution, a coin was tossed for ground advantage, and when then penny landed it was United's preference of the Old Showground that was chosen.

The replay took place on a warm evening, and after the initial cautionary thrusts the game turned into a real cracker, particularly in its final phase. United's trump cards turned out to be their wide men, O'Connor and Wadsworth. Not only did they cause havoc by running at their nervous defenders, but each thumped a goal apiece. McCaffery pulled one back to set up a cliff-hanger at the end. Both back lines took a pummelling, but both refused to be beaten again. United went through to take on Notts County, but even given the tie in their own backyard, they could not outsmart the Second Division team.

It was not until the leaves were falling from the trees that Scunthorpe United got their bandwagon rolling in Division Four. They put smiles on to the faces of their supporters with a series of wins, starting with a four goal margin against Crewe. There was even the sight of the football programme notes recording consecutive wins, over Hartlepool and Halifax, which lifted the team into eighth position. At that time it was said the team was so high up in the table that supporters were getting nose bleeds!

Unfortunately, as the freezing weather approached, so United ran into a cold spell. Everything started to go wrong under the floodlights at Oakwell against a mid-table Barnsley. Although Stuart Pillings goal from range might have been the pick of the bunch, the 5-1 defeat proved they had been asleep most of the night. It was no excuse that this mining area was not a happy hunting ground for the Iron at that time. This loss was quickly followed by an exit out of the F.A.Cup to Chesterfield, and again the opposition seemed to have no trouble in outclassing the Scunthorpe side. United continued to lose their footing and slid down the table, once they resumed Fourth Division duties. Wins became scarce as did goals, but a hat-trick at Plainmoor by Dougy O'Connor brightened a dark Saturday evening when the news came through from Torquay that United had won 3-1. Into Christmas, Scrooge brought nothing in the way of presents. The seven thousand crowd who came to view the fare served up by Scunthorpe against Doncaster did initially have something to cheer. Rick Green rifled home the first goal, but the United could not hang on to the lead. Full-back Stan Brookes saw Rovers save a point when he supported his forwards and scored.

In February, Scunthorpe United received a bid for their talented goalscorer Rick Green. The fee of £20,000 was from Chesterfield, who had been pleasantly impressed by the hammering he had given their defenders in the F.A.Cup. Since taking the big step out of non-League football, Rick had scored once in every three games, in a team that was under continuous pressure. United supporters could only wish this brave player the very best of luck in the future.

The ink was barely dry on the cheque they had just banked when Ron Ashman decided to make a small investment in another local lad who was scoring goals. He was the former Mariner, Jimmy Lumby, who was in the black and white strikes of the Zebras at Brigg Town. Jim was a completely different player to Green, for his stature was smaller, but he chased every half chance. Goals came via shots and headers, and once in the first team he continued his trade.

The signing of Lumby coincided with the blooding of another forward from local sources, when Kevin Kilmore, a Scunthorpe-born youngster, also found first team fame. Kilmore and Lumby linked up to do most of the Scunthorpe attacking.

Unfortunately, in the Spring, as the tender flowers bloomed, so the team continued to wilt. Ron Ashman refused to throw in the towel and gave his team a mixture of encouragement and the occasional rollicking.

There were fleeting glimpses of form and the best forty-five minutes of the whole season took place at home to Exeter City. Perhaps it was the long journey from Devon that sapped the visitors strength, but at the halfway point United had virtually won with a 3-1 score in their favour. They went on to add another for an invigorating performance. It was one of the last worthwhile gestures in a season which was slipping away, leaving a touch of emptiness amongst supporters.

Ron Ashman did bring back the memories to Scunthorpe followers with a part-time signing everyone approved of. He decided to offer Geoff Barnard the chance of another swan-song to assist the back order in the last half a dozen games of the year. Geoff may not have been as agile as he was in full-time training, but his positional sense was still there. The two thousand regulars that were still in attendance applauded his efforts.

Fortunately there was sufficient space between the team and the danger of the bottom four re-election positions. However, a lean spell of three draws and no victories in the last five games saw them sail very close to the wind. A resting place of twentieth hardly had anyone in raptures at the team's overall performance. It was a great pity, because at one stage this term did promise so much, but had fulfilled so little.

~ 1977-78 ~

The close season before the campaign of 1977-78 started was the time to get on with making changes and improvements, and Ashman was not a man to dwell on the past. Instead he used the limited resources at his disposal to attract new discoveries. Ron had done his homework, and when Workington's abysmal record lined them up for the firing squad at the League's A.G.M., to be replaced by Wimbledon, he pounced for one of their men. This was the slim Eamon Kavanagh who had scored against the Iron at Borough Park in the first match of the 1974-75 season. Kavanagh was to add his skills to the midfield, alongside another newcomer, Bernard Bridges.

Doncaster-born Bridges came up through the junior channels at the Old Showground, and had actually made his debut in January 1977. For the attack a contract was offered to Scotsman Brian Heron from Oxford United. Heron had recovered from a broken leg but could not get back into the Second Division side at the Manor Ground, and this career change at Scunthorpe provided a refreshing boost all round. The puzzle was completed with the inclusion of a very sound goalkeeper, another Scotsman, Graeme Crawford. With his safe hands the question on this position was answered when he joined from Third Division York City.

Inevitably, there were the usual casualties on the way out of the door at the Old Showground as the result of the new acquisitions. It was with deep regret that the heavy moustache of Angus Davidson would not be seen in the thick of the action again after more than three hundred games.

Also gone was Clive Wiggington, off to Lincoln City for a fee, and Graham Collier who went over to Yorkshire to have a spell at Barnsley. There would also be no place for Doug O'Connor, Mike Wadsworth and Peter Markham.

The 1977-78 campaign began in a positive fashion for Scunthorpe United, just for a change, and two draws plus a win put them in fifth position in the table after the first three games. Although nothing could be deduced at this early stage, it did make United supporters smile to apparently see the club 'in contention'. Perhaps if they were still there in another forty matches time it would be worth looking at the League ladder again. There was better news from the League Cup games, for Darlington were held goalless in the North East, and then were beaten 3-1 on aggregate. The reward was a trip half way to the Capital to play Peterborough United at London Road. Stuart Pilling gave the Iron a real chance of meeting one of the big boys in round three, when he earned a draw with his goal. Unfortunately, a single goal defeat spoiled the party in the replay.

The few decent results at the start of the season were followed by more of what supporters had become used to over the years, and a run of three League defeats surrounded the exit from the Cup competition. United's turning point happened against the new boys of Wimbledon. At that time in the season the London Dons were still trying to get a grip on life in the Fourth Division. It was not a strong side that they brought with them, and the only mystery was how Scunthorpe could play so badly and still come up with a comfortable 3-0 result. There was also the delight of two goals from Bob Oates, whose career total would only reach fifteen.

It was around this time that United brought back John Kaye to the club as Assistant manager. Kaye had played football at the top level at West Bromwich Albion winning major honours. His career then took him into the management structure at Hull City, and for a number of years he kept the Tigers sailing along in the Second Division. He would now be expected to help take some of the weight off Ron Ashman's shoulders, particularly in the coaching department.

Throughout the first-half of the season the results did not improve. Richard Money was doing his best to shore up the back-quarters, and Jim Lumby continued to supply the goals whenever possible. Then a disastrous performance at Torquay finally saw the Club put one foot in the grave, when they slumped to a 4-2 defeat. Their lean performance could have been worse, but for the generosity of the penalty by Jim Lumby, and an own goal by the Devon defender Mike Green. The end of this troubled run saw them three places off the bottom of the Fourth Division table.

The Torquay United match had another significance in that it marked the debut of the long-haired Ron Wigg from Barnsley. Wigg had already scored twice against Scunthorpe that season when the Iron visited Oakwell, now this will o' the wisp character would be using his spells to mesmerize opposition defences at the Old Showground.

Scunthorpe were to enjoy an upturn in fortunes for a short while, that coincided with Ron Wigg's arrival, which saw the club hover just above the re-election zone but in touch with the middle of the table. The first victims of the resurgence were the Shaymen of Halifax Town, who set Scunthorpe United off in the right direction with a penalty. This was promptly dispatched by Jim Lumby, who was becoming a role model for the tense situations. Not since the days of Jack Brownsword had so many penalty kicks been hammered home. At the far end of the season seven had been harvested by the same player.

In November a lot of interest had been directed in the direction of Richard Money, a rare diamond in the mine. Everything came to a head at the end of that month when United were scheduled to play Stockport County at Edgeley Park. When the players trotted out of the tunnel Richard Money could not be counted among the United men. It was later disclosed that he was involved in negotiations with Fulham in London. United could have done with him, because they were comfortably eased out of the reckoning by three goals without reply. It was disclosed on 1st December that Richard would go for a fee of £50,000 to Craven Cottage. Later he was transferred to Liverpool and as a climax to his career Money played in the Semi-Final of the European Cup.

The loss of Richard Money did not have too profound effect on Scunthorpe United, as Mike Czuczman shuffled across to cover in the central position. United then gave credence to the ability of former West Ham United junior Steve Davey who moved into the vacancy left by Czuczman. This was not the only activity Ron Ashman indulged in, for he decided to contract the services of Yorkshireman John O'Donnell, a utility player for the right side of the field, from Hartlepool United.

By the time O'Donnell made his debut at Belle Vue on Boxing Day, Scunthorpe had cheered their supporters by a couple of wins at home to Rochdale and Darlington. The encounter with the Quakers was particularly pleasing because a goal by Bob Oates, and a couple by Jim Lumby made the game cut and dried by half-time. Indeed home form was not the problem. Thus, when Ron Wigg danced through the Rovers defence to secure a Boxing Day equalizer, the Christmas spirit gave travelling Irons a warmer glow.

There was news on the grapevine that United might be out to make another couple of signings around the middle of Winter. The rumours proved to be right, and when supporters learned who it was, it brought broad beams to their faces. Ashman had made soundings as to the availability of Scunthorpe born forward Vinny Grimes, who was at Hull City. Vinny had been recommended by John Kaye, who had brought him into first team duty, through the junior ranks, while he was manager at Boothferry Park.

It was to be a very popular signing as did the other man, who needed no introduction to supporters at the Old Showground. Ron Ashman had sounded out Steve Deere, languishing in non-League football at Scarborough. It must be said the team from the seaside were no mugs, and Steve was with them when they won the F.A.Challenge Trophy in 1977 at Wembley.

The first opportunity that Vinny Grimes and Steve Deere were able to combine was at Northampton on their three sided County Ground. It was the first outing out for the team for a couple of weeks, following a spell of inclement weather which had frozen them out.

Despite the new characters and lack of preparation, the one hundred or so travelling supporters were privileged to see, a much improved performance from United. Lumby scattered the defenders with a shot drilled through an ineffective covering of defending bodies, and Steve Deere raced in from close in to bundle the ball over the line for the winner in a commanding 2-1 victory.

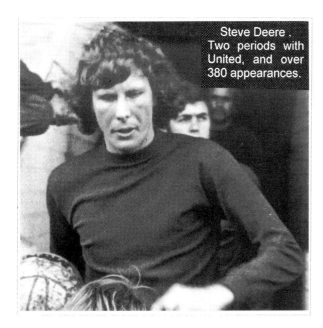

Steve Deere.
Two periods with United, and over 380 appearances.

This result was just the tonic they needed to set their minds focused to break the hoodoo of Grimsby Town at the Old Showground seven days later. The Mariners were threatening promotion, but Steve Deere's involvement put a block on their forward motions. Jim Lumby was very well supported by Grimes, and this was the contributing factor which eventually separated the teams. A goal in each half, one from the penalty spot, by the former Mariner, Limby, gave United clear water in front of their local derby rivals. Grimsby did pull one goal back through Donovan, but it was too little too late. Most of the seven and a half thousand spectators agreed the points went where they were most deserved.

It was not long before Scunthorpe United was to reap some reward for the investment of faith they had sowed in taking Lumby out of non-League soccer at Brigg Town. Early in April, Carlisle United made a generous offer in the region of £30,000 to sign the highly rated goalscorer. On the last Saturday of the season, Jim's second game with his new club from Cumbria was marked by his first goal against Swindon.

The loss of Lumby was a blow to the Iron and its supporters, but they bowed to the inevitable. At least the team had produced a spurt in the last two months of the season.

They were to finish the season in fourteenth table position, one which before Christmas everyone would have been satisfied with. It was no surprise that Jim Lumby had registered twenty times on the score sheet, while Kevin Kilmore notched eight. A surprise goalscorer was Bob Oates, who had wandered up front on foraging missions, and had also been successful on eight occasions.

~ 1978-79 ~

The late flurry of transfer activity at the end of the 1977-78 season meant Ron Ashman had a more relaxing Summer, without having to chase after too many new signings. The only significant player of foreign import was another from Hull, who had been recommended by John Kaye from the Boothferry Park academy of football skills. He was Dave Gibson, a man for the forward line, which was supplemented with Geoff Couch and Brian Bloomer. Geoff came from local club Crowle United, while Brian Bloomer was from the Brigg Town stable. It was another example of seeing what local players could do when given the right opportunity. Of these two, Geoff Couch was to have the biggest impact.

It was still early in August, when the United were geared up ready for a two-legged League Cup battle with Notts County. This tie turned out to be an easy passage for Second Division County, winning the tussle with a 4-0 aggregate score. But considering Manager Jimmy Sirrel almost won them promotion at the end of the campaign, it went to show that Scunthorpe hadn't performed that badly.

At Vale Park the team snatched a point from a 2-2 draw against Port Vale thanks to a very late Stuart Pilling shot at goal, and this was followed by consecutive home wins against Bournemouth and Huddersfield. It put the team in a strong position from the start, but the latter two opponents were only of average quality. This took the side into September, where five games were notable with an absence of Scunthorpe goals. The direct consequence was that the Club were installed around midpoint in the League ladder. A knee injury at Doncaster had seen Nolan Keeley limp out of the game and a six week lay off only went to exasperate the situation. However, one of the goalless draws was at Portsmouth, where a once mighty club had fallen from grace.

In October there were further frustrations which started with a home loss to the Welsh raiders of Newport County. Once the men in black and amber went ahead United were always playing catch up, and at 3-2 the groans of the crowd signalled that time had run out on them. Good form away from home was also sparse. During the month United had only the blessing of beating Bradford City at the Showground to comfort them. Ron Ashman could not have enjoyed the inept way the team was performing, and a further three goal loss at home to Reading, the eventual champions, was not entirely unexpected. Then a two goal lead at Huddersfield was squandered completely in the second-half, and ended in defeat. This sent the Iron spiralling down the League into twentieth position.

Scunthorpe United's next appointment was at home to Sheffield Wednesday in the F.A.Cup. It was not to be the same as the 1970 shoot-out at Hillsborough, for Wednesday were by now only of mediocre Third Division stock.

The nature of the F.A.Cup tournament and the extra support that arrived from Sheffield did inflate the attendance to eight and a half thousand paying spectators. A typical Cup-tie was slogged out in the sticky conditions of the Old Showground and the players gave the supporters full value. On the hour Stuart Pilling ran at speed towards the Owls goalmouth and volleyed the Iron ahead. While everyone was still celebrating Ian Nimmo stole in to equalize.

In midweek, on a bitterly freezing night, United repelled raid after raid. It looked as if the crowd of just below ten thousand would have to endure the Northern wind for another thirty minutes. Then, with about a minute to play, Ian Nimmo again became a thorn in the Scunthorpe side, with his goal which left no way back for United.

The lack of success ensured Ashman was not about to stand idly by as the slide continued, but he was hampered by a total lack of money, and opted instead to look to local football. Steve Earl had been getting rave reviews, scoring goals with works side Appleby-Frodingham. It was now the time to offer Earl the chance to distinguish himself at National level. The inclusion of Earl was shortly to see the last of Ron Wigg, who drifted out of senior football. Most encouragingly, United's form began to pick up, as at last they bottomed out.

A penalty goal by Kilmore sealed a win at Torquay, and Hereford United were sent sprawling by a four goal pulse at the Old Showground. This saw Steve Earl score his first goal for the club. A point was picked up at Darlington before Christmas, as Kevin Kilmore scored twice in a purple patch of five goals in three games. It was with this frame of mind that the club entered a Boxing Day clash with Grimsby Town, who were on the verge of a real promotion push.

Before the match the rival supporters made it clear they did not love each other; the Grimsby Town radio announcer gleefully rubbed his hands expecting blood, while in a more reserved mode his Scunthorpe counterpart wished for a modest draw. On the field of play United would settle for nothing short of a victory. The Mariners looked like getting something out of the game when Eamon Kavanagh cut the ball into his own goal. At half-time another Kilmore penalty saw the sides disappear into the darkness of the tunnel all square. In the second period, the eight thousand present hailed a cracking shot by Vinny Grimes and the scoring was complete. The rest of the match was not without its 'backs to the wall' entertainment, but the Iron held out.

Four days later heavy snow was falling onto a pitch already three inches deep. Rochdale were changed and ready for the game, when inexplicably the official blessing was given for the game to go ahead. Rochdale had not won a game away from home up to that point, but they won the equivalent of a Whithall farce 4-0.

Football at the Old Showground was abandoned until the beginning of March, due to the build up of snow. Local lanes had piles of the infernal white stuff, some higher than the tallest of the hedgerows. When they did get back into harness, Kevin Kilmore became the next player to convert two penalties in one match, when he beat Joe Neenan in the

visiting York City goal. He did in fact have the opportunity to put his name in the record books whilst taking a third spot kick. This attempt was foiled as Neenan guessed the right way and saved. The miss was costly as United lost 3-2.

Football was now moving its rusty wheels after the big freeze up and Scunthorpe United continued with yet another defeat at Barnsley. The 4-1 result at Oakwell was not a total surprise, for the faster opponents had promotion on their minds, and had only lost twice at home to that point. United's consolation was a long low drive for a Vinny Grimes strike. It did not augur well for the team's Friday evening journey into Berkshire to test the reputation of Reading, who were leading the race at the top of the Division. The Royals had used Elm Park as a fortress, and no team had outgunned them on their own territory. A great deal of activity was needed to clear the pitch of snow, which was only just declared fit at kick-off.

In the event Nolan Keeley stole an audacious breakaway goal at a very early stage in the game. Reading did not seemed too flustered with this set-back, and started hammering away at their target, which was defended stoutly by Graeme Crawford. The game turned out to be a non-stop stream of pressure on the Scunthorpe goal, but try as they may the continuous domination counted for nought. The Iron showed true grit and frustrated all efforts by the Champions-elect. A reflection on the balance of the game was that United had to defend twenty-two corners, whereas Steve Death in Reading's goal required an extra vest to keep warm. At 1-0 the incredulous defeat was the only one sustained by Reading, at home, all season.

The inconsistency of the team continued to come to light when in their next game the side confounded the Old Showground supporters by losing by three clear goals to Northampton. It appeared to be a lack of concentration throughout the ranks that had resulted in this poor showing. The manager dipped into his second team squad to promote David Hall, an apprentice at the club, from Doncaster. The newcomer's efforts assisted the Iron to overcome the immediate problems, and a slight flurry of activity toward the end of the season increased the points input.

The late run enjoyed by United started with a hard earned point in the electric atmosphere of Grimsby's Blundell Park. United held their focus on the game and at 1-1 they could not be broken. More than ten thousand supporters were in the tightly packed ground to cheer the teams on. By contrast gates which plunged well below two thousand at the Showground were commonplace, especially so in the crowded run-in to the finishing point of the campaign.

The colossal number of postponements meant that the players could not fly off on their holidays until after mid-May. It was then, in the last three games of the season, that United had an upturn in fortunes, and finished in a respectable midway position. At Crewe, Geoff Couch had his best game for the club thus far, and scored twice. Wimbledon arrived brimming full of promotion hopes, but left with their tails between their legs having been beaten 2-0, and the culmination of forty-six matches was at Halifax.

A pinch over one thousand spectators saw Dave Gibson hit United's last goal of the season, one more than the Shaymen. The 3-2 result gave a maximum of six points from six .

~ 1979-80 ~

A shorter time to re-charge the batteries was experienced during the close season in the summer of 1979. It was soon time for the agonies and slog of pre-season training, and United were back in the harness. The playing staff had been depleted by the exit of Mike Czuczman to Stockport County, but there were two noted additions, both of which had been given a remit to enhance the attack. The first was the much travelled Mal-colm Partridge from down the road at Grimsby Town. This tall unruffled man could fit into most positions around the park, but initially he would adopt an aggressive left-sided approach with good effect. On the opposite side, utilized as a busy skilled winger, was the dark-haired Paul O'Berg. Fresh out of non-League football at Bridlington, his non-stop industry was something the supporters appreciated, but in his first season injuries did his career no favours at all. Why no other League clubs had given Paul an opportunity is still a mystery.

United met with an early demise in the League Cup against a rejuvenated Grimsby Town. Two goals down from the first leg, United showed good spirit to hold the seafarers to no goals in Scunthorpe, but this it left little as consolation. The misery continued with three straight League defeats, the last of which was a harrowing 6-1 affair on the South Coast at Portsmouth. Harry Pilling scored the one goal for the Iron in the thrashing, and the Saturday Telegraph bugled the last post as United plunged into bottom place.

The reaction was to reach for the cheque book, and overstretch the accounts by a further £25,000, to recall Rick Green back to the fold, who was firing the shots at Notts County. For United the money was well spent. Rick repaid some of his fee scoring the first goal for his side in the overthrow of Bournemouth. It was only a shame that just 1,471 were there to welcome him home. Within a fortnight there was to be more frantic activities on the transfer trail. The announcement came on the 14th September that the money for Rick Green had been recouped when Kevin Kilmore was snapped up for £60,000 by Grimsby Town. Of this £15,000 had been invested extremely wisely in the acquisition of striker Steve Cammack from Chesterfield. Steve was an instant hit, and would go on to write his own individual page in the history of Scunthorpe United.

Once installed the new crew soon proved their value by thwarting the attempts of a Huddersfield Town side, whose visit resulted in a goal apiece scoreline. It was an accomplished performance supporters watched against the Terriers, who were destined to be promoted as top dogs.

This result was immediately followed by a dazzling display that blinded another set of Yorkshire visitors, York City. It marked the first goal for the club by Steve Cammack, plus a brace by Rick Green, and a hat-trick from Malcolm Partridge; one of Partridge's trio was a penalty conversion. A lot of local interest was in City's Peter Lorimer, the ex-Leeds United striker, and at the end of the game York did pull one back.

Despite the new men on board, United were still not able to climb free of the bottom four re-election places just yet. Even at York, for the away fixture two weeks later, they struggled to raise their game and failed to win. The Minstermen contained several changes and took a 2-0 revenge. It led to United changing their goalkeeper, and Crawford gave way to Jimmy Gordon from Reading. There were two other additions as the bumpy ride continued with more League uncertainty, and a Cup exit at Rochdale. David Dall, a tall Scottish central defender was lifted from Grantham Town for a small fee. Then Chelsea allowed them to take David Stewart, an attacking midfielder out of their reserve squad. Stewart was a Northern Ireland International who had been known by John Kaye from the time the young lad had been at Hull City.

It was not until the New Year before the situation began to improve. At this time, twentieth position in the table was hardly satisfactory, before yet another new signing made his debut against Portsmouth at the Old Showground. The newcomer was ex-Sheffield Wednesday star Graham Pugh, who had won an F.A.Cup Finalist's medal with the Owls when they lost to Everton. United picked him up from Barnsley. The performance in this game with Pompey was in marked contrast to the one at the beginning of the 1979-80 season. This time United were far more organized in each department. Portsmouth kept knocking on the door, but the Iron would not let them in. In the second-half Malcolm Partridge scored another important goal and United won both points. They should have done the same to Bradford City, but as the home fans waved their scarves in celebration, United went from 3-1 up, to only eventually squeeze a draw.

In February United started a long run with far more positive results which would see them out of the woods completely. It started after a real kick up the backside at Doncaster, when they felt the pain of going down 5-0, but only two more defeats were to be inflicted on them in the remaining sixteen games. The team began to fire on all cylinders and in this spell goals were never a problem. Unfortunately, attendances had trickled to no more than two thousand.

Mindful of the effect that the media had around the country, United managed something of a coup, when they courted favour with Ian Botham, the England Cricket Captain. Botham had been a supporter of the club for sometime, and Ashman had encouraged him to train with the players. He proved to be a willing front runner and reserve football had provided him with a chance. When he signed for the Iron on a non-contract basis Ashman decided to throw him in at the deep end as a substitute in the attack.

At Bournemouth he replaced Eamon Kavanagh and the cameras recorded the moment. From United's point of view it was more important that they pulled the game round to a draw from being three goals down at one stage. Botham had not been overawed, and was to be around for a couple of years to lend his weight to United's cause.

The euphoric rise of the team late in the campaign was nothing short of a miracle. There was even the startling event of a win on foreign soil, at Rochdale, as the season slipped away.

Undoubtably, most of the Club's troubles at the dawn of the year's events would have faded into insignificance if they had not suffered from stage fright on their travels. Ashman also had time to blood a new goalkeeper at the end of the season. Having had a number of looks at Joe Neenan of York, United agreed to enter into an exchange deal that took the reliable Graeme Crawford back to his familiar locker at Bootham Crescent. Before the season was completed Joe made two appearances for the Iron. In his first game the 'keeper kept a clean sheet, as Northampton were crushed 3-0. A trip to Hereford, ending in a 1-1 draw thanks to a ranging effort by Stuart Pilling, marked the culmination of the season.

Ian Botham

Division programme opened in dazzling sunshine at home to Aldershot. Vinny Grimes announced his fitness to the supporters by scoring the first goal of the season. United then dropped back into their familiar reverse gear finding goalscoring difficult and winning impossible, that is until they visited Darlington halfway through September. The Quakers were having problems of their own, particularly in putting the ball away. Neenan kept a clean pair of gloves, while Cammack weaved his way through the home defence, and a twenty-sixth minute strike won the points at last.

There was also another novelty for Scunthorpe United setting a 'first'. At the end of September the Old Showground played hosts to a different sport. Ian Botham brought a cricket eleven to play Scunthorpe Town Cricket Club in a limited overs game. More than five hundred spectators turned out to see Botham's colleagues win an exciting game in the last over, under the pylons of United's lights late in the evening. This was one of a number of fundraisers. Indeed, when only fourteen shareholders turned up in the 1500 club bar, along with the board for the A.G.M., Mr Empson suggested a public meeting to invite all supporters to make revenue-raising proposals.

To everyone's astonishment the red shirts of Scunthorpe United had staged a remarkable comeback. Up until the end of March, United had never risen to higher than nineteenth in the table. For the majority of the time they were candidates for re-election, but then they surged forward into a highly unlikely position of fourteenth; two more points would have seen them enter the top ten. The canny transfer dealings of Ashman once again helped to restore respectability to the balance sheet, but poor turnstile numbers were threatening the existence of the club. The Chairman, Mr Jack Empson, always looked a worried man, and it was said that on numerous occasions he was bailing the club out with cash injections. Scunthorpe United's supporters may have not realised it, but they owed the gentleman a lot for the club's survival, and he was not the only one to lend a hand.

The win against Darlington was a prelude to a six match unbeaten run, the height of which took the club to tenth in the table. At home to Stockport County the Scunthorpe legions inflicted the Cheshire side's first defeat of the season. Steve Cammack's opening goal on the twenty minute mark was already hailed the 'goal of the season' by the Evening Telegraph. He controlled an awkward ball, rounded a defender, left him sprawling on the floor wrong-footed, then shaped up the perfect shot to score. The game was sorted out as early as the first half hour, with a second shot from Paul O'Berg. Such a performance had the crowd cheering them into the tunnel at half-time, and at the end of the match as 2-0 winners.

~ 1980-81 ~
It was decided to exercise a little pruning of the playing staff during the close season in view of the tight restraints due to the cash flow. The contracts not being renewed would allow Ron to stock up once again.

Among the men to set off into the sunset were Dave Gibson, Steve Early, Geoff Chouch, David Hall, John O'Donnell and Steve Deere. Steve Deere had decided to opt for a change of career, and was retiring from the senior game. In addition, Nolan Keeley had left for Lincoln City late in the old campaign. The room created brought recognition for local man Chris Cowling, who already had a handful of games under his belt. Vinny Grimes was also to be involved after a catastrophic time with injury. New signings were Nicky Jarvis from Grantham and London-born Alan Boxall from Barton Town, both for the defence. Then for midfield, Phil Ashworth, a lean man with as many clubs as a golfer, came from Portsmouth, while Anton Lambert left Long Eaton to come to the Old Showground. All four of the new lads made a contribution of just over twenty appearances each.

The August nights were already drawing in when Scunthorpe knew they would not win the League Cup! Barnsley had already done the dirty on them by the time their Fourth

Steve Cammack and his goals were the catalyst of the team's success at this time in the season. He was on the target twice when Darlington turned up in Scunthorpe for the return match. Either side of Steve's strikes Malcolm Partridge slotted in a penalty after a harsh handball decision, but United were good value for their win.

In the F.A.Cup, United were hoping to jump the first hurdle for the first time in seven years. Their lot was against high flying Hartlepool United from their own division. Scunthorpe had already conceded three points to them in the League, and they knew the threat posed by Newton and Houchen in the 'Pool attack. When the game kicked off the five thousand spectators numbered twice the normal expectation. They would not be disappointed by the bustle put in by both busy sets of players.

Scunthorpe stamped their authority on the initial stages and went ahead when work by Rick Green created space for Vinny Grimes to hammer home. Hartlepool responded by delving into the advanced regions of Scunthorpe's territory, and a delightful chip had the ball in the net for the equalizer.

In the second-half the game could have gone either way. On the hour Rick Green rose high to nod the Iron in the lead again, swaying the initiative towards the home side. Full control was taken on the match when a foul was awarded for a dubious penalty, duly dispatched by Malcolm Partridge. The only incident to spoil an otherwise first class footballing day was crowd trouble during the ninety minutes, but the local constabulary took the necessary firm steps.

The progress United had made was rewarded with the gift of a sticky tie at home to the Alliance Premier team, Altrincham. Altrincham were renowned Cup fighters, and were as good as several of the company in the Fourth Division. The Cheshire men had already beaten Burscough away from home, and it may not have been the draw Scunthorpe would have chosen.

When the game kicked-off Altrincham adopted some hard tackling tactics, with the first visiting player being booked as early as the second minute. On another occasion Joe Neenan was knocked to the ground and required treatment. Chances were at a premium in the blustery conditions but United's best player, Vinny Grimes, should have scored, when he burst through, and hit the side netting with a cross shot.

On the following Monday all eye were focused on Moss Lane. It was to be another night when United were to have to deal with a robust style of play. The vital moment which decided the game was when they were cast as the villains, and were mugged. In the twenty-ninth minute, Neenan caught the ball as an Altrincham forward rushed at him. Having been left prostrate in the first game, Neenan rather rashly defended himself by raising his knee. The man hit the knee and collapsed in a writhing heap. Gilbert Napthine, the referee, pointed to the spot, and in a storm of controversy United made an exit from the competition. Altrincham went on to play Liverpool.

Attention was focussed back on the soap opera of Division Four, where Christmas brought its highs and lows, to keep the United anchored in the middle of the bunch. At the Old Showground the sixteen hundred supporters who avoided the temptation of visiting Santa in the stores down High Street, did right to be at the Tranmere Rovers match. Lambert may have headed them in front against the run of play, but they had worked hard enough for victory when Dave Stewart came on as substitute and scored five minutes from time.

It prompted the Telegraph to comment, *"United give Christmas Cheer to the Faithful"*. Unfortunately, on Boxing Day, a loss against Mansfield did not go down too well with the whisky at the end of play. It was a similar story when Bury visited the next day, and a 2-0 lead was reduced to a draw. At least there was not the same concerns as other years at this time, but the team did have room for improvement on the half term report.

The continuation of League matches in the New Year was delayed due to the F.A.Cup duties of opponents, and United did not carry on until an extra week had passed. Their opening gambit was against Peterborough, which saw them trail from the third minute. It could have been more if Joe Neenan had not been in fine form. The points were split down the middle when Cammack distributed to Green. Green side-stepped his defender and placed a low shot beyond the Posh custodian.

United were playing some sound soccer, but the response of the local public was thin to say the least, although there was a hard core of two thousand spectators who were terrific with their loyalty and praise for the club. Unfortunately football clubs could not run on such sparse crumbs and a loss of up to two thousand pounds per week was a worrying prospect. It therefore came as no surprise to learn of the sacking of John Kaye purely for financial reasons in February. Also that month, United received a visit from Lincoln City, whose promotion push was in full swing. The gate increased to a figure just in excess of five thousand people, many supporting the Imps. One of the Sincil Bank men was Nolan Keeley, enjoying the pressures at the top of the League with his new club. Those persons who turned up in the bright Winter sunshine were present for an excellent fixture. The main ingredients of the game were the influence of Gordon Hobson for the green-shirted City side, and United's refusal to lay down and die.

Lincoln City soon stamped their authority on the game and Hobson put them ahead on eleven minutes. O'Berg had Scunthorpe supporters waiting until the hour before he clipped in the equalizer. This set up a grandstand finish, and Hobson looked to have stolen the win two minutes from time. The City supporters were still pointing fingers of derision at the sickened Scunthorpe fans when Stuart Pilling thrust himself forward, and hit a ball on the run with his trusty left peg to secure a dramatic last chance equalizer.

Stuart Pilling had a habit of scoring important goals, and was considered a little gem by those on the terraces. Another outstanding match was in March for the visit of the team keeping Lincoln off the championship spot, Southend United. A notable aspect at this time was the experiment of a Sunday afternoon kick-off. An extra thousand was added to the normal expected crowd for a Saturday match. It was good to see Scunthorpe play as well as against Lincoln. Pilling scored with a similar left-footed drive on fifty-one minutes after a sneaky back heel from Steve Cammack. Paul O'Berg flicked on to Rick Green, six minutes later, and Rick chipped home for number two. The champions did pull one back, but all too late.

The campaign was slipping away for United, when it was announced the club was looking to let Ron Ashman go 'upstairs' as the General Manager and a younger party be sought to take over team matters in a player/manager role. Meanwhile, as Ron Ashman's time ebbed away, so too did the season. The more memorable moments toward the end included the total domination of Doncaster at Belle Vue, which finished with Billy Bremner's men committing a burglary of the two points with a 1-0 score.

Stuart Pilling scores the winner against Champions-elect Southend United. March 1981

York City were beaten in a frenzied first-half, when all five goals were scored to produce the 3-2 result. At the final curtain United truly became the division's draw specialists with their twentieth sharing of the spoils in the Wigan match at the Old Showground. The Latics had been a bogie side which the Iron could never conquer. United led their rivals 3-1 and 4-2 at various stages. Then, right at the death Wigan pulled two goals out of the hat to draw level.

At the end of the 1980-81 campaign United finished in sixteenth place. The sixty goals they had scored was slightly more than usual. Steve Cammack was top marksman on sixteen in all first team competitions, while Paul O'Berg on ten also reached double figures. However, the main cause of concern was the way United were losing money hand over fist. It was still no consolation that other clubs were in a worst dilemma than Scunthorpe.

~1981-82 ~

The big news in the Summer was the signing of John Duncan, a Scotsman who had risen to fame when he left Dundee to join Tottenham Hotspur. From there he moved to Derby County, and it was from the Baseball Ground that he came to Scunthorpe as player/manager. He soon made his first signing, bringing Andy Keeley, a former Tottenham apprentice, off the books of Sheffield United. Andy's job was to strengthen the back four. They also took on board David Hughes, a midfielder. He had been previously with Lincoln City, and within a couple of weeks of football starting Paul Moss brought more weight to add to the attack when he left Hull City. There were also terms offered to apprentices Vince Duffy and Neil Pointon. At first Duffy was used more often, but Pointon's impact in seasons to come would be more effective.

To make way for the new recruits six players were placed on the not retained list, with the big news being that leading goalscorer Steve Cammack had decided to try his luck at Lincoln City. Other players making their way into non-League football included Graham Pugh, leaving for Matlock, Nick Jarvis, returning to Grantham, Phil Ashworth to Cambridge City, and Jimmy Gordon, off to play for Boston United.

Scunthorpe United played a pre-season friendly against Liverpool to ease the depressing financial problems, which it was announced amounted to £140,000 in the red, and the supporters had now to pay more to watch the team as the cost of ground admission rose by 20p to £1.50. Old Age Pensioners and Boys would cost 80p. The club did not get far into the season, when Mr David Wraith was promoted to Vice-Chairman. Mr Wraith was a dynamic businessman not prepared to let the club go under, and he added a lot of drive to the board in an effort to get the club moving again.

On the field of play United started with draws at Northampton and at home to Blackpool. Mansfield Town continued with their familiarization with the Iron in the League Cup, and just as a familiar exit was shown to United at the first round stage. Despite this handicap, two straight home wins against Tranmere Rovers and Hartlepool United set a course for calmer waters, and it was good to see David Moss scoring in both of these encounters. After this minor success everything started to go wrong. The team found it impossible to win and in the next couple of months they failed to pick up another victory. It sent them tumbling down the League and only just off the bottom position. The only match of note in all that time was a game of sweat and toil which ended in a goal bonanza against Hull City. United were behind three times, and at the end equally shared eight goals, although at one time being 4-2 down. The key to United's revival was two penalty conversions by big Malcolm Partridge.

It was not until November before the tide turned for the Iron. BBC Television cameras caught up with them at Halifax for a lower division 'Match of the Day' glimpse. Although Town scored first, Chris Cowling headed United back on track by half-time. The winner arrived a quarter of an hour from the end of the game. Paul O'Berg put Paul Moss through, and his shot entered the back of the net via the underside of the bar.

United drew Bradford City in the F.A.Cup, a club who were on a roll at the top of Division Four, and they had already comfortably scored a victory over Scunthorpe in the League at the Old Showground. John Duncan urged his local supporters to get behind their team, for with home soil favouring them, they might come up with a different result than expected. Indeed, this proved to be the case, but Scunthorpe had to call on all their reserves of character to get through. As early as the second minute Paul O'Berg was a victim of a high tackle and eventually had to be substituted. In the seventeenth minute Dave Stewart found Chris Cowling on the edge of the penalty area, and he drilled a low shot into the net. Not long into the second-half David Dall was subjected to a vicious tackle and finished as a limping passenger, but somehow United hung on for the win.

At the start of the Winter, United made two more signings. Tony Arins decided to drop down the divisions after precious little first team exposure at Leeds United. Meanwhile ex-Everton man George Talfer came from football in the United States with San Diego Sockers. The pair were both on duty for the goalless draw with Port Vale, but bad weather throughout the month of December meant that this home match was the only one played for four weeks.

It was not until the first Saturday in the New Year that soccer lifted its nose from under the warm blankets. This should have been the date on the schedule for the third round F.A. Cup-tie, but instead United had to travel to Crewe for the second round. Crewe were one of the few teams below Scunthorpe in the Fourth Division and they only managed six wins all season; in all but one of these, victory was by the odd goal. The sixth result was by three goals without reply versus Scunthorpe. Fortunately there was not to be a repetition, and goals by Cowling, Telfer and O'Berg, the last two in the second-half, earned a 3-1 win.

Scunthorpe United had hoped for a First Division side in the third round, so with all due respect, a visit from Fourth Division Hereford United did not exactly light up the sky, and the opportunity to make progress was thrown away at the Old Showground. When they fell behind in the first-half they always knew it was going to be difficult, but David Stewart's equalizer did give them a second chance.

A fortnight later their next bite of the cherry was fruitless. The 4-1 result spoke volumes and severed Scunthorpe from the competition. In the rest of the fragmented competition Hereford entertained Leicester City on their Edgar Street ground before a five figure crowd. The question was how much would that have replenished Scunthorpe's empty coffers if they had won the day?

At the end of January there was a srun of form which caused some optimism. Three successive victories over Northampton, Tranmere and Mansfield, the second away from home, did lift the team within striking distance of safety, but they were still flirting with disaster, and on the spectator front, the average gate in the League was only just hovering above two thousand. During that month United did ease the finances by playing Nottingham Forest in a friendly game, as the pressure from creditors threatened to pull them under. Over four thousand turned up to view a 2-2 draw.

It was on 11th February 1982 that United called a press conference. The situation was so acute that they were forced to adopt a number of unpleasant and austere measures in an effort to keep the club afloat.

Firstly, the position of Chairman was to be taken on by Mr David Wraith, whilst Mr Jack Empson would move across as his Vice-Chairman. There would be a number of casualties, who regrettably would lose their positions at the football club. These included General Manager Ron Ashman, Secretary Sheila Louth, and Physiotherapist Charlie Strong. Mr Wraith set the ball rolling on a fighting fund to raise £50,000 for the immediate future.

Supporters rallied round to pledge small amounts out of their wages, and within a short period two cheques rolled in, one for £100, the proceeds from a disco evening, and another for £740 for a sponsored walk to the away game at Peterborough. The Supporters Club were not long in coming forward and threw in over £3,000. Money was also realized from other sources, in order to keep the ship afloat.

One new face to cheer the situation in the offices was that of Don Rowing, to oversee the secretarial work. Don always had a smile on his face, and over the years had to be responsible as a front for the Club to oversee a number of decisions which did not always suit everyone. Whatever he did, Don did for the good of Scunthorpe United, and he could be relied upon to make an honest judgement at all times. The Iron was to be all the richer for his service.

Don Rowing rolled up for work on his first morning and was confronted by an individual he did not recognize. It turned out to be a bailiff who had come for a payment. Mr Wraith duly wrote a cheque for the sum demanded and the Club was able to carry on. It was on the following Saturday that United paid host to Sheffield United, a mile in front of everyone in the League race.

A stream of expectant supporters made their way from the Steel City swelling the attendance to in excess of eight thousand spectators. The extra numbers meant a welcome pile of coinage to be counted, but just as Don and the ladies in the office started to tally the amount, all the lights failed. Hastily they went to the corner shop for candles, and continued their totalling under candlelight. After that incident, Don was always frugal with cash.

Sheffield United entered the arena in strange yellow and brown striped shirts. They no doubt expected to steam roller the lowly Iron into the ground, but Scunthorpe had other ideas. The Iron's players raised their game and produced the best display of the season. The visiting hordes were stunned into silence on the Fox Street terrace, after Scunthorpe's mobility, first seen in the fifth minute, had a Vinny Grimes free-kick curl over the defence to give Paul Moss a simple header. All attempts to get back on terms by the costly Sheffield side were thwarted, as Scunthorpe paraded a complete team of heros.

On the sixty-sixth minute the Iron's George Telfor produced another trump card. His shot on the run went high into the roof of the net. Only a penalty goal by Kenworthy spoiled a brilliant day, but finally it was the Blades that were blunted. In total Sheffield United only lost four games all season. The result against the Blades raised hopes of prosperity on the pitch, but when a run of form needed to be put together to keep the interest of home supporters, so the opposite

Dave Stewart and George Telfer pressurise Rochdale's Crawford - the former United 'keeper.

of second from bottom in the Fourth Division. For only the second time in their history the Club had the indignation of seeking re-election. Fortunately this was secured without any problem, but it went to serve as a warning to all concerned. Before the season was wrapped up Jack Brownsword brought a star-studded eleven to play a friendly against United. The exercise attracted over four thousand supporters to the Old Showground to go one more step nearer to survival. Jack's team included star performing old boy Kevin Keegan, and World Cup 1966 winner Jack Charlton.

happened. It did not help that a number of team members had been shown their cards, and Malcolm Partridge joined Stuart Pilling in the dole office in Station Road. However, it was not expected that the Club would plunge down the table losing the next six matches, and being unable to win for a further three. Ian Botham even made himself available, but when he made his full debut against Wigan the news cameras saw United lose at home by a record 7-2 score.

There was precious little to applaud for supporters as the team struggled in the bottom four places. John Duncan tried a last gamble by making a number of short term contract signings. These included Gordon Boyd, Alan Thompson, Stuart Hamill and Ronnie Goodlass, but none was retained at the end of the season. Ronnie Goodlass was the best known of the quartet, being the ex-Evertonian who had played at the top level, and who, remarkably, became the first one-handed footballer to represent the Club. There was also an exchange deal set up with Lincoln City. Steve Cammack had never settled at Sincil Bank, and rushed at the chance of a return when swapped for Dave Hughes.

Despite all of the last minute alterations, what had gone on before in the season doomed United to re-election. It was confirmed when United could only draw at home to Bury. Even then it needed a last gasp equalizer from Steve Cammack to guarantee the point.

The season finished with a sequence of three draws, starting with the Bury match, which meant a final League table place

New man Steve Baines, who, after his playing days became a Football League referee.

The game against Jack Brownsword's eleven was to bring to the end an era of Scunthorpe United playing in an all red kit with white facings. For the forth-coming term, United would be wearing their original colours of claret and blue, by popular demand of their supporters. To be tech-nically correct it was originally to be blue with claret facings, including a broad claret vee along the neckline. One year later a more recognisable version of the colours went on display, followed by variations on the modern vogue.

~ 1982-83 ~

Between seasons, John Duncan had worked unceasingly to attract a higher quality set of players to the Club. His early efforts were rocked by the news that Tony Arins and Paul Moss would not be available because they were pursuing careers outside the game. Contracts would not be renewed in the case of Steve Davy and David Dall, but supporters could expect plenty of new additions to the squad.

The first of the fresh men was a towering defender from Chesterfield. Les Hunter was 6'2", and a tremendous competitor. He would be joined in the back station by Steve Baines, a much travelled man from Walsall. In midfield Noel Parkinson was small in comparison, but the ex-Ipswich and Mansfield Town midfielder would bolster the team with plenty of energy. There was also the addition of the stockily built Martin Fowler from Stockport, who operated from the right-hand side.

The advanced ranks were to benefit from the arrival of another man who was on the small side, Dennis Leman. Leman was to inject pace and skill to the left hand side of the park after his signature completed a move from Sheffield Wednesday. There was also a prolonged period on loan for Mike Angus from Middlesbrough, while Peter Cartwright similarly arrived, from Newcastle, for a month. Duncan also promoted youngsters Chris Cowling and Neil Pointon making them regular fixtures in the first team squad.

Before the season properly kicked off, ex-Scunthorpe player Keith Burkinshaw, by then a household name managing Tottenham Hotspur, assisted the Club by bringing the famous 'Spurs to the Old Showground. Among the team was the rather long-haired Glen Hoddle, a person who was to leave an indelible mark on Football. Tottenham had just won the Cup by beating Queens Park Rangers at Wembley, and paraded the trophy in front of five thousand Scunthonians. The visitors strolled through the game with majestic grace, winning 5-0, but leaving a vivid impression.

The start of football in earnest was a goalless draw at Hartlepool, which gave no true indications of what was ahead, and the League Cup brought Dave Booth's strong Grimsby Town side to the stadium on Doncaster Road. They were always too good for the Iron, but their poorer neighbours gave them a run for their money. Chris Cowling equalized in the eighty-fifth minute, but while the lads were celebrating, the Mariners snatched the late winner. After a home draw against Aldershot, battle recommenced at Blundell Park. It was to Scunthorpe's great credit that another goalless draw was recorded, but it was not quite enough.

Scunthorpe supporters did not have to wait long for their first win. It was a victory that swept a bewildered Stockport County away by 3-0. Telfer and Cowling virtually had the job sealed at the interval, but a second strike by Telfer put the icing on the cake, and life for John Duncan was much sweeter. As the early part of the League season continued the unbeaten run was extended. There was the unusual sight of Scunthorpe United rubbing shoulders with the top runners in the Division. It was not until the derby with Hull City that United lost their first game in the Fourth Division, at the tenth attempt. The Tigers massed bands of supporters exploded into a great wave of noise five minutes from time when Les Mutrie scored the only goal, but Scunthorpe were never disgraced.

United were playing very well as a compact unit, with Steve Cammack, who was the main spearhead of the attack, becoming a regular goalscorer. The beauty of this forward line was that goals were also arriving from a number of other sources. It was pleasing to see that the side was not derailed by the initial loss to Hull, and they eked out revenge at Mansfield Town, then Tranmere Rovers at the Showground, in consecutive matches.

The team was even treated to an unusual trip to play Torquay. Normally it was the tedious six hour journey down to Plainmoor that tired the team out before they played the game. This time the players and officials went in a private aircraft from Hallgate Airport near Gainsborough. They returned with a hard earned point.

United were making steady progress all the time. The stiff opposition of Potteries team Port Vale posed a threat, but Cammack's goal saw them off. Then came a championship performance against Northampton. The Iron were steaming. Two goals by Paul O'Berg, followed by a hat-trick from Steve Cammack, did the speaking for them as they won 5-1. The reward for this cracking serving to the supporters was the side's elevation on to the top of Division Four.

United maintained full throttle with another victory, at Crewe, before the welcome break of playing in the F.A.Cup. Fate had them paired in the North-East with Darlington. They had already taken the League points from a 1-0 result, and John Duncan's men went off in confident mood. They did have to work hard, but when Steve Cammack rose gracefully to head a copybook goal in the fifty-second minute, there was only one winner.

The second round tie, three weeks later, was against non-League Northwich Victoria, who had been one of the original Second Division teams in the last century. Before the Cup-tie, a home defeat to fellow promotion hopefuls, Bury had cost United their position at the peak of the Division. When the green-shirted Northwich Victoria ran onto the field, United knew they would have to be on their best behaviour.

The team did not disappoint their supporters and dominated the early proceedings. Chris Cowling saw United ahead, but on the stroke of half-time Victoria levelled, due to some defensive hesitation in the home back line. A stiff talk from Duncan at the interval sorted the job out, and Scunthorpe rolled into the next phase after Paul O'Berg's goal. There was a sigh of relief when the game finished because of the potential banana skin Northwich had threatened.

During the final part of 1982 Scunthorpe slipped down the Fourth Division table to fifth position, but still well within contention. The reason for their slide could be found in two 3-1 reverses, at Blackpool and Halifax Town, where the usual high standards had not been maintained. Lapses at the back caused Joe Neenan to be unreasonably exposed.

The excitement of the New Year was the chance to topple the Mariners, who had been drawn again, this time in the F.A.Cup third round. Grimsby Town were in fine form and their recent victory over Carlisle United saw them soar to seventh place in Division Two. When the teams squared up to each other, both thought they could outdo the other. A huge eleven thousand crowd streamed into the Old Showground to see a blood and thunder tussle, but at the end of ninety minutes no goals were registered and no superiority gained.

The draw meant a night of sea air, plus fish and chips for United supporters over in Cleethorpes. Unfortunately there would be no fairytale ending. Tony Ford caught Scunthorpe cold in the first couple of minutes and then Joe Waters stuck away a penalty. Worse, was when United had their own opportunity from twelve yards, but Noel Parkinson missed his chance. Generally speaking the whole team had not come up to expectations, and the Chairman blew his top.

The simmerings that resulted from the Cup elimination by the sword of Grimsby Town continued at the Old Showground between David Wraith and John Duncan.

It appeared that not all was well between them, and despite maintaining a position on the top rungs of the ladder an uncomfortable truce prevailed. Eventually the sensational news broke from the Old Showground that John Duncan had been sacked on 2nd February, and that thirty-six year-old former Leeds United and England striker Allan Clarke was immediately appointed as a replacement.

Clarke saw his new charges two days later at home to Bristol City, but United were not the fluent well oiled machined of the past. It required a precision strike direct from a Noel Parking free kick to grind out a draw. Clarke implied that the squad he had inherited was not strong enough to be serious promotion contenders. He was probably judged to be correct when his next three games in charge ended all square. To be fair, one of these was before fourteen thousand at Hull City and it was the home side that fought in desperation for the point at the end. This run was finished in winning ways when Tranmere Rovers were slaughtered 4-0 at Prenton Park, where three goals came in the first forty-five minutes. The following week, halfway through the second period, Torquay United were stunned into submission by two Les Hunter headers.

Scunthorpe United entered April still in contention with the leaders, but far enough away from the number one spot to realize the championship was out of their grasp. They then received blows which would rock most clubs. Noel Parkinson broke a leg in training to rule him out for almost a year, then a home defeat by bottom club Hereford United was followed by the hammer blow of a 5-1 crucifixion at Colchester United. For a moment all the efforts of the past months appeared to be in tatters.

It was Clarke's job to lift his men. In the next game Blackpool's visit proved to be a fascinating affair, but not one for the fainthearted. Blackpool twice took the lead, and the Iron twice equalized. Cowling put United ahead on the hour, only for Greenall to make it 3-3 on seventy eight-minutes. This see-saw encounter could have gone either way, but Steve Cammack played the last trick. In the eightieth minute Neil Pointon took a free kick. The defence headed it out, but only as far as Cammack, who returned the ball at speed into the net.

This win was the prelude to the final run into the last phase of the season and included two late signings to boost United's promotion drive. The pair were the much travelled Mike Lester from Bradford City, and Tommy Graham, a Scotsman from Doncaster Rovers, whose incentive was to prove himself and earn a full contract. Allan Clarke had also brought the quietly spoken Frank Barlow to the Old Showground as his second in command.

The final months of the season started when Steve Cammack and Mike Lester shot down Swindon Town at the Old Showground, with a goal in each half. It meant that promotion was still a possibility, but more likely in the third or fourth spot, depending on the results of other teams.

United's next appointment was a meeting with Darlington, low in the table and only average travellers. The three points for a win were vital, and at two nil up with ten minutes to play everything seemed to be on course for success. Then came the 'Rocky Horror' show. Two lapses of concentration and two points were lost in a draw. United's supporters were devastated. When David Wraith left the ground he was ashen-faced, knowing promotion was almost certainly blown.

The facts of the matter were that United had to win both their remaining away games and hope that Bury lost their last test, which was at home. If there was to be any hope of salvation, it was that Bury had to play Wimbledon, who were guaranteed the championship. The first hurdle was a midweek match in the Potteries against Port Vale. Vale were celebrating promotion themselves in front of six thousand fans, who wanted a party at United's expense. It was all or nothing for Scunthorpe, and they pulled out a display from the bottom of the locker that reached meteoric heights. Every man played a star role, and when Chris Cowling rose like a giant to head home the winner, Scunthorpe had completed the first leg of the impossible double.

A string of buses lined up outside the Old Showground on the Saturday morning, ready to take the hopeful supporters to see United's final game at Chester. The players were waved off, and went into the game with the best wishes of former manager John Duncan. To add a little more intrigue into the equation Paul O'Berg had injured himself at Port Vale, and the ligament damage sustained ruled him out of the encounter. United were down to the bare bones of the playing staff, and short of playing himself, the manager called up Ian Webster to make his debut and Simon Snow to sit on the bench. Both were Scunthorpe apprentices.

At kick-off, Scunthorpe United knew that if they were successful, an agonising fifteen minutes would have to be waited at the end, because of the difference in the kick-off time at Bury. However, a couple of mass invasions by Scunthorpe Supporters in fancy dress, were chased by the local Cheshire constabulary, and seemed to last exactly a quarter of an hour. In the fifteenth minute of play Tommy Graham had the one thousand visiting fans partying when he was first to react to a loose ball from Cammack's shot. The lead was shortlived, because Chester scrambled the ball into Scunthorpe United's net in the twenty-fourth minute. The sparse home terraces did show some signs of life at the goal, but Chester fans were, in the main, anywhere except at Sealand Road and getting behind their team.

Meanwhile, with no prompting, Scunthorpe United's supporters started jumping up and down in wild excitement. Ears pressed against transistor radios had taken in news of first one, and then another Wimbledon goal against Bury.

The latest news of the score continued to be passed on amongst the crowd, and eventually to the players. It meant that the Iron needed to beat Grenville Millington, the Seals Welsh International 'keeper again, and Scunthorpe's defence had to remain firm. The second-half saw no real threats to the United back line, but the illusive goal would not come.

Time was running out for the team and also on promotion. Then came the moment of drama all Scunthonians wanted to see. United forced their opponents into conceding a corner in the eighty-second minute. Ian Webster looped the ball over into the penalty box. Les Hunter charged in with a meaty header. Millington parried it, but again Tommy Graham got a foot to it and poked it home. Suddenly the tension burst like a multi-coloured firework lighting up the sky. The shear emotion of the crowd carried the team through the last few moments of the game.

When it was learned that Bury had lost 3-1, at Sealand Road all hell was let loose. Scunthorpe supporters went wild with delirium. Grown men were see to cry. At last United were promoted. Allan Clarke was delighted his prediction that the team would probably not win promotion was incorrect. He saluted all their hard work and endeavours. There were scenes of wild celebrations in front of the Directors box by the players and fans alike as the triumph was celebrated.

Les Hunter rises above the Torquay defenders to head home in the vital 2-0 victory at the Old Showground in March 1983.

Tommy Graham rises after scoring the winning goal at Chester that clinched promotion. Steve Baines, Chris Cowling and Steve Cammack join in the celebrations.

Nobody wanted to go back to the buses for the journey home. When the players coach did finally arrive back at a late hour, everyone on board made for the Royal Hotel outside the Old Showground to crack open the champagne. The bottom line was that Allan Clarke could do nothing but offer the hero of the day, Tommy Graham, a full contract. Scunthorpe United would now be playing in Division Three in the 1983-84 season.

CHAPTER 12

THE LAST YEARS OF THE OLD SHOWGROUND

The success of the 1982-83 promotion campaign brought with it the increased financial pressures demanded by a bigger wage bill and transfer fees to maintain the position. It was learned that to offset the costs they would occur if they did finish in the top four, David Wraith and his fellow directors had taken out an insurance to cover the possibility of promotion. Promotion meant an extra pay out of £50,000, and although the premiums may have been high, the dividend was justified.

It meant that Allan Clarke had a little cash in hand to pay for new blood, and some would be brought to the Club at the start of the season. The defence saw the acquisition of a young Yorkshire lad, Paul Longden, from Barnsley. Paul had played a handful of games at Oakwell, but over the years he would become part of the furniture at Scunthorpe United. His position was usually on either flank of the back four. He was joined by a very strong central pivot in John Green from Rotherham United, who was certainly worth the fee, playing in all but one of the forty-six fixtures.

In midfield, or as a wide man, the bearded Mike Brolly signed as an ex-Mariner from Derby County. His skill level was just what was required in this higher grade of football. He was joined further up the field by teenagers Geoff Dey and Julian Broddle from Sheffield United. There was also occupation from the junior ranks for Ian Webster, Robbie Holden, Simon Snow, and Dave Hill, but only in a limited capacity.

Promotion had resulted in a termination for some men who had done the spadework to haul the Club into the Third Division, and it may have been rough justice to see them shown the back door. Supporters would see no more of Andy Keeley, Martin Fowler, George Telfer, Steve Baines and above all Bob Oates. Bob had toiled through over three hundred appearances and in that time had played his entire career for the Iron in Division Four. All supporters wished him the best at his new club, Rochdale. It would not be long before we would be joined on the way out by Dennis Leyman, Andy Boxall and Les Hunter, who had all played a roll in the year's new challenges.

~ 1983-84 ~

Scunthorpe United started the season with another 'first'., for their shirts sported a sponsor for the first time. The breast of the garment advertised the legend 'Scunthorpe E.Z.', which referred to the Scunthorpe Enterprise Zone set up by the local council. The novelty stocked the bank account with some extra pennies, but this was the initial tentative steps in a venture which in years to come would become big business.

The season proper started on the huge pitch at Vale Park against Port Vale. A goalless draw set both promoted sides off in the right direction.

Then there was even better news at home, for Exeter City tired, particularly in the second-half, after a long trek from Devon. Mike Lester set the ball rolling before the interval, then strikes by Steve Cammack and Tommy Graham helped make it a first win of 3-1. Another point came when Oxford United were held to a goalless draw, and the overall impression at the initial stages was satisfactory.

Meanwhile, the League Cup threw up a local derby with Doncaster Rovers. The teams served up yet another goalless draw, but at Belle Vue in torrential rain, Rovers stepped up a gear and cracked in three without reply. It was from here that the going started to get tough.

At the end of September Scunthorpe had gradually slipped to the fringe relegation positions, just above the bottom four in the table. One of their problems lay in their inability to score, but things came to a head for the visit of Southend United. The game marked the Club's seven hundred and fiftieth home League game. Allan Clarke made a number of team changes and a very youthful side trotted out of the tunnel. The outcome was that Southend United, ran riot and decimated the Scunthorpe side with a 6-1 scoreline; The Iron goal came from a Robbie Holden penalty. It brought shades of Blundell Park in 1966 to the memories of Scunthorpe's hard pressed supporters.

During the Autumn there continued to be some ups and downs as Scunthorpe United struggled to accumulate points for their safety in the Third Division. It was more important to turn the draws into wins, due to the incentive of three points for a win, which was first instigated two years earlier. The side went down the roller coaster at Eastville against third placed Bristol Rovers, when United felt hard done by. The 4-1 defeat included a questionable penalty, and an own goal conceded by John Green. In a next game they produced the best result of the season, 5-1 at home to Wimbledon. In this encounter luck changed places and it was they who received the rub of the green. One of the goalscorers was from on loan player Danny Wilson, in a class of his own, who had come via Nottingham Forest for a month. One of his two goals was from the penalty spot, and Wimbledon gifted an own goal. In the next match, United played with spirit under the lights of Brammall Lane against Sheffield United, but lost 5-3.

The F.A. Cup brought them face to face with fellow Third Division competitors Preston North End in the first round at the Old Showground and there was little difference between the teams, but Steve Cammack settled it by converting a second-half penalty.

In the second round, Scunthorpe found themselves pitched with Bury, who were having problems in maintaining the same momentum for another promotion drive. This did not stop The Shakers causing United some work to get past them in the competition, but a 2-0 result was a fair reflection of the Iron superiority.

Before Allan Clarke could concentrate his thoughts on another F.A.Cup sortie he had more in the way of League matches to consider. A hard fought game in wet conditions brought three points against Gillingham, to raise the team into nineteenth in the Division. The 2-0 score was the last victory in the Third Division that the Club would enjoy until March. United did have the sight of Ian Botham lending his weight to try and achieve better results, and nobody would deny this man's efforts.

Phil McLoughlin, United's physio., attends a wounded Paul Longden, while Neil Pointon, Joe Neenan, Les Hunter and John Green stand by - in the match versus Rotherham in October.

Allan Clarke also brought out the cheque book to bring Micky Matthews into the team. He had been a contributing factor in Wolverhampton Wanderers' promotion push to Division One, and he fitted instantly into United's midfield. Unfortunately the newcomer's first few games all ended in sorry defeats. Preston North End gained revenge by winning 5-1 at the Old Showground, and four days later, on New Years Eve, United crashed 5-0 at Turf Moor against Burnley. The back line conceded four more to Brentford on New Year Monday, but thanks to a brace of goals by Cammack, and others from O'Berg and Graham, they did manage to take a precious point.

Once the New Year was in, Scunthorpe United turned their attention to a lucrative F.A.Cup draw away to Second Division Leeds United. For Allan Clarke it could not be a better game, because it was at Elland Road, as a player, that he had won the nation's top footballing honours, and this did not prevent him wishing to put one over his old club. Even though the Peacocks were going through tough times by their standards, the Yorkshire element in the seventeen thousand crowd expected them to make progress. When Tommy Wright shot Leeds into a first-half lead everything looked to be on course for the team in white. Scunthorpe United were not to be outdone and forced the pace from the break. Late in the game Cammack grabbed the equaliser through a crowd of bodies, making a lunge at the ball from the edge of the goalmouth.

The replay on the following Tuesday saw ninety minutes of deadlock unable to separate the teams. Leeds United again took the lead through Tommy Wright after twelve minutes of extra time, but two minutes later teenager Geoff Dey shot Scunthorpe level, and the thirteen thousand crowd warmed to the efforts of those concerned. At the end of all the honest sweat there was still no decisive result. The policy dictated that the clubs would toss a coin to choose the privilege of staging the second replay. Luckily, the Scunthorpe camp called correctly, and a week later the exercise was recommenced.

Steve Cammack scores the equaliser in the Cup match at Leeds.....
.....Paul O'Berg, arm raised, shows his approval.

On the Thursday evening gales swept the county and caused major structural damage. The Old Showground did not escape the havoc and the roof of the East Stand was ripped to shreds. After an inspection it was declared safe, but supporters who sat there for the Cup game were able to gaze up and contemplate the stars.

At the sounding of the referee's first whistle, a second gate of thirteen thousand ensured another bumper pay-day. It was not long before the rising atmosphere on the terraces reached melting point. United had the gusty conditions to thank for a little assistance in their first goal in the twelfth minute. Mike Brolly crossed from deep on the right but the ball caught the wind. In goal, ex-Scottish International David Harvey could only help it over the line and into the net. Leeds were soon on terms when Scunthorpe's defence made one of its few errors to let Wright in for his third goal in the trilogy. Scunthorpe United did not let the setback stifle their play, for they got stuck in straight away, and the classy Steve Cammack baffled the Yorkshire defence with a low drive beyond the stretch of the bemused Harvey.

There was no let up in the second-half, for Mike Lester had the claret and blue scarves waving again only a minute after the restart. His shot from the left of the penalty box was rifled high over Harvey and into the net at the Doncaster Road end, to make it 3-1. Scunthorpe were on fire and continued to take the game to the visitors. Twenty minutes remained when Tommy Graham shot in a similar drive from almost the same spot as the previous goal. At 4-1, the tie was virtually over, and when The Iron took their foot off the pedal, Leeds United sneaked one back, but it was too little too late. Little Scunthorpe has won the right to travel to First Division West Bromwich Albion.

Returning to sanity, Allan Clarke had a dabble in the transfer market to ease the critical situation in the Third Division. During a drawn match against The Iron, The Manager took a shine to the huge Brentford central defender Alan Whitehead. Initially the player was taken on loan, and after negotiations he signed permanently in March, when the asking price was dropped from £60,000 to £34,000. Clarke also enticed Derek Bell from Chesterfield to add power to the forward line. Bell had played at a few local Northern clubs including Lincoln City.

The demand for F.A.Cup tickets to West Bromwich was tremendous, and a stream of supporters queued patiently to pay at the box office. It was estimated that four thousand would made their way to the Midlands, but bad weather caused a postponement, and the match had to wait until the following Tuesday. Scunthorpe equalled the Albion in every department and could have gone ahead if it had not been for Jim Barrow in goal. The vital moment occurred in the fifty-seventh minute, when a corner, which clearly should have been a goalkick, was awarded to West Brom. The ball was swung over, but the United defence could not clear it from the resulting melee, and Noel Luke forced it home. Battling Scunthorpe looked to have been robbed, but there was nothing that could be done about it, and Albion entertained Plymouth in the next round.

Work would now have to be done on improving the Club's poor Third Division record, and the points shared against Brentford was the start of a run of six consecutive draws which failed to elevate the Iron up the League. The first win of 1984 did not come along until mid-March, when Bradford City were narrowly defeated 2-1. Micky Matthews' winner was his debut goal in claret and blue, and the team included Richard Prateley on a two month loan from Derby County, who played in midfield. Generally, though, victories were sporadic, and the loss of points was the norm.

A number of results worth a special mention included the 3-0 score over Plymouth Argyle. Remarkably, seven days after playing at the Old Showground, the Pilgrims met Watford in the F.A. Cup Semi-Final. Then, over Easter, Hull City lost 2-0 at Scunthorpe. This result came by way of a goal in each half by Derek Bell, a penalty, and Steve Cammack. It was a result the Tigers would have not have wished for, because it virtually ended their chances of promotion. Finally, in the last home game of the season a 4-0 thrashing of Burnley exacted an away defeat. The Iron had to look at Simon Steele, on loan from Brighton until the end of the campaign, to keep a clean sheet in their goal.

Unfortunately the rest of the picture was much blacker. Only nine wins had been recorded all season, and no victories had been achieved away from home. Two matches were left, and both had to be played on foreign soil. The Iron had to win one of them to stand a realistic chance of avoiding the drop. At Gillingham, Chris Cowling gave them hope with a first-half strike, but the Kent side later drew level, and the one point did not look to be sufficient. United's only solution was a high scoring win at Millmoor against Rotherham United. To give Scunthorpe credit, they did make a fight of it, but unfortunately this left the back door open and Rotherham exploited it three times. It resulted in the Iron finishing fourth from bottom of the Third Division, and the following season they would have to face life in the Fourth Division, again exactly where they had started from twelve months before.

~ 1984-85 ~

Allan Clarke didn't have time to feel sorry for himself, for he was too professional for that. He immediately set about preparations for regaining the lost status by changing his pack. Unfortunately a number of circumstances did not let his ideas go according to plan. During the close season his attempts to sign a number of players were all thwarted, and there were disagreements voiced about the Manager by the Board. John Green and Steve Cammack put in transfer requests, while Paul O'Berg left for Wimbledon. David Wraith announced he was to resign as Chairman because of business commitments, but he would remain a Director. The Club was then put up for sale to see if that would bring any more cash in. If that was not enough, a dry summer caused the Old Showground pitch to be unfit for the pre-season matches. When football did get underway, the friendly fixtures produced a poor set of results.

A Board meeting on Friday 24th August was called, principally to elect a new Chairman, when Mr Tom Belton was proposed by Mr Cooper and seconded by Mr Alston. The motion was carried unanimously, but Tom Belton's conditions were that Mr Wraith should resign from the Board and Allan Clarke leave the Club. This also came to pass, and immediately the sale of Scunthorpe United was withdrawn. Assistant manager, Frank Barlow, took charge at Chester to see the team through a 1-1 draw, and then on the eve of the Milk Cup tie, at home to Mansfield Town, he was officially confirmed as the new boss. Later in the year Allan Clarke received an unconfirmed sum for unfair dismissal.

until their seventh match for that illusive first win, and at one stage dropped to second to bottom in the table, but the visit of a poor Halifax Town team changed all that. Three first-half goals made the points safe by half-time, and another in the period after the interval made for a happy 4-0 success. United may have lost at Peterborough United in the next match, but they remained unbeaten throughout October. It was around the end of October and into the next month that a purple patch saw them win three consecutive games, at home to Torquay United and Aldershot, while sandwiched between them came a trip to Bury.

Alan Whitehead typically rises above the packed Chesterfield defence for a power header, during the September 1984 encounter.

It was only a pity that Scunthorpe United could not provide their new Manager with a winning start, but Frank Barlow had only just enough players to make a team. In the end they went down by an only goal to the Stags.

A week later they pulled back the deficit with a 2-1 result, and hence brought the scores level. A period of thirty minutes extra time was played, with no further scoring, then because of the two away goals, scored by Mike Lester and Steve Cammack, Frank Barlow's men went through.

Scunthorpe United found themselves up against Aston Villa in the second round of the competition. There was very little chance of making progress against the sophisticated giants of the First Division, but in each of the two legs the team did themselves credit. An aggregate score of 6-3 in Villa's favour saw the Midlands side comfortably through, but for lowly Scunthorpe United to score three times in the tie was an extraordinary feat.

Meanwhile, the lack of new signings and the number of injuries picked up was causing a headache. United's physio, Phil McLoughlin, was one of the Club's busiest staff members. On the Fourth Division scene, United had to wait

There had been better news on the transfer market front. Frank Barlow was hesitant in rushing to buy any player, just to satisfy the demands of the expectant supporters. However, they were appeased when he signed Terry Lees, a much travelled full-back of Midlands origin. Lees' previous League club had been Blackpool, and his final League appearance had been at Newport County. There was also the signing of Paul Gregory as goalkeeping cover for the ginger-haired Joe Neenan. Gregory was small for a goalkeeper, but made up for it with an approach that was as keen as mustard. A jaw injury to the first choice custodian let the newcomer in, and he grabbed his chance to make the majority of the year's games between the Scunthorpe posts.

When it came to the F.A.Cup Scunthorpe had drawn a real hot potato. Their lot was an away tie at Nuneaton, one of the country's top non-League lights. Barlow emphasised caution, for he knew it would not be easy, and so it proved. United took the lead in a scramble of a goal, with Chris Cowling claiming the last touch, although it could have been an own goal. Nuneaton roared back and were level at half-time, but Scunthorpe, playing in a change strip of green and yellow, managed to hang on to the end.

At the Old Showground the Nuneaton side sprung an early upset, going ahead within five minutes. It took a long time for the Iron to turn their engine over, and the local crowd had some anxious moments to sweat out. They had to wait until the sixty-ninth minute before United got their minds in gear, when Mike Lester found space on the left hand side of the box, and his low left-footed cross shot crept inside the post. Madam chance extended a hand to both teams, but her advances were scorned. The result was a further thirty minutes of torture for both sets of supporters. In the end it was Steve Cammack who resolved the impasse four minutes into the resumption with a poached close range header.

Cammack was certainly the hero of all the Iron fans, but before more Cup duties could be performed he scored a hat-trick in the League match on familiar soil against the Welshmen from Wrexham. The visitors were never in the hunt. Micky Matthews and Alan Whitehead notched other strikes to send a little more than two thousand patrons home, happy with a resounding 5-2 win.

It was only a pity that this could not be done a week later when United visited Port Vale for a rare Friday evening second round Cup fixture. The Iron may have scored first with an own goal assist, but from then on they were never at the races. Vale tore into them, and after unusually slack defending, at 1-4 down, the side had received what it deserved. If the team had performed to their true capabilities they could have been on their way to play West Ham United at Upton Park.

Ironically, in Scunthorpe's next League match, they drew 1-1 at Vale Park in late December. Much of that month's schedule had been wiped out by inclement weather, and only two more games were played, both at the Old Showground, either side of the away fixture in the Potteries. The first home encounter was a highly entertaining friendly match for Ian Botham's Testimonial. Four thousand supporters turned up to watch Ron Atkinson bring a Manchester United eleven to Scunthorpe. It was great fun for all concerned, and the evening was summed up by the 5-5 draw. On a more serious note, football for 1984 passed by with an important single goal victory over Stockport County. Who else, but Steve Cammack supplied the winner!

The remainder of the Fourth Division programme saw Scunthorpe United never quite in the promotion hunt, but always able to score a bag full of goals. With so much drama on the field going on, it was hard to understand why the Scunthorpe public did not respond through the turnstiles. There was also the added bonus of a host of young players making the grade, with Dave Hill, playing in the advance stages of midfield, a prime example. His career had developed like a sprinter out of the blocks. To a lesser degree Steve Shutt, Willy Ferry, Sean Stubart and Mark Atkins also played their parts. Of these Doncaster-born Atkins was to make the greatest impact.

The visit of Exeter City in mid-March under the Old Showground floodlights only managed to lever one and a half thousand people away from their firesides.

Those warming themselves by the flickering flames missed a cracker. Scunthorpe murdered the distant travellers from Devon 7-1, but the man who took the applause was Steve Cammack again. This mud splattered hero not only scored twice on the night, but he wrote his name into the record books. His second goal took his career total at Scunthorpe United to ninety-seven, thus beating the previous proud achievement of Barry Thomas. Whilst leaving the field he was mobbed by excited supporters who rushed to congratulate him. A few weeks later he hit another goal, in the 6-2 beating of Swindon Town, when eight different men scored. Just into April, Cammack reached the one hundred mark with a brace against Tranmere Rovers, when United served up another treat, winning 5-2.

The season gradually dwindled away in a series of three scoring draws. They may have been pleasing to watch, but could not raise the team near to where they needed to be to win promotion. Frank Barlow would have been able to sleep easier than a lot of Managers as his team settled in at ninth position in the table. Cammack continued to be the ace up Barlow's sleeve, scoring seven goals in the last five matches. Once again Steve Cammack was the leading goalscorer, and he made up his total for the season to twenty-five. This set the Club's stall out for a far more prosperous future.

~ 1985-86 ~

The Summer sun brought the expectancy of new players, and Frank Barlow obliged with two very strong defenders to plug the holes which had cost them points. In the central pivot position, United supporters would come to enjoy the services of Steve Lister. Lister was a well proportioned back-line player who had appeared more than two hundred times for Doncaster Rovers.

On his left hand side he was to be joined by the nimble Scotsman Billy Russell, who also came from Belle Vue. Russell had a tough pedigree, starting his football career as an apprentice at Glasgow Celtic. Along with Neil Pointon, Paul Longden and Alan Whitehead in front of Paul Gregory the low numbered shirts looked to be sorted.

The only other new player would not arrive until a couple of matches into the season, in John Hawley, an experienced forward from Bradford City. Hawley's other clubs included Leeds United and Arsenal. It meant that, as far as Scunthorpe United were concerned, the death knell had sounded on the careers of John Neenan, Derek Bell, Chris Cowling and Terry Lees. In particular it was sad to see Joe Neenan go, but he made good at Burnley. Chris Cowling was to retire from full-time football, but would still be seen round the parks in the local League's. To his credit, Cowling later attended matches as a spectator on the terraces to watch the Iron.

There was another new face at the Club, but not amongst the playing staff, for Frank Barlow had chosen Bill Green as his Assistant Manager. Bill had a similar attitude to Barlow, unruffled and firm. He had played for a number of clubs including Doncaster Rovers, West Ham United and Carlisle United, where he had been a member of the Cumbrian club's only First Division sortie, during the 1974-75 season.

Scunthorpe United began the 1985/86 season in full flow at home to Torquay United, which was played in humid conditions. Unlike the opposition, the team refused to wilt in the heat. Each half saw two goals, and a 4-0 win was quite convincing. Unfortunately the season was put on temporary hold, for there was no more victories in the next eight League matches, and Darlington beat them in the League Cup, 3-2 on aggregate. On the first day of October the mould was broken. The team achieved success against Crewe, but another loss in London against Orient followed five days later. This slump landed the Club in familiar territory at the base of the Division.

Thankfully, this was as bad as it would get, and their stay at the bottom was temporary. To strengthen the team, United paid a fee to Portsmouth for the return of their former protégé, Richard Money, to steady the midfield. This brought the ship back on course before October was out, with three consecutive draws and a victory over Hereford United. During the next month, United's travels found them heading in a Westerly direction for a Fourth Division match, played on firework night, against Preston North End. United won the game 1-0, but the crowd at a pinch more than two thousand, was the smallest ever to watch a first team match at Deepdale.

After the game, Everton stepped in with a £75,000 cheque for Neil Pointon; a record amount going into Scunthorpe United's coffers at a much needed time. For young Pointon it was the start of a first class career at the top level.

Later in the Autumn, Barlow was beset with more problems as a result of injuries to Steve Cammack and Mike Brolly. The gap was bridged when he dipped into the loan market to bring Bobby Barnes for a month from West Ham United as a tricky right winger specialist. This move helped to ease the crisis until the stresses and strains cleared up.

November saw Scunthorpe travel to Halifax to meet the Shaymen in the F.A.Cup first round. The conditions for playing football were perfect, but the awkward arrangements for viewing from the terraces were not ideal for the visiting assembly from Humberside. Honours ran out even at one goal each by half-time, and it was Dave Hill who secured United's goal. Shortly after the restart, Julian Broddle fired Scunthorpe into the lead, and from then on United were firmly in the driving seat. Steve Lister went up to support the attack and rounded it off at 3-1.

A home tussle with Rochdale in round two should have made it easy to gain a place in the third stage of the competition alongside the big boys. Tommy Graham gave United the lead, but a fighting second-half by Rochdale left Scunthorpe thankful with a 2-2 draw. That evening it was learned that the winners would face Manchester United in the hallowed Theatre of Dreams, but perhaps the thoughts of the prize stifled Scunthorpe. In the replay the Iron never got out of first gear and Rochdale were full value for a 2-1 victory. Scunthorpe United were left to rue the missed opportunities in the first game, as Dale went on to claim the pot of gold.

At the turn of the year the Fourth Division programme had shown signs of an improvement. However, the mildly spoken Frank Barlow did have to kick some backsides when Halifax Town called by the Old Showground. At one stage United trailed 0-3, but thanks to an amazing fight-back, and a hat-trick by John Hawley, the team managed a draw.

A radical improvement began to take place from Boxing Day, when the Iron played Hartlepool. The victory in front of their own supporters started a home game sequence of six matches, when only two points were squandered. If the team's away form had not been so barren they would have reached a position above halfway up the League. Instead they just had their noses clear of trouble as the Spring approached.

It was during this run to the end of the season that Frank Barlow took on another loan player to assist in this mini-revival. Kevin Dixon was the player, who operated on the right side of midfield. Although Kevin was not taken on permanently, his name was noted for future reference when he returned to his parent club Hartlepool United. Dixon was not the only man to see a Scunthorpe debut in the late stages of the fixtures, for Dave Travis, from Doncaster Rovers, came as a lithe player in the forward line, and he was joined by Keith Houchen. Houchen was a tall strong player from York City, who was used as an out and out striker. There was also a welcome return for Les Hunter, who left Chesterfield and filled his old back four position. Les slotted in exactly where he had left off, dominating the back as though he had never been away. Finally the goalkeeper's sweater changed hands, allowing Scunthorpe-born Paul Johnson to show his paces until the end of the season. This early shopping trip did not stop Frank getting the purse out again when the Summer sales were around a few months later.

Scunthorpe United rallied in the last month of the season, and with the new men on board an upturn in fortunes moved them up the table. During April, only lowly Preston North End, making a concerted effort to avoid the wooden spoon, beat them in Humberside, while on their travels the single loss was at Wrexham. Keith Houchen made his mark, demonstrating his extremes of class with three goals in nine games. Two of these helped to put down Burnley at Turf Moor. The season was finally curtailed with an excellent all-round performance against promoted Chester City, when a large number of visiting fans watched in silence as their team were licked 2-0. Steve Cammack had the honour of scoring the final goal of the season, and what a classic it was. His diving header sent the ball full-blooded into the back of the Doncaster Road goal net. This parting shot hoisted the Club into fourteenth place in Division Four.

During the break between campaigns, Frank Barlow was not happy with the goalkeeping situation, and he decided to offer a contract to Ron Green of Bristol Rovers. Green had also played at Walsall and Shrewsbury Town. The new man was immediately pressed into first team duty and proved to be a reliable sort of character. Barlow also decided on bringing in new recruits for further up the field. Among the influx were Alan Birch from Rotherham United, David McLean of Darlington, and Steve Johnson, late of Bristol City.

Alan Birch was to operate on the right hand side of the field to support the forward line, while David McLean operated in a midfield roll. Steve Johnson was well developed for the wear and tear required against tough tackling defenders.

~ 1986-87 ~

The 1986-87 season would see home grown players expected to perform in the boiling pot of the Fourth Division. Andy Stevenson, Mark Atkin and Paul Nichol all were handed the chance to show their paces. The experience did them no harm at all and, like Paul Longden and Dave Hill had done before them, young players coming through the ranks proved the value of the junior teams.

On the way out United would see no more of Tommy Graham, John Hawley, Mike Brolly and Keith Houchen. Scunthorpe United had been approached by First Division Coventry City regarding the availability of Houchen. The financial situation was not improving significantly, and when a substantial fee was offered, he left the Old Showground for Highfield Road.

Scunthorpe United opened the season at home to Northampton. The players shared four goals, but what would turn out to be the most significant factor was Steve Cammack's goal, which was to be his last. Unfortunately injuries were catching up on him and three matches later he wore the claret and blue for the last time at Orient. His final tally of goals for United set the record for others to improve upon, at hundred and twenty-one.

The beginning of the year brought League Cup battles against Darlington, and in the first leg, at home, the team took a giant stride with their 2-0 victory. There was more joy for the loyal band that set off towards the North-East, for the two goals supplied by Steve Lister allowed a 2-1 victory, and a comfortable aggregate score. At the end of September and crossing over into October, in the same competition, United had to play a useful Ipswich Town side who were now operating in Division One. It was never going to be easy, and a defeat by the odd goal in three in the home leg left the team with an uphill task. At Portman Road Ipswich took control again and scored twice more. There was meaningful applause for Scunthorpe when they left the field, because a great deal had been contributed by the lads from the lower Division.

At the time of this League Cup exit, United were in their usual position in the table just hovering below the halfway position. This season, supporters had to adjust to a new situation in their Division, for the bottom club would be replaced by the top non-League Conference side, and the teams who took up positions from fourth to seventh would play-off for promotion. Scunthorpe United's next opponents hoped to be involved further up the table to make sure of automatic promotion in the first three places. Wolverhampton Wanderers were once a household name associated with major trophies, but had now fallen from grace. They brought upwards of a thousand supporters with them, waving the club's gold and black colours. On the field of play the Wolves snarled their way through to a two goal victory, scoring once in each half.

The Wolves defeat was the middle match of a sequence of five consecutive home games. The run started when Preston North End were beaten 4-0, and finished with victories over Swansea City and Torquay United. These results did have the effect of a small rise up the table for the Club.

Before the Winter set in, United lost the services of Alan Whitehead to York City, who had not been too happy over the circumstances surrounding Keith Houchen's transfer. On the other hand Scunthorpe did give a debut to Ian Richardson, who played against the Iron for his old club, Chester City, in the ultimate game of the previous season. There was also the signing of a dynamo for midfield in David Harle from Bristol City, whose origins were in Yorkshire. David would play so hard that he would bleed for his cause. Sometimes this dedicated approach found him in trouble with the men in the black on the field.

In the F.A.Cup, United had drawn former Football League club, Southport, at home, on paper a game that Scunthorpe ought to have had not too much trouble in dealing with. On the other hand these sort of ties had seen many over-confident League sides slip up. Certainly, the Conference team started with their tails up, but with a calm professional approach the home team took control and wore them down. A goal in each half, by Dave Hill and Julian Broddle, ensured there was to be no shocks at the Old Showground.

The second round was to be a similar affair, and this time it was Runcorn who paid the Iron a formal visit. It was difficult to judge the strength of the side from the Wirral, because their passage into this part of the competition was only in the beating of Boston United away from home after a replay. Once again the opposition was given full respect by Frank Barlow. A goalless first-half had Runcorn dreaming of a top club in round three, but United would have none of it, winning 1-0 when Julian Broddle struck. This was a goal worth a king's ransom, because the third round was to take little Scunthorpe into the capital to play the mighty Tottenham Hotspur.

Into December and over the New Year, Scunthorpe United enjoyed the company of two loan signings. The first was striker David Reeves from Sheffield Wednesday, who made his mark, immediately before Christmas, by scoring twice on his debut against Exeter City. No doubt Frank Barlow would have loved to have signed the player, but the asking price was beyond his budget. Reeve's final game of his month's stay coincided with the arrival of Ken De Mange on New Year's Day. De Mange came from Liverpool where he was good enough to make an appearance for the Republic of Ireland, but not good enough to get in the Anfield team. Liverpool were gracious enough to allow him to play in the F.A.Cup game at White Hart Lane, and that was the subject preoccupying everyone at that time.

On 10th January 1987, a posse of buses filed off from Henderson Avenue to make the journey South to London. At kick-off, almost twenty thousand supporters had paid through the turnstiles. Most of the noise came from the visiting supporters, who were sporting their claret and blue favours, on what was the most bitter cold of Winter days.

As they stamped their feet to keep warm the teams lined up as follows:-

Tottenham H.: Clemence, D.Thomas, M.Thomas, Hodge, Gough, Mabbutt, C.Allen, P.Allen, Waddle, Hoddle, Claesen.
Scunthorpe Utd..: Green, Money, Longden, De Mange, Lister, Atkins, Russell, McLean, Johnson, Broddle, Hill.

was asked to step down. Frank had done his duties in a dignified manner and won many friends for being a gentleman. Unfortunately the buck had to stop with him, and he fell to the inevitable. Scunthorpe United's Board were in no hurry to appoint a successor to Frank Barlow, and Richard Money was put in temporary charge of team affairs, with Bill

Julian Broddle shoots from just outside the penalty area, in the end of season match with Rochdale. In May 1987.

United won 2-0

The game kicked-off at a fast pace, and Scunthorpe gave a brave account of themselves. They showed they could give as good as they took and were generally cool under pressure. Garry Mabbutt, the Spurs captain, gave Tottenham the lead, but Steve Johnson forced an equaliser before half-time. In the second-half the Cockerel of the London club began to crow as Claesen and Waddle put the game beyond the reach of Scunthorpe. The Waddle goal was the pick of the bunch, when he hit a vicious swerving shot from distance which Ron Green could be forgiven for not seeing.

United continued to press forward, and Ken De Mange made the scoreline looked respectable at 3-2. At the end of the game there was generous praise for the visitors. Tottenham went on to Wembley, but were undone by Scunthorpe old boy Keith Houchen. Houchen's famous diving header helped Coventry lift the F.A.Cup for the first time.

Scunthorpe United now had to concentrate on the League programme, where the team was not able to make any sort of impression on the leading pack. The Club did pursue their policy of obtaining loan players once again, and took Mark North for a month from Luton Town. The highlight of his stay was without doubt the 6-0 thrashing of Tranmere Rovers at home. North did not score in that game, but he hit both goals in the next one, when Aldershot paid a visit and lost 2-0. This thin wedge of good form was followed by an eight match spell without a win.

Scunthorpe United's poor showing in the Winter, and lack of tangible success, meant the Board could not stand by and allow the situation to continue. At the turn of March, Chairman Tom Belton regrettably informed Frank Barlow that his contract with the Club would not be renewed, and he

Green keeping a weather eye on the situation at the same time. It was during this state of limbo that Andy Flounders, a cheeky goal poacher, came from Hull City. It was one of the most astute signings of the decade, and he was to become a regular goalscorer for a number of years to come. There was even time for Scunthorpe to earn a line in the National Press. Julian Broddle hit the headlines with a goal after ten seconds in the 3-0 beating of Southend United.

Eventually it was announced, on 15th April, that the former Huddersfield Town boss, Mick Buxton, had accepted the position of Manager. He was a determined sort of a man who did not suffer fools gladly. Once he had introduced himself it was straight down to work. Buxton had only seven games left to impress, and his formula produced six wins and a draw. Suddenly, United rocketed up the table and finished miraculously in eighth position, their highest position all season. The question was how far would the Iron have got if Buxton had signed earlier in the season?

~ 1987-88 ~

Those seven matches in charge gave Mick Buxton plenty of time to assess the playing staff. During the ten week break until the battle royal recommenced he had decided on his strategy. In defence he had chosen another towering central defender in Tony Brown from Doncaster Rovers. It meant that with Brown, Russell, Lister, Harle and Assistant Manager Bill Green, United could almost field a team of Rovers' old boys. Kevin Dixon had become available at Hartlepool, and this time Buxton took him on a permanent contract. There was also the quick-flighted Tony Daws, a slightly built youngster from Sheffield United. It would take a little while, but Daws and Flounders became synonymous with goal-scoring at Scunthorpe, like Toshack and Keegan at Liverpool.

Mick Buxton decided that there would be no room for Paul Gregory, Dave Travis and Les Hunter in his plans. Les incredibly went back to Chesterfield, signing for the Derbyshire club for a third spell.

The sensational news released from Scunthorpe United in the Summer was the confirmation by the Board of Directors that the Club would be leaving the Old Showground at the end of the season. In charge of overseeing the operation was their new Chairman, Graham Pearson, who had taken over from Tom Belton. Mr Belton was still in the picture but had opted for the Assistant Chairman's position. A number of public meetings took place to explain the Club's situation. The main point was that negotiations had been entered into with the Safeway Supermarket chain to buy the land on which the Old Showground stood. Cash raised from the sale would pay off the Club's crippling debts and allow them to build a completely new showpiece stadium. There might even be a small surplus to put by for team building.

The construction firm of Birse and Company had been consulted to build the new structure. This was not a case of choice, for United had to follow this scheme through, or the Club would fold. This statement won the supporters over immediately with minimum opposition, albeit much sadness.

At future meetings there were discussions as to where the new ground should be sited. Eventually an area of farm land outside the town boundary, in Glanford, was purchased. It was difficult for supporters to visualise the new stadium from the plot of ground situated between Doncaster Road and the main railway line to Doncaster. Once the corn had been harvested, the construction workers moved in and gradually the area was pegged out and walls were put together to mark the outside boundaries of the ground. The phoenix was rising, with a distant glance at the forlorn floodlights of the condemned Old Showground.

On the playing field, Mick Buxton's men got off to the positive start they would have wished for, when they beat Tranmere Rovers 3-0. All the goals came in the second-half, after a cagey first forty-five minutes. The team even progressed in the League Cup, now sponsored by Littlewoods. Hartlepool United were the Scunthorpe victims, beaten in both legs of the competition. The next step was to engage Leicester City, then residing in the Second Division. At Filbert Street United put up a plucky display but lost 2-1. Andy Flounders' running up field, plus a well taken goal was a feature of the game. In the second phase at the Old Showground a similar score gave Leicester an easy 4-2 aggregate, but Buxton's men had made them fight for it.

At the conclusion of the Club's sojourn in the League Cup, United supporters were introduced to a new half-back, Kevin "Ticker" Taylor. Kevin was a Yorkshire son, who signed from Crystal Palace. His vision and distribution were light years in front of that normally expected in the Fourth Division. Buxton had unearthed a real gem. The Manager also dipped into the loan system to bring David Reeves for another month, and Dave Cowling from his old club Huddersfield.

In the Fourth Division, there were smiles as Scunthorpe United gradually climbed towards the top area of the League. Only high-flying Wolverhampton Wanderers and Carlisle managed to lower United's colour before the end of October, both games taking place away from home. Perhaps they enjoyed their best forty-five minutes of football in the second-half at Darlington, where they advanced from a goal each to score three more through Kevin Dixon, Steve Lister and Andy Flounders. The climax of this treat for supporters was when they remarkably reached the dizzy heights of second place, following a 2-1 result at the Old Showground against Cardiff City. Unfortunately, that was as far as it would go and throughout the rest of the Autumn there was a gradual easing back on the throttle.

One of the team's problems happened when Scarborough, freshly promoted into the League at the expense of Lincoln City, made a first appearance since Midland League days. It was very unfortunate that the Boro goalkeeper had to be stretchered off with a broken leg. The visiting club's motto on their crest stated "No battle, no victory", and that is something for which the seaside team could be credited. A sterling tussle was fought, and they became the first team to win a Fourth Division match at the Old Showground that term.

The Scarborough 1-0 reserve did not put United off their stride in the F.A.Cup game that came along seven days later. Scunthorpe had to face a Bury side bristling with form, who lay towards the sharp end of Division Three. The paying customers at the Old Showground were to witness a remarkable hat-trick by Billy Russell. This was the only trio ever recorded by a Scunthorpe United full-back, with one of the goals coming from a penalty spot-kick.

Scunthorpe United's second round opponents were to be Sunderland. The North-Eastern giants had slid for a temporary drop into the Third Division, but were top of the pile when they were selected to travel South to Humberside. It was a tie that struck the right chord with Mick Buxton who had connections in the area. On the day of the game the Rokerites poured into the Showground, filling the Fox Street end. When the turnstile returns were worked out more than twice the Bury gate had attended the game, and a figure of 7,178 was announced. Sunderland took the honours in the first period of play and went ahead through the quick-witted Eric Gates, once of Ipswich Town. Buxton rallied his troops for the second-half as they attacked the Doncaster Road goal, behind which their own faithful were massed. Suddenly the tables turned on the visitors, when United's own mid-field powerhouse, Kevin Taylor, scored the equalising goal and David Harle showed the forwards how to capitalise by hitting the winner. The Scunthorpe United fans took every opportunity to cock a snook at their deposed opponents.

During the last month of 1987, United only completed one win in their Fourth Division programme. This particular event rounded off the double over Darlington. However, the Quakers made life for Scunthorpe a lot more difficult, and only a poached strike from Andy Flounders registered on the goalscoring sheet. The situation improved over the first two days of the New Year, when Scunthorpe United became one of only a few teams to take six points in forty-eight hours. A 3-0 victory on New Years day, thanks to Tony Daw's first brace for the Club, and another by Steve Lister, made a most rewarding journey to Colchester United.

The second week of 1988 found the Club on F.A.Cup duty against yet another Third Division club. This time it was Blackpool and ground advantage brought back fond memories of the 6-2 victory in 1961. The game that ensued saw no such high jinx, but instead the sweat and graft resulted in a scoreless match. In midweek fans froze at the seaside, and those from Scunthorpe who suffered in the cold were disappointed when the men in tangerine scored a single goal in the second period.

Scunthorpe United now had to concentrate on their Fourth Division fixtures and were helped in the interim by another loan player. Martin Taylor arrived from Derby County, and took the goalkeeper's gloves for eight consecutive League games up to the end of January. When he returned to his parent club, United had slipped to eleventh place, but that was the furthest down the ladder they would reach. A successful February began with Joe Neenan back between the posts and Dave Shearer, a Scotsman, taken on as an all out attacker. Shearer had an impressive scoring record, particularly during his time at Middlesbrough and Gillingham, but United unloaded him from Bournemouth.

Dave Shearer's debut was a most remarkable event against Leyton Orient. The Londoners went in at half-time a goal up, even though Scunthorpe had fought with them tooth and nail all the way. Later in the second-half the 'O's' made it 2-0, something that had the Iron's honest endeavours pale into the mist. Then came three last astonishing minutes of the game. David Harle fired in two goals and Shearer netted on his debut. Visiting London supporters held their heads in shock and disbelief.

The match against Leyton Orient began the run to the finishing line, and so focused were Buxton's men that only Wrexham were able to torpedo them into defeat. The team won the next two matches outright, one of which was at home to Peterborough. The London Road boys were scuppered 5-0 and Andy Flounders did his reputation no harm with a trio of strikes. He was in excellent form, but he was not monopolising the goals, for it was a great delight to see them flying in from all angles. A point in case was the beauty Dave Shearer scored at Cardiff City's Ninian Park. The sparse crowd in the stadium's vast bowl looked on awestruck when the player made the most of a defensive mix-up, and scored from the acutest angle imaginable, to delight a hundred or so visiting fans. This lifted the Club into the second place in the table for the second time.

There was even hopes of an automatic promotion place at this stage in the season. The way the Club were playing they deserved to have some sort of award, but unfortunately, a run of four consecutive draws put the prize in jeopardy. The last of these was to celebrate the final game at the Old Showground against Exeter City. There was a recall of dozens of old favourite players to parade before the crowd which numbered 6,736, and a souvenir programme was printed. The party spirit was spoiled somewhat when Exeter scored a controversial goal two minutes from time, which the United team appealed against. The 1-1 result meant that Scunthorpe had to beat fellow promotion candidates Torquay United in Devon to put them out of the reckoning, and Bolton Wanderers had to lose at Wrexham.

At the time, Torquay United as the home club, were enforcing a ban on away supporters due to alleged trouble caused when Wolverhampton Wanderers played them earlier. As a result a number of ingenious methods were used to smuggle Scunthorpe supporters incognito into the ground, all using Devon accents with heavy northern undertones. At the kick-off the near capacity five thousand crowd were treated to a cloudburst, and those persons packed into exposed places had to endure the torrents of water that trickled down their necks and into their boots.

Scunthorpe United set about the match in the right frame of mind, with a goal by Flounders before the break, and a decisive winner by Ian Richardson gave United a vital 2-1 victory. This was achieved despite the biased cries against the visitors' every move from large sections of the home support. Then came the crushing news from Wrexham. The Wrexham team had been reduced to ten men, and Bolton won the third automatic promotion spot with a late winner from midfielder Bob Savage.

This situation put United in fourth place in the table, and they were obliged to enter the dreaded play-offs. Ironically their opponents would be Torquay United, who had settled in seventh spot. This meant an eleventh hour reprieve for the Old Showground, while the last promotion option was decided.

There was some more controversy before the game at Plainmoor in the play-off semi-final first leg, for the Devon club did not want Scunthorpe supporters at the game. United appealed to the Football League to have the decision reversed. The League came down on Scunthorpe's side, but to counteract this, the Torquay club arranged a mid-day kick-off, in an effort to minimise the number of travelling fans.

This did not deter the Iron supporters setting off at four in the morning to shout for their team. There was also the question of Torquay United's striker Caldwell playing in the play-off game. The Devon club appealed against a lengthy ban that was imposed for his alleged disciplinary problems, and with their plea successful, it meant Caldwell could play in the next two matches.

It must be said that the first leg of the Semi-Final was an 'x-rated' affair, with both teams fiercely committed. Scunthorpe felt hard done by when Paul Nichol was given a red card for a challenge which left an opponent apparently playing possum. Other incidents included a mystery offside flag to disallow a Scunthorpe goal when the offending man appeared nowhere near the play to interfere. Then the Torquay manager was sent away from the pitch, after running on to make a one man protest, following the flattening in the second-half of Mr Caldwell.

The facts of the matter were that Torquay led at the interval by 2-0, through Caldwell and Dobson. In the second-half, Flounders capitalised on a howler by Kenny Allen in the Gulls defence, to pull one back. At this point the door was still ajar on promotion, but a lot of work was still needed if it was to be prized open.

It was in a mood of sadness on the one hand, and with the desire for revenge on the other, that the last game took place at the Old Showground. After almost ninety years of use by the Club, almost six and a half thousand spectators turned out for what was the end of an era, and visiting supporters were made most welcome. Injuries and a suspension depleted the Scunthorpe team to the bare bones. The final line-ups on Wednesday 18th 1988 were as follows:-

breaking up this proud part of Scunthorpe United's history. So keen were the contractors, that Barnes had to rescue some of his groundsman's equipment from being scrapped. Eventually the pillars were cut from the stands and the pylons of the floodlights brought to their knees. The burners torch reduced the stadium to dust. There had been talk of taking the country's first cantilever stand to Doncaster Rugby club, but this too fell victim to the cutting flame.

Many a tear was shed. Within twelve months shoppers would be buying groceries on the site in the Safeway supermarket. The legend would now continue on a completely new ground. United's history was as strong as ever, but it would now continue down the road at the new pristine stadium of Glandford Park.

The first leg of the Play-off Semi-Final. Flounders heads the ball in an attack on the Torquay United goal.

Scunthorpe Utd: Green, Stevenson, Longden, Taylor, Lister, McLean, Richardson, Shearer, Daws, Flounders, Hill. Torquay United: Allen, McNichol, Kelly, Haslegrave, Cole, Impey, Pearce, Lloyd, Loram, Dobson, Gibbins.

Scunthorpe used Atkin and Dixon as substitutes for Longden and Richardson. Torquay swapped Pearce for Sharpe, and in turn Sharpe gave way for Caldwell. The game at the Old Showground was no less full of passion, but players did behave themselves a little better. A goalless first-half saw plenty of work, but it was Torquay United's band of travellers that cheered first when Mark Loram shot them into the lead. Scunthorpe knew their chance of promotion was over. There was a slight flicker of light when Steve Lister scored from the penalty spot at the Doncaster Road end with eight minutes left, and although the team rallied, the legs had gone. There was to be no promotion for the Club this time. The Scunthorpe players sunk to the ground drained as the Devon men celebrated. For Torquay United talk of playing in the Third Division was to be terminated when Swansea City leapfrogged in front in the final, winning 5-4 on aggregate.

Once the Torquay game was over Ronnie Barnes, United's groundsman, had the task of dismantling the goal posts after the Old Showground lights had shone for the last time. Supporters took parts of the seats and lumps of the pitch home as souvenirs. The firm of Churchills, in which Chairman Mr Pearson was involved, moved in early to start

The last goal ever scored at the Old Showground. Steve Lister nets the ball from the penalty spot in the Play-off second leg versus Torquay United on the 18th May 1988.

## CHAPTER 13

THE GLANFORD PARK SAGA...
....AND A CENTENARY PROMOTION

Scunthorpe United now had a proud new stadium at Glanford Park. The Club had been pathfinders in the project of ground development in the wake of the Bradford City fire and other football disasters, and this was the role model for building a completely fresh arena from a green field site. It was the first time since Port Vale moved to Vale Park, midway through the 1950's, that a club had opted to leave their old ground and start again. Other sides would consult the Scunthorpe board in future with a view to following suit. Within ten years there would be a least ten other similar schemes that had been built, planned or contemplated.

Scunthorpe United had to wait until the 27th August for their first home game in the Fourth Division to start the season. During that time they tried to gain clearance for Dutchman Rob De Lang from amateur club D.A.C. in Dan Haag. Rob did play in the opening friendly game, but it was a great disappointment that he was never granted papers for a permanent stay and had to return. Another player who would not stop long was Paul Rumble. His loan spell from Watford lasted through September but was not extended. A player that did stay the course was a tall young goalkeeper, Paul Musslewhite, who had been a second choice for his native Portsmouth.

History is made! The first kick-off at Glanford Park on 14th August 1988.

~ 1988-89 ~

The stadium that opened its door on Sunday 14th August 1988, brought gasps of disbelief from supporters, for generally speaking everyone was impressed with the product. It was given Royal approval by the Princess Alexandria and her husband Angus Ogilvy. Other VIP guests included Football League Secretary Graham Kelly and civic dignitaries from the district. The opening game was a star-studded Football League eleven, headed by Graham Taylor, against a Scunthorpe United side, supplemented by old boy Kevin Keegan. United looked very smart in claret and blue striped shirts, with the 'Brikenden' sponsor's name across the front. A crowd of close to five thousand watched in shirtsleeves and summer dresses, as the Football League XI turned on the style. They strolled to a 5-1 victory, as was to be expected with the array of the country's top talent on display. Dave Shearer had the honour of scoring Scunthorpe United's first goal at the Park twelve minutes from time. The result was not the important factor, it was the introduction to this splendid stadium with a capacity for 11,266. All the crowd had been thrilled with what they had seen and generous applause was afforded to the players as they left the field to sign autographs.

When Mick Buxton pitched him in at the deep end from the very start he responded in the manner expected and by the end of the season he had appeared in all but five games. Other newly arrived men were Andy Hodkinson, Julian Winter and Dave Cowling. Signing from Stockport County, Hodkinson took up in the number seven shirt as support for the attacking players. Julian Winter was another loan man, coming from Huddersfield, but like Rumble he did not last long. On the other hand former loanee, Dave Cowling, decided to take up the option for a contract with his old mentor at Glanford Park. Paul Smalley, a no nonsense full-back from Notts County, was to soon join the new men.

The move to Glanford Park did not materialise for a handful of the previous season's workhorses. United decided not to offer terms to Ron Green, Billy Russell, David McLean, Kevin Dixon, Alan Birch and Steve Johnson. In addition Ipswich Town took a shine for Dave Hill and came in with a substantial fee. Then Mark Atkins left for Blackburn Rovers in strained circumstances; his transfer was fixed by a tribunal at £45,000 plus a sell on clause.

On 27th August 1988, Scunthorpe United filed out of the tunnel at Glanford Park, hoping to get off to a winning start.

Goalmouth action in the first League game at the new venue - 27 August. Tony Daws, Andy Flounders, Andy Hodkinson and Steve Lister are the United players in stripes attacking the Hereford goal

The teams for this historic occasion lined up as follows:-
Scunthorpe Utd: Musslewhite, Longden, Rumble, Taylor, Lister, Brown, Hodkinson, Winter, Shearer, Flounders, Cowling.
Hereford Utd: Rose, M.Jones, Crane, Pejic, Steves, Maddy, Campbell, R.Jones, Stant, Devine, McLaughlin.

Scunthorpe used Daws for Shearer on thirty-one minutes, while Stevenson was the other substitute who did not play. Hereford changed Campbell for Bowyer and R.Jones for Benow.

Scunthorpe started the game cautiously in their new £2½ million home, not wishing to make a mistake to begin with. The forward line was disrupted when Dave Shearer was forced to retire through injury, but Tony Daws, with his darting runs, was more than a capable deputy. United's supporters in the official gate of 3,663, announced by secretary Don Rowing, had to wait until after the interval for the real action. The first goal came in the forty-seventh minute from Dave Cowling. Julian Winter delivered the ball into a crowded goalmouth, and Cowling forced it in, past Kevin Rose, from close range. The next strike was four minutes later, and came as a solo effort from substitute Tony Daws, who took the ball from the halfway line and steered a delightful shot low to the left hand side of Rose.

Hereford United did manage to pull one back through McLaughlin, but generally they played second fiddle to a rampant Scunthorpe side. Five minutes from time 'Ticker' Taylor made it 3-1. A corner was only cleared to Taylor on the edge of the box, and his sweet volley found its way through a pack of players into the net, where the local supporters were massed. Scunthorpe were off to the flying start they had wished for.

The floodlights were used for the first time on the following Tuesday evening. Buxton had the dilemma of finding a full squad to play against his old side, Huddersfield Town, in the League Cup. Eventually a patched up team was assembled to play the Terriers, whose eleven included former England International Peter Withe.

The gate of just short of four thousand were to see a dazzling performance from both camps. Huddersfield took the initiative as early as the fourth minute, although Flounders equalised fifteen minutes into the second-half. Huddersfield went ahead with twenty-five minutes remaining. Then came the sting in the tail. Two goals in the last ten minutes, from Lister and Hodkinson set the Scunthorpe crowd buzzing and gave United a strong chance in the second leg.

At Leeds Road the drama continued. Andy Flounders looked to have secured the tie for the Iron, scoring before the interval, then the worm turned and Maskell and Trevitt put the celebrations on hold. Scunthorpe supporters had to suffer the tension of extra time, but another goal from Flounders put them through 5-4 on aggregate, and two apiece on the night.

This result was to see a money-spinning game materialise against the blue city slickers of the King's Road from Chelsea. Chelsea were residents of the Second Division, and would top the Division at the end of the season, with just one League point short of the ton. There were fears of crowd trouble from the excitable Londoners followers, but those who attended in the five thousand crowd behaved impeccably. These fans would not have enjoyed the way Scunthorpe ripped into the smooth Chelsea runners, and after forty-five minutes United had scored twice, but an earlier error by Steve Lister resulted in an own goal. Then came a half of whirlwind football that cruised Scunthorpe into an unlikely 4-1 lead at the end of the first leg.

The second part of this tussle caused another problem for those who wished to see the match. A play-off game between Chelsea and Middlesbrough had seen a flare up between rival supporters at the end of the previous season, and incredibly all away travellers were banned from Stamford Bridge. It was an ingredient to keep Scunthorpe United's loyal hordes from attending. This did not stop some fans secreting themselves into the Bridge with tickets begged from various local Southern sources. The attendance of less than 6,000 was one of the smallest ever to watch any Chelsea match. Those supporters who did make it were astonished to see Scunthorpe hold their own and draw 2-2.

In the Fourth Division League programme, six thousand people watched the first Glanford Park derby with Grimsby Town, a week after Prime Minster Margaret Thatcher had given the stadium her blessing. There was probably more interest in the 1-1 draw than in the honourable lady, and Scunthorpe should have buried the opposition. Then in October the fans had the horror of a huge 3-0 defeat by a useful Scarborough team who, for a short time, would be considered a bogie side. This saw the team tumble into thirteenth place in the League. From there on the results began to improve, especially as three consecutive wins were strung together at the end of the month.

There was the unusual situation of United still in two cup competitions when November broke. In the early part of the month the team went off for a skirmish with Bradford City in the League Cup. The stadium had been rebuilt from the tragic days of the horrific fire, and eight thousand spectators made their way into the spacious ground of a team midway in the Second Division. The hero and villain for Scunthorpe was Paul Musslewhite. He brought off a procession of fine saves, but could not hold on to the ball for Bradford's thirty-sixth minute goal. Five minutes into the second-half, Tony Daws struck from close range to beat Litchfield in the City goal. There were several anxious moments before the replay was won, but thanks to Lister and Longden at the back, United survived.

The replay had to be postponed, ironically because of England International duties, not that too many Scunthorpe players had to fear being called up! It meant that United could fit in an F.A.Cup first round game on the West Coast against Blackpool. Scunthorpe United ran their legs-off but had nothing other than a David Harle penalty to show for their efforts. Blackpool struck twice earlier in the match and went on to play Bury in round two, after their 2-1 success.

Three days later Glanford Park had another large attendance for the return of Bradford City, when unfortunately there was to be a second exit from a knockout tie. Leonard scored the only vital goal of the evening but it was a highly contentious point. A Scunthorpe shot was scrambled away from the line, and those in attendance vowed that it was the net side of the base line and a goal should have stood. The officials were not in a position to confirm the action, and play was waved on.

On Boxing Day, United introduced a new player to the Glanford Park faithful, for the home visit of Hartlepool, in Ian Hamilton from Cambridge United. Hamilton, a very educated footballer and a shrewd signing, was to make the engine room tick and frequently would make an impact in the forward position. In his first game, United looked to be beaten until the last few minutes, when a fist rose out of the Hartlepool defence to punch the ball clear. There was no green sleeve on the end of the hand, and Harle dispatched the penalty.

The Hartlepool game was one of three consecutive draws, which were followed by two defeats, and had Mick Buxton frowning. Tranmere Rovers won 1-0 at Glanford Park with the most amazing own goal ever seen on the field.

Steve Lister was under no pressure when he looped a header back to Paul Musselwhite from twenty-five yards. The problem was that Musselwhite was unable to reach this doubtful pass back.

Two days into the New Year, Mick Buxton was further angered by his subordinates when they visited Halifax Town. Not only was the 5-1 reverse the worst result of the campaign, but it was an affront to the Scunthorpe supporters who had paid hard earned cash to travel with their team. Buxton made up his mind to immediately improve the situation from the back with the loan signing of 'keeper David Brown from Preston North End for a month. Within two weeks the manager also took on board David Cork for the defence role from West Bromwich Albion. The effect was immediately seen in results. On the next Saturday morning after losing to Halifax Town, United dismantled Stockport County at Edgeley Park, with the duo of Flounders and Daws producing the goals in the 2-1 win. These two worked as a formidable combination, and although they lacked inches in height, they made up with dash and an uncanny instinct to poach in front of the posts. It was a partnership to rival Brown and Gregory, or Thomas and Godfrey, of earlier years.

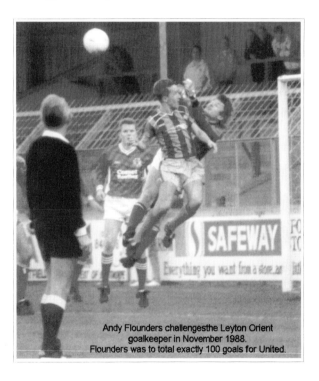

Andy Flounders challenges the Leyton Orient goalkeeper in November 1988. Flounders was to total exactly 100 goals for United.

Scunthorpe enter the last third of the season in virtually unstoppable form. Throughout the Winter and into the Spring their results were encouraging. On a handful of occasions positive scores had them jostling with the leaders, as high as second in the table. Twice they achieved heartening 3-0 away victories, at Carlisle and Cambridge, the same score at home to Peterborough brought Andy Flounders a hat-trick. To supporters dismay two very important matches in the final phase did not produce the wins they wanted. Over ten thousand supporters watched the match at Tranmere in a continuous downpour, but the drenched Scunthorpe fans on an open bank had to suffer losing 2-1.

Later, at home to Rotherham United, the eventual champions, a record 8,775 crowd saw a tight defensive guard on both sides prevent any goals being scored on May day.

The empty seats give a false impression of the crowd numbers for the Rotherham match in May!

Only two games remained. The first was a simple thrashing of Darlington 5-1 at Glanford Park, which not only lifted Scunthorpe into the automatic promotion spot of second, but it relegated the poor visitors to the Vauxhall Conference. It was difficult to watch the weeping Darlington supporters. All that remained was a trip to Leyton Orient, where a draw could have been sufficient. In the event a couple of thousand Scunthorpe travellers saw a disastrous crash when the team lost 4-1. Anxious hearts missed many a beat as other results were waited for around the country. The worst fears were confirmed when Dario Gradi took a necessary point at Tranmere, and United were condemned once again to the play-offs.

The dubious treat was to be a visit to Wrexham which had not been a happy hunting ground in recent times, and already they had lost 2-0 at the Racecourse Ground. This next episode would be just as harrowing, for Wrexham raced into the lead and completely dominated the affair. Dave Cowling did give the Iron some hope, but at 3-1 down they needed a piece of devine inspiration in the home leg at Glanford Park. The five and a half thousand watched mainly in silence, as two goals by Russell for the Welsh dragons sealed United's fate by half-time. The game finished at 2-0 in the visitors favour. This sweat and toil would be repeated in the Fourth Division the following season when Leyton Orient sneaked promotion through the back door, beating Wrexham in the final.

There had been valuable lessons learned from the 1988-89 season, with the new surroundings at Glanford Park. Now, twelve months later, they had to make it into an impregnable fortress that teams feared to visit, and not find it a novelty to take advantage of. Further use had to be made of the diamond set in Flounders and Daws, for their strikes had totalled twenty and twenty-seven goals respectively. The disappointments of the play-offs had to be put behind them, and then surely promotion would come.

In an attempt to solve the goalkeeping situation Mike Buxton went to Bradford City to sign the custodian who had kept them out in the League Cup, Peter Litchfield, who had represented Preston North End before his move to Valley Parade. The healthy competition between Litchfield and Musslewhite kept both men on their toes, and both would have a share in the position. Buxton went back to Huddersfield where he knew the ability of midfielder Gordon Tucker. There was a chance given to Ian Knight of Sheffield Wednesday, who was trying to regain his standing after a tragic broken leg. Scunthorpe took him on loan but the move broke down after a couple of games. Likewise Martin Bulter was given a couple of games but failed to win a contract as a forward player. However, New Zealander Perry Cotton, another front quarters man, did win extended opportunities, but usually for only part of most games. The signing to gain star status was that of Gary Marshall, a winger for the left side of the park. United forked out a record £50,000 to gain his services, and it was expected that the Daws and Flounders story would flourish under his influence.

Mick Buxton was continuously searching for the right talent refusing to sign any clubs' castoffs and old crocks. Before September was out he dipped into the wallet again and made a brilliant signing in Mark Lillis, another of his Huddersfield Town discoveries, whose immense skills had caused Manchester City, Derby County and Aston Villa to court his services. For Scunthorpe United this signature was a tremendous boost.

To make way for the new talents there were the inevitable condemned men. Tony Brown decided to head into Lancashire with Rochdale, and David Cork found an appointment with Darlington in the Conference. Cork was to assist this club back into the League within a year as the non-League champions. Dave Shearer also went with his colleague to Feethams, while David Harle found a niche at Peterborough. Finally Ian Richardson went out of League football altogether to play for Staines Town.

~ 1989-90 ~
Scunthorpe United's start to the 1989-90 season was not the most auspicious in their history. They lost the local derby in the first game at Sincil Bank 1-0, and then repeated the same score at home to Rochdale. At the end of that game Tony Brown in the Dale strip was wearing the biggest smile. There was disappointment, too, when Scarborough continued to cast an evil spell over the Iron and knocked them out of

the League Cup. In the away leg a couple of sendings off did not helped the team, and an aggregate score of 3-1 saw the chances perish.

The early part of the season did have a stop/go stutter about it. Gillingham were thwarted at the Priestfield stadium by a three goal barrage in the second-half, after a void initial period. Scarborough continued to haunt the Scunthorpe dreams, and they returned to lever away the points with a 1-0 score, although United recovered sufficiently to beat the champions-to-be, Exeter City, by the odd goal in nine. It was a tremendous exhibition of attacking football which advertised Fourth Division football at its best; conversely it was a defenders nightmare. The game saw Mark Lillis pump the air twice, as he celebrated goals on his debut. Then came two results that found Scunthorpe in contrasting theatres. At home to Colchester a 4-0 pommelling of the visitors had the Iron on their metal. Seven days later they trailed 4-1 at the interval to Cambridge and eventually lost 5-3. One of the Cambridge goals was rather bizarre, for the wind caught a forward directed ball and dropped it from distance high over Litchfield into the back of the Scunthorpe net.

At Cambridge, United brought on a new signing as substitute, in Paul Ward, a midfielder from Leyton Orient. Ward had originally been a Chelsea apprentice, but played his first League games for Middlesbrough. Immediately Buxton drafted him into the engine room with good effect.

November brought an interesting number of matches in three different modes. Nothing has been mentioned of the Associated Members Cup as yet. It is always thought of as a second class competition by the public, until the final round where Wembley beckons. The value of a brief mention in 1989 is merited, for at long last United were able to break the hoodoo against Scarborough. It may have only been a 1-0 win but the psychological victory was the most important factor. Days later there was the unusual arrangement of a morning kick-off against Burnley. This was instigated by the police to beat the possible drinking problems which might materialise with the large travelling

element from Turf Moor. In the event both sets of supporters were immaculately behaved, and United turned up the heat in the first forty-five minutes with three winning goals.

Midway through the month, United were at loggerheads with H.F.S. League team Matlock Town in the F.A.Cup first round. The contest did not last long, and when Lillis headed in a flick from Ward on seven minutes, the game was made to feel secure. Lillis forced another on twenty-four minutes at close range, from Marshall's pass. Seconds after the interval and a left-footed shot by Hodkinson made it 3-0. There was a brief response from the brave non-Leaguers when they pulled one back with their only effort on target, but when they lost a man for a second bookable offence there was no possibility of a comeback. Finally, another Marshall/Lillis combination rounded off a fine hat-trick by the Manchester-born forward. Statisticians noted that this was only the fifth F.A.Cup trio by a Scunthorpe player since they went into League football in 1950.

The saga of the F.A.Cup continued when Mick Buxton found his present club drawn against Burnley, his former one. Confidence should have been high when bearing in mind the other claret and blues had already been demolished in the Fourth Division. But there was a problem to overcome, for physio Phil McLaughlin was working overtime on the queue of players wanting treatment. As it happened, Scunthorpe scored a couple of goals either side of two by Burnley, although Buxton was not totally happy with the way Scunthorpe had performed. The manager looked forward to a more committed team effort in the replay, which might see them indulge themselves with an away tie in round three against Blackpool.

The replay brought a much better display from Scunthorpe at Turf Moor. Although they fell behind to a Roger Eli goal on twenty seven minutes, Tony Daws restored the balance on the hour. But their fight was compounded by the sending-off of Andy Stevenson for two bookable offences. Due to this second draw another replay was required, in Burnley.

Richard Hall (later sold for £250,000 to Southampton), in a heading dual, made his debut in the Grimsby Town match.

Unfortunately United were to be stream rollered by the home side who were in a rampant mood, and everything they did had the Midas touch about it. The Iron were crushed 5-0, and were left bemused by three goals between the forty-fourth and fiftieth minute of the game. It did not stop the pack of Scunthorpe supporters giving the bedraggled losers a standing ovation for the 'never stop chasing' play the team had put in during the frustrating ninety minutes.

Back to the day-to-day chores of Division Four, United were to let their momentum slide through a series of draws and defeats. The first of these matches was a highly entertaining affair against the Mariners, before the second biggest crowd at Glan-ford Park, of 8,384 spectators. It was a Boxing Day fixture which Scunthorpe looked to have sewn up by the mid-point, through goals by Daws and Marshall.

The rest of the match brought a gradual recovery by the Town team, who were perched just below the Iron in the table. Eventually they pulled the score back, scoring the killer blow with less than ten minutes on the watch. Team selection problems had forced Buxton to promote Richard Hall from the reserves for his debut, which the young lad administered from a central defensive position with honour. Later, this tall player would play solidly enough to keep more experienced men out of the team.

Mark Lillis scores United's goal, at home to Lincoln. Lillis was destine to become the Assistant manager, while his opponent, Matt Carmichael, would also wear the claret and blue.

To deal with the injury crisis for the time being, Mick Buxton went to Halifax Town to buy John Bramhall. Bramhall's service was as a back line man where his height was of great advantage. Already he had played over four hundred matches as far afield as Bury, Tranmere Rovers and Rochdale. His inclusion would stem the flow of goals into the Scunthorpe net, after signing in January. Supporters on the terraces nicknamed him "whoosh", because of the distances he could kick the ball, particularly from a deal ball situation.

Scunthorpe United's run without a League win extended to ten matches, but only Chesterfield and Rochdale beat them during this time, as there were to be five goalless draws to endure, including four in consecutive games. This left fans exasperated with their tongues hanging out waiting for an illusive goal. The famine ended in great style. Stockport County were the lambs to the slaughter, losing by five goals, Paul Ward netting the last, to give the starved Glanford Park fans something to cheer about at last.

The Stockport County result began a sequence which was in contrast to their struggling inconsistency, whereby four games on the trot ended with three points each time. Once again United were in contention for a play-off spot. The rules of the competition reminded everyone that a late acceleration to secure the seventh League place could poach promotion through 'the back door'. Their second-half onslaught at Torquay produced three goals and took them up to ninth in the division. It was unfortunate that poor returns towards the end of March blew all their chances away.

When Doncaster Rovers visited on the last day of the season, Scunthorpe supporters knew they would be staying in Division Four next season, and the same old mundane teams in the main had to be faced again. It could have been worse, because Colchester United's fans would not have League fixtures to enjoy, for they were guaranteed Conference soccer for the immediate future. At least a match with the Iron's Yorkshire cousins was an eventful afternoon's entertainment, as both sets of supporters embraced themselves with verbal abuse. The Doncaster following soon wondered why they had bothered coming, after Scunthorpe ran up a four goal lead by half-time.

The name of Andy Flounders was on everyone's lips for a smartly taken hat-trick, while Tony Daws did not want to miss out and scored his last of the season. The rest of the game was a case of going through the motions, and Grant Morrow pulled one back for a Rovers consolation strike. United's three points lifted them to a slightly disappointing eleventh resting place, no doubt a position not good enough for the ambitious Mick Buxton.

During the year there were a couple of significant changes at the Glanford Park Stadium. Against Aldershot, early in March, a new electronic scoreboard had pride of place high above the away end goal for all Scunthonians attending games to be kept informed with up to the minute information. The next stage of development was the installation of seats in the railway end terraces at a cost of £40,000. It meant two thousand visitors could be seated in comfort the following season after the work was completed in the Summer recess. This resulted in a drop in capacity to an abstract figure of 9,183.

The last act of the 1989-90 season was to award Paul Longden with the player of the season trophy for services rendered, and then, as the players dispersed for annual holidays it was time to flick through the register of available talent released by unimpressed employers. Top of United's captures was a very solid and reliable defender Stuart Hicks, a player from the University of honest endeavours, who was signed from Colchester United. There was also a winger off the books of Port Vale, namely Ian Miller.

Miller was a Scotsman with delicate ball skills, but his stay with the Club was very brief. Buxton also instigated promotion on a regular basis for the exciting Richard Hall and later Neil Cox. Both players knew each other well, having been coaxed through United's youth team nursery.

~ 1990-91 ~

On the way out along the M181 was to be Alan Hodkinson, Gordon Tucker and Richard Money. Money had quit the game as a player and started his apprenticeship in management by accepting the first run of the ladder having taken the youth coach position at Aston Villa. It would not be long before the likes of Peter Litchfield and Paul Smalley wore the claret and blue for the last time and joined their former colleagues up the road.

Once Mick Buxton had put the side through the gruelling paces of pre-season training, United started in the sunshine at Glanford Park with a difficult League game against Blackpool. This time it was the Claret and Blues who gained the upper hand. On seventeen minutes Andy Flounders' tantalising lob was fingered by Steve McIhargey in the Seasiders goal, but the shot had enough power in it to reach the back of the net, and was then scooped out by the overjoyed Mark Lillis in celebration. Right at the end, while the referee checked his timepiece, Ian Hamilton cracked the winner, to launch what supporters hoped would be a successful term. This result was a false dawn and poor returns followed in the next half a dozen matches. First Carlisle United ended any League Cup prosperity by knocking the Iron out of the competition, then a couple of defeats were climaxed by a 6-1 defeat to Maidstone United in Dartford, their chosen abode in their latter nomadic days. This was to become the 'Stones' record League victory.

The agitated Scunthorpe United supporters were not happy with the running of the Club and directed their venom in the direction of the board and management, and at the end of September changes took place at the top of the pyramid. Mr Pearson stepped aside as Chairman and Mr Belton took the post for a second time.

On the field of play, United gradually calmed the ship, but not at first. The inclusion of Musselwhite in place of Litchfield and Neil Cox to replace the injured Dave Cowling did have a bearing on the recovery, with two 3-0 wins to halt the progress of Scarborough and Stockport County. The effect was to raise Scunthorpe into a position above halfway, but the excitement associated with a real promotion challenge was nothing but a distant dream.

Scunthorpe United managed to draw Rochdale in the annual knockout provided by the F.A.Cup. It was their task to head West in the direction of the Pennines. They had a fair idea of what to expect because the Lancastrians had lost 2-1 at Glanford Park on the previous Saturday. United held a generous amount of sway, and came away with a replay from Stuart Hicks' goal.

On the following Tuesday the affray recommenced, and local supporters had a scare when Costello repeated his act in the Spotland match, by opening the scoring under the Glanford Park lights.

Andy Flounders saved the blushes, shooting into the base of the net to force extra time. It was while Scunthorpe were attacking the Railway End that Mick Lillis lashed the ball into the target from close range, saluting the crowd in triumph as he wheeled away in celebration.

Scunthorpe United's next clash was a difficult one, for they drew Tranmere Rovers at home. Rovers had received a massive injection of cash and were riding high at the top of the Third Division; they were destined to take the play-off place at Wembley in June. The Cup game at Scunthorpe was to produce a bubbling cauldron of pacey football, where no quarter was given and none asked for. At times United rode their luck but always managed to keep one stride in front of their classy opponents. At half-time they led 2-1, through strikes by Paul Ward and Mark Lillis. Then the Iron made sure with a third goal supplied by Andy Flounders. Life was not made easy with the absence of Tony Daws, out for a couple of months with injury, nevertheless sticking to the task in sight, United deserved to win through a sustained team effort.

Supporters were still not totally happy with the Club's direction. The debate over the manager was now coming to the fore. Rumblings that they would favour a change were being discussed, but Mick Buxton was made of sterner fibre, and continued with the affairs of the team. A four match run without a victory up to Christmas did not help his position, but before United engaged the power of Second Division Brighton and Hove Albion in the Cup, they did manage to dispose of Carlisle United.

The third round draw at the Goldstone Ground against the South Coast club was not the money-spinner desired, for a crowd of less than eight thousand arrived to take their places by kick-off. It turned out to be a near mirror image of the Tranmere game, but this time Scunthorpe were on the back foot. They found themselves trailing on forty-five minutes by the odd goal in three, then shared two goals with the Seagull's in the last part of the match. At 3-2 the Cup trail had hit the stop blocks for another term, but there was no disgrace from the team's efforts.

When United returned to the Fourth Division there was to be a brief respite from their bad patch, when they played host to Aldershot. In the 'Shots' goal was Peter Hucker who kept goal for Queens Park Rangers in the League Cup Final against Oxford United. The keeper' was now more used to humble pickings, and probably wished he had not visited Glanford Park that Saturday. Andy Flounders was the instigator of the slaughter, notching another hat-trick in the 6-2 result, but this was a rare oasis in a metaphorical dessert. The calls for Buxton's head increased and following a loss at Blackpool the Board of Directors decided to terminate his employment.

Scunthorpe United did the usual soul searching before promoting from within the ranks. A new era began when Bill Green took charge at the start of February, yet before he had time to rearrange the desk, Green had to sell his two prized assets, Neil Cox and Richard Hall. Aston Villa paid £350,000 for Neil Cox who would have a career at top level with not only Villa, but later Middlesbrough and Bolton

Wanderers. Richard Hall went South to the Dell and Southampton for around £250,000. Both players would play for England at Junior International level, but Hall's career was to be dogged by injury, and he eventually found his way to West Ham United, to play in a different shade of claret and blue.

Bill Green's next job was to strengthen the team before the year was out. His first choice was the 'Old Head' full-back Joey Joyce who had the legs of a deer, even though he was almost thirty when he signed from Barnsley. He blended with his contemporaries which proved to be a steadying influence at the rear of the team. Within a month Glen Humphries took up residence in the midfield, having been bought for a record £55,000 fee from Bristol City. Humphries was the type of player that would run through a brick wall if his manager requested it. The new manager also brought back Dave Hill on a loan visit from Ipswich Town. A broken leg had hampered his career, but now he had recovered United took a look at him with a view for a permanent transfer. This would come to fruition, ready for the battles of the coming season. Finally Green introduced the pint-sized Mark Hine from Peterborough to the squad as another midfield option .

Late in the campaign there was better news of Steve Lister whose back injury threatened to terminate his career. Fortunately there had been a positive response to treatment, and Steve returned adding strength to the defending pack, which had been sorely missed him in his absence.

There was still plenty that Green was able to do for his short time at the helm in the 1990-91 season, allowing him to turn the course of events. A defeat at Rochdale may have seen the team tumble into sixteenth place in the table, but Green did have a wild card up his sleeve. Alterations in the structure of the Football League resulted for this one season, in four automatic promotion places, and four teams below this hierarchy playing off for an additional place. The play-off finalists would have the bonus of a day out at Wembley to decide the winner of this lottery. From that time on the team played with revitalised zest. Five straight wins later in February and into March relaunched United's statement of intent. A stutter as Spring approached did not help the team, but they continued to fight hard for Bill Green, whose unflustered approach seemed to make his men deliver their best.

April was to be a crucial time for the team. It started with consecutive 3-0 wins, first at home to Hereford United, then, more significantly, in the cold planes of Cumbria, against Carlisle United at Brunton Park. The winning streak could not continue and defeats had to be coped with against Hartlepool in the North-East, and by play-off minded Burnley at Glanford Park. If the Club did have an advantage it was that only one draw was taken in all this time, from a visit to Peterborough United. It meant that they were going for gold, and trying for three points instead of one. Often this left an exposed defence, and they received no reward at all, but that was life!

The last part of the crusade left United with three home games, then a visit to Stockport County's Edgeley Park. All went well when they successfully dealt with Chesterfield, Darlington and Wrexham. The Darlington 2-1 victory was the most exhilarating, for the Quakers had not only returned to the League as Conference Champions, but went on to win the Fourth Division at the first attempt. The Champions-elect posed plenty of questions that afternoon, but Scunthorpe United answered them all. There was also excitement on the terraces, where the fun came from watching the local constabulary stretch their legs keeping the visiting supporters in check. Finally it was off to Stockport. United, where really at least a point was required. Stockport County needed three to guarantee automatic promotion, and they ripped into Scunthorpe, showing no mercy. The result was an embarrassing 5-0 defeat, but anxious glances at the Saturday Telegraph showed a table where the Iron had sneaked the last play-off place.

Scunthorpe United would probably have hoped for a better moral booster to the last promotion push, than that they had just received at Stockport, and they may not have wished to have Blackpool as their opponents for this next hurdle. The first encounter against the tangerine shirts was at Glanford Park, but the dismissal of Steve Lister, due to comments to the linesman, seemed a minor affair for the red card, when it appeared to be no more than a protest at an official's decision. This hampered United throughout the game and the six and a half thousand crowd were relieved to see a second-half equaliser by Lillis save the day. In the second leg United had the boost of an early strike by Dave Hill, but as the game wore on Blackpool ground them down. David Eyres hit two goals in the second-half and once again Scunthorpe United's bubble had burst. For Bill Green and his players it was back to the drawing board again.

~ 1991-92 ~

A number of changes were required in areas where the manager wanted to alter the strategy. Initially he had a goalkeeping problem to solve. Paul Musselwhite was not available for the opener at Gillingham and it was suggested by Dave Moore, now promoted to Assistant Manager, that Nigel Batch be hired for one match. Moore knew Batch from his Grimsby Town days, where the goalkeeper had been a legend after almost four hundred first team games.

In the middle of the park United had already given Graham Alexander a run out as a substitute. Now the young Y.T.S. student, born in Coventry, was to be thrown in at the deep end. Not only did he stay the course, but had scouts flocking to note his progress. There was another player added to the engine room when Dean Martin from Halifax Town was added to the squad. Scunthorpe supporters commented that, although he could play well enough, with à name like Dean Martin, they were disappointed with his voice!

In the front lines United had a number of new faces. The most noteworthy was the towering Ian Helliwell, whose £80,000 expense once again raised United's record outlay. When he was taken from York City, Helliwell was the ideal target man to pump balls upfield to, and his heading power was phenomenal.

He would be joined by left flank player John Buckley from Partick Thistle. John was a Scotsman who started at Queen's

Park, but he had been employed at a number of Yorkshire clubs, including Doncaster Rovers, Leeds United and Rotherham United. There was also a young black forward Jason White, whose previous club, Derby County, introduced him to the game as a trainee. Jason was such a willing workhorse that he immediately won favour with the crowd, despite an initial ungainly style. There was another fringe man for the pool in Gary Hyde who started as a junior at Wolverhampton Wanders, but had most of his League experience at Darlington. United lifted him from Leicester where he was unable to break into the first team. These additions, plus the full time settlement of Dave Hill's contract made up the bulk of the newcomers.

The change in attitude, to fall in line with what Bill Green wanted, required some unfortunate redundancies. Men who had seen the Club through critical periods were to leave. The list included Dave Cowling, shortly to go into management, Mark Lillis off to Stockport County, John Bramhall who went to Hyde United and Paul Ward whose next stop was Lincoln City. Inexplicably Kevin Taylor's talent was allowed to drift away into obscurity at Frickley Athletic, and the enormous loss of Andy Flounders had its repercussions for years. Flounders could not agree terms with Scunthorpe United and he was allowed to wander off, for a fee, to Rochdale. It was a move that benefitted neither club particularly, but perhaps the biggest loser was Andy himself. The man was a fond favourite of everyone at Glanford Park, and his total number of goals set him within site of breaking all Scunthorpe scoring records.

Scunthorpe United set off towards Gillingham via the notorious M25 motorway, in good time, ready for the start of the season. Nigel Batch was installed between the posts but by full-time the novelty of a return to League Football may have worn off. A scintillating display of football increased a single goal lead by the Kent side, to 4-0 in the final act.

It was a long journey home to contemplate how easily they had been dressed down. Bill Green demanded more, and a midweek loss at Wrexham in the League Cup did produce a display more characteristic of what he was expecting. Scunthorpe supporters had to wait until the first home game before they had any joy. United met neighbours Doncaster Rovers, and always did sufficient to keep one step ahead in the entertaining 3-2 result. Doncaster were no yardstick to judge how well the Iron played, for only once did they leave the bottom four all season. At the end of the opening month, Scunthorpe found themselves close to the bottom of the table after a defeat at Blackpool, but a convincing second-half display against Wrexham brought goals from Glen Humphries, Graham Alexander, and Ian Helliwell. The booty for this League Cup success was two games in round two with the famous white shirts of Leeds United.

The Scunthorpe public had a rare treat brought to them once the season was underway. Graham Taylor had just been appointed the England manager, and he had plenty of links with the area. He went to school in the town and his proud father had been Scunthorpe United's Evening Telegraph reporter in the post-war years. It was a tremendous privilege that through his influence an England under twenty-one game was staged at Glanford Park on 10th September 1991.

Ian Helliwell, United's new record signing, in acrobatic action in the Hereford goalmouth during the October 1991 home match.

Over seven thousand spectators turned up to give the England team a rousing welcome for a game against Germany, which they won 2-1. The England team for the night lined-up: James, Dodd, Vinnicombe, Ebbrell, Tiler, Warhurst, Johnson, Draper (Matthew), Shearer, P.Williams and Campbell.

September also saw a rise in the right direction for Scunthorpe United. There were three excellent victories all of which saw Paul Musselwhite keep clean sheets. The most outstanding of these was the victory at Saltergate against Chesterfield. United's whole team made a full contribution to the win, which was secured from Glen Humphries' drive. A midweek game in London took Scunthorpe to uncharted territory at Underhill, against Barnet. Barnet were the fresh faces in the League, and although they won the match 3-2, Scunthorpe pointed to a strange penalty decision in the last few moments as their downfall. Substitute Jason White provided the highlight of the game with a solo effort from a shot on the run in this, his League debut.

In the League Cup the whole town was buzzing with talk of the visit of Leeds United. There was also great demand from Scunthorpe people, with dubious Yorkshire connections, to buy tickets for the away end of the ground. The total ticket sales produced the second largest attendance at Glanford Park, to date, of 8,392. Supporters who turned up on a pleasant evening, ideally suited for football, may not have seen any goals, but they were thoroughly entertained. The Scunthorpe team raised their standard to match the illustrious Peacocks in every department and it was a privilege to see the abundance of skill from the First Division club.

In the second-leg at Elland Road, played two weeks later, United gave a good account of themselves against their Yorkshire Counterparts.

Talk at the interval was of a possible upset because the expected torrent of goal had not materialised. It needed the intervention of a referee to award a mystery penalty to spur Leeds United into action. Mel Sterling put the conversion away, before Lee Chapman and Gary Speed added a respectable look to the aggregate score of 3-0.

On League duty, United were not yet in top gear, and the struggle continued. As the dark nights closed in and the clocks were put back, Scunthorpe were only just above halfway up the table. It was not until 5th November that folks saw the real fireworks at Glanford Park, when Rochdale were the visitors, and once again United gave a cordial welcome to old boy Tony Brown. At half-time the contest was over at 3-0, and Brown had obliged with an own goal for Scunthorpe's second. The end product turned out to be a lively 6-2 affair, and of all the goalscorers, only John Bowden managed more than one, for Rochdale. The evenings fireworks must have been like damp squibs in comparison!

There was hardly time to breath when Rotherham United called in for a visit three days after the slamming of Rochdale for another League game. Interest in this encounter centred on the fact that the Millers would also be in town one week later to contest the F.A.Cup. As was to be expected the men from Millmoor proved to be a stern test. Little could be found between the teams as they matched each other like chess champions. It was not until the Iron attacked the home supporters end that a chink of light briefly appeared as a flaw in the Rotherham defence. Tony Daws picked up the ball near the halfway line, and ran hard at the back line, rounding them as they committed themselves. Then in full flight Daws fashioned a tremendous shot which left 'keeper Billy Mercer groping the air. It was a fitting goal to claim all three points.

Fingers were crossed for a repeat in the F.A.Cup, but after Tony Cunningham scored in the first period, United knew there would be an uphill battle to win the game outright. In the end they were happy to settle for a draw, when Helliwell saw Scunthorpe safe. It had been usual for replays to be played in the next week, however, new regulations to allow time for policing arrangements would now put the second game on hold for more than a week. What was more the replay was to be the deciding factor, for if no result came after ninety minutes, half an hour of extra time was on offer, followed by a penalty shootout.

United were soon locking horns in a tremendous head to head with the Millers in an intriguing contest. Twice Rotherham led and twice the Iron fought back. Then the trench warfare went into extra-time. Jason White looked as though he had fired the visitors into the next round with eleven minutes remaining. But with seven minutes left Don Page hit his second of the night with a cleanly taken shot and once again brought the scores equal at 3-3. After one hundred and twenty minutes the two teams stood side by side dripping in sweat. Nobody wanted a penalty shoot-out, but history dictated that these two teams would be involved in the first in the F.A.Cup to be decided by the dreaded spot-kick. At the end of each club's allocation the scores could not be separated.

Hearts pounded when both sides shaped up for the last moments of the action. Four more goals went in, then there was anguish amongst the Scunthorpe supporters when Billy Mercer pushed Ian Helliwell's shot wide. Ally Pickering took hold of the ball for the Millers, placed it on the twelve yard spot and netted the winning goal. Rotherham had triumphed seven-six on penalties and went on to play Burnley at Turf Moor. Scunthorpe United were wretched with disappointment, as were the supporters.

Bill Green's therapy was to quickly get the lads back in action again. One of the problems identified was the effect of too much pressure on United's young goalkeeper Paul Musselwhite. Paul's confidence had suffered in recent weeks and abuse from sections of the crowd did not help. Bill's solution was to rest Musselwhite and bring in Phil Whitehead on loan from Barnsley. The first game after losing the Cup-tie was against York City, who were a stiff test, but United overcame the challenge with an Ian Hamilton goal.

The exit from the F.A.Cup did have the advantage of giving everyone a free week. Don Rowing, now adorned with the celebrated title of chief executive would rather have been counting gate receipts no doubt, but a strong run by the team up to the Christmas period had extra revenue rolling in through the claret turnstiles. Consecutive matches brought wins against Doncaster at Belle Vue, then Gillingham and Blackpool at Glanford Park. The Blackpool score of 2-1 saw Scunthorpe's black bomber, Jason White smack two timely goals and lift the team into fifth place in the Division.

New Year did not start too well, for it found Scunthorpe United still suffering from a hangover, and they were stuffed 4-1 at Scarborough. Supporters wondered why the Iron always fell for the sucker punch against the Boro. The next game did not take place until two weeks later, and Scunthorpe had recovered sufficiently to inflict the same score on a poor Halifax Town side at the Shay. Hero of the hour was Jason White, after he scored a hat-trick that afternoon, and then went on to net eight goals in five games around this time.

During the next couple of months United maintained their pressure at the right end of the table, mainly thanks to a first class home record. Their away results were poor and four games on opponents territory in consecutive visits yielded no points. The worst of the quartet was the trip to Millmoor when they crashed 5-0, and this was followed by the loss of three points at home to Lincoln City.

The run to the end of the season was to be assisted by the signing of two players as the board strengthened Bill Green's hand for a promotion push. Mark Samways was taken on loan from Doncaster Rovers as a goalkeeping deputy for Musselwhite. The new man was a veteran of more than one hundred and twenty games and had already played two games against United that season.

Next was the giant blond Matt Elliott, who was also taken on loan. His club was Torquay United, who were going through a sticky patch at the base of Division Three. Both signatures were to be made permanent at the end of the playing activities, but for the meantime the pair made their Scunthorpe debuts together in a 2-0 victory at Glanford Park against Chesterfield.

United now had a defensive set-up which was virtually impregnable. As the end of the season loomed, supporters would be treated to another seven unbeaten matches, where one goal was the most Samways would have to pick out the ball from the net in a single game. It was this time of year when almost every man chose to enter his name on the scoresheet. Only the ever reliable Paul Longden opted out, but he had slotted in one of the penalties in the F.A.Cup shootout. The general synopsis was that an automatic promotion place was just beyond their grasp, but another play-off spot was a distinct possibility. The confirmation came to pass on the last Saturday of the season, when Carlisle United were comprehensively dispatched 4-0 with a brace of goals in each half.

The task now was to check the rest of the table to see who fifth place Scunthorpe United would meet in the Semi-Finals, and fate dictated Crewe Alexandra who had finished sixth. The first part of the competition was played at Gresty Road, where a crowd of just in excess of six thousand left little space in any of the corners. For those supporters with faint hearts the message was to keep away, because these sort of games were certain to be nerve-racking affairs. Scunthorpe got off to the worse possible start, when Craig Hignett steered a right foot shot into the corner of the net after only six minutes. It was then Ian Helliwell's turn to pay back part of his £50,000 transfer fee, falling backwards as he poked in the equaliser on seventeen minutes. He was there again ten minutes before the interval, scoring with a powerful header. Four minutes later Tony Naylor shot on the run to make parity at two goals each. This effort was the last as far as goal-scoring was concerned, but it left Scunthorpe's camp the happier of the two.

make it to the match, and this raised the attendance to a few short of eight thousand. Once again it was going to be a close fought tussle. Samways was called into the action making sure that efforts from Hignett and Naylor were cancelled out, while at the other end Helliwell was causing all sorts of problems, but no goals were on the board by half-time. Bill Green reassured his team that they had the ability to win, but the stalemate lasted until late into the game.

Dean Martin then emerged as the Scunthorpe hero. Buckley put in a great cross to the far post in the eighty-third minute allowing Daws to rifle in a shot. Gariner of Crewe cleared it to the edge of the box, from where Martin came steaming in, to crack home a glorious right foot shot. Crewe had little option but to attack and left gaps at the back. Only a minute of the game remained when another Buckley cross curled into the far post and from close range Hamilton beat the defence, leaving Edwards with no chance as the ball rocketed into the net. The ecstatic Scunthorpe supporters rushed onto the pitch at the end of the match to demand an encore from their gallant troops. United's triumphant players were only too pleased to oblige and drink in the applause. It would be they who would be playing Blackpool, who had beaten Barnet, in the final of the Fourth Division Play-Off Final at Wembley.

Victory over Crewe Alexandra, 4-2 on aggregate, resulted in the Club's first ever visit to the hallowed twin towers of Wembley. For Don Rowing and the hard-working ladies in the office there was the delight - a labour of love - supplying the Scunthorpe public with tickets and all varieties of souvenirs. The phone never stopped ringing and the name of the Club was on everyone's lips. In total over nine thousand tickets were sold for the Scunthorpe section in the enormous stadium. Eventually an army of over forty coaches filed out of Glanford Park as well as other starting points around the town. Tangerine was not the favourite colour that day.

A proud moment, as Scunthorpe emerge from the Wembley tunnel with rivals Blackpool for the 1992 Play-off Final.

Scunthorpe were the County's first side to grace the hallowed turf

The return was scheduled for the next Wednesday at Glanford Park. Bill Green relaxed his team, and put them in the right mind for another important night of high drama. Every supporter worth his or her salt made sure they could

The historic Blackpool game took place on Saturday 23th May 1992. United's supporters were in fine voice throughout the arena which had a 22,741 attendance at the kick-off. Bill Green led the Iron out on to the lush pitch holding the hand of the Scunthorpe Mascot, his daughter Victoria, who was dressed in United's kit. The teams lined up at kick-off as follows:-

Scunthorpe Utd: Samways, Joyce, Longden, Hill, Elliott, Humphries, Martin, Hamilton, Daws and Buckley.

Blackpool: McIlhargey, Burgess, Cook, Groves, Davies, Gore, Rodwell, Horner, Bamber, Garner and Eyres. Murphy replaced Davies and Sinclair replaced Horner.

Scunthorpe started in fine style as a brilliant atmosphere presided around the ground. They worked well as a unit and caused lots of problems for the Blackpool back lines. Blackpool were just as tight and chances were at a premium. Despite the pressure the Iron exerted, it was the Seasiders who took the lead forty minutes into the game. Blackpool pressure caused the ball to be lost and it was seized upon, then crossed to the far post. The opponent's leading goalscorer, Dave Bamber, rose to squeeze a header into the unguarded side of the goal.

This setback rocked Scunthorpe, but Bill Green steadied the ship at half-time with a reassuring talk. His words did the trick, for United came out of the tunnel raring to get back on terms. They did not have long to wait. The equalising strike was one of the best goals to have been scored at Wembley all season. It started with Dean Martin feeding the ball through to John Buckley. Buckley pushed a perfect pass to Tony Daws, who hit a sweet left-footed shot high into he net. The match had now run fifty-two minutes of its course. Scunthorpe went for the jugular, and for long periods looked to be the better of the two sides on view. Ninety minutes of pressure resulted in an impasse, as did the next half hour of extra time.

Keith Hackett, the match day official, then had to indicate another frustrating penalty shoot-out. Substitutions had put Daws and Buckley out of the picture and understandably some of the seasoned professionals did not want to volunteer to take the kicks. In the event Ian Hamilton, Paul Longden and Matt Elliott all scored from their attempts. Blackpool matched them shot for shot. Next came Graham Alexander's shot. To the horror of all the folk from Humberside, Steve McIlhargey saved the firmly struck effort. Young Alexander was grief-stricken after making such a generous contribution to the game. Eyres made it 4-3 with the next kick. It all hinged on Jason White. He put some real body into his strike but the ball went sailing over the bar. It was all over. Jason sank to his knees in disbelief. Joey Joyce, the captain, was first to console the lad for his miss. Graham Alexander was doing his best to hold back the tears.

To a person, everyone applauded the shattered Scunthorpe team from the field. The whole town was proud of the Club and full of admiration for what had been achieved. Up the motorways the claret and blue flags and scarves still fluttered in the breeze, as the subdued thousands made their way home.

Talk was kept to a minimum but the general tone was of total praise for everyone at Scunthorpe United. The pain of defeat was not to go away overnight, but once the Summer came and the batteries were recharged it was soon time to start again.

~ 1992-93 ~

During the close season there was some anxiety as to whether or not Samways and Elliott would sign for the Club, but eventually the situation over contracts was settled. It solved a big headache for Bill Green, and he was to stick to the same first team structure which had done the Club proud at Wembley. Fringe players were added to the pool including Sammy Goodacre, Steve Greaves and Paul McCullough. Each of these players gave a limited contribution to the team, but without making a solid impact. There was to be a couple of loan signings to supplement affairs shortly into the start of the season, and United made a further investment in borrowing Paul Whitehead again, while a much more mature Julian Broddle was taken for a spell from Partick Thistle. Green may have wished to have added Broddle to the squad, but the price demanded was considered poor value for money.

There were the usual crop of departures during the summer. It was decided not to renew the contract of Steve Lister, who at the height of his playing career had been a rock. The player had saved the day for United on so many occasions, but his back injury problems had put a halt to his appearances for the Club. In the end he left the Football League for Boston United. Paul Musselwhite had taken up with John Rudge, manager of Port Vale, and the small fee paid would make him a basement bargain buy. Mark Hine left for Gateshead, whilst Steve Hicks continued a nomadic career, where his next stop was Doncaster Rovers. The last departure was the important loss of Ian Hamilton for some serious money, at £170,000, to West Bromwich Albion. Hamilton had been the prime mover in seeing that United's middle order was firing on all cylinders, and of all the players leaving, his absence was to be felt the most. For years to come the Club would not find a replacement in the same league as Hamilton.

The Football Association had negotiated to take over the First Division, and at the start of the 1992-93 season it was relaunched, with backing from Sky Television, as the Premiership. It meant a promotion in name only of all other Divisions in the Football League. Thus, instead of watching Fourth Division football, Scunthorpe supporters were to view Third Division entertainment.

Before a ball was kicked, it was noticed that Scunthorpe United's squad was a little on the thin side in terms of numbers, but it did not seem to effect early season form. They started off under the gaze of the moors of Yorkshire at Halifax Town, where less than two thousand spectators, many from Scunthorpe, bothered to turn up for a drab goalless muddle. The team continued to make progress, with victory in the League Cup over Darlington on aggregate, and did not lose in the Third Division until a trip to Lincoln in the fourth match. Battle stations were again called against Crewe Alexandra. The visit of the railwaymen saw a thrilling six goal charge by both sides, and a point apiece was about the right outcome. It marked the first goal for United in Sammy Goodacre's career.

In the League Cup, Scunthorpe once again drew Leeds United, who months before had lifted the last of the old First Division Championships. The first game was at Leeds, and the Premiership side had no trouble in marking their superiority. Strachen and Chapman saw the mean Leeds United machine step up a gear to edge 2-0 ahead at the interval, and Speed and Shutt later added two more. The biggest cheer of all came from a couple of thousand Scunthorpe supporters when Helliwell scored for the Iron.

The replay did not take place at Glanford Park until five weeks later, due to the European commitments of Leeds United and International duties by their players. Business for tickets was brisk, and another large crowd of almost seven and a half thousand headed for the game on the day. Very few of those persons attending the match thought that United had a realistic chance of recouping the three goal difference, but there was an opportunity to cause the Elland road club an embarrassment if possible, and that is what Scunthorpe attempted to do. At the halfway point Ian Helliwell had bagged two goals, and the Iron were playing with confidence which remained intact. In the end Scunthorpe were obliged to settle for a draw on the night, and their name was removed from the competition.

At this stage of the Third Division season, United had made no real progress towards a promotion position. Indeed, a place just below the middle of the table was the norm. It did not take long to find sections of the crowd voicing their discontent at Glanford Park, for they had hoped to see the team storm up into a dominating position, but the Club was not even able to reach anywhere near the standard of the 1991-92 season. A stop gap measure was introduced into the side with the signing of Steve Charles on loan from Mansfield, but the improvements, as a whole, were minimal.

In the F.A.Cup, United took on the might of Huddersfield Town. The Terriers were well represented on the terraces for support, and both teams went hammer and tongs at each other. Defences held firm and the crowd had to be content with lots of endeavour but no goals. Eleven days later and the decider took place on the Leeds Road ground. The star of the show turned out to be Gary Barnett, playing in Huddersfield Town's blue and white stripes, when he nosed the Yorkshire club in front. Scunthorpe managed to hang on through a John Buckley strike, which put the game into extra time. Thoughts of a penalty shootout did not go down well in the Scunthorpe dug out, but they did not need to worry, for Barnett scored his second goal and United had exited another Cup competition.

Scunthorpe United could only look to the Third Division for any success now, but they would have to improve dramatically if it was to mature. The pressure on Bill Green continued to mount in December, when the only win of the month came against lowly Hereford United. It was the game against Gillingham, the League's bottom club at the time, which was a deciding factor, that was played three days after Christmas Day. This match was to be a personal disaster for Paul Longden who broke his leg, and it was such a bad injury that after four hundred appearances Paul's career was effectively terminated. He would return to Glanford Park years later as mine host at the new 'Iron Bar' built on the ground. Meanwhile his colleagues struggled to get to grips with the game, and needed a last minute penalty by Tony Daws to salvage a point from a 2-2 draw.

The result was the last straw for the Board of Directors. They could not see the Club going anywhere after the previous season's success, and it was with regret that Bill Green was made yet another managerial casualty in the first week of the New Year. He could count himself unlucky because a number of bosses had been in far more serious positions with their clubs, and survived. Bill was a man of dignity. He cleared his desk immediately and disappeared into history. All fairminded football followers would afford the gentleman a moment to reflect on the good he had done the Glanford Park team in taking them to Wembley. His name had been the one chanted by thousands of fans just seven months previously.

During the same week a press meeting announced former player, Richard Money, as the new appointment. Money had been schooled at Aston Villa in the youth department, firstly under Dr. Jozef Venglos, and later with Ron Atkinson. He was a fresh face and possessed new ideas, and it was likely that his methods would bring young players into the first team reckoning. In his first match in charge at Glanford Park he impressed supporters with his frankness as he walked round the perimeter of the ground, shaking hands and chatting to people on the terraces.

It took Money some time to settle down, for after two months he only had one win to show for his efforts, a 4-1 result at home to the eventual wooden spoon team Halifax Town. The new manager brought in a few of the players that he had become acquainted with in his days as a coach, some of whom were from the Midlands, and others were non-contract. Names to appear for brief periods on the team sheet included David Foy, Shaun Constable, Richard Wilmot, Darrell Duffy, Jason Maxwell and Richard Crisp. Unfortunately, none made the grade and would not make it until the start of the following season. On the other hand Nicky Platnauer from Leicester City, taken on a short term contract until the Summer, was more of a prospect and had seen life in a defensive roll further up the League. The Club also persuaded the strong Ian Thompstone to leave the sinking Halifax ship to support the Scunthorpe front line.

Money had to take care of dealings in the other direction, too. Supporters were sorry to find John Buckley making a new start in February at Rotherham United. They later learned that he suffered a serious head injury at Millmoor whilst playing, and was last heard of at Buxton Town assisting Bill Green, his old boss. United received a £20,000 fee for his transfer. Within a month Tony Daws decided to accept a change of direction, and to move up the League with Grimsby Town. Scunthorpe United were sorry to see him go, but needed the £50,000 cash injection to pay their way. Tony Daws had been an integral part of Scunthorpe's goal machinery for the past six years, and only a handful of men had registered in excess of his seventy-one strikes for the Club.

Once Money had got his house in order, the right results began to flow. The beginning of March brought a ten match undefeated run which hoisted the Club as high as eleventh at one stage. They even went nap on two occasions, both at home, beating Northampton 5-0 and Rochdale 5-1. Supporters started to believe again, and if it was not for a bruising end to the season, when United ran up a number of defeats, they could have finished higher than fourteenth in the table. This was not the yardstick to measure Richard Money by as yet, but now the honeymoon was over he would be expected to make his mark in the coming twelve months.

Number 12, Ian Thompstone, gets a header in on the Torquay United goal during the match in March. Other Scunthorpe players on hand are Glen Humphries, Sammy Goodacre and Matt Elliott.

Before the 1992-93 season was finally wound up, Scunthorpe United had to play Cardiff City in the last match of the season at Glanford Park. Cardiff City needed one point to make certain of the Championship and police warned of a mass invasion from more than five thousand Welsh fans who were in high spirits on the day of the game. United's Board of Directors made a decision to offer Cardiff City's supporters both ends of the ground, but this was a great affront to Scunthorpe followers who thought it was an invasion of their rightful territory. Some never forgave the Club and stayed away on a permanent basis. The Directors claimed it was purely a financial move which gave the extra income of many thousands of pounds. Even a seat at standing prices was insufficient for many local fans, and a long debate raged at the merits of that 'which had been decided. In the event Cardiff City won the game 3-0, and the visiting clans celebrated in a well behaved manner.

~ 1993-94 ~
The news that greeted supporters at the start of the 1993-94 season was the signing of almost a complete new team by manager Richard Money. In defence Paul Mudd was drawn away from Scarborough to replace the critical hole left by Paul Longden. Mudd was joined across the back four by two tall youngsters whose presence was to be a vital factor in the team's survival in the matches to come. The pair were Russell Bradley from Halifax Town and Chris Hope who was taken from Nottingham Forest's second team. Hope was to stay with the Club, giving yeoman service for a number of years, winning the praise of the home supporters with the dedication he gave. Bradley was more experienced at the time, and linked up well with his new colleagues. In midfield United had brought Yorkshireman Steve Thornber from Blackpool, who, whilst earlier at Swansea, had won a Welsh Cup winners medal.

There were a number of players for the forward line, some of whom would be considered to be utility men. The first was Mark Smith of Grimsby Town origins, who at the start of his career had made one appearance for Scunthorpe as a trainee in the days of the Old Showground. Other men included Andy Toman, a tricky ball player from Darlington, Ian

Juryeff who had scored goals at half a dozen clubs, and soldier Neil Trebble a non-Leaguer at Stevenage Borough. Finally, room was made for Matt Carmichael who was given a free transfer from Lincoln City. What Lincoln discarded, turned out to be a tremendous boost to Scunthorpe United's goalscoring department, and to a large degree made up for the loss of Tony Daws.

The new signings inevitably meant others were outward bound. Dave Hill was to swap places with Carmichael as part of a package, and Ian Helliwell was given leave to play for Rotherham United, recouping part of his record cost with a £50,000 fee. Glen Humphries dropped out of League football to take up with Frickley, while Andy Stevenson stayed nearer home to play for Brigg Town at the Hawthornes.

Richard Money was eager to see his selected side get off to the right start and they did so by taking their first ever win in League Football against Wigan Athletic at Springfield Park, after eight attempts on that ground. Indeed all of the first four Third Division games yielded points. The only setback was in the League Cup, sponsored for the second year by Coca Cola. Shrewsbury Town beat them narrowly 2-1 on aggregate, but this disappointment did not have an adverse effect at all. It was a joy to see the team strong on their travels, and from then until the end of September, the first failure only came on an opponent's ground, when they lost on the tiresome journey to Gillingham.

By now the team's diligence had eked out three wins. One of the victories was at Chester City, where United soon got used to their first ever visit to the new Deva Stadium. Toman and Juryeff gave the Iron a comfortable win.

Into the Autumn, October provided a mixed bag of fortunes. Two of the five games were won, but by an aggregate of ten goals to none. Northampton Town felt the hardest done by, when they lost 7-0, while Darlington were the other losers. During the Cobblers walkover, there was the welcome sight of Matt Carmichael milking the applause for his hat-trick.

All this activity took the Iron to as high as third place in the division, but gradually there was a slip-back as the New Year approached.

F.A.Cup action was delayed for a day until the Sunday, for opponents Accrington Stanley had chosen to play their tie against the Iron at Turf Moor, Burnley, and on the Saturday Burnley needed the ground for their own game with York City. Andy Toman gave Scunthorpe the lead, but Accrington sought to make sure the Iron had a good chasing. Richard Money was forced to bring on the slightly built Sammy Goodacre who scored twice, but his second goal was vital, a couple of minutes from time, to sneak a hard fought 3-2 victory.

Matt Carmichael scores one of his brace, in the Carlisle United home victory in September 1993.

Alan Knill, a former Welsh International, for an undisclosed fee from Bury.

In the second round of the F.A.Cup, Walsall were to stage the tie on their new Bescot Stadium. United had played there before and felt quite at home because it was almost an exact clone of Glanford Park on which it was based. Walsall were in the same division as the Iron but still expected to win. Richard Money decided to keep the defence in tight order and United earned a replay from a 1-1 draw. Both moments of elation came in the first forty minutes. Scunthorpe's goal arrived when Carmichael drilled the ball past the reach of Jimmy Walker in the Walsall goal.

Ian Thompstone is in the thick of the action again, flanked by Ian Trebble and Dean Martin, after scoring in the first home League match of the 1992-93 season. The dejected Bury player on the deck is Alan Knill who was to become a United player three months later.

The non-Leaguers took the accolades for an excellent second-half, but it was Scunthorpe United who went on to play Walsall. One absentee from the team was Matt Elliott, who was transferred to Oxford United on the 5th November, for a fee of £150,000 plus a sell-on clause. He made his debut in London for Oxford against Millwall the next day. Elliott's elimination from team affairs at Glanford Park was to be compensated by the arrival of the tall central defender

At the press interviews at the end of the game Kenny Hibbitt, Walsall's forthright manager, was scathing in his attack on Scunthorpe United's tactics. Richard Money smiled and said that he was looking forward to the replay. Certainly Scunthorpe had shown plenty of resolve, but they were never robust. The replay at Glanford Park was even more of a chess game, for chances were few and far between.

Standing firm in front of Samways, the whole back line played with distinction, particularly Knill. His safety first policy was mimicked by the rest of the side and at the conclusion of the allotted hour and a half no score was on the electronic scoreboard. The position had not changed after extra time, and both sets of supporters had to steal themselves for the dreaded penalties. At the end of all the tension it was the Scunthorpe camp that were jumping up and down with excitement when they won 7-6 from the shootout.

Although Scunthorpe United had been making progress in the F.A.Cup, little headway had been made in the Third Division programme to put them up with the leaders. Indeed, the situation as Autumn turned to Winter saw a fallow period. To alter the trend, United brought in a number of new men to introduce to supporters. To begin the changes, Richard Money used the strapping figure of Damian Henderson from Scarborough as an injection into the forward area. Part of this agreement took Jason White and Andy Toman to Seamer Road on the East coast of Yorkshire in the other direction. Room was made in the team for Hull-born Christian Sansam, one of Scunthorpe's own trainees. Christian had an abundance of potential, and it was felt that he had the ability to make the grade. Then there was the signing of ex-Manchester United apprentice Wayne Bullimore, from Stockport County. This midfield youngster had enormous ball skills and fitted straight into the first team.

The Christmas game on the calendar was to take place against Lincoln City at Sincil Bank. If United were poor in the first-half, they were only fractionally better in the second period. City adapted far more positively to the muddy conditions, and a goal in each session of play made them thoroughly worth the three points. Scunthorpe played to a much higher standard the next day, when Chesterfield journeyed up from Derbyshire. Paul Mudd scored only his second goal in the claret and blue, for the Iron's first goal. Then Matt Carmichael converted a penalty to earn a draw, in what had proved to be an uphill battle. Carmichael's goal was the first in a record-breaking sequence, for he was to score in eight consecutive League games, and hence set a new record at the Club.

To start the New Year Scunthorpe had to travel to 'Proud Preston', where the North End club were up where it mattered. United raised their game and ignored the monotony of the sound of drums pounding a dirge from the terraces. At 2-1 in the lead they claimed to have been cheated when the ball clearly went out for a Scunthorpe throw. A Preston player rushed in to take it as the United men protested, and from the throw Preston levelled the score, an injustice sanctioned by the referee. This was followed on the Monday evening by another visit to Glanford Park by Walsall. The Fourth Division fixture brought an astonishing 5-0 success to United. In the F.A.Cup the Saddlers defence had been rock solid, but this time it crumbled to dust. The result made Kenny Hibbitt dislike the Iron even more, as he left tight lipped to set off back to the Midlands.

Attention now turned back to the Cup, where fate had Scunthorpe on the road to London town to play unfashionable Wimbledon, who were waiting at Selhurst Park. Wimbledon were the only Premiership club to guarantee there would be no big pay day from their gate receipts. At kick-off there were less than five thousand spectators present, and over one thousand of those wore the claret and blue colours of Scunthorpe United. The Don's support might have been thin, but the reception they gave the Iron was not. One man dominated the match and that was Dean Holdsworth, for his hat-trick completely destroyed Scunthorpe. If there was a disappointment it was that Scunthorpe afforded the Dons too much respect, and they did not put enough fight into the game. The highlight in the 3-0 defeat came when Wimbledon's charismatic Chairman Sam Hamman stood shoulder to shoulder with Scunthorpe fanatics on the terraces, giving away Wimbledon Tee-shirts.

Once Scunthorpe United were out of the F.A.Cup they entered a very lean spell. Supporters again became agitated with what they had been witnessing, and the board were unhappy in a number of aspects with life on the field of play. At the beginning of March, United's Chairman, Keith Wagstaff, who had succeeded Tom Belton, informed Richard Money he was being given a break from duties as a rest to recharge his batteries. Money could not accept this situation and tendered his resignation. From 12th March, Dave Moore, United's physio, was put in charge as the temporary manager for the trip to Carlisle United. It was too late for Dave Moor to make any new signings, but he was able to turn the problems around for the team and restore the players faith.

Once Moore had introduced his ideas and system there was a healthy improvement in the situation. Revenge was exacted over Lincoln City, reversing the score of the previous encounter. The afternoon saw the Iron take the bait and show far more authority than in the recent previous weeks. Preston were another visitor to sample United's newly acquired hostility, for the North End club had their promotion aspirations dinted with a 3-1 destruction of the Lilywhites rear guard, which again shut that drummer up.

Towards the end of April, the Iron found themselves treading on new territory, when they set course for Adams Park, in pleasant Spring sunshine, to play Wycombe Wanderers. A 2-2 result turned out to be a fair reflection of the endeavours from both sides, and it eased the Chairboys a step nearer promotion via the play-offs in their first League season. This left two matches to play, the first of which was a swan-song for the season in front of United's own supporters. Calling into Glanford Park was Shrewsbury Town, who needed to win to guarantee them top spot. From the onset they exerted their authority on the play, and Scunthorpe found them in a class beyond any another club in the Third Division that term. The Shrews became deserved 4-1 winners, and at the end of the match both sets of supporters stood to applaud the Champions.

All that remained was a quick trip across the Pennines to settle matters at Rochdale. In the past Spotland had been something of a graveyard for Scunthorpe United teams, and the last six League games had all ended in sorry defeats. This time the table was turned. Goals by Thornber and Juryeff had seen the Iron level at the break, and looking to take at least a point from the proceedings. In the second section a shot by Juryeff was deflected by Lancaster, an earlier scorer for Rochdale, past Martin Hodge, the former Sheffield Wednesday goalkeeper, and into the net. It did not matter who had scored this effort, but what was important was that United had signed off with a win. The points gleaned were to raise Scunthorpe into eleventh place in the table, two slots behind Rochdale.

~ 1994-95 ~

Scunthorpe United's board were highly satisfied with Dave Moore's contribution to management affairs, and for his troubles they offered him the manager's job on a regular basis. In May, everything was made official and another new day in the history of the Club was dawning under the charge of Moore. He did not have much time to dwell on his achievements in the short time he had been in control, before the start of another campaign was upon him.

The 1994-95 season started with only one new face in the first team pool, this was Tony Ford, a former long term colleague of the manager at Grimsby Town. Ford was one of football's ageless group of players who just refused to retire, and he became an excellent buy when discarded by the Mariners, at the end of his second Blundell Park spell. At the same time Moore thought it only necessary to dispense with Neil Trebble, who went off to Preston North End, before eventually returning to his roots at Stevenage.

Scunthorpe United had an early August start on their hands, and for those supporters who made the trip to Barnet there was the possibility of a look round the capital after the game if they wished. Damian Henderson had the fans singing at a very early stage, after running on to a through ball and steering it past Phillips in the Bees goal. Juryeff looked to have made certain of the points with another firm shot, before it was time to pause for a half-time read of the matchday programme. Cooper may have pulled one back, but the policing policy of the likes of Ford, Knill and Bradley, meant there was only a remote chance of losing the lead.

This away visit was followed by a four match home set of fixtures in the League, only briefly interrupted by a pair of games against Huddersfield in the League Cup, which continued to be sponsored by Coca Cola. A first leg win of 2-1 was a slender advantage, and the question was, had Dave Moores men done enough? All answers came at a half completed Alfred McAlpine Stadium. It was a magnificent venue even with only the sides able to accommodate spectators, and this was only the second first class game to be staged there. Huddersfield set off at a devastating pace leaving Scunthorpe to clutch at straws. Samways was left exposed on too many occasions, and by half-time Jepson had scored a brace, and Reid added another. At 3-0 it was game set and match to the Terriers, and Scunthorpe were out.

In the Third Division, United surrendered their home record on the occasion of the first Glanford Park League match against Fulham, whose supporters expected a lot. Juryeff put the Iron on a course for victory, but it was clawed back, and two minutes from time Fulham squeezed in the winner. It was not until the visit of Gillingham, when Thornber,

Henderson and Smith all scored in the second-half, that the Glanford Park faithful were able to welcome a positive result on home soil.

One very remarkable score was registered at the beginning of September. Scunthorpe were to play hosts to Carlisle United, who were top of the pile at that stage. From the kick-off, United played with style and panache which baffled the opposition. Juryeff and Thornber put Scunthorpe into an apparent unassailable lead, and nothing Carlisle could do made any impact. Then came the last throw of the dice from the visitors director of coaching, Mick Wadsworth, when he brought on Thorpe and Robinson as substitutes to change his beleaguered troops, with some ten minutes remaining. Suddenly the tables turned, starting with a lone strike by Tony Callimore. Then trainee Jeff Thorpe plundered two quick goals to send the Carlisle United players into an exited heap, as they all piled on top of each other. At the other end of the pitch Scunthorpe's shattered side held their heads in utter dejection. Thankfully it was not all bad news during the month, and consecutive wins at Darlington, then at home to Barnet and Wigan Athletic restored confidence.

In the F.A.Cup, United again found themselves in line for a difficult time when they were pulled out of the draw to face Bradford City at Valley Parade. Not many gamblers would have taken a bet on Scunthorpe United to win, but the old cliche about the Cup being a great leveller rang true again. It would have seemed as if the Iron were in for some punishment when Neil Tolson shot the Bantams ahead in twenty-six seconds, while the rest of the attack had strolled through the Scunthorpe back line. Three minutes later and United were back on par. A cross was dropped by Paul Tomlinson in the Bradford goal, and the ball rolled invitingly to Chris Hope for an easy tap in. Scunthorpe United were quite at home for the rest of the tie, and with a little more fortune could have settled it then. In the event Dave Moore was not ungrateful for the replay.

The second and deciding game at Glanford Park hinged on a reckless tackle which had a huge baring on the events. Keeper Tomlinson ran out of his area in the sixth minute and made an horrific challenge on Christian Sansam. Sansam was left writhing and in need of attention. Tomlinson walked to the dressing room at the insistance of the referee.

The score sheet remained blank until Matt Carmichael fired in a close range shot when Ian Juryeff's header came back off the underside of the bar. Graham Alexandra made it 2-0 with a tremendous powerhouse drive from thirty yards after a little more than an hour. Then came a Bradford fightback from their ten men team. They pulled back both of the arrears, and actually kept in the tie with a ninetieth minute equaliser from Dean Richards.

The dramatic all important winner came six minutes into extra time, as City began to run out of steam. Paul Mudd made an excellent high cross, where substitute Ian Thompstone met it before stand-in goalkeeper Ian Bowling, and guided a header into the unguarded net. The result meant that Scunthorpe had played twenty-six F.A.Cup games at home since 1976 without defeat.

In between the two F.A. Cup-ties United had given a debut to blond forward Max Nicholson from Torquay. Nicholson only played once for the Devon club, but had appeared more often for Doncaster Rovers and Hereford. His Scunthorpe debut provided a goal at home to Mansfield Town, but sloppy defending cost United the points in a 4-3 thriller.

The news of the F.A.Cup was much better, as United had drawn Birmingham City for their first ever competitive game at St. Andrews. Sky Television had taken a shine to the tie, and broadcast the match live, bringing it forward to the Friday night. Don Rowing announced that with a television fee from the Sky people of £48,000, the receipts United would receive as a whole could exceed £75,000. It was certainly a great boost to the Clubs coffers now that the cost of running a football team had reached astronomical heights.

Once the match got underway United became settled, controlling the game with accurate passing. Birmingham City's manager was full of admiration at the way Scunthorpe played. If it was not for a couple of World class saves from Ian Bennett, Scunthorpe might have gone through to the third round where the winners would be in line to meet Liverpool. The Birmingham team may have been in the Second Division briefly, but they had cost a very large sum to assemble, and United had given them a real fight. At the end of the frantic ninety minutes that both sides were pleased not to have lost, the scoreboard showed no goals.

Sky were so impressed with what they saw that they put up the cameras again to see the re-run at Glanford Park twelve days later. This time Birmingham turned on the style, looking to be a very classy outfit. Scunthorpe United resisted the pressure for an hour, then two goals in two minutes virtually ended the tie as a contest. First Steve McGavin, then Gary Cooper pressed home the City case for supremacy. United did pull one back straight from a direct free kick, taken by Wayne Bullimore, but by then it was too late. The Scunthorpe coffers had filled up again, but the unbeaten home run in the Cup was gone.

The day after the replay, Scunthorpe took on loan a young Hull-born player from Oldham Athletic. John Eyre was a twenty year old with pace and accuracy, and in his two months stay at the Club he made a vivid impression. Eyre made his debut in the number ten shirt as a striker at the new Sixfields Stadium against Northampton. Scunthorpe won the game when Alan Knill forced in from close range early in the proceedings. In his next match Eyre scored his first goal for the Club against derby rivals Lincoln City.

It was the second goal of the evening and guaranteed a win. Halfway through Eyre's loan period, United took on board Stuart Young from Scarborough. These two players combined very well, enabling John Eyre to total seven goals in eight games. There had been memorable contests during his stay, especially those at home to Rochdale and Hartlepool United away, when 4-1 results had favoured United. Against Exeter City, Eyre scored two of the goals in the 3-0 success. In the last game of his stay he netted the final Scunthorpe goal of three before being substituted. United then proceeded to throw it all away and incredibly lost 4-3 at home.

Dave Moore experimented with other signings as the season continued into the Spring. Roger Eli, who caused a lot of trouble in F.A.Cup-ties with Burnley, was taken for a trial period but was rejected. Then Lee Turnbull was given a two month loan spell from Wycombe Wanderers until the end of the season. This North-East born midfield player was considered up to scratch, and during the Summer his efforts won him a full-time contract.

Then came Neil Gregory from Ipswich Town and Andy Kiwomya, both men taken on for forward duties. In each case United would have liked to have signed these players but nothing materialised. Neil Gregory was a keen goalscorer and almost had as much success as John Eyre. Unfortunately the attempted deal never got off the ground. In Kiwomya's case, his dazzling ball skills provided many chances for his colleagues, but unfortunately he was snatched from under Dave Moore's nose by Bradford City, and was given a larger pay packet.

There was however, the launching of two young careers which pleased local supporters, because they had come up from the junior ranks and nurtured through Scunthorpe United's school of excellence. The pair were Gainsborough-born Steve Housham and Michael Walsh, whose family came from Rotherham. The two of them made such an early impression that from the following season they were considered permanent members of the first team squad.

While the football season was rapidly disappearing, Scunthorpe were desperately trying to make the top six which would qualify them for a play-off place. The alteration of the League structure higher up meant that, for just this one season, only two teams would win an automatic place in the division above, and the next four would fight it out for the third spot. Two home games in the final approach showed how Scunthorpe could play in peaks and troughs. When Doncaster Rovers arrived, United expected to beat their neighbours, but Rovers ran riot. At the end of play they had savaged the Iron with a humiliating 5-0 scoreline.

It was probable that this result ended the local supporters' dreams of promotion. Then in the last game of the season, Preston were once again knocking on the door. Playing with far more authority, Scunthorpe curbed the Lancastrians spirits with a much better performance in a 2-1 win. This left the manager to rue the day his team gave away precious points to teams they were capable of beating, as only seventh League position was attained.

On the shopping list for the Summer of 1995, Dave Moore had included defender Paul Wilson from York City. In the forward position United had invested in the tall black target man Andy McFarlane from Swansea City, but perhaps the most notable news of new men was the fixing of the career of John Eyre at Glanford Park. Eyre had only been given a limited chance in Oldham's colours, and he was pleased to be guaranteed first team football by Dave Moore.

~ 1995-96 ~

To make way for the new players Scunthorpe United had already accepted late in the previous season, a small fee for unsettled Matt Carmichael from Preston.

Chris Hope challenges Preston's 'keeper, with half the opposition in attendance, plus Alan Knill and Andy Kiwomya. Chris, signed from Nottingham Forest, became a very influential defender in the division.

They also allowed Graham Alexander to join Luton Town for £100,000. United would miss the enthusiasm and skills of this young man who had matured since the day of his debut. This was not the only cheque received for this value, because a sell-on clause in the deal had yielded a similar bonus, when former player Mark Atkin moved to Wolverhampton Wanderers. Other transfers took Paul Mudd to Lincoln City, Damian Henderson to Hartlepool United, while Mark Smith and Ian Juryeff left League football altogether.

Cambridge United were the first team to roll up outside the Glanford Park stadium, ready to lock horns with the Iron. Scunthorpe initially got the bit between their teeth, and John Eyre was the first man to be featured on the electronic scoreboard, with a thirty-sixth minute strike. All seemed well until Cambridge sneaked an equaliser. Then came their killer blow in the dying minutes and the late goal sickener gave Scunthorpe insufficient time to pull the deficit back.

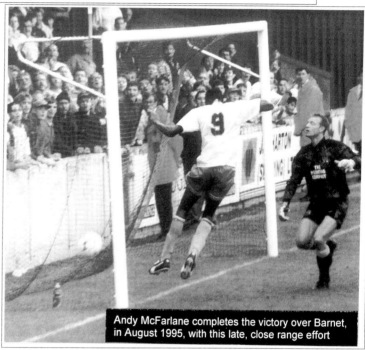

Andy McFarlane completes the victory over Barnet, in August 1995, with this late, close range effort

In midweek, Scunthorpe United looked to have sorted themselves out and received deafening applause as they left the field having devastated Rotherham United 4-1 in the League Cup first round first leg. One week later they were crying in their beer, for a 2-1 defeat at Wigan Athletic, influenced by a Scunthorpe sending off, was topped in misery by defeat at Rotherham.

It was not only the manner of the reverse but the shear size that mattered. Scunthorpe allowed the Millers to equal the tie in normal time, and in the thirty minutes extra played they took the score to 5-0, and overhauled United. Scunthorpe had been dumped out of the competition when they were odds on to progress.

It had been a frustrating match, with Moore having to bring the team back to basics, and they started the road to recovery by beating Barnet 2-0. An own goal by Thomas early in the

second-half did provide a generous start, but the numbers on the terraces dropped to below two thousand in protest. Dave Moore continued to do his best, but September was not a good month for either him or the team. It was not until the last game of the month that another victory was taken, and that was only a single goal beating of Colchester United. At one stage Scunthorpe had sunk to as low as third from bottom of the table.

The big talking point of the season arrived when the team went to Torquay. The Gulls were not the most formidable of opponents, being second off the foot of the division, three positions below the Iron. On the afternoon Torquay United's defence was non-existent, and this left the astonished Scunthorpe attack with the easy option to keep on scoring. At half-time Scunthorpe had gone 4-1 in the lead and incredibly set up a record 8-1 away win by the end. Andy McFarlane joined a select few players to have scored four goals in a game for the Club, while others came from John Eyre (two), Alan Knill and Tony Ford. Regrettably the enormity of the defeat cost Don O'Riordan, Dave Moore's former Grimsby colleague, his job as the Torquay manager.

Included in the Scunthorpe side facing Torquay was Jamie Patterson, playing his third game for the Club, having been given the chance after leaving Falkirk. He was a fiery Scot, with a lot of ball skills, who was able to link up with loan signing Phil Clarkson from Crewe. The next game was won 1-0 under less dramatic circumstances at Ninian Park Cardiff. United gave Clarkson the benefit of the doubt and came back for the goalscoring midfielder, signing him full-time in February.

When the time arrived for F.A.Cup duties, Scunthorpe United were handed the task of sorting out Northwich Victoria at their ancient Drill Field ground in Cheshire. Despite their much earlier Football League pedigree, Victoria were now of more humble stock enjoying mid-table comfort in the Vauxhall Conference.

Scunthorpe gave them the respect they deserved, but on a wet afternoon in November the gloom fell on the home dressing room. All the action came in the second-half, and was started by Tony Ford and Andy McFarlane putting the Iron two goals up. Later, there might have been some anxious moments, when Northwich pulled one back, but a misdirected clearance was intercepted and squared to Andy McFarlane to side foot home, and make the tie safe.

Scunthorpe United's next obstacle was Shrewsbury Town, who had caused them so much trouble in all competitions in the past. This was going to be no exception, although at Glanford Park, John Eyres' goal was just sufficient to eke out a replay. At Gay Meadow it was not long before events went wrong for United and they trailed back to the dressing rooms having exposed Samways to a strike by Richard Scott, then a penalty from Darren Rowbottom. Jamie Paterson may have reduced the lead, but the Shrews deserved their victory, and a shot at Fulham in the next round.

Throughout November and December, Scunthorpe frustrated their supporters with a poor run of six matches which only yielded a harvest of three points from a trio of draws. The most annoying result of this sequence was the home match against Scarborough, when Ford, Clarkson and Bullimore gave United a healthy advantage, which was frittered away to eventually earn only a 3-3 share. It was this result that induced Dave Moore to approach the Seasiders and persuade them to part with their midfield dynamo David D'Auria. He was to bring some delicate ball artistry to the middle of the park where it was needed most. Originally D'Auria had been signed by Scarborough from his home town club of Swansea.

To solve the problem United were experiencing during the poor run up to the New Year, Moore went to Sheffield Wednesday to take Ryan Jones on loan for two months. The improvement was immediate. Wigan Athletic were United's 3-1 victims and Jones led the way, firing Scunthorpe's first goal on his debut. Another 'first' was United's second goal of the game, which happened to be David D'Auria's initial strike for his new club. This began an inspired four match glut of victories, three on their travels, which had an about turn effect on the Iron's march in the League table; Unfortunately, such rich fruits soon dried up, and a barren run was to follow.

Throughout the whole of February and into the first three games in March, Scunthorpe United could find little in the way of scoring power and managed only two points from a possible twenty-one. The team had hit another spell of inconsistency and the Board of Directors once again had to get their heads together, making the difficult decision that Dave Moore had to leave the manager's seat. Dave Moore had been a likable sort of man who was popular with the players. Even when times were hard, the morale in the dressing room appeared to be high, but all managers live on results. Moore's Midas touch had deserted him and he had to suffer the consequences.

Shortly after Dave Moore packed his kit bag the directors made an announcement of his replacement. The man to take over was familiar to everyone, Mick Buxton. Mick knew the ropes inside out and wasted no time in getting down to work. His first game in charge was against Doncaster Rovers which ended in a two goal reverse. It did serve its purpose because Buxton knew where he stood with the team. One of his earliest assessments was that a different system of training and fitness needed to be introduced. He soon had the team having a stricter defensive attitude, while the forwards were encouraged to be far sharper in the box. Buxton's shrewd methods soon put the wheels in motion again, and his second spell in charge was almost a mirror image of his first. From when he took over in mid-March, Buxton was to see his charges only lose once more, and that was for the visit of promotion minded Bury.

During the later stages of the season United introduced two players from the loan system. Mark Samways confidence had suffered because of the pressures of results, and Gary Germaine, a Scottish 'keeper, came from West Bromwich Albion to good effect. There was also a couple of months given to Keith O'Holloran from Middlesbrough in the back half of the field. As time wore on supporters waited to see if full-time signings would be made for these two men, but nothing was forthcoming.

The end of season report showed that Scunthorpe United completed the season in twelfth position. Under Mick Buxton there had been a couple of outstanding performances, which were more in keeping with what supporters had hoped for. The visit of Exeter City saw the team in masterful form and able to crush the Devonshire men 4-0. Then in the last away match of the season they were off to the North-East coast of Yorkshire for the annual trek to play Scarborough. This time there was not the same amount of resistance from the Boro, and Scunthorpe swamped them with a 4-1 scoreline.

~ 1996-97 ~

When United lined up for the team photograph at the beginning of the 1996-97 season, Scunthorpe had another Paul Wilson in the frame. He was Paul D. Wilson, who was taken on as the youth development coach. The new man was joined by Nigel Adkins, a former Wigan goalkeeper as the Physio. Buxton also took on utility man Mark Sertori, a hard tackling no nonsense player, usually playing in the back lines, from Bury. Sertori had seen other service at Wrexham, Lincoln and Stockport. David Moss was also in the frame, and he looked to be an excellent acquisition from Chesterfield, but in September he left full-time football for a job outside the game in Scotland. However, he did continue in Scottish football at Partick Thistle.

There was another contract given to the much travelled Mark Gavin from Exeter City, but he never was able to hold down a full time first team place. A number of other men made short stays at Glanford Park in the senior squad without being regular members. These included Kirk Jackson, John Francis, Ian Dunn and John Borland, although in Borland's case he did play for a longer period with the reserves.

On the way out of the door were Tony Ford and Max Nicholson. Any hopes of seeing the last of Ford were quickly dashed as he picked up the threads of his career at Mansfield Town. To his credit he kept in the peak of condition and was to play for the Stags a number of times against Scunthorpe United in the years to come. Also gone, but at various dates during the past season, were Steve Thornber, Stuart Young and Wayne Bullimore. Bullimore was the most inspirational of the trio, leaving for the richer fields of Bradford City.

Scunthorpe United started the season with another Jeckle and Hyde performance. They started off with three consecutive wins, something that had not happened since the men of the Midland League days had been playing. Phil Clarkson hit the only goal of the game with twenty minutes left in London against Leyton Orient, and on the following Tuesday evening, supporters were treated to a battling Cup performance against Blackpool, who were still in the Second Division after winning promotion at Wembley in the play-offs against the Iron. Between the twelfth and eighteenth minute United went from a goal down to lead 2-1. The pace never dropped but the goalscoring stopped at that point. Phil Clarkson scored the winner, and he did so again at the home end at Glanford Park against Torquay a few days later.

Blackpool then took charge in the League Cup first round second leg. United were unlucky to lose 2-0, but it put the Club out of the competition. Bloomfield Road had been the nightmare of all Scunthorpe United's visits and no United team had been able to return home with even the morsel of a draw. This result introduced supporters to the start of an eight match spell which only saw a single victory against Cambridge United as any tangible reward.

To introduce some bite into the team Buxton went to Torquay where he signed the tall forward Paul Baker. Baker had already played against the Iron earlier in the season, but although he had not scored that day his new manager knew he was the type of player who was able to score goals anywhere.

His debut coincided with that of another debutant, the Spanish midfielder Alex Calvo-Garvia. The first game for both men was in a rough and tumble derby at Boothferry Park against Hull City. The Tigers had set off at a fast early pace up the table, but United matched them every inch of the way on this particular afternoon. All the real drama was reserved for the last two minutes, once Calvo-Garvia had been given his first taste of English football as substitute. First Clarkson and then Baker had the Iron fans dancing with delight at the late night final 2-0 show.

United continued with another victory over local opponents in the next contest, when a similar score beat Lincoln City. The most important factor in this game was the first goal

scored by the rapidly improving discovery Steve Hoksham. It was a great introduction for Scunthorpe United's next signing, Mark Lillis, who would not be taking up first team duties. He was joining the coaching staff, and his innovative ideas made a refreshing change to the training routines. The backroom compliment of Wilson, Adkin and Lillis was one of the best ever assembled by a Scunthorpe manager.

The final phase of October saw United's form wane somewhat, but when it came round to F.A.Cup action, the Club had the chance of a welcome break. There was to be plenty of interest in the game, for Rotherham United were plucked out of the hat for a journey to Glanford Park. This brought a crowd of close on four thousand, around a thousand more than the average Third Division attendance. Two quick goals brought joy to each section of the ground within the initial quarter of an hour. Then after half and hour David D'Auria stung the Millers, and Scunthorpe went in at the interval singing the loudest. A couple more strikes in the second section of the match for Scunthorpe left the Iron's supporters happy and ready to fight in round two, following the 4-1 success.

Scunthorpe United's next Cup battle took them to Wales to play Wrexham, a division higher in the League. On the day United were magnificent, twice taking a lead through Paul Baker, and when he struck the second effort, a penalty, past Andy Marriott in the home goal, around twenty five-minutes remained on the clock. It was not until the very last moment of the game that Scunthorpe gave way to the continual bombardment.

The replay was given the extra incentive of a money spinning home visit of West Ham United in front of the Sky Television cameras for the winners. Scunthorpe confirmed their desire to win, when in less than ten minutes Paul Baker shot them ahead, and this lead lasted until the seventieth minute. Two minutes later and Phil Clarkson looked to have won the tie at last. Little time remained on the watch when Samways made a mess of a clearance, gifting a second Wrexham leveller for Morris to stroke home from a couple of yards out. There was disbelief in the Scunthorpe camp, but everyone had to feel for the stricken home goalkeeper. Extra time was ordered, and United's players could not raise themselves against their rejuvenated opponents. Eventually the inevitable happened, and Scunthorpe tragically lost 3-2.

The repercussions of this costly misjudgement was that Mick Buxton took Preston's England Junior International 'keeper, David Lucas on loan, and Mark Samways was sidelined. It was felt that a career change would do the man who represented Scunthorpe at Wembley the world of good, and after a trial period Samways settled back in the groove at York City. At the same time, United signed Brian Laws, the ex-Grimsby Town manager, as a player. Laws was trying to re-establish his career, following some unfortunate circumstances which forced him to leave Blundell Park.

Coinciding with these alterations in Club personnel, Scunthorpe received some welcome news. Matt Elliott, the Club's former defender, had left Oxford in the middle of January for Leicester City. The fee was a cool £1.6 million, and a proportion of this would become a welcome windfall to the Iron, which would cover all expenses United had incurred that season. In the first week in February there was another cheque for £80,000 that came their way, but at enormous cost, with the loss of Phil Clarkson to Blackpool.

Scunthorpe United needed something to cheer them up through the darkest nights of the Winter because the middle of the season was filled with a combination of frustrating postponements and poor results. A run of eight matches that began at Christmas had only the scraps of a 5-1 win at home to Hereford United to keep them going. There was restlessness from the terraces, and supporters began to shout for the manager's head. In February Scunthorpe put up a feeble account of themselves for a midweek loss against Chester City. This was the third consecutive defeat, and was to prove to be Mick Buxton's last game in charge of the team.

United's board gave temporary charge to Mark Lillis, who threw his hat into the ring as a contender for the job. He immediately went out and signed two men, who were ready to play in the following Saturday's contest at home to Colchester United. While Samways had gone to York, United had taken from them their towering 'keeper Tim Clarke. Then from Notts County, Gary Jones was loaned to do one job, and that was to score goals. In his two months stay, until the end of the season, he had a fifty precent per game strike rate. Lillis lived and died every moment of the Colchester game, and a great roar of relief greeted a 2-1 victory at the final whistle.

It was now the responsibility of the board to make the decision as to who would lead the team towards the twenty first century. When the announcement came as to the identity of the new boss, the finger of fate did not point at Lillis. Instead the choice was someone equally close to United's affairs, for it was Brian Laws who would lead the Iron on to what they hoped was much needed glories. For Lillis there was still important work to be completed as Laws' assistant. The two men, plus Wilson and Adkin in support were to make the Scunthorpe United tradition continue. Once Laws took over the reins he lost no time in imprinting his ideals on the team structure. Like his predecessor, Mick Buxton, Laws was a disciplinarian who stood no nonsense.

This was reflected in his approach to the game and in what was expected of his players. There was a complete turnaround in results, and he was quite happy to pursue Lillis' thoughts over Clarke and Jones, but decided on three other reinforcements of his own. There was no doubting the touch of class, when he brought the dashing Jamie Forrester to score goals for the Iron, from Grimsby Town. Forrester had been part of the Leeds United junior squad which had won the Youth F.A.Cup.

In midfield, Laws took Justin Walker from one of his old clubs, Nottingham Forest. Walker was still a raw recruit, but given a first team opportunity he quickly adapted. Finally the new manager did business with Hartlepool for Sean McAuley in a deal which let Paul Baker go back to the North-East. McAuley was taken to fill in on the left side of the defensive set up.

Before United completed their fixtures, they gave a unique and important debut to a player on their books. The debutant was Youth Development Officer Paul Wilson who had always kept himself in trim appearing regularly in the reserves. When Brian Laws was short, Wilson had been included on the substitutes bench. At Cardiff, United suffered an injury to John Eyre, and the sub. took up his position to replace him. Paul Wilson hence became the oldest player this century to make his debut for a first class professional club, being thirty six years of age at the time.

There was little time for Scunthorpe United to influence the promotion situation, but by the end of the campaign they were pleased to settle for thirteenth place in the Third Division. Despite his move in February to Blackpool, Phil Clarkson was United's leading scorer on sixteen goals, followed by Paul Baker on fourteen, five of which were in the F.A.Cup. Brian Laws was not concerned that neither of these men were on the books anymore.

His strike force of Eyre and Forrester was still not fully matured, and he had plenty of plans for the future of his new club. After all this turmoil, United's supporters were again pleased to see calm prevail once more.

Jamie Forrester connects with the ball from Chris Hope's cross, while Ayre (no.9), Setori (no.40) and Knill (no.6) are on hand for any mistake by the Hull City 'keeper in the April 1997 local derby.

The Summer months gave Laws little time for a suntan, as he scrutinized the list of available bloodstock. It was not long before the Evening Telegraph was publishing a list of new faces to introduce supporters to the men that would be carrying their aspirations. In defence United were to offer places to Russ Wilcox and Jimmy Neil. Wilcox was a very strong signing from Preston North End. It was United's second attempt to acquire him, and he was to prove to be arguably the best of all the newcomers. His ability was as a centre lynch pin, and he was a real boon. On the left side of the rearguard, Scunthorpe looked to Jimmy Neil, who had a couple of first team games under his belt at Grimsby Town, the club he departed from. Neil went straight into the first team but was unable to maintain a regular position.

In the middle of the park, Scunthorpe took the services of Craig Shakespeare, a vastly experienced Birmingham born player whose clubs had included Walsall, Sheffield Wednesday and West Bromwich Albion, but again it was from Grimsby Town that he was signed. Despite a concerted effort he only played a minimum number of games for the Iron.

Up with the front runners, United started with a short term contract for Dave Regis, a black player, who had represented at least ten different clubs. He put himself about effectively, but after looking the part he was not retained. In the second-half of the season Laws had another think about him and he was offered a second chance. Unfortunately, just when he was becoming established, his career with Scunthorpe was ended with a serious injury at Lincoln City. Another forward to be injury prone was the huge six feet five inches tall Ian Ormanroyd; he is believed to be the tallest Scunthorpe United player of all time. Ian turned out to be a great trier, but never stamped his authority on team affairs as expected.

Laws best signings during the close season were his junior players who could not be denied first team prospects. This younger element included Paul Harsley, a Scunthonian rejected by Grimsby Town, Lee Marshall, an ex-Nottingham Forest trainee, and Darryn Stamp, who came from Beverley and had no previous League club experience. Also in an advance stage of development were Michael Walsh, Steve Housham and Alex Calvo-Garvia. It was particularly encouraging to see Alex brought on under the eye of the coaching staff, and as his English improved he began to adapt extremely well to life in the town.

Packing cases, and moving elsewhere, were Alan Knill, going to Rotherham, Paul Wilson, who would make Cambridge United his home following a successful loan period, while Mark Gavin went to Hartlepool to join Russell Bradley who had left late in the previous season. Lee Turnbull was given another chance at Darlington and John Borland left the Football League altogether.

United would see Andy McFarlane from time to time in a Torquay United shirt, and Jamie Paterson went back to Halifax Town, where his enthusiasm helped them back into the Third Division. Like Bradley, McFarlane and Paterson were away before the previous campaign concluded.

It was blistering hot sunshine that greeted the players on the opening day of the 1997-98 season at London Road against a very much fancied Peterborough, under the management of the irrepressible Barry Fry. Scunthorpe were raring to go, and at the same time make a favourable impression on their own manager. Both camps shed buckets of sweat, but when Jamie Forrester fired the Iron into the lead on the hour, there was to be only one winner. This fine form continued with a similar 1-0 result at home to Leyton Orient and a welcome double against Scarborough in the League Cup.

One of the most exciting players to make the team in latter years, the amicable Spanish midfielder Alex Calvo-Garcia, about to make a tackle in the opening home fixture.

The triumph over the Yorkshire side in the Cup competition was to lead to another massive payday when the second round brought them in line for a pair of games with Everton from the Premiership. More money was guaranteed from Sky Television who wanted to broadcast the match nationwide. The local population were keen to see these illustrious visitors, who were led by Scotsman Duncan Ferguson.

On the evening of the game the crowd of over seven thousand provided a marvellous atmosphere, although it was predictable that a number of the supporters wearing Evertonian shirts had local accents. From the kick-off, Scunthorpe United put themselves about in a busy fashion, and caused more than a nuisance. At the back of the Merseysides defensive wall Dave Watson was a rock which proved to be immovable, and it was his side that made the all important move to win the match. A slip in the Scunthorpe midfield allowed the ball to go out wide to Gareth Farrelly, who shunted forward and hit a raging shot beyond Tim Clarke at the home end of the ground.

Before Scunthorpe could make the replay they were involved in a home match with Hull City, which had a significant bearing on events. In the League visit of the Tigers, United repelled all advances by the Amber and Blacks. Forrester had given the Iron an early lead, but it was an incident in the second-half that caused a lot of concern. Tim Clarke raced out of his goal to relieve the ball from the foot of a Hull City attacker, and there was a sickening thud as the two collided, leaving Clarke prostrate on the floor. It was obvious that the brave 'keeper could take no further part in the proceedings. Chris Hope took the green jersey and went on to make a string of saves like a natural. Instead of looking after the stand-in, the rest of the team pressed forward and Alex Calvo-Garcia scored a second goal. This was Scunthorpe United at their most prolific.

Meanwhile, the League Cup at Goodison Park brought a stream of hopeful supporters across the M62 to follow the Iron in the second round second leg. The consequences of Clarke's injury forced Brian Laws to give a debut to the young second team goalkeeper, Tom Evans, who had been signed from Crystal Palace. Evans responded magnificently and while his outfield colleagues were having a torrid time, he became the Scunthorpe man of the match, despite a 5-0 scoreline in Everton's favour.

Throughout the Autumn Scunthorpe United kept in touch with the positions in the top half of the table. Against Exeter City, United became the first team to win at St. James Park that season. Colchester United thought they had beaten Scunthorpe when they went 3-0 up before half-time, and then almost lost the game in the last minute after Scunthorpe drew level. This draw was one of four matches without a decision for either side as United ran up to the time when they were ready for more action in the F.A.Cup.

Scunthorpe United were not displeased with another Cup-tie that would see them facing Scarborough. Laws was to make sure there was no complacency in the team and he knew the psychological advantage lay with his camp after beating them on League Cup duty. The game was to be the fiercest confrontation so far, and Scarborough played on a much higher plane than had been witnessed before. United also stepped up the pace, and both sets of supporters cheered a typical blood and thunder knockout tie. Just on half-time Wilcox headed in from close range through a crowded goalmouth, but Robinson restored the balance with a goal for the visitors seven minutes into the second phase. The winner did not arrive until twenty minutes from time, and as Alex Calvo-Garcia shot into the net past Kevin Martin, he stood hands aloft in front of the Scunthorpe fans to milk the applause. United took the match with a 2-1 result but late in the game a linesman's flag twice ruled out Boro goals for clear off-side decisions, much to the players anger.

Scunthorpe returned to Third Division action with the delight of two outstanding away wins at Rotherham and Torquay, winning 3-1 and 4-2 respectively. At this stage the Iron was up to fifth in the table, well on course for at least a place among the play-offs. Then a slide started with a visit of Brighton & Hove Albion, the team with only Doncaster Rovers below them in the table. United played like complete strangers, and subsequently lost 2-0. There would be worse to come!

In the F.A.Cup Scunthorpe had the pleasure of entertaining Ilkeston Town from the Midlands Division of the Dr. Martens League. The Derbyshire club were no mugs, and would finish as runners-up in their League at the end of the season. Ilkeston completely dominated the proceedings and had the audacity to take the lead in front of a large following of supporters in the fifty-second minute. Scunthorpe United were too professional to allow an upset to happen, and respectability came a quarter of an hour from time when Jamie Forrester forced the ball home. It was certainly a relief, because the non-Leaguers had given them a fright.

Snow swept through the country on the afternoon of the replay date, and the match was in doubt due to the freezing conditions, right up until kick-off. Finally, on a carpet of wet slush, the referee sanctioned the start, with a bright orange ball. This time there was to be no slip-ups, and Scunthorpe played with far more authority. By half-time the game was virtually sewn up. Forrester scored after ten minutes, with a low drive in the net behind which the Scunthorpe supporters were massed on a concrete terrace. Then on the half-hour, Wilcox notched another as he went in support of his attack. There were a number of pockets of resistance, but nothing that could not be dealt with. It was not until the seventy-second minute, when Moore, standing in an offside position central to the play, received the ball from a colleague and stabbed the ball home to make it 2-1. Scunthorpe cursed their luck but would have wished for similar fortune for themselves. The goal was not significant and it was to be the Iron who would be travelling South to London in January for a third round encounter with Crystal Palace.

While United's attention focused on the F.A.Cup, the misery of defeat was evident in the bread and butter affairs of the Third Division, and with vital refereeing decisions regularly going against them. The concern started growing as not a single point was won out of the four games in December. Consolation could be found in some good performances in defeat, especially at home to Notts County who were sprinting away at the head of the table. County's winning goal looked to be offside when Gary Jones, once scoring for the Iron, hit one from almost on the goal line.

Booking at the box office for tickets to see the Crystal Palace match was quite heavy, and Scunthorpe were to have a large contingent to roar them on at Selhurst Park. United really got stuck into their Premiership opponents who had not won a League match at home all season. It was difficult to see which team came from the top flight, and Scunthorpe fans did all the cheering, especially when Steve Housham let fly with a tremendous strike which hit the woodwork. The theme of play was of continuous Scunthorpe pressure throughout, but as is often the case, Palace had two shots on goal and scored twice. United even had the ball in the net from Forrester but it was mysteriously disallowed, for reasons that even the home side could not understand. At the end of the match Crystal Palace were humble in their apology to Scunthorpe for beating them, when on the balance of play it was the Lincolnshire side that deserved success.

Brian Laws' immediate priority was to deal with the team's diabolical deterioration in the League. United were sliding to defeat after defeat. The Board must have been very concerned at what was going on, and eventually the situation was so bad that the team lost the eighth match on the trot, at Macclesfield on a pitch as hard as rock and was barely playable. Scunthorpe appeared like an amorphous mess, and throughout the ninety minutes could not count on one effort that resembled a shot. Macclesfield scored twice in the first-half and should have had more in the second. Laws was a very angry man and let his players know.

The rehabilitation started slowly and surely at home to Swansea City. Tom Evans was brought back in goal for the game and Lee Marshall was promoted into the attack. David D'Auria had been a substitute at Macclesfield, but went straight into the starting line-up. After twenty minutes he scored and to everyone's relief the rot had at last been stopped. If they thought they were having a hard time it was worse for Doncaster who played them on the following Friday night. Poor old Rovers were anchored at the bottom of the Third Division, and fighting for their very survival. Scunthorpe were not at their best, but came from a goal down to scramble a winner near the end, from Steve Housham's second attempt at close range.

Once Scunthorpe United had got over their cold they began to play with a more reassured air. Laws produced a better blend in the team with a series of loan players or those taken on short contracts. These new faces included Martin Phillips, from Manchester City, Neil Woods of Grimsby, and Matt Murphy who came from Oxford United. There was another short spell for Dave Regis, while Martin Pemberton tried his hand for six games from luckless Doncaster. Promotion from Paul Wilson's junior ranks meant that there was to be first team groomings for Wayne Graves, Steve Nottingham, Gareth Sheldon, James Featherstone and Nathan Stanton. The morale amongst the players had improved, and no doubt the pre-match involvement of Mark Lillis and Nigel Adkins had a positive effect. Certainly United started to put an extra spring in their step.

The final part of the season saw the team edge nearer the top positions of the table as time went on. Only three defeats were to be suffered after the disaster in February against Macclesfield Town, until the fixtures ran out. There were some successes, such as four consecutive wins in home matches, including a 1-0 victory over the Silkmen of Macclesfield, Cheshire. On the other hand there were also setbacks, such as a defeat at Gillingham, where lowly Brighton were playing their home matches. Brighton only won six matches all year, but completed the double over the Iron. The United team could also look at a draw at home to Cardiff City as two lost points. Alex Calvo-Garcia fired them into the lead four minutes from time, but the defence caused Laws to deliver some curt comments, as they managed to give the Bluebirds a last gasp equaliser.

United finished the campaign in eighth place in the Third Division table, one point and five goals short of the play-offs. Support was up on average at exactly four hundred spectators per game, and they had seen the best and worst of the team over the last twelve months. Jamie Forrester was the leading goalscorer on thirteen strikes, but D'Auria, Eyres and Calvo-Garcia all edged into double figures. Much information was gleaned during the season, and if the younger element could develop, United's future was secure. The manager would also have admitted that he was a wiser man for his first full campaign in charge.

~ 1998-99 ~

During the Summer Brian Laws was busy attracting the quality players he wanted, ready for a promotion push at the start of the 1998-99 season. Laws selected two newcomers for the back four. The first, the nimble-footed Ashley Fickling, who impressed with the reserves, when he came for a trial from Grimsby Town earlier in 1998. Joining Fickling was Richard Logan, a Yorkshireman signed from Plymouth Argyle, and he proved himself to be a real tough customer. Unfortunately, a facial injury in a Lincolnshire Cup game delayed his debut for a short while.

In attack, United would enjoy the services of two new men. John Gayle was a towering black player, signed from Northampton Town, who was to become very popular with the crowd, and his huge frame often took the weight off the likes of Eyre and Forrester. Also making a presence up front was the vastly experienced Gary Bull, once of Barnet, but lately of York City. United were to bring him on from the substitutes bench towards the end of most games.

The new additions to the side meant that it was the end of the line for others. Ian Ormanroyd was forced to retire through injury, and Craig Shakespeare went into non-League football after a distinguished career. Port Vale swooped for Michael Walsh, who would make an acquaintance in the Potteries with former Scunthorpe 'keeper Paul Musselwhite. The two clubs could not agree on the transfer fee, and this was decided upon by tribunal. Finally Mark Sertori found new digs at Halifax Town, who had just come back into the Football League after an exile in the Conference.

The League season began early in August, and the computer gave the same start at Shrewsbury as had ended the previous campaign. This time round it was Forrester who put the Iron in front, but late in the game Shrewsbury came back with two, including an unlucky own goal by Ashley Fickling. It was a cruel blow to the side who deserved some reward for their valiant efforts. Fortunately there was a victory to be savoured at home seven days later, when United made comfortable work of beating Carlisle United. Chris Hope set the ball rolling with the first, while others came from Eyre and Gayle. Late on the visitors scored a consolation to make it 3-1. United supporters did not have long to see their team win on its travels either, for this came in the next match, at Hartlepool, where Richard Logan came on as a substitute to rattle in the vital goal, and Scunthorpe ran out 2-1 winners. By the end of the month the team had risen to seventh in the table, a position which would have been higher if not for a set-back at home to Plymouth.

In the meantime, Scunthorpe United played two League Cup games, a competition now sponsored by Worthington, against Blackpool. The first match was in front of a sparse 1,873 crowd at Bloomfield Road, and it was the home supporters who had the joy of cheering the only goal. One week later it was the referee who made all the headlines. Scunthorpe did far more than the 1-1 result suggested, but they had a goal disallowed, a penalty turned down, and a Blackpool player received a yellow card for an offence which other officials surely would have given a red. Later the referee made an apology to the club.

While the warmth of the Summer sun slipped away in September, Scunthorpe United went from strength to strength, gradually creeping further up the table. Although they started on a winning note in this period, at home to Torquay United, it was the next home game, played in midweek under floodlights against Cambridge United that gave most satisfaction. Cambridge had taken an early lead, but this was cancelled out before the interval by Jamie Forrester. After the break it was the Iron who surged forward looking for the advantage. The breakthrough came when a Sean McAuley free kick was touched on by Richard Logan through a mass of players. Scunthorpe looked to have stolen the points when John Gayle headed on a Justin Walker corner for Forrester to score his second goal from close in. However, the visitors were of an excellent pedigree and when they made it 3-2 the home followers had ten minutes of nail biting ahead.

Throughout the rest of September Scunthorpe United remained unbeaten, and a 3-1 win against Brighton in an away match, on the borrowed Priestfield Stadium ground of Gillingham, saw the unprecedented site of Scunthorpe top of the Division for the first time since the 1982-83 season. Into the bargain Brian Laws was named the Division's manager of the month. Later in the week, results by the reserves and the juniors meant that they, too, went to the top of their respective Leagues, making a unique treble.

Once the Iron were flying high on the crest of a wave the only place to go was down. Halifax Town became the first club to successfully lower their colours, and they did so in some style. Scunthorpe were uncharacteristically quiet, and the Eyre, Gayle and Forrester combination never managed to get out of first gear. Although the Iron survived the first-half, the Shaymen hit the back of the net four times after the break. This was the theme throughout the rest of this Autumn month, when the Iron never quite repeated the form which had taken them to the summit of the table. One casualty of this dip in fortunes was Sean McAuley, who lost his place for a time to Steve Housham, who was now back in contention after a long injury lay off. It was not until the last Saturday in October when another three points were collected. The visitors to Glanford Park were a very useful Rotherham United side who found themselves 4-0 down before they awoke from their slumbers. Then the Millers fired in three quick strikes to give a slightly generous 4-3 look to the score. The Iron earned their corn, thanks to goals by Wilcox, Eyre, a penalty, Knill a generous own goal against his old club, and a finale by Richard Logan. This result reinstated the club briefly at the top of the League again.

Once the clocks had been put back Scunthorpe hit patchy League form, winning one week and losing the next. At least the sparse number of draws meant that this vein of form still kept them in contention with the top of the table. Perhaps the best result of November was before the season's biggest home League crowd of 5,633, against Hull City. Passions were high and United were generally one step ahead of the lowly placed Tigers. Twice the Iron went in front, and twice the men from Boothferry Park rallied to equalise. Then came the dramatic moment as John Gayle received a second yellow card, and Scunthorpe found themselves in for a real fight. But they rose to the occasion, and substitute Lee Marshall squeezed in the winner just inside the post.

In the meantime the club had been called up for F.A.Cup duty. This season there was no segregation of the Northern teams from those in the South. The draw saw Scunthorpe having to travel South to play Woking from the Conference. On paper United knew that they could be in for a bumpy ride, and an injury to John Eyre could have been part of the ingredient to assist a shock result. However, the players on the park put in a professional performance and in truth Woking never had the opportunity to threaten Scunthorpe's control. The vital moment came halfway through the first-half when Tim Clarke kicked the ball out of his hands to Jamie Forrester. Forrester controlled the ball, beat two men as he advanced, and then delightfully lobbed over the marooned 'keeper.

At the beginning of December, the F.A.Cup brought the Club a home tie against Bedlington Terriers from the North-East. The non-Leaguers had caused something of an upset as they beat Second Division Colchester and the T.V. cameras were at Glanford Park looking for another shock. Local football supporters had to inspect the road map to see where Bedlington was actually situated, but Brian Laws had relatives living in the town, and his spies gave him valuable information on the visitors.

The game produced plenty of interest, and the away end was at near capacity with supporters, producing a gate of 4,917. United weathered the storm the gallant Terriers threw at them, urged on by the deafening vocal support. Most of the meaningful action came in the second-half, after Scunthorpe survived a good case for a penalty. However, it was a cheeky chipped penalty conversation by John Eyre which gave the Iron the advantage. Ten minutes remained, when Lee Marshall's shot was parried into the path of Jamie Forrester. Forrester made no mistake and effectively stopped the Terriers tails wagging at 2-0. There was just a moment to reflect on the draw for the next round, conducted live on television by Graeme Souness and Kenny Dalglish, which rather unkindly gave the Iron a tie at Second Division Wrexham.

When United returned to League action, consecutive defeats by Cardiff City at home, and Darlington away, saw United tumble to their lowest table position of ninth. Against Cardiff the only bright spot was a substitution appearance of the promising Natham Stadon who would be chosen again in future. At Darlington the outstanding player was full-back Andy Dawson making his loan debut from Nottingham Forest. Andy was to become a regular first team choice, and after some anxiety he was secured permanently in the Spring for £50,000.

Those two defeats were just the kick in the pants United needed. Brian Laws decided to give Tom Evans a chance in goal to regain confidence and the team went on to record five straight League wins, including 4-1 and 5-1 victories against Scarborough, away and at home respectively. Two goals at Scarborough by leading scorer Jamie Forrester, and another pair by the mercurial Spanish player Alex Calvo-Garcia, at Glanford Park, did much of the damage to the seasiders record. The match at home to Scarborough saw Gareth Sheldon make his first appearance of the season. His hard running on defenders and accurate shooting was a key part of the success the Iron's second string were having, and it was obvious that it was now the right time to give the youngster more of an opportunity in the first team squad.

Into the New Year, the F.A.Cup took precedence over the League on the first Saturday in January, and close on a thousand Scunthorpe supporters proudly displayed the claret and blue colours of the club. Wrexham had struggled at home in the bread and butter of their Second Division campaign, and United knew they could take advantage of this factor.

Initially the teams could only spar with each other and it took an unfortunate own goal by Richard Logan to give the Welshmen the lead on twenty-two minutes, as the ball cannoned off him into the net. However, it was in the second-half when the game came to the boil. In the first quarter of an hour, Connolly twice increased the Wrexham lead to 2-0, then to 3-1. Between times, Scunthorpe's substitute Steve Housham had scored near the left-hand post from within a crowded box. From then on it was all Scunthorpe as they descended on the home goal. Chris Hope was discharged up front to increase the Iron's aerial threat. Meanwhile John Eyre fired in United's second, and a tremendous lob on the run by Paul Harsley levelled the match at 3-3. In the time added for stoppages Alex Calvo-Garcia broke through to confront the 'keeper, but as he poised to shoot he was brought down from behind. All of the Scunthorpe camp appealed for a penalty. The referee waved play on, and in the blink of an eye Connelly completed his hat-trick and United were beaten 4-3.

Brian Laws had to be restrained seconds later when the match finished. The vocal protest from the visitors end was damning. A series of three photographs of the 'penalty' incident published in the Monday edition of the Evening Telegraph pointed to an emphatic case for a spot kick. It was now too late and Scunthorpe had to get on with matters in Division Three.

John Eyre completes his hat-trick against Brighton.

claim any three point games. Of four matches played, three saw them fail to score, although the draw at Cambridge United was a result many other sides would have settled for.

This match coincided with the debut of a lean black player, Tony Witter, late of Welling United, but formerly of Q.P.R., Millwall and Northampton. Witter had gazelle-like pace, and with the compliment of Dawson on the other defensive flank, United had a pair of the Division's fastest full-backs.

However, during this dismal spell the most inept display came at home to Rochdale. United never left the starting blocks and went down 0-1. It was not until the arrival of the nomadic Brighton and Hove Albion in the first week in March that spirits were lifted and Scunthorpe produced a performance Brian Laws knew his team was capable of. The Iron won 3-1, and the crowning glory belonged to John Eyre for a superb hat-trick. The only real debate was, which goal was the best. Perhaps it might have been the third down at the end where the home supporters were massed. Eyre burst through the defence on the right hand side of the field and shot home hard on the run past the Albion custodian.

Supporters were by this time appreciating the way Scunthorpe United were playing and foll- owing an appeal by Brian Laws they came to Glanford Park in greater numbers. The Brighton match, for example, was attended by 4,148

Alex Calvo-Garcia wheels away after scoring United's first goal against Leyton Orient..... John Gayle looks equally happy!

Once Scunthorpe United's bright run of consecutive wins was finished they found the month of February impossible to

paying customers, and after the beating of Chester City at the Deva Stadium, this figure was main-tained for the visit of

Leyton Orient in the next fixture at home. Orient arrived as the fourth placed club in the table, having lost least games than any other side to date. It was always going to be a tight struggle, but United capitalised in the second-half with scores by Calvo-Garcia and Forrester, without reply. This result meant that the Iron leap-frogged into the 'O's' place on the League ladder.

Scunthorpe United were to maintain their fourth spot in the League, despite losing the next two matches. First they went down 2-1 to a tall Swansea City side at Glanford Park, in a game re-arranged when the Welshmen had been involved on F.A.Cup duty on the original date. It was probable that the reason for this defeat was lack of concentration, especially as Justin Walker had fired them into an early lead. Certainly they should have cleared the ball which led to a corner from which the winning goal was scored near to full-time. Then at Plymouth, the Devon men completed the double with a 5-0 drubbing, on a night when they had little more than those five shots at the target all evening.

It was not long before Laws instilled confidence back in his men and led them back on course. Easter proved to be an excellent time, and six points were picked up against Exeter City at home and Southend United away. The trip to Roots Hall was particularly rewarding for Gareth Sheldon who won the game with his first senior goal in a 1-0 result. His cross shot from the right beat at least three stretching boots of the home defenders. It was a score which set the scene for the visit of Brentford, who, along with Cambridge United and Cardiff City, were Scunthorpe's main contenders for promotion. Naturally the interest brought a large crowd, numbering 5,604, the second highest of the season, to witness the event. The only missing factory over the intriguing ninety minutes was a goal, as each side equalled the other.

Scunthorpe United were well and truly on the run in to the end of the season. Peterborough were next in Town for a scheduled night game, and the Iron were desperately unlucky not to win. The Posh equalised from a direct free kick with one of their few meaningful attacks on the Scunthorpe target. This result was enhanced by a performance from the top draw against Hull City at Boothferry Park. During the first forty-five minutes United were devastating. Jamie Forrester fired home the first. Then Darryn Stamp turned on a sixpence and hit the second close to the goal line. In the second period John Eyre wrapped the points up with another tremendous strike near the penalty spot, to send almost two thousand visiting Scunthonians into joyful celebration. Hull did pull two goals back in the last seven minutes to give them a flattering look to the scoreline, but during the match they had been embarrassed by the slick Scunthorpe eleven.

The team continued to play some excellent football in their next game, at home to Barnet. The North Londoners came to Lincolnshire as a form team, even though they occupied a middle of the road table position, with no danger of relegation, and no prospect of promotion or play-offs. The Southern challenge was dealt effectively with a 3-1 result in bright sunshine. The only problem for the Iron was that as they continued to gather points, so too did all of their rivals. It was imperative that they win their next game, a twice postponed fixture at Halifax.

The Tuesday evening event saw a tough match with little in the way of changes. Richard Logan and Chris Hope were outstanding in the yellow and navy away strip emblazoned with United's Motek sponsors name. However, when the vital break came it was Halifax Town whom Lady Luck pointed towards, and they scored the only goal from close range.

With two fixtures remaining, Brian Laws was left with the situation where he had to make sure his troops won both, the next taking them to promotion rivals Cardiff City. If six points were not obtained, it would definitely mean another venture into the play-offs. At least there was some good news in mid-week, when the reserves lifted the Championship of the Pontins Division Three League. The two strikes made by Gareth Sheldon in the vital 2-1 win over Walsall Reserves earned him a place as a starter in the eleven chosen first team men. He was not to let his side down, and although Scunthorpe had most of the play, the 0-0 result guaranteed that Cardiff would have Division Three football, and the Iron would enter the lottery of the play-offs.

Unfortunately there were repercussions from the Ninian Park clash, for Tony Witter had the misfortune to tear a cartilage and was ruled out for the rest of the campaign, while Richard Logan had been sent off late on for a professional foul. These two incidents would seriously effect Scunthorpe United's selection options in the immediate future. Certainly they went through the motions in the final home game against Darlington, eventually losing 1-0 to a Gabbiadini goal six minutes from time. However, draws by Rotherham United, at Chester, and Leyton Orient, at home to Barnet, preserved the Iron's fourth standing in the League table. The interesting news from Scunthorpe United's point of view was that a late rally by Swansea City, who beat Hull City, meant the Swans were seventh and would face them in the play-off semi-finals.

Disturbances during the Swansea-Hull match led to the local Welsh Constabulary demanding a 12.30 p.m. kick-off. But despite the inconvenience, over six hundred hardy souls journeyed from Scunthorpe to the South-West. At the start supporters may have been surprised to see big Tim Clarke replace Tom Evans in goal for the first time since Christmas. There was also a call up for Steve Housham and Ashley Fickling, but it was apparent that Brian Laws was selecting for a specific game, not downgrading others.

The match turned out to be a real 'cup-tie' game, with Swansea City using their tall men to good effect, and they were particularly threatening at set pieces. Scunthorpe impressed the crowd by playing the purer football, and Captain Chris Hope led by example. As it happened, Matthew Bound headed the only goal of the ninety minutes right on half-time, from a free kick that was taken from just inside the Scunthorpe half of the pitch. Swansea had other chances to make the result safe, as did Housham and Calvo Garcia have opportunities for the Iron, but at 1-0, both clubs were happy with the score and were confident of a Wembley date.

On the following Wednesday more than seven thousand supporters passed through the turnstiles to create an electric atmosphere. The noise was deafening, while everyone found their heartbeats racing. Brian Laws came on to the pitch to urge the home supporters to get solidly behind the team, and

Rule Britannia boomed out from the tannoy as Mark Lillis paraded the flag of St.George. Even United's mascot 'Scunny Bunny' banged a drum.

On the field Richard Logan returned from suspension, and Paul Harsley took over from Steve Housham, who joined Gary Bull and Gareth Sheldon on the bench. Within two minutes of the kick-off, Scunthorpe raised the stakes with the vital goal they wanted. John Gayle flicked on the ball to Andy Dawson, who advanced and drilled it low and hard to the left of the goal behind which over a thousand visitors watched in disbelief. The rest of the ground erupted like a cannon blasting off. This gave the team the assurance it needed, but no further goals came despite the Iron's pressure. Swansea were always a force to be reckoned with, but they too could not find a breakthrough, despite having the better of the second period.

The game was fast developing into a tense stalemate, and at 1-0 extra-time beckoned. Five minutes before the referee's final whistle, Brian Laws played a trump card, when he replaced Forrester with Sheldon. This was to prove the turning point of this intriguing tussle which reached a climax in the first period of extra-time. In the ninety-second minute, Scunthorpe pressed forward, and John Gayle knocked the ball into the path of Gareth Sheldon who side-footed it home. The explosion of noise must have been heard in neighbouring Yorkshire. But six minutes after the second United goal it was Swansea's turn to celebrate, when a corner, taken from Clarke's left in front of the Iron supporters. The heads all went up, and Bird claimed the last touch as the ball narrowly crossed the line. At 2-2 on aggregate, Swansea City were in the driving seat due to the all important away goal counting double in the event of a tie. Scunthorpe surged forward as shattered Iron fans wondered if their dreams were over. It only took four minutes for the men in claret and blue to find an answer, and it was the hero of the hour, Gareth Sheldon, who took the accolade. In the heat of an attack, Dawson weaved his magic on the left before crossing to Sheldon, and the youngster's shot found the far side of the net.

Before the referee sounded the whistle for the mid-point of the extra period, he just had time to show John Eyre a second yellow card for a mistimed tackle, unfortunately caused by tired legs. It meant a 'backs to the wall' job for the remaining ten men, but John Gayle came into his own, shielding the ball with his huge frame, from the attentions of the frustrated visitors. Eventually the sands of time ran out and the referee ended one of the most exciting games ever witnessed at Glanford Park. Even more important Scunthorpe were at Wembley and the door of promotion was still open.

The whole town was buzzing with the prospect of a second visit to the twin towers of the World's most famous football ground. Scunthorpe United were inundated with demands for match tickets and bus travel, while calls for merchandise from the souvenir shop reached record levels. At the club, the management were quietly confident of victory, the mountain to climb this time being the challenge of London's Leyton Orient who had beaten Rotherham United on penalties after two goal-starved games.

On Saturday the 29th of May 1999, 15,000 Scunthorpe supporters made their way to the capital in eighty buses, dozens of mini-buses, and an endless stream of cars. All passengers were suitably clad in different versions of claret and blue. Unlike 1992, this body of supporters went believing the team would win, not just hoping for the right result. At kick-off, 36,985 fans rose from their seats to hail the combatants. The teams lined up as follows:
Scunthorpe United: Evans, Harsley, Dawson, Logan, Wilcox, Hope, Walker, Forrester, Sheldon, Gayle, Calvo-Garcia. Subs: Housham, Stamp and Bull.
Leyton Orient: Barrett, Joseph, Lockwood, Smith, Hicks, Clark, Ling, Richards, Watts, Simba, Beal. Subs: Maskell, Inglethorpe, Stimpson.

Both clubs were forced into changes as a result of suspension, and Lincolnshire supporters hoped that Sheldon would carry on where he left off against Swansea, while standing in for John Eyre. Evans was recalled in front of Clarke, and Paul Harlsey could have no better way of celebrating his twenty-first birthday. There was also the sight of Scunthorpe playing in their away strip colours.

Once the match started, in a boiling temperature, United knew that their belief in themselves was not to be underestimated. Only six minutes was on the clock when Gareth Sheldon took the ball close to the Orient goal-line, jinxed past his bemused defender, and put in the perfect cross for Alex Calvo-Garcia to glance home inside the far post. Garcia took off his shirt and waved it excitedly at the ecstatic Scunthorpe supporters, as his team-mates mobbed him in triumph. There should have been more by half-time, as Hope and Dawson went close, and the forwards ran the London defenders ragged. After forty-five minutes there was only one team in the game. Orient's manager made two changes at half-time, bringing on Maskell and Inglethorpe. The complexity of the affair altered immediately, and the Iron had some anxious moments. On two occasions, Tommy Evans must be given 'mentions in dispatches', and he was well supported by Hope, Logan and Wilcox. In the dying minutes of the play-off final, Scunthorpe could have increased the lead, but shots by Harsley and substitute Stamp were cleared off the line by the desperate Orient defence. As the minutes ticked away Brian Laws gave all his substitutes a taste of Wembley, roared on by the jubilant claret and blue army.

At the final whistle, the Scunthorpe section of the crowd went wild as the Iron players milked the applause and received their trophy and medals. It was the first promotion for sixteen years and it was well deserved. The press pundits could not decide whether Andy Dawson or Jamie Forrester should be named as 'The Man of the Match'. It mattered not. The fact was that ninety-nine years and exactly nine months after its birth, the Club had won a game at football's mecca. Now was the time to party, because after the reconvening of the new season, the task in front would be of the stiffest order. Even torrential rain on the journey home could not dampen the Scunthorpe spirits. While the club celebrated victory, a new chapter in their history was about to begin, as Scunthorpe United approached its centenary.

 **UP THE IRON!**

Scunthorpe United Managers

TOM CRILLY

Tom Crilly was Scunthorpe and Lindsey United's first deviation from the Directors themselves picking the team in favour of a team manager. He took over as Player-Manager in the Summer of 1935. It was probably his credentials as a defender at Hartlepool, Derby County, and Crystal Palace which swayed Scunthorpe's board into believing that Crilly could guide them to a second Midland League championship.

On the field, Crilly made twenty-five appearances as left-back in his initial season of 1935-36. At 5'9" and weighing 11st 7lbs, he was not the biggest of men, but could be nimble against some of the more robust forwards. During that campaign Scunthorpe United finished eleventh of twenty-one teams, gathering forty points from forty games.

Success during that time will be remembered, not in the moderate displays in the Midland League, but in a thrilling F.A.Cup run, when Scunthorpe reached the second round of the F.A.Cup, after beating high-flying Coventry City. Crilly also launched the Scunthorpe careers of Mal Millington and local man Jeff Barker.

Little was seen of Crilly on the park during the 1936-37 campaign, and after six appearances in the side his name ceased to be a feature in the team selection. At the end of his second twelve months, Scunthorpe finished in twelfth position of twenty-two starters. This result did not inspire the Directors to retain Crilly's services, and it wasn't until after the Second World War that the board took it upon themselves to employ another manager.

BERNARD HARPER

Barnard Harper was signed by the Board of Directors as Player-Manager for the 1946-47 Midland League season. Like many of his contemporaries, the hostilities had cut short his official playing career. However, Harper had continued to enjoy football at Barnsley throughout most of the War in a half-back position, and he had even been selected to represent England on one occasion.

In his two years at the Old Showground, Bernard Harper represented the team in eighty-seven League and Cup games, almost exclusively wearing the number six shirt, from where he was able to muster his troops and use his huge frame to good effect. It was under Harper's leadership that Scunthorpe signed Timmy Bowers for the forward line and Jack Brownsword in defence.

United were relatively successful during Harper's time, and he steered the club beyond the qualifying round of the F.A.Cup competition on two occasions. In 1946, they beat York City at Bootham Crescent, the only time, as a non-league outfit, that a Football League team was beaten away from home. Additionally, the Knuts made improvements in their League position. However, at the end of his two year contract, Bernard Harper parted company with the club.

Once again the United Board did not seem to be in any hurry to appoint a successor, despite having ambitions to join the Football League. Harper never succeeded to a position of authority in charge of a club in the Football League, and Scunthorpe United remained managerless until 1950.

LESLIE JONES

Leslie Jones had the honour of becoming Scunthorpe United's first Football League Manager, in June 1950. He made no rash promises of success, but instead gave the assurance that his side would work hard to consolidate the Club's position in the higher sphere of football.

Jones had started his career in his home town of Aberdare in the 1920's, where as a butcher's boy the youngster's skills had been developed on the local park. In his early days, Jones took up as a left-sided inside man and found goalscoring no problem.

In August 1929 he went to Cardiff City for four years and then on to Coventry City, before his transfer to Arsenal, in November 1937. At Highbury he reached the zenith of his playing days, winning a First Division Championship medal as well as topping up his Welsh International caps to a total of eleven.

After the War Leslie Jones had a number of coaching and scouting jobs at SwanseaTown, Barry Town, and Brighton & Hove Albion, and from the latter he joined the staff at the Old Showground.

Jones blended the best of the 1949-50 Midland League team with an influx of new men, many of whom were fellow Welshmen. Amongst his signings were former West Bromwich Albion and England International Wally Boyes, and Ted Gorin, who had previously been at Cardiff City; Gorin became the club's leading goalscorer. Jones proved to be a shrewd tactician, particularly at the Old Showground, where only York City won, and just nine goals were conceded. United's final League placing of twelfth was the best of all the four newcomers to the two Third Divisions. Unfortunately relationships between some Board members and the Manager turned sour towards the end of the season, and as a result of certain criticisms Jones resigned in the Summer of 1951.

BILL CORKHILL

The Board of Directors at Scunthorpe continued to have a half-hearted view on the subject of Managers, and when Leslie Jones left, Bill Corkhill was only put in temporary charge. It was not until an unrecorded date in 1952 that he officially took over as the Manager.

Corkhill was Belfast-born, but started his football at Northern Nomads, and then Marine. Whilst at Marine he was spotted by Notts County scouts, and from 1931 spent most of the next twenty years at Meadow Lane. He did enjoy a brief spell immediately before the War at Cardiff City, but when he finished his days at County, in 1951, he was the oldest outfield player to have represented the Magpies.

In Management, Corkhill turned out to be an honest man, well liked by his playing staff, and knowledgable in the game. He brought a string of excellent recruits to the Old Showground, the best of which included Jack Gregory, Gordon Brown, Merfyn Jones and Jack Haigh.

It was Bill Corkhill's game plan that saw the Iron through the mid-1950's, where in particular they earned a reputation as F.A.Cup fighters. In 1954 the three epic battles against First Division Portsmouth are well documented, and two years later his team reached the fourth round of the Cup for the first time.

Bill Corkhill enjoyed success in the Third Division North, twice taking the club to the brink of promotion, but unfortunately, he never achieved the ultimate prize. It was, therefore, with great reluctance that his resignation was accepted in May 1956, when he chose to take up a similar position at Bradford Park Avenue. His legacy turned out to be the foundation of a Championship winning side adopted and groomed by his successor.

Life at Bradford was a struggle, and he never enjoyed the same level of fulfilment as at Scunthorpe. He left in November 1957, later returning to Nottingham as a licensee, and died in 1978.

RON SUART

When Bill Corkhill resigned, the Board of Directors uncharacteristically acted without hesitation. Within a matter of a week or so, thirty-six year old, Kendall born Ron Suart was announced as the new man at the helm. For Suart it was his first appointment as Manager of a Football League side, having made his baptism at non-League Wigan Athletic twelve months earlier.

Suart's playing career started at Blackpool, but was halted after less than a year, due to the start of the War. In January 1946 he continued to wear a Blackpool shirt, where he established himself as a strong tackling full-back. In 1949 he moved to Blackburn for six years, before he became Player-Manager at Wigan.

Suart took a full season at Scunthorpe to assess the playing staff around him, gradually changing faces as necessary, before adding the finishing touches in the summer of 1957 to what would be a squad to take United into the Second Division. Among his signings were goalkeeper Ken Hardwick, captain and half-back Frank Marshall, Jack Marriott, the return of a local lad, plus forwards Eric Davis and Ronnie Waldock.

It was the 1957-58 season that made Suart arguably the most successful Manager in Scunthorpe United's history, when the team stormed to the Third Division North Championship by a handsome margin. Into the bargain United progressed to the fifth round of the F.A.Cup, overcoming Newcastle United en route, and winning the Sunday Pictorial Giant Killers Cup. Before he could savour the full fruits of his victory, Suart left at the end of the campaign to manage Blackpool. His football career continued into the early 1990's, at such places as Chelsea and Wimbledon, but in different roles.

TONY McSHANE

Tony McShane was the second Belfast-born Manager of the club. His appointment as successor to Ron Suart may have been something of a surprise, because his only previous management skills had been learned at Goole Town during the 1957-58 season. Nevertheless, he had managed to secure Goole a place in the first round of the Cup, ironically against Scunthorpe, which may have influenced the Board to offer him the job at the Old Showground in May 1958.

As a player, McShane had enjoyed his playing days as a wing-half at Plymouth Argyle from the end of 1949 (helping Argyle to the Third Division South Championship in 1952), to mid-1955, when he joined Swindon Town. During a managership that lasted a little less than a full season, McShane did his best to see that the Club staved off relegation to the newly created Third Division.

United rarely left the lower regions of the table, but always looked to be odds-on to beat the drop, and they finished five places off the bottom.

Generally speaking McShane had vindicated his appointment without setting a blazing trail. He did have some notable successes in the transfer market, including Welsh under-23 international 'keeper Ken Jones' signing from Cardiff City. He also brought in Peter 'Noddy' Neale from Oldham, and later, goalscorer Peter Harburn from Everton.

April 1959 saw McShane leave Scunthorpe United to take a post outside the game, however, he was back in football as Manager of Chesterfield from 1963 until May 1967 when he left the game for good.

BILL LAMBTON

Bill Lambton's contribution to Scunthorpe United's history is infinitesimal as it lasted only three days. It was said that he gave Scunthorpe a verbal agreement in April 1959 but decided to take up a coaching job instead. United would not have been pleased by the embarrassing situation, and had to start the selection process all over again, before Frank Soo took the reigns.

Lambton had been a player on the books of his home city club, Nottingham Forest before the War, but joined Exeter City in 1946. A goalkeeper, his career lasted only a matter of months in Devon, before he moved North to Doncaster in October 1946. It is not certain how long he wore the number one shirt, but during the 1950's he took up coaching in such diverse places as Grimsby and Denmark. Leeds United took him on as trainer-coach in November 1957,

and he was elevated to Manager thirteen months later. It was he who brought Don Revie to Elland Road, as a player.

If Ron Suart was the most successful Manager of Scunthorpe United, then statistically, Bill Lambton had the worst record. His only game in charge is thought to be the final game of the 1958-59 season, at home to Huddersfield Town. His counterpart was Shankley, who included Dennis Law in the Terriers' team. The youngster's dazzling skills brought two goals and an overall 3-0 defeat for Lambton.

Two years following his brief sojourn in Scunthorpe, Bill Lampton became Manager at Chester where his tenure lasted a little short of two seasons. In July 1963 he left the game, and died in Nottingham aged sixty-one.

FRANK SOO

Scunthorpe United needed to quickly re-establish a reliable new Manager after the three day debacle involving the previous incumbent Bill Lambton. The man chosen was Frank Soo who was appointed in June 1959. Frank Soo, real name Hong Y Soo, was of Chinese extraction and born in Liverpool. He made his way through non-League circles at Prescot Cables before signing for Stoke City at the beginning of 1933.

During the War he guested for a number of teams, including Everton and Chelsea, and during this period he represented England in nine unofficial Internationals. Once the hostilities were over Leicester City and Luton Town enjoyed his services, until he drifted out of League Football, moving to Chelmsford City in 1948, and later to St. Albans

City as Manager, before taking up the same position in Scunthorpe.

At the Old Showground, Frank Soo found there was little room for error between relegation and safety. However, the signings of Harry Middleton, Dennis John, Martin Bakes and the legendary Barry Thomas made life a lot easier. Thomas and Middleton blended very well with Jack Haigh, at the twilight of his career. Each of these goalscorers reached double figures to help Frank Soo's squad to a slightly improved table placing of fifteenth.

In early May 1960, Frank Soo resigned, wishing to seek pastures new. He accepted a number of coaching jobs in Sweden and Denmark, and the Old Showground was to be his only senior managerial position in the Football League.

DICK DUCKWORTH

When Scunthorpe United invited Dick Duckworth to become Manager in May 1960, there was no denying they had taken a very experienced man on board. He had played for a string of clubs including, Carlisle United, Rochdale, Oldham Athletic, Chesterfield, Southport, Chester, Rotherham United and finally York City before the War.

His first post-war position as a Manager was in the humble surroundings of Newark Town, followed by a spell scouting for Birmingham City and Sheffield United. In 1950, Duckworth took charge of his first Football League club when he returned to York City, and then beat a path to Stockport where he was at the helm from October 1952 until the end of the 1955-56 season. When he parted company with the Cheshire club Duckworth returned to Bramall Lane as Chief Scout. Prior to his Scunthorpe appointment this interesting character spent from October 1957 as Darlington's Manager, taking them to the F.A.Cup fifth round in 1958.

There can be no doubt that Duckworth took Scunthorpe to both their Zenith and Nadir, the Iron finishing fourth in Division Two in 1962, their best position to date. Two years later his team was relegated to Division Three.

Whilst Duckworth was in charge, United sold Barry Thomas for an equivalent fee of £40,000, and little more than a year later John Kaye moved for a similar figure. Although these dealings made the club a lot of money, it was claimed that this was soon spent, with inadequate player replacements. It was suggested that the sale of these top quality players cost the team promotion to the First Division, and a tremendous amount of support was lost from the terraces within a short period of time. In any event, Duckworth left the Old Showground in November 1964, with many loyal supporters disgruntled at the way affairs had been handled. The Scunthorpe position was the last official job Duckworth had in football, and he died in Sheffield, in April 1983 aged 76.

FREDDIE GOODWIN

Freddie Goodwin followed as Scunthorpe United's Manager in December 1964, one month after his predecessors contract had been terminated. He joined the Club at a time of disquiet, but despite the many problems he soothed the situation with a firm and quiet, but positive, approach to matters. His reassuring manner quickly won supporters over, as the team gradually improved.

Freddie Goodwin was a towering figure at over six foot, and stockily built. He made his way from schools football straight into the youth team at Old Trafford as one of the Busby Babes with Manchester United. Chances in the first team were few at that time, and it was not until the tragic events of the Munich air disaster that he gained a foothold on a more regular basis. During 1958 he was a member of the heroic United team that lost 2-0 to Bolton in the F.A.Cup Final.

Goodwin next went to Leeds United, but a broken leg put paid to his notable career as a half-back at top level. Once he had regained his mobility, Freddie chose to go into management as a Player-Manager at Scunthorpe, although the injury limited him to only a handful of appearances. He soon brought a number of his own players into the first team to good effect, including Ray Clemence, who was nursed through the junior ranks into first eleven prominence. He was also responsible for other signings such as Geoff Sidebottom, Keith Burkinshaw, Frank Burrows, Brian Bedford and Bobby Smith. When the old hands failed he was not frightened to blood youngsters. On one infamous occasion, Goodwin put too many inexperienced men in the side and they were overwhelmed by Grimsby Town, but Freddie was humble enough to make a public apology.

Under Goodwin's control Scunthorpe enjoyed a fourth spot in the 1965-66 season, and gained a record 8-1 home triumph over Luton Town.

In October 1967, Goodwin left to take over as Manager of the New York generals, later moving on to Brighton and Hove Albion and Birmingham City. One little known fact about Freddie Goodwin is that he played eleven times for Lancashire at cricket, and took twenty-seven wickets.

RON ASHMAN

If ever there was a man that Scunthorpe United owe a great debt to it is Ron Ashman. Ron was responsible for two stints in charge at the Old Showground, first in October 1967 and secondly from January 1976. On each of those occasions Scunthorpe United were in trouble and he managed to turn the tide.

Ron Ashman began his career as an amateur with Norwich City in 1944, and between 1946 and 1963 made 662 appearances for the Canaries as a professional. During his days at Carrow Road this excellent club man normally played at left-half, captaining City to the F.A.Cup semi-final in 1959, and taking them into the Second Division in 1960. His roll in the 1960-61 season F.A.Cup fourth round tie was instrumental in the downfall of the Iron. Ron took over the managerial duties at Carrow Road from 1962, until parting company with his beloved Norfolk club in 1966.

Norwich City's loss definitely became Scunthorpe United's gain, when he became the Iron's Manager in October 1967. Ashman's predeccessor, Freddie Goodwin, eased the Club's severe financial position by buying some of United's players for his American adventure. Ashman's answer was to plug the holes with a number of former East Anglian men including Bill Punton, Mel Blyth, Geoff Barnard and Steve Deere. Unfortunately this was not sufficient to stave off relegation, but it formed the basis of a more stable structure for the club. Ashman, a man well liked by his players, also recruited George Kerr and Terry Heath. But the trump card was the discovery of one Kevin Keegan, who made his debut for the Iron at Peterborough in 1968.

Ron Ashman brought a moderate degree of success to the Old Showground in the early seventies, first by reaching the fifth round of the F.A.Cup in February 1970, then by winning promotion to the Third Division two years later. This austere period prevented him from strengthening the squad, with relegation following twelve months later, and Ron moved on to Grimsby Town July 1973.

Ron Ashman never enjoyed the same admiration he had gained in Scunthorpe in his two seasons at Blundell Park and lost his job in February 1975. Meanwhile, Scunthorpe United were lurching through a number of crises, and non-League football was a strong possibility when he answered the call again in January 1976. Immediately Ron tightened up the defence and instilled more confidence into the front runners. The effect was instantaneous, and from a seemingly impossible League position, anchored in the bottom four, Ashman clawed the side into a position of safety.

Ron Ashman never had the resources he would have liked, to benefit in the transfer market, instead having to rely on a 'make do and mend' policy at which he was nothing short of brilliant. He kept United's head just above water until 1981, when he went upstairs as General Manager, only to be succeeded by John Duncan. Early in 1982 the acute financial situation claimed his job along with others.

However, Ron always kept close to the town, and for a number of years ran a popular travel agency on the High Street. In recognition of his loyal service he was made a Vice-President, and still attends virtually all Scunthorpe home matches at all levels.

RON BRADLEY

Staffordshire-born Ron Bradley came to Scunthorpe United in 1972 as Coach under Ron Ashman. When Ashman departed for Grimsby Town Bradley seemed to be the natural successor, and was promoted in June 1973.

Bradley's early football days began as an amateur in 1954 at West Bromwich Albion, where he operated as a wing-half. Two years later he was a professional at the Hawthorns where he enjoyed a further eight seasons. In 1964 he was transferred to Norwich City, and became acquainted with Ron Ashman. Ironically in all the years he was in the game he only made seventeen first team appearances. This lack of high level experience may have influenced his decision to take up coaching when he moved to Wolverhampton Wanderers in October 1966. Bradley's next move was to coach in Greece with Olympiakos, where he won recognition for his services, after his club won the 1971 Greek Cup Final. At the end of his two year Greek escapade Bradley returned to England and joined the staff at the Old Showground in 1972.

His first season in charge, 1973-74, was marked by an F.A.Cup run which saw the Iron reach the fourth round of the competition and enjoy a couple of epic games against Newcastle. United's League form in those twelve months was only moderate and they could only manage a final eighteenth place in the table. A disastrous run in the following season left the Board in a difficult position of having to part company with Ron Bradley as the team struggled in the bottom four re-election spots.

However, it was he who blooded Richard Money into first team football, although with Money's Lowestoft background Ron Ashman's influence must have also been present. Bradley also gave debuts to Stuart Pilling, Ken Houghton and Chris Simpkin.

Post-Scunthorpe, Ron Bradley coached in countries within two continents, first with the Libyan National Squad, and then a spell in the United States, before a return to England, at Derby County. In 1986 be became an FA Coach.

DICKIE ROOKS

Dickie Rooks was a Sunderland-born man, who, at the age of seventeen, signed for his home town club in the Summer of 1957. His chances at the centre-half position were limited because of the dominating presence of Charlie Hurley. This was the main reason for Rooks' move to neighbouring Middlesbrough in August 1965, for £20,000, which gave him instant first team football over the next four years.

Early in the Summer of 1969 he moved to Bristol City for a fee of £17,000, well away from his North-Eastern roots. This transfer was rumoured to have resulted from certain disagreements with his former club. Whatever the real reasons, many Middlesbrough supporters were unhappy at the final outcome. After his playing days were finished at Ashton Gate, Rooks returned to the North-East, and took up a coaching role with Willington.

In November 1974, Rooks was successful in obtaining the Scunthorpe United Manager's job. At the time United were in a stricken position in the bottom four, with little or no cash available, and the new man could do nothing to push them up the League with new signings. Indeed by the end of March it was plain they were a re-election certainty, and the bottom place for the Club's one and only time resulted. Bob Oates was the only player given a debut during this time, and he was from the junior ranks.

Scunthorpe United were re-elected for the 1975-76 season, and Rooks signed Clive Wiggington, Archie Irvine, and Dudley Roberts amongst others, to try to revive fortunes, he even gave a chance to striker Rick Green from local football. Despite the fresh faces Scunthorpe United once again slumped to the depths of Division Four.

Dickie Rooks made great efforts to turn the tide, but the Board of Directors decided to terminate his contract and he was dismissed in January 1976. He probably considered his tough baptism in football management was enough, and the position at Scunthorpe was therefore his last known salaried job in football.

JOHN DUNCAN

John Duncan succeeded Ron Ashman, as Player-Manager, although at this time he had no managerial experience, but was known for a distinguished playing career both North and South of the border. His enthusiasm for the game and fresh ideas no doubt won him the approval of the Board of Directors.

John Duncan was born in Lochee, Scotland, in 1949, and made his way through junior football to eventually sign for Dundee in April 1966. During the next eight years he gained Scottish League representative honours, and a Scottish League Cup winner medal in 1974.

He was lured away to Tottenham Hotspur in 1974, for a £125,000 fee, and then left for Derby County in 1978 for £150,000.

Sadly, Duncan's career became dogged by injury and Derby had to suffer a financial loss when he left for the Manager's seat at the Old Showground im 1981. The legacy of his injuries were such that he played little in Scunthorpe United's colours. The Iron were just about holding their own, but the 1981-82 season was a time of crises and upheaval. There was virtually nothing in hand to buy new players, and old contracts meant that Duncan had to soldier on with that available.

United slumped as the end of the season approached, and not until the last couple of months was Duncan able to bring in a number of men on short term contracts. Alas, this could not save the club from finishing next to bottom in Division Four.

Duncan's managerial career began to blossom in the 1982-83 season when he brought in a number of new players, including Steve Baines, Les Hunter, Neil Pointon, Dennis Leman, Martin Fowler and Noel Parkinson. Overnight the team was transformed as they headed towards the top of the League. A good F.A.Cup run plus a potential promotion place looked to have secured Duncan's future at the Old Showground.

Unfortunately it all turned sour after defeat in the F.A.Cup third round replay at Grimsby, when it would appear that there were differences between the Manager and Chairman which led to the shock dismissal of Duncan in February 1983.

Many considered that Scunthorpe had lost an excellent young Manager, and his departure was mourned on the terraces of the Old Showground. However, John Duncan went on to control the affairs of Hartlepool United, Ipswich Town and Chesterfield, twice, where he steered his Second Division team to the F.A.Cup Semi-Finals in the 1996-97 season.

ALLAN CLARKE

Allan Clarke came to Scunthorpe United in February 1983, when Chairman David Wraith introduced him to supporters as the Club's big name signing, to replace John Duncan. Clarke was experienced at all levels of the game and looked to be the answer to Scunthorpe's prayers. At last the Iron looked as though they might be on a winner.

Allan Clarke's career had started fairly low key at Walsall, with further progression at Fulham, before Leicester City paid £150,000 for this phenomenal goalscorer. After thirteen months at Filbert Street he moved on to Leeds for £165,000 in July 1969. At Elland Road he reached the pinnacle of his playing days, winning nineteen England Caps, as well as medals for the F.A.Cup plus League Championship victories, and eventually spent nearly nine years at the club.

In May 1978, Allan Clarke became the Player-Manager at Barnsley, and led them to promotion from Division Four in 1979. This, no doubt, encouraged Leeds United to offer Clarke the Manager's job at his old club in October 1982, but his lack of success there led to his dismissal in June 1982.

Clarke appreciated, in the Winter of 1983, that the Scunthorpe team might not be good enough for promotion, and strengthened the squad with the much travelled Like Lester and

Tommy Graham; the latter scored twice in the last day of the season promotion clincher.

During the Summer break of 1983 Clarke made a number of signings, including Paul Longden, Mike Brolly, Julian Broddle and John Green, and during the season he brought in others such as Micky Matthews and Alan Whitehead.

Unfortunately the squad was not strong enough to fight off relegation, due mainly to a poor away record. However, there was one compensation that season, for United won through to the fourth round of the F.A.Cup, after ironically beating Clarke's old club, Leeds United in round three, after a trio of epic battles.

Before the team had time to settle back in the Fourth Division, a number of boardroom changes took place, and the power struggle upstairs led to the Chairman and Manager leaving the club. It was a great shock to supporters who were unprepared for the sudden departures.

Allan Clarke returned to manage Barnsley in July 1985 for more than four years, before taking charge of Lincoln City for four months in 1990. The Sincil Bank position was his last in football, but he still lives with his family in the Scunthorpe area.

FRANK BARLOW

Frank Barlow was always thought of as a gentleman, quietly spoken and with good ideas. He came to the club as assistant under Allan Clarke, and succeeded him in the Manager's post. The Scunthorpe policy of promoting from within thrust Frank into the limelight for his second period in charge of a League club.

Frank Barlow's career as a player started as a highly rated youngster at Sheffield United, where he operated as a wing-half, winning England International honours at schoolboy level. At Bramall Lane, Barlow made more than 100 appearances in seven years, before a transfer to Chesterfield in August 1972 for a record £15,000 Saltergate transfer fee. His career as a player was dramatically cut short through injury, in 1975, but on his recovery he continued as a Coach. When the Manager, Arthur Cox, moved to Newcastle, Barlow took the reigns but lost his

job in 1983 after the Spireites were relegated to Division Four. At Scunthorpe, Barlow enjoyed three years in charge of team affairs. During that time he brought in the likes of Billy Russell, Steve Lister and Steve Johnson, and also arranged the return of several players including Richard Money, Dave Hill and Les Hunter. Julian Broddle also came for a second spell, but on loan, and this move never materialized into a full contract. Under Frank Barlow's charge, Scunthorpe had memorable games against Aston Villa in the League Cup, and Tottenham Hotspur in the F.A.Cup, but the bread and butter Fourth Division programme rarely saw the Iron threaten promotion, and inevitably his tenure of office was terminated, in March 1987. After leaving Scunthorpe Frank remained in the game, notably as Assistant-Manager at Barnsley, and he also spent some time coaching at Sheffield Wednesday.

MICK BUXTON

Mick Buxton's association with Scunthorpe United began in April 1987 when he succeeded Caretaker-Manager Richard Money, who had taken charge at the end of Frank Barlow's term in March. This was to be the beginning of two spells at United, the first of which bridged the transition period between the move between Grounds. Buxton soon stamped his authority on team matters, displaying a no nonsense approach which soon gained positive results.

Mick Buxton started as a player at Burnley, making nineteen appearances in nine years from 1960. In June 1960 he moved to Halifax Town as their Player-Coach, playing only thirty-five games, where a serious leg injury was the main reason for his limited outings. Buxton then had seven years coaching at Southend United, until 1978, when he moved back North to take a similar position at Huddersfield Town.

Before long, the Terriers parted company with Manager Tom Johnston, and Buxton took over. He was an instant success, gaining promotion for the club in 1980 as Division Four Champions, and three years later moving up to the old Second Division. Although the team remained at this level for sometime Buxton departed in 1986.

At Scunthorpe, Mick Buxton soon built up a very forceful team which flirted on occasions with the play-offs but could not quite win promotion.

Among his signings were Paul Musselwhite, Tony Daws, Richard Hall, Neil Cox, Mark Lillis, Stuart Hick, Paul Ward and Kevin Taylor. It was under his management that the Tony Daws/Andy Flounders goalscoring partnership developed into one of the deadliest of United goalscoring duos. Another Buxton signing was that of Bill Green as his assistant, but in January 1991, pressure from the terraces was probably a factor towards his loss of the Manager's job.

After leaving Scunthorpe United Mick Buxton took a number of positions in the game, before becoming the Sunderland Manager, where he was initially successful, saving them from relegation to the new Second Division. Mick Buxton was dismissed when the Rokerites could not make it to the Premiership under his guidance in March 1995.

It was something of a surprise to Scunthorpe supporters when Buxton was reappointed to manage Scunthorpe in March 1996, following a poor run of form and the sacking of Dave Moore. Buxton returned with his strict disciplinary methods and expectations of high work rates from players, and once again the immediate results were of a high standard. Two of his signings were Brian Laws and Mark Lillis, the former an experienced player, and the latter as Assistant-Manager. In February 1997, when Buxton's team failed to produce, Lillis, originally became Caretaker-boss, before Laws took over permanently, with the former continuing as his assistant.

BILL GREEN

acquainted with Frank Barlow.

Bill Green became Manager after a long apprenticeship as assistant to both Mick Buxton and Frank Barlow. His succession came in February 1991, and Green immediately won the favour of the local supporters by taking the Club to the play-offs. This was quite an achievement for the tall Newcastle-born Manager, who had an air of authority, despite his softly spoken voice and unhurried ways.

Bill Green started his football nearer his home city, at Hartlepool United in 1969. Four years later he was transferred to Carlisle United for £15,000, where he represented the Cumbrian side in their only season in the old First Division. In 1976 he moved South for £100,000 to play for West Ham United, and after two years moved to Peterborough United for £90,000, in the Summer of 1978. After 12 months, Green moved on to Chesterfield as Player-Coach under Arthur Cox, and during his four year period there he became well

In June 1983, Green made his last move as a player to Doncaster Rovers, before being snapped up by Barlow as his Assistant-Manager at the Old Showground in October 1984.

During Bill Green's first week, his initial task was to oversee the transfers of Neil Cox and Richard Hall, for a total fee of £650,000, and these dealings did not help to stabilize the team selection. Green's most notable early success was a very strong run at the end of March and into April 1992, when the team achieved a play-off place and a first Wembley appearance. During the next campaign, Green never quite reached the same heights, although this may well have been due to an overstretched team where there was not enough strength in depth to cover injuries. The expected promotion push never materialized, and as the fans patience ran thin, he inevitably became yet another football managerial casualty, in January 1993.

RICHARD MONEY

Richard Money originally came to Scunthorpe as one of many who made their way up from East Anglia under the watchful eye of Ron Ashman. He started at Lowestoft and made his Scunthorpe United debut against Peterborough in 1973. In his second spell at the Old Showground, he was made Caretaker-Manager between the periods of office of Frank Barlow and Mick Buxton, and hence gained his first managerial experience, but he did not attain the Manager's job until January 1983, when he succeeded Bill Green.

Money enjoyed four seasons at the Old Showground, and soon developed into a talented defender, before Fulham stepped in with a £50,000 cheque for his transfer. His valuation increased to £333,333 when Liverpool took him to Anfield in the Summer of 1980.

At Anfield, Money's chances were limited, but he did play in the European Cup Semi-Final, and in December 1981 he was loaned to Derby County before being transferred to Luton in the following March for a fee of £100,000.

His next move was to Portsmouth, in the 1983 Summer break, but injury reduced the number of appearances he was able to make for Pompey. In October 1985, his career turned full circle when he returned to the Old Showground for the remainder of his playing days. Richard Money went on to play more than three hundred games for Scunthorpe, and later, during his brief time as Manager, he made the important signing of Andy Flounders. Towards the end of Money's playing days he also coached the junior side, which eventually led him to becoming Youth Development Officer at Aston Villa in 1992.

When Money became Scunthorpe's Manager in 1993, he brought in Colin Morris as his assistant, while Dave Moore continued with Youth Development and Physio duties.

It was still a learning process for Money, and during his initial managerial period he made a number of somewhat insignificant signings, although other players he brought in helped to boost confidence.

Players of the calibre of Ian Thompstone, Matt Carmichael, Russell Bradley, Steve Thornbor, Alan Knill and Paul Mudd formed the backbone of Richard Money's side. Unfortunately, after a poor run of form into March 1994, the Board suggested that Richard should take time off to recuperate from the pressure of the job, but he found this unacceptable, and it led to the parting of the ways. Richard Money continued in football with a number of coaching appointments, including those at Nottingham Forest, Manchester City and Coventry City.

DAVE MOORE

Dave Moore had been on the backroom staff at Glanford Park for some time when the opportunity arose to take over from Richard Money. Moore was initially Caretaker-Manager, and after an improvement in team results, took over in a permanent role.

Dave Moore was a Grimsby-born man who made his way through Grimsby Town's junior ranks. His first team debut came during the 1978-79 season and he enjoyed five seasons with the Mariners until the Summer of 1983. The stockily built defender moved to Carlisle United, but his stay was only a brief one, for Blackpool stepped in for him in January 1984. He played over one hundred games for the tangerine shirts until 1986, before returning to Grimsby Town in November that year. Unfortunately, his career was not entirely injury free, and this led to a termination of his contract in 1988. He then went into coaching, moving to Scunthorpe in 1990, initially under Mick Buxton as a Youth Development Officer, but in the 1993-94 season he took on the physio' duties.

Once Dave Moore was occupying the Manager's chair, he took the team on a run of eleven games with only two defeats until the end of the campaign. The 1994-95 season, his first full term at the helm, is well remembered for two epic F.A.Cup-ties against Birmingham City, and at this period, Moore took John Eyre on loan from Oldham Athletic, leading to a permanent move at the start of the 1995-96 season. He also gave debuts to Steve Housham and Mick Walsh, and brought the likes of Tony Ford, Andy McFarlane, Lee Turnbull and Paul Wilson to the club at various times.

The 1995-96 season was to prove to be the last of Dave Moore's reign, when United could not maintain a promotion bid, although they did produce a record 8-1 victory at Torquay. The winter of 1996 was to be Moore's downfall, and a lean spell through February and March cost him his position. However, he was well liked by his players, and had an unruffled air about him.

BRIAN LAWS

When Brian Laws was brought to Scunthorpe United as a player by Mick Buxton he was not aware that this experienced and knowledgable football brain would eventually succeed him. The opportunity came in February 1997 when Buxton was dismissed. Mark Lillis, the United second in command, took charge in a temporary capacity and it must have been a close run contest as to who should take the Manager's job. Laws was successful, but the two set up a first class partnership, ably assisted by Paul Wilson and Nigel Adkins as Youth Development Officer and Physiotherapist, respectively.

Brian Laws began as a Burnley apprentice, making his debut in the number two shirt for the last game of the 1979-80 season at Watford. He quickly established himself at Turf Moor, but left for Huddersfield in the Summer of 1983, where he stayed for two years, before a move to Middlesbrough. In July 1988 he was transferred to Nottingham Forest and enjoyed the most prosperous days of his playing career. Laws spent more than six years at Forest until he applied successfully to become the Player-Manager at Grimsby Town. He was Town's Manager for exactly two years from November 1994, when an incident involving Italian import Bonetti led to Laws leaving the East Coast club. He spent a short time as a player at Darlington, before arriving at Glanford Park early in the

1997 New Year. Soon after signing as a player he was able to continue with a career in football management, and demonstrate his strict authority, yet whenever the call came to put on the claret and blue shirt, he never shirked from the responsibility, often showing younger men how it should be done.

Among the players Brian Laws brought to Glanford Park were those that were a reflection of his days at Nottingham Forest and Grimsby Town in particular, for these included Justin Walker, Andrew Dawson, Jamie Forrester, Paul Harsley and Craig Shakespear. Laws was also quick to use players from his rapidly expanding junior ranks when the opportunity arose. During Brian Laws' first full season as Manager, United finished one point off the play-off places, and if it had not been for an indifferent spell in the Winter months they might have fared better. However, Cup progress earned much needed cash towards survival as Laws' team took on Everton and Crystal Palace. In the 1998-99 season he continued to make improvements in the strength of the side, making a determined bid for promotion from the Third Division. This was realised when the Club finished fourth in the final table and qualified for the play-offs. After overcoming Swansea City in the Semi-Final, Scunthorpe beat Leyton Orient 1-0 at Wembley, and hence were promoted to the Second Division.

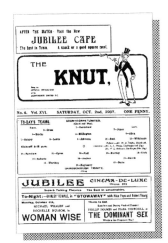

1937-38

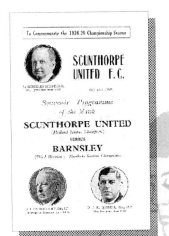

1945-46

PROGRAMME
PARADE

1949-50

1950-51

1954-55

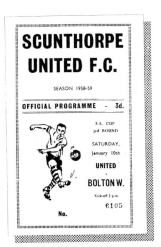

1958-59

1960-61

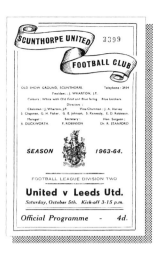

1963-64

1964-65

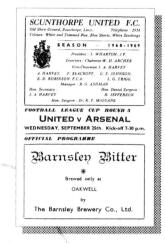

1968-69

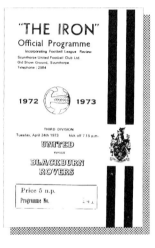

1972-73

1976-77

1978-79

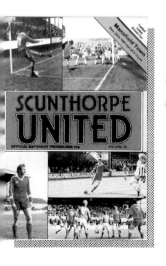

1981-82

1984-85

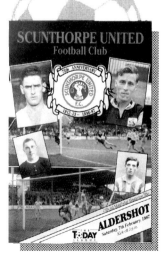

1986-87

1987-88

The Old Showground 'The Last'

18 May 1988

1988-89

1990-91

Glanford Park - 'The First'

14 August 1988

1993-94

1994-95

29 May 1999...............

1998-99

The last as a Division 3 club

Sheet no.1   **Agnew to Clarke**

Player		D.O.B	Place of Birth	Previous Club		Scunthorpe	Debut	Next Club		Appearances				Goals			
										League	FAC	FLC	AMC	League	FAC	FLC	AMC
Agnew	David	04/08/39	Kilwinning	Leicester City	6/61	Brighton	(H) 3-3 19/8/61	Notts County	6/62	1	0	0	0	0	0	0	0
Alexander	Graham	10/10/71	Coventry	YTS	3/90	Chesterfield	(H) 3-0 27/4/91	Luton Town	7/95	159	12	12	15	18	1	2	3
Allen	Bill	22/10/17	Newburn	York City	6/50	Shrewsbury	(H) 0-0 19/2/50	Retired	5/52	64	2	0	0	1	0	0	0
Anderson	Alan	21/12/39	Edinburgh	Millwall	7/62	Sunderland	(A) 0-0 27/9/62	Hearts	11/63	6	0	4	0	0	0	0	0
Anderson	Terry	11/03/44	Woking	Baltimore Comets	9/74	Shrewsbury	(A) 0-5 28/9/74	Crewe Alexandra	11/74	10	0	0	0	0	0	0	0
Andrews	Les	29/10/53	Dudley	Wolves (loan)	3/74	Brentford	(A) 1-2 9/3/74			9	0	0	0	1	0	0	0
Angus	Mike	28/01/60	Middlesbrough	Middlesbrough (loan)	9/82	Bristol City	(A) 2-0 25/9/82			20	4	0	0	2	0	0	0
Arblaster	Brian	06/06/43	Kensington	Chesterfield	6/67	Peterborough	(H) 2-1 19/8/67	Barnsley	5/68	10	0	2	0	0	0	0	0
Arins	Tony	26/10/58	Chesterfield	Leeds United	11/81	Halifax	(A) 2-1 28/11/81			20	0	0	0	1	0	0	0
Armstrong	Keith	11/10/57	Corbridge	Sunderland (loan)	10/78	Hartlepool	(A) 1-1 17/10/78			1	0	0	0	0	0	0	0
Ash	Micky	04/09/43	Sheffield	Sheffield Utd.	9/65	Oldham	(A) 3-1 2/10/65	New York Generals	5/67	49	2	1	0	7	0	0	0
Ashworth	Phil	04/04/53	Burnley	Portsmouth	7/80	Rochdale	(A) 0-4 19/8/80	Gais (Sweden)	6/81	23	1	0	0	3	0	0	0
Atkin	Mick	14/02/48	Scunthorpe	Local	9/69	Lincoln	(A) 2-1 18/10/69	Gainsborough Tr.	7/75	122	16	2	0	0	0	0	0
Atkins	Mark	14/08/68	Doncaster	Jnrs.	7/86	Wrexham	(A) 1-2 27/4/85	Blackburn Rovers	6/88	50	5	4	6	2	0	0	0
Atkinson	Graeme	11/11/71	Hull	Brighton	11/98	Darlington	(A) 1-3 19/12/98	Scarborough	2/99	1	0	0	1	0	0	0	0
Babes	John	20/11/29	Lurgan	Arsenal	9/50	Carlisle	(A) 1-3 23/9/50			9	0	0	0	0	0	0	0
Baines	Steve	23/06/54	Newark	Walsall	8/82	Wimbledon	(A) 2-2 11/9/82	Chesterfield	7/83	38	4	0	0	1	0	0	0
Baker	Paul	05/01/63	Newcastle	Torquay	10/96	Hull	(A) 2-0 5/10/96	Hartlepool	3/97	21	3	0	2	9	5	0	0
Bakes	Martin	08/02/37	Bradford	Bradford City	6/59	Charlton	(A) 1-1 22/8/60	Retired	5/63	77	3	3	0	5	2	0	0
Bannister	Jack	26/01/42	Chesterfield	West Bromwich A.	6/64	Bristol City	(H) 5-2 22/8/64	Crystal Palace	7/65	9	0	6	0	0	0	0	0
Barker	Jeff	16/10/15	Scunthorpe	Huddersfield T	8/48	Shrewsbury	(H) 0-0 19/8/50	Retired	5/52	73	14	0	0	1	1	0	0
Barker	John	04/07/48	Huddersfield	App.	7/66	Bournemouth	(A) 2-1 23/4/66	Scarborough	7/75	263	28	13	0	6	2	0	0
Barley	Peter	25/04/36	Scunthorpe	Leeds United	10/53	Hartlepool	(H) 0-0 1/10/53			5	0	0	0	0	0	0	0
Barnard	Geoff	23/03/46	Southend-on-Sea	Norwich City	7/68	Rochdale	(A) 2-3 10/8/68	Scarborough	7/75	262	25	13	0	0	0	0	0
				Scarborough	9/76			Retired	5/77								
Barnes	Bobby	17/12/62	Kingston	West Ham Utd. (loan)	11/85	Burnley	(H) 1-1 30/11/85			6	0	0	0	0	0	0	0
Barrett	John	26/03/31	Birmingham	Aston Villa	6/54	York	(H) 1-2 1/1/55	Bradford P.A.	10/59	17	1	0	0	0	0	0	0
Barton	Frank	22/10/47	Barton-on-Humber	App.	8/65	Barnsley	(H) 2-3 5/2/65	Carlisle Utd.	1/68	93	4	3	0	26	2	2	0
Batch	Nigel	09/09/57	Huddersfield	Stockport Co.	8/91	Gillingham	(A) 0-4 17/8/91	Retired	8/91	1	0	0	0	0	0	0	0
Bedford	Brian	24/12/33	Ferndale	QPR	9/65	Exeter	(A) 0-4 4/9/65	Brentford	9/66	37	1	0	0	23	0	0	0
Bell	Derek	30/10/56	Wyberton	Chesterfield	1/84	Southend	(A) 0-0 3/2/84	Boston Utd.	3/86	22	0	1	3	7	0	0	3
Bennett	Bobby	29/12/51	Harrow	Southend U (loan)	10/73	Stockport	(A) 1-3 2/11/73			3	1	0	0	0	0	0	0
Benson	Joe	07/01/33	Misterton	Local	8/55	Stockport	(A) 2-3 26/8/55			2	0	0	0	0	0	0	0
Betts	Barry	18/09/32	Barnsley	Manchester City	8/64	Bristol City	(H) 5-2 22/8/64	Lancaster City	6/65	7	0	2	0	0	0	0	0
Birch	Alan	12/08/56	West Bromwich	Rotherham Utd.	6/86	Northampton	(H) 2-2 23/8/86	Stockport Co.	10/87	23	1	6	1	2	0	0	0
Bloomer	Brian	03/05/52	Cleethorpes	Brigg Town	8/78	Port Vale	(A) 2-2 19/8/78	Brigg Town	7/79	7	0	0	0	1	0	0	0
Blyth	Mel	28/07/44	Norwich	Gt. Yarmouth	11/67	Shrewsbury	(H) 0-0 17/11/67	Crystal Palace	7/68	27	0	0	0	3	0	0	0
Bond	Len	12/02/54	Ilminster	Bristol City (loan)	12/75	Southport	(H) 1-2 6/12/75			8	0	0	0	0	0	0	0
Bonson	Joe	19/06/36	Barnsley	Cardiff City	6/60	Charlton	(A) 1-1 20/8/60	Doncaster Rovers	2/62	52	2	2	0	11	3	1	0
Borland	John	28/01/77	Lancaster	Burnley	8/96	Cardiff	(H) 0-1 14/9/96	Accrington Stanley	6/97	2	0	0	0	0	0	0	0
Botham	Ian	24/11/55	Heswall	Somerset C.C.C.	3/80	Bournemouth	(A) 3-3 25/3/80	Yeovil Town	3/85	11	1	0	2	0	0	0	0
Bowen	Danny	16/11/21	Ynysybwl	Treharris	7/50	Mansfield	(A) 1-1 26/8/50	Hastings Utd.	7/51	5	0	0	0	0	0	0	0
Boxall	Alan	11/05/53	Woolwich	Barton Town	8/80	Bradford City	(A) 0-0 23/8/80	Chesterfield	11/83	54	3	3	3	1	0	0	0
Boyd	Gordon	27/03/58	Glasgow	Barnsley	3/82	Aldershot	(H) 1-1 23/3/82	Goole Town	7/82	11	0	0	0	0	0	0	0
Boyes	Wally	05/01/13	Killamarsh	Notts County	8/50	Shrewsbury	(H) 0-0 19/8/50	Retford T (p/m)	7/51	13	0	0	0	2	0	0	0
Bradley	Russell	28/03/66	Birmingham	Halifax Town	6/93	Wigan Athletic	(A) 2-0 14/8/93		7/97	119	11	6	9	5	0	0	0
Bramhall	John	20/11/56	Warrington	Halifax Town	1/90	Lincoln	(H) 1-1 20/1/90	Hyde United	7/91	32	3	0	0	0	1	0	0
Bramley	Stuart	19/04/46	Scunthorpe	App.	4/64	Walsall	(A) 2-0 20/10/64	Plymouth Argyle	8/67	35	0	0	0	3	0	0	0
Bridges	Bernard	28/02/59	Doncaster	Jnrs.	7/36	Brentford	(H) 2-1 25/1/77	Barton Town	7/78	23	0	4	0	0	0	0	0
Broadley	Les	10/08/30	Goole	Goole Town	8/52	Grimsby	(H) 0-1 28/8/52			5	0	0	0	2	0	0	0
Broddle	Julian	01/11/64	Laughton	Sheffield Utd.	8/83	Port Vale	(A) 0-0 27/8/83	Barnsley	9/87	144	11	11	6	32	4	1	1
				St.Mirren (loan)	9/92					5	0	0	0	0	0	0	0
Brolly	Mike	06/10/54	Galston	Derby County	8/83	Port Vale	(A) 0-0 27/8/83	Scarborough	7/86	95	9	8	5	15	1	1	2
Brown	Tony	17/09/58	Bradford	Doncaster Rovers	7/87	Tranmere	(H) 3-0 15/8/87	Rochdale	8/89	54	3	8	3	2	0	0	0
Brown	David	28/01/57	Hartlepool	Preston NE (loan)	1/89	Stockport	(A) 2-1 7/1/89			5	0	0	0	0	0	0	0
Brown	Gordon	30/06/33	Ellesmere Port	Wolves	12/52	Workington	(H) 2-1 21/3/53	Derby County	1/57	164	11	0	0	68	7	0	0
Brown	Monty	07/09/43	Grimsby	Jnrs.	7/63	Barnsley	(A) 0-2 25/9/64	Corby Town	1/66	19	0	1	0	6	0	0	0
Brownsword	Jack	15/05/23	Campsall	Hull City	7/47	Shrewsbury	(H) 0-0 19/8/50	(Trainer)	7/65	597	56	10	0	50	3	0	0
Buckley	John	10/05/62	Glasgow	Partick Thistle	8/91	Gillingham	(A) 0-4 17/8/91	Rotherham Utd.	2/93	43	4	6	4	8	1	0	0
Bull	Gary	12/06/66	West Bromwich	York City	7/98	Blackpool	(A) 0-1 11/8/98			22	1	2	1	0	0	0	0
Bullimore	Wayne	12/09/70	Sutton-in-Ashfield	Stockport Co.	11/93	Chesterfield	(H) 2-2 28/12/93	Bradford City	12/95	67	7	4	5	11	1	1	1
Burkinshaw	Keith	23/06/35	Barnsley	Workington	5/65	Hull	(A) 2-3 21/8/65	Newcastle U(coach)	6/68	108	4	4	0	3	0	0	0
Burrows	Frank	30/01/44	Larkhall	Raith Rovers	6/65	Hull	(H) 2-4 29/1/66	Swindon Town	7/68	106	4	3	0	4	1	0	0
Bushby	Alan	15/01/32	Doncaster	Local	8/52	Gateshead	(H) 0-0 27/9/52	Rochdale	7/59	218	23	0	0	10	2	0	0
Butler	Lee	30/05/66	Sheffield	Barnsley (loan)	2/96	Plymouth	(H) 1-1 10/2/96			2	0	0	0	0	0	0	0
Butler	Martin	03/03/66	Hull	Carlisle Utd.	8/89	Rochdale	(H) 0-1 26/8/89	Macclesfield Town	9/89	2	0	1	0	0	0	0	0
Callaghan	Robert	05/10/31	Glasgow	Duntocher H.	8/55	Oldham	(H) 2-1 27/8/55	Barrow	10/56	19	1	0	0	6	0	0	0
Calvo-Garcia	Alex	01/01/72	Crdizia	Eibar (Spain)	10/96	Hull	(A) 2-0 5/10/96			100	9	6	4	16	0	4	1
Cammack	Steve	20/03/54	Sheffield	Chesterfield	9/79	Huddersfield	(H) 1-1 14/9/79	Lincoln City	7/81	245	18	10	6	110	6	3	2
				Lincoln City	3/82			Scarborough	10/86								
Carmichael	Matt	13/05/64	Singapore	Lincoln City	7/93	Wigan Athletic	(A) 2-0 14/8/93	Preston NE	3/95	62	7	2	5	20	2	0	5
Cartwright	Peter	23/08/57	Newcastle	Newcastle U (loan)	12/82	Hereford	(A) 2-0 4/12/82			4	0	0	0	1	0	0	0
Cassidy	Nigel	07/12/45	Sudbury	Norwich City	12/68	Halifax	(A) 0-2 26/12/68	Oxford Utd.	11/70	88	7	2	0	35	4	0	0
Charles	Steve	10/05/60	Sheffield	Mansfield Town (loan	11/92	Torquay	(A) 1-0 21/11/92			4	0	0	2	0	0	0	0
Charleswort	Terry	13/07/33	Scunthorpe	Local	6/52	Mansfield	(A) 0-1 11/4/53			19	2	0	0	0	0	0	0
Charnley	Derek	07/05/54	Doncaster	Jnrs.	2/73	Charlton	(A) 0-2 10/2/73	Bridlington Trin.	7/76	38	0	1	0	3	0	0	0
Clarke	Tim	19/09/68	Stourbridge	York City	2/97	Colchester	(H) 2-1 22/2/97			78	5	6	3	0	0	0	0

Player		D.O.B	Place of Birth	Previous Club		Scunthorpe	Debut	Next Club		Appearances				Goals			
										League	FAC	FLC	AMC	League	FAC	FLC	AMC
Clarkson	Phil	13/11/68	Hambleton	Crewe Alexandra (loa	10/95	Hartlepool	(A) 0-2 14/10/95			24	0	0	0	6	0	0	0
				(Permanent)	2/96			Blackpool	2/97								
Clelland	David	18/03/24	Netherburn	Weymouth	7/50	Lincoln	(A) 1-2 23/8/50	Met. Police	7/51	16	0	0	0	8	0	0	0
Clemence	Ray	05/08/48	Skegness	Notts County	8/65	Swansea	(H) 1-1 2/4/66	Liverpool	6/67	48	2	0	0	0	0	0	0
Coatsworth	Fred	05/07/48	Lincoln	Jnrs.	7/65	Swindon	(A) 0-0 7/5/66	Rugby Town	7/67	15	0	0	0	2	0	0	0
Collard	Bruce	21/08/53	Hetton-le-Hole	West Bromwich A.	7/73	Lincoln	(A) 0-1 25/8/73	Dunstable Town	7/74	22	4	1	0	0	0	0	0
Collier	Graham	12/09/51	Nottingham	Nottm. Forest	3/72	Swansea	(H) 1-0 12/8/72	Barnsley	8/77	161	11	11	0	19	2	0	0
Colquhoun	John	03/06/40	Stirling	Oldham Athletic	8/65	Hull	(A) 2-3 21/8/65	Oldham Athletic	11/68	149	5	7	0	23	1	0	0
Comley	Len	25/01/22	Swansea	Newport County	3/51	Hartlepool	(A) 2-4 17/3/51	Llanelly	7/51	12	0	0	0	5	0	0	0
Conde	Jim	19/07/44	Creswell	Wolves	6/63	Charlton	(A) 1-0 23/11/63	Bangor City	7/64	4	1	0	0	1	0	0	0
Conroy	Maurice	26/04/19	Bradford	Accrington Stanley	8/50	Tranmere	(A) 1-0 5/5/51	(trainer)		1	0	0	0	0	0	0	0
Constable	Shaun	21/03/68	Maidstone	Leeds University	2/93	Lincoln	(H) 1-0 13/2/93	Halifax Town	7/93	7	0	0	0	0	0	0	0
Cooper	Terry	11/03/50	Croesyceiliog	Lincoln City (loan)	11/77	Watford	(A) 1-4 12/11/77			4	0	0	0	0	0	0	0
Cork	David	28/10/62	Doncaster	Huddersfield Town	2/89	Colchester	(H) 2-3 18/2/89	Darlington	7/89	15	0	0	0	0	0	0	0
Cotton	Perry	11/11/65	Chislehurst	Nelson U (NZ)	12/88	Stockport	(H) 1-1 4/4/89	Kettering Town	7/91	33	5	1	6	2	0	0	1
Couch	Geoff	03/04/53	Crowle	Crowle	3/78	Watford	(H) 0-1 8/4/78			26	0	2	0	5	0	0	0
Cowling	Chris	19/09/62	Scunthorpe	App.	12/79	Doncaster	(H) 0-0 28/9/79			134	13	9	4	26	4	2	0
Cowling	Dave	27/11/58	Doncaster	Huddersfield T (loan)	11/87	Scarborough	(H) 0-1 7/11/87			90	5	8	5	5	0	0	0
				Reading	8/88												
Cox	Neil	08/10/71	Scunthorpe	Trainee	3/90	Halifax	(A) 0-0 6/10/90	Aston Villa	2/91	17	4	0	5	1	0	0	0
Cox	Sam	30/10/20	Mexborough	Accrington Stanley	7/52	Barrow	(A) 1-2 23/8/52	Retired	5/53	3	0	0	0	0	0	0	0
Crawford	Graeme	07/08/47	Falkirk	York City	8/77	Southport	(A) 1-1 20/8/77	York City	1/80	104	3	8	0	0	0	0	0
Crawford	Ian	14/07/34	Edinburgh	West Ham Utd.	2/63	Huddersfield	(A) 0-2 23/3/63	Peterborough U	7/64	35	1	3	0	2	0	1	0
Crisp	Richard	23/05/72	Wordsley	Aston Villa (loan)	3/93	Lincoln	(H) 1-1 13/2/93			8	0	0	0	0	0	0	0
Cumner	Horace	31/03/18	Cwmaman	Watford	9/50	Accrington S.	(H) 3-0 30/9/50	Bradford City	8/53	102	4	0	0	21	0	0	0
Currie	Jim	06/08/48	Stirling		9/68	Southend	(H) 4-1 12/5/69	Ashby Town	7/70	6	0	0	0	0	0	0	0
Czuczman	Mike	27/05/53	Carlisle	Grimsby Town	8/76	Rochdale	(H) 0-1 21/8/76	Stockport County	5/79	116	3	10	0	1	0	0	0
Dale	Alan	20/09/58	Thorne	App.	9/76	Exeter	(A) 4-5 29/4/76			3	0	0	0	0	0	0	0
Daley	Alan	11/10/27	Mansfield	Boston United	7/52	Barrow	(A) 1-2 23/8/52	Corby Town	7/53	35	4	0	0	8	1	0	0
Dall	David	10/10/57	St Andrews	Grantham	10/79	Newport	(H) 1-3 20/10/79	East Fife	7/82	77	4	0	0	2	0	0	0
Danzey	Mike	08/02/71	Widnes	Cambridge U (loan)	2/94	Torquay	(H) 1-3 5/2/94			3	0	0	0	0	0	0	0
D'Auria	David	26/03/70	Swansea	Scarborough	12/95	Mansfield	(H) 1-0 9/12/95	Hull City	7/98	107	6	6	4	18	1	0	0
Davidson	Angus	02/10/48	Dundee	Grimsby Town	7/69	Southend	(A) 0-3 15/8/69			321	28	13	0	45	0	1	0
Davidson	Ian	31/01/47	Goole	Hull City (loan)	9/68	York	(H) 1-2 14/9/68			35	1	1	0	0	0	0	0
Davies	John	26/09/33	Portsmouth	Portsmouth	7/57	Bradford	(A) 0-2 20/8/55	Walsall	1/59	67	9	0	0	10	7	0	0
Davis	Eric	26/02/32	Stonehouse, Devo	Plymouth Argyle	7/57	Oldham	(A) 1-2 23/11/57	Chester	2/59	40	2	0	0	20	2	0	0
Davy	Steve	09/04/55	Norwich	West Ham Utd.	8/77	Stockport	(A) 0-3 26/11/77	App. Frodingham	7/82	134	8	6	0	1	0	0	0
Daws	Tony	10/09/66	Sheffield	Sheffield Utd.	6/87	Darlington	(A) 1-3 19/12/98	Grimsby Town	3/93	183	9	16	15	63	2	4	2
Dawson	Andrew	20/10/78	Northallerton	Nottingham F.	7/87	Tranmere	(H) 3-0 15/8/87			24	0	0	1	0	0	0	0
Deere	Steve	31/03/48	Burnham Market	Norwich City	11/67	Stockport	(H) 0-2 3/11/67	Hull City	6/73	343	26	12	0	22	4	2	0
				Scarborough	2/78												
De Mange	Ken	03/09/64	Dublin	Liverpool (loan)	12/86	Colchester	(A) 0-1 3/1/87			3	1	0	1	2	1	0	0
DeVries	Roger	25/10/50	Hull	Blackburn Rovers	10/81	Crewe	(A) 0-3 10/10/81			6	0	0	0	1	0	0	0
Dey	Geoff	11/01/64	Chesterfield	Sheffield Utd.	8/83	Port Vale	(A) 0-0 27/8/83			17	5	4	2	1	1	0	0
Dixon	Kevin	27/07/60	Blackhill	Hartlepool Utd(Loan)	1/86												
				Hartlepool Utd.	8/87	Torquay	(A) 0-1 18/1/86	Hartlepool Utd.	6/88	55	4	4	5	6	0	0	0
Donnelly	Peter	22/09/36	Hull	Doncaster Rovers	7/58	Lincoln	(H) 3-1 30/3/59	Cardiff City	6/60	39	2	0	0	19	0	0	0
Drake	Steve	27/08/48	Goole	Huddersfield T	7/67	Walsall	(H) 2-5 9/10/67	Goole Town	7/70	23	1	0	0	0	0	0	0
Duffy	Darrell	18/01/71	Birmingham	Moor Green	2/93	Lincoln	(H) 1-1 13/2/93	Tamworth	10/93	4	0	0	0	0	0	0	0
Duffy	Vince	21/09/62	Nottingham	Nottm. Forest	12/80	Port Vale	(H) 1-1 24/2/81	Heanor Town	3/82	8	0	0	0	0	0	0	0
Duncan	John	22/02/49	Dundee	Derby County	6/81	Crewe	(H) 0-1 28/2/82	(manager)		9	0	1	2	0	0	0	0
Dunn	Iain	01/04/70	Derwent	Huddersfield T (loan)	9/96	Chester	(A) 0-1 21/9/96			3	0	0	0	0	0	0	0
Earl	Steve	31/08/56	Scunthorpe	App. Frodingham	9/74	Darlington	(A) 1-3 14/9/74	App. Frodingham	7/75	39	0	2	0	10	0	0	0
				App.Frodingham	11/78			App. Frodingham	7/80								
Eli	Roger	11/09/65	Bradford	Burnley	2/95	Chesterfield	(H) 0-1 18/2/95	Partick Thistle	3/95	2	0	0	0	0	0	0	0
Elliott	Matt	01/11/68	Wandsworth	Torquay United (loan)	3/92	Chesterfield	(H) 2-0 31/3/92	Oxford United	11/93	61	2	6	5	8	0	0	0
Ellis	Keith	06/11/35	Sheffield	Sheffield Wed.	3/64	Preston N.E.	(H) 1-0 7/3/64	Cardiff City	9/64	10	0	0	0	5	0	0	0
Evans	Tommy	31/12/76	Doncaster	Crystal Palace	8/97	Everton	(A) 0-5 1/10/97			29	1	1	1	0	0	0	0
Eyre	John	09/10/74	Humberside	Oldham Athletic (loan)	12/94	Northampton	(A) 1-0 16/12/94	Hull City	6/99	173	12	9	6	51	3	2	3
Farrell	David	11/11/71	Birmingham	Aston Villa (loan)	1/93	Shrewsbury	(A) 1-2 26/1/93			5	0	0	2	1	0	0	0
Farrell	Mick	13/03/59	Ilkley	App.	3/77	Workington	(H) 3-0 8/11/75			9	1	0	0	1	0	0	0
Fawcett	Brian	14/02/32	Doncaster	Bentley Colliery	2/55	Rochdale	(A) 0-2 5/3/55	Bradford	7/56	1	0	0	0	0	0	0	0
Featherstone	Jamie	12/11/79	Wharfedale	Blackburn R.	3/98	Exeter	(H) 2-1 25/4/98			1	0	0	0	0	0	0	0
Ferguson	Ron	09/02/57	Accrington	Sheffield Wed. (loan)	12/75	Reading	(A) 0-1 13/12/75			3	0	0	0	0	0	0	0
Ferry	Willie	21/11/66	Sunderland	Trainee	9/84	Mansfield	(A) 1-0 24/4/85	Barnsley	11/86	5	1	2	0	0	0	0	0
Fickling	Ashley	15/11/72	Sheffield	Grimsby Town	6/98	Shrewsbury	(A) 1-2 8/8/98			29	2	2	1	0	0	0	0
Finney	Shaun	05/10/66	Dinnington	Nottm. Forest	10/84	Hartlepool	(H) 2-0 19/4/85	Gainsborough Trin.	7/85	2	0	0	1	0	0	0	0
Fletcher	Doug	17/09/30	Sheffield	Bury	7/56	Darlington	(H) 1-2 18/8/56	Darlington	7/58	54	6	0	0	26	1	0	0
Fletcher	Rod	23/09/45	Preston	Lincoln City	6/71	Grimsby	(A) 1-4 14/8/71	Grimsby Town	11/73	98	7	6	0	30	2	0	0
Flounders	Andy	13/12/63	Hull	Hull City	3/87	Cardiff	(H) 1-3 7/3/87	Rochdale	7/91	196	13	14	13	87	3	6	3
Foley	Peter	28/06/44	Glasgow	Workington	7/67	Peterborough	(A) 1-1 19/8/67	Chesterfield	8/69	17	0	3	0	3	0	1	0
Ford	Tony	14/05/59	Grimsby	Grimsby Town	8/94	Barnet	(A) 2-1 13/8/94	Barrow	6/96	76	7	4	4	9	1	1	0
Forrester	Jamie	01/11/74	Bradford	Grimsby Town	3/97	Torquay	(A) 2-1 22/3/97	F.C.Utrecht	6/99	101	7	6	4	37	4	1	0
Fowler	Martin	17/01/57	York	Stockport Co.	9/82	Hartlepool	(H) 0-0 28/8/82			18	4	2	3	0	0	0	0
Foxon	Neil	10/07/48	Nottingham	Notts County	8/65	Bristol Rovers	(H) 3-1 24/4/67	Wisbech Town	7/68	22	1	1	0	1	1	0	0
Foxton	Graham	02/10/49	Harrogate	Jnrs.	10/67	Grimsby	(H) 0-3 20/1/68	Brigg Town	7/73	154	17	6	0	1	0	0	0
Foy	David	20/10/72	Coventry	Birmingham City	3/93	Wrexham	(H) 0-1 20/3/93	Stafford Rangers	10/93	3	0	0	0	0	0	0	0
Francis	John	12/11/63	Dewsbury	Burnley	8/96	Leyton Orient	(A) 1-0 17/8/96	Halifax Town	10/96	4	0	1	0	0	0	0	0

Player		D.O.B	Place of Birth	Previous Club		Scunthorpe	Debut	Next Club		Appearances				Goals			
										League	FAC	FLC	AMC	League	FAC	FLC	AMC
Gannon	Mick	02/02/43	Liverpool	Everton	5/62	Southampton	(H) 2-1 18/8/62	Crewe Alexandra	10/64	15	0	1	0	0	0	0	0
Gavin	Mark	10/12/63	Baileston	Exeter	8/96	Wigan Athletic	(A) 0-3 7/9/96	Hartlepool U.	9/97	11	0	1	2	0	0	0	0
Gayle	John	30/07/64	Bromsgrove	Northampton T.	6/98	Shrewsbury	(A) 1-2 08/08/98			37	1	2	1	4	0	0	0
Germaine	Gary	02/08/76	Birmingham	West Brom. (loan)	3/96	Hereford	(H) 0-1 9/3/96			11	0	0	0	0	0	0	0
Gibson	Archie	30/12/33	Girvan	Leeds United	7/60	Charlton	(A) 1-1 20/8/60	Barnsley	9/64	138	6	10	0	5	0	1	0
Gibson	David	14/02/58	Seaham	Hull City	7/78	Notts County	(H) 0-1 12/8/78			21	0	2	0	1	0	0	0
Gilbert	David	22/06/63	Lincoln	Lincoln City	8/82	York	(H) 0-0 19/9/82	Boston United	10/82	1	0	1	2	0	0	0	0
Gleadall	Ted	21/08/31	Sheffield	Bury	3/57	Bradford City	(A) 1-3 9/3/57	Weymouth	7/58	6	0	0	0	2	0	0	0
Godfrey	Brian	01/05/40	Flint	Everton	6/60	Charlton	(A) 1-1 20/8/60	Preston NE	10/63	87	5	7	0	24	1	2	0
Goodacre	Sam	01/12/70	Sheffield	Sheffield Wed.	7/91	Northampton	(A) 0-1 12/9/92	Stalybridge Celtic	6/95	44	2	5	3	12	2	0	1
Goodlass	Ronnie	06/09/53	Liverpool	Fulham	3/82	York	(A) 1-3 26/3/82	Happy Valley (H.Kong)	5/83	9	0	0	0	0	0	0	0
Goodwin	Freddie	28/06/33	Heywood	Leeds United	12/64	Peterborough	(H) 1-1 11/9/65	New York Generals	11/67	6	1	0	0	1	0	0	0
Goodwin	Steve	23/02/54	Chadderton	Norwich City (loan)	9/73	Hartlepool	(H) 1-1 29/9/73			2	0	0	0	0	0	0	0
Gordon	Jimmy	03/10/55	Stretford	Reading	9/78	Lincoln	(A) 0-4 13/10/79	Gainsborough Trinity	8/81	34	1	0	0	0	0	0	0
Gorin	Ted	02/02/24	Cardiff	Cardiff City	7/50	Shrewsbury	(H) 0-0 19/8/50	Shrewsbury Town	1/51	26	1	0	0	12	0	0	0
Graham	Deiniol	04/10/69	Cannock	Stockport Co.	8/95	Lincoln	(A) 2-2 28/8/95	Dagenham & Red.	9/95	3	0	0	0	1	0	0	0
Graham	Tommy	31/03/58	Glasgow	Doncaster Rovers	3/83	Torquay	(H) 2-0 12/3/83	Scarborough	8/86	109	8	5	7	21	2	0	1
Grant	Jim	10/06/40	Chapelhall	Larkhall Thistle	11/58	Huddersfield	(H) 0-3 25/4/59			1	0	0	0	0	0	0	0
Graves	Wayne	18/09/80	Scunthorpe	Trainee	7/97	Macclesfield	(H) 1-0 11/4/98			3	0	0	0	0	0	0	0
Gray	George	06/10/29	Glasgow	Sligo Rovers	8/51	Hartlepool	(A) 1-3 25/8/51	Kettering Town	7/52	9	0	0	0	3	0	0	0
Greaves	Steve	17/01/70	Chelsea	Ipswich Town	8/92	Northampton	(A) 0-1 12/9/92	Dagenham & Red	7/93	15	2	1	3	0	0	0	0
Green	John	07/08/58	Rotherham	Rotherham Utd.	9/83	Exeter	(H) 3-1 3/9/83	Darlington	10/85	100	9	6	5	4	0	0	0
Green	Rick	23/11/52	Scunthorpe	App. Frodingham	9/75	Swansea	(A) 0-2 27/9/75	Chesterfield	2/77	137	6	6	0	38	2	0	0
				Notts County	8/79			Brigg Town	4/82								
Green	Ron	03/10/56	Birmingham	Bristol Rovers	8/86	Northampton	(H) 2-2 23/8/86	Wimbledon	8/88	78	5	7	2	0	0	0	0
Gregory	Jack	24/09/26	Shoreditch	West Ham Utd.	6/53	Grimsby	(A) 1-0 22/8/53	Aldershot	6/57	147	18	0	0	63	6	0	0
Gregory	Neil	07/10/72	Zambia	Ipswich Town (loan)	3/95	Bury	(H) 3-2 11/3/95			10	0	0	0	7	0	0	0
Gregory	Paul	26/07/61	Sheffield	Doncaster Rovers	10/84	Southend	(A) 1-1 19/10/84	Goole Town	7/87	69	3	2	6	0	0	0	0
Grimes	Vince	13/05/54	Scunthorpe	Hull City	1/78	Southend	(A) 0-2 3/2/78	Gainsborough Trin.		143	7	6	0	12	2	0	0
Haigh	Jack	10/09/28	Rotherham	Liverpool	8/52	Barrow	(A) 1-2 23/8/52	Doncaster Rovers	7/60	329	31	0	0	66	5	0	0
Hall	Arthur	23/11/25	Sheffield	Goole Town	8/51	Bradford City	(H) 1-0 18/8/51	Grantham	7/52	15	1	0	0	5	0	0	0
Hall	David	26/09/60	Doncaster	App.	9/78	Crewe	(H) 0-1 31/3/79	Frickley Athletic	7/80	17	0	0	0	0	0	0	0
Hall	Richard	14/03/72	Ipswich	Trainee	3/90	Grimsby	(H) 2-2 26/12/89	Southampton	2/91	22	3	2	4	3	0	0	0
Hamill	Stewart	22/01/60	Glasgow	Leicester City (loan)	3/82	York	(A) 1-3 26/3/82			4	0	0	0	0	0	0	0
Hamilton	Ian	14/12/67	Stevenage	Cambridge Utd.	12/88	Hartlepool	(H) 1-1 26/12/88	West Bromwich A.	6/92	145	7	6	11	18	0	0	2
Harburn	Peter	18/06/31	Shoreditch	Everton	1/59	Derby	(A) 1-3 17/1/59	Workington	10/59	20	0	0	0	8	0	0	0
Hardwick	Ken	01/01/24	West Auckland	Doncaster Rovers	4/57	Gateshead	(H) 1-2 19/4/57	Barrow	6/59	96	6	0	0	0	0	0	0
Harle	David	15/08/63	Denaby	Bristol City	11/86	Hereford	(A) 2-2 29/11/86	Peterborough U	3/89	89	5	8	6	10	2	1	2
Harney	David	02/03/47	Jarrow	Grimsby Town	7/67	Peterborough	(H) 1-1 19/8/67	Brentford	10/69	25	0	2	0	1	0	0	0
Harper	Ian	23/11/44	Scunthorpe	Jnrs.	7/62	Sunderland	(H) 1-1 9/9/63	Gainsborough Trin.	7/65	21	0	0	0	0	0	0	0
Harsley	Paul	29/05/78	Scunthorpe	Grimsby Town	7/97	Barnet	(A) 1-0 20/9/97			49	3	2	1	1	1	0	1
Hawley	John	08/05/54	Patrington	Bradford City	7/85	Peterborough	(A) 0-1 31/8/85	Retired	5/86	21	2	2	3	7	0	0	4
Heath	Michael	07/02/74	Hull	Tottenham H	12/93	Chesterfield	(A) 1-1 4/4/94	N Ferriby Utd.	7/94	2	0	0	0	0	0	0	0
Heath	Terry	17/11/43	Leicester	Hull City	3/68	Colchester	(H) 5-1 9/3/68	Lincoln City	2/73	176	20	8	0	49	3	0	0
Helliwell	Ian	07/11/62	Rotherham	York City	8/91	Gillingham	(A) 0-4 17/8/91	Rotherham Utd.	8/93	80	4	8	6	22	2	5	0
Hemmerman	Jeff	25/02/55	Hull	Hull City (loan)	9/75	Hartlepool	(A) 2-1 13/9/75			5	0	0	0	1	0	0	0
Hemstead	Derek	22/05/43	Scunthorpe	Jnrs.	5/60	Luton	(A) 0-0 29/4/61	Carlisle Utd.	7/69	248	11	11	0	2	0	0	0
Henderson	Damian	12/05/73	Leeds	Scarborough	12/93	Bury	(A) 0-1 11/12/93	Hartlepool U.	3/95	37	1	2	1	4	0	1	0
Heron	Brian	19/06/48	Dumbarton	Oxford United	7/77	Southport	(A) 1-1 20/8/77	Retired	5/78	20	5	0	4	1	0	0	0
Heward	Brian	17/07/35	Lincoln	Jnrs.	3/54	Gateshead	(A) 0-1 12/11/55	Lincoln City	7/61	137	12	0	0	0	0	0	0
Heyes	Darren	11/01/67	Swansea	Nottm. Forest	7/87	Bolton	(H) 1-1 15/9/87	Shepshed Chart.	7/88	3	0	1	3	0	0	0	0
Hicks	Stuart	30/05/67	Peterborough	Colchester Utd.	8/90	Blackpool	(H) 2-0 25/8/90	Doncaster Rovers	8/92	67	4	4	6	1	1	0	0
Hill	David	06/06/66	Nottingham	Trainee	2/85	Southend	(H) 1-6 30/9/83	Ipswich Town	7/88	205	11	12	10	16	3	1	0
				Ipswich Town	3/91			Lincoln City	7/93								
Hine	Mark	18/05/64	Middlesbrough	Peterborough Utd.	3/91	Northampton	(A) 1-2 30/3/91	Doncaster Rovers	6/92	22	1	3	0	2	0	0	0
Hodgson	Ken	19/01/42	Newcastle	Newcastle United	12/61	Brighton	(A) 3-0 16/12/61	Bournemouth	6/64	88	4	2	0	30	0	0	0
Hodkinson	Andy	04/11/65	Ashton-under-Lyne	Stockport Co.	8/88	Hereford	(H) 3-1 27/8/88	Hyde United	7/90	62	5	7	4	8	1	1	0
Holden	Robbie	28/10/65	Sunderland	Sunderland	9/83	Bolton	(H) 1-0 16/9/83			7	0	1	0	1	0	0	0
Holt	Ray	29/10/39	Thorne	Halifax Town	7/68	Rochdale	(A) 2-3 10/8/68	Worksop Town	7/70	50	1	4	0	0	0	0	0
Holyoak	Phil	22/05/59	Sunderland	Tottenham H (loan)	2/78	Wimbledon	(A) 0-0 11/2/78			1	0	0	0	0	0	0	0
Hope	Chris	14/11/72	Sheffield	Nottm. Forest	7/93	Wigan Athletic	(A) 2-0 14/8/93			243	17	12	14	16	1	0	2
Horsfall	Tommy	07/01/51	Hamilton	Southend Utd. (loan)	11/73	Mansfield	(H) 5-3 8/12/73			5	0	0	0	2	0	0	0
Horstead	Barry	08/05/35	Brigg	Jnrs.	5/56	Hull	(A) 2-2 29/12/56			320	21	13	0	3	0	1	0
Houchen	Keith	25/07/60	Middlesbrough	York City	3/86	Hartlepool	(A) 1-0 1/4/86	Coventry City	6/86	9	0	0	0	2	0	0	0
Houghton	Ken	18/10/39	Rotherham	Hull City	6/73	Lincoln	(A) 0-1 25/8/73	Scarborough	5/74	33	7	4	0	5	2	0	0
Housham	Steve	24/02/76	Gainsborough	Trainee	12/93	Chesterfield	(A) 1-1 8/11/94			106	8	4	7	4	1	0	3
Howells	Ron	03/08/35	Ferndale	Portsmouth	6/61	Brighton	(H) 3-3 19/8/61	Walsall	7/63	69	3	1	0	4	0	0	0
Hubbard	Jack	24/03/25	Wath-on-Dearne	Scarborough	8/50	Mansfield	(A) 1-8 26/8/50	Wombwell	7/60	359	31	0	0	12	0	0	0
Hughes	David	19/03/58	Birmingham	Lincoln City	6/81	Northampton	(A) 1-1 29/8/81	Lincoln City	3/82	20	1	1	0	0	0	0	0
Humphries	Glenn	11/08/64	Hull	Bristol City	3/91	Doncaster	(A) 3-2 8/3/91	Frickley Athletic	7/93	72	4	5	4	5	0	1	1
Hunter	Les	15/01/58	Middlesbrough	Chesterfield	7/82	Hartlepool	(A) 0-0 28/8/82	Chesterfield	1/84	110	6	6	6	13	0	0	2
				Chesterfield	3/86			Lincoln City	7/87								
Hussey	Malcolm	11/09/33	Darfield	Rotherham Utd.	8/56	Darlington	(H) 1-2 18/8/56	Rochdale	3/59	23	0	0	0	0	0	0	0
Hutchinson	David	25/09/41	Grimsby	Brigg Town	7/71	Aldershot	(A) 1-1 25/9/71	Gainsborough Trin.	7/72	9	0	0	0	0	0	0	0
Hutton	Jack	23/04/44	Bellshill	Hamilton Acad.	6/63	Northampton	(H) 1-2 27/8/63	St. Mirren	7/66	54	7	0	0	7	0	0	0
Hyde	Gary	28/12/69	Wolverhampton	Leicester City	8/91	Wrexham	(H) 3-0 27/8/91	Whitby Town	7/92	8	1	1	3	0	0	0	0
Irvine	Archie	25/06/46	Coatbridge	Doncaster Rovers	7/75	Darlington	(H) 0-2 16/8/75			23	0	1	0	1	0	0	0

Player		D.O.B	Place of Birth	Previous Club		Scunthorpe	Debut	Next Club		Appearances				Goals			
										League	FAC	FLC	AMC	League	FAC	FLC	AMC
Jackson	Kirk	16/10/76	Barnsley	Sheffield Wed.	7/96	Chester	(A) 0-1 21/1/96	Chesterfield	8/97	4	0	0	1	1	0	0	0
Jackson	Nigel	27/06/50	Pudsey	App.	7/68	Workington	(H) 0-1 28/1/69	Bridlington Trin.	7/73	118	2	5	0	5	0	1	0
Jarvis	Nick	19/09/55	Mansfield	Grantham	7/80	Aldershot	(H) 2-2 16/8/80	Grantham	7/81	21	3	2	0	0	0	0	0
Jobling	Kevin	01/01/68	Sunderland	Grimsby Town (L)	12/93	Scarborough	(A) 2-0 1/12/93			0	0	0	1	0	0	0	0
John	Dennis	27/01/35	Swansea	Swansea Town	8/59	Bristol City	(H) 1-1 22/8/59	Millwall	6/62	88	4	2	0	0	0	0	0
Johnson	Paul	10/05/63	Scunthorpe	App.	5/81	Bradford City	(A) 0-0 14/2/82			14	2	0	3	0	0	0	0
Johnson	Steve	23/06/57	Liverpool	Bristol City	7/86	Northampton	(H) 2-2 23/8/86	Chester City	8/88	72	6	7	6	20	1	3	0
Jones	Gary	06/04/69	Huddersfield	Notts County (loan)	2/97	Colchester	(A) 2-1 22/2/96			11	0	0	0	5	0	0	0
Jones	Ken	02/01/36	Aberdare	Cardiff City	12/58	Bristol Rovers	(H) 0-0 3/1/59	Charlton Ath.	9/64	168	9	9	0	0	0	0	0
Jones	Merfyn	30/04/31	Bangor	Liverpool	8/53	Grimsby	(A) 1-1 22/8/53	Crewe Alexandra	6/59	240	23	0	0	27	6	0	0
Jones	Ron	27/02/26	Rhondda	Swansea Town	8/50	Bradford City	(H) 0-0 18/4/51			3	0	0	0	0	0	0	0
Jones	Ryan	23/07/73	Sheffield	Sheffield Wed. (loan)	1/96	Wigan Athletic	(H) 3-1 13/1/96			11	0	0	0	3	0	0	0
Joyce	Joe	18/03/61	Consett	Barnsley	2/91	Rochdale	(H) 1-2 23/2/91	Carlisle United	8/93	91	0	5	6	2	0	0	0
Juryeff	Ian	24/11/62	Gosport	Darlington	8/93	Bury	(H) 1-1 21/8/93	Farnborough Town	2/95	44	5	2	3	13	0	0	0
Kavanagh	Eamonn	05/01/54	Manchester	Workington	8/77	Peterbrough	(A) 1-1 30/8/77			77	4	4	0	3	0	0	0
Kaye	John	03/03/40	Goole	Goole Town	9/60	Liverpool	(H) 2-3 4/2/61	West Bromwich A.	6/63	77	3	2	0	25	0	0	0
Keegan	Kevin	14/02/51	Armthorpe	App.	12/68	Peterborough	(A) 2-3 16/9/68	Liverpool	5/71	124	14	3	0	17	3	1	0
Keeley	Andy	16/09/56	Basildon	Sheffield Utd.	7/81	Northampton	(A) 1-1 29/8/81			77	6	4	3	1	0	0	0
Keeley	Nolan	24/05/51	Barsham	Gt. Yarmouth	4/73	Walsall	(A) 1-1 28/4/73	Lincoln City	1/80	259	15	20	0	37	3	4	0
Kerr	George	09/01/43	Alexandria	Oxford United	2/68	Walsall	(A) 0-0 24/2/68	Lincoln C (coach)	7/73	157	10	6	0	32	4	2	0
Kilmore	Kevin	11/11/59	Scunthorpe	Jnrs.	1/77	Bournemouth	(H) 0-0 19/2/77	Grimsby Town	9/79	102	3	8	0	28	0	1	0
Kirk	Harry	25/08/44	Saltcoats	Hartlepool Utd.	11/70	Northampton	(H) 2-2 28/11/70	Stockport County	9/73	112	10	3	0	16	3	0	0
Kirkman	Alan	21/06/36	Bolton	Newcastle United	12/63	Manchester City	(A) 1-8 26/12/63	Torquay United	7/65	32	0	8	0	5	0	0	0
Kisby	Chris	07/11/52	Horsforth	App.	10/70	Bournemouth	(A) 2-0 30/9/70	Workington	8/73	39	4	0	0	2	0	0	0
Kiwomya	Andy	01/10/67	Huddersfield	Halifax Town	3/95	Carlisle	(A) 1-2 25/3/95	Bradford City	7/95	9	0	0	0	3	0	0	0
Knight	Ian	26/10/66	Hartlepool	Sheffield Wed. (loan)	8/89	Lincoln	(A) 0-1 19/8/89			2	0	0	0	0	0	0	0
Knill	Alan	08/10/64	Slough	Bury	11/93	Wycombe	(H) 0-0 6/11/93	Rotherham Utd	7/97	131	10	5	8	8	0	0	0
Krzywicki	Dick	02/02/47	Penley	Huddersfield T (loan)	2/73	Port Vale	(H) 0-1 24/2/73			2	0	0	0	0	0	0	0
Lamb	Harry	20/04/28	Stourbridge	Aston Villa	6/54	Grimsby	(A) 4-1 24/8/54			36	5	0	0	0	0	0	0
Lambert	Anton	29/11/59	Nottingham	Long Eaton	7/80	Aldershot	(H) 2-2 16/8/80	Ilkeston Town	3/82	39	3	3	0	3	0	0	0
Lavery	Jim	13/12/48	Glasgow	Juniors	8/66	Oxford	(A) 3-2 30/12/67	Brigg Town	7/68	26	1	1	0	0	0	0	0
				Brigg Town	8/74												
Laws	Brian	14/10/61	Wallsend	Darlington	1/97	Doncaster	(A) 1-1 1/2/97	Manager		18	2	2	0	0	0	0	0
Lawther	Ian	20/10/39	Belfast	Blackburn Rovers	7/63	Swindon	(A) 0-3 24/8/63	Brentford	11/64	60	11	12	0	22	1	0	0
Lee	Robert	23/12/57	Newcastle	Doncaster Rovers	7/76	Watford	(H) 0-0 5/2/77	Ashby Town	7/78	19	1	0	0	0	0	0	0
Lees	Terry	30/06/52	Stoke-on-Trent	Stafford Rangers	9/84	Halifax	(H) 4-0 28/9/84	(Sweden)	6/85	31	3	1	1	0	0	0	0
Leman	Dennis	01/12/54	Newcastle	Sheffield Wed.	8/82	Hartlepool	(A) 0-0 28/8/82	Burton Albion	7/84	38	2	2	3	3	0	0	0
Lester	Mike	04/08/54	Manchester	Bradford City	3/83	Crewe	(H) 2-0 25/3/83	Stockport County	9/86	106	9	7	3	9	2	1	0
Letheran	Glan	01/05/56	Llanelli	Leeds United (loan)	8/76	Rochdale	(H) 0-1 21/8/76			27	0	4	0	0	0	0	0
Lewis	Kenny	12/10/29	Bangor	Worcester City	8/56	Carlisle	(H) 1-2 10/11/56	Boston United	7/57	1	0	0	0	0	0	0	0
Lillis	Mark	17/01/60	Manchester	Aston Villa	9/89	Exeter	(H) 5-4 23/9/89	Stockport County	9/91	68	8	1	3	23	5	1	2
Lindsey	Barry	17/04/44	Scunthorpe	App.	5/61	Sunderland	(A) 0-4 23/9/61			217	13	12	0	13	0	0	0
Lindsey	Keith	25/11/46	Scunthorpe	App.	12/64	Hull	(A) 2-3 21/8/65	Doncaster Rovers	7/66	15	1	1	0	0	0	0	0
Lister	Steve	18/11/61	Doncaster	Doncaster Rovers	7/85	Torquay	(H) 4-0 17/8/85	Boston United	7/92	182	16	17	11	30	1	5	1
Litchfield	Peter	27/07/56	Manchester	Bradford City	7/89	Lincoln	(A) 0-1 19/8/89			25	4	3	1	0	0	0	0
Lloyd	Stan	01/10/24	Newcastle	Worksop Town	7/54	Gateshead	(A) 0-2 13/11/54			1	1	0	0	0	0	0	0
Lockwood	Edward	04/08/25	Barnburgh	Denaby United	6/51	Gateshead	(H) 1-1 15/9/51			9	0	0	0	4	0	0	0
Logan	Richard	24/05/69	Barnsley	Plymouth Argyle	6/98	Carlisle	(H) 3-1 15/8/98			41	3	1	1	6	0	0	0
Longden	Paul	28/09/62	Wakefield	Barnsley	8/83	Port Vale	(A) 0-0 27/8/83	Retired		368	29	31	27	0	0	0	0
Lucas	David	23/11/77	Preston	Preston N.E. (loan)	12/96	Wigan Athletic	(H) 2-3 28/12/96			6	0	0	2	0	0	0	0
Luke	George	20/10/32	Lanchester	Sheffield Utd.	5/56	Workington	(A) 2-2 8/9/56	King's Lynn	7/57	18	1	0	0	0	0	0	0
Lumby	Jim	02/10/54	Grimsby	Brigg Town	3/77	Southend	(H) 1-0 5/3/77	Carlisle United	4/78	55	1	4	0	28	0	1	0
Lynch	Barry	08/06/51	Birmingham	Grimsby Town	7/73	Lincoln	(A) 0-1 25/8/73	Portland Timbers	5/75	64	7	5	0	0	0	0	0
McAuley	Sean	23/06/72	Sheffield	Hartlepool Utd.	3/97	Leyton Orient	(H) 1-2 29/3/97			51	5	5	2	1	0	0	0
McCormick	Joe	15/07/16	Holywell	Boston United	7/49	Shrewsbury	(H) 0-0 19/8/50			7	1	0	0	0	0	0	0
McCullagh	Paul	06/02/74	Brigg	Trainee	7/92	Carlisle	(A) 2-0 26/8/92	Brigg Town	10/93	5	2	2	2	1	0	0	0
McDonald	Colin	15/05/50	Norwich	Norwich City	7/70	Southend	(H) 3-0 22/8/70	Brigg Town	7/72	86	6	0	0	11	0	0	0
McDowall	James	25/10/40	Glasgow	Boston United	12/61	Southampton	(A) 4-6 3/3/62			1	0	0	0	0	0	0	0
McFarlane	Andy	30/11/66	Wolverhampton	Swansea City	8/95	Cambridge	(H) 1-2 12/8/95	Torquay United	1/97	60	4	4	3	16	2	1	2
McGill	Andy	11/07/24	Glasgow	Bradford City	7/52	Barrow	(A) 1-2 23/8/52			183	22	0	0	15	2	0	0
McGuigan	John	29/10/32	Motherwell	Newcastle United	1/62	Rotherham	(A) 1-0 2/1/62	Southampton	8/63	57	2	4	0	17	1	2	0
McLaren	Bobby	05/08/29	Chryston	Barry Town	8/51	Chester	(A) 1-3 22/8/51	Barry Town	7/52	6	0	0	0	0	0	0	0
McLean	David	24/11/57	Newcastle	Darlington	7/86	Northampton	(H) 2-2 23/8/86	Whitley Bay	7/88	24	2	4	2	0	0	0	0
Mahy	Barry	21/01/42	Doncaster	Jersey	5/63	Barnsley	(A) 0-2 25/4/64	New York Generals	4/67	22	2	5	0	2	1	0	0
Malan	Norman	23/11/23	South Africa	Darlington	6/50	New Brighton	(A) 2-1 18/11/50	Bradford Park Ave.	7/56	136	18	0	0	0	0	0	0
Mann	Jimmy	15/12/52	Goole	Barnsley	1/83	York	(A) 1-2 23/1/83	Doncaster Rovers	2/83	2	0	0	0	0	0	0	0
Markham	Peter	18/03/54	Scunthorpe	App.	3/72	Aldershot	(H) 1-0 4/4/72			122	8	4	0	1	0	0	0
Marples	Chris	03/08/64	Chesterfield	York City (loan)	2/92	Burnley	(H) 2-2 15/2/92			1	0	0	0	0	0	0	0
Marriott	Jack	01/04/28	Scunthorpe	Huddersfield T	6/57	Chesterfield	(A) 1-1 24/8/57	Retired	12/63	212	11	3	0	26	0	0	0
Marshall	Brian	20/09/54	Bolton-on-Dearne	Huddersfield T (loan)	10/74	Cambridge	(H) 2-0 12/10/74			3	0	0	0	0	0	0	0
Marshall	Frank	26/01/29	Sheffield	Rotherham Utd.	7/57	Chesterfield	(A) 1-1 24/8/57	Doncaster Rovers	10/59	80	6	0	0	0	0	0	0
Marshall	Gary	20/04/64	Bristol	Carlisle Utd.	7/89	Lincoln	(A) 0-1 19/8/89	Exeter City	10/90	41	4	4	2	3	0	0	0
Marshall	Lee	01/08/75	Nottingham	Eastwood Town	6/97	Hull	(A) 2-0 27/9/98			40	4	1	1	2	0	0	0
Marshall	Peter	05/12/34	Worksop	Worksop Town	9/54	Barrow	(H) 3-0 22/11/55			64	5	0	0	0	0	0	0
Martin	Dean	09/09/67	Halifax	Halifax Town	7/91	Gillingham	(A) 0-4 17/08/91	Rochdale	1/95	106	7	8	11	7	0	1	0
Mason	Cliff	27/11/29	York	Leeds United	2/64	Plymouth	(A) 1-3 29/2/64	Chesterfield	7/64	12	0	0	0	1	0	0	0
Matthews	Mike	25/09/60	Hull	Wolves	2/84	Hull	(A) 0-1 26/12/83	N Ferriby Utd.	7/86	58	5	4	8	5	0	0	3

Player		D.O.B	Place of Birth	Previous Club		Scunthorpe	Debut	Next Club		Appearances				Goals			
										League	FAC	FLC	AMC	League	FAC	FLC	AMC
Matthews	Neil	19/09/66	Grimsby	Grimsby Town (loan)	11/85	Swindon	(H) 0-2 9/11/85			1	0	0	0	0	0	0	0
Maw	John	22/12/34	Scunthorpe	Local	6/57	Workington	(H) 2-2 1/2/58			1	0	0	0	0	0	0	0
Maxwell	Jason	01/09/72	Scunthorpe	App. Frodingham	1/93	Colchester	(A) 0-1 1/5/93	App. Frodingham	7/93	2	0	0	0	0	0	0	0
Middleton	Harry	18/03/37	Birmingham	Wolves	9/59	Ipswich	(A) 2-2 10/10/59	Portsmouth	6/61	29	2	2	0	11	1	0	0
Miller	Ian	13/05/55	Perth	Port Vale	8/90	Aldershot	(A) 2-3 1/9/90	Stafford Rangers	7/91	12	4	1	1	0	0	0	0
Minton	Albert	22/09/37	Walsall	Blackpool	7/57	Bradford City	(A) 3-2	Doncaster Rovers	12/58	5	0	0	0	2	0	0	0
Money	Richard	13/10/55	Lowestoft	Lowestoft Town	7/73	Peterborough	(A) 0-1 8/9/73	Fulham	12/77	279	14	21	9	4	0	0	1
				Portsmouth	10/85			(Youth coach)									
Mosby	Harold	25/06/26	Kippax	Rotherham Utd.	7/50	Shrewsbury	(H) 0-0 19/8/50	Worksop Town	7/55	149	18	0	0	21	2	0	0
Moss	David	15/11/68	Doncaster	Chesterfield	7/96	Leyton Orient	(A) 1-0 17/8/96	Partick Thistle	9/96	4	0	1	0	0	0	1	0
Moss	Paul	02/08/57	Birmingham	Hull City	9/81	Tranmere	(H) 2-1 19/9/81	Worcester City	7/82	42	4	0	0	7	0	0	0
Mountford	Bob	23/02/52	Stoke-on-Trent	Port Vale (loan)	10/74	Southport	(H) 3-3 15/10/74			3	0	0	0	0	0	0	0
Mudd	Paul	13/11/70	Hull	Scarborough	7/93	Wigan Athletic	(A) 2-0 14/8/93	Lincoln City	7/95	68	8	4	5	4	0	0	0
Muldoon	Terry	10/08/51	Ashington	Local	8/70	Workington	(A) 0-0 26/9/70	App. Frodingham	7/71	1	0	0	0	0	0	0	0
Mulholland	John	07/12/28	Dumbarton	Grimsby Town	10/50	Halifax	(A) 3-3 2/10/50			6	1	0	0	1	0	0	0
Mullen	Andy	28/07/28	Newcastle	South Shields	8/55	Southport	(A) 2-2 17/3/56	Goole Town	7/57	10	0	0	0	1	0	0	0
Murfin	Andrew	26/11/76	Doncaster	Juniors	8/95	Exeter	(A) 0-1 2/9/95			1	0	0	0	0	0	0	0
Murphy	Matt	20/08/71	Northampton	Oxford United (loan)	12/97	Scarborough	(H) 1-3 13/12/97			3	0	0	1	0	0	0	0
Musselwhite	Paul	22/12/68	Portsmouth	Portsmouth	3/88	Hereford	(H) 3-1 27/8/88	Port Vale	7/92	132	7	11	9	0	0	0	0
Mynard	Les	19/12/25	Bewdley	Derby County	8/52	Barrow	(A) 1-2 23/8/52	Worcester City	7/53	18	1	0	0	3	0	0	0
Naylor	Geoff	28/12/49	Goole	App.	9/67	Stockport	(H) 0-2 3/11/67	Alfreton Town	7/68	10	2	0	0	0	0	0	0
Neale	Peter	09/04/34	Chesterfield	Oldham Athletic	10/58	Brighton	(H) 2-3 18/10/58	Chesterfield	10/66	226	10	9	0	7	0	1	0
Needham	Tony	04/01/41	Scunthorpe	Jnrs.	7/59	Lincoln	(A) 1-2 23/4/60	Corby Town	7/65	33	3	3	0	0	0	0	0
Neenan	Joe	17/03/59	Manchester	York City	1/80	Northampton	(H) 3-0 25/4/80	Burnley	7/85	191	20	12	5	0	0	0	0
Neil	Jimmy	28/02/76	Bury St.Edmunds	Grimsby Town	8/97	Peterborough	(A) 1-0 9/8/97	Gainsborough Trin.	12/98	7	0	1	0	0	0	0	0
Nicholson	Max	03/10/71	Leeds	Torquay United	11/94	Mansfield	(H) 3-4 18/11/94	Gainsborough Trin.	6/96	51	3	2	3	5	0	0	0
Nicol	Paul	31/10/67	Scunthorpe	Trainee	7/86	Swansea	(A) 2-1 11/10/86	Kettering Town	7/90	75	3	6	7	2	0	1	0
Norris	Mike	27/02/57	Retford	App.	2/75	Exeter	(A) 0-4 22/4/74	Scarborough	7/76	25	0	2	0	0	0	0	0
North	Marc	29/05/66	Ware	Luton Town (loan)	1/87	Crewe	(A) 2-2 24/1/87			5	0	0	1	2	0	0	0
Nottingham	Steve	21/02/80	Peterborough	Trainee	7/97	Exeter	(H) 2-1 25/4/98	Kings Lynn	2/99	1	0	0	0	0	0	0	0
O'Berg	Paul	08/05/58	Hull	Bridlington Town	7/79	Torquay	(A) 0-3 18/8/79	Wimbledon	8/84	132	16	6	4	23	2	0	0
O'Connor	Doug	29/04/54	Barnsley	Mansfield Town	7/75	Mansfield	(A) 0-4 20/8/75			31	2	3	0	9	0	1	0
O'Donnell	Jon	21/03/54	Leeds	Hartlepool Utd.	7/77	Doncaster	(A) 1-1 26/12/77	Cambridge City	7/80	60	2	4	0	0	0	0	0
O'Halloran	Kevin	10/11/75	Dublin	Middlesbrough (loan)	3/96	Exeter	(H) 4-0 26/3/96			7	0	0	0	0	0	0	0
O'Meara	Alan	15/12/58	Grantham	App.	7/76	Crewe	(A) 0-1 18/10/75			41	2	0	0	0	0	0	0
O'Riley	Paul	17/10/50	Prescot	Hull City (loan)	3/71	Chesterfield	(A) 0-2 17/3/71			11	0	0	0	4	0	0	0
Oates	Bob	26/07/56	Leeds	Ashley Road	8/74	Rochdale	(A) 2-4 22/2/75	Rochdale	8/83	315	14	19	0	16	0	1	0
Ormond	Ian	26/08/26	Greenock	Barrow	8/58	Ipswich	(H) 1-1 23/8/58	Weymouth	6/59	3	0	0	0	0	0	0	0
Ormondroyd	Ian	22/09/64	Bradford	Oldham Athletic	9/97	Notts County	(A) 1-2 7/9/97	Retired	5/98	30	3	0	3	0	0	0	0
Ottewell	Syd	23/10/19	Horsley	Mansfield Town	3/52	Bradford P.A.	(H) 0-0 8/3/52	Whitstable Town	7/53	30	2	0	0	12	0	0	0
Parkinson	Noel	16/11/59	Hull	Mansfield Town	8/82	Hartlepool	(A) 0-0 22/8/82	Colchester Utd.	8/84	41	3	2	4	7	0	0	0
Parrott	John	05/06/34	Scunthorpe	Local	12/55	Chesterfield	(H) 2-0 3/12/55			1	1	0	0	0	0	0	0
Partridge	Malcolm	28/08/50	Calow	Grimsby Town	7/79	Torquay	(A) 0-3 18/8/79	Retired	2/82	97	3	6	0	21	1	0	0
Pashley	Robert	09/09/37	Sheffield	Gainsborough Trin.	5/59	Stoke	(A) 3-1 26/3/60	Barrow	6/60	3	1	0	0	1	0	0	0
Passmore	Tom	12/02/37	Chester-le-Street	South Shields	5/59	Sunderland	(A) 0-1 9/4/60	Carlisle Utd.	12/63	27	1	2	0	0	0	0	0
Paterson	Jamie	26/04/73	Dumfries	Falkirk	10/95	Hartlepool	(A) 0-2 14/10/95	Halifax Town	6/97	55	5	0	3	2	1	0	0
Payne	Irving 'Joe'	29/06/21	Briton Ferry	Newport County	7/50	Shrewsbury	(H) 0-0 19/8/50	Northampton Town	8/51	40	1	0	0	2	0	0	0
Peacock	John	27/03/56	Leeds	Jnrs.	8/74	Workington	(A) 1-1 17/8/74	Boston United	7/80	190	4	16	0	1	0	0	0
Pearce	David	19/12/34	Scunthorpe	Local	7/56	Grimsby	(H) 1-3 14/3/59			2	0	0	0	0	0	0	0
Pemberton	Martin	01/02/76	Bradford	Doncaster Rovers	3/98	Torquay	(H) 2-0 28/3/98	Harrogate Town	10/98	6	0	0	0	0	0	0	0
Phillips	Martin	13/03/76	Exeter	Manchester C.(loan)	1/98	Peterborough	(H) 1-3 10/1/98			3	0	0	1	0	0	0	0
Pilling	Stuart	26/03/51	Sheffield	Hull City	5/73	Lincoln	(A) 0-1 25/8/73	Retired	3/82	262	16	14	0	26	3	2	0
Platnauer	Nicky	10/06/61	Leicester	Leicester City	3/93	Bury	(H) 2-0 9/3/93	Mansfield Town	8/93	14	0	0	0	2	0	0	0
Platts	Peter	14/01/28	Dinnington	Local	7/51	Darlington	(A) 3-2 8/9/51			2	0	0	0	2	0	0	0
Pointon	Neil	28/11/64	Church Warsop	App.	8/82	Torquay	(H) 0-2 6/3/82	Everton	11/85	159	13	9	7	2	0	1	0
Powell	Gary	02/04/69	Hoylake	Everton (loan)	11/90	Wrexham	(A) 0-1 24/11/90			4	0	0	2	1	0	0	0
Powell	Ray	05/08/24	Swansea	Swansea Town	8/51	Bradford City	(H) 1-0 12/8/51	Kettering Town	7/52	31	4	0	0	14	4	0	0
Pratley	Dick	12/01/63	Banbury	Derby County (loan)	3/84	Wigan Athletic	(A) 0-2 3/3/84			10	0	0	2	0	0	0	0
Pugh	Graham	12/02/48	Hoole	Barnsley	1/80	Portsmouth	(H) 1-0 26/1/80	Matlock Town	7/81	55	2	2	0	0	0	0	0
Punton	Bill	04/05/34	Glenkindie	Sheffield Utd.	1/68	Gillingham	(H) 2-1 26/1/68	Gt. Yarmouth	7/69	45	0	2	0	2	0	0	0
Ratcliffe	Barrie	21/09/41	Blackburn	Blackburn Rovers	5/64	Bristol City	(H) 5-2 22/8/64	Rochdale	7/65	26	0	11	0	7	0	0	0
Rees	Mal	21/04/24	Neath	Barry Town	7/50	Shrewsbury	(H) 0-0 19/8/50	Aberystwyth T	7/51	18	1	0	0	1	0	0	0
Regis	Dave	03/03/64	Paddington	Barnsley (loan)	8/97	Peterborough	(A) 1-0 9/8/97			9	0	0	0	2	0	0	0
				Lincoln City	2/98			Retired	5/98								
Reeves	David	19/11/67	Birkenhead	Sheffield Wed. (loan)	12/86	Exeter	(H) 3-1 19/12/86			10	0	0	0	6	0	0	0
				Sheffield Wed. (loan)	10/87												
Reeves	Brian	18/02/39	Skelmersdale	Blackburn Rovers	4/62	Norwich	(H) 3-1 26/4/62	Southport	7/65	38	1	1	0	0	0	0	0
Reid	Tony	09/05/63	Nottingham	Derby County (loan)	2/83	Hull	(A) 1-1 26/2/83			6	0	0	0	0	0	0	0
Richardson	Ian	09/05/64	Ely	Chester City	10/86	Wrexham	(H) 3-3 1/11/86	Staines Town	7/89	18	3	3	1	4	0	0	0
Richardson	Russell	21/10/64	Sheffield	Trainee	8/83	Southend	(H) 1-6 30/9/83	Worksop Town	7/84	2	1	0	1	0	0	0	0
Roberts	Dudley	16/10/45	Derby	Mansfield Town	2/74	Doncaster	(A) 0-1 2/3/74	Retired	5/76	59	2	3	0	17	0	0	0
Roberts	Harry	12/01/20	Liverpool	Shrewsbury Town	7/53	Workington	(H) 4-1 19/9/53	Gresley Rovers	7/55	17	0	0	0	1	0	0	0
Robinson	Alan	02/12/55	Grantham	Sheffield Wed.	8/75	Darlington	(A) 0-2 16/8/75			1	0	0	0	0	0	0	0
Rudd	Jimmy	25/10/19	Dublin	Rotherham Utd.	10/51	Wrexham	(A) 2-1 6/10/51	Workington	9/52	32	4	0	0	4	1	0	0
Rumble	Paul	14/03/69	Hemel Hempstead	Watford (loan)	8/88	Hereford	(H) 3-1 27/8/88	Maidstone Utd.	9/89	8	0	0	0	1	0	0	0
Rusling	Graham	04/04/48	Keadby	Local	1/67	Swansea	(A) 4-3 14/1/67	Goole Town	7/71	81	11	1	0	17	4	0	0
Russell	Billy	14/09/59	Glasgow	Doncaster Rovers	8/85	Torquay	(H) 17/8/85	Rotherham Utd.	8/88	117	10	10	8	7	3	1	0
Ryan	Tim	10/12/74	Stockport	Trainee	4/93	Hereford	(A) 2-1 29/3/94	Buxton	10/94	2	0	0	0	0	0	0	0

Player		D.O.B	Place of Birth	Previous Club		Scunthorpe	Debut	Next Club		App League	FAC	FLC	AMC	Goals League	FAC	FLC	AMC
Samways	Mark	11/11/68	Doncaster	Doncaster R	3/92	Chesterfield	(H) 2-0 31/3/92	York City	7/97	155	13	8	3	0	0	0	0
Sansam	Christian	26/12/75	Hull	Trainee	12/93	Wigan Athletic	(H) 1-0 18/12/93	Halifax Town	1/96	21	3	0	5	1	0	0	0
Sargent	Gary	11/09/52	Turvey	Norwich City	7/72	Charlton	(A) 0-2 16/9/72	Bedford Town	7/73	15	0	0	0	1	0	0	0
Scott	Dick	26/10/41	Thetford	Cardiff City	9/64	Workington	(H) 1-1 29/9/64	Lincoln City	7/66	47	10	1	0	8	0	0	0
Sertori	Mark	01/09/67	Manchester	Bury	7/96	Leyton Orient	(A) 1-0 17/8/96	Halifax Town	7/98	83	7	6	6	2	0	0	0
Shakespeare	Craig	26/10/63	Birmingham	Grimsby Town	7/97	Swansea	(A) 0-2 23/8/97	Telford United	3/98	4	1	2	1	0	0	0	0
Sharpe	Len	29/11/32	Scunthorpe	Jnrs	5/50	Crewe	(A) 2-2 22/9/51	Hull City	6/62	185	13	1	0	6	0	0	0
Shearer	David	16/10/58	Caol	Bournemouth	2/88	Leyton Orient	(H) 3-2 13/2/88	Darlington	12/88	16	0	0	1	7	0	0	0
Sheldon	Gareth	31/01/80	Birmingham	Trainee	7/97	Shrewsbury	(A) 2-0 2/5/98			12	0	0	1	1	0	0	0
Shutt	Steve	29/11/64	Barnsley	Goole Town	2/85	Crewe	(A) 1-1 16/2/85	Goole Town	7/85	2	0	0	0	1	0	0	0
Sidebottom	Geoff	29/12/36	Mapplewell	Aston Villa	1/65	Southend	(A) 1-0 23/1/65	New York Generals	4/67	59	1	2	0	0	0	0	0
Simpkin	Chris	24/04/44	Hull	Blackpool	10/73	Bradford City	(A) 1-2 3/10/73	Huddersfield T	8/75	61	9	4	0	2	0	0	0
Skipper	Peter	11/04/58	Hull	Hull City (loan)	2/80	Doncaster	(A) 0-5 16/2/80			1	0	0	0	0	0	0	0
Sloan	David	28/10/41	Lisburn	Bangor	11/63	Swansea	(A) 1-4 16/11/64	Oxford United	2/68	136	11	14	0	42	0	0	0
Smalley	Paul	17/11/66	Nottingham	Notts County	9/88	Scarborough	(H) 0-3 1/10/88	Leeds United	12/90	86	5	5	2	1	0	0	0
Smillie	Andy	15/03/41	Minster, Sheppey	Crystal Palace	7/63	Northampton	(A) 0-3 24/8/63	Southend Utd.	9/64	13	0	1	0	2	0	1	0
Smith	Brian	27/10/66	Sheffield	Sheffield Utd. (loan)	3/87	Cardiff	(H) 1-3 7/3/87			6	0	0	0	1	0	0	0
Smith	Mark	19/12/61	Sheffield	Gainsborough Trin.	9/85	Aldershot	(A) 1-2 28/9/85	Kettering Town	10/85	63	7	4	6	8	0	0	0
				Grimsby Town	8/93			Boston United	6/95								
Smith	Bobby	14/03/44	Prestbury	Manchester Utd.	3/65	Carlisle	(A) 1-3 6/3/65	Grimsby Town	1/67	82	3	2	0	12	1	0	0
Snow	Simon	03/04/66	Sheffield	App.	8/83	Chester	(A) 2-1 14/5/83	Sutton Town	7/84	2	0	0	0	0	0	0	0
Sowden	Maurice	21/10/54	Doncaster	App.	10/72	Brentford	(H) 1-0 7/10/72			3	1	0	0	0	0	0	0
Sproates	Alan	30/06/44	Hetton-le-Hole	Darlington	8/74	Workington	(A) 1-1 17/8/74	(Australia)	7/75	24	0	1	0	0	0	0	0
Stamp	Darryn	21/09/78	Beverley	Hessle	7/97	Hull	(A) 2-0 27/9/97			35	2	3	0	5	0	0	0
Stanley	Paul	12/04/66	Chesterfield	Sheffield Utd.	7/84	Nuneaton Boro'	(A) 1-1 17/11/84	Buxton	1/85	0	2	0	0	0	0	0	0
Stanton	Nathan	06/05/81	Nottingham	Trainee	7/97	Scarborough	(A) 0-0 13/4/98			5	0	0	0	0	0	0	0
Steele	Simon	29/02/64	Liverpool	Brighton	3/84	Leyton Orient	(H) 3-1 1/5/84	Worthing	7/84	5	0	0	0	0	0	0	0
Stevenson	Andy	29/09/67	Scunthorpe	Jnrs.	1/86	Port Vale	(A) 1-3 3/2/86	Brigg Town	6/93	103	6	11	14	4	0	1	1
Stewart	Dave	20/05/58	Belfast	Chelsea	11/79	Rochdale	(H) 2-0 30/11/80	Goole Town	7/82	97	7	4	0	19	1	0	0
Stirland	Cec	15/07/21	Ardwick	New Brighton	8/51	Bradford City	(H) 1-0 1/8/51	Retired	5/52	17	0	0	0	0	0	0	0
Stobart	Sean	31/07/66	Wolverhampton	Jnrs.	7/84	Rochdale	(A) 3-3 6/5/85	Dudley Town	7/86	2	0	0	0	1	0	0	0
Stokes	Albert	26/01/33	Darnall	Grimsby Town	7/57	Rochdale	(H) 2-0 3/10/57	Southport	2/59	5	0	0	0	2	0	0	0
Talbot	Jason	26/10/68	Gainsborough			Runcorn	(H) 1-0 6/12/86			0	1	0	0	0	0	0	0
Taylor	Edward	17/05/56	Irvine	Ipswich Town	8/74	Barnsley	(A) 2-2 3/9/74			7	0	1	0	0	0	0	0
Taylor	Kevin	22/01/61	Wakefield	Crystal Palace	10/87	Halifax	(H) 1-0 10/10/87	Frickley Athletic	7/91	157	11	8	10	25	3	1	2
Taylor	Martin	09/12/66	Tamworth	Derby County (loan)	12/87	Torquay	(H) 2-3 18/12/87			8	0	0	0	0	0	0	0
Taylor	Roy	02/04/33	Hoyland	Denaby United	1/53	Workington	(H) 2-1 21/3/53			2	0	0	0	0	0	0	0
Taylor	Dick	09/04/18	Wolverhampton	Grimsby Town	5/48	Shrewsbury	(H) 0-0 19/8/50	Trainer/coach	7/54	131	16	0	0	2	0	0	0
Taylor	Stewart	06/04/46	Owston Ferry	Local	8/65	Swansea	(H) 1-1 2/4/66	Ashby Town	7/69	67	4	0	0	0	0	0	0
Telfer	George	06/07/55	Liverpool	San Diego Sockers	12/81	Port Vale	(H) 0-0 5/12/81	Altrincham	3/83	36	4	2	2	11	1	0	0
Thomas	Barrie	19/05/37	Measham	Mansfield Town	9/59	Sheffield Utd.	(H) 1-1 26/8/59	Newcastle United	1/62	143	6	4	0	93	3	0	0
				Newcastle United	11/64			Barnsley	11/66								
Thompson	Allan	20/01/52	Liverpool	Bradford City	3/82	York	(A) 1-3 26/3/82			11	0	0	0	0	0	0	0
Thompson	Dennis	19/07/34	Bolsover	Chesterfield	7/55	Workington	(A) 2-1 3/9/55			3	0	0	0	0	0	0	0
Thompstone	Ian	17/01/71	Manchester	Halifax Town	3/93	Torquay	(H) 2-2 27/3/93	Rochdale	7/95	60	6	2	2	8	1	0	0
Thornber	Steve	11/10/65	Dewsbury	Blackpool	7/93	Wigan Athletic	(A) 2-0 14/8/93	Halifax Town	2/96	77	5	4	5	7	0	0	0
Thorpe	Arthur	31/07/39	Lucknow, India	Ossett Town	9/60	Stoke	(A) 0-2 4/3/61	Bradford City	7/63	27	0	1	0	5	0	0	0
Toman	Andy	07/03/62	Northallerton	Darlington	8/93	Bury	(H) 1-1 21/8/93	Scarborough	12/93	15	2	1	1	5	1	0	0
Travis	David	04/07/64	Doncaster	Doncaster Rovers	2/86	Leyton Orient	(H) 2-2 8/3/86	Chesterfield	8/87	13	1	0	1	1	0	0	0
Trebble	Neil	16/02/69	Hitchin	Stevenage Boro.	7/93	Wigan Athletic	(A) 0-4 14/8/93	Preston NE	7/94	14	1	1	2	2	0	0	0
Tucker	Gordon	05/01/68	Manchester	Huddersfield T	7/89	Lincoln	(A) 0-1 19/8/89	Goole Town	7/90	15	1	2	1	1	0	0	0
Turnbull	Lee	27/09/67	Stockton	Wycombe Wand.	3/95	Bury	(H) 3-2 11/3/95	Darlington	7/97	47	2	2	1	7	0	0	0
Turner	Joe	21/03/31	Barnsley	Darlington	6/60	Southampton	(A) 2-0 18/2/61	Barnsley	11/61	22	0	1	0	0	0	0	0
Turner	Phil	20/02/27	Chester	Bradford	6/54	Accrington S.	(H) 4-0 2/10/54	Accrington Stanley	10/55	5	0	0	0	2	0	0	0
Tutty	David					Grimsby	(A) 0-2 21/8/82			0	0	0	1	0	0	0	0
Underwood	George	06/09/25	Sheffield	Sheffield Wed.	6/53	Accrington S.	(A) 1-0 1/1/54	Rochdale	6/54	8	0	0	0	0	0	0	0
Varadi	Imre	08/07/59	Paddington	Mansfield Town	9/95	Colchester	(H) 1-0 30/9/95	Boston United	9/95	2	0	0	0	0	0	0	0
Verity	David	21/09/49	Halifax	App.	9/67	Doncaster	(A) 0-3 5/5/67	Halifax Town	9/68	5	0	0	0	0	0	0	0
Wadsworth	Mick	03/11/50	Barnsley	Gainsborough Trin.	8/76	Rochdale	(H) 0-1 21/8/76	Frickley Athletic	7/77	28	0	3	0	3	0	1	0
Wainwright	Lewis	15/12/30	Kirton-in-Lindsey	Brigg Town	5/51	Chester	(H) 2-1 21/4/56			2	0	0	0	0	0	0	0
Waldock	Ronnie	06/12/32	Heanor	Sheffield Utd.	2/57	Workington	(H) 1-0 2/2/57	Plymouth Argyle	9/59	97	6	0	0	45	0	0	0
Walker	Dean	18/05/62	Newcastle	Burnley	3/82	Aldershot	(A) 0-4 1/5/82	North Shields	7/82	1	0	0	0	0	0	0	0
Walker	Justin	06/07/75	Nottingham	Nottingham Forest	3/97	Leyton Orient	(H) 1-2 29/3/97			79	5	6	4	2	0	0	1
Wallace	George	18/04/20	Aberdeen	Army	3/46	Hartlepool	(A) 1-3 25/8/51			33	3	0	0	8	2	0	0
Walsh	Michael	05/08/77	Rotherham	Trainee	7/95	Scarborough	(H) 3-1 22/4/95	Port Vale	7/98	104	11	6	4	1	0	0	0
Walton	Ian	17/04/58	Goole	Grimsby Town	3/76	Southport	(A) 1-2 12/4/77			1	0	0	0	0	0	0	0
Ward	Richie	16/09/40	Scunthorpe	Jnrs	5/58	Fulham	(H) 1-2 21/2/59	Northampton Town	6/59	1	0	0	0	0	0	0	0
Ward	Paul	15/09/63	Sedgefield	Leyton Orient	10/89	Cambridge	(A) 3-5 28/10/89	Lincoln City	3/91	55	5	2	4	6	1	0	0
Warnock	Neil	01/12/48	Sheffield	Hartlepool Utd.	2/72	Rochdale	(A) 2-0 11/11/72	Aldershot	3/75	72	10	5	0	7	1	0	0
Watson	John	14/04/74	South Shields	Newcastle United	7/93	Carlisle	(H) 2-1 18/9/93	Gateshead	1/94	5	1	2	1	0	0	0	0
Webster	Alan	03/07/44	Melton Mowbray	Local	7/66	Swindon	(A) 1-2 24/9/66	Kettering Town	7/68	6	0	0	0	1	0	0	0
Webster	Ian	30/12/65	Askern	Trainee	7/83	Chester	(A) 2-1 14/5/83	Goole Town	7/86	18	5	1	2	1	0	0	0
Welbourne	Don	12/03/49	Scunthorpe	App.	3/67	Bournemouth	(A) 0-1 3/9/66	App. Frodingham	7/76	254	26	12	0	5	1	1	0
White	Jason	19/10/71	Meriden	Derby County	9/91	Barnet	(A) 2-3 17/9/91	Scarborough	12/93	68	6	2	7	16	1	0	1
White	Dick	18/08/31	Scunthorpe	Scunthorpe SC	7/49	Oldham	(H) 1-0 6/9/50	Liverpool	11/55	133	12	0	0	7	1	0	0

Player		D.O.B	Place of Birth	Previous Club		Scunthorpe	Debut	Next Club		Appearances				Goals			
										League	FAC	FLC	AMC	League	FAC	FLC	AMC
Whitehead	Alan	20/11/56	Bury	Brentford	1/84	Bolton	(A) 0-0 21/1/84	York City	10/86	108	6	8	5	8	0	1	1
Whitehead	Phil	17/12/69	Halifax	Barnsley (loan)	11/91	York	(H) 1-0 30/11/91			16	0	2	2	0	0	0	0
				Beverley	9/92												
Whiteside	Billy	24/09/35	Belfast	Portadown	8/56	Darlington	(H) 1-2 18/8/86	Rotherham Utd	12/56	2	0	0	0	0	0	0	0
Whitfield	Jimmy	18/05/19	Hull	Grimsby Town	4/49	Lincoln	(A) 1-2 23/8/50	Southport	8/51	120	14	0	0	31	5	0	0
				Southport	2/52			Boston United	7/55								
Whitnall	Brian	25/05/33	Doncaster	Hull City	5/56	Oldham	(H) 0-0 27/4/57	Exeter City	7/58	3	0	0	0	0	0	0	0
Wigg	Ron	18/05/49	Great Dunmow	Barnsley	10/77	Torquay	(A) 2-4 22/10/77			50	3	2	0	6	0	0	0
Wigginton	Clive	18/10/50	Sheffield	Grimsby Town	7/75	Darlington	(A) 0-2 16/8/75	Lincoln City	9/77	88	2	6	0	7	0	1	0
Wilcox	Russ	25/03/64	Hemsworth	Preston N.E.	7/97	Peterborough	(A) 1-0 9/8/97			57	6	5	3	3	2	0	0
Williams	Ivor	29/05/35	Scunthorpe	Local	8/59	Ipswich	(H) 2-2 10/10/59			8	0	0	0	0	0	0	0
Williams	Mike	23/10/44	Hull	Workington	7/70	Colchester	(A) 0-2 22/3/71	Scarborough	7/74	28	5	0	0	0	0	0	0
Wilmott	Richard	29/08/69	Matlock	Stevenage Boro.	3/93	Northampton	(H) 5-0 30/3/93	Halifax Town	7/93	3	0	0	0	0	0	0	0
Wilson	Andy	27/09/40	Rotherham	Sheffield Utd.	6/61	Swansea	(A) 1-2 7/10/61	Doncaster Rovers	7/65	112	15	12	0	14	1	1	0
Wilson	Andy P.	13/10/47	Maltby	Rotherham Utd.	9/68	Port Vale	(A) 1-4 28/9/68	Corby Town	7/69	23	1	0	0	4	0	0	0
Wilson	Danny	01/01/60	Wigan	Nottm. Forest (loan)	10/83	Bradford City	(A) 2-2 8/10/83			6	0	0	0	3	0	0	0
Wilson	Paul	02/08/68	Bradford	York City	8/95	Cambridge	(H) 1-2 12/8/95	Cambridge Utd.	3/97	77	6	4	4	2	0	0	0
Wilson	Paul D.	16/11/60	Doncaster	Yeovil Town	2/96	Cardiff	(A) 0-0 15/4/97	Youth Dev.Officer		1	0	0	0	0	0	0	0
Winter	Julian	06/09/65	Huddersfield	Huddersfield T (loan)	8/88	Hereford	(H) 3-1 27/8/88			4	0	0	0	0	0	0	0
Witter	Tony	12/08/65	London	Welling	2/99	Cambridge Utd	(A) 0-0 13/2/99			14	0	0	0	0	0	0	0
Wood	Barrie	05/12/36	Doncaster	Doncaster Rovers	7/58	Rotherham	(H) 2-0 20/9/58	South Shields	7/59	3	0	0	0	1	0	0	0
Wood	Hugh	16/11/60	Bellshill	Grantham	9/80	Southend	(A) 0-2 17/10/80	Shepshed Chart.	7/81	1	0	0	0	0	0	0	0
Woods	Eddie	29/07/51	Pentre	Bristol City (loan)	10/73	Colchester	(A) 0-2 19/10/73			4	0	0	0	2	0	0	0
Woods	Neil	30/07/66	York	Grimsby Town (loan)	1/98	Macclesfield	(A) 0-2 20/1/98			2	0	0	0	0	0	0	0
Woodward	John	16/01/47	Stoke-on-Trent	Port Vale	7/75	Hartlepool	(A) 2-1 13/9/75	Ostend	7/76	19	0	0	0	5	0	0	0
Woolmer	Tony	25/03/46	Swardeston	Bradford Park Ave.	11/70	Lincoln	(A) 1-4 7/11/70	King's Lynn	7/72	40	5	1	0	3	1	0	0
Young	Stuart	16/12/72	Hull	Scarborough	12/94	Rochdale	(H) 4-1 31/12/94	Blyth Spartans	2/96	28	1	2	3	3	0	0	0

PLAY-OFFS - SEMI-FINALS AND FINALS:
Additional appearances and goals should be added to the following players' records.

Player:	App.	Goals:	Player:	App.	Goals	Player:	App.	Goals	Player:	App.	Goals
Alexander G.	2	0	Elliott M.	3	0	Hodkinson A.	2	0	Nicol P.	3	0
Atkins M.	1	0	Eyre J.	2	0	Hope C.	3	0	Richardson I.	3	0
Buckley J.	3	0	Fickling A.	1	0	Housham S.	3	0	Samways M.	3	0
Bull G.	1	0	Flounders A.	6	1	Humphries G.	3	0	Shearer D.	2	0
Calvo-Garcia A.	3	1	Forrester	3	0	Joyce J.	5	0	Sheldon G.	2	2
Clarke T.	2	0	Gayle J.	3	0	Lillis M.	2	1	Smalley P.	2	0
Cork D.	2	0	Green Ron	2	0	Lister S.	3	0	Stamp D	1	0
Cotton P.	1	0	Hamilton I.	5	1	Logan R.	2	0	Stevenson A.	3	0
Cowling D.	2	1	Harle D.	2	0	Longdon P.	9	0	Taylor K.	6	0
Daws T.	9	1	Helliwell I.	3	2	Martin D.	3	1	Walker J.	3	0
Dawson A.	3	1	Hicks S.	2	0	McLean D.	2	0	White J.	1	0
Dixon K.	1	0	Hill D.	7	1	Money R.	1	0	Wilcox R.	3	0
			Hine M.	2	0	Musselwhite P.	4	0			

NOTES:
PLAYERS WHO'S WHO SECTION:
This preceding section is generally self-explanatory. Every player who has made a first team competitive match appearance (to the end of the 1989/99 season) is included, with date of birth (D.O.B.) Where known. 'Previous Club' and 'Next Club' transfer dates (month/year are included where known). Where a player has played for Scunthorpe United in more than one separate period, the total appearances and goals only are shown. Appearances include those as a substitute.

SEASONAL STATISTICS SECTION:
The following section is also generally self-explanatory. 'Home' games are shown by the opponents name in upper case (capital letters), and 'Away' games in lower case. Scunthorpe United score is always given first. Full team line-ups are given for every Football League season (1949-50 to 1998-99 inclusive), plus the Midland League season 1949-50 only. Substitutes (only when used) are given the numbers 12,13,14 (where applicable) regardless of the actual shirt number used. '12' is used where only one substitute was used, and '14' is used for the second used substitute up to the 1994/95 season. From 1995/96, '13' refers to the second subtitute, and '14' for the third. The player(s) substituted are shown underlined. Unused subtitutes have not been included.

Cup matches - Typical abbreviations: P = Preliminary round, Q = Qualifying, rep = replay, R1/2 = 1st round,second replay, SF1 = Semi-final 1st leg, etc. Additional pre-League abbreviations are shown on the appropriate pages.

Pre-Scunthorpe United: 1885 - 1899

The following are the (Friendly) matches traced of the forerunners:

SCUNTHORPE TOWN

1885-86

1	Oct	31	Brigg Town Res.	1-5
2	Feb	5	ASHBY	6-0
3		6	FERRIBY SLUICE	5-0
4		13	Crowle	0-1
5		20	Ashby	7-0
6		27	Barton	2-3
7	Mar	13	CROWLE	7-1

1886-87

1	Oct	10	Gainsborough Trinity	0-18
2	Nov	6	BARTON	4-4
3		13	Winterton	8-0
4		20	CROWLE	7-1
5	Mar	11	Brigg Ancholme	1-6

1887-88

1	Sep	3	CLEETHORPES	1-1
2	Dec	6	Brigg Swifts	1-2

1888-89

1	Apr	20	Brigg Swifts	3-5

1889-90

1	Jan	11	Barton	0-4
2	Feb	6	BRIGG TOWN UNITED	0-4

1890-91

1	Dec	13	Barton	1-0
2	Jan	10	Brigg Town United	1-0
3		17	BRIGG TOWN UNITED	0-5 *
4		31	MARKET RASEN	6-1
5	Feb	14	NOTTINGHAM ST.GEORGE'S	3-1
6		21	Barton Town	1-0
7	Mar	7	Brigg Town	2-2
8		14	GRIMSBY WEST END	0-1
9		21	GAINSBOROUGH TRINITY	2-2

1891-92

1	Sep	19	DONCASTER ROVERS RES.	2-1
2	Oct	31	GRIMSBY ALL SAINTS	1-2
3	Nov	7	Barton Town	3-0
4		14	Brigg Town United	0-1
5	Dec	26	GRIMSBY AMATEURS	3-0
6	Mar	5	GRIMSBY WEST END	4-1
7	Apr	9	FRODINGHAM ROVERS	0-0

1892-93

1	Sep	3	GAINSBOROUGH ASHCROFT	4-1
2	Oct	1	GAINSBOROUGH TRINITY RES.	1-4
3		8	GRIMSBY WEST END	2-1
4		22	GAINSBOROUGH TRINITY RES.	0-4
5		29	Barton Town	3-1
6	Nov	5	GRIMSBY ALL SAINTS	0-1
7		12	Brigg Brittania	1-2
8		26	GAINSBOROUGH AMATEURS	5-2
9	Dec	24	GRIMSBY TOWN RES.	0-1
10	Jan	14	DONCASTER ROVERS RES	2-0
11		21	BRIGG BRITTANIA	1-1
12		28	Doncaster Rovers Res.	3-4
13	Feb	4	Gainsborough Trinity Res.	0-12
14		11	Brigg Brittania	3-1
15	Mar	4	BRIGG TOWN	1-0
16		25	Cleethorpes	0-3
17	Apr	1	GAINSBOROUGH AMATEURS	6-0
18		3	FRODINGHAM IRON WORKS	1-0
19		15	CLEETHORPES	2-1

1893-94

1	Sep	16	MR. F. ADAMS XI	2-1
2		30	GAINSBOROUGH TRINITY RES	2-1
3	Oct	7	FRODINGHAM ROVERS	5-1
4		14	Gainsborough Trinity Res.	2-3
5		21	GAINSBOROUGH PARISH CHURCH	4-1
6		28	Barton Town +	0-0
7	Nov	4	Brigg Town	1-1
8		11	MORTON	3-1
9	Dec	2	FRODINGHAM ROVERS	3-1
10		9	GAINSBOROUGH AMATEURS	1-0
11		16	Gainsborough Athletic	0-3
12	Jan	13	BRIGG SWIFTS	3-0
13		27	BARTON	2-2
14	Mar	3	GRIMSBY ALL SAINTS	0-7
15		10	GAINSBOROUGH ATHLETIC	5-0
16		24	STEELWORKS	3-3
17	Apr	14	Gainsborough Parish Church	3-0
18		21	BRIGG SWIFTS	5-1

1894-95

1	Sep	8	GAINSBOROUGH ATHLETIC	2-2
2		15	SCUNTHORPE UNITED #	10-1
3	Oct	13	GAINSBOROUGH TRINITY RES.	0-5
4	Nov	3	GAINSBOROUGH ST. JOHNS	0-10
5		10	GRIMSBY ALL SAINTS	6-0
6	Dec	1	CLOWNS	2-7
7		8	GAINSBOROUGH TRINITY RES.	3-3
8		26	DONCASTER ROVERS RES.	2-1
9	Jan	30	BRIGG	0-1
10	Mar	2	HEXTHORPE WANDERERS	1-0
11		9	SCUNTHORPE AMATEURS	2-6
12		30	SCUNTHORPE AMATEURS	6-3
13	Apr	13	STEELWORKS XI	1-2
14		15	FRODINGHAM UNITED	3-0

1895-96

1	Sep	7	WINTERTON	16-0
2		21	FRODINGHAM UNITED	3-0
3		28	GAINSBOROUGH TRINITY RES.	0-3
4	Oct	5	GAINSBOROUGH JARDINES	3-3
5		16	GRIMSBY ALL SAINTS	0-3
6		30	GAINSBOROUGH TRINITY RES.	0-2
7	Dec	14	GAINSBOROUGH PARISH CHURCH	0-3
8		26	GRIMSBY ROVERS	3-2
9		28	BARTON ROVERS	10-0
10	Jan	4	BARTON	5-0
11		11	GAINSBOROUGH PARISH CHURCH	1-2
12		18	Caistor	7-0
13	Feb	28	FRODINGHAM UNITED	11-1
14	Mar	28	Spilsby	2-1
15	Apr	4	GRIMSBY HUMBER ROVERS	2-1

1896-97

1	Sep	12	Grimsby Town Res.	1-7
2		26	GAINSBOROUGH TRINITY RES.	1-3
3	Oct	10	FRODINGHAM UNITED	7-1
4		17	GRIMSBY TOWN RES.	1-1
5		24	Brigg Rovers	2-2
6	Nov	21	GRIMSBY ALL SAINTS	3-3
7		28	BARTON	5-1
8	Jan	6	Grimsby Rovers	1-5

BRUMBY HALL

1895-96

1	Sep	28	SCUNTHORPE TOWN RES.	1-7
2	Nov	2	Winterton Rovers	3-1
3	Jan	18	Scunthorpe Rangers	1-2
4	Feb	8	Brigg Rovers	5-0
5	Apr	4	KIRTON	1-3

1896-97

1	Sep	19	GAINSBOROUGH ST. JOHNS	1-1
2	Oct	3	Frodingham United	0-5
3	Nov	7	Ashby Town	1-3
4		14	MR. T.B. MENNEL'S XI	2-0
5	Dec	12	KIRTON	0-2
6		19	Scunthorpe Trilby	1-2
7	Jan	2	ASHBY	5-1
8		23	KEELBY	2-3

1897-98

1	Jan	15	Winterton	2-1
2		22	MARSHGATE	2-1
3	Feb	5	Broughton West End	1-3
4		26	Frodingham & Bromby Utd.	0-2
5	Apr	23	GAINSBOROUGH ST. JOHNS	1-2

1898-99

1	Sep	3	ASHBY CLUB	6-0
2		17	Kirton	5-1
3	Nov	5	Gainsborough St. Johns	2-0
4		12	MORTON	2-2
5		17	BARTON ROVERS	5-0
6		31	MORTON	6-1
7	Jan	7	Grimsby Humber Trinity	0-4
8		21	GRIMSBY ALL SAINTS	1-2
9	Feb	21	2nd VOLUNTEER BATT. DONCASTER	11-0
10	Mar	11	GRIMSBY HUMBERS	0-3
11	Apr	8	DONCASTER MARSH GATE	5-1

Note:
* Lincolnshire Challenge Cup match.
+ Charity Match: Combined Scunthorpe Town and Frodingham United team.
# 'Town' Reserve match. 'United' a Junior team not related to later club.

Competitions: The following is a complete listing of all matches traced, with details of competition, where known.
(Where no competition is shown, these are most likely League matches of Friendly games)
GL = Gainsborough & District League. LL = Lindsey League. BC = Bellamy Cup. FA = F.A.Amateur Cup. FAC = F.A.Cup
F = Friendly. FC = Frodingham Charity Cup. GC = Grimsby Charity Cup. HC = Hull Charity Cup. HC = Horncastle Charity Cup.
IC = Ironstone Cup. LJ = Lincolnshire Junior Cup. LS = Lincolnshire Shield. MC = Moreing Cup. SN = Scunthorpe Nursing Cup.

SCUNTHORPE UNITED

1899-1900

1	Sep	16	CROWLE	4-1	
2	Oct	21	MORTON	3-0	
3	Nov	12	GAINSBOROUGH BLUE STAR	3-1	
4	Dec	16	FRODINGHAM UNITED	3-2	LS rep
5	Mar	24	Gainsborough W.M.C.& I.	0-7	

1900-01

1	Oct	21	Ashby Town	1-3	
2	Dec	26	TINDSLEY (SHEFFIELD)	5-0	
3		27	GAINSBOROUGH ROVERS	1-1	LS
4	Feb	9	Frodingham United	4-2	HC
5		16	Ashby Town	3-5	
6		23	FRODINGHAM UNITED	0-2	
7	Mar	2	ASHBY	6-2	
8		9	BRIGG	10-1	LL
9		23	GRIMSBY ALL SAINTS *	1-3	HC S/F
10		30	FRODINGHAM UNITED	1-1	

Note:
* At Brumby Hall
** Local side, correct name unknown
+ Tie drawn away, played at home for extra 'gate'.
# Played at Frodingham
3-3 after 90 minutes

1901-02

1	Sep	14	Hull **	1-1	
2		22	BRIGG TOWN	4-0	LL
3	Oct	12	SCUNTHORPE CENTRALS	5-1	LS R1
4		19	GRIMSBY UNITED	1-2	F
5		26	GAINSBOROUGH W.M.C.& I.	4-2	
6	Nov	2	BROUGHTON	18-0	LL
7		9	GAINSBOROUGH CENTRALS	3-2	F
8		14	FRODINGHAM UNITED	4-1	LS R2
9		23	BURTON ST. CHADS	1-1	HC R2
10		30	H.M.S. GALATICA XI	2-0	F
11	Dec	7	SCUNTHORPE CENTRALS	8-1	LL
12		14	GAINSBOROUGH WEDNESDAY	3-4	LS R3
13		21	Barton St. Chads	3-0	HC R2 rep
14	Jan	4	Scunthorpe Centrals	9-0	LL
15		11	Scunthopre St. Johns	2-1	LL
16		25	GRIMSBY ST. JOHN +	3-2	GC
17	Feb	8	Frodingham United	0-1	LL
18		15	FRODINGHAM UNITED	1-1	HC R3
19		22	Frodingham United	1-1	HC R3 rep
20	Mar	1	Grimsby Tradesmen #	1-5	GC S/F
21		8	Broughton	6-1	LL
22		15	FRODINGHAM UNITED ##	3-4	HC R3 2rep
23		29	FRODINGHAM UNITED	0-1	LL
24	Apr	23	SCUNTHORPE ST. JOHNS	3-1	

Season 1901/02 - Scunthorpe United Junior Section,
Known as 'The Centrals', this is the oldest known team group of any Scunthorpe club.
(Back) Lawson,Symes,E.Hollingsworth,Bones,Floyd,Kennington,Jacques. (Middle) Northall (capt.),Lings,Todd
(Front) Laird, Walker, Dustin, J. Hollingsworth, Bray

SCUNTHORPE UNITED

1902-03

#					
1	Sep	27	North Lindsey Utd	1-2	LL
2	Oct	11	GRIMSBY UNITED	3-2	
3		25	Frodingham United	2-4	LL
4	Nov	1	GRIMSBY TRADESMEN	1-4	
5		8	NORTH LINDSEY UTD	2-2	LS
6		15	North Lindsey Utd	0-2	LS rep
7		29	BARTON ST. CHADS	1-0	HC R1
8	Dec	6	NORTH LINDSEY BEES	11-1	LL
9		13	FRODINGHAM UNITED	2-4	
10	Jan	10	Crowle	10-1	
11		17	FRODINGHAM ROVERS	4-1	
12		24	North Lindsey Utd	?	HC R2
13		31	Broughton	3-3	
14	Feb	21	NORTH LINDSEY UTD	4-1	LL
15		28	NORTH LINDSEY BEES	9-1	LL
16	Apr	19	ATTERCLIFFE	0-3	F

1903-04

#					
1	Sep	5	ASHBY RISING STARS	8-0	LL
2		12	Ashby Town	5-1	
3		19	BROUGHTON	4-1	
4		26	FRODINGHAM ROVERS	2-2	
5	Oct	10	Frodingham United	0-10	
6		24	Broughton	1-2	LL
7	Jan	9	Frodingham United	0-3	GL
8		16	FRODINGHAM UNITED	2-5	HC
9		30	FRODINGHAM UNITED	0-7	LL
10	Feb	13	NORTH LINDSEY UTD	1-2	GL
11		20	NORTH LINDSEY BEES	7-1	GL
12	Mar	12	ASHBY TOWN	4-0	FC

1904-05

Individual Results not traced,
but records show the following:
Lindsey League Champions.
Winterton Charity Cup winners.
Frodingham Charity Cup winners.

NORTH LINDSEY UNITED

1902-03

#					
1	Sep	27	SCUNTHORPE UTD	2-1	LL
2	Nov	1	NORTH LINDSEY BEES	4-1	
3		8	Scunthorpe United	2-2	LS
4		15	SCUNTHORPE UNITED	2-0	LS rep
5		29	FRODINGHAM UNITED	0-3	LS
6	Jan	3	Frodingham United	0-1	
7		10	NORTH LINDSEY BEES	2-1	
8		17	Crowle Parish Institute	3-3	
9		24	SCUNTHORPE UNITED	1-0	HC
10		31	FRODINGHAM ROVERS	6-0	
11	Feb	7	GRIMSBY ST. JOHNS	1-6	GR
12		21	Scunthorpe United	1-4	LL
13		28	Frodingham Rovers	3-3	
14	Mar	21	GRIMSBY ST. JOHNS	1-3	HC F

1903-04

#					
1	Sep	12	Ashby Rising Stars *	5-1	LL
2		26	BARNETBY	15-0	
3	Oct	10	Broughton	1-0	GL
4	Nov	21	Broughton	3-4	
5	Jan	9	ASHBY RISING STARS	2-0	LL
6		23	Frodingham United	6-1	GL
7		30	Ashby Town	3-1	
8	Feb	6	NORTH LINDSEY BEES	7-1	GL
9		13	Scunthorpe United	2-1	GL
10		20	FRODINGHAM UNITED	2-1	LL
11		27	Winterton Rovers	13-1	FC
12	Mar	12	FRODINGHAM ROVERS	3-0	HC

* Abandoned - crowd disturbances.

1904-05

#					
1	Oct	1	Broughton	2-1	
2		8	Ashby Town	2-1	
3	Nov	19	BROUGHTON	3-0	
4	Dec	24	Winterton	2-0	
5		31	FRODINGHAM	2-1	GL
6	Mar	4	Broughton	6-1	

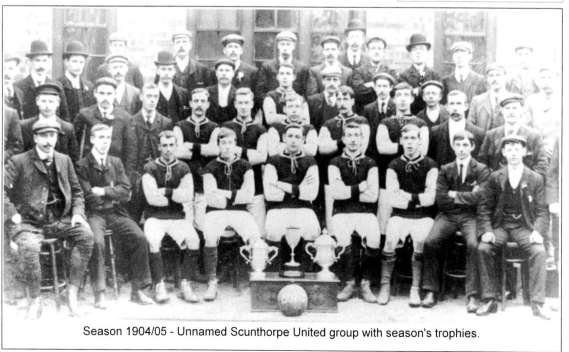

Season 1904/05 - Unnamed Scunthorpe United group with season's trophies.

SCUNTHORPE UNITED

1905-06

1	Sep	23	FRODINGHAM UNITED	3-1	
2	Nov	25	BROUGHTON	3-2	
3	Dec	2	Broughton	4-0	
4		16	Broughton	1-1	GL
5		23	GRIMSBY ROVERS	0-2	HC

1906-07

1	Oct	13	ASHBY RISING STARS	2-2	GL
2	Nov	3	GRIMSBY ROVERS	1-1	HN
3	Jan	5	ASHBY RISING STARS	8-0	
4		12	Frodingham United	1-1	FC
5		19	GRIMSBY ST. JOHNS	0-0	HC
6		26	GRIMSBY HAYCROFT ROV.	1-0	HN
7	Feb	2	Frodingham United	2-4	
8		9	Grimsby St. Johns	3-2	HC S/F
9		16	Frodingham United	2-4	SN S/F
10	Mar	2	FRODINGHAM UNITED	1-3	GL
11		9	North Lindsey United	2-1	LL
12		16	NORTH LINDSEY UTD	0-1	LL
13		23	GRIMSBY ROVERS	3-4	HC F
14	Apr	13	Barton Town	0-3	LL
15		20	Broughton	2-0	LL

1907-08

1	Sep	21	GRIMSBY HAYCROFT R.	1-6	
2		28	Frodingham & Brumby Utd	1-1	LL
3	Oct	5	Ashby Rising Stars	4-0	
4		12	FRODINGHAM & BRUMBY	2-1	HN
5		19	FRODINGHAM & BRUMBY	2-0	
6		26	GAINSBOROUGH AMATEURS	10-1	
7	Nov	2	Kirton	6-1	
8		9	North Lindsey United	0-1	
9		16	SCUNTHORPE ALL SAINTS	4-2	LIC
10		23	SCUNTHORPE WMC	4-3	FC
11	Dec	7	Barton	4-1	GL
12		?	Frodingham & Brumby Utd	won	HC
13		11	SCUNTHORPE ALL SAINTS	4-2	FC
14		18	Frodingham & Brumby Utd	1-2	HC
15	Feb	8	Lincoln St. Catherines	3-1	LIC (aet)
16		15	GRIMSBY ROVERS	2-0	
17		22	Frodingham & Brumby Utd *	2-2	FC
18		29	SPALDING	2-2	LIC
19	Mar	14	North Lindsey Utd	1-0	
20		21	Broughton Rangers	2-1	LL
21		28	Frodingham & Brumby Utd	1-2	FC
22	Apr	17	CLEETHORPES	2-0	LIC F
23		18	Frodingham & Brumby Utd	0-0	GL
24		25	GAINSBORO' TRINITY INST.	1-2	MC

* Abandoned after 75 minutes.

NORTH LINDSEY UNITED

1905-06

1	Oct	14	BARNETBY	23-1	
2	Dec	16	GRIMSBY HAYCROFT ROVS	1-2	HC

1906-07

1	Jan	5	Broughton	1-2	GL
2		12	Scunthorpe All Saints	1-2	
3		19	FRODINGHAM UTD	2-4	GL
4		26	FRODINGHAM UTD	1-0	LL
5	Feb	2	Gainsborough Trinty Institute	0-7	LS
6		9	SCUNTHORPE ALL SAINTS	1-5	FC
7	Mar	2	Barton	*	
8		9	Scunthorpe United	1-2	LL
9		16	SCUNTHORPE UNITED	1-0	LL

* Game awarded to Barton
(North Lindsey failed to appear)

1907-08

1	Sep	21	Frodingham & Brumby Utd	0-0	GL
2		28	SCUNTHORPE ALL SAINTS	2-2	LL
3	Oct	5	Barton Town	0-0	
4		26	Gainsborough Trinity & Inst.	1-3	LIC
5	Nov	2	ASHBY RISING STARS	3-1	
6		9	SCUNTHORPE UNITED	1-0	
7		16	ASHBY RISING STARS	2-1	
8		23	GAINSBOROUGH WMCI	6-1	
9	Dec	14	ASHBY RISING STARS *	1-2	
10	Jan	4	Frodingham & Brumby Utd	0-1	LL
11		18	Broughton Rangers	3-2	LL
12	Feb	1	Frodingham & Brumby Utd	0-2	HC
13		15	Scawby Swifts	1-0	F
14		29	Frodingham & Brumby Utd	4-1	LL
15	Mar	14	Scunthorpe United	0-1	
16		21	Frodingham & Brumby Utd	1-4	

* Abandoned after 75 minutes - bad light

Season 1907/08 - Unnamed North Lindsey United group, many of whom were, two years later, to be associated with Scunthorpe United

SCUNTHORPE UNITED

1908-09

#	Date		Opponent	Score	Note
1	Sep	12	GRIMSBY ROVERS	3-1	
2		19	LINCOLN CITY	0-2	Lincs Cup
3		?	GRIMSBY RANGERS	2-0	
4		26	Grantham	0-2	
5	Oct	3	WORKSOP	4-0	
6		10	BROUGHTON RANGERS	4-0	
7		17	North Lindsey United	2-1	
8		24	GRIMSBY HAYCROFT ROV.	2-2	SN
9		31	FRODINGHAM & BRUMBY U	3-1	LL
10	Nov	7	Hull City Reserves	0-1	Friendly
11		14	GRIMSBY VICTORIA	2-0	
12		21	GAINSBORO' TRINITY RES.	1-1	Friendly
13		28	GRIMSBY HAYCROFT ROVS	2-0	
14	Dec	5	NORTH LINDSEY UTD	1-1	
15		12	GRIMSBY VICTORIA	4-1	HC
16		19	Frodingham & Brumby Utd	1-3	
17		25	LINDSEY WMC	7-1	
18	Jan	2	GRIMSBY RANGERS	1-1	
19		9	North Lindsey Utd	2-1	GL
20		16	Ashby Rising Stars	3-0	
21		23	Grimsby Rovers	1-2	HN
22		?	ASHBY RISING STARS	7-0	GL
23		30	FROD. & BRUMBY UNITED	3-1	
24	Feb	6	GRIMSBY ROVERS	1-3	IC
25		13	Frodingham & Brumby Utd	2-2	
26		20	NORTH LINDSEY UTD	4-0	
27		27	Gainsboro' Trinity Reserves	3-4	
28	Mar	13	CLEETHORPES	5-3	SN
29		20	Frodingham & Brumby Utd	3-0	
30		27	ASHBY RISING STARS	0-1	FC
31	Apr	3	Scawby Swifts	4-1	
32		17	NORTH LINDSEY UTD	3-3	
33		24	NORTH LINDSEY UTD	1-2	
34		29	Frodingham & Brumby Utd	1-2	LL

1909-10

#	Date		Opponent	Score	Note
1	Sep	4	GRIMSBY ROVERS	3-2	
2		11	HULL DAY STREET O.B.	1-1	
3		18	WITHERNSEA	8-0	FAC Prelim
4		25	FRODINGHAM & BRUMBY U.	2-0	LJC Rnd 1
5	Oct	2	York City	0-4	FAC Q1
6		9	GRIMSBY TOWN RES	1-1	Friendly
7		23	Broughton Rangers	3-1	LJC Rnd 2
8		30	NORTH LINDSEY MIDGETS	7-0	LL
9	Nov	6	NORTH LINDSEY UTD	1-1	LL
10		13	GRIMSBY HUMBER ROVERS	1-2	LJC Rnd 3
11		20	HULL CITY RES.	0-8	Friendly
12		27	NORTH LINDSEY UTD	5-1	HC
13	Dec	4	FRODINGHAM & BRUMBY U.	2-2	LL
14		11	GRIMSBY HUMBER ROVERS	2-3	IC
15		18	North Lindsey United	3-3	LL
16		25	GAINSBORO' TRINITY RES.	2-3	Friendly
17		27	GRIMSBY RANGERS	1-2	SN
18	Jan	8	BRIGG BRITANNIA	6-1	LL
19		15	Brigg Britannia	1-3	
20	Feb	5	FRODINGHAM & BRUMBY U.	2-5	LL
21		12	Scunthorpe Midgets	1-2	LL
22	Mar	5	ASHBY RISING STARS	2-3	LL
23		12	Frodingham & Brumby Utd	1-1	HC
24		19	BROUGHTON RANGERS	4-0	LL
25		25	Broughton Rangers	2-5	
26		27	FRODINGHAM & BRUMBY U.	0-2	HC
27	Apr	4	NORTH LINDSEY UTD	3-3	

NORTH LINDSEY UNITED

1908-09

#	Date		Opponent	Score	Note
1	Sep	12	Frodingham & Brumby Utd	1-1	
2	Oct	3	NORTH LINDSEY MIDGETS	6-0	GL
3		10	FROD. & BRUMBY UTD	3-1	
4		17	SCUNTHORPE UNITED	1-2	
5		24	BROUGHTON RANGERS	6-2	LJC
6		31	Broughton Rangers	3-3	GL
7	Nov	7	GRIMSBY RANGERS	1-2	SN
8		14	FRODINGHAM & BRUMBY U	2-1	LJC
9		21	Scawby Swifts	2-1	LL
10	Dec	5	Scunthorpe United	1-1	
11		12	Immingham	6-0	IC
12		19	ASHBY RISING STARS	1-0	
13		25	Lincoln South End	0-3	
14	Jan	2	Frodingham & Brumby Utd	1-1	FC
15		9	SCUNTHORPE UNITED	1-2	
16		23	FRODINGHAM & BRUMBY U	1-3	
17	Feb	6	FRODINGHAM & BRUMBY U	0-1	FC
18		13	GRIMSBY ROVERS	3-1	IC
19		20	Scunthorpe United	0-4	
20		27	ASHBY RISING STARS	2-1	GL
21	Mar	13	GRIMSBY ROVERS	1-1	
22		20	Ashby Rising Stars	0-2	
23		27	Frodingham & Brumby Utd	0-0	
24	Apr	3	Grimsby Rovers	1-7	IC
25		17	Scunthorpe United	3-3	HC
26		?	Scunthorpe United	2-1	

1909-10

#	Date		Opponent	Score	Note
1	Sep	4	Frodingham & Brumby Utd	3-2	
2		11	ASHBY RISING STARS	3-5	
3		18	SCUNTHORPE MIDGETS	1-2	
4		25	BROUGHTON RANGERS	6-1	LJC Rnd 1
5	Oct	2	Grimsby Rangers	2-5	
6		9	FRODINGHAM & BRUMBY U.	1-3	
7		23	NORTH LINDSEY MIDGETS	2-2	
8		30	Broughton Rangers	0-2	
9	Nov	6	Scunthorpe United	1-1	LL
10		27	Scunthorpe United	1-5	HC
11	Dec	4	Broughton Rangers	1-1	
12		11	Frodingham & Brumby Utd	2-2	
13		18	SCUNTHORPE UNITED	3-3	
14	Jan	1	Grimsby Haycroft Rovers	1-3	GC
15		8	BROUGHTON RANGERS	3-1	FC
16		15	Grimsby Rovers	1-7	SN
17	Feb	12	Frodingham & Brumby Utd	1-10	FC
18	Mar	5	BRIGG BRITANNIA	9-0	LL
19		12	Ashby Rising Stars	0-2	
20	Apr	4	Scunthorpe United	3-3	
21		16	GRIMSBY RANGERS	0-1	IC

1910: North Lindsey United merged with Scunthorpe United, to become Scunthorpe and Lindsey United

1910-11

#	Mon	Day	Opponent	Score	Comp	Scorers
1	Sep	3	HULL CITY JUNIORS	3-2	F	Cox (3)
2		10	GRIMSBY ROVERS	2-3	F	Brown, Hollin
3		17	Denaby	0-6	FAC P.	
4		24	ASHBY RISING STARS	6-2		Morley(3),Tune,Fenwick,Unknown
5	Oct	1	SCUNTHORPE MIDGETS	4-2	LIC R1	Morley(2), Leaning, Hollin
6		8	FROD & BRUMBY UTD	2-1	HN	Parrott, Cox
7		15	GRIMSBY ROVERS	2-2	IC	Unknown, Hollin
8		22	Brigg Britannia	6-2	LIC R2	Barrick (2), Unknown (4)
9		29	Grimsby Rovers	1-5	HC	Morley
10	Nov	5	Grimsby Rovers	0-2	IC	
11		12	Barton United	4-1		Unknown (4)
12		19	ASHBY RISING STARS	6-0	LL	Harrison, Carr,(3), Leaning, Oates
13		26	Scunthorpe Midgets	0-2		*
14	Dec	3	BARTON TERRIERS	9-0	LIC R3	Holland(4),Carr,Leaning,Tell,Parrott
15		10	CLEETHORPES	0-0	SN	
16		17	LINCOLN LIBERAL CLUB	3-1	LIC R4	Barrick, Fisher, Leaning
17		24	Ashby Rising Stars	1-2	LL	Unknown
18		26	SCUNTHORPE MIDGETS	5-2	F	Cox,Fisher,Fewster,Leaning,Unknown
19	Jan	7	CLEETHORPES	1-1	SN rep	Fewster
20		28	FROD & BRUMBY UTD	2-0	LL	Unknown (2)
21	Feb	11	Scunthorpe Midgets	2-2	LL	Harrison, Holland
22		18	NORTH LINDSEY MIDGET	1-1	FC	Unknown
23		25	CLEETHORPES	1-0	F	Hollin
24	Mar	3	Cleethorpes		United Defaulted	
25	Apr	1	SCUNTHORPE TERRIERS	7-2	FC	Unknown (7)
26		8	Grimsby Rovers (1)	1-2	LIC F	Barrick
27		15	NORTH LINDSEY MIDGET	2-0	LL	Unknown (2)
28		18	Cleethorpes	1-1	SN rep 2	Hollin
29		25	Frod & Brumby Utd. (2)	2-1	FC F	Holland, Hollin
30		29	GRIMSBY RANGERS	4-3	SN F	Parrott, Holland, Unknown (2)

* Abandoned after 79 minutes.
(1) Played at Blundell Park, Cleethorpes.
(2) Played at Brumby Hall, Scunthorpe.

1911-12

#	Mon	Day	Opponent	Score	Comp	Scorers
1	Sep	9	GRIMSBY ROVERS	3-1		Blanchard (2), Tune
2		16	York City	2-1	FAC P	Blanchard (2)
3		23	BENTLEY	3-3	F	Long, Sylvester (2)
4		30	Mexborough	2-3	FAC Q1	Ibbotson (2)
5	Oct	7	NETHEREDGE (SHEFFIELD)	0-1	FA	
6		14	Grimsby St. Johns	2-0	SN	Harris (2)
7		21	WINTERTON	8-0	LL	Unknown (8)
8		28	ASHBY RISING STARS	2-1	IC	Ibbotson, Tune
9	Nov	4	GRIMSBY ST. JOHNS	3-1	GC	Harris (2), Ibbotson
10		11	FRODINGHAM & BRUMBY U	2-2	LIC R3	Ibbotson (2)
11		18	Frodingham & Brumby Utd	1-0	LIC rep	Blanchard
12		25	Ashby Rising Stars	0-0	LL	
13	Dec	2	YORKSHIRE DRAGOONS	6-2	F	Ibbotson (4), Harris (2)
14		9	Grimsby St. Johns	1-0	SN	Cox
15		16	ASHBY RISING STARS	4-2	LIC R4	Parrott, Cox, Blanchard, Ibbotson
16		25	FRODINGHAM & BRUMBY U	2-2	LL	Ibbotson (2)
17		31	Broughton Rangers	4-2	LL	Blanchard (2), Harris, Hollin
18	Jan	6	Frodingham & Brumby Utd	0-0	LL	
19		13	BROUGHTON RANGERS *	1-0	LL	Blanchard
20		27	SPALDING	2-0	LIC R5	Harris, Cox
21	Feb	3	ASHBY RISING STARS	4-0	LL	Blanchard (2), Hollin, Ibbotson
22		10	BROUGHTON RANGERS	10-2	FC	Ibbotson(3),Blanchard(4),Bowers(og),Harris, Brown
23		17	FROD & BRUMBY UTD	4-0	SN S/F	Ibbotson, Blanchard, Harris, Parrott
24		24	Lincoln South End	1-5	LIC R6	Blanchard
25	Mar	2	GRIMSBY HAYCROFT ROV.	5-1	F	Hollin (2), Ibbotson (2), Parrott
26		9	GRIMSBY ROVERS	2-3	HC	Blanchard, Hill S.
27		16	Grimsby St. Johns	4-1	IC	Blanchard (2), Ibbotson, Brown
28		23	NORTH LINDSEY JUNIORS	7-0	LL	Holland,Hobson(3),Barrick,Parrott,Edinbro
29		30	Grimsby Rovers	1-1	BC	Holland
30	Apr	6	CLEETHORPES	4-0	GC	Hill S., Rusling, Ibbotson (2)
31		8	GRIMSBY ROVERS	2-0	BC rep	Hill S., Rusling
32		8	Winterton	6-2	LL	Unknown
33		13	FRODINGHAM & BRUMBY U	1-0	FC F	Rusling
34		15	NORTH LINDSEY JUNIORS	0-0	LL	
35		17	GRIMSBY HAYCROFT ROV.	4-0	BC	Hill S.(3), Blanchard
36		20	GRIMSBY HAYCROFT ROV.	4-0	IC	Hill S.(2), Blanchard, Rusling
37		27	CLEETHORPES	2-0	SN F	Rusling (2)
38		29	Cleethorpes	0-3	BC F	

* Abandoned at half-time - result stood.

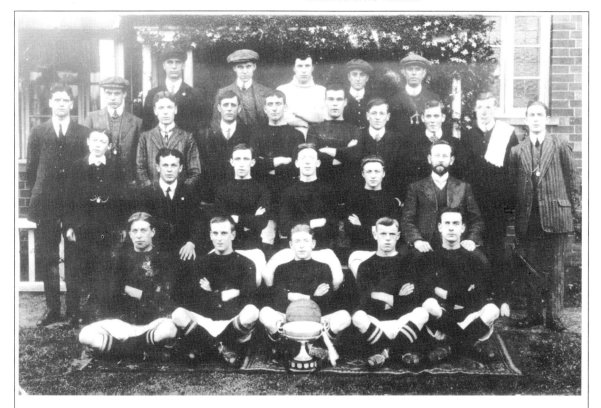

Season 1910/11 - The first group photograph of the new 'Scunthorpe and Lindsey United F.C.'
R.A.C Symes, is on the far right (seated, with beard), one of the prime movers in the Club's formation.

SEASON 1911-12
(Players only)   Back: Wogin. Second Row: Parrott, Long
Third Row: Cox, Holland, Brown.   Front: Hollin, Rusling, Hill, Blanchard, Ibbotson, Harrison

Season 1912/13
Standing: Parrott, Hall, Henderson, Wogin, Drury, Burkhill, Pearce, Brown
Seated: Hill, Walden, Bell

1912/13 — 15th in Midland League

				Score	Scorers
1	Sep	7	Leeds City Res.	0-1	
2		14	NOTTS COUNTY RES.	0-1	
3		21	Lincoln City Res.	1-7	Bell
4	Oct	3	CHESTERFIELD TOWN	0-1	
5		5	LEEDS CITY RES.	1-2	Henderson
6		10	Notts County Res.	1-9	Henderson
7		19	MEXBOROUGH TOWN	5-3	Walden 3, Bell 2
8		26	GAINSBOROUGH TRINITY	2-2	Bell, Pearce
9		28	Rotherham Town	1-2	Higgins
10	Nov	9	YORK CITY	4-3	Bell, Walden 3
11		11	DONCASTER ROVERS	1-3	Walden
12		23	THE WEDNESDAY RES.	1-3	Pearce
13	Dec	14	Mexborough Town	0-3	
14		25	HALIFAX TOWN	3-0	Spelvins, Pearce, Walden
15		26	Grimsby Town Res.	1-1	Wagstaffe
16		28	Halifax Town	1-4	Spelvins
17	Jan	18	ROTHERHAM TOWN	3-3	Jackson 2, Spelvins
18		25	York City	0-4	
19		30	HULL CITY RES.	3-2	Jackson 2, Barrick
20	Feb	1	Goole Town	0-2	
21		8	GRIMSBY TOWN RES.	2-2	Oates, Spelvins
22		20	WORKSOP TOWN	3-1	Spelvins 2, Walden
23		22	Sheffield United Res.	2-3	Bell, Walden
24		27	ROTHERHAM COUNTY	1-5	Walden
25	Mar	1	GOOLE TOWN	1-1	Walden
26		8	Doncaster Rovers	2-2	Cox, Walden
27		13	Castleford Town	0-0	
28		15	LINCOLN CITY RES.	2-1	Cox, Spelvins
29		22	Hull City Res.	1-0	Walden
30		26	Gainsborough Trinity	1-0	Cox
31		29	Denaby United	3-1	Bell 3
32	Apr	3	Worksop Town	0-0	
33		7	Rotherham County	0-3	
34		12	SHEFFIELD UTD RES.	3-1	Walden, Bell, Higgins
35		16	Chesterfield Town	4-2	Higgins, Walden, Hill, Roberts
36		19	DENABY UNITED	3-0	Walden, Bell, Higgins
37		24	CASTLEFORD TOWN	1-0	Walden
38		26	The Wednesday Res.	0-1	

F.A.Cup

P	Sep	28	Brodsworth Colliery	3-0	Pearce 2 (1 pen), Walden
Q1	Oct	12	GOOLE TOWN	2-1	Walden 2
Q2	Nov	2	YORK CITY	2-2	Bell, Walden
rep		6	York City	4-5	Rusling, Walden 2, Hill

1912/13

	P	W	D	L	F	A	Pts.
Rotherham County	38	28	5	5	111	37	61
Chesterfield Town	38	20	11	7	78	41	51
Gainsborough Trinity	38	22	6	10	84	40	50
Doncaster Rovers	38	21	7	10	67	43	49
Leeds City Res.	38	18	7	13	68	52	43
Goole Town	38	14	14	10	52	49	42
The Wednesday Res.	38	16	7	15	78	69	39
Grimsby Town Res.	38	15	9	14	65	67	39
Sheffield United Res.	38	15	8	15	68	57	38
York City	38	16	6	16	69	80	38
Rotherham Town	38	17	4	17	55	67	38
Hull City Res.	38	17	3	15	65	73	37
Lincoln City Res.	38	16	3	19	81	73	35
Halifax Town	38	14	7	17	68	67	35
SCUNTHORPE UNITED	38	13	8	17	55	78	34
Castleford Town	38	12	9	17	55	56	33
Worksop Town	38	12	5	21	47	91	29
Notts County Res.	38	10	6	22	67	85	26
Mexborough Town	38	11	3	24	42	77	25
Denaby United	38	7	4	27	39	112	15

1913/14 — 7th in Midland League

				Score	Scorers
1	Sep	1	Lincoln City Res.	0-0	
2		6	LEEDS CITY RES.	2-1	Bradbury, Root
3		13	Rotherham County	0-7	
4		20	CHESTERFIELD TOWN	4-0	Bradbury, Root, Mulholland, Smelt (OG)
5	Oct	4	Mexborough Town	1-1	Bradbury
6		18	THE WEDNESDAY RES.	1-2	Walden
7		25	The Wednesday Res.	0-1	
8	Nov	1	ROTHERHAM TOWN	3-1	Root, Walden 2
9		8	Leeds City Res.	4-1	Bradbury 2, Walden, Mulholland
10		15	WORKSOP TOWN	3-1	Morris, Walden, Mulholland
11		22	MEXBOROUGH TOWN	3-1	Root, Walden, Mulholland
12		29	CASTLEFORD TOWN	2-0	Bradbury, Clark
13	Dec	6	Castleford Town	3-2	Root 2, Mulholland
14		13	Worksop Town	0-1	
15		20	GOOLE TOWN	1-0	Bradbury
16		25	Hull City Res.	1-0	Mulholland
17		26	Chesterfield Town	0-6	
18		27	SHEFFIELD UTD RES.	2-2	Mulholland 2
19	Jan	3	York City	1-2	Mulholland
20		10	Halifax Town	3-1	Goates 3
21		17	GAINSBOROUGH TRINITY	1-1	Morris
22	Feb	14	Doncaster Rovers	1-0	Roberts
23		21	DONCASTER ROVERS	1-0	Roberts
24		28	HALIFAX TOWN	2-1	Walden, Hollin
25	Mar	7	Rotherham Town	1-2	Wood
26		14	Sheffield Utd Res.	3-2	Wood 3
27		21	YORK CITY	4-1	Wood 3, Roberts
28		28	ROTHERHAM COUNTY	0-2	
29	Apr	2	Goole Town	0-1	
30		4	GRIMSBY TOWN RES.	3-4	Wood, Clark 2
31		10	Gainsborough Trinty	0-2	
32		11	Grimsby Town Res.	1-2	Thompson
33		13	HULL CITY RES.	1-3	Thompson
34		18	LINCOLN CITY RES.	4-2	Wood 2, Thompson, Root

F.A.Cup

				Score	Scorers
P	Sep	27	Mexborough Town	2-2	Mulholland, bradbury
rep	Oct	1	MEXBOROUGH TOWN	3-0	Morris, Bradbury, Walden
Q1		11	York City	1-2	Walden

1913/14

	P	W	D	L	F	A	Pts.
Rotherham County	34	25	2	7	92	38	52
Gainsborough Trinity	34	22	6	6	76	36	50
Chesterfield Town	34	19	4	11	80	43	42
The Wednesday Res.	34	17	6	11	68	50	40
Goole Town	34	16	6	12	52	39	38
Grimsby Town Res.	34	16	6	12	68	56	30
SCUNTHORPE UNITED	34	16	4	14	55	55	36
Castleford Town	34	15	4	15	54	51	34
Rotherham Town	34	13	8	13	46	61	34
Sheffield United Res.	34	11	10	13	60	62	32
Lincoln City Res.	34	11	9	14	49	60	31
York City	34	13	5	16	48	60	31
Worksop Town	34	13	3	18	51	61	29
Halifax Town	34	11	6	17	38	51	28
Hull City Res.	34	11	5	15	37	55	27
Doncaster Rovers	34	12	2	20	30	51	26

Note: For convenience the Club is generally referred to as 'Scunthorpe United' (rather than 'Scunthorpe & Lindsey United'), however, the later name was not adopted until 1954.

SEASON 1913-14
Back: Dixon (Asst. Trainer), H.P.Roberts, Blackwell, Wogin, Clarke, Burkhill, Marsden (Trainer)
Middle: A.Roberts, Hill, Morris, Fuljames
Front: Thompson, Mulholland, Bradbury, Walden, Root

SEASON 1914-15   (Players only)
Back: Hill, Cownley, Wogin, Pinch, Taylor, Burkhill, Jaques
Front: Mahon, Robinson, Wood, Clark, Platts

1	Sep	3	GRIMSBY TOWN RES.	3-2 Wood, Clark, Platts
2		5	Leeds City Res.	0-5
3		12	ROTHERHAM COUNTY	1-1 Hill
4		19	HULL CITY RES.	3-0 Robinson, Clark, Monaghan
5	Oct	3	York City	0-0
6		8	HECKMONDWIKE	4-0 Robinson, Rusling, Ibbotson, Hill
7		17	SHEFFIELD UTD RES.	2-2 Robinson, Clark
8		19	Mexborough Town	1-1 Robinson
9		31	Castleford Town	2-6 Robinson, Armitage
10	Nov	21	Worksop Town	2-0 Robinson, Armitage
11		28	Rotherham Town	1-3 Platts
12	Dec	5	WORKSOP TOWN	1-1 Robinson
13		10	The Wednesday Res.	1-3 Platts
14		12	GAINSBOROUGH TRINITY	2-0 Robinson, Armitage
15		19	Bradford Park Ave Res.	1-5 Robinson
16		25	GOOLE TOWN	0-0
17		26	Goole Town	0-4
18	Jan	2	LINCOLN CITY RES.	2-5 Wood 2
19		9	Gainsborough Trinity	0-5
20		14	Halifax Town	1-2 Wood
21		16	CHESTERFIELD TOWN	3-1 Wood, Monaghan, Platts
22		23	Hull City Res.	4-1 Wood, Robinson, Hill, Leaning
23	Feb	6	Sheffield United Res.	0-3
24		20	Rotherham County	1-4 Wood
25		27	BRADFORD PARK AVE RE	2-3 Robinson 2
26	Mar	6	Chesterfield Town	2-2 Robinson, Wood
27		13	YORK CITY	2-0 Wood 2
28		15	Heckmondwike	6-0 Wood 2, Ibbotson2, Rusling 2
29		20	THE WEDNESDAY RES.	2-3 Wood, Platts
30		27	LEEDS CITY RES.	2-2 Wood, Rusling
31	Apr	2	Grimsby Town Res.	0-1
32		3	DONCASTER ROVERS	3-2 Robinson, Ibbotson 2
33		5	Doncaster Rovers	0-2
34		10	HALIFAX TOWN	2-1 Ibbotson, Hill
35		17	Lincoln City Res.	0-4
36		24	ROTHERHAM TOWN	5-5 Root, Taylor, Ibbotson 2, Chantry
37		29	MEXBOROUGH TOWN	5-0 Root, Ibbotson 2, Chantry, Leaning
38	May	1	CASTLEFORD TOWN	4-0 Ibbotson, Root, Platts, Wood

F.A.Cup

P	Sep	26	HULL OLD BOYS *	5-1 Robinson, Armitage, Clark 3
Q1	Oct	10	GRIMSBY ROVERS	4-0 Robinson, Clark 2, Ibbotson
Q2		24	DONCASTER ROVERS	1-0 Robinson
Q3	Nov	14	GOOLE TOWN	1-1 Robinson
rep		19	Goole Town	1-5 Platts

* Tie drawn 'away', but played at Scunthorpe for guaranteed gate receipt.

1914/15

	P	W	D	L	F	A	Pts.
Rotherham County	38	23	13	7	104	42	54
Leeds City Res.	38	24	5	9	99	42	53
Chesterfield Town	38	20	10	8	76	41	50
Goole Town	38	20	7	11	103	58	47
The Wednesday Res.	38	20	7	11	92	56	47
Gainsborough Trinity	38	19	8	11	78	46	46
Grimsby Town Res.	38	21	3	14	73	54	45
Worksop Town	38	17	11	10	70	55	45
Rotherham Town	38	20	4	14	112	65	44
Halifax Town	38	16	9	13	49	57	41
Bradford P.A. Res.	38	16	6	16	83	66	38
Sheffield United Res.	38	15	6	17	57	46	36
SCUNTHORPE UNITED	38	13	9	16	70	79	35
Lincoln City Res.	38	12	9	17	76	74	33
Doncaster Rovers	38	14	3	21	58	82	31
York City	38	12	7	19	45	72	31
Mexborough Town	38	10	13	20	37	89	28
Castleford Town	38	9	9	20	50	103	27
Hull City Res.	39	13	2	28	39	105	18
Heckmondwike	38	5	1	32	30	169	11

1	Aug	30	ROTHERHAM COUNTY RE	4-1 Spavin 2, Butler, Hobson
2	Sep	6	Rotherham County Res	1-3 Charlesworth
3		13	Halifax Town	1-2 Spavin
4		20	SHEFFIELD UTD RES	0-0
5	Oct	4	CASTLEFORD TOWN	1-0 Mahon
6		18	Grimsby Town Res	2-1 Spavin, Lemon
7	Nov	1	Sheffield Utd Res.	1-1 Butler
8		8	HALIFAX TOWN	4-1 Spavin, Butler, Lemon, Booth
9		15	Castleford Town	1-3 Mahon
10		22	WORKSOP TOWN	1-0 Butler
11		29	Barnsley Res.	3-3 Booth 2, Cox
12	Dec	6	HULL CITY RES.	4-1 Butler, Lemon 2, Cox
13		13	Gainsborough Trinty	4-1 Booth, Robson, Butler, Spavin
14		20	Notts County Res.	1-1 Wield
15		25	LINCOLN CITY RES	6-0 Spavin 4, Lemon 2
16		26	Lincoln City Res.	2-0 Lemon, Cox
17	Jan	3	GRIMSBY TOWN RES	4-1 Spavin, Amos, Robinson, Booth
18		10	Worksop Town	1-3 Spavin
19		31	GAINSBOROUGH TRINITY	5-0 Spavin, Butler, Lemon, Booth, Atkinson
20	Feb	7	SILVERWOOD COLLIERY	5-1 Spavin 2, Amos 2, Lemon
21		14	BARNSLEY RES.	4-0 Spavin 2, Atkinson 2
22		21	Hull City Res.	1-2 Butler
23		28	Silverwood Colliery	3-0 Lemon 2, Atkinson
24	Mar	6	Mexborough	0-1
25		13	MEXBOROUGH	0-0
26		20	Rotherham Town	1-3 Mahon
27		27	THE WEDNESDAY RES.	1-0 Mahon
28	Apr	3	CHESTERFIELD MUNICIPA	1-2 Broadhead
29		5	Chesterfield Municipal	1-3 Mahon
30		8	LEEDS UNITED	3-2 Lemon 2, Butler
31		10	ROTHERHAM TOWN	3-2 Lemon 2, Atkinson
32		17	The Wednesday Res.	1-1 Lemon
33		24	NOTTS COUNTY RES	1-0 Lemon
34		28	Leeds United	0-0

F.A.Cup

P	Sep	27	GOOLE TOWN	7-0 Butler,Spavin3, Mahon2, Millington
Q1	Oct	11	BRODSWORTH M.	2-1 Butler, Brown
Q2		25	CLEETHORPES	0-1 Brown

1919/20

	P	W	D	L	F	A	Pts.
Chesterfield Municipal	34	24	5	5	78	35	53
Sheffield United Res.	34	20	11	3	73	28	51
SCUNTHORPE UNITED	34	15	7	9	71	39	43
Worksop Town	34	20	3	11	71	52	43
Mexborough	34	18	6	10	60	45	42
The Wednesday Res.	34	16	6	12	50	44	38
Rotherham Town	34	14	a	12	83	71	36
Castleford Town	34	14	8	12	53	46	36
Hull City Res.	34	16	2	16	74	59	34
Grimsby Town Res.	34	14	5	15	66	64	33
Rotherham County Res.	34	13	5	16	60	57	31
Leeds United	34	11	9	14	56	56	31
Notts County Res.	34	10	11	13	50	56	31
Halifax Town	34	13	4	17	52	70	30
Lincoln City Res.	34	8	7	19	43	83	23
Barnsley Res.	34	6	9	19	46	72	21
Silverwood Colliery	34	6	7	21	38	89	19
Gainsborough Trinity	34	7	3	24	37	95	17

1915 to 1919 - Midland league Fixtures Suspended (War)

SEASON 1919-20
Back: Moran (Trainer), Hill, Robson, Pattison, Hannah, Bullivant, Wield, Dixon (Asst. Trainer)
Front: Butler, Spavin, Brown, Lemon, Booth, Allcock (Secretary)

SEASON 1920-21
Back: Betts, Hargreaves, Davey, Hill, Crooks, Blackwell, Monteith, J.H.Harvey, unknown,
Dixon (Asst.Trainer), Moran (Trainer).   Front: Butler, Leggitt, J.Harvey, Cox, Sylvester

			Score	Scorers
1	Aug	28	NOTTS COUNTY RES	1-3	Lemon
2	Sep	4	Sheffield United Res.	1-0	J.Duffus
3		11	GAINSBOROUGH TRINITY	1-1	Lemon
4		18	ROTHERHAM TOWN	2-0	J.Duffus 2
5	Oct	2	DONCASTER ROVERS	1-0	J.Duffus
6		16	SHEFFIELD UNITED RES	1-1	J.Duffus
7		30	LEEDS UNITED RES	2-0	Tunstall, Simpson
8	Nov	13	NOTTM FOREST RES	4-0	Lemon, Tunstall, Simpson 2
9		27	The Wednesday Res.	2-3	Lemon, Harvey
10	Dec	4	Rotherham Town	1-3	Harvey
11		11	CHESTERFIELD	1-2	Broadhead
12		18	Chesterfield	3-3	Mayo 2, Lloyd
13		25	Hull City Res.	3-1	Roebuck, Harvey, Simpson
14		27	HULL CITY RES.	4-1	Ackroyd, Jenkins, Simpson 2
15		30	Nottm Forest Res.	5-3	Roebuck 2, Jenkins, Robson, Simpson
16	Jan	1	Gainsborough Trinity	4-1	Roebuck 3, Simpson
17		8	Rotherham County Res.	1-0	Lemon
18		15	WORKSOP TOWN	0-0	
19		29	Denaby United	2-0	Roebuck, Lemon
20	Feb	5	DENABY UNITED	4-1	Roebuck, Lemon, Crofts 2
21		12	CASTLEFORD TOWN	1-3	Butler
22		19	Halifax Town	0-1	
23		26	Castleford Town	0-0	
24	Mar	5	MEXBOROUGH	3-0	Lemon 2, Ackroyd
25		10	Worksop Town	0-0	
26		12	Leeds United Res.	1-0	Ackroyd
27		19	Lincoln City	0-2	
28		26	GRIMSBY TOWN RES	3-1	Lemon, Jones, Broadhead
29		28	Grimsby Town Res.	0-1	
30	Apr	2	LINCOLN CITY	1-0	Jenkins
31		9	Doncaster Rovers	1-1	Roebuck
32		14	THE WEDNESDAY RES.	0-2	
33		16	ROTHERHAM COUNTY RES	1-1	Lemon
34		21	Barnsley Res.	1-0	Meredith
35		23	Mexborough	0-0	
36		27	Notts County Res.	3-5	Lemon, Harvey 2
37		30	BARNSLEY RES.	1-3	Broadhead
38	May	7	HALIFAX TOWN	5-0	Lemon 2, Broadhead 2, Meredith

F.A.Cup

				Score	Scorers
P	Sep	25	HULL BRUNSWICK INST.	6-0	J.Duffus2, Lemon, Tunstall, Ackroyd, Bell
Q1	Oct	9	BENTLEY COLLOIERY	3-0	J.Duffus, Simpson, Ackroyd
Q2		23	Grimsby Charltons	4-1	Simpson, Lemon 2, Harvey
Q3	Nov	6	BRODSWORTH MAIN	1-1	J.Duffus
rep		?	Brodsworth Main	0-0	
re2		15	Brodsworth Main *	3-1	Harvey, Simpson, Moore
Q4		20	Mansfield Town	0-1	

* Played at Bramall Lane, Sheffield

1920/21	P	W	D	L	F	A	Pts.
Lincoln City	38	27	3	8	95	40	57
Notts County Res.	38	22	9	7	80	45	53
Chesterfield	38	15	11	9	70	46	47
SCUNTHORPE UNITED	38	15	9	11	64	43	45
Rotherham Town	38	18	8	12	68	48	44
Sheffield United Res.	38	16	10	12	73	63	42
Rotherham C. Res.	38	16	9	13	57	37	41
Castleford Town	38	17	6	15	61	56	40
The Wednesday Res.	38	16	7	15	66	50	39
Worksop Town	38	16	7	15	62	55	39
Halifax Town	38	17	5	16	54	62	39
Leeds United Res.	38	15	8	15	49	51	38
Gainsborough Trinity	38	14	8	16	58	60	36
Nottingham F. Res.	38	13	10	15	69	77	36
Hull City Res.	38	12	9	17	52	68	33
Doncaster Rovers	38	11	10	17	38	54	32
Mexborough	38	10	11	17	39	61	31
Grimsby Town Res.	38	11	6	21	45	72	28
Barnsley Res.	38	9	13	21	55	86	26
Denaby United	38	4	6	28	37	118	14

				Score	Scorers
1	Aug	27	ROTHERHAM COUNTY RES	2-2	Maycock 2
2	Sep	3	WATH ATHLETIC	2-1	Gibson 2
3		8	Nottm Forest Res.	1-0	Maycock
4		10	HULL CITY RES.	2-0	Richards, Maycock
5		17	Gainsborough Trinity	0-3	
6		20	Wombwell	1-1	Gibson
7	Oct	1	Barnsley Res.	2-3	Witham, Gibson
8		15	Mexborough	0-2	
9		27	MANSFIELD TOWN	3-1	Gibson, Reed, Maycock
10		29	WORKSOP TOWN	2-2	Ackroyd, Witham
11	Nov	12	Rotherham Town	1-5	Gibson
12		19	Denaby United	3-4	Duke, Broadhead, Maycock
13		26	NOTTS COUNTY RES	1-2	Clark
14	Dec	3	Boston	0-2	
15		10	Hull City Res.	1-3	Lloyd
16		17	THE WEDNESDAY RES.	3-1	Lloyd, Meredith, Whitham
17		24	BARNSLEY RES.	4-1	Whittingham, Whitham, Maycock 2
18		26	LINCOLN CITY RES	4-1	Whittingham, Whitham, Maycock, Meredith
19		28	Lincoln City Res.	1-0	Lloyd
20		31	DONCASTER ROVERS	2-1	Whitham, Maycock
21	Jan	7	Doncaster Rovers	1-0	Whittingham
22		14	GRIMSBY TOWN RES	6-0	Meredith, Chambers, Whitham, Lloyd, Mycock2
23		26	Notts County Res.	3-1	Whitham, Lloyd, Maycock
24		28	NOTTM FOREST RES	5-3	Lloyd, Ackroyd, Whitham 2, Maycock
25	Feb	4	Worksop Town	3-4	Ackroyd, Whittingham, Maycock
26		11	BOSTON	4-1	Meredith, Ackroyd, Whittingham, Whitham
27		15	Wakefield City	1-1	Maycock
28		18	DENABY UNITED	3-0	Meredith, Whittingham, Maycock
29		25	Wath Athletic	4-1	Whitham 2, Maycock 2
30		27	Rotherham County Res.	3-0	Lloyd, Whitham, Maycock
31	Mar	4	Grimsby Town Res.	1-1	Lloyd
32		8	WAKEFIELD CITY	3-0	Crooks, Whitham 2
33		18	WOMBWELL	4-0	Meredith 2, Ackroyd, Lloyd
34		22	Mansfield Town	1-3	Ackroyd
35		25	MEXBOROUGH	1-1	Maycock
36	Apr	1	The Wednesday Res.	0-5	
37		8	GAINSBOROUGH TRINITY	2-1	Whitham 2
38		15	CASTLEFORD TOWN	3-0	Yarrow, Maycock 2
39		17	Castleford Town	0-0	
40		22	ROTHERHAM TOWN	3-1	Whitham 2, Yarrow
41		29	Harrogate	0-1	
42	May	6	HARROGATE	1-1	Broadhead

F.A.Cup

				Score	Scorers
P	Sep	24	Retford Town	2-1	Calthorpe 2
Q1	Oct	8	HULL HOLDERNESS	10-0	Calthorpe 4, Witham 3, Richards 2, Meredith
Q2		22	BRODSWORTH MAIN	4-1	Witham 2, Lloyd, Meredith
Q3	Nov	5	Gainsborough Trinity	0-2	

1921/22	P	W	D	L	F	A	Pts.
Worksop Town	42	26	9	7	70	41	61
Grimsby Town	42	24	9	9	87	56	57
The Wednesday Res	42	23	10	9	99	49	56
SCUNTHORPE UNITED	42	22	9	12	87	60	52
Barnsley Res.	42	20	9	13	81	50	49
Mexborough	42	19	9	14	67	40	47
Castleford Town	42	18	11	13	69	54	47
Mansfield Town	42	20	7	15	68	57	47
Nottingham F. Res.	42	19	6	17	69	60	44
Rotherham C. Res.	42	17	8	17	80	79	42
Rotherham Town	42	15	11	16	65	66	41
Wombwell	42	16	9	17	60	66	41
Doncaster Rovers	42	17	6	19	52	66	40
Denaby United	42	14	11	17	67	67	39
Gainsborough Trinity	42	15	9	18	63	65	39
Notts County Res.	42	15	7	20	64	57	37
Boston	42	15	7	20	66	73	37
Wath Athletic	42	13	8	21	50	71	34
Harrogate	42	14	6	22	49	88	34
Hull City Res.	42	10	8	24	55	83	28
Wakefield City	42	9	9	24	39	103	27
Lincoln City Res.	42	6	13	23	53	97	25

SEASON 1921-22
Back: White (Trainer), Smith, Lloyd, Wogin, Ackroyd, Duke, Broadhead, Richards
Front: Meredith, Whittingham, Witham, Maycock, Chambers

SEASON 1922-23
Back: Allcock (Secretary), Sanderson, Smith, Lloyd, Hargreaves, Wogin, Betts, White (Trainer)
Front: Meredith, Whitham, Retford, Talbot, Maycock

1922/23 — 6th in Midland League

1	Aug	26	NOTTS COUNTY RES	2-0	Whitham, Hargreaves
2	Sep	2	HULL CITY RES.	1-2	Whitham
3		9	Rotherham County Res	2-1	Whitham, Talbot
4		16	ROTHERHAM COUNTY RES	2-1	Rushby, Maycock
5		23	Castleford Town	0-0	
6		25	The Wednesday Res.	0-2	
7	Oct	9	Denaby United	0-6	
8		14	Gainsborough Trinity	2-2	Gittos 2
9	Nov	11	WOMBWELL	3-0	Rushby 2, Gittos
10		25	BARNSLEY RES.	1-1	Gittos
11	Dec	9	NOTTM FOREST RES	3-0	Lloyd, Talbot, Hill
12		16	Boston	0-3	
13		23	WORKSOP TOWN	3-2	Gittos 3
14		25	DONCASTER ROVERS	2-2	Gittos, Whitham
15		26	Lincoln City Res.	2-1	Meredith, Gittos
16		30	Mexborough	0-0	
17	Jan	1	Rotherham Town	2-1	Gittos, Whitham
18		7	MANSFIELD TOWN	2-1	Gittos, Rushby
19		13	Wombwell	2-2	Gittos, Whitham
20		17	York City	2-2	Gittos, Meredith
21		20	LINCOLN CITY RES.	2-0	Moore, Smith
22		27	Wath Athletic	0-4	
23	Feb	3	GRIMSBY TOWN RES	4-2	Gittos 3, Meredith
24		8	Nottm Forest Res.	2-2	Whitham, Maycock
25		10	Chesterfield Res.	0-0	
26		15	Hull City Res.	4-3	Gittos, Crooks, Meredith, Rushby
27		17	MEXBOROUGH	4-0	Rushby 2, Whitham, Maycock
28		24	Mansfield Town	1-1	Maycock
29	Mar	1	Notts County Res.	1-1	Maycock
30		3	GAINSBOROUGH TRINITY	3-0	Meredith, Gittos 2
31		10	Grimsby Town Res.	0-3	
32		12	Barnsley Res.	0-3	
33		17	WATH ATHLETIC	2-1	Meredith, Maycock
34		31	ROTHERHAM TOWN	5-0	Talbot 3, Gittos 2
35	Apr	2	Doncaster Rovers	0-0	
36		7	BOSTON	0-0	
37		14	THE WEDNESDAY RES.	0-1	
38		19	YORK CITY	3-0	Whitham, Gittos, Thorpe (og)
39		21	Worksop Town	0-3	
40		26	DENABY UNITED	0-3	
41		28	CASTLEFORD TOWN	0-2	
42	May	5	CHESTERFIELD RES.	3-0	Meredith, Whitham, Talbot

F.A.Cup

Q1	Oct	7	GRIMSBY CHARLTONS	3-0	Gottos, Rushby 2
Q2		21	Gainsborough Trinity	2-1	Rushby, Moore
Q3	Nov	4	Boston United	1-0	Maycock
Q4		18	Worksop Town	2-4	Meredith, Gittos

1922/23

	P	W	D	L	F	A	Pts.
The Wednesday Res.	42	28	7	7	88	37	63
Doncaster Rovers	42	26	9	7	72	28	61
Worksop Town	42	26	5	11	86	45	57
Denaby United	42	24	9	9	76	49	57
Grimsby Town Res.	42	21	9	12	77	58	51
SCUNTHORPE UNITED	42	18	13	11	65	58	49
Wath Athletic	42	18	10	14	59	38	46
Notts County Res.	42	16	12	14	76	55	44
Boston	42	18	8	16	61	46	44
Nottingham F. Res.	42	to	11	15	74	60	43
Rotherham C. Res.	42	18	6	18	56	52	42
Hull City Res.	42	14	13	15	63	63	41
Mansfield Town	42	17	6	19	79	64	40
Barnsley Res.	42	14	12	16	67	65	40
Wombwell	42	12	14	16	50	63	38
Castleford Town	42	15	6	21	61	70	36
Chesterfield Res.	42	14	8	20	56	79	36
Mexborough	42	11	13	18	44	63	35
York City	42	11	12	19	56	70	34
Gainsborough Trinity	42	8	8	26	42	111	24
Rotherham Town	42	8	6	28	45	105	22
Lincoln City Res.	42	7	7	28	39	114	21

1923/24 — 6th in Midland League

1	Aug	25	York City	0-0	
2	Sep	1	DENABY UNITED	1-2	Burkinshaw
3		8	Gainsborough Trinity	2-2	White, Foster
4		13	Notts County Res.	1-4	Kitchen
5		15	SUTTON TOWN	2-1	Burkinshaw, Kitchen
6		29	YORK CITY	4-1	Kitchen 2, Raby 2
7	Oct	13	NOTTS COUNTY RES	0-0	
8		27	BARNSLEY RES.	0-0	
9	Nov	10	GRIMSBY TOWN RES.	3-0	White, Kitchen 2
10		24	HULL CITY RES.	1-2	Wilson
11	Dec	8	NOTTM FOREST RES	2-0	Kitchen 2
12		15	CASTLEFORD TOWN	3-1	Kitchen 2, Ashmore
13		22	Wombwell	0-0	
14		25	LINCOLN CITY RES.	1-0	Raby
15		26	Lincoln City Res.	3-1	Burkinshaw, Kitchen, Raby
16		29	Mexborough	0-3	
17	Jan	1	Barnsley Res.	1-0	Raby
18		5	MEXBOROUGH	0-2	
19		12	Rotherham Town	3-0	Raby 3
20		19	ROTHERHAM TOWN	2-0	Raby 2
21		26	Hull City Res.	2-0	Raby 2
22	Feb	2	CHESTERFIELD RES.	2-0	Green, Kitchen
23		9	Chesterfield Res.	1-0	Ashmore
24		16	Worksop Town	0-3	
25		18	Nottm Forest Res.	1-0	Raby
26		23	WATH ATHLETIC	1-0	Kitchen
27		25	Denaby United	1-5	Raby
28	Mar	1	GAINSBOROUGH TRINITY	3-0	Raby 3
29		8	Rotherham County Res.	1-1	Burkinshaw
30		13	ROTHERHAM COUNTY RES	1-0	Bradbury
31		15	WOMBWELL	1-0	Raby
32		22	Boston	0-1	
33		27	Doncaster Rovers Res.	0-4	
34		29	BOSTON	2-0	Raby, Foster
35	Apr	5	Sutton Town	1-3	Raby
36		9	Castleford Town	1-1	Ashmore
37		12	Wath Athletic	0-3	
38		19	MANSFILED TOWN	0-2	
39		21	Grimsby Town Res.	0-1	
40		22	Mansfiled Town	0-6	
41		26	WORKSOP TOWN	4-0	Burkinshaw, Kitchen, Raby 2
42	May	3	DONCASTER ROVERS RES	4-0	Broksom, Kitchen, Raby 2

F.A.Cup

P	Sep	22	GRIMSBY ROVERS	5-1	Burkinshaw 2, Meredith, Raby, Kitchen
Q1	Oct	6	CLEETHORPES	5-0	Kitchen 3, Raby, Thorpe
Q2		20	GAINSBOROUGH TRINITY	2-0	Kitchen, Skull
Q3	Nov	3	BOSTON UNITED	2-0	White 2
Q4		17	ROTHERHAM TOWN	0-0	
rep		22	Rotherham Town	1-0	Kitchen
R1	Dec	1	ROTHERHAM COUNTY	1-1	Kitchen
rep		6	Rotherham County	0-2	

1923/24

	P	W	D	L	F	A	Pts.
Mansfield Town	42	31	6	5	98	31	68
Grimsby Town Res.	42	25	6	11	99	46	56
Worksop Town	42	25	4	13	93	54	54
Mexborough	42	22	7	13	78	64	51
Notts County Res.	42	21	8	13	83	51	50
SCUNTHORPE UNITED	42	21	7	14	55	49	49
Sutton Town	42	21	6	15	86	68	48
Denaby United	42	21	6	15	78	62	48
Hull City Res.	42	19	8	15	70	48	46
Nottingham F. Res.	42	18	9	15	52	52	45
Chesterfield Res.	42	19	5	18	64	64	43
Boston	42	15	11	16	64	62	42
Gainsborough Trinity	42	16	11	15	55	62	40
Barnsley Res.	42	15	9	to	58	57	39
Doncaster R. Res.	42	14	9	19	58	63	37
Rotherham C. Res.	42	15	7	20	60	75	37
Wath Athletic	42	14	8	20	57	85	36
Wombwell	42	12	10	20	47	74	34
York City	42	10	13	19	48	71	33
Lincoln City Res.	42	13	3	26	46	81	29
Castleford Town	42	8	5	29	39	116	21
Rotherhom Town	12	7	4	31	42	95	18

SEASON 1923-24
Back: Kitchen, Bradbury, Forbes, Reynolds, Crooks, Hargreaves, White (Trainer)
Front: Meredith, Hill, Bukinshaw, Raby, Foster

SEASON 1925-26
Standing: Skull, Glennie, Wogin, Shearsmith, Hooper, White (Trainer)
Seated: Dawson, Whitham, Evans, Briggs, Cawley, Clarkson

1924/25   7th in Midland League

1	Aug	30	Wombwell	0-1	
2	Sep	4	CASTLEFORD TOWN	0-3	
3		6	DENABY UNITED	1-0	Needham
4		10	York City	0-1	
5		13	GAINSBOROUGH TRINITY	2-1	Cammack, Shaw
6		27	Lincoln City Res.	0-1	
7	Oct	11	Gainsborough Trinity	2-2	Lees, Fenwick
8		25	Sutton Town	5-0	Shaw 3, Fenwick, Lees
9	Nov	8	WATH ATHLETIC	1-0	Shaw
10		15	Worksop Town	0-3	
11		22	WORKSOP TOWN	1-1	Burnham
12		29	Mansfield Town	0-3	
13	Dec	6	MANSFIELD TOWN	2-3	Shaw 2
14		13	Frickley Colliery	4-1	Shaw 3, Green
15		20	BOSTON	2-4	Shaw 2
16		25	WOMBWELL	3-0	Shaw, Skull, Dawson
17		26	MEXBOROUGH	3-1	Shaw, Geaves, Dawson
18		27	ROTHERHAM TOWN	3-2	Shaw 2, Burnham
19	Jan	3	SUTTON TOWN	0-0	
20		10	Mexborough	3-1	Shaw 2, Green
21		17	FRICKLEY COLLIERY	2-0	Shaw 2,
22		24	Rotherham Town	1-3	Shaw
23		31	Boston	1-3	Shaw
24	Feb	7	YORK CITY	1-1	Shaw
25		14	LINCOLN CITY RES	2-0	Shaw 2
26		16	Denaby United	1-2	Rhodes (og)
27		21	Castleford Town	0-0	
28		28	Wath Athletic	5-4	Shaw 4, Todd

Subsidiary Competition

	Mar	12	SUTTON TOWN	1-1	Woulds
		14	Lincoln City Res.	0-2	
		21	BOSTON	1-2	J.Hill
		28	Boston	0-2	
	Apr	4	GAINSBOROUGH TRINITY	0-2	
		6	SUTTON TOWN	3-0	Shaw, Green, Burnham
		11	WORKSOP TOWN	1-0	Shaw
		13	Worksop Town	1-2	McDonald
		20	LINCOLN CITY RES	1-3	J.Hill
		23	MANSFIELD TOWN	0-1	
		25	Gainsborough Trinity	0-2	
	May	2	Mansfield Town	3-4	Shaw, Skull, Burnham

F.A.Cup

P	Sep	20	BARTON TOWN	2-1	Fenwick 2
Q1	Oct	4	BOSTON UNITED	0-0	
rep		9	Boston United	0-3	

1924/25

	P	W	D	L	F	A	Pts.
Mansfield Town	28	20	4	4	82	27	44
Boston	28	17	5	6	56	36	39
Gainsborough Trinity	28	14	7	7	47	38	35
Worksop Town	28	14	4	10	51	42	32
Lincoln City Res.	28	14	4	10	40	40	32
York City	28	10	10	8	39	36	30
SCUNTHORPE UNITED	28	12	5	11	45	41	29
Mexborough	28	9	9	10	49	49	27
Denaby United	28	9	8	11	41	38	26
Wath Athletic	28	10	4	14	43	49	24
Castleford Town	28	9	6	13	47	61	24
Rotherham Town	28	10	2	16	43	46	22
Frickley Colliery	28	5	10	13	35	61	20
Sutton Town	28	7	4	17	40	66	18
Wombwell	28	5	8	15	31	59	18

1924/25 Subsidiary Competition

	P.	W.	D.	L.	F.	A.	Pts
Lincoln City Res.	12	8	2	2	25	10	18
Mansfield Town	12	9	0	3	23	15	18
Boston	12	7	1	4	18	9	15
Gainsborough Trinity	12	4	2	6	12	14	10
Worksop Town	12	4	1	7	15	17	9
Sutton Town	12	3	2	7	12	28	8
SCUNTHORPE UNITED	12	2	1	9	11	21	5

1925/26   7th in Midland League

1	Aug	29	ALFRETON TOWN	2-1	Dawson, Briggs
2	Sep	2	Alfreton Town	1-4	Briggs
3		5	Gainsborough Trinity	0-0	
4		12	GAINSBOROUGH TRINITY	0-0	
5		14	Frickley Colliery	3-1	Witham, Volwes
6		24	FRICKLEY COLLIERY	5-0	Lawrie, Volwes 3, Clarkson
7		26	MANSFIELD TOWN	3-0	Whitham, Volwes, Cawley
8	Oct	10	Mansfield Town	1-3	Volwes
9		24	LINCOLN CITY RES.	1-1	J.Hill
10		31	Mexborough	1-4	Whitham
11	Nov	7	Denaby United	0-0	
12		21	WATH ATHLETIC	4-1	Whitham, Cawley 2, Wilson
13		28	Newark Town	0-4	
14	DEc	5	DENABY UNITED	3-1	Volwes, Cawley 2
15		12	York City	1-1	Volwes
16		19	YORK CITY	2-1	Whitham, Cawley
17		25	Long Eaton	1-5	Volwes
18		26	LONG EATON	5-3	Whitham 2, Volwes 2, Cawley
19		28	Wath Athletic	2-6	Volwes 2
20	Jan	9	LOUGHBOROUGH COR.	3-0	Lawrie, Whitham, Cawley
21		16	Lincoln City Res.	2-9	Whitham, Volwes
22		23	WOMBWELL	3-1	Whitham, Cawley 2
23		30	Loughborough Corinthians	1-6	Kemp
24	Feb	6	Castleford Town	5-1	Volwes 4, Cawley
25		13	MEXBOROUGH	1-2	Lawrie
26		20	SHIREBROOK	4-1	Whitham, Volwes 3
27		27	SUTTON TOWN	5-0	Lawrie, Whitham 2, Clarkson 2
28	Mar	6	GRANTHAM	1-1	Volwes
29		13	BOSTON	1-1	Volwes
30		20	Boston	1-5	Lawrie
31		22	Ilkeston United	1-1	Volwes
32		27	Grantham	2-1	Volwes 2
33	Apr	3	WORKSOP TOWN	2-1	Volwes 2
34		5	Worksop Town	2-1	Cawley, Marsh (og)
35		10	Shirebrook	2-5	Volwes, Whitham
36		15	ILKESTON UNITED	4-1	Volwes, Whitham, Green 2
37		17	Sutton Town	1-1	Green
38		22	CASTLEFORD TOWN	5-2	R.Webb, Volwes, Cawley 2, G.Webb
39		24	Wombwell	0-2	
40	May	1	NEWARK TOWN	5-0	Volwes 3, Whitham 2

F.A.Cup

P	Sep	19	Cleethorpes	4-0	Vowles 3, Cawley
Q1	Oct	3	GRIMSBY HAYCROFT ROVER	5-1	Vowles, Cawley 4
Q2		17	GAINSBOROUGH TRINITY	2-2	Vowles, Cawley
rep		22	Gainsborough Trinity	0-1	

1925/26

	P	W	D	L	F	A	Pts.
Mexborough	40	25	7	8	111	53	57
Mansfield Town	40	23	7	10	120	54	53
Boston	40	21	10	9	98	43	52
Lincoln City Res.	40	20	10	10	102	57	50
Denaby United	40	20	7	13	95	63	47
Wath Athletic	40	19	9	12	98	72	47
SCUNTHORPE UNITED	40	19	9	12	86	78	47
Newark Town	40	16	9	15	94	88	41
Alfreton Town	40	17	7	16	99	102	41
Loughborough Corins.	40	17	5	18	86	82	39
Worksop Town	40	14	10	16	82	82	38
Wombwell	40	14	9	17	73	89	37
Long Eaton	40	14	8	18	82	94	36
Grantham	40	15	6	19	71	94	36
Sutton Town	40	15	6	19	68	102	36
York City	40	14	7	19	74	94	35
Gainsborough Trinity	40	13	8	19	58	85	34
Shirebrook	40	14	4	22	81	106	32
Ilkeston United	40	12	7	21	57	91	31
Frickley Colliery	40	11	7	22	61	99	29
Castleford Town	40	10	2	28	62	130	22

1926/27 — 1st in Midland League

#	Date		Opponent	Score	Scorers
1	Aug	28	FRICKLEY COLLIERY	3-1	Allen, Hunter, Smith
2	Sep	4	Heanor Town	2-0	Thompson 2
3		11	Mexborough Athletic	0-4	
4		13	LINCOLN CITY RES.	4-1	Johnson, Simms 3
5		20	Wombwell	2-0	Johnson, Hunter
6		25	GAINSBOROUGH TRINITY	0-0	
7	Oct	9	NEWARK TOWN	1-0	Simms
8		23	Newark Town	1-1	Allen
9	Nov	6	WATH ATHLETIC	3-0	Simms 2, Allen
10		20	ILKESTON UNITED	5-3	Johnson 2, Simms, Allen 2
11		27	Alfreton Town	6-1	Johnson 2, Simms 2, Allen, Alford
12	Dec	4	LONG EATON	6-1	Johnson 2, Simms 2, Allen, Smith
13		11	Sutton Town	3-2	Johnson, Simms, Allen
14		18	MEXBOROUGH ATHLETIC	5-2	Johnson, Simms 3, Allen
15		25	YORK CITY	2-2	Allen 2
16		27	York City	2-1	Simms 2
17	Jan	1	Grantham	3-0	Johnson, Simms 2
18		8	WOMBWELL	5-1	Johnson, Simms 3, Allen
19		15	Gainsborough Trinity	1-0	Simms
20		22	SHIREBROOK	8-1	Johnson 2, Simms 3, Allen 3
21	Feb	5	GRANTHAM	7-1	Simms 4, Allen 3
22		12	Loughborough Corinthians	3-2	Johnson, Simms, Allen
23		19	LOUGHBOROUGH COR.	3-0	Johnson, Simms 2
24		24	Frickley Colliery	3-4	Johnson, Allen, Hunter
25		26	Lincoln City Res.	2-0	Johnson, Simms
26	Mar	5	BOSTON	2-1	Johnson, Allen
27		12	Denaby United	2-3	Simms, Alford
28		19	ALFRETON TOWN	6-1	Skull, Johnson, Simms 2, Smith, Allen
29		26	Long Eaton	0-1	
30	Apr	2	SUTTON TOWN	10-0	Simms 6, Johnson, Allen, Alford, Smith
31		9	Boston	2-1	Simms 2
32		16	WORKSOP TOWN	6-1	Johnson, Simms 2, Allen 2, Smith
33		18	Worksop Town	2-2	Johnson, Alford
34		19	Shirebrook	1-2	Allen
35		23	Wath Athletic	1-2	Moore
36		27	Ilkeston United	3-1	Simms 3
37		30	DENABY UNITED	1-0	Allen
38	May	6	HEANOR TOWN	5-1	Simms 2, Allen 3

F.A.Cup

	Date		Opponent	Score	Scorers
P	Sep	18	HULL HOLDERNESS	10-0	Skull, Johnson2, simms3, Allen2, Alford
Q1	Oct	2	GRIMSBY HAYCROFT ROVER	7-2	Johnson2, Simms2, Allen2, Smith
Q2		16	Selby Olympic	0-0	
rep		21	SELBY OLYMPIC	1-0	Allen
Q3		30	Gainsborough Trinity	3-3	Johnson 2, Alford
rep	Nov	4	GAINSBOROUGH TRINITY	1-0	Simms
Q4		13	KETTERING	1-2	Johnson

1926/27

	P	W	D	L	F	A	Pts.
SCUNTHORPE UNITED	38	28	4	6	121	44	60
Boston	38	21	7	10	128	64	49
Gainsborough Trinity	38	22	5	11	85	63	49
Wath Athletic	38	21	4	13	76	63	46
Mexborough Athletic	38	20	6	12	97	81	46
York City	38	16	13	9	96	68	45
Loughborough Corns	38	20	5	13	94	76	45
Lincoln City Res.	38	18	7	13	94	70	43
Denaby United	38	18	4	16	88	59	40
Shirebrook	38	19	2	17	112	96	40
Worksop Town	38	17	5	16	95	87	39
Frickley Colliery	38	14	9	15	80	84	37
Ilkeston United	38	13	7	15	73	95	33
Grantham	38	12	8	18	84	76	32
Heanor Town	38	13	6	19	70	99	32
Newark Town	38	13	6	19	67	95	32
Long Eaton	38	12	7	19	72	105	31
Alfreton Town	38	8	5	25	59	143	21
Wombwell	38	7	5	25	57	111	20
Sutton Town	38	6	4	26	67	136	20

1927/28 — 9th in Midland League

#	Date		Opponent	Score	Scorers
1	Aug	27	Newark Town	5-2	Simms, Brooks 2, Allen 2
2	Sep	1	SCARBOROUGH	2-3	Simms, Wainwright
3		3	NOTTM FOREST RES.	2-1	Simms, Brooks
4		10	GAINSBOROUGH TRINITY	4-2	Simms 2, Wainwright, Vincent (og)
5		19	Heanor Town	7-4	Simms 3, Brooks 2, Allen 2
6		24	Gainsborough Trinity	1-1	Green
7		26	WOMBWELL	3-0	Allen 2, Brooks
8	Oct	8	Scarborough	2-3	Simms, Brooks
9		15	STAVELEY TOWN	7-2	Simms, Brooks 2, Allen 3, Hunter
10		20	Wombwell	4-2	Simms, Brooks, Allen 2
11		22	Lincoln City Res.	2-2	Simms 2
12		29	HEANOR TOWN	5-0	Simms 4, Brooks
13	Nov	5	Mansfield Town	1-5	Allen
14		12	LINCOLN CITY RES	1-3	Brooks
15		19	Grantham	5-4	Simms, Brooks, Allen 2
16		26	Staveley Town	1-2	Foster
17	Dec	3	Ilkeston United	1-4	Simms
18		10	BOSTON	4-2	Simms 2, Allen, Noble
19		17	Boston	2-2	Allen, Foster
20		24	NOTTS COUNTY RES.	4-4	Simms, Maw 2, Moore
21		26	GRIMSBY TOWN RES.	0-1	
22		27	Grimsby Town Res.	1-3	Moore
23		31	GRANTHAM	2-0	Maw, Foster
24	Jan	2	Shirebrook	0-3	
25		7	Nottm Forest Res.	0-4	
26		14	NEWARK TOWN	7-2	Simms 3, Maw 2, Allen, Skull
27		21	WATH ATHLETIC	0-2	
28	Feb	11	York City	1-2	Maw
29		16	Frickley Colliery	2-0	Hunter, Skull
30		18	MEXBOROUGH ATHLETIC	5-0	Maw, Allen 2, Foster 2
31		25	Mexborough Athletic	1-4	Bowers
32	Mar	3	YORK CITY	0-1	
33		8	FRICKLEY COLLIERY	2-1	Bowers, Maw
34		10	Denaby United	0-1	
35		24	Wath Athletic	2-3	Bowers, Wainwright
36		31	LOUGHBOROUGH COR.	4-0	Bowers 2, Maw, Holland
37	Apr	7	WORKSOP TOWN	4-1	Bowers, Maw, Wainwright 2
38		9	Worksop town	0-3	
39		10	Loughborough Corinthians	2-1	Maw, Allen
40		14	ILKESTON UNITED	4-1	Maw 2, Holland, Green
41		19	MANSFIELD TOWN	5-1	Maw 2, Allen 2, Green
42		23	Notts County Res.	3-2	Bowers 2, Maw
43		26	SHIREBROOK	7-1	Bowers 3, Maw 3, Johnson
44	May	3	DENABY UNITED	3-1	Bowers 3

F.A.Cup

	Date		Opponent	Score	Scorers
P	Sep	17	CLEETHORPES	5-2	Simms 4, Hunter
Q1	Oct	1	Gainsborough Trinity	0-3	

1927/28

	P.	W.	D.	L.	F.	A.	Pts
Gainsborough Trinity	44	29	7	8	141	62	65
Scarborough	44	26	7	11	108	61	59
Nottingham For. Res.	44	23	8	13	127	84	54
Notts County Res.	44	24	5	15	143	81	53
Lincoln City res.	44	23	7	14	126	99	53
Wath Athletic	44	24	4	16	94	74	52
York City	44	22	7	15	97	73	51
Shirebrook	44	23	5	16	108	89	51
SCUNTHORPE UNITED	44	23	4	17	118	85	50
Mansfield Town	44	19	11	14	118	97	49
Worksop Town	44	20	9	15	97	101	49
Grimsby Town Res.	44	20	8	16	93	83	48
Grantham	44	17	11	16	88	102	45
Denaby United	44	19	6	19	76	82	44
Boston	44	16	11	17	79	87	43
Staveley Town	44	16	10	18	98	109	42
Mexborough Athletic	44	14	9	21	84	112	37
Frickley Colliery	44	15	5	24	84	107	35
Loughborough Corinth.	44	14	7	23	76	104	35
Wombwell	44	12	7	25	70	107	31
Heanor Town	44	10	5	29	66	155	25
Ilkeston United	44	8	5	31	75	133	21
Newark Town	44	8	4	32	60	139	20

SEASON 1926-27 (Players only)
Standing: Smith, Skull, Reynolds, Hunter, Moore
Seated: Thompson, Johnson, Simms, Allen, Alford   Kneeling: McKenzie, Holland

SEASON 1927-28
Back: Skull, Severn, Murphy, Wogin, Holland, Hunter
Front: Wainwright, Brooks, Simms, Allen, Foster

1928/29 — 11th in Midland League

#	Date		Opponent	Score	Scorers
1	Aug	25	HULL CITY RES.	0-0	
2		30	NEWARK TOWN	1-2	Allen
3	Sep	1	DONCASTER ROVERS	5-1	King 3, Allen, Moore
4		5	Shirebrook	0-7	
5		8	Gainsborough Trinity	0-2	
6		22	GAINSBOROUGH TRINITY	2-2	Brandon 2
7	Oct	3	York City	1-3	Webb
8		6	Lincoln City Res.	1-2	Maw
9		20	FRICKLEY COLLIERY	2-1	Skull, Allen
10	Nov	3	CHESTERFIELD RES.	4-0	Wadsworth, Allen, Maw, Webb
11		12	Rotherham Utd Res.	2-3	King, Whaley
12		17	STAVELEY TOWN	6-1	Drury 3, Allen, Maw 2
13		24	DENABY UNITED	2-0	Wadsworth, Maw
14	Dec	1	SCARBOROUGH	2-2	Maw 2
15		8	Hull City Res.	1-1	Wadsworth
16		15	GRANTHAM	2-1	Wadsworth, Allen
17		22	BARNSLEY RES.	3-1	Allen, Maw, Bailey
18		25	**GRIMSBTOWN RES.**	**2-1**	**Allen 2**
19		26	Grimsby Town Res.	2-1	Wadsworth, Goy
20		29	MEXBOROUGH ATHLETIC	4-2	Allen 2, Hall 2
21	Jan	1	Mexborough Athletic	0-0	
22		5	Mansfield Town	0-5	
23		12	BOSTON	1-2	Allen
24		16	Chesterfield Res.	1-0	Allen
25		19	Denaby United	2-2	Wadsworth, Maw
26		26	WOMBWELL	2-2	Wadsworth, Brandon
27		31	YORK CITY	3-2	Mooney, Smalley, Maw
28	Feb	2	Wombwell	1-1	Allen
29		9	MANSFIELD TOWN	0-3	
30		14	ROTHERHAM UTD RES	1-1	Smalley
31		16	Doncaster Rovers Res.	1-3	Webb
32		23	NOTTM FOREST RES	3-1	Smith, Maw, Webb
33		28	Notts County Res.	2-6	Maw, Allen
34	Mar	2	Grantham	2-3	Maw, Allen
35		7	Frickley Colliery	3-3	Smith, Maw 2
36		9	NOTTS COUNTY RES	3-1	Smith 2, Maw
37		14	SHIREBROOK	1-1	Smith
38		16	Newark Town	2-1	Wadsworth, Maw
39		23	Barnsley Res.	1-1	Webb
40		25	Loughborough Corinthians	1-5	Courtney
41		30	WORKSOP TOWN	4-0	Smith 2, Whaley, Naylor
42	Apr	1	Worksop Town	1-0	Smith
43		2	Wath Athletic	0-4	
44		11	LOUGHBOROUGH COR.	3-1	Smith 2, Mooney
45		13	Boston	2-4	Smith 2
46		17	Nottm Forest Res.	1-1	Smith
47		20	Lincoln City Res.	5-2	Smith 2, Wadsworth 2, Webb
48		27	Scarborough	2-2	Smalley 2
49	May	1	Staveley Town	1-4	Smith
50		4	WATH ATHLETIC	7-2	Smith 3, Calladine 3, Allen

F.A.Cup

	Date		Opponent	Score	Scorers
P	Sep	15	Barton Town	3-2	Webb, King, Pearson
Q1		29	Spalding United	3-0	Haywood 2, Maw
Q2	Oct	13	CLEETHORPES	4-3	Reid 3, Maw
Q3		27	Boston United	1-0	Wadsworth
Q4	Nov	10	Grantham	1-2	Maw

1928/29

	P.	W.	D.	L.	F.	A.	Pts
Mansfield Town	50	31	10	9	133	72	72
Gainsborough Trinity	50	25	13	12	94	54	63
Lincoln City Res.	50	29	5	16	118	86	63
Hull City Res.	50	26	10	14	101	84	62
Grantham	50	25	10	15	113	79	60
Boston	50	27	5	18	96	72	59
Scarborough	50	25	8	17	115	91	58
Notts County Res.	50	21	15	14	91	75	57
York City	50	22	13	15	106	99	57
Grimsby Town Res.	50	24	6	20	109	95	54
SCUNTHORPE UNITED	50	20	14	16	98	96	54
Barnsley Res.	50	18	17	15	95	79	53
Nottingham For. Res.	50	20	12	18	101	74	52
Frickley Colliery	50	22	8	20	93	87	52
Denaby United	50	22	7	21	86	86	51
Chesterfield Res.	50	19	9	22	69	81	47
Shirebrook	50	19	8	23	112	113	46
Doncaster Rovers	50	19	7	24	92	97	45
Wath Athletic	50	16	12	22	97	104	44
Mexborough Athletic	50	15	12	23	81	105	42
Newark Town	50	16	9	25	82	118	41
Rotherham United Res.	50	18	4	28	99	125	40
Staveley Town	50	15	8	27	102	142	38
Loughborough Corinth.	50	13	6	31	75	117	32
Wombwell	50	12	8	30	80	136	32
Worksop Town	50	10	6	34	69	140	26

1929/30 — 7th in Midland League

#	Date		Opponent	Score	Scorers
1	Aug	31	HULL CITY RES.	3-1	Smalley, Calladine 2
2	Sep	5	Newark Town	1-1	Bailey
3		7	Lincoln City Res.	0-2	
4		14	GAINSBOROUGH TRINITY	5-0	Stringfellow, Smalley, Calladine 2, Beynon
5		25	Shirebrook	3-1	Smalley 2, Bailey
6		28	ROTHERHAM UTD RES	4-0	Simmons, Smalley, Calladine, Beynon
7		30	Staveley Town	1-1	Simmons
8	Oct	7	LOUGHBOROUGH COR.	2-0	Calladine 2
9		12	Gainsborough Trinity	1-4	Hackett
10		26	Rotherham Utd Res.	1-3	Beynon
11	Nov	11	Chesterfield Res.	2-3	Kennedy, Beynon
12		18	Wombwell	5-1	Stringfellow, Kennedy, Calladine 2, Beynon
13		23	Grantham	1-2	Beynon
14	Dec	7	Worksop Town	5-3	Simmons, Beynon, Cross, Stanyon, Calladine
15		21	HULL CITY RES.	4-1	Cross, Calladine 3
16		25	GRIMSBY TOWN RES	1-1	Simmons
17		26	Grimsby Town Res.	2-6	Baldwin 2
18		28	MEXBOROUGH ATHLETIC	6-0	Simmons, Stringfellow, Baldwin, Calladine 2, Cooke
19	Jan	1	Frickley Colliery	5-1	Baldwin 2, Calladine 2, Cooke
20		4	WOMBWELL	4-1	Simmons, Calladine, Baldwin, Cooke
21		11	CHESTERFIELD RES.	3-0	Stringfellow, Baldwin, Calladine
22		16	Nottm Forest Res.	3-5	Stringfellow, Baldwin, Beynon
23		18	Barnsley Res.	1-5	Stringfellow
24		23	DENABY UNITED	5-1	Stringfellow, Baldwin 3, Calladine
25		25	NOTTS FOREST RES	5-3	Baldwin 2, Calladine, Beynon 2
26		30	NOTTS COUNTY RES	1-2	Baldwin
27	Feb	1	Scarborough	1-1	Stringfellow
28		8	GRANTHAM	4-1	Baldwin, Calladine, Beynon 2
29		10	Denaby United	2-0	Cross, Calladine
30		15	BARNSLEY RES.	2-2	Baldwin, Calladine
31		20	WATH ATHLETIC	3-0	Stringfellow, Calladine, Beynon
32		22	Doncaster Rovers Res	0-3	
33		27	Wath Athletic	1-3	Osborne
34	Mar	1	WORKSOP TOWN	3-0	Crawford, Calladine, Beynon
35		8	Boston	1-1	Baldwin
36		12	Loughborough Corinthians	1-7	Calladine
37		15	BOSTON	3-5	Baldwin, Calladine, Beynon
38		17	FRICKLEY COLLIERY	2-0	Baldwin, Beynon
39		22	Mansfield Town	3-1	Calladine, Beynon 2
40		24	DONCASTER ROVERS RES	4-0	Whittingham, Crawford, Beynon 2
41		27	Notts County Res.	0-3	
42		29	LINCOLN CITY RES	2-1	Whittingham, Hackett
43	Apr	3	SHIREBROOK	1-0	Stringfellow
44		5	Mexborough Athletic	1-3	Kennedy
45		10	STAVELEY TOWN	9-0	Staniforth 2, Moore 2, Baldwin 3, Shaw, Beynon
46		12	MANSFIELD TOWN	2-1	Stringfellow, Baldwin
47		19	BRADFORD PARK AVE RES	2-5	Baldwin, Beynon
48		21	Bradford Park Avenue Res	0-9	
49		26	SCARBOROUGH	1-4	Kennedy
50	May	3	NEWARK TOWN	2-0	Simmons, Beynon

F.A.Cup

	Date		Opponent	Score	Scorers
P	Sep	21	Selby Town	3-1	Smalley, Bailey, Cooke
Q1	Oct	5	SELBYOLYMPIC	1-0	Simmons
Q2		19	GOOLE TOWN	2-1	Simmons 2
Q3	Nov	2	BROUGHTON RANGERS	7-0	Kennedy 4, Smalley 2, Simmons
Q4		16	South Kirkby Colliery	6-1	Smalley, Simmons 2, Stringfellow 2
R1		30	HARTLEPOOLS UNITED	1-0	Smalley
R2	Dec	14	ROTHERHAM UNITED	3-3	Smalley, Calladine 2
rep		19	Rotherham United	4-5	Beynon 2, Smalley, Calladine

1929/30

	P.	W.	D.	L.	F.	A.	Pts
Scarborough	50	36	9	5	143	44	81
Barnsley Res.	50	33	9	8	137	69	75
Bradford P. A. Res.	50	33	5	12	163	83	71
Grimsby Town Res.	50	28	9	13	160	88	65
Lincoln City Res.	50	27	9	14	131	83	63
Loughborough Corinth.	50	25	11	14	113	74	61
SCUNTHORPE UNITED	50	26	6	18	124	98	58
Gainsborough Trinity	50	25	6	19	117	99	56
Nottingham Forest (Res.)	50	24	8	18	117	103	56
Mansfield Town	50	25	4	21	126	98	54
Notts County Res.	50	22	9	19	136	114	53
Boston	50	23	7	20	102	94	53
Grantham	50	23	6	21	100	93	52
Chesterfield Res.	50	21	8	21	123	102	50
Rotherham United Res.	50	22	4	24	101	122	48
Hull City Res.	50	20	7	23	109	105	47
Shirebrook	50	16	13	21	87	109	45
Newark Town	50	17	11	22	93	125	45
Frickley Colliery	50	16	9	25	83	129	41
Mexborough Athletic	50	14	12	24	90	132	40
Wombwell	50	15	9	26	76	116	39
Denaby United	50	15	7	28	90	123	37
Doncaster Rovers Res.	50	12	12	26	85	118	36
Worksop Town	50	13	6	31	114	162	32

SEASON 1928-29
Back: Severn, Skull, Ashford, Unwin, Saxton, Mooney, Lloyd (Trainer)
Seated: Phillips, Maw, Dixon, Allan, Webb

SEASON 1929-30
Back: Severn, Skull, Bromage, Cooke, Bailey, Baynham, Lloyd (Trainer)
Seated: Simmons, Stringfellow, Smalley, Calladine, Beynon

1930/31 — 11th in Midland League

1	Aug	30	Wombwell	1-3	Rawlings
2	Sep	1	WOMBWELL	2-1	Rawlings, Beynon
3		6	BARNSLEY RES.	0-2	
4		13	Lincoln City Res.	4-4	Whittingham, Green, Beynon, Oakton
5		18	SCARBOROUGH	1-1	Green
6		20	ROTHERHAM UTD RES	7-2	Rawlings2,Stringfellow,Green2,Pattison,Oakto
7		27	GAINSBOROUGH TRINITY	2-1	Stringfellow, Richards
8	Oct	4	Doncaster Rovers Res	2-0	Rawlings, Stringfellow
9		9	NEWARK TOWN	0-2	
10		11	DENABY UNITED	4-0	Stringfellow, Whittingham 2, Green
11		18	Barnsley Res.	2-6	Stringfellow, Oakton
12		22	Gainsborough Trinity	0-4	
13		25	LOUGHBOROUGH COR.	4-2	Pattison 2, Stringfellow, Beynon
14	Nov	1	Scarborough	4-2	Pattison 2, Stringfellow, Green
15		8	NOTTS COUNTY RES	5-1	Pattison 3, Oakton, Beynon
16	Dec	6	Chesterfield Res.	4-4	Pattison 3, Foster
17		13	SHIREBROOK	1-0	Beynon
18		25	GRIMSBY TOWN RES	2-2	Pattison, Beynon
19		27	Frickley Colliery	6-0	Pattison 4, Green, Oakton
20	Jan	1	Rotherham Utd Res.	2-2	Pattison, Green
21		10	HULL CITY RES	1-2	Pattison
22		17	LINCOLN CITY RES	0-5	
23		24	Newark Town	0-1	
24		31	BRADFORD PARK AVE RES	1-0	Beynon
25	Feb	7	DONCASTER ROVERS RES	3-1	Wainwright, Beynon 2
26		12	Grimsby Town Res.	4-3	Rawlings 2, Wainwright, Stringfellow
27		14	Boston	3-0	Oakton, Johnson, Beynon
28		19	Hull City Res.	2-2	Rawlings 2
29		21	BOSTON	1-1	Rawlings
30		26	Mexborough Athletic	3-3	Rawlings 2, Pattison
31	Mar	5	Nottm Forest Res.	0-9	
32		7	NOTTM FOREST RES	1-0	Pattison
33		12	MEXBOROUGH ATHLETIC	5-2	Pattison 3, Stringfellow, Oakton
34		14	Shirebrook	0-3	
35		18	Bradford City Res.	1-4	Pattison
36		21	GRANTHAM	2-2	Rawlings, Oakton
37		23	Denaby United	2-2	Oakton 2
38		28	Notts County Res.	2-6	Rawlings 2
39		30	Grantham	1-3	Johnson
40	Apr	4	Bradford Park Ave Res.	1-1	Cross
41		6	Mansfield Town	4-3	Rawlings, Johnson 3
42		11	Loughborough Corinthians	1-1	Pattison
43		18	BRADFORD CITY RES	3-1	Stringfellow, Pattison 2
44		20	FRICKLEY COLLIERY	3-1	Rawlings, Pattison 2
45		25	CHESTERFIELD RES.	1-2	Pattison
46	May	2	MANSFIELD TOWN	0-2	

F.A.Cup

Q4	Nov	15	WORCESTER CITY	3-0	Pattison 2, Beynon
R1		29	Gainsborough Trinity	0-1	

1931/32 — 9th in Midland League

1	Aug	29	MANSFIELD TOWN RES	3-2	Adams 2, Dawson
2		31	BOSTON	2-1	Dawson, Isaac
3	Sep	5	SCARBOROUGH	0-2	
4		7	Denaby United	2-2	Smith, Elding
5		12	NOTTS COUNTY RES	0-3	
6		19	Gainsborough Trinity	0-3	
7		21	MEXBOROUGH ATHLETIC	4-1	Adams 2, Reed, Baynham
8		26	GAINSBOROUGH TRINITY	2-4	Methven, Hubbard
9	Oct	3	Rotherham Utd Res.	4-0	Methven, Reed 2, Welbourne
10		10	FRICKLEY COLLIERY	4-2	Methven 2, Hubbard 2
11		17	BARNSLEY RES.	4-2	Methven, Dawson, Baynham, Smith(og)
12		24	Notts County Res.	0-3	
13		31	LINCOLN CITY RES	1-0	Dawson
14	Nov	7	Mexborough Athletic	6-1	Dawson, Reed 3, Daws 2
15		21	Barnsley Res.	1-6	Hubbard
16	Dec	5	Lincoln City Res.	4-4	Cross, Reed, Daws 2
17		19	NOTTM FOREST RES	2-1	Baynham, Osbourne
18		25	GRIMSBY TOWN RES	2-4	Stimpson, Whittingham
19		26	Grimsby Town Res.	0-3	
20	Jan	1	Wombwell	3-5	Cross, Baynham, Reed
21		2	Bradford Park Ave Res.	0-6	
22		9	Frickley Colliery	3-2	Methven 2, Dawson
23		16	GRANTHAM	4-1	Cross, Hubbard 3
24		23	CHESTERFIELD RES	3-1	Hubbard 2, Reed
25		30	DONCASTER ROVERS RES	1-3	Reed
26	Feb	6	Grantham	0-3	
27		13	ROTHERHAM UTD RES	3-0	Smelt, Dawson, Reed
28		20	Doncaster Rovers Res	0-3	
29		27	Bradford City Res	3-1	Methven 2, Reed
30	Mar	5	LOUGHBOROUGH COR	0-0	
31		9	York City Res.	0-6	
32		12	Boston	2-3	Methven, Reed
33		19	BRADFORD CITY RES	2-2	Hubbard 2
34		25	Hull City Res.	1-1	Methven
35		26	BRADFORD PARK AVE RES	1-0	Hubbard
36		28	HULL CITY RES	3-2	Methven, Hubbard 2
37	Apr	2	Nottm Forest Res.	1-3	Hubbard
38		9	NEWARK TOWN	1-0	Smelt
39		11	Loughborough Corinthians	1-1	Smelt
40		13	Mansfield Town Res.	0-0	
41		16	Chesterfield Res.	2-4	Methven, Hubbard
42		23	Scarborough	0-1	
43		25	WOMBWELL	2-2	Cross, Meadows
44		30	DENABY UNITED	3-3	Methven, Hubbard, Tucker
45	May	5	YORK CITY RES.	2-0	Methven, Hubbard
46		7	Newark Town	1-2	Hubbard

F.A.Cup

Q4	Nov	14	SUTTON JUNCTION	7-1	Hubbard3, Methven2, Grainger,Dawson
R1		28	ROCHDALE	2-1	Hubbard, Methven
R2	Dec	12	QUEENS PARK RANGERS	1-4	Baynham (pen)

1930/31

	P.	W.	D.	L.	F.	A.	Pts
Grimsby Town Res.	46	32	6	8	174	73	70
Bradford City Res.	46	32	6	8	141	76	70
Bradford P. A. Res.	46	20	4	12	138	63	64
Barnsley Res.	46	25	7	14	126	78	57
Nottingham For. Res.	46	25	7	14	152	108	57
Lincoln City Res.	46	22	10	14	124	80	54
Grantham	46	21	10	15	85	85	52
Hull City Res.	46	20	11	15	105	88	51
Gainsborough Trinity	46	22	5	19	131	117	49
Mansfield Town	46	19	11	16	103	95	49
SCUNTHORPE UNITED	46	19	11	16	98	101	49
Newark Town	46	18	8	20	74	89	44
Boston	46	16	11	19	79	92	43
Denaby United	46	17	9	20	84	104	43
Chesterfield Res.	46	17	8	21	91	111	42
Scarborough	46	16	9	21	93	110	41
Notts County	46	17	6	23	119	121	40
Shirebrook	46	15	10	21	100	116	40
Loughborough Corinth.	46	14	8	24	80	116	36
Mexborough Athletic	46	13	8	25	84	129	34
Rotherham United Res.	46	14	6	26	85	145	34
Doncaster Rovers Res.	46	10	13	23	54	95	33
Wombwell	46	9	9	28	74	129	27
Frickley Colliery	46	8	9	29	64	137	25

1931/32

	P.	W.	D.	L.	F.	A.	Pts
Bradford P. A. Res.	46	36	3	7	189	63	75
Grimsby Town Res.	46	36	3	7	178	60	75
Nottingham For. Res.	46	30	7	9	117	62	67
Notts County Res.	46	24	11	11	115	81	59
Bradford City Res.	46	20	11	15	111	93	51
Scarborough	46	22	7	17	81	83	51
York City Res.	46	20	8	18	99	99	48
Chesterfield Res.	46	18	9	19	100	98	45
SCUNTHORPE UNITED	46	18	9	19	83	99	45
Mansfield Town Res.	46	16	12	18	86	86	44
Newark Town	46	18	8	20	85	90	44
Gainsborough Trinity	46	17	10	19	76	86	44
Loughborough Corinth.	46	18	8	20	88	113	44
Doncaster Rovers Res.	46	16	11	19	96	100	43
Boston	46	16	10	20	87	112	42
Mexborough Athletic	46	18	5	23	92	121	41
Hull City Res.	46	17	7	22	76	112	41
Barnsley Res.	46	14	12	20	97	108	40
Lincoln City Res.	46	15	7	24	103	112	37
Wombwell	46	14	9	23	81	99	37
Denaby United	46	10	14	22	101	127	34
Grantham	46	12	9	25	80	121	33
Frickley Colliery	46	13	7	26	86	135	33
Rotherham United Res.	46	12	7	27	59	106	31

200

SEASON 1930-31
Standing: Lloyd (Trainer), Pattison, Webster, Bromage, Richards, Bailey, Baynham, Hilton
Seated: Oakton, Stringfellow, Rawlings, Green, Wainwright

SEASON 1931-32
Standing: Lloyd (Trainer), Cross, Staniland, Grainger, Bromage, Stimpson, Baynham
Seated: Dawes, Elding, Adams, Dawson, Isaac

1932/33 8th in Midland League

1	Aug	27	Wombwell	3-2	Tucker 2, Chapman
2		29	WOMBWELL	3-0	Tucker, Patton, Chapman
3	Sep	3	SCARBOROUGH	0-4	
4		10	Scarborough	0-6	
5		17	GAINSBOROUGH TRINITY	3-0	Hubbard, Baynham, Murfin
6		24	Chesterfield Res.	3-3	Price 2, Chapman
7		26	BRADFORD PARK AVE RES	3-0	Price, Hubbard, Murfin
8	Oct	1	Mansfield Town Res.	2-1	Hubbard, Chapman
9		8	NOTTS COUNTY RES.	2-2	Hubbard, Milson
10		12	Bradford Park Ave Res.	0-7	
11		15	Gainsborough Trinity	4-4	Price 2, Baynham, Murfin
12		22	Doncaster Rovers Res.	3-1	Price, Hubbard, Murfin
13		29	Rotherham Utd Res.	2-2	Price 2
14	Nov	5	Barnsley Res.	1-4	Sumpter
15		19	YORK CITY RES.	2-3	Price, Murfin
16	Dec	3	ROTHERHAM UTD RES	5-0	Hubbard, Murfin, Chapman (3)
17		10	York City Res.	4-2	Price, Hubbard 2, Murfin
18		17	Lincoln City Res.	1-7	Hubbard
19		24	BRADFORD CITY RES	4-2	Price, Chapman 2, Murfin
20		27	Grimsby Town Res.	0-1	
21		31	GRANTHAM	4-1	Price 2, Hubbard, Baynham
22	Jan	2	Mexborough Athletic	3-2	Sharman, Baynham, Murfin
23		21	BARNSLEY RES.	4-1	Price 3, Chapman
24		28	Grantham	3-2	Price, Oates, Chapman
25	Feb	2	Frickley Colliery	3-1	Price, Hubbard, Chapman
26		4	LINCOLN CITY RES	1-2	Price
27		16	DENABY UNITED	3-1	Price, Chapman, Tucker
28		18	Boston	2-5	Chapman, Tucker
29		25	DONCASTER ROVERS RES	4-1	Hubbard 2, Chapman, Murfin
30	Mar	4	BOSTON	3-2	Hubbard, Tucker 2
31		6	Denaby United	1-5	Hubbard
32		11	Notts County Res.	0-4	
33		18	MEXBOROUGH ATHLETIC	3-1	Hubbard, Chapman, Price
34		22	Loughborough Corinthians	1-5	Chapman
35		25	Bradford City Res.	0-2	
36	Apr	3	LOUGHBOROUGH COR	3-1	Hubbard 2, Chapman
37		8	MANSFIELD TOWN RES	0-1	
38		14	Hull City Res.	3-1	Price, Hubbard, Tucker
39		15	FRICKLEY COLLIERY	0-0	
40		17	HULL CITY RES.	6-0	Hubbard 4, Chapman 2
41		22	Newark Town	6-3	Price, Hubbard 2, Oates, Tucker, Murfin
42		27	GRIMSBY TOWN RES	0-1	
43		29	CHESTERFIELD RES.	2-5	Hubbard, Chapman
44	May	6	NEWARK TOWN	4-2	Oates 3, Chapman

F.A.Cup

Q4	Nov	12	BURTON TOWN	4-1	Murfin 3, Hubbard
R1		26	Workington	1-5	Tucker

1932/33

	P.	W.	D.	L.	F.	A.	Pts
Grimsby Town Res.	44	36	1	7	184	66	73
Lincoln City Res.	44	30	6	8	161	73	66
Bradford P. A. Res.	44	28	8	8	146	52	64
Chesterfield Res.	44	28	4	12	131	67	60
Scarborough	44	25	9	10	137	81	59
Bradford City Res.	44	24	10	10	112	63	58
Barnsley Res.	44	24	5	15	116	83	53
SCUNTHORPE UNITED	44	23	5	16	104	100	51
Notts. County Res.	44	20	10	14	104	76	50
Gainsborough Trinity	44	18	10	16	95	90	46
Denaby United	44	20	5	19	78	93	45
Doncaster Rovers Res.	44	16	12	16	83	89	44
Mansfield Town Res.	44	16	9	19	108	97	41
Frickley Colliery	44	16	7	21	80	118	39
Loughborough Corinth.	44	14	10	20	92	110	38
Hull City Res.	44	17	4	23	104	131	38
Grantham	44	12	11	21	91	110	35
Boston	44	15	4	25	94	109	34
Newark Town	44	14	4	26	92	132	32
York City Res.	44	13	4	27	74	129	30
Mexborough Athletic	44	11	6	27	73	139	28
Rotherham United Res.	44	9	4	31	66	153	22
Wombwell	44	2	2	40	32	196	6

1933/34 7th in Midland League

1	Aug	26	BARNSLEY RES.	5-0	Pattison 3, Smalley, Allen
2		30	Scarborough	2-2	Pattison 2
3	Sep	2	Boston United	2-0	Pattison, Sumpter
4		9	Gainsborough Trinity	2-1	Pattison, Smalley
5		16	CHESTERFIELD RES.	6-0	Pattison 2, Barry 2, Swain, Allen
6		23	Rotherham Utd Res.	0-2	
7	Oct	7	GAINSBOROUGH TRINITY	2-1	Smalley, Starkey
8		21	DENABY UNITED	3-0	Smalley, Mills 2
9	Nov	4	Lincoln City Res	3-1	Pattison 3
10		18	ROTHERHAM UTD RES	8-1	Pattison,Sumpter 3,Oates 2,Nicholson,Mills
11	Dec	2	BRADFORD CITY RES	3-2	Pattison 2, Mills
12		9	Notts County Res.	2-4	Pattison, Sumpter
13		23	Doncaster Rovers Res	2-4	Smalley, Allen
14		25	Grimsby Town Res.	1-5	Pattison
15		26	GRIMSBY TOWN RES	3-9	Pattison, Reed, Mills
16	Jan	13	DONCASTER ROVERS RES	1-1	Pattison
17		20	YORK CITY RES.	6-1	Pattison 2, Sumpter, Allen, Reed 2
18		27	Denaby United	1-1	Pattison
19	Feb	3	NOTTS COUNTY RES	3-1	Pattison, Allen
20		10	Lincoln City Res.	2-2	Pattison, Reed
21		17	Barnsley Res.	2-3	Cross 2
22	Mar	3	Mexborough Athletic	2-6	Barry, Smalley
23		17	BOSTON UNITED	1-0	Burton
24		24	SCARBOROUGH	1-1	Oates
25		30	Hull City Res.	0-4	
26		31	BRADFORD PARK AVE RES	5-3	Sumpter 2, Allen, Mills, Roberts
27	Apr	2	HULL CITY RES.	0-3	
28		7	Chesterfield Res.	0-4	
29		14	Bradford City Res.	1-4	Barry
30		21	Bradford Park Avenue	0-3	
31		26	York City Res.	1-4	Smalley
32		28	MEXBOROUGH ATHLETIC	6-0	Sumpter 3, Davidson, Allen, Reed

F.A.Cup

Q1	Sep	30	SELBY TOWN	4-1	Sumpter, Cross, Barry, Fenwick
Q2	Oct	14	HUMBER UNITED	5-0	Mills, Smalley, Allen, Reed, Nicholson
Q3		28	LOUTH TOWN	4-1	Nicholson, Oates, Mills, Smalley
Q4	Nov	11	HEANOR TOWN	4-2	Pattison 2, Sumpter, Cross
R1		25	ACCRINGTON STANLEY	1-1	Sumpter
rep		30	Accrington Stanley	0-3	

1933/34

	P.	W.	D.	L.	F.	A.	Pts
Grimsby Town Res.	32	25	4	3	127	47	54
Bradford City Res.	32	23	3	6	107	47	49
Bradford P. A. Res.	32	21	2	9	90	43	44
Chesterfield Res.	32	15	4	13	66	56	34
Lincoln City Res.	32	14	6	12	83	75	34
Hull City Res.	32	15	3	14	74	70	33
SCUNTHORPE UNITED	32	14	5	13	76	73	33
Scarborough	32	12	8	12	57	67	32
Denaby United	32	11	9	12	58	76	31
Barnsley Res.	32	12	5	15	71	80	29
Notts County Res.	32	13	2	17	64	64	28
York City Res.	32	10	7	15	69	88	27
Doncaster Rovers Res.	32	10	5	17	57	58	25
Boston United	32	11	3	18	54	96	25
Gainsborough Trinity	32	10	4	18	54	79	24
Mexborough Athletic	32	10	2	20	53	85	22
Rotherham United Res.	32	8	4	20	46	102	20

SEASON 1932-33
Standing: Cross, Staniland, Millson, Young, Sharman, Baynham, Lloyd (Trainer)
Seated: Tucker, Pashley, Hubbard, Chapman, Murfin

SEASON 1933-34
Standing: Cross, Hill, Nicholson, Young, Davidson, Staniland
Seated: Sumpter, Fenwick, Smalley, Allen, Barry

1934/35 11th in Midland League

1	Aug	25	Mexborough Athletic	3-1	Pattison, Allen, Lax
2	Sep	3	PETERBOROUGH UNITED	0-0	
3		8	DENABY UNITED	4-2	Fenwick, Pattison, Cross, Lax
4		15	GAINSBOROUGH TRINITY	2-3	Barley, Lax
5		22	Lincoln City Res.	1-1	Roberts
6		29	NOTTS COUNTY RES.	2-1	Pattison, Lax
7	Oct	6	Denaby United	4-1	Mills 2, Allen 2
8		13	BRADFORD CITY RES	0-1	
9		20	BOSTON UNITED	4-2	Barley, Lynch 2, Barkley
10		27	Gainsborough Trinity	0-2	
11	Nov	3	CHESTERFIELD RES.	4-2	Lynch, Pattison 2, Lax
12		17	Bradford City Res.	0-1	
13	Dec	1	LINCOLN CITY RES	1-1	Roberts
14		8	Norwich City Res.	0-5	
15		15	BRADFORD PARK AVE RES	1-1	Noble
16		22	Hull City Res.	1-7	Barkley
17		25	GRIMSBY TOWN RES	1-0	Allen
18		26	Grimsby Town Res.	0-3	
19		29	NORWICH CITY RES	3-2	Barley, Rushby, Barkley
20	Jan	5	ROTHERHAM UTD RES	2-0	Mills, Lax
21		12	MEXBOROUGH ATHLETIC	4-1	Barkley, Mills, Allen, Lax
22		26	Doncaster Rovers Res	1-2	Noble
23	Feb	2	Boston United	2-1	Pattison, Lax
24		9	Barnsley Res.	0-4	
25		16	DONCASTER ROVERS RES	0-2	
26		23	Frickley Colliery	0-4	
27		28	Notts County Res.	1-0	Barley
28	Mar	2	Rotherham Utd Res.	1-4	Noble
29		16	Chesterfield Res.	0-4	
30		21	GRANTHAM	2-0	Pattison 2
31		30	BARNSLEY RES.	2-3	Mills, Nicholson
32	Apr	4	Peterborough United	0-2	
33		9	Grantham	0-5	
34		19	Scarborough	5-3	Mills 3, Allen, Lax
35		20	HULL CITY RES.	4-2	Noble 2, Fenwick, Allen
36		23	SCARBOROUGH	6-2	Barley, Noble 3, Fenwick 2
37		27	Bradford Park Ave Res	1-3	Noble
38	May	4	Frickley Colliery	5-1	Barley, Pattison 2, Mills 2

F.A.Cup

Q4	Nov	10	KETTERING TOWN	2-2	Allen, Lax
rep		15	Kettering Town	3-1	Lax 2, Barley
R1		24	Coventry City	0-7	

1934/35	P.	W.	D.	L.	F.	A.	Pts
Barnsley Res.	38	28	5	5	120	56	61
Norwich City Res.	38	22	8	8	97	36	52
Grimsby Town Res.	38	20	8	10	114	54	48
Bradford Park Avenue Res.	38	19	9	10	94	64	47
Boston United	38	19	8	11	85	71	46
Bradford City Res.	38	19	7	12	104	65	45
Notts County Res.	38	17	11	10	69	59	45
Gainsborough Trinity	38	18	8	12	80	73	44
Grantham	38	15	11	12	86	67	41
Peterborough United	38	15	10	13	81	84	40
SCUNTHORPE UNITED	38	17	3	18	67	82	37
Doncaster Rovers Res.	38	14	8	16	64	70	36
Chesterfield Res.	38	14	7	17	77	76	35
Lincoln City Res.	38	15	5	18	83	89	35
Mexborough Athletic	38	14	4	20	69	96	32
Hull City Res.	38	13	5	20	73	91	31
Rotherham United Res.	38	6	13	19	65	97	25
Denaby United	38	8	8	22	67	104	24
Frickley Colliery	38	5	11	22	57	137	21
Scarborough	38	2	11	25	32	113	15

1935/36 11th in Midland League

1	Aug	31	MEXBOROUGH ATHLETIC	2-2	Snaith, Roberts
2	Sep	7	Gainsborough Trinity	0-3	
3		14	BRADFORD CITY RES.	2-0	Snaith, Roberts
4		16	GAINSBOROUGH TRINITY	2-1	Barker, Davies
5		21	Lincoln City Res.	8-5	Kilsby 2, Barker, Snaith 3, Roberts, Davies
6		23	Burton Town	1-6	Roberts
7		28	ROTHERHAM UTD RES	3-3	Kilsby 2, Barker
8	Oct	5	BOSTON UNITED	2-0	Roberts, Davies
9		12	Notts County Res.	0-3	
10		19	BARNSLEY RES.	1-2	Lewis
11		26	Chesterfield Res.	3-2	Lewis, Snaith 2
12	Nov	2	NOTTS COUNTY RES.	0-2	
13		9	PETERBOROUGH UNITED	1-0	Snaith
14		23	NORWICH CITY RES	2-0	Snaith, Roberts
15	Dec	7	Bradford City Res.	1-2	Allen
16		21	Denaby United	1-5	Davies
17		25	GRIMSBY TOWN RES	5-0	Kilsby, Lewis, Snaith 2, Roberts
18		26	Grimsby Town Res.	3-2	Kilsby, Lewis, Roberts
19		28	Barnsley Res.	2-6	Allen 2
20	Jan	1	Frickley Colliery	3-3	Snaith 2, Roberts
21		4	LINCOLN CITY RES.	1-4	Snaith
22		11	DENABY UNITED	1-1	Allen
23		25	DONCASTER ROVERS RES	0-0	
24	Feb	1	Rotherham Utd Res	2-2	Roberts, Allen
25		8	Grantham	0-2	
26		15	SCARBOROUGH	2-0	Barker, Allen
27		22	Mexborough Athletic	8-3	Kilsby, Noble 2, Snaith 3, Roberts, Allen
28		29	CHESTERFIELD RES.	2-3	Snaith, Roberts
29	Mar	14	GRANTHAM	1-0	Kilsby
30		21	Peterborough United	1-3	Noble
31		25	Norwich City Res.	2-2	Kilsby, Noble
32		28	Doncaster Rovers Res.	1-0	Allen
33	Apr	2	Boston United	1-3	Kilsby
34		4	BRADFORD PARK AVE RES	4-1	Kilby, Lewis 3
35		10	Hull City Res.	0-1	
36		11	FRICKLEY COLLIERY	2-1	Snaith, Oates
37		13	HULL CITY RES.	0-0	
38		18	Scarborough	1-0	Snaith
39		25	BURTON TOWN	2-3	Chapman 2
40	May	2	Bradford Park Ave Res	0-1	

F.A.Cup

Q4	Nov	16	DENABY UNITED	4-1	Snaith 2, Lewis 2
R1		30	Coventry City	1-1	Snaith
rep	Dec	9	COVENTRY CITY	4-2	Davies, Roberts, Lewis, Kilsby
R2		14	Tranmere Rovers	2-6	Lewis, Allen

1935/36	P.	W.	D.	L.	F.	A.	Pts
Barnsley Res.	40	28	3	9	127	59	59
Bradford Park Avenue Res.	40	22	8	10	107	51	52
Gainsborough Trinity	40	24	4	12	92	49	52
Grantham	40	20	7	13	83	60	47
Doncaster Rovers Res.	40	20	6	14	73	70	46
Norwich City Res.	40	17	10	13	92	59	44
Boston United	40	19	4	17	64	69	42
Grimsby Town Res.	40	16	8	16	88	70	40
Rotherham United Res.	40	16	8	16	71	70	40
Burton Town	40	15	10	15	95	94	40
SCUNTHORPE UNITED	40	16	8	16	73	77	40
Notts County Res.	40	14	11	15	68	69	39
Scarborough	40	15	9	16	61	70	39
Chesterfield Res.	40	16	5	19	99	91	37
Bradford City Res.	40	14	7	19	74	77	35
Denaby United	40	12	10	18	73	111	34
Peterborough United	40	13	8	19	52	86	34
Lincoln City Res.	40	15	3	22	85	106	33
Frickley Colliery	40	14	5	21	76	109	33

1936/37 — 14th in Midland League

1	Aug	29	Newark Town	1-3	Porter
2		31	HULL CITY RES.	1-1	Barker
3	Sep	5	GAINSBOROUGH TRINITY	2-0	Porter, Beckett
4		7	Denaby United	3-1	Porter, Norris, Barker
5		16	Scarborough	1-2	Moore
6		19	NOTTM FOREST RES.	1-3	Norris
7		26	MANSFIELD TOWN RES.	2-1	Norris, Barker
8	Oct	3	Gainsborough Trinity	0-3	
9		12	NEWARK TOWN	0-2	
10		17	Burton Town	1-3	Norris
11		24	Grimsby Town Res.	0-3	
12		29	Nottm Forest Res.	1-2	Smithson
13		31	GRIMSBY TOWN RES.	0-3	
14	Nov	7	FRICKLEY COLLIERY	5-1	Chapman, Pattison, Smithson 2, Bartley
15		21	SCARBOROUGH	2-0	Norris, Allen
16	Dec	12	Peterborough United	5-3	Norris, Smithson 4
17		19	CHESTERFIELD RES.	0-0	
18		25	BURTON TOWN	2-0	Porter, Smithson
19	Jan	2	Grantham	0-7	
20		9	Bradford Park Ave Res.	1-6	Smithson
21		23	BRADFORD PARK AVE RES	1-0	Moses
22		30	Mansfield Town Res.	1-4	Porter
23	Feb	6	BARNSLEY RES.	2-1	Norris 2
24		11	Doncaster Rovers Res	0-2	
25		13	Barnsley Res.	2-1	Porter, Jones
26		20	GRANTHAM	1-1	Norris
27		27	Boston United	0-1	
28	Mar	6	DENABY UNITED	7-2	Porter 4, Gardiner, Moses 2
29		15	Chesterfield Res.	2-3	Porter, Horton
30		20	BRADFORD CITY RES	3-2	Porter 2, Norris
31		26	Lincoln City Res.	2-3	Porter, Norris
32		27	PETERBOROUGH UNITED	4-0	Porter 2, Norris, Horton
33		29	LINCOLN CITY RES	3-2	Porter 2, Moses
34		30	Rotherham Utd Res.	1-6	Porter
35	Apr	3	BOSTON UNITED	3-0	Norris, Moses 2
36		5	DONCASTER ROVERS RES	1-4	Norris
37		10	Bradford City Res.	4-1	Smithson 4
38		15	Hull City Res.	0-2	
39		17	Notts County Res.	5-2	Smithson 3, Horton 2
40		21	Frickley Colliery	0-2	
41		24	NOTTS COUNTY RES.	3-1	Smithson, Norris, Horton
42	May	1	ROTHERHAM UTD RES	3-2	Smithson, Bett, Horton

F.A.Cup

Q4	Nov	14	Gainsborough Trinity	1-0	Norris
R1		28	Walsall	0-3	

1936/37

	P.	W.	D.	L.	F.	A.	Pts
Barnsley Res.	42	27	7	8	121	68	61
Bradford Park Avenue Res.	42	26	8	8	124	62	60
Grimsby Town Res.	42	23	7	12	108	61	53
Chesterfield Res.	42	23	4	15	117	79	50
Bradford City Res.	42	23	4	15	104	75	50
Doncaster Rovers Res.	42	21	8	13	84	63	50
Nottingham Forest Res.	42	23	3	16	109	67	49
Gainsborough Trinity	42	22	5	15	110	82	49
Grantham	42	19	7	16	91	72	45
Boston United	42	19	7	16	85	76	45
Rotherham United Res.	42	20	5	17	94	94	45
Hull City Res.	42	19	6	17	64	62	44
Burton Town	42	17	8	17	75	89	42
SCUNTHORPE UNITED	42	19	3	10	77	136	41
Notts County Res.	42	17	5	20	92	106	39
Peterborough United	42	16	6	20	75	97	38
Lincoln City Res.	42	16	4	22	77	85	36
Newark Town	42	15	4	23	80	97	34
Mansfield Town Res.	42	11	9	22	57	100	31
Denaby United	42	12	4	26	73	134	28
Scarborough	42	10	6	26	55	99	26
Frickley Colliery	42	3	2	37	39	157	8

1937/38 — 6th in Midland League

1	Aug	28	DENABY UNITED	5-0	Johnson 2, Bett 2, Wilkinson
2	Sep	1	NOTTM FOREST RES	3-2	Norris, Bett, Wilkinson
3		4	Peterborough United	3-3	Whittaker, Stocks, Wilkinson
4		6	SCARBOROUGH	1-2	Lewis
5		11	GRIMSBY TOWN RES	3-0	Lewis 2, Stocks
6		16	Grantham	0-0	
7		18	BARNSLEY RES.	4-3	Lewis, Johnson 2, Bett
8		25	Gainsborough Trinity	0-1	
9		27	PETERBOROUGH UNITED	5-0	Lewis, Johnson 2, Bett (2)
10	Oct	2	GAINSBOROUGH TRINITY	2-3	Baldry, Bett
11		6	Lincoln City Res.	3-4	Johnson 3
12		9	Denaby United	3-2	Lewis, Proctor, Wilkinson
13		16	Grimsby Town Res.	3-2	Baldry 2, Wilkinson
14		23	Boston United	3-6	Baldry, Johnson 2
15	Nov	6	Frickley Colliery	1-2	Johnson
16		20	ROTHERHAM UNITED RES	6-0	Baldry 2, Lewis, Johnson 2, Bett
17	Dec	4	MANSFIELD TOWN RES	4-1	Baldry, Johnson, Lewis, Butler
18		11	Barnsley Res.	2-4	Wilkinson 2
19		18	Bradford Park Ave Res	0-3	
20		27	DONCASTER ROVERS RES	1-2	Wilkinson
21		27	SHREWSBURY TOWN	2-1	Norris, Allen
22	Jan	1	Newark Town	5-2	Norris 2, Johnson 3,
23		15	FRICKLEY COLLIERY	4-0	Baldry, Johnson, Allen, Wilkinson
24		22	Mansfield Town Res.	1-1	Johnson
25		29	Bradford City Res.	6-4	Norris, Lewis 2, Johnson, Stocks, Wilkinson
26	Feb	12	BOSTON UNITED	3-0	Baldry, Johnson 2
27		19	Rotherham United Res	0-0	
28		26	Notts County Res.	2-2	Johnson 2
29	Mar	5	BURTON TOWN	4-3	Lloyd 2, Stocks, Wilkinson
30		12	Shrewsbury Town	1-5	Johnson
31		19	NOTTS COUNTY RES	4-0	Johnson 2, Wilkinson 2
32		26	BRADFORD CITY RES	1-3	Lloyd
33	Apr	2	BRADFORD PARK AVE RES	3-1	Johnson 3
34		7	LINCOLN CITY RES	4-2	Lewis 3, Johnson
35		9	Burton Town	1-2	Johnson
36		15	Hull City Res.	2-1	Wilkinson 2
37		18	HULL CITY RES.	7-1	Norris, Lewis, Johnson 3, Clarvis, Wilkinson
38		21	Doncaster Rovers Res	0-1	
39		23	Scarborough	1-1	Lewis
40		30	NEWARK TOWN	2-1	Lewis, Wilkinson
41	May	2	GRANTHAM	4-3	Johnson 2, Proctor, Wilkinson
42		7	Nottm Forest Res.	0-1	

F.A.Cup

Q4	Nov	13	GRANTHAM	4-2	Johnson, Wilkinson
R1		27	Hull City	0-4	

1937/38

	P.	W.	D.	L.	F.	A.	Pts
Shrewsbury Town	42	25	9	8	111	50	59
Grantham	42	25	6	11	89	63	56
Scarborough	42	23	7	12	70,	46	53
Doncaster Rovers Res.	42	21	9	12	80	48	51
Grimsby Town Res.	42	22	5	15	87	57	49
SCUNTHORPE UNITED	42	22	5	15	109	78	49
Lincoln City Res.	42	22	5	15	107	90	49
Barnsley Res.	42	19	10	13	93	59	48
Boston United	42	20	8	14	79	74	48
Frickley Colliery	42	19	8	15	77	79	46
Burton Town	42	18	8	16	74	66	44
Notts County Res.	42	16	9	17	70	72	41
Nottingham Forest Res.	42	16	8	18	90	81	40
Bradford Park Avenue Res.	42	16	7	19	95	72	39
Mansfield Town Res.	42	18	3	21	69	67	39
Gainsborough Trinity	42	16	7	19	90	109	39
Hull City Res.	42	17	4	21	73	83	38
Bradford City Res.	42	16	6	20	81	105	38
Peterborough United	42	7	13	22	67	105	27
Newark Town	42	10	7	25	57	106	27
Rotherham United Res.	42	10	7	25	51	107	27
Denaby United	42	6	5	31	57	159	17

SEASON 1937-38
Standing: Lloyd (Trainer), Millington, Stocks, Cross, Earnshaw, Allen, W.Jones
Seated: Whittaker, Norris, Johnson, Bett, Wilkinson

SEASON 1938-39
Standing: Allcock (Secretary), Stocks, Millington, Thorpe, Poxton, T.Jones, Allen, Cliff (Chairman)
Seated: Norris, Fleetwood, Johnson, Nightingale, Wilkinson, Lloyd (Trainer)

1938/39 1st in Midland League

1	Aug	27	Mansfield Town Res.	2-0	Johnson, Fleetwood
2		29	NEWARK TOWN	10-3	Johnson 5,Norris, Fleetwood 2,Nightingale, Hunt(og)
3	Sep	5	MANSFIELD TOWN RES	3-1	Norris, Allen, Nightingale
4		10	Bradford Park Ave Res	3-3	Johnson 2, Nightingale
5		15	Grantham	3-1	Johnson 3
6		17	SHREWSBURY TOWN	3-1	Johnson 2, Norris
7		19	Gainsborough Trinity	1-1	Wilkinson
8		24	GAINSBOROUGH TRINITY	2-0	Johnson, Fleetwood
9		28	Scarborough	2-2	Johnson 2
10	Oct	8	GRANTHAM	4-1	Johnson 2, Norris, Nightingale
11		20	NOTTM FOREST RES	2-3	Fleetwood 2
12		22	Peterborough United	3-0	Johnson, Norris 2
13	Nov	5	Newark Town	3-0	Johnson, Fleetwood, Nightingale
14		19	GRIMSBY TOWN RES.	5-0	Johnson 3, Oxley, Nightingale
15	Dec	3	NOTTS COUNTY RES.	8-0	Johnson2, Norris2, Fleetwood, Nightingale(2), Oxley
16		17	Bradford City Res.	0-5	
17		24	BRADFORD PARK AVE RES	5-2	Johnson 2, Nightingale 2, Wilkinson
18		27	DENABY UNITED	9-1	Johnson 6, Fleetwood, Lacy, Nightingale
19		31	Shrewsbury Town	2-4	Fleetwood, Nightingale
20	Jan	2	Denaby United	10-0	Johnson2, Norris2, Fleetwood2, Nightingale2, Wilkinson2
21		14	LINCOLN CITY RES	4-1	Johnson, Norris, Wilkinson 2
22		28	BOSTON UNITED	3-1	Johnson, Wilkinson, Nightingale
23	Feb	4	Barnsley Res	4-3	Johnson, Fleetwood, Nightingale, Staniland
24		9	BARNSLEY RES.	5-1	Johnson 3, Fleetwood 2
25		11	Doncaster Rovers Res.	0-0	
26		16	Notts County Res.	2-2	Johnson, Wilkinson
27		18	ROTHERHAM UTD RES	0-0	
28		25	Grimsby Town Res.	2-2	Fleetwood, Nightingale
29	Mar	4	DONCASTER ROVERS RES	5-2	Johnson 4, Nightingale
30		6	PETERBOROUGH UNITED	2-1	Fleetwood, Nightingale
31		18	Nottm Forest Res.	2-1	Fleetwood, Wilkinson
32		22	Burton Town	1-2	Nightingale
33		25	BRADFORD CITY RES	4-0	Norris, Nightingale 2, Wilkinson
34	Apr	1	LINCOLN CITY RES	1-0	Harris
35		7	HULL CITY RES.	2-0	Harris, Nightingale
36		8	Boston United	4-3	Johnson 2, Harris, Nightingale
37		10	Hull City Res.	2-4	Harris, Norris
38		15	BURTON TOWN	2-0	Johnson, Wilkinson
39		17	SCARBOROUGH	0-1	
40		24	FRICKLEY COLLIERY	4-2	Johnson 2, Fleetwood, Harris
41		27	Rotherham Utd Res.	2-2	Fleetwood, Nightingale
42		29	Frickley Colliery	2-1	Nightingale 2

F.A.Cup

Q1	Oct	1	BARTON TOWN	9-1	Johnson 5, Fleetwood 2, Norris 2
Q2		15	APPLEBY FRODINGHAM	4-1	Johnson 3, Stocks
Q3		29	LYSAUGHTS SPORTS	11-3	Johnson5,Nightingale4, Norris, Fleetwood
Q4	Nov	12	BOSTON UNITED	2-1	Nightingale, Johnson
R1		26	LANACASTER CITY	4-2	Nightingale, Fleetwood 2, Johnson
R2	Dec	10	WATFORD	1-2	Jones (pen)

1938/39

	P.	W.	D.	L.	F.	A.	Pts
SCUNTHORPE UNITED	42	28	8	6	133	57	64
Barnsley Res.	42	27	4	11	130	73	68
Shrewsbury Town	42	25	5	12	125	65	55
Nottingham Forest Res.	42	21	13	8	102	70	55
Grimsby Town Res.	42	23	6	13	120	74	52
Burton Town	42	22	6	14	115	75	50
Bradford City Res.	42	20	7	15	107	77	47
Boston United	42	21	5	16	95	90	47
Scarborough	42	18	10	14	79	81	46
Peterborough United	42	20	4	18	99	77	44
Rotherham United Res.	42	17	9	16	76	83	43
Lincoln City Res.	42	18	5	19	93	90	41
Doncaster Rovers Res.	42	18	4	20	95	87	40
Grantham	42	17	6	19	103	118	40
Gainsborough Trinity	42	18	3	21	102	92	39
Bradford Park Avenue Res.	42	18	3	21	91	83	39
Frickley Colliery	42	19	1	22	96	111	39
Hull City Res.	42	15	3	24	76	90	33
Mansfield Town Res.	42	11	7	24	80	112	29
Notts County Res.	42	11	6	25	60	121	29
Newark Town	42	11	5	26	82	149	27

1939/40 Midland League Abandoned

1	Aug	26	Rotherham Utd Res.	3-1	Campbell, Maw, J.Millington
2		28	SHREWSBURY TOWN	4-2	Campbell 2, Maw, Rickards
3	Sep	1	GRIMSBY TOWN RES	1-2	Campbell

(Unofficial Competition) Part 1

1	Oct	28	Newark Town	5-2	Nightingale 2, Maw, Norris 2
2	Nov	4	GRANTHAM	5-2	Nightingale 3, Swain, Maw
3		11	Frickley Colliery	3-5	Maw, Norris 2
4		18	NEWARK TOWN	2-1	Robertshaw, Fleetwood
5		25	BOSTON UNITED	7-0	Nightingale 5, Maw, Norris
6	Dec	9	FRICKLEY COLLIERY	3-0	Nightingale 2, Norris
7		16	Grantham	2-2	Maw, Fleetwood
8		23	DENABY UNITED	6-1	Nightingale 2, Johnson, Fleetwood 3
9		25	GAINSBOROUGH TRINITY	7-3	Night'gale2,Johnson,Maw,Norris,Fleetwood
10		26	Gainsborough Trinity	8-2	Nightingale 6, Norris, Fleetwood
11		30	Boston United	1-0	Nightingale
12	Jan	6	Peterborough United	1-1	Nightingale
13		13	PETERBOROUGH UNITED	3-6	Nightingale 2, Fleetwood
14		20	Denaby United	2-2	Nightingale, Fleetwood

Part 2

1	Feb	24	BOSTON UNITED	8-2	Night'gale2,Maw2,Fleet'd 2,Johns'n,Greaves
2	Mar	2	Boston United	0-2	
3		9	DENABY UNITED	3-0	Nightingale 2, Johnson
4		16	Frickley Colliery	3-1	Johnson 3
5		22	GAINSBOROUGH TRINITY	5-1	Nightingale, Maw, Johnson 2, Greaves
6		25	Gainsborough Trinity	3-2	Nightingale, Johnson, Carter (og)
7		30	Peterborough United	3-5	Johnson 2, Fleetwood
8	Apr	6	PETERBOROUGH UNITED	4-1	Nightingale 2, Fleetwood 2
9		13	Grantham	8-0	Nightingale 4, Johnson 2, Swain, Fleetwood
10		27	FRICKLEY COLLIERY	3-3	Nightingale, Johnson, Swain
11	May	4	Newark Town	2-1	Maw, Johnson
12		11	GRANTHAM	5-0	Nightingale,Johnson2,Swain,Archer(og)
13		13	Denaby United	2-0	Johnson 2

Part 2 Fixtures not completed
Part 1 Fixtures - subsequently
considered the unofficial Championship

Friendly Fixtures

1	Sep	23	BARNSLEY RES.	5-3	Norris, Maw, Fleetwood 2, Nightingale
2		30	GAINSBOROUGH TRINITY	3-2	Maw, Johnson, Norris
3	Oct	7	Gainsborough Trinity	2-1	Maw, Norris
4		14	LINCOLN CITY	5-2	Nightingale 3, Norris, Fleetwood
5		21	GRIMSBY TOWN RES	5-2	Maw 2, Nightingale 2, Fleetwood
6	Dec	12	BRADFORD PARK AVENUE	2-1	Nightingale, Stephens (og)
7	May	18	Peterborough United	2-3	Johnson 2

Last match considered as the 'Champions versus Runners-up'

1939/40 (Unofficial) Part 1

	P.	W.	D.	L.	F.	A.	Pts.
SCUNTHORPE UNITED	14	9	3	2	55	27	21
Peterborough United	14	8	3	3	49	29	19
Frickley Colliery	13	7	2	4	45	30	16
Newark Town	14	6	2	6	45	51	16
Boston United	14	6	2	6	45	51	16
Denaby United	14	4	4	6	30	39	12
Grantham	14	3	3	8	28	43	9
Gainsborough Trinity	13	2	1	10	25	45	5

1939/40 (Unofficial) Part 2

	P.	W.	D.	L.	F.	A.	Pts.
Peterborough United	13	10	2	1	54	23	22
SCUNTHORPE UNITED	13	10	1	2	49	18	21
Denaby United	12	5	2	5	24	23	12
Newark Town	11	5	0	6	28	20	10
Boston United	10	5	0	5	24	30	10
Frickley Colliery	9	1	3	5	17	24	5
Grantham	8	1	0	7	6	40	2
Gainsborough Trinity	6	0	0	6	7	31	0

1945/46 — 6th in Midland League

#		Date	Opponent	Score	Scorers
1	Aug	25	MANSFIELD TOWN RES	6-1	Marriott, Leeman 2, Carver 3
2	Sep	1	Notts County Res.	0-3	
3		8	Lincoln City Res.	3-0	Fleetwood 2, Redhead
4		15	GAINSBOROUGH TRINITY	4-1	Leeman 3, Carver
5		22	BRADFORD PARK AVE RES	3-1	Fleetwood, Carver 2
6		29	Gainsborough Trinity	2-3	Johnson, Marriott
7	Oct	6	NOTTS COUNTY RES	3-3	Johnson 2, Proctor
8		13	RANSOME & MARLES	1-2	Johnson
9		27	Barnsley Res.	3-1	Leeman, Carver 2
10	Nov	10	BARNSLEY RES.	2-1	Gratton, Carver
11		17	OLLERTON COLLIERY	5-1	Marriott, Fleetwood, Swain, Carver 2
12		24	Boston United	2-1	Leeman, Swain
13	Dec	1	Ransome & Marles	0-2	
14		15	Rotherham United Res	1-1	Carver
15		22	ROTHERHAM UTD RES	1-1	Redhead
16		25	GRIMSBY TOWN RES	2-2	Carver 2
17		26	Grimsby Town Res.	3-4	Marriott, Sheen 2
18		29	Lincoln City Res	4-2	Johnson 3, Wilson
19	Jan	5	Frickley Colliery	4-5	Johnson 2, Wilson, Marriott
20		12	PETERBOROUGH UNITED	1-0	Sheen
21		19	Shrewsbury Town	0-0	
22		26	Denaby United	4-2	Carver 4
23	Feb	2	GRANTHAM	3-1	Stewart, Carver 2
24		9	NOTTM FOREST RES	2-0	Heath 2
25		16	Peterborough United	1-3	Heath
26	Mar	2	SHREWSBURY TOWN	2-3	Sheen, Robertshaw
27		16	Nottm Forest Res.	4-0	Priestley 3, Robertshaw
28		23	FRICKLEY COLLIERY	3-1	Sheen 3
29		30	Grantham	0-3	
30	Apr	6	Bradford Park Ave Res	0-4	
31		10	Mansfield Town Res.	0-4	
32		13	DENABY UNITED	4-1	Burton 3, Wallace
33		19	Donacster Rovers Res	4-1	Stocks, Empson, Leeman, Wallace
34		22	DONCASTER ROVERS RES	1-3	Johnson
35		27	BOSTON UNITED	2-2	Robertshaw 2
36		28	Ollerton Colliery	2-3	Robertshaw 2

F.A.Cup

Q3	Oct	20	LYSAUGHTS SPORTS	4-1	Johnson 2, Allen, Marriott
Q4	Nov	3	YORKSHIRE AMATEURS	1-2	Fleetwood

1945/46

	P.	W.	D.	L.	F.	A.	Pts
Shrewsbury Town	36	25	6	4	133	43	58
Ransome & Marles (Newark)	36	26	5	5	90	39	57
Barnsley Res.	36	23	6	7	91	50	52
Rotherham United Res.	36	15	11	10	85	62	41
Grantham	36	18	5	13	85	62	41
SCUNTHORPE UNITED	36	17	5	13	82	65	40
Frickley Colliery	36	16	6	14	83	75	38
Boston United	36	16	6	14	76	80	38
Peterborough United	36	17	3	16	63	74	37
Grimsby Town Res.	35	15	4	16	59	64	34
Doncaster Rovers Res.	36	13	8	15	65	88	34
Gainsborough Trinity	36	15	3	18	100	95	33
Lincoln City Res.	36	12	6	18	81	101	30
Denaby United	36	10	9	17	70	94	29
Bradford P.A. Res.	36	8	10	18	83	116	26
Nottingham Forest Res.	35	9	7	19	76	81	25
Ollerton Colliery	36	10	4	22	71	114	24
Notts. County Res.	36	6	11	19	59	110	23
Mansfield Town Res.	36	7	8	21	66	104	22

1946/47 — 4th in Midland League

#		Date	Opponent	Score	Scorers
1	Aug	31	·MANSFIELD TOWN RES	5-4	Bowers, Wynne 3, Wallace
2	Sep	5	SCARBOROUGH	4-1	Marriott, Bowers, Wynne, Robertshaw
3		7	Shrewsbury Town	1-3	Wallace
4		14	BARNSLEY RES.	2-3	Marriott, Wynne
5		19	Boston United	2-2	Bowers, Wynne
6		23	Gainsborough Trinity	2-0	Bowers, Wallace
7		28	DONCASTER ROVERS RES	3-3	Bowers, Robertshaw 2
8	Oct	12	GAINSBOROUGH TRINITY	0-3	
9		26	Rotherham United Res	2-0	Wallace 2
10	Nov	9	Bradford Park Ave Res	1-3	Marriott
11		23	NOTTS COUNTY RES	6-1	Bowers 3, Wynne 3
12	Dec	7	FRICKLEY COLLIERY	9-0	Marriott, Bowers 4, Wynne 3, R.Jones
13		21	Lincoln City Res.	3-0	Wynne, Robertshaw 2
14		25	GRIMSBY TOWN RES	3-3	Bowers 3
15		26	Grimsby Town Res.	1-1	Wynne
16		28	Mansfield Town Res.	3-3	Bowers 2, Robertshaw
17	Jan	1	Denaby United	2-3	Norris, Robertshaw
18		4	Notts County Res.	5-1	Bowers, Harper, R.Jones
19		11	BRADFORD PARK AVE RES	5-1	Norris 2, Bowers, Rodi, Wallace
20		16	DENABY UNITED	7-1	Norris 3, Bowers 2, Rodi, Harper
21		18	Barnsley Res.	1-2	Bowers
22		25	Scarborough	2-1	Bowers, Marriott
23	Feb	1	PETERBOROUGH UNITED	3-0	Bowers, Marriott, Wilson (og)
24		20	BOSTON UNITED	1-0	Bowers
25	Mar	6	RANSOME & MARLES	5-1	Bowers 2, Robertshaw 3
26		29	SHREWSBURY TOWN	6-2	Bowers 3, Norris 2, Hydes
27	Apr	4	Hull City Res.	2-0	Robertshaw 2
28		5	NOTTM FOREST RES	1-1	Bowers
29		7	HULL CITY RES.	3-3	Bowers 2, Wynne
30		12	ROTHERHAM UTD RES	6-1	Bowers 3, Norris 2, Hydes
31		19	Grantham	1-0	Bowers
32		21	OLLERTON COLLIERY	1-0	Wynne
33		26	Bradford City Res.	4-1	Bowers 3, Robertshaw
34	May	3	BRADFORD CITY RES	4-0	Bowers 3, Robertshaw
35		10	GRANTHAM	5-2	Bowers 2, Hydes 3
36		15	Doncaster Rovers Res	0-2	
37		17	Peterborough United	0-1	
38		24	LINCOLN CITY RES	3-0	Norris, Hydes, Robertshaw
39		26	Ransome & Marles	2-1	Hydes, Robertshaw
40		31	Frickley Colliery	1-3	Bowers
41	Jun	2	Nottm Forest Res.	2-2	Bowers, Wallace
42		14	Ollerton Colliery	1-3	Bowers

F.A.Cup

P	Sep	21	NORTON WOODSEATS	5-2	Bowers 3, Fleetwood, Wallace
Q1	Oct	5	HAWORTH COLLIERY	5-2	Bowers 2, Robertshaw, Wallace 2
Q2		19	Rawmarsh Welfare	3-0	Robertshaw, Marriott, Wallace
Q3	Nov	2	Wombwell Athletic	5-2	Bowers, Wynn 3, Marriott
Q4		16	BOSTON UNITED	4-1	Bowers 2, Robershaw, Wallace
R1	Dec	4	York City	1-0	Marriott
R2		14	Rotherham United	1-4	Bowers

1946/47

	P.	W.	D.	L.	F.	A.	Pts
Grimsby Town Res.	42	29	8	5	133	54	66
Nottingham Forest Res.	42	26	8	8	119	60	60
Bradford Park Avenue Res.	42	28	2	12	131	68	58
SCUNTHORPE UNITED	42	24	9	9	121	61	57
Barnsley Res.	42	24	8	10	100	57	56
Shrewsbury Town	42	25	4	13	117	77	54
Doncaster Rovers Res.	42	21	8	13	101	71	50
Grantham	42	19	10	13	102	71	48
Peterborough United	42	18	12	12	90	77	48
Gainsborough Trinity	42	19	9	14	96	79	47
Ransome & Marles (Newark)	42	19	6	17	79	75	44
Denaby United	42	19	6	17	107	104	44
Boston United	42	16	10	16	96	107	42
Scarborough	42	15	9	18	73	83	39
Rotherham United Res.	42	15	6	21	93	109	36
Notts County Res.	42	16	4	12	90	113	36
Hull City Res.	42	12	7	23	68	108	31
Lincoln City Res.	42	13	4	25	77	113	30
Ollerton Colliery	42	8	5	29	68	130	21
Mansfield Town Res.	42	7	6	29	84	126	20
Bradford City Res.	42	7	5	30	66	150	19

SEASON 1946-47
Standing: Lloyd (Trainer), Millington, Staniland, Harper, Poxton, Reed, Burnip, Douglas (Groundsman)
Seated: Marriott, Wynn, Bowers, Wallace, Robertshaw

SEASON 1947-48
Standing: Johnson (Masseur), Lloyd (Trainer), Leeman, Watford, Rymer, Harper, Brownsword,
Millington, Douglas (Groundsman), Allcock (Secretary)
Seated: Smith, Rowney, Bowers, Wallace, Robertshaw, Norris

1947/48 — 2nd in Midland League

#		Date	Opponent	Score	Scorers
1	Aug	23	Bradford City Res	4-3	Bowers2, Wallace, Norris
2		28	SCARBOROUGH	1-0	Brownsword (pen)
3		30	BRADFORD CITY RES	3-1	Hydes 2, Norris
4	Sep	1	Denaby United	2-4	Wynne, Pinchbeck
5		6	Notts County Res.	2-2	Robertshaw, Wallace
6		10	GAINSBOROUGH TRINITY	3-1	Bowers, Rowney, Norris
7		13	Shrewsbury Town	1-1	Bowers
8		22	Gainsborough Trinity	1-2	Robertshaw
9		27	Nottm Forest Res.	1-2	Bowers
10	Oct	11	York City Res.	1-1	Bowers
11		25	NOTTS COUNTY RES	3-0	Bowers 2, Pinchbeck
12	Nov	8	Rotherham United Res	2-1	Pinchbeck, Robertshaw
13	Dec	6	OLLERTON COLLIERY	7-1	Bowers 6, Rowney
14		13	Lincoln City Res.	1-2	Crack
15		20	Mansfield Town Res	1-1	Bowers
16		25	GRIMSBY TOWN RES	2-1	Bowers, Robertshaw
17		26	Grimsby Town Res.	1-2	Robertshaw
18		27	PETERBOROUGH UNITED	7-1	Norris, Rowney 2, Wallace, Bowers 3
19	Jan	3	Scarborough	1-1	Bowers
20		10	Ransome & Marles	2-2	Robertshaw, Wallace
21		17	Donacster Rovers Res.	2-1	Rowney, Bowers
22		24	Bradford Park Ave Res	2-1	Bowers 2
23		31	GRANTHAM	1-0	Robertshaw
24	Feb	7	Peterborough United	1-2	Rowney
25		14	BRADFORD PARK AVE RES	1-0	Smith
26		19	ROTHERHAM UTD RES	3-2	Rowney 2, Smith
27		28	NOTTM FOREST RES	0-0	
28	Mar	6	BOSTON UNITED	2-1	Wallace, Rowney
29		13	Ollerton Colliery	5-1	Smith, Bowers 2, Johnson 2
30		18	DENABY UNITED	0-0	
31		20	Grantham	1-5	Bowers
32		26	Hull City Res.	1-3	Rowney
33		27	RANSOME & MARLES	4-3	Johnson, Bowers 2, Wallace
34		29	HULL CITY RES.	2-0	Rowney 2
35	Apr	1	MANSFIELD TOWN RES	1-1	Bowers
36		3	Shrewsbury Town	2-0	Johnson 2
37		10	YORK CITY RES.	3-0	Andrews (og), Rowney, Wallace
38		14	Frickley Colliery	3-1	Johnson 2, Bowers
39		17	Boston United	2-3	Johnson, Wallace
40		22	FRICKLEY COLLIERY	2-0	Wallace, Bowers
41		24	DONCASTER ROVERS RES	3-0	Johnson 2, Norris
42		26	LINCOLN CITY RES	2-4	Robertshaw, Rowney

F.A.Cup

		Date	Opponent	Score	Scorers
P	Sep	20	THE SHEFFIELD CLUB	5-1	Bowers2, Rowney, Robershaw, Norris
Q1	Oct	4	RAWMARSH WELFARE	8-0	Bowers 5, Wallace 2, Turner
Q2		18	DENABY UNITED	1-0	Rowney
Q3	Nov	1	NORTON WOODSEATS	2-1	Pinchbeck 2
Q4		15	GAINSBOROUGH TRINITY	4-2	Pinchbeck, Rowney, Robertshaw, Bowers
R1		29	Runcorn	2-4	Bowers, Rowney

1947/48

	P.	W.	D.	L.	F.	A.	Pts
Shrewsbury Town	42	28	6	8	98	51	62
SCUNTHORPE UNITED	42	23	9	10	89	57	55
Nottingham Forest Res.	42	23	8	11	112	59	54
Bradford Park Avenue Res.	42	25	2	15	138	97	52
Lincoln City Res.	42	22	5	15	97	53	49
Peterborough United	42	22	4	16	88	78	48
Gainsborough Trinity	42	19	10	13	88	50	48
Ransome & Marles (Newark)	42	19	9	14	85	76	47
Grimsby Town Res.	42	18	10	14	101	88	46
Grantham	42	10	6	16	110	99	46
Boston United	42	21	4	17	89	32	46
Doncaster Rovers Res.	42	17	11	14	93	66	45
Hull City Res.	42	19	6	17	86	71	44
Denaby United	42	16	9	17	82	84	41
Notts County Res.	42	16	6	20	72	95	38
York City Res.	42	13	10	19	69	109	36
Scarborough	42	12	9	21	67	85	33
Mansfield Town Res.	42	12	9	21	63	82	33
Rotherham United Res.	42	12	8	22	75	93	32
Frickley Colliery	42	11	9	22	85	119	31
Bradford City Res.	42	9	5	28	59	111	23
Ollerton Colliery	42	7	1	34	57	168	15

1948/49 — 4th in Midland League

#		Date	Opponent	Score	Scorers
1	Aug	21	Lincoln City Res	4-1	J.Taylor 2, Murphy 2
2		25	Scarborough	3-0	Murphy 2, Little
3		28	RANSOME & MARLES	1-0	Wallace
4	Sep	4	SHREWSBURY TOWN	0-1	
5		6	Gainsborough Trinity	2-5	Rowney, Wallace
6		11	Nottm Forest Res.	5-0	Murphy 2, Watford, J.Taylor, Whitehead
7		18	York City Res.	4-3	Murphy 2, J.Taylor, Barker
8		23	GAINSBOROUGH TRINITY	7-0	Murphy 4, J.Taylor 2, Wallace
9		30	FRICKLEY COLLIERY	2-1	J.Taylor, Barker
10	Oct	2	NOTTM FOREST RES	3-1	Murphy 2, Rowney
11		9	Mansfield Town Res	0-2	
12		14	GOOLE TOWN	3-0	Murphy 2, Wallace
13		16	NOTTS COUNTY RES	3-0	Murphy 2, J.Taylor
14		23	Boston United	2-1	Rowney, Wallace
15		30	MANSFIELD TOWN RES	5-1	Little, Rowney, Murphy, Wallace, Barker
16	Nov	6	Denaby United	2-0	Murphy 2
17		20	Doncaster Rovers Res	3-1	Murphy, Rowney, Barker
18	Dec	18	LINCOLN CITY RES	3-3	Little, Rowney, Barker
19		25	GRIMSBY TOWN RES	0-1	
20		27	Grimsby Town Res.	1-1	Rowney
21	Jan	1	Notts County Res.	0-1	
22		8	PETERBOROUGH UNITED	4-1	Murphy, Little 2, Barker
23		15	DENABY UNITED	4-1	Murphy 2, Little, Dale
24		22	Rotherham United Res	1-2	Lindley
25		29	GOOLE TOWN	3-2	Little, J.Taylor 2
26	Feb	5	BRADFORD APRK AVE RES	5-1	Murphy 3, J.Taylor 2
27		12	Grantham	1-2	Whitehead
28		19	Bradford Park Ave Res	2-4	Murphy 2
29		26	YORK CITY RES.	3-0	Murphy 2, Bowers
30	Mar	5	Peterborough United	3-4	Whitfield, Bowers 2
31		19	ROTHERHAM UTD RES	1-1	Bowers
32		26	Raansome & Marles	4-1	Little, Whitfield, Bowers, J.Taylor
33		30	Frickley Colliery	5-0	Whitfield, Bowers 2, J.Taylor, R.E.Taylor
34	Apr	2	GRANTHAM	1-3	Barker
35		9	Bradford City Res.	1-1	Whitfield
36		15	HULL CITY RES.	3-0	Whitfield 2, Bowers
37		16	DONCASTER ROVERS RES	0-0	
38		18	Hull City Res.	1-1	Watson
39		23	Shrewsbury Town	1-5	Bowers
40		28	SCARBOROUGH	2-1	Bowers, Whitfield
41		30	BRADFORD CITY RES	5-0	Bowers 3, Dale, Watson
42	May	2	BOSTON UNITED	1-2	Bowers

F.A.Cup

		Date	Opponent	Score	Scorers
Q4	Nov	13	SELBY TOWN	2-1	Murphy 2
R1	Dec	4	Halifax Town	0-0	
rep		6	HALIFAX TOWN	1-0	Barker
R2		11	STOCKPORT COUNTY	0-1	

1948/49

	P.	W.	D.	L.	F.	A.	Pts
Gainsborough Trinity	42	26	8	8	93	69	60
Bradford Park Avenue Res.	42	26	4	12	117	67	56
Nottingham Forest Res.	42	25	5	12	116	53	55
SCUNTHORPE UNITED	42	24	6	12	104	56	54
Grimsby Town Res.	42	21	9	12	86	65	51
Notts County Res.	42	18	14	10	79	60	50
Rotherham United Res.	42	21	7	14	81	60	49
Shrewsbury Town	42	19	7	16	82	70	45
Hull City Res.	42	16	12	14	86	67	44
Goole Town	42	19	6	17	86	86	44
Lincoln City Res.	42	18	7	17	89	86	43
Grantham	42	15	12	15	89	79	42
Boston United	42	15	10	17	83	108	40
York City Res.	42	15	10	17	68	98	40
Ransome & Marles (New'k)	42	15	7	20	82	98	37
Peterborough United	42	15	6	21	58	83	36
Bradford City Res.	42	12	10	20	72	84	34
Doncaster Rovers Res.	42	13	8	21	47	63	34
Scarborough	42	11	9	22	49	90	31
Denaby United	42	13	4	25	67	96	30
Mansfield Town Res.	42	9	8	25	49	81	26
Frickley Colliery	42	8	7	27	51	115	23

1949/50 3rd in Midland League

No	Date		Opponent	Score	Scorers	Thompson G	Barker	Brownsword	Conroy	Taylor	McCormick	Deniff	Whitfield	Heseltine	Wallace	Malcolm	Wilson A	Bowers T	Pigdon	Stanham	Lindley	Poole	Dixon	Barkas	Kirk	Sharpre	Lodge	Thompson E	Wright	Watson	Lemmon	Camm	Ward	Nagy	Millington
1	Aug 20		LINCOLN CITY RES	3-	Barker 2, Heseltine	1	2	3	4	5	6	7	8	9	10	11																			
2	27		Shrewsbury Town	1-	Whitfield	1	2	3	4	5			8	9	10	11	7																		
3	Sep 1		GAINSBOROUGH TRINITY	3-	Bowers 2, Conroy	1	2	3	4	5	6		8		10	11	7	9																	
4	3		GRANTHAM	5-	Bowers 3, Wallace, Barker	1	2	3	4	5			8		10	11	7	9	6																
5	8		GOOLE TOWN	5-	Wilson, Bowers 4	1	2	3	4	5			8		10	11	7	9	6																
6	10		Denaby United	1-	Whitfield	1	2	3	4	5			8		10	11	7	9	6																
7	14		Gainsborough Trinity	1-	Whitfield	1	2	3	4	5			10				7	9	6	11	8														
8	17		NOTTS COUNTY RES	1-	Whitfield	1	2	3	4	5			10		11			6	9		8	7													
9	24		York City Res.	0-1		1	2	3	4	5	6		8		10	8	9								7										
10	28		Goole Town	1-	Wallace	1	2	3	4	5	6		8		10	11	7	9																	
11	Oct 1		BRADFORD CITY RES	1-	Malcolm	1	2	3	4	5	6				10	11	7	9			8														
12	8		Lincoln City Res.	2-	Lindley, Wilson	1		3	4	5	6				10	11	7	9			8		2												
13	13		Notts County Res.	2-	Wallace, Whitfield	1		3	4	5	6		9		10	11	7				8		2												
14	15		YORK CITY RES.	1-	Wilson	1	2	3	4	5	6		9		10	11	8								7										
15	22		Bradford P.A.Res	2-	Whitfield 2	1	2	3	4	5	6		9		10	11	7									8									
16	27		Nottm Forest Res.	3-	Wallace, Barkas, Wilson	1	2	3	4	5	6		9		10	11	7						6	8											
17	29		MANSFIELD TOWN RES	5-	Barkas 2, Whitfield 2, Wilson	1	2	3	4	5	6		9		10									8				7							
18	Nov 5		DONCASTER R. RES	7-	Barkas 2, Whitfield 3, Wilson, Conroy	1	2	3	4	5	6		9		10	11	7							8											
19	26		NOTTM FOREST RES	0-2		1	2	3	4	5					10	11								8		7	4								
20	Dec 3		Frickley Colliery	1-	Whitfield	1	2	3	4	5			9			8	11									7	6						10		
21	10		HALIFAX TOWN RES	2-	Whitfield, Lodge	1	2	3	4	5			9		10									8		7	6	11							
22	17		Rotherham United Res	1-	Sharpre	1	2	3	4	5			9		10	11										7	6		8						
23	26		GRIMSBY TOWN RES	2-	Bowers, Whitfield	1	2	3	4	5	6		9		10			7								8					11				
24	27		Grimsby Town Res.	0-1		1	2	3	4	5	6		9		10			7								8					11				
25	31		Grantham	2-	Whitfield, Lodge	1	2	3	4	5	6		9		10											8	7				11				
26	Jan 7		PETERBOROUGH UNITE	1-	Conroy	1	2	3	4	5	6		9		10	11	7									8									
27	14		DENABY UNITED	1-	Whitfield	1	2	3	4	5	6		9			11	7										8				10				
28	21		Bradford City Res.	0-3		1	2	3	4	5	6		9		10	11	7									8	6								
29	28		BRADFORD P. A. RES	6-	McCormick, Wilson, Whitfield 3, Lennon	1	2	3	4	5	6		9			11	7										6				8				
30	Feb 4		RANSOME & MARLES	3-	Whitfield 2, McCormick	1		3	4	5	6		9			11						2					6				8	7			
31	11		SCARBOROUGH	1-	Whitfield	1	2	3	4	5	6		9			11											6				8	7			
32	18		Peterborough United	1-	Lennon	1	2	3	4	5	6		9		10	11											6				8	7			
33	28		BOSTON UNITED	3-	Lennon, Whitfield 2	1	2	3	4	5	6		9			11											6				8	7			
34	Mar 4		Mansfield Town Res.	0-1		1	2	3	4	5	6		9			11											6				8	7			
35	16		Halifax Town Res.	3-	Wallace, Barker, Heseltine	1	2	3	4	5			8	9	10	11	7										6								
36	18		Worksop Town	3-	Wallace, Heseltine 2	1	2	3		5	6		8	9	10	11	7										6								
37	25		ROTHERHAM UTD RES	2-	Whitfield, Wallace	1	2	3		5	6		8	9	10	11	7										6								
38	Apr 1		Ransome & Marles	5-	Heseltine 3, Wilson 2	1	2	3		5	6		8	9	10	11	7										6								
39	10		HULL CITY RES.	5-	Heseltine, Wilson 3, Lodge	1	2	3		5	6		8	9	10	11	7										6								
40	14		Hull City Res.	0-1		1	2	3		5	6		8	9	10	11	7										6								
41	15		SHREWSBURY TOWN	4-	Wallace 2, Heseltine, Brownsword (pen)	1	2	3	4	5	6		8	9	10	11	7																		
42	20		FRICKLEY COLLIERY	1-	Heseltine	1	2	3	4	5	6		8	9	10	11	7																		
43	22		Doncaster Rovers Res	2-	Whitfield 2	1	2	3		5	6		8	9		11	7																	10	
44	26		Scarborough	2-	Wilson, Malcolm	1	2	3		5	6		9		10	11	7																		4
45	29		Boston United	2-	Heseltine, Whitfield	1	2	3		5	6		8	9	10	11	7										8								4
46	Ma 3		WORKSOP TOWN	2-	Malcolm, McCormick	1	2	3		5	6		8	9	10	11	7																	4	
		Apps				42	39	42	33	42	30	1	39	13	33	37	26	12	6	1	5	2	3	6	2	7	21	1	2	4	6	5	2	1	2
		Goals				0	4	1	3	0	3	0	29	11	9	3	13	10	0	0	1	0	0	5	0	1	3	0	0	0	3	0	0	0	0

F.A.Cup

	Date		Opponent	Score	Scorers	Thompson G	Barker	Brownsword	Conroy	Taylor	McCormick	Deniff	Whitfield	Heseltine	Wallace	Malcolm	Wilson A	Bowers T	Pigdon	Stanham	Lindley	Poole	Dixon	Barkas	Kirk	Sharpre
Q4	Nov 12		GOOLE TOWN	0-0		1	2	3	4	5			9		10	11	7		6							8
rep	22		Goole Town	1-3	Barker	1	6	3	4	5			9		10	11		9				2				8

1949/50

1950/51 12th in Division 3(N)

#	Date	Opponent	Score	Scorers	Att	Thompson GH	Barker Jeff	Brownsword NJ	Allen W	Taylor RE	McCormick JM	Mosby H	Payne IEH	Gorin ER	Rees MJF	Boyes WE	Whitfield J	Clelland D	Hubbard J	Bowen D	White R	Babes J	Cumner RH	Mulholland JR	Malan NF	Comley LG	Jones RJ	Conroy RM
1	Aug 19	SHREWSBURY TOWN	0-0		11847	1	2	3	4	5	6	7	8	9	10	11												
2	23	Lincoln City	1-2	Gorin	16908	1	2	3	4	5	6	7		9	10		8	11										
3	26	Mansfield Town	1-1	Whitfield	11637	1	2	3	6	5				9	10	11	8		4	7								
4	30	LINCOLN CITY	1-1	Whitfield	14840	1	2	3	6	5				9	10	11	8		4	7								
5	Sep 2	ROTHERHAM UNITED	0-0		14687	1	2	3	6	5		11		9	10		8		4	7								
6	6	OLDHAM ATHLETIC	1-0	Whitfield	7994	1	2	3		5		11		9	10		8		4	7	6							
7	9	Barrow	0-1		10004	1	2	3		5		11		9	10		8		4	7	6							
8	12	Oldham Athletic	4-3	Gorin 2, Whitfield, Mosby	11980	1	2	3		5	6	11	7	9	10		8		4									
9	16	YORK CITY	0-1		12101	1	2	3		5	6	11	7	9	10		8		4									
10	23	Carlisle United	1-3	Gorin	11167	1	4	3	6	5		11		10	9		8		7				2					
11	30	ACCRINGTON STANLEY	3-0	Gorin 3	7861	1	2	3	6	5		7		10	9		8		4				11					
12	Oct 7	Gateshead	0-1		11167	1	2	3	6	5		7		10	9		8		4				11					
13	14	CREWE ALEXANDRA	1-1	Gorin	11307	1	2	3	6	5		7		10	9		8		4				11					
14	21	Halifax Town	3-3	Mulholland, Cumner, Rees	9512	1	2	3	6	5				10	9		8		4				11	7				
15	28	HARTLEPOOLS UNITED	0-0		10657	1	2	3	6	5				10	9		8		4				11	7				
16	Nov 4	Darlington	2-3	Gorin, Barker (p)	5253	1	2	3	6	5		11		10	9		8		4					7				
17	18	New Brighton	2-1	Gorin 2	3250		2	3	4		6	7	10	9			8	5					11	1				
18	Dec 2	Rochdale	0-2		5336	1	2	3	4		6	7	10	9			8	5					11					
19	9	CHESTER	2-0	Mosby, Boyes	7089	1	2	3	6	5		7	10	9			8		4				11					
20	16	Shrewsbury Town	1-3	Gorin	7368	1	2	3	6	5		7	10	9			8		4				11					
21	23	MANSFIELD TOWN	0-0		7459	1	2	3	6	5		7	10	9			8		4				11					
22	25	WREXHAM	2-0	Cumner, Own goal (Turney)	8933	1	2	3	6	5		7	10	9			8		4				11					
23	26	Wrexham	1-3	Mosby	9652	1	2	3	6	5		7	10	9			8		4				11					
24	30	Rotherham United	1-4	Cumner	10169	1		3	6	5		7	10	9			8		4		2		11					
25	Jan 6	BRADFORD PARK AVE.	1-1	James (og)	6760	1		2	6	5			8	9		10			4		3		11	7				
26	13	BARROW	1-0	Boyes	7850	1	2	3	6	5		7	8	9		10			4				11					
27	20	York City	0-0		7159	1	2	3	6	5		7	8			10		9	4				11					
28	27	Bradford Park Avenue	2-2	Clelland 2	10246	1	2	3		5		7	8			10		9	4	6			11					
29	Feb 3	CARLISLE UNITED	1-1	Clelland	9247	1	2	3		5		7	8		10			9	4		6		11					
30	10	TRANMERE ROVERS	1-1	Payne	10495	1	2	3	6	5		7	8		10			9	4				11					
31	17	Accrington Stanley	0-0		3433	1	2	3	6	5		7	8			10		9	4				11					
32	24	GATESHEAD	2-1	Cumner, Whitfield	9688	1	2	3	6	5		7				10	8	9	4				11					
33	Mar 3	Crewe Alexandra	0-2		6390	1	2	3	6	5		7				10	8	9	4				11					
34	10	HALIFAX TOWN	2-2	Mosby, Cumner	8447	1	2	3	6	5		11		9			8		4				10	7				
35	17	Hartlepools United	2-4	Comley, Whitfield	5365	1	2	3		5	6	7	8				9		4				11			10		
36	23	Southport	2-2	Comley, Clelland	8206	1	2	3	6	5		7	8					9	4				11			10		
37	24	DARLINGTON	2-0	Clelland, Mosby	8888	1	2	3	6	5		7	8					9	4				11			10		
38	26	SOUTHPORT	0-0		5083	1	2	3	6	5		7	8				9		4				11			10		
39	31	Stockport County	2-1	Cumner, Clelland	6401	1	2	3	6	5		7	8					9	4				11			10		
40	Apr 7	NEW BRIGHTON	6-0	Clelland 2, Comley 2, Payne, Cumner(p)	8588		2	3	6	5		7	8					9	4				11		1	10		
41	14	Bradford City	0-2		13001		2	3	6	5		7	8					9	4				10		1	11		
42	18	BRADFORD CITY	0-0		10287	1		3	6	5		7	8						4		2		11			10	9	
43	21	ROCHDALE	3-0	Cumner 2, Comley	9209	1		3	6	5		7	8						4		2		11			10	9	
44	28	Chester	1-4	Cumner	3778	1	2	3	6	5		7			8				4				11			10		
45	30	STOCKPORT COUNTY	3-0	Mosby, Hubbard, White	9175		2	3	6	5		7					9		4		8		11			10		
46	May 5	Tranmere Rovers	0-1		6990		2	3	6	5								9	4				11			10		8
		Apps				41	42	46	39	44	7	37	40	26	18	13	16	16	42	5	9	3	35	6	5	12	3	1
		Goals					1					6	2	12	1	2	6	8	1		1		10	1		5		

Two own goals

F.A. Cup

#	Date	Opponent	Score	Att																							
Q4	Nov 11	Hereford United	0-1	10527		2	3	4	5	6	11	10	9	8									7	1				

		P	W	D	L	F	A	W	D	L	F	A	Pts
1	Rotherham United	46	16	3	4	55	15	15	6	2	48	25	71
2	Mansfield Town	46	17	6	0	54	19	9	6	8	24	29	64
3	Carlisle United	46	18	4	1	44	17	7	8	8	35	33	62
4	Tranmere Rovers	46	15	5	3	51	26	9	6	8	32	36	59
5	Lincoln City	46	18	1	4	62	23	7	7	9	27	35	58
6	Bradford Park Ave.	46	15	3	5	46	23	8	5	10	44	49	54
7	Bradford City	46	13	4	6	55	30	8	6	9	35	33	52
8	Gateshead	46	17	1	5	60	21	4	7	12	24	41	50
9	Crewe Alexandra	46	11	5	7	38	26	8	5	10	23	34	48
10	Stockport County	46	15	3	5	45	26	5	5	13	18	37	48
11	Rochdale	46	11	6	6	38	18	6	5	12	31	44	45
12	SCUNTHORPE UNITED	46	10	12	1	32	9	3	6	14	26	48	44
13	Chester	46	11	6	6	42	30	6	3	14	20	34	43
14	Wrexham	46	12	6	5	37	28	3	6	14	18	43	42
15	Oldham Athletic	46	10	5	8	47	36	6	3	14	26	37	40
16	Hartlepools United	46	14	5	4	55	26	2	2	19	9	40	39
17	York City	46	7	12	4	37	24	5	3	15	29	53	39
18	Darlington	46	10	8	5	35	29	3	5	15	24	48	39
19	Barrow	46	12	3	8	38	27	4	3	16	13	49	38
20	Shrewsbury Town	46	11	3	9	28	30	4	4	15	15	44	37
21	Southport	46	9	4	10	29	25	4	6	13	27	47	36
22	Halifax Town	46	11	6	6	36	24	0	6	17	14	45	34
23	Accrington Stanley	46	10	4	9	28	29	1	6	16	14	72	32
24	New Brighton	46	7	6	10	22	32	4	2	17	18	58	30

SEASON 1950-51
Standing: Barker, Brownsword, Allen, Thompson, Taylor, McCormick
Seated: Mosby, Payne, Gorin, Rees, Boyes

SEASON 1951-52
Standing: Corkhill (Manager), Hubbard, unknown, Brownsword, Barker, Thompson, Taylor, Sharpe, Johnson (Trainer)
Seated: five players unknown.

1951/52 14th in Division 3(N)

Player columns (left to right): Thompson GH, Barker Jeff, Brownsword NJ, Stirland CJ, Taylor RE, Allen W, Mosby H, Hubbard J, Powell R, Hall A, Cumner RH, McLaren R, Gray G, Wallace G, Babes J, Platts P, Malan NF, Lockwood E, Sharpe LT, Rudd JJ, White R, Whitfield J, Ottewell S

#	Date	Opponent	Score	Scorers	Att.
1	Aug 18	BRADFORD CITY	1-0	Cumner	10315
2	22	Chester	1-3	Hall	7045
3	25	Hartlepools United	1-3	Powell	9028
4	30	CHESTER	2-2	Cumner 2	6042
5	Sep 1	OLDHAM ATHLETIC	2-2	Cumner, Wallace	10389
6	6	LINCOLN CITY	1-3	Allen	12967
7	8	Darlington	3-2	Cumner, Platts, Wallace	6169
8	12	Lincoln City	1-4	Platts	14220
9	15	GATESHEAD	1-1	Hall	8539
10	22	Crewe Alexandra	2-2	Hall, Gray	5650
11	29	SOUTHPORT	1-1	Gray	9297
12	Oct 6	Wrexham	2-1	Powell 2	8172
13	13	CHESTERFIELD	1-1	Powell	9833
14	20	Bradford Park Avenue	2-2	Wallace 2	11203
15	27	HALIFAX TOWN	2-1	Wallace, Powell	8729
16	Nov 3	Mansfield Town	1-4	Mosby	10300
17	10	ROCHDALE	3-1	Powell, Cumner, Taylor (p)	8374
18	17	Accrington Stanley	2-2	Martin(og), Powell	6381
19	Dec 1	Stockport County	1-1	Wallace	10398
20	8	WORKINGTON	3-1	Mosby, Rudd, Powell	7113
21	22	HARTLEPOOLS UNITED	2-0	Powell, Cumner	7320
22	25	Grimsby Town	2-3	Powell 2	19351
23	26	GRIMSBY TOWN	1-3	Powell	15734
24	29	Oldham Athletic	0-2		16332
25	Jan 5	DARLINGTON	5-2	Hall 2, Powell, Mosby, Rudd	7223
26	17	YORK CITY	1-1	Rudd	4046
27	19	Gateshead	1-2	Cumner	5586
28	26	CREWE ALEXANDRA	2-0	Cumner, Powell	6404
29	Feb 9	Southport	1-5	Gray	4592
30	16	WREXHAM	0-0		6924
31	23	Barrow	1-2	Hubbard	7062
32	Mar 1	Chesterfield	0-3		10307
33	8	BRADFORD PARK AVE.	0-0		8445
34	15	Halifax Town	1-2	Whitfield	8418
35	22	MANSFIELD TOWN	4-1	Mosby, Cumner, Ottewell, Rudd	7352
36	26	Bradford City	0-1		3825
37	29	Rochdale	2-1	Ottewell, Wallace	1226
38	Apr 5	ACCRINGTON STANLEY	3-1	Cumner, Whitfield, Ottewell	4801
39	11	Tranmere Rovers	1-3	Ottewell	9075
40	12	Carlisle United	0-3		6981
41	14	TRANMERE ROVERS	2-0	Ottewell, Wallace	8066
42	19	Stockport County	1-1	Ottewell	8305
43	24	CARLISLE UNITED	1-1	Ottewell	7453
44	26	Workington	0-0		5133
45	28	York City	1-0	Ottewell	7827
46	May 1	BARROW	0-0		7103

Appearances and Goals

	Thompson GH	Barker Jeff	Brownsword NJ	Stirland CJ	Taylor RE	Allen W	Mosby H	Hubbard J	Powell R	Hall A	Cumner RH	McLaren R	Gray G	Wallace G	Babes J	Platts P	Malan NF	Lockwood E	Sharpe LT	Rudd JJ	White R	Whitfield J	Ottewell S
Apps	36	31	46	17	28	25	27	36	31	15	44	6	9	29	6	2	10	1	28	32	19	14	14
Goals					1	1	4	1	14	5	11		3	8		2				4		2	8

One own goal

F.A. Cup

	Date	Opponent	Score	Scorers	Att.
R1	Nov 24	BILLINGHAM SYNTH.	5-0	Wallace 2, Powell 2, Hubbard	9861
R2	Dec 15	Millwall	0-0		22702
rep	20	MILLWALL	3-0	Powell 2, Rudd	13580
R3	Jan 12	TOTTENHAM HOTSPUR	0-3		22652

Final Division 3(N) table

		P	W	D	L	F	A	W	D	L	F	A	Pts
1	Lincoln City	46	19	2	2	80	23	11	7	5	41	29	69
2	Grimsby Town	46	19	2	2	59	14	10	6	7	37	31	66
3	Stockport County	46	12	9	2	47	17	11	4	8	27	23	59
4	Oldham Athletic	46	19	2	2	65	22	5	7	11	25	39	57
5	Gateshead	46	14	7	2	41	17	7	4	12	25	32	53
6	Mansfield Town	46	17	3	3	50	23	5	5	13	23	37	52
7	Carlisle United	46	10	7	6	31	24	9	6	8	31	33	51
8	Bradford Park Ave.	46	13	6	4	51	28	6	6	11	23	36	50
9	Hartlepools United	46	17	3	3	47	19	4	5	14	24	46	50
10	York City	46	16	4	3	53	19	2	9	12	20	33	49
11	Tranmere Rovers	46	17	2	4	59	29	4	4	15	17	42	48
12	Barrow	46	15	5	3	33	19	4	7	12	24	42	46
13	Chesterfield	46	15	7	1	47	16	2	4	17	18	50	45
14	SCUNTHORPE UNITED	46	10	11	2	39	23	4	5	14	26	51	44
15	Bradford City	46	12	5	6	40	32	4	5	14	21	36	42
16	Crewe Alexandra	46	12	6	5	42	28	5	2	16	21	54	42
17	Southport	46	12	6	5	36	22	3	5	15	17	49	41
18	Wrexham	46	14	5	4	41	22	1	4	18	22	51	39
19	Chester	46	13	4	6	46	30	2	5	16	26	55	39
20	Halifax Town	46	11	4	8	31	23	3	3	17	30	74	35
21	Rochdale	46	10	5	8	32	34	1	8	14	15	45	35
22	Accrington Stanley	46	6	8	9	30	34	4	4	15	31	58	32
23	Darlington	46	10	5	8	39	34	1	4	18	25	69	31
24	Workington	46	8	4	11	33	34	3	3	17	17	57	29

1952/53 15th in Division 3(N)

#	Mon	Date	Opponent	Score	Scorers	Att	Thompson GH	Cox S	Brownsword NJ	McGill A	White R	Sharpe LT	Mosby H	Haigh I	Mynard LD	Cumner RH	Daley AJ	Hubbard J	Broadley L	Ottewell S	Taylor RE	Whitfield J	Wallace G	Bushby A	Malan NF	Taylor R	Brown GA	Lockwood E	Charlesworth T
1	Aug	23	Barrow	1-2	Mynard	6254	1	2	3	4	5	6	7	8	9	10	11												
2		28	GRIMSBY TOWN	0-1		18974	1		3	4	5	6		8	7	10	11	2	9										
3		30	Stockport County	2-2	Broadley, Ottewell	8871	1		3	4	5	6		8	7		11	2	9	10									
4	Sep	3	Grimsby Town	0-1		22213	1		3	4				8			11	2	9	10	5	6							
5		6	Bradford City	0-0		11525	1		3	4				8			11	2	9	10	5	6	7						
6		11	CHESTER	1-1	Broadley	6695	1		3	4			7	8			11	2	9		5	6							
7		13	ROCHDALE	5-1	McGill, Mynard, Whitfield, Mosby, Haigh	7381	1		3	4		6	7	8	9		11	2			5	10							
8		17	Chester	1-1	Haigh	5004	1		3	4		6	7	8	9		11	2			5	10							
9		20	Darlington	0-1		5850	1		3	4		6	7	8	9	10	11	2			5								
10		25	MANSFIELD TOWN	0-1		7252	1		3	4		6	7	8	9		11	2			5	10							
11		27	GATESHEAD	0-0		6940	1		3	4			7	8	9		11	2			5	10		6					
12	Oct	2	SOUTHPORT	3-0	Daley, Haigh, Whitfield	5105	1		3	4			7	8		11	10	2			5	9		6					
13		4	Hartlepools United	1-1	Daley	9060	1		3	4			7	8		11	10	2			5	9		6					
14		11	YORK CITY	2-0	Daley, Brownsword (p)	7849	1		3	4				8		11	7	2		10	5	9		6					
15		18	Tranmere Rovers	1-0	Mynard	9156	1		3	4				8		11	7	2		10	5	9		6					
16		25	CHESTERFIELD	1-0	Daley	8319			3	4				8		11	7	2		10	5	9		6	1				
17	Nov	1	Workington	3-0	Whitfield, Haigh, McGill	7348			3	4	9			8		11	7	2			5	10		6	1				
18		8	ACCRINGTON STANLEY	5-2	White 2, Daley 2, Brownsword (p)	7334			3	4	9			8		11	7	2			5	10		6	1				
19		15	Halifax Town	1-2	White	7247			3	4	9			8		11	7	2			5	10		6	1				
20		29	Oldham Athletic	1-0	Daley	14344			3	4	9			8	11		7	2			5	10		6	1				
21	Dec	13	Wrexham	3-2	Hubbard, Haigh, Brownsword (p)	9266			3	4	9			8	11		7	2			5	10		6	1				
22		20	BARROW	1-2	White	5434		3		4	9			8	11		7	2			5	10		6	1				
23		25	Carlisle United	0-8		9489		2	3	4	9			8	11		7				5	10		6	1				
24		27	CARLISLE UNITED	1-2	White	7325			3	4	9		7	8		11		2			5	10		6	1				
25	Jan	1	Southport	3-2	Haigh, Mosby, Ottewell	4727			3	4			7	8			11	2		9	5	10		6	1				
26		3	Stockport County	1-1	Whitfield	7999			3	4			7	8			11	2		9	5	10		6	1				
27		17	BRADFORD CITY	4-0	Haigh 2, Whitfield, Daley	7356			3	4			7	8			11	2		9	5	10		6	1				
28		24	Rochdale	2-2	Ottewell, Brownsword (p)	5050			3	4			7	8			11	2		9	5	10		6	1				
29		31	PORT VALE	1-2	Mosby	9684			3	4			7	8			11	2		9	5	10		6	1				
30	Feb	7	DARLINGTON	2-0	Haigh, Whitfield	5938			3	4			7	8		11		2		9	5	10		6	1				
31		18	Gateshead	1-1	Ottewell	3980			3	4			7	8		11		2		9	5	10		6	1				
32		21	HARTLEPOOLS UNITED	0-0		7076			3	4			7	8		11		2		9	5	10		6	1				
33		28	York City	2-0	Haigh, Brownsword (p)	7532			3	4			7	8		10	11	2			5	9		6	1				
34	Mar	7	TRANMERE ROVERS	2-0	Haigh, Daley	6796			3	4			7	8		10	11	2			5	9		6	1				
35		14	Chesterfield	1-1	Whitfield	8340			3	4			7	8		10	11	2			5	9		6	1				
36		16	Port Vale	0-4		11371			3	4			7	8		11		2		9	5	10		6	1				
37		21	WORKINGTON	2-1	Bushby 2	6529			3	4				8		10	11	2			5	9		6	1	7			
38		26	BRADFORD PARK AVE.	1-2	Haigh	6117			3	4				8	11	10		2			5	9		6	1	7			
39		28	Accrington Stanley	1-2	Brown	2903				4				8	11	10		2			5	9		6	1	7	3		
40	Apr	3	Crewe Alexandra	0-2		9379				4				8	11	10		2			5	9		6	1	7	3		
41		4	HALIFAX TOWN	1-1	Whitfield	6451				4				8	11			2			5	9	10	6	1		7	3	
42		6	CREWE ALEXANDRA	2-0	Haigh, Brown	5989				4				8	11			2			5	9	10	6	1		7	3	
43		11	Mansfield Town	0-1		7314		11		4				8				2			5	9	10	6			7	3	1
44		18	OLDHAM ATHLETIC	1-1	Bushby	10399				4		6		8				2			5	9		10	1		7	3	
45		25	Bradford Park Avenue	1-1	Brown	8571				4		6		8	9	11		2			5			10	1		7	3	
46		27	WREXHAM	1-2	Brown	4250				4		6		8	9	11		2			5			10	1		7	3	
					Apps		15	3	38	46	11	10	24	46	18	23	35	44	5	16	43	40	4	36	27	2	10	8	2
					Goals				5	2	5		3	13	3		9	1	2	4		8		3			4		

F.A. Cup

Rnd	Mon	Date	Opponent	Score	Scorers	Att	Brownsword NJ	McGill A	White R	Mosby H	Haigh I	Cumner RH	Daley AJ	Hubbard J	Ottewell S	Taylor RE	Whitfield J	Bushby A	Malan NF
R1	Nov	22	CARLISLE UNITED	1-0	Whitfield	9028	3	4	9		8	11	7	2		5	10	6	1
R2	Dec	6	Hereford United	0-0		8765	3	4	9		8	11	7	2		5	10	6	1
rep		11	HEREFORD UNITED	2-1	White, Whitfield	10631	3	4	9		8	11	7	2		5	10	6	1
R3	Jan	10	Sunderland	1-1	McGill	56507	3	4		7	8		11	2	9	5	10	6	1
rep		15	SUNDERLAND	1-2	Daley	21624	3	4		7	8		11	2	9	5	10	6	1

		P	W	D	L	F	A	W	D	L	F	A	Pts
1	Oldham Athletic	46	15	4	4	48	21	7	11	5	29	24	59
2	Port Vale	46	13	9	1	41	10	7	9	7	26	25	58
3	Wrexham	46	18	3	2	59	24	6	5	12	27	42	56
4	York City	46	14	5	4	35	16	6	8	9	25	29	53
5	Grimsby Town	46	15	5	3	47	19	6	5	12	28	40	52
6	Southport	46	16	4	3	42	18	4	7	12	21	42	51
7	Bradford Park Ave.	46	10	8	5	37	23	9	4	10	38	38	50
8	Gateshead	46	13	6	4	51	24	4	9	10	25	36	49
9	Carlisle United	46	13	7	3	57	24	5	6	12	25	44	49
10	Crewe Alexandra	46	13	5	5	46	28	7	3	13	24	40	48
11	Stockport County	46	13	8	2	61	26	4	5	14	21	43	47
12	Tranmere Rovers	46	16	4	3	45	16	5	1	17	20	47	47
13	Chesterfield	46	13	6	4	40	23	5	5	13	25	40	47
14	Halifax Town	46	13	5	5	47	31	3	10	10	21	37	47
15	SCUNTHORPE UNITED	46	10	6	7	38	21	6	8	9	24	35	46
16	Bradford City	46	14	7	2	54	29	0	11	12	21	51	46
17	Hartlepools United	46	14	6	3	39	16	2	8	13	18	45	46
18	Mansfield Town	46	11	9	3	34	25	5	5	13	21	37	46
19	Barrow	46	16	6	2	48	20	1	6	16	18	51	44
20	Chester	46	10	7	6	39	27	1	8	14	25	58	37
21	Darlington	46	13	4	6	33	27	1	2	20	25	69	34
22	Rochdale	46	12	5	6	41	27	2	0	21	21	56	33
23	Workington	46	9	5	9	40	33	2	5	16	15	58	32
24	Accrington Stanley	46	7	9	7	25	29	1	2	20	14	60	27

1953/54 3rd in Division 3(N)

#		Date	Opponent	Score	Scorers	Att	Malan NF	Hubbard J	Brownsword NJ	McGill A	Taylor RE	Bushby A	Brown GA	Haigh J	Whitfield J	Gregory JE	Jones JM	Roberts H	Barley PJ	Sharpe LT	White R	Mosby H	Underwood GR	Heward B
1	Aug	22	Grimsby Town	1-0	Gregory	18246	1	2	3	4	5	6	7	8	9	10	11							
2		24	Gateshead	0-0		7864	1	2	3	4	5	6	7	8	9	10	11							
3		29	YORK CITY	3-0	Brown 2, Bushby	7494	1	2	3	4	5	6	7	8	9	10	11							
4	Sep	3	GATESHEAD	1-1	Brownsword (p)	11288	1	2	3	4	5	6	7	8	9	10	11							
5		5	Southport	3-4	Brown, Haigh, Whitfield	5640	1	2	3	4	5	6	7	8	9	10	11							
6		7	Workington	3-1	Whitfield 2, Haigh	7367	1	2	3	4	5	6	7	8	9		11	10						
7		12	CHESTER	1-0	Whitfield	10210	1	2	3	4	5	6	7	8	9		11	10						
8		17	WORKINGTON	4-1	Brown, Taylor, Roberts, Jones	10013	1	2	3	4	5	6	7	8	9		11	10						
9		19	Crewe Alexandra	1-1	Haigh	8486	1	2	3	4	5	6	7	8	9		11	10						
10		21	Hartlepools United	2-3	McGill, Jones	5924	1	2	3	4	5	6	7	8	9		11	10						
11		26	PORT VALE	0-2		12630	1	2	3	4	5	6	7	8	9		11	10						
12	Oct	1	HARTLEPOOLS UNITED	0-0		9102		2	3			6	7	8	9		11	10	1		4	5		
13		3	Bradford Park Avenue	2-2	Jones, Gregory	13686		2	3			6		8	9	10	11		1	7	4	5		
14		10	Rochdale	1-1	Mosby	7873		2	3			6		8	9	10	11		1	7	4	5		
15		17	WREXHAM	3-1	Whitfield 2, Gregory	8402		2	3			6		8	9	10	11		1	7	4	5		
16		24	Mansfield Town	1-2	Brownsword (p)	8539		2	3			6		8	9	10	11		1	7	4	5		
17		31	BARROW	3-2	Jones 2, Sharpe	6982	1	2	3			6		8	9	10	11			7	4	5		
18	Nov	7	Bradford City	3-1	Jones, Whitfield, Brownsword (p)	8039	1	2	3			6		8	9	10	11			7	4	5		
19		14	CHESTERFIELD	2-1	Whitfield, Brownsword (p)	8247	1	2	3			6		8	9	10	11			7	4	5		
20		28	HALIFAX TOWN	3-2	Jones, Brownsword (p), Bushby	8151	1	2	3			6		8	9	10	11			7	4	5		
21	Dec	5	Carlisle United	1-5	Gregory	6550	1	2	3			6		8	9	10	11			7	4	5		
22		19	GRIMSBY TOWN	2-1	Whitfield, Gregory	9985	1	2	3			6		8	9	10	11			7	4	5		
23		25	DARLINGTON	1-1	Brownsword (p)	8035	1	2	3			6		8	9	10	11			7	4	5		
24		26	Darlington	0-3		4518	1	2	3			6	7	8	9	10	11				4	5		
25	Jan	1	Accrington Stanley	1-0	Gregory	8729	1		3	4	5	6	7	8	9	10	11						2	
26		2	York City	0-2		5226	1		3	4		6	7	8	9	10	11					5	2	
27		16	SOUTHPORT	1-1	Brownsword (p)	6870	1	2	3	4		6		8	9	10	11			7		5		
28		23	Chester	0-0		5186	1	2	3	4		6		8	9	10	11			7		5		
29	Feb	6	CREWE ALEXANDRA	2-2	Mosby, Haigh	7914	1	2	3	4		6		8	9	10	11			7		5		
30		13	Port Vale	0-0		17240	1	2	3			6		8	9	10	11			7	4	5		
31		20	BRADFORD PARK AVE.	4-1	Brown 2, Mosby, Wright (og)	8097	1	2	3	4		6	9	8		10	11			7		5		
32		27	ROCHDALE	1-1	Brown	7264	1	2	3	4		6	9	8		10	11			7		5		
33	Mar	6	Wrexham	1-3	Gregory	6522	1	2	3	4		6	9	8		10	11			7		5		
34		10	Stockport County	1-1	Brownsword (p)	2939	1	2	3	4	5	6	7	8	9	10						11		
35		13	MANSFIELD TOWN	2-2	Gregory, Haigh	6516	1	2	3	4		6	9	8		10	11			7		5		
36		18	ACCRINGTON STANLEY	1-2	McGill	5187	1	2	3	4	5	6		8	9	10	11			7				
37		20	Barrow	2-1	Gregory 2	4486	1	2	3	4				8	9	10	11			7		5		6
38		27	BRADFORD CITY	2-1	Haigh, Mosby	7035	1	2	3			6		8	9	10	11			7		5		
39	Apr	1	STOCKPORT COUNTY	2-0	Mosby, Jones	5849	1	2	3	4	5	6		8	9	10	11			7				
40		3	Chesterfield	0-1		5769	1	2	3	4		6	9	8		10	11			7		5		
41		10	TRANMERE ROVERS	3-1	Gregory 3	6180	1		3	4		6	9	8		10	11			7		5	2	
42		16	BARNSLEY	6-0	Gregory 2, Haigh, Brown, Jones, Thomas (og)	9975	1	6	3	4			9	8		10	11	7				5	2	
43		17	Halifax Town	3-0	Brown 2, Haigh	4674	1	6	3	4			9	8		10	11	7				5	2	
44		19	Barnsley	1-0	Haigh	10685	1	6	3	4			9	8		10	11					5	2	
45		24	CARLISLE UNITED	2-1	Hubbard, Gregory	7722	1	6	3	4			9	8		10	11	7				5	2	
46		27	Tranmere Rovers	1-1	Jones	4826	1	6	3	4			9	8		10	11					5	2	
				Apps			41	44	46	28	16	40	30	43	38	39	44	13	5	14	30	26	8	1
				Goals				1	8	2	1	2	10	10	9	16	9	1		1		5		

Two own goals

F.A. Cup

		Date	Opponent	Score	Scorers	Att	Malan NF	Hubbard J	Brownsword NJ	McGill A	Bushby A	Brown GA	Haigh J	Whitfield J	Gregory JE	Jones JM	Sharpe LT	White R	Mosby H
R1	Nov	21	BOSTON UNITED	9-0	Haigh 3, Whitfield 2, Jones 2, Mosby, Gregory	8894	1	2	3		6		8	9	10	11	7	4	5
R2	Dec	12	BOURNEMOUTH	1-0	Brown	12005	1	2	3		6	7	8	9	10	11		4	5
R3	Jan	9	Wrexham	3-3	Bushby 2, Mosby	17287	1	2	3	4	6		8	9	10	11	7		5
rep		14	WREXHAM	3-1	Whitfield, Gregory, Brownsword (p)	12862	1	2	3	4	6		8	9	10	11	7		5
R4		30	PORTSMOUTH	1-1	Jones	23735	1	2	3	4	6		8	9	10	11	7		5
rep	Feb	3	Portsmouth	2-2	Jones 2	30247	1	2	3	4	6		8	9	10	11	7		5
rep2		8	Portsmouth	0-4		24556	1	2	3	4	6		8	9	10	11	7		5

R4 replay a.e.t. R4 replay 2 at Highbury.

		P	W	D	L	F	A	W	D	L	F	A	Pts
1	Port Vale	46	16	7	0	48	5	10	10	3	26	16	69
2	Barnsley	46	16	3	4	54	24	8	7	8	23	33	58
3	SCUNTHORPE UNITED	46	14	7	2	49	24	7	8	8	28	32	57
4	Gateshead	46	15	4	4	49	22	6	9	8	25	33	55
5	Bradford City	46	15	6	2	40	14	7	3	13	20	41	53
6	Chesterfield	46	13	6	4	41	19	6	8	9	35	45	52
7	Mansfield Town	46	15	5	3	59	22	5	6	12	29	45	51
8	Wrexham	46	16	4	3	59	19	5	5	13	22	49	51
9	Bradford Park Ave.	46	13	6	4	57	31	5	8	10	20	37	50
10	Stockport County	46	14	6	3	57	20	4	5	14	20	47	47
11	Southport	46	12	5	6	41	26	5	7	11	22	34	46
12	Barrow	46	12	4	7	46	26	4	5	14	26	45	44
13	Carlisle United	46	10	8	5	53	27	4	7	12	30	44	43
14	Tranmere Rovers	46	11	4	8	40	34	7	3	13	19	36	43
15	Accrington Stanley	46	12	7	4	41	22	4	3	16	25	52	42
16	Crewe Alexandra	46	12	6	5	36	26	5	5	13	19	41	41
17	Grimsby Town	46	14	5	4	31	15	2	4	17	20	62	41
18	Hartlepools United	46	10	8	5	40	26	3	6	14	19	44	40
19	Rochdale	46	12	5	6	40	20	3	5	15	19	57	40
20	Workington	46	10	9	4	36	22	3	5	15	23	58	40
21	Darlington	46	11	3	9	31	27	1	11	11	19	44	38
22	York City	46	8	7	8	39	32	4	6	13	25	54	37
23	Halifax Town	46	9	6	8	26	21	3	4	16	18	52	34
24	Chester	46	10	7	6	39	22	1	3	19	9	45	32

SEASON 1952-53
Standing: Hubbard, Brownsword, McGill, Malan, Taylor, Bushby, Johnson (Trainer)
Seated: Daley, Haigh, White, Whitfield, Mosby

SEASON 1953-54
Standing: Hubbard, McGill, White, Malan, Bushby, Brownsword
Seated: Mosby, Haig, Brown, Gregory, Jones

1954/55 — 3rd in Division 3(N)

No	Date		Opponent	Score	Scorers	Att	Malan NF	Hubbard J	Brownsword NJ	McGill A	White R	Bushby A	Mosby H	Haigh J	Brown GA	Gregory JE	Jones JM	Lamb HT	Roberts H	Turner PS	Whitfield J	Lloyd WS	Sharpe LT	Barrett J	Marshall PW	Fawcett B
1	Aug	21	HALIFAX TOWN	2-2	Haigh 2	10388	1	2	3	4	5	6	7	8	9	10	11									
2		24	Grimsby Town	4-1	Brown 2, McGill, Gregory	19736	1	6	3	4	5		7	8	9	10	11	2								
3		28	York City	3-2	Gregory 3	12911	1	6	3	4	5		7	8	9	10	11	2								
4	Sep	2	GRIMSBY TOWN	1-0	Jones	15547	1	6	3	4	5		7	8	9	10	11	2								
5		4	SOUTHPORT	2-0	Brown 2	9406	1	6	3	4	5		7	8	9	10	11	2								
6		9	BARNSLEY	1-0	Gregory	12158	1	6	3	4	5		7	8	9	10	11	2								
7		11	Barrow	3-1	Gregory, Brown, Haigh	6307	1	6	3	4	5		7	8	9	10	11	2								
8		15	Barnsley	0-1		16431	1	6	3	4	5		7	8	9	10	11	2								
9		18	WORKINGTON	1-1	Haigh	9403	1	6	3	4	5		7	8	9	10	11	2								
10		22	Wrexham	1-0	Gregory	8139	1	6	3	4	5		7	8	9	10		2		11						
11		25	Mansfield Town	1-2	McGill (p)	11809	1	6	3	4	5		7	8	9	10		2		11						
12		30	WREXHAM	1-0	Gregory	8810	1		3	4	5	6	7	8	9	10	11	2								
13	Oct	2	ACCRINGTON STANLEY	4-0	Brown 2, Turner, Haigh	11370	1	2		4	5	6		8	9	10	11		3	7						
14		9	Bradford Park Avenue	0-0		14402	1	2	3	4	5	6		8	9	10	11				7					
15		16	ROCHDALE	2-2	Brown 2	10331	1	2	3	4	5	6		8	9	10	11				7					
16		23	Tranmere Rovers	2-1	Brown, Haigh	5493	1	2	3	4	5	6	7	8	9	10	11									
17		30	STOCKPORT COUNTY	3-0	Brown, Bushby, Brownsword (p)	9956	1	2	3	4	5	6	7	8	9	10	11									
18	Nov	6	Hartlepools United	2-4	Gregory 2	7621	1	2	3	4	5	6	7	8	9	10	11									
19		13	GATESHEAD	0-2		9159	1	2	3	4	5	6		8	9	10	11					7				
20		27	CHESTERFIELD	2-1	Brown, Brownsword (p)	8739	1	2	3	4	5	6	7	8	9	10	11									
21	Dec	4	Crewe Alexandra	1-1	Gregory	3651	1	2	3	4	5	6	7	8	9	10	11									
22		18	Halifax Town	1-3	McGill	10981	1	2	3	4	5	6	7	8	9	10	11									
23		25	Bradford City	4-2	Brown 2, Gregory, Mosby	12587	1	2	3		5	6	7	8	9	10	11						4			
24		27	BRADFORD CITY	1-0	Brown	11016	1	2	3		5	6	7	8	9	10	11						4			
25	Jan	1	YORK CITY	1-2	Brownsword (p)	10593	1	2	3		5	6	7	8	9	10	11							4		
26		8	Chester	4-2	Whitfield 3, Brown	4083	1	2	3	4	5	6	7	8	9		11				10					
27		22	BARROW	3-0	Whitfield 2, Mosby	7348		2	3	4	5	6	7		9	10	11				8				1	
28		29	CHESTER	1-1	Brown	8328		2	3	4	5	6	7	8	9		11				10				1	
29	Feb		Workington	1-1	Gregory	8601		2	3	4	5	6	7		9	10	11				8				1	
30		12	MANSFIELD TOWN	2-0	Jones, Gregory	7132		2	3	4	5	6	7		9	10	11				8				1	
31		19	Accrington Stanley	1-2	Turner	10763		2	3	4	5	6			9	10	11		8	7					1	
32	Mar	5	Rochdale	0-2		6078		2	3	4	5	6			9	10	11		8						1	7
33		12	TRANMERE ROVERS	1-2	Gregory	7817	1	2	3	4	5	6			9	10	11		8	7						
34		19	Stockport County	2-4	Gregory, Brown	7005	1	6	3	4	5		7	8	9	10	11	2								
35		26	HARTLEPOOLS UNITED	5-1	Hubbard 4, Gregory	4155	1	8	3	4	5	6	7		9	10	11	2								
36	Apr	2	Gateshead	1-0	Brown	4217	1	8	3	4	5	6	7		9	10	11	2								
37		8	Oldham Athletic	1-1	Hubbard	9396	1	8	3	4	5	6	7		9	10	11	2								
38		9	DARLINGTON	1-0	McGill	8268	1	8	3	4	5	6	7		9	10	11	2								
39		11	OLDHAM ATHLETIC	6-1	Brown 2, Hubbard 2, Gregory 2	8471	1	8	3	4	5	6	7		9	10	11	2								
40		16	Chesterfield	0-2		7314	1	8	3	4	5	6	7		9	10	11	2								
41		18	Carlisle United	1-1	Gregory	7263	1	8	3	4	5	6	7		9	10	11	2								
42		23	CREWE ALEXANDRA	3-1	Gregory, Brown, McGill	5316	1	8	3	4	5	6			9	10	11	2			7					
43		27	Darlington	1-1	Whitfield	3395	1	8	3	4	5	6			9	10	11	2			7					
44		30	Carlisle United	2-1	Brown, Brownsword (p)	4636	1	2	3	4	5	6	7		9	10	11				8					
45	May	5	BRADFORD PARK AVE.	1-1	Gregory	5136	1	2	3	4	5	6	7		9	10	11				8					
46		7	Southport	1-1	Mosby	2407	1	2	3	4	5	6	7		9	10	11				8					
			Apps				40	45	45	43	46	36	35	28	46	44	44	22	4	5	12	1	2	1	6	1
			Goals					7	4	5		1	3	6	23	22	2			2	6					

F.A. Cup

No	Date		Opponent	Score	Scorers	Att	Malan NF	Hubbard J	Brownsword NJ	McGill A	White R	Bushby A	Mosby H	Haigh J	Brown GA	Gregory JE	Jones JM	Lamb HT	Roberts H	Turner PS	Whitfield J	Lloyd WS	Sharpe LT	Barrett J	Marshall PW	Fawcett B
R1	Nov	20	Horden Colliery	1-0	McGill	5949	1	2	3	4	5		7	8	10	9	11					6				
R2	Dec	11	Coventry City	0-4		21360	1	2	3	4	5	6	7	8	9	10	11									

		P	W	D	L	F	A	W	D	L	F	A	Pts
1	Barnsley	46	18	3	2	51	17	12	2	9	35	29	65
2	Accrington Stanley	46	18	2	3	65	32	7	9	7	31	35	61
3	SCUNTHORPE UNITED	46	14	6	3	45	18	9	6	8	36	35	58
4	York City	46	13	5	5	43	27	11	5	7	49	36	58
5	Hartlepools United	46	16	3	4	39	20	9	2	12	25	29	55
6	Chesterfield	46	17	1	5	54	33	7	5	11	27	37	54
7	Gateshead	46	11	7	5	38	26	9	5	9	27	43	52
8	Workington	46	11	7	5	39	23	7	7	9	29	32	50
9	Stockport County	46	13	4	6	50	27	5	8	10	34	43	48
10	Oldham Athletic	46	14	5	4	47	22	5	5	13	27	46	48
11	Southport	46	10	9	4	28	18	6	7	10	19	26	48
12	Rochdale	46	13	7	3	39	20	4	7	12	30	46	48
13	Mansfield Town	46	14	4	5	40	28	4	5	14	25	43	45
14	Halifax Town	46	9	9	5	41	27	6	4	13	22	40	43
15	Darlington	46	10	7	6	41	28	4	7	12	21	45	42
16	Bradford Park Ave.	46	11	7	5	29	21	4	4	15	27	49	41
17	Barrow	46	12	4	7	39	34	5	2	16	31	55	40
18	Wrexham	46	9	6	8	40	35	4	6	13	25	42	38
19	Tranmere Rovers	46	9	6	8	37	30	4	5	14	18	40	37
20	Carlisle United	46	12	1	10	53	39	3	5	15	25	50	36
21	Bradford City	46	9	5	9	30	26	4	5	14	17	29	36
22	Crewe Alexandra	46	8	10	5	45	35	2	4	17	23	56	34
23	Grimsby Town	46	10	4	9	28	32	3	4	16	19	46	34
24	Chester	46	10	3	10	23	25	2	6	15	21	52	33

SEASON 1954-55
Standing: Barrett, Brownsword, Mosby, Marshall, Bushby, Taylor, Hubbard
Seated: Gregory, Turner, Whitfield, Brown, Haig, Jones, Lamb

SEASON 1955-56
Standing: Barrett, Hubbard, Marshall, White, Brownsword, Sharpe, Hobson (Trainer)
Seated: Davis, Haig, Brown, Gregory, Jones

1955/56   9th in Division 3(N)

Results

#	Date	Opponent	Score	Scorers	Att.
1	Aug 20	Bradford Park Avenue	0-2		12604
2	Aug 22	Mansfield Town	2-3	Haigh, Gregory	9730
3	Aug 27	OLDHAM ATHLETIC	2-1	Haigh, Callaghan	8839
4	Aug 31	MANSFIELD TOWN	3-0	Gregory 2, Plummer (og)	8923
5	Sep 3	Workington	2-1	Callaghan, Gregory	7087
6	Sep 7	WREXHAM	1-1	Brown	9566
7	Sep 10	YORK CITY	1-1	Callaghan	9720
8	Sep 14	Wrexham	1-0	Brownsword (p)	8902
9	Sep 17	Derby County	2-2	Callaghan 2	18237
10	Sep 21	HALIFAX TOWN	1-0	Davies	8434
11	Sep 24	CREWE ALEXANDRA	1-1	Brown	8271
12	Sep 26	Stockport County	2-3	Brown, Jones	4146
13	Oct 1	Hartlepools United	2-0	Gregory, Jones	8170
14	Oct 8	CARLISLE UNITED	4-0	Gregory 2, Davies, Haigh	8623
15	Oct 15	Rochdale	2-3	Brown, Gregory	6110
16	Oct 22	BARROW	2-0	Gregory, Brownsword (p)	7030
17	Oct 29	Accrington Stanley	0-2		7443
18	Nov 5	DARLINGTON	0-1		7642
19	Nov 12	Gateshead	0-1		3765
20	Nov 26	Tranmere Rovers	1-2	Brown	4748
21	Dec 3	CHESTERFIELD	2-0	Jones, Brownsword (p)	7114
22	Dec 17	BRADFORD PARK AVE.	4-2	Brown 3, Gregory	5942
23	Dec 24	Oldham Athletic	1-2	Jones	5852
24	Dec 26	Bradford City	3-4	Gregory 2, Brown	7896
25	Dec 27	BRADFORD CITY	2-0	Haigh, McGill	7978
26	Dec 31	WORKINGTON	3-1	Brown 2, Davies	7446
27	Jan 21	DERBY COUNTY	0-2		10361
28	Feb 4	Crewe Alexandra	2-1	Gregory, Jones	2432
29	Feb 11	HARTLEPOOLS UNITED	5-1	Jones 2, Brown, Bushby, McGill (p)	5614
30	Feb 18	Carlisle United	2-1	Haigh, Gregory	4928
31	Mar 3	Barrow	2-2	Callaghan, Haigh	4001
32	Mar 10	ACCRINGTON STANLEY	2-3	Brown 2	10049
33	Mar 17	Southport	2-2	Brown, Mullen	5610
34	Mar 22	ROCHDALE	1-2	Gregory	4865
35	Mar 24	GATESHEAD	1-1	Brown	4702
36	Mar 30	Grimsby Town	1-0	Brown	23399
37	Mar 31	Darlington	0-1		4797
38	Apr 2	GRIMSBY TOWN	0-1		19067
39	Apr 7	TRANMERE ROVERS	2-1	Brown, Gregory	4443
40	Apr 9	York City	0-0		9045
41	Apr 14	Chesterfield	0-2		5592
42	Apr 18	SOUTHPORT	0-1		4452
43	Apr 21	CHESTER	2-1	Gregory, Haigh	4333
44	Apr 26	STOCKPORT COUNTY	1-5	Gregory	3780
45	Apr 28	Halifax Town	3-0	Haigh, Gregory, Brown	2839
46	May 2	Chester	5-3	Brown 2, Gregory, McGill (p), Bushby	3253

Appearances / Goals (shirt numbers)

Player columns (left to right): Malan NF, Hubbard J, Brownsword NJ, McGill A, White R, Bushby A, Davies JR, Haigh I, Brown GA, Gregory JE, Jones JM, Barrett J, Callaghan R, Marshall PW, Thompson D, Sharpe LT, Benson JR, Lamb HT, Heward B, Parrott JF, Mullen A, Wainwright L

Apps	13	42	45	31	18	28	31	44	40	45	36	16	19	33	3	6	2	14	28	1	9	2
Goals			3	3		2	3	8	21	20	7		6								1	

One own goal

F.A. Cup

Round	Date	Opponent	Score	Scorers	Att.
R1	Nov 19	SHILDON COLLIERY	3-0	Davies, Brown, Gregory	8868
R2	Dec 10	Bishop Auckland	0-0		13500
rep	Dec 15	BISHOP AUCKLAND	2-0	Davies, Hubbard	9923
R3	Jan 7	Rotherham United	1-1	Brown	16144
rep	Jan 12	ROTHERHAM UNITED	4-2	Brown 3, Davies	13262
R4	Jan 28	Liverpool	3-3	Davies 2, Gregory	53393
rep	Feb 6	LIVERPOOL	1-2	Davies	19612

R4 replay a.e.t.

Division 3 (N) Final Table

		P	W	D	L	F	A	W	D	L	F	A	Pts
1	Grimsby Town	46	20	1	2	54	10	11	5	7	22	19	68
2	Derby County	46	18	4	1	67	23	10	3	10	43	32	63
3	Accrington Stanley	46	17	4	2	61	19	8	5	10	31	38	59
4	Hartlepools United	46	18	2	3	47	15	8	3	12	34	45	57
5	Southport	46	12	9	2	39	18	11	2	10	27	35	57
6	Chesterfield	46	18	1	4	61	21	7	3	13	33	45	54
7	Stockport County	46	16	4	3	65	22	5	5	13	25	39	51
8	Bradford City	46	16	5	2	57	25	2	8	13	21	39	49
9	SCUNTHORPE UNITED	46	12	4	7	40	26	8	4	11	35	37	48
10	Workington	46	13	4	6	47	20	6	5	12	28	43	47
11	York City	46	12	4	7	44	24	7	5	11	41	48	47
12	Rochdale	46	13	5	5	46	39	4	8	11	20	45	47
13	Gateshead	46	15	4	4	56	32	2	7	14	21	52	45
14	Wrexham	46	11	5	7	37	28	5	5	13	29	45	42
15	Darlington	46	11	6	6	41	28	5	3	15	19	45	41
16	Tranmere Rovers	46	11	4	8	33	25	5	5	13	26	59	41
17	Chester	46	10	8	5	35	33	3	6	14	17	49	40
18	Mansfield Town	46	13	6	4	59	21	1	5	17	25	60	39
19	Halifax Town	46	10	6	7	40	27	4	5	14	26	49	39
20	Oldham Athletic	46	7	12	4	48	36	3	6	14	28	50	38
21	Carlisle United	46	11	3	9	45	36	4	5	14	26	59	38
22	Barrow	46	11	4	6	44	25	1	3	19	17	58	33
23	Bradford Park Ave.	46	13	4	6	47	38	0	3	20	14	84	33
24	Crewe Alexandra	46	9	4	10	32	35	0	6	17	18	70	28

1956/57 14th in Division 3(N)

#		Date	Opponent	Score	Scorers	Att	Marshall PW	Hubbard J	Brownsword NJ	McGill A	Hussey FM	Bushby A	Whiteside WR	Haigh I	Brown GA	Fletcher D	Jones JM	Gregory JE	Sharpe LT	Luke GB	Heward B	Lewis K	Charlesworth T	Davies JR	Horstead JB	Waldock R	Mullen A	Gleadall E	Hardwick K	Whitnall B
1	Aug	18	DARLINGTON	1-2	Brown	7923		2	3	4	5	6	7	8	9	10	11													
2		21	Southport	2-2	Brown 2	6625		2	3	4	5	6	7	8	9	10	11													
3		25	Barrow	2-1	Brown, Fletcher	8455		2	3	4	5	6		8	9	10	11	7												
4		30	SOUTHPORT	1-0	Brown	7768		2	3	4	5	6		8	9	10	11	7												
5	Sep	1	HULL CITY	1-1	Brown	11004		2	3		5	6		8	9	10	11	7	4											
6		3	Bradford Park Avenue	2-1	Haigh, Gregory	8564		2	3		5	6		8	9	10	11	7	4											
7		8	Workington	2-2	Haigh, Jones	11073		2	3		5	6		8	7	10	11		4	9										
8		13	BRADFORD PARK AVE.	2-2	Brown, Luke	7855		2	3		5	6		8	7	10	11		4	9										
9		15	HALIFAX TOWN	6-1	Luke 2, Jones 2, Fletcher, Brown	7143		2	3		5	6		8	7	10	11		4	9										
10		19	Crewe Alexandra	1-2	Luke	5425		2	3		5	6		8	7	10	11		4	9										
11		22	Rochdale	0-3		6320		2	3		5	6		8	7	10	11		4	9										
12		27	CREWE ALEXANDRA	5-1	Gregory 2, Haigh, Fletcher, Brown	5776		2	3	4	5	6		8	7		11	10		9										
13		29	MANSFIELD TOWN	0-1		7774		2	3	4	5	6		8	7		11	10		9										
14	Oct	6	Chesterfield	0-1		9017		2	3	4		6		8		11	7	10		9	5									
15		13	CHESTER	3-0	Brown, McGill, Gill (og)	6377		2	3	4		6		8	7	11		10		9	5									
16		20	York City	2-0	Gregory, Hubbard	8881		2	3	4		6		8	7	11		10		9	5									
17		27	BRADFORD CITY	1-1	Brown	6837		2	3	4		6		8	7	11		10		9	5									
18	Nov	3	Stockport County	3-1	Brown, Bushby, Jones	12313		2	3	4		6		8	7	11		10		9	5									
19		10	CARLISLE UNITED	1-2	Luke	5564		2	3	4		6		8		11		10		9	5		7							
20		24	TRANMERE ROVERS	1-4	Gregory	5228		2	3	4		6		8	7	11		10		9	5									
21	Dec	1	Hartlepools United	0-0		7881		2	3	4		6		8		10	11			9	5		1	7						
22		15	Darlington	2-1	Fletcher 2	3421		2	3			6		8	9		11	10	4		5		1	7						
23		22	BARROW	1-1	Haigh	3324		2	3			6		8	9		11	10	4		5		1	7						
24		25	Derby County	0-4		11266		2	3	4		6		8	9	7	11	10			5		1							
25		26	DERBY COUNTY	1-4	McGill (p)	4103		2	3	4		6		8	9	7	11	10			5		1							
26		29	Hull City	2-2	Fletcher 2	12873			3	4		6		8	9	7	11	10			5		1		2					
27	Jan	1	Accrington Stanley	1-0	Brown	8880	3					6		8	9	7	11	10			5		1		2					
28		12	WORKINGTON	2-1	Brown, R Brown (og)	5707			3	4		6		8	9	7	11	10			5		1		2					
29		19	Halifax Town	0-1		4496			3	4		6		8	9		11	10			5		1	7	2					
30	Feb	2	ROCHDALE	1-0	Haigh	6080			3	4		6		10	9						5			7	2	8	11			
31		9	Mansfield Town	1-1	Davies	8823			3	4		6		10	9						5			7	2	8				
32		16	CHESTERFIELD	5-1	Waldock 3, Fletcher, McGill	6854			3	4		6		10	9	11					5		1	7	2	8				
33		23	Chester	2-2	Waldock, Haigh	2691			3	4		6		10	9	11					5		1	7	2	8				
34	Mar	2	YORK CITY	2-1	Davies, Jones	7848			3	4	5	6		10	9	11								7	2	8				
35		9	Bradford City	1-3	Waldock	13475			3	4		6		10	9	11					5				2	8			7	
36		16	STOCKPORT COUNTY	2-3	Waldock, Bushby (p)	6829			3	4	5	6		10	9	11							1		2	8			7	
37		23	Carlisle United	0-0		8165	3					6			9	11							1	7	2	10		8		
38		30	ACCRINGTON STANLEY	2-3	Fletcher, Haigh	6602			3	4		6		10	9	11							1	7	2	8				
39	Apr	4	WREXHAM	4-3	Haigh, Waldock, Fletcher, Davies	4196	3			4	5	6		10	9	11							1	7	2	8				
40		6	Tranmere Rovers	2-4	Waldock, Haigh	5491	9		3	4	5	6		10		11							1	7	2	8				
41		10	Wrexham	1-1	Luke	4340		2	3	4	5	6		10						9			1	7		8				
42		13	HARTLEPOOLS UNITED	1-2	Fletcher	4599			3	4	5	6		10	9	11								7	2	8				
43		19	GATESHEAD	1-2	Waldock	4044			3	4	5	6		10	9	11								7	2	8		1		
44		20	Oldham Athletic	1-1	Fletcher	5897		2	3	4		6		10	9	11					5			7		8		1		
45		22	Gateshead	0-0		3324		2	3			6		10	9	11			4		5			7		8		1		
46		27	OLDHAM ATHLETIC	0-0		3903	3		2			6		10	9	11			4		5			7		8			1	3

	Marshall PW	Hubbard J	Brownsword NJ	McGill A	Hussey FM	Bushby A	Whiteside WR	Haigh I	Brown GA	Fletcher D	Jones JM	Gregory JE	Sharpe LT	Luke GB	Heward B	Lewis K	Charlesworth T	Davies JR	Horstead JB	Waldock R	Mullen A	Gleadall E	Hardwick K	Whitnall B
Apps	1	32	43	35	22	46	2	45	38	28	38	19	11	18	24	1	17	19	17	17	1	3	4	1
Goals		1		3		2		9	14	12	5	5		6				3		9				

Two own goals

F.A. Cup

		Date	Opponent	Score	Scorers	Att	Marshall PW	Hubbard J	Brownsword NJ	McGill A	Hussey FM	Bushby A	Whiteside WR	Haigh I	Brown GA	Fletcher D	Jones JM	Gregory JE	Sharpe LT	Luke GB	Heward B	Lewis K	Charlesworth T	Davies JR
R1	Nov	17	ROCHDALE	1-0	Brown	8655	1	2	3	4		6		8	7	11		10		9	5			
R2	Dec	8	WREXHAM	0-0		9153		2	3	4		6		8		10	11			9	5		1	7
rep		11	Wrexham	2-6	Gregory 2	11549		2	3	4		6		8	9	11		10			5		1	7

R2 replay a.e.t.

		P	W	D	L	F	A	W	D	L	F	A	Pts
1	Derby County	46	18	3	2	69	18	8	8	7	42	35	63
2	Hartlepools United	46	18	4	1	56	21	7	5	11	34	42	59
3	Accrington Stanley	46	15	4	4	54	22	10	4	9	41	42	58
4	Workington	46	16	4	3	60	25	8	6	9	33	38	58
5	Stockport County	46	16	3	4	51	26	7	5	11	40	49	54
6	Chesterfield	46	17	5	1	60	22	5	4	14	36	57	53
7	York City	46	14	4	5	43	21	7	6	10	32	40	52
8	Hull City	46	14	6	3	45	24	7	4	12	39	45	52
9	Bradford City	46	14	3	6	47	31	8	5	10	31	37	52
10	Barrow	46	16	2	5	51	22	5	7	11	25	40	51
11	Halifax Town	46	16	2	5	40	24	5	5	13	25	46	49
12	Wrexham	46	12	7	4	63	33	7	3	13	34	41	48
13	Rochdale	46	14	6	3	38	19	4	6	13	27	46	48
14	SCUNTHORPE UNITED	46	9	5	9	44	36	6	10	7	27	33	45
15	Carlisle United	46	9	9	5	44	36	7	4	12	32	49	45
16	Mansfield Town	46	13	3	7	58	36	4	7	12	33	52	44
17	Gateshead	46	9	6	8	42	40	8	4	11	30	50	44
18	Darlington	46	11	5	7	47	36	6	3	14	35	59	42
19	Oldham Athletic	46	9	7	7	35	31	3	8	12	31	43	39
20	Bradford Park Ave.	46	11	2	10	41	40	5	1	17	25	53	35
21	Chester	46	8	7	8	40	35	2	6	15	15	49	33
22	Southport	46	7	8	8	31	34	3	4	16	21	60	32
23	Tranmere Rovers	46	5	9	9	33	38	2	4	17	18	53	27
24	Crewe Alexandra	46	5	7	11	31	46	1	2	20	12	64	21

1957/58 Champions Division 3(N)

#	Date	Opponent	Score	Scorers	Att	Hardwick K	Horstead IB	Brownsword NJ	Marshall F	Heward B	Bushby A	Marriott IL	Waldock R	Fletcher D	Haigh J	Jones JM	Hussey FM	Hubbard J	Stokes AW	Whitnall B	Sharpe LT	Davies JR	Gleadall E	Davis EWC	Maw J	Minton AE
1	Aug 24	Chesterfield	1-1	Marriott	10768	1	2	3	4	5	6	7	8	9	10	11										
2	26	Tranmere Rovers	4-1	Waldock 3, Fletcher	13197	1	2	3	4	5	6	7	8	9	10	11										
3	31	DARLINGTON	5-0	Marriott 2, Waldock 2, Fletcher	8506	1	2	3	4	5	6	7	8	9	10	11										
4	Sep 5	TRANMERE ROVERS	1-0	Fletcher	10480	1	2	3	4	5	6	7	8	9	10	11										
5	7	Gateshead	2-1	Waldock, Fletcher	5666	1	2	3	4	5	6	7	8	9	10	11										
6	12	CREWE ALEXANDRA	3-2	Marriott, Haigh, Brownsword (p)	9679	1	2	3	4	5	6	7	8	9	10	11										
7	14	MANSFIELD TOWN	3-3	Haigh, Brownsword(p), Chamberlain(og)	9533	1	2	3	4		6	7	8	9	10	11	5									
8	18	Crewe Alexandra	2-0	Haigh, Williams (og)	4159	1	5	3	4		6	7	8	9	10	11		2								
9	21	Workington	2-3	Haigh, Fletcher	8839	1	5	3	4		6	7	8	9	10	11		2								
10	25	Rochdale	4-1	Haigh, Waldock, Marriott, Fletcher	5278	1	5	3	4		6	7	8	9	10	11		2								
11	28	BRADFORD CITY	0-2		9576	1	5	3	4		6	7	8	9	10	11		2								
12	Oct 3	ROCHDALE	2-0	Haigh, Stokes	11636	1	5	3	4		6	7		8	10	11		2	9							
13	5	Hull City	0-2		12009	1	5	3	4		6	7		8	10	11			9	2						
14	12	Accrington Stanley	1-2	Fletcher	7388	1	5		4		6	7		8	10	11		3	9		2					
15	19	BRADFORD PARK AVE.	6-2	Davies 2, Fletcher 2, Brownsword 2(2p)	7591	1	5	3	4		6	11	8	9	10			2				7				
16	26	Carlisle United	4-3	Gleadall 2, Fletcher, Marriott	10579	1	5	3	4		6	11		9	10			2				7	8			
17	31	HALIFAX TOWN	1-1	Davies	9373	1	5	3	4		6	11		9	10			2				7	8			
18	Nov 2	SOUTHPORT	1-0	Fletcher	8305	1	5	3	4		6	11	8	9	10			2				7				
19	9	York City	0-0		8276	1	5	3	4		6	11	8	9	10			2				7				
20	23	Oldham Athletic	1-2	Davis	8150	1	5	3	4		6		8		10	11		2				7		9		
21	30	BURY	1-0	Waldock	10926	1	5	3	4		6	7	8	9	10	11		2								
22	Dec 14	Chester	2-1	Fletcher 2	4604	1	5	3	4		6	7	8	9	10	11		2								
23	21	CHESTERFIELD	1-1	Fletcher	7741	1	5	3	4		6		8	9	10	11		2				7				
24	26	Halifax Town	1-0	Waldock	9942	1	5	3	4		6		8	9	10	11		2				7				
25	28	Darlington	1-1	Waldock	7833	1	5	3	4		6		8		10	11		2				7		9		
26	Jan 11	GATESHEAD	2-1	Waldock 2	7750	1	5	3	4		6	7	8		10	11		2						9		
27	18	Mansfield Town	5-3	Davis 2, Waldock, Haigh, Marriott	8415	1	5	3	4		6	7	8		10	11		2						9		
28	Feb 1	WORKINGTON	2-2	Davis	9060	1	5	3	4		6	7	8		10	11		2						9		
29	20	HULL CITY	2-0	Davis, Feasey (og)	11408	1	5	3	4		6	7	8		10	11		2						9		
30	22	OLDHAM ATHLETIC	1-1	Waldock	10036	1	5	3	4		6		8		10	11		2				7		9		
31	Mar 1	Bradford Park Avenue	2-1	Waldock 2	13467	1	5	3	4		6		8		10	11		2				7		9		
32	13	STOCKPORT COUNTY	4-0	Waldock 2, Davis 2	8446	1	5	3	4	6			8		10	11		2				7		9		
33	15	Southport	2-1	Waldock, Davis	3366	1	5	3	4	6			8		10	11		2				7		9		
34	22	ACCRINGTON STANLEY	1-0	Davis	11304	1	5	3	4	6			8		10	11		2				7		9		
35	29	Barrow	1-0	Davies	5261	1	5	3	4	6			8		10	11		2				7		9		
36	Apr 4	Wrexham	0-1		14280	1	5	3	4	6			8		10	11		2				7		9		
37	5	HARTLEPOOLS UNITED	2-0	Davis 2	8684	1	5	3	4				8		10	11		2			6	7		9		
38	7	WREXHAM	1-0	Brownsword (p)	9879	1	5	3	4				8		10	11		2			6	7		9		
39	12	Bury	1-2	Haigh	12508	1	5	3	4				8		10	11		2			6	7		9		
40	17	BARROW	1-0	Stokes	9609	1	5	3	4				8			11		2	10		6	7		9		
41	19	YORK CITY	1-2	Davis	10083	1	5	3	4				8			11		2	10		6	7		9		
42	21	Stockport County	1-2	Davis	14005	1	5	3	4				8		10	11		2			6	7		9		
43	24	Bradford City	3-2	Minton 2, Davis	18240	1	5	3	4						10	11		2			6	7		9		8
44	26	CHESTER	2-1	Haigh, Davis	10403	1	5	3	4						10	11		2			6	7		9		8
45	28	Hartlepools United	2-1	Davis 2	8159	1	5	3	4						10	11		2			6	7		9		8
46	May 1	CARLISLE UNITED	3-1	Davis, Haigh, Brownsword (p)	12555	1	5	3	4				8		10	11		2			6	7		9		
				Apps		46	46	44	46	11	31	34	33	26	45	41	1	33	5	1	16	17	3	23	1	3
				Goals				6				7	21	14	10				2			4	2	17		2

Three own goals

F.A. Cup

R	Date	Opponent	Score	Scorers	Att	Hardwick K	Horstead IB	Brownsword NJ	Marshall F	Heward B	Bushby A	Marriott IL	Waldock R	Fletcher D	Haigh J	Jones JM	Hussey FM	Hubbard J	Stokes AW	Whitnall B	Sharpe LT	Davies JR	Gleadall E	Davis EWC	Maw J	Minton AE
R1	Nov 16	GOOLE TOWN	2-1	Fletcher, Davies	8931	1	5	3	4		6	11	8	9	10			2				7				
R2	Dec 7	BURY	2-0	Waldock, Jones	12106	1	5	3	4		6	7	8	9	10	11		2								
R3	Jan 4	BRADFORD CITY	1-0	Haigh	11645	1	5	3	4		6	7	8	9	10	11					2					
R4	25	Newcastle United	3-1	Davis 2, Haigh	33407	1	5	3	4		6	7	8		10	11					2			9		
R5	Feb 15	LIVERPOOL	0-1		23000	1	5	3	4		6	7	8		10	11					2			9		

		P	W	D	L	F	A	W	D	L	F	A	Pts
1	SCUNTHORPE UNITED	46	16	5	2	46	19	13	3	7	42	31	66
2	Accrington Stanley	46	16	4	3	53	28	9	5	9	30	33	59
3	Bradford City	46	13	7	3	42	19	8	8	7	31	30	57
4	Bury	46	17	4	2	61	18	6	6	11	33	44	56
5	Hull City	46	15	6	2	49	20	4	9	10	29	47	53
6	Mansfield Town	46	16	3	4	68	42	6	5	12	32	50	52
7	Halifax Town	46	15	5	3	52	20	5	6	12	31	49	51
8	Chesterfield	46	12	8	3	39	28	6	7	10	32	41	51
9	Stockport County	46	15	4	4	54	28	3	7	13	20	39	47
10	Rochdale	46	14	4	5	50	25	5	4	14	29	42	46
11	Tranmere Rovers	46	12	6	5	51	32	6	4	13	31	44	46
12	Wrexham	46	13	8	2	39	18	4	4	15	22	45	46
13	York City	46	11	8	4	40	26	6	4	13	28	50	46
14	Gateshead	46	12	5	6	41	27	3	10	10	27	49	45
15	Oldham Athletic	46	11	7	5	44	32	3	10	10	28	52	45
16	Carlisle United	46	13	3	7	56	35	6	3	14	24	43	44
17	Hartlepools United	46	11	6	6	45	26	5	6	12	28	50	44
18	Barrow	46	9	7	7	36	32	4	8	11	30	42	41
19	Workington	46	11	6	6	46	33	3	7	13	26	48	41
20	Darlington	46	15	3	5	53	25	2	4	17	25	64	41
21	Chester	46	7	10	6	38	26	6	3	14	35	55	39
22	Bradford Park Ave.	46	8	6	9	41	41	5	5	13	27	54	37
23	Southport	46	8	3	12	29	40	3	3	17	23	48	28
24	Crewe Alexandra	46	6	5	12	29	41	2	2	19	18	52	23

SEASON 1956-57
Standing: Hubbard, Hussey, McGill, Marshall, Bushby, Brownsword
Seated: Gregory, Haigh, Fletcher, Brown, Jones

SEASON 1957-58
Standing: Hubbard, Marshall, Horstead, Hardwick, Sharpe, Brownsword
Seated: Marriott, Minton, Davis, Haigh, Jones

1958/59 — 18th in Division 2

#		Date	Opponent	Score	Scorers	Att.	Hardwick K	Hubbard J	Brownsword NJ	Marshall F	Horstead JB	Sharpe LT	Marriott IL	Waldock R	Davis EWC	Haigh J	Ormond W	Jones JM	Heward B	Wood BW	Minton AE	Neale P	Jones K	Harburn PAP	Ward JR	Bushby A	Pearce DG	Donnelly P	Grant J
1	Aug	23	IPSWICH TOWN	1-1	Davis	13317	1	2	3	4	5	6	7	8	9	10	11												
2		28	Swansea Town	0-3		21056	1	2	3	4	5	6	7	8	9	10	11												
3		30	Bristol Rovers	0-4		24221	1	2	3	4	5	6	7	8	9	10	11												
4	Sep	4	SWANSEA TOWN	3-1	Davis 2, Waldock	13592	1	2	3	4	5	6	7	8	9	10		11											
5		6	DERBY COUNTY	2-2	Marriott, Haigh	13318	1	2	3	4	5	6	7	8	9	10		11											
6		10	Stoke City	3-4	Waldock, Sharpe, M Jones	17824	1	2	3	4	5	6	7	8	9	10		11											
7		13	Leyton Orient	1-2	Waldock	15955	1	2	3	4	5	6	7	8	9	10		11											
8		18	STOKE CITY	1-1	M Jones	14159	1	2	3	4	10	6	7	8	9			11	5										
9		20	ROTHERHAM UNITED	2-0	Wood, Brownsword (p)	13959	1	2	3	4		6	7		9	8		11	5	10									
10		27	SHEFFIELD WEDNESDAY	1-4	Brownsword (p)	17488	1	2	3	4		6	7		9	8		11	5	10									
11	Oct	4	Fulham	1-1	Bentley (og)	24569	1	2	3				7		10	8		11	5		9								
12		11	Sheffield United	1-4	M Jones	22084	1	2	3	4		6	7	10	9	8		11	5										
13		18	BRIGHTON & HOVE ALB	2-3	Waldock, Haigh	11921	1		3			2	7	8	9	4		11	5			10	6						
14		25	Grimsby Town	1-1	Waldock	16753	1	2	3		5	6	7	8	9			11	4			10							
15	Nov	1	BARNSLEY	1-0		12956	1	2	3			6	7	8	9	4		11	5			10							
16		8	Middlesbrough	1-6	Neale	23020	1	2	3			6	7	8	9	4		11	5			10							
17		15	CHARLTON ATHLETIC	3-3	Waldock, Hewie (og), Brownsword (p)	11023	1	2	3	4	5	6	7	8	9			11				10							
18		22	Bristol City	1-0	Marriott	20306	1	2	3	4	5	6	7	8	9			11				10							
19	Dec	6	Huddersfield Town	1-0	Marriott	13888	1	2	3	4	5	6	7	8	9			11				10							
20		13	LIVERPOOL	1-2	Waldock	11194	1	2	3	4	5	6	7	8	9			11				10							
21		18	CARDIFF CITY	1-0	Marriott	10365	1	2	3	4	5	6	7	8	9			11				10							
22		20	Ipswich Town	1-3	Waldock	13204	1	2	3		5	4	7	10	9	8		11					6						
23		26	SUNDERLAND	3-2	Ashurst (og), Neale, Sharpe	14509	1	2	3	4	5	6	7		9	8		11				10							
24		27	Sunderland	1-3	Neale	27550	1	2	3	4		6	7		9	8		11	5			10							
25	Jan	3	BRISTOL ROVERS	0-0		11130		2	3	4	5	6	7		9	8		11				10	1						
26		17	Derby County	1-3	Harburn	13941	1	2	3	4	5	6	7	10		8		11						9					
27		31	LEYTON ORIENT	2-0	Harburn, Waldock	10259	1	2	3	4	5	6	7	10		8		11						9					
28	Feb	7	Rotherham United	0-1		9843	1	2	3	4	5	6	7	10		8		11						9					
29		14	Sheffield Wednesday	0-2		21801	1	2	3	4	5	6	7	10		8		11											
30		21	FULHAM	1-2	Waldock	10080		2	3	4	5	6	7			8		11				10	1	9					
31		28	MIDDLESBROUGH	0-3		11171		2	3	4	5	6	7	10		8		11					1	9					
32	Mar	7	Brighton & Hove Albion	1-2	Haigh	17795		2	3	4	5		7		9	8		11				10	1			6			
33		14	GRIMSBY TOWN	1-3	Marriott	13539		2	3		5		7		9	8		11	6			10	1				4		
34		21	Barnsley	1-0	Harburn	6032	1	2	3	4	5		7	8		10		11					6	9					
35		27	Lincoln City	3-3	Harburn, Waldock, Jones M	14679	1	2	3	4	5		7	8		10		11					6	9					
36		28	SHEFFIELD UNITED	1-3	Harburn	12353	1	2	3	4			7	8		10		11	5			6		9					
37		30	LINCOLN CITY	3-1	Donnelly 2, Harburn	13742	1	2	3				7	8		4		11	5			6		9				10	
38	Apr	4	Charlton Athletic	3-2	Harburn 2, Waldock	15285	1	2	3	4			7	8		10		11	5			6		9					
39		11	BRISTOL CITY	3-3	Donnelly 2 (1 p), McCall (og)	11101	1	2	3				7	8		4			5			6		9				10	
40		18	Cardiff City	2-0	Haigh, Waldock	13003	1	2	3	4			7	8		10			5		11	6		9					
41		22	Liverpool	0-3		13976	1	2	3	4			7	8		10			5		11	6		9					
42		25	HUDDERSFIELD T	0-3		9035	1		3	4				8		10			5			6		9			2		7
			Apps				35	40	42	34	27	30	39	38	17	40	3	37	19	3	2	26	7	15	1	1	2	3	1
			Goals						3			2	5	14	3	4		4		1		3		8				4	

Four own goals

F.A. Cup

	Date		Opponent	Score		Att.	Hardwick K	Hubbard J	Brownsword NJ	Marshall F	Horstead JB	Sharpe LT	Marriott IL	Waldock R	Davis EWC	Haigh J	Ormond W	Jones JM	Neale P
R3	Jan	10	BOLTON WANDERERS	0-2		23706	1	2	3	4	5	6	7	9		8		11	10

		P	W	D	L	F	A	W	D	L	F	A	Pts
1	Sheffield Wed.	42	18	2	1	68	13	10	4	7	38	35	62
2	Fulham	42	18	1	2	65	26	9	5	7	31	35	60
3	Sheffield United	42	16	2	3	54	15	7	5	9	28	33	53
4	Liverpool	42	15	3	3	57	25	9	2	10	30	37	53
5	Stoke City	42	16	2	3	48	19	5	5	11	24	39	49
6	Bristol Rovers	42	13	5	3	46	23	5	7	9	34	41	48
7	Derby County	42	15	1	5	46	29	5	7	9	28	42	48
8	Charlton Athletic	42	13	3	5	53	33	5	4	12	39	57	43
9	Cardiff City	42	12	2	7	37	26	6	5	10	28	39	43
10	Bristol City	42	11	3	7	43	27	6	4	11	31	43	41
11	Swansea Town	42	12	5	4	52	30	4	4	13	27	51	41
12	Brighton & Hove A.	42	10	9	2	46	29	5	2	14	28	61	41
13	Middlesbrough	42	9	7	5	51	26	6	3	12	36	45	40
14	Huddersfield Town	42	12	3	6	39	20	4	5	12	23	35	40
15	Sunderland	42	13	4	4	42	23	3	4	12	22	52	40
16	Ipswich Town	42	12	4	5	37	27	5	2	14	25	50	40
17	Leyton Orient	42	9	4	8	43	30	5	4	12	28	48	36
18	SCUNTHORPE UNITED	42	7	6	8	32	37	5	3	13	23	47	33
19	Lincoln City	42	10	5	6	45	37	1	2	18	18	56	29
20	Rotherham United	42	9	5	7	32	28	1	4	16	10	54	29
21	Grimsby Town	42	7	7	7	41	36	2	3	16	21	54	28
22	Barnsley	42	8	4	9	34	34	2	3	16	21	57	27

SEASON 1958-59
Back: Hubbard, Stokes, Bushby, Hardwick, Wood, Brownsword
Middle: Pearce, Haigh, Marshall, Horstead, Davies, Sharpe, Minton
Seated: Marriott, Malcolm, Davis, Waldock, Jones

SEASON 1959-60
Standing: John, Haigh, Jones, Heward, Sharpe, Brownsword
Seated: Marriott, Thomas, Middleton, Donnelly, Bakes

1959/60 15th in Division 2

#	Date		Opponent	Score	Scorers	Att	Hardwick K	John DCJ	Brownsword NJ	Sharpe LT	Horstead JB	Neale P	Marriott JL	Waldock R	Harbury PAP	Haigh J	Donnelly P	Heward B	Bakes MS	Thomas BEB	Williams I	Middleton H	Jones K	Pashley R	Passmoor T	Hubbard J	Needham A
1	Aug	22	BRISTOL CITY	1-1	Brownsword (p)	10863	1	2	3	4	5	6	7	8	9	10	11										
2		24	Plymouth Argyle	0-4		25888	1	2	3	4	5	6	7	8	9	10	11										
3		29	Huddersfield Town	0-2		14730	1	2	3	6	5	10	7	11	9	8		4									
4	Sep	3	PLYMOUTH ARGYLE	2-0	Sharpe, Haigh	12165	1	2	3	6	5		7	8	9	10		4	11								
5		5	Rotherham United	1-1	Haigh	10764	1	2	3	6	5		7	8	9	10		4	11								
6		9	Liverpool	0-2		31713	1	2	3	6	5	9	7	8		10		4	11								
7		12	Cardiff City	1-2	Haigh	10933	1	2	3	6	5	9	7	8		10		4	11								
8		17	LIVERPOOL	1-1	Donnelly	11822	1	2	3	4		6	7	8		10	9	5	11								
9		19	Hull City	2-0	Waldock, Donnelly	18459	1	2	3	4		6	7	8		10	9	5	11								
10		26	SHEFFIELD UNITED	1-1	Marriott	15384	1	2	3	4		6	7			10	9	5	11	8							
11	Oct	3	Middlesbrough	1-3	Thomas	27979	1	2	3	4		6	7			10	9	5	11	8							
12		10	IPSWICH TOWN	2-2	Middleton, Thomas	11408		2	3	4		6	7			10	11	5		8	1	9					
13		17	Bristol Rovers	1-1	Donnelly	15225		2	3	4		6	7			8	10	5	11		1	9					
14		24	SWANSEA TOWN	3-1	Marriott, Donnelly, Middleton	9675		2	3	4		6	7			8	10	5	11		1	9					
15		31	Brighton & Hove Albion	1-0	Middleton	18927		2	3	4		6	7			8	10	5	11		1	9					
16	Nov	7	STOKE CITY	1-1	Haigh	10827		2	3	4		6	7			8	10	5	11		1	9					
17		14	Portsmouth	0-4		14949		2	3	4		6	7			8	10	5	11	8	1	9					
18		21	SUNDERLAND	3-1	Donnelly 2, Thomas	11682		2	3	6			7			4	10	5	11	8	1	9					
19		28	Aston Villa	0-5		37367		2	3	6			7			4	10	5	11	8		9					
20	Dec	5	LINCOLN CITY	5-0	Middleton 2, Thomas, Bakes, Brownsword (p)	13945		2	3	6			7			4	10	5	11	8		9	1				
21		12	Leyton Orient	1-1	Haigh	9588		2	3	6			7			4	10	5	11	8		9	1				
22		19	Bristol City	2-0	Marriott, Middleton	9099		2	3	6			7			4	10	5	11	8		9	1				
23		26	DERBY COUNTY	3-2	Middleton 2, Donnelly	13342		2	3	6			7			4	10	5	11	8		9	1				
24		28	Derby County	0-3		17677		2	3	6			7			4	10	5	11	8		9	1				
25	Jan	2	HUDDERSFIELD T	0-2		12228		2	3	6			7			4	10	5	11	8		9	1				
26		16	ROTHERHAM UNITED	2-1	Donnelly, Middleton	12745		2	3	6			7			4	10	5	11	8		9	1				
27		23	Cardiff City	2-4	Thomas, Middleton	16759		2	3	6			7			4	10	5	11	8		9	1				
28	Feb	6	HULL CITY	3-0	Middleton, Thomas, Donnelly	10885		2	3	6			7			4	10	5	11	8		9	1				
29		13	Sheffield United	1-2	Thomas	16460		2	3	6			7			4	10	5	11	8		9	1				
30		20	MIDDLESBROUGH	1-1	Thomas	10817		2	3	6			7			4	10	5	11	8		9	1				
31		27	Ipswich Town	0-1		12829		2	3	6			7			4	10	5	11	8		9	1				
32	Mar	5	BRISTOL ROVERS	3-4	Thomas 2, Donnelly	9277		2	3	6			7			4	10	5	11	8		9	1				
33		12	Swansea Town	1-3	Donnelly	11646		2	3	6			7				10	5	11	8		9	1				
34		19	ASTON VILLA	1-2	Marriott	13084		2	3	4		6	7				9	5	11	10				1	8		
35		26	Stoke City	3-1	Marriott, Pashley, Bakes	6234		2	3	4		6	7				9	5	11	10				1	8		
36	Apr	2	PORTSMOUTH	1-0	Donnelly	8675		2	3	4		6	7				9		11	10				1	8	5	
37		9	Sunderland	0-1		16952		2	3	4		6	7				8		11	9		10	1		5		
38		15	CHARLTON ATHLETIC	1-1	Haigh	8741		2	3	4		6	7			8		10	11	7		9	1		5		
39		16	LEYTON ORIENT	2-1	Bakes, Brownsword (p)	8192		2	3	4		6				8	10		11			9	1		5		
40		18	Charlton Athletic	2-5	Bakes, Donnelly	10787		2	3	4		6	7			8	10	5	11			9	1				
41		23	Lincoln City	1-2	Donnelly	12691		2	3				7			8	10	5	11			9	1			4	6
42		30	BRIGHTON & HOVE ALB	1-2	Donnelly	6537			3	8	2	10				4	11	5	7			9	1				6

	Hardwick K	John DCJ	Brownsword NJ	Sharpe LT	Horstead JB	Neale P	Marriott JL	Waldock R	Harbury PAP	Haigh J	Donnelly P	Heward B	Bakes MS	Thomas BEB	Williams I	Middleton H	Jones K	Pashley R	Passmoor T	Hubbard J	Needham A
Apps	11	41	42	41	8	23	40	9	5	38	36	36	38	25	8	28	23	3	4	1	2
Goals			3	1			5	1		6	15		4	10		11		1			

F.A. Cup

	Date		Opponent	Score	Scorers	Att	John DCJ	Brownsword NJ	Sharpe LT	Marriott JL	Waldock R	Haigh J	Donnelly P	Heward B	Bakes MS	Thomas BEB	Middleton H	Jones K	Hubbard J	Needham A
R3	Jan	9	CRYSTAL PALACE	1-0	Middleton	12651	2	3	6	7		4	10	5	11	8	9	1		
R4		30	PORT VALE	0-1		14043	2	3	4	7		10	9	5		8			1	11

		P	W	D	L	F	A	W	D	L	F	A	Pts
1	Aston Villa	42	17	3	1	62	19	8	6	7	27	24	59
2	Cardiff City	42	15	2	4	55	36	8	10	3	35	26	58
3	Liverpool	42	15	3	3	59	28	5	7	9	31	38	50
4	Sheffield United	42	12	5	4	43	22	7	7	7	25	29	50
5	Middlesbrough	42	14	5	2	56	21	5	5	11	34	43	48
6	Huddersfield Town	42	13	3	5	44	20	6	6	9	29	32	47
7	Charlton Athletic	42	12	7	2	55	28	5	6	10	35	59	47
8	Rotherham United	42	9	9	3	31	23	8	4	9	30	37	47
9	Bristol Rovers	42	12	6	3	42	28	6	5	10	30	50	47
10	Leyton Orient	42	12	4	5	47	25	3	10	8	29	36	44
11	Ipswich Town	42	12	5	4	48	24	7	1	13	30	44	44
12	Swansea Town	42	12	6	3	54	32	3	4	14	28	52	40
13	Lincoln City	42	11	3	7	41	25	5	4	12	34	53	39
14	Brighton & Hove A.	42	7	8	6	35	32	6	4	11	32	44	38
15	SCUNTHORPE UNITED	42	9	7	5	38	26	4	3	14	19	45	36
16	Sunderland	42	8	6	7	35	29	4	6	11	17	36	36
17	Stoke City	42	8	3	10	40	38	6	4	11	26	45	35
18	Derby County	42	9	4	8	31	28	5	3	13	30	49	35
19	Plymouth Argyle	42	10	6	5	42	36	3	3	15	19	53	35
20	Portsmouth	42	6	6	9	36	36	4	6	11	23	41	32
21	Hull City	42	7	6	8	27	30	3	4	14	21	46	30
22	Bristol City	42	8	3	10	27	31	3	2	16	33	66	27

						Jones K	John DCJ	Brownsword NJ	Gibson A	Heward B	Neale P	Marriott IL	Godfrey BC	Thomas BEB	Bonson J	Bakes MS	Horstead JB	Sharpe LT	Middleton H	Kaye J	Turner J	Thorpe AW	Passmoor T	Needham A	Hemstead DW
1	Aug	20	Charlton Athletic	1-1	Thomas	12590	1	2	3	4	5	6	7	8	9	10	11								
2		25	IPSWICH TOWN	4-0	Marriott, Neale, Thomas, Godfrey	11130	1	2	3	4	5	6	7	8	9	10	11								
3		27	LEYTON ORIENT	2-2	Thomas 2	10107	1	2	3	4	5	6	7	8	9	10	11								
4		30	Ipswich Town	0-2		12426	1	2	3	4	5	6	7	8	9	10	11								
5	Sep	3	Derby County	5-2	Bonson 2,Thomas,Godfrey,Brownsword(p)	16944	1	2	3	4	5	6	7	8	9	10	11								
6		10	BRISTOL ROVERS	2-1	Thomas 2	10262	1	2	3	4	5	6	7	8	9	10	11								
7		15	MIDDLESBROUGH	1-1	Thomas	13852	1	2	3	4	5	6	7	8	9	10	11								
8		17	Liverpool	2-3	Thomas, Marriott	23797	1	2	3	4	5	6	7	8	9	10	11								
9		21	Middlesbrough	3-1	Thomas 2, Bonson	19744	1	2	3	4	5	6	7	8	9	10	11								
10		24	ROTHERHAM UNITED	1-1	Marriott	12724	1	2	3	4	5	6	7	8	9	10	11								
11	Oct	1	Southampton	2-4	Thomas 2	17464	1	2	3	4	5	6	7	8	9	10	11								
12		8	Sheffield United	0-2		14160	1	2	3	4	5	6	7	8	9	10	11								
13		15	STOKE CITY	1-1	Godfrey	8777	1	2	3	4	5	6	7	8	9	10	11								
14		24	Swansea Town	2-2	Bonson 2	9599	1	2	3	4			7	8	9	10	11	5	6							
15		29	LUTON TOWN	1-0	Thomas	8643	1	2	3	4			7	8	9	10	11	5	6							
16	Nov	5	Lincoln City	2-0	Godfrey, Thomas	10262	1	2	3	4			7	8	9	10	11	5	6							
17		12	PORTSMOUTH	5-1	Thomas 2, Godfrey 2, Sharpe	8335	1	2	3	4			7	8	9	10	11	5	6							
18		19	Huddersfield Town	2-1	Thomas, McGarry(og)	8617	1	2	3			4	7	8	9	10	11	5	6							
19		26	SUNDERLAND	3-3	Thomas, Bonson, Brownsword (p)	9156	1	2	3			4	7	8	9	10	11	5	6							
20	Dec	3	Plymouth Argyle	1-3	Sharpe	11925	1	2	3	4			7	8	9	10	11	5	6							
21		10	NORWICH CITY	2-1	Thomas, Godfrey	8444	1	2	3	4			7	8	9	10	11	5	6							
22		23	BRIGHTON & HOVE ALB	2-2	Brownsword 2 (2p)	9277	1	2	3	4			7	8	9	10	11	5	6							
23		27	Brighton & Hove Albion	1-1	Godfrey	20602	1	2	3	4			7	8	9	10	11	5	6							
24		31	Leyton Orient	1-2	Bonson	8450	1	2	3	4			7	8	9	10	11	5	6							
25	Jan	14	DERBY COUNTY	1-2	Godfrey	10067	1	2	3	4				8	9	10	11	5	6	7						
26		21	Bristol Rovers	3-3	Thomas 2, Marriott	11276	1	2	3			4	7	8	9	10	11	5	6							
27	Feb	4	LIVERPOOL	2-3	Thomas, Bonson	7970	1	2	3	4	6		7		9	10	11	5			8					
28		11	Rotherham United	0-4		8225	1	2	3	4	6		7		9	10	11	5			8					
29		18	SOUTHAMPTON	2-0	Thomas, Godfrey	8268			3	4	5		7	8	9	10	11	2	6			1				
30		25	SHEFFIELD UNITED	1-1	Godfrey	10873			3	4	5		7	8	9	10	11	2	6			1				
31	Mar	4	Stoke City	0-2		12667			3	4	5		7	8	9	10		2	6			1	11			
32		11	SWANSEA TOWN	1-2	Brownsword (p)	7926			3	4			7	8	9			2			10	1	11	5	6	
33		18	Norwich City	1-0	Godfrey	20598		2	3	4			7	8	9	10	11	5	6			1				
34		25	LINCOLN CITY	3-1	Bonson 2, Marriott	6981		2	3	4			7	8	9	10		5	6			1	11			
35	Apr	1	Sunderland	0-2		18242		2	3	4			7	8	9	10		5	6			1	11			
36		3	LEEDS UNITED	3-2	Godfrey, Thomas, Bakes	8725		2	3	4			7	8	9	10	11	5	6			1				
37		8	HUDDERSFIELD T	0-1		8352		2	3	4			7	8	9	10	11	5	6			1				
38		11	CHARLTON ATHLETIC	0-0		7303		2	3	4			7	8	9		11	5	6		10	1				
39		15	Portsmouth	2-2	Kaye, Godfrey	15223		2	3	4	5			7	9	8	11		6		10	1				
40		22	PLYMOUTH ARGYLE	2-0	Thomas, Bonson	5762		2	3	4	5		7	8	9	10	11		6			1				
41		25	Leeds United	2-2	Godfrey, Thorpe	6975		2	3	4			6	7	8	9	10	5				1	11			
42		29	Luton Town	0-0		8373		2					6	7		9	10	5	4		8	1	11			3
					Apps		28	38	41	38	18	20	40	39	42	40	36	27	25	1	6	14	6	1	1	1
					Goals			5			1	5	15	26	11	1		2			1		1			

One own goal

							Jones K	John DCJ	Brownsword NJ	Gibson A			Marriott IL	Godfrey BC	Thomas BEB	Bonson J	Bakes MS	Horstead JB	Sharpe LT
R3	Jan	7	BLACKPOOL	6-2	Thomas 3, Bonson 3	19303	1	2	3	4				8	9	10	11	5	6	7
R4		28	Norwich City	1-4	Bakes	15485	1	2	3	4			7	8	9	10	11	5	6	

							Jones K	John DCJ	Brownsword NJ	Gibson A	Heward B	Neale P	Marriott IL	Godfrey BC	Thomas BEB	Bonson J	Bakes MS		Sharpe LT	Middleton H
R1	Oct	10	Rochdale	1-1	Bonson	4274	1	2	3	4	5	6	7	11	9	10			8	
rep		20	ROCHDALE	0-1		5727	1	2	3	4	5		7	8	9		11		6	10

		P	W	D	L	F	A	W	D	L	F	A	Pts
1	Ipswich Town	42	15	3	3	55	24	11	4	6	45	31	59
2	Sheffield United	42	16	2	3	49	22	10	4	7	32	29	58
3	Liverpool	42	14	5	2	49	21	7	5	9	38	37	52
4	Norwich City	42	15	3	3	46	20	5	6	10	24	33	49
5	Middlesbrough	42	13	6	2	44	20	5	6	10	39	54	48
6	Sunderland	42	12	5	4	47	24	5	8	8	28	36	47
7	Swansea Town	42	14	4	3	49	26	4	7	10	28	47	47
8	Southampton	42	12	4	5	57	35	6	4	11	27	46	44
9	SCUNTHORPE UNITED	42	9	8	4	39	25	5	7	9	30	39	43
10	Charlton Athletic	42	12	3	6	60	42	4	8	9	37	49	43
11	Plymouth Argyle	42	13	4	4	52	32	4	4	13	29	50	42
12	Derby County	42	9	6	6	46	35	6	4	11	34	45	40
13	Luton Town	42	13	5	3	48	27	2	4	15	23	52	39
14	Leeds United	42	7	7	7	41	38	7	3	11	34	45	38
15	Rotherham United	42	9	7	5	37	24	3	6	12	28	40	37
16	Brighton & Hove A.	42	9	6	6	33	26	5	3	13	28	49	37
17	Bristol Rovers	42	13	4	4	52	35	2	3	16	21	57	37
18	Stoke City	42	9	6	6	39	26	3	6	12	12	33	36
19	Leyton Orient	42	10	5	6	31	29	4	3	14	24	49	36
20	Huddersfield Town	42	7	5	9	33	33	6	4	11	29	38	35
21	Portsmouth	42	10	6	5	38	27	1	5	15	26	64	33
22	Lincoln City	42	5	4	12	30	43	3	4	14	18	52	24

1961/62 4th in Division 2

#	Date	Opponent	Score	Scorers	Att	Jones K	John DCJ	Agnew DY	Gibson A	Horstead JB	Howells R	Marriott IL	Godfrey BC	Thomas BEB	Bonson J	Thorpe AW	Brownsword NJ	Turner J	Hemstead DW	Kaye J	Neale P	Lindsey B	Bakes MS	Wilson A	Sharpe LT	Hodgson K	McGuigan JJ	McDowall JC
1	Aug 19	BRIGHTON & HOVE ALB	3-3	Marriott (p), Godfrey, Thomas	7965	1	2	3	4	5	6	7	8	9	10	11												
2	23	Norwich City	2-2	Thomas 2	27407	1	2		4	5	6	7	8	9	10	11	3											
3	26	Bury	1-4	Gibson	11236		2		4	5	6	7	8	9	10	11	3	1										
4	29	NORWICH CITY	2-0	Thomas 2	8803				4	5	6	7	8	9	10	11	3	1	2									
5	Sep 1	CHARLTON ATHLETIC	6-1	Godfrey 2,Thomas,Marriott,Thorpe,Brownsword(p)	9639				4	5	6	7	8	9	10	11	3	1	2									
6	5	BRISTOL ROVERS	2-1	Godfrey, Thomas	9558				4	5	6	7	8	9	10	11	3	1	2									
7	9	Liverpool	1-2	Godfrey	46837				4	5	6	7	8	9	10	11	3	1	2									
8	15	ROTHERHAM UNITED	5-2	Thomas 2, Godfrey 2, Thorpe	11823	1			4		6	7	10	9		11	3			2	8	5						
9	18	Bristol Rovers	1-2	Thomas	14107	1			4		6	7		9	10	11	3			2	8	5						
10	23	Sunderland	0-4		35112				4		6	7		9			3	1		2	8	5	10	11				
11	29	STOKE CITY	2-2	Thomas, Kaye	10347				4	5	6	7		9	10	11	3	1		2	8							
12	Oct 7	Swansea Town	1-2	Thomas	12479				4	2	6	7		9	10		3	1		8	5			11				
13	13	SOUTHAMPTON	5-1	Thomas 2,Wilson,Kaye,Davies(og)	10638	1			4	2	6	7	10	9			3			8	5			11				
14	21	Luton Town	2-1	Thomas, Kaye	9766	1			4	2	6	7	10	9			3			8	5			11				
15	27	NEWCASTLE UNITED	3-2	Thomas 2, Brownsword (p)	13988	1			4	2	6	7	10	9			3			8	5			11				
16	Nov 4	Middlesbrough	2-1	Thomas 2	12142	1			4	2	6	7	10	9			3			8	5			11				
17	11	PLYMOUTH ARGYLE	5-1	Thomas 4, Thorpe	8780	1			4	2	6	7	10	9		11	3			8	5							
18	18	Derby County	2-2	Brownsword (p), Wilson	21134	1			4	2		7	10	9			3			8	5			11		6		
19	24	LEYTON ORIENT	0-2		11812	1			4	2	6	7	10	9			3			8	5			11				
20	Dec 2	Preston North End	1-4	Thomas	8326	1			4	2	6		7	9			3			10	5	8		11				
21	16	Brighton & Hove Albion	3-0	Thomas, Kaye, Sitford(og)	9377	1			4	5	6	11		9	10		3			2	8					7		
22	22	BURY	1-2	Thomas	8287	1			4	5	6	11	8	9	10		3			2						7		
23	26	Leeds United	4-1	Thomas 4	19481	1			4	5	6	11	10	9			3			2	8					7		
24	Jan 13	Charlton Athletic	3-3	Thomas, Hodgson, Hinton(og)	13672	1			4	2	6	11	10	9			3			8	5					7		
25	20	LIVERPOOL	1-1	Howells	11162	1			4	2	6	7	8				3			9	5			11		10		
26	Feb 2	Rotherham United	1-0	Kaye	12528	1			4	2	6	7	8				3			9	5					11	10	
27	10	SUNDERLAND	3-1	McGuigan, Kaye, Godfrey	11436	1			4	2	6	7	8				3			9	5					11	10	
28	17	Stoke City	0-1		16578	1			4	2	6	7					3			9	5			11		8	10	
29	20	LEEDS UNITED	2-1	Hodgson, McGuigan	9011	1			4	2	6	11	8				3			9	5					7	10	
30	23	SWANSEA TOWN	2-0	McGuigan	8246	1			4	2	6	11	8				3			9	5					7	10	
31	Mar 3	Southampton	4-6	McGuigan,Marriott,Brownsword (p),Kaye	10455				4	2	6	7					3			9	5			11		8	10	
32	6	WALSALL	2-1	McGuigan, Hodgson	7028	1			4	2	6	7					3			9	5			11		8	10	
33	10	LUTON TOWN	2-0	McGuigan, Kaye	7709	1	2		4		6	7				11	3			9	5					8	10	
34	17	Newcastle United	1-2	McGuigan	37931	1	2		4		6	11					3			9	5				7	8	10	
35	23	MIDDLESBROUGH	1-1	McGuigan	7978	1			4	2	6	7	8				3			9	5			11			10	
36	31	Plymouth Argyle	1-3	Kaye	15913	1	2		4				8				3			9	5			11	6	7	10	
37	Apr 6	DERBY COUNTY	2-0	Kaye, McGuigan	6981	1	2		4		6	7	8				3			9	5			11			10	
38	14	Leyton Orient	1-0	McGuigan	16867	1	2		4		6	7	8				3			9	5			11			10	
39	20	PRESTON NORTH END	2-1	Hodgson 2	11147	1			4		6	7					3		2	9	5			11		8	10	
40	23	Huddersfield Town	2-1	Wilson, Gibson	12397	1			4		6	7					3		2	9	5			11		9	10	
41	24	HUDDERSFIELD T	1-3	Hodgson	10573	1	2		4		6	7	8				3				5			11		9	10	
42	28	Walsall	1-4	McGuigan	7173	1			4	2	6	7					3			8	5			11		9	10	
				Apps		33	9	1	41	31	41	40	29	24	12	12	39	8	15	32	31	3	1	21	2	19	17	1
				Goals					2		1	3	8	31			3	4		11				3		7	10	

Three own goals

F.A. Cup

	Date	Opponent	Score	Att																							
R3	Jan 6	Charlton Athletic	0-1	20694	1			4	5	6	11	10	9			3			2	8					7		

F.L. Cup

	Date	Opponent	Score	Att																							
R1	Sep 13	Newcastle United	0-2	14340				4	5	6	7	8	9	10	11	3	1	2									

		P	W	D	L	F	A	W	D	L	F	A	Pts
1	Liverpool	42	18	3	0	68	19	9	5	7	31	24	62
2	Leyton Orient	42	11	5	5	34	17	11	5	5	35	23	54
3	Sunderland	42	17	3	1	60	16	5	6	10	25	34	53
4	SCUNTHORPE UNITED	42	14	4	3	52	26	7	3	11	34	45	49
5	Plymouth Argyle	42	12	4	5	45	30	7	4	10	30	45	46
6	Southampton	42	13	3	5	53	28	5	6	10	24	34	45
7	Huddersfield Town	42	11	5	5	39	22	5	7	9	28	37	44
8	Stoke City	42	13	4	4	34	17	4	4	13	21	40	42
9	Rotherham United	42	9	6	6	36	30	7	3	11	34	46	41
10	Preston North End	42	11	4	6	34	23	4	6	11	21	34	40
11	Newcastle United	42	10	5	6	40	27	5	4	12	24	31	39
12	Middlesbrough	42	11	3	7	45	29	5	4	12	31	43	39
13	Luton Town	42	12	1	8	44	37	5	4	12	25	34	39
14	Walsall	42	11	7	3	42	23	3	4	14	28	52	39
15	Charlton Athletic	42	10	5	6	38	30	5	4	12	31	45	39
16	Derby County	42	10	7	4	42	27	4	4	13	26	48	39
17	Norwich City	42	10	6	5	36	28	4	5	12	25	42	39
18	Bury	42	9	4	8	32	36	8	1	12	20	40	39
19	Leeds United	42	9	6	6	24	19	3	6	12	26	42	36
20	Swansea Town	42	10	5	6	38	30	2	7	12	23	53	36
21	Bristol Rovers	42	11	3	7	36	31	2	4	15	17	50	33
22	Brighton & Hove A.	42	7	7	7	24	32	3	4	14	18	54	31

SEASON 1960-61
Standing: John, Gibson, Jones, Turner, Horstead, Sharpe, Strong (Masseur)
Seated: Middleton, Godfrey, Thomas, Bonson, Bakes, Brownsword

SEASON 1961-62
Back: Bonson, Neale, Gibson, Hemstead, Bakes, Godfrey, Brownsword
Middle: Strong (Masseur), Passmoor, Horstead, Turner, unknown, unknown, Barker (Trainer)
Seated: Marriott, John, Duckworth (Manager), Wharton (Chairman), Sharpe, Middleton, Thomas

1962/63 9th in Division 2

No	Date	Opponent	Score	Scorers	Att	Jones K	Gannon MJ	Brownsword NJ	Gibson A	Neale P	Howells R	Marriott IL	Godfrey BC	Kaye J	McGuigan JJ	Hodgson K	Hemstead DW	Wilson A	Lindsey B	Horstead JB	Anderson AA	Bakes MS	Thorpe AW	Crawford I	Passmoor T	Reeves TB
1	Aug 18	SOUTHAMPTON	2-1	Hodgson, Knapp(og)	9583	1	2	3	4	5	6	7	8	9	10	11										
2	22	Chelsea	0-3		18190	1	2	3	4	5	6	7	8	9	10	11										
3	25	Grimsby Town	0-3		16303	1		3	4	5	6	7	8	9	10	11	2									
4	28	CHELSEA	3-0	Kaye 3	10976	1		3	4	5	6			9	10	11	2	7	8							
5	Sep 1	Bury	2-0	Kaye, Lindsey	8418	1		3	4	5	6			9	10	11		7	8	2						
6	4	NEWCASTLE UNITED	2-1	Wilson, McGuigan	14053	1		3	4	5	6			9	10	11		7	8	2						
7	8	ROTHERHAM UNITED	1-0	Kaye	12911	1		3	4	5	6			9	10	11		7	8	2						
8	11	SWANSEA TOWN	1-0	Hodgson	10468	1		3	4	5	6			9	10	11		7	8	2						
9	15	Charlton Athletic	0-1		13259	1		3	4	5	6			9	10	7		11	8	2						
10	18	Swansea Town	0-1		10793	1		3	4	5	6		8	9	10	11		7		2						
11	22	STOKE CITY	0-0		11683	1		3	4	5	6		8	9		11		7	10	2						
12	29	Sunderland	0-0		42980	1		3	4	5			7		10	9		11	8	2	6					
13	Oct 6	PLYMOUTH ARGYLE	2-2	Godfrey, Hodgson	8497	1			4	5			7	9	10	11	3		8	2	6					
14	13	Preston North End	1-3	Kaye	9919	1		3	4	5			7	9					8	2	6		11			
15	19	PORTSMOUTH	1-2	Brownsword (p)	8375	1		3	4	5			7	9	10				8	2	6		11			
16	27	Cardiff City	0-4		11883	1		3	4	5			8	9	10			7		2	6		11			
17	Nov 2	HUDDERSFIELD T	2-2	Hodgson 2	8695	1		3	4	5	6		8	9	10			7		2			11			
18	10	Middlesbrough	3-4	Thorpe, McGuigan, Brownsword (p)	10536	1		3	4	5	6	7		9	10	8				2			11			
19	16	DERBY COUNTY	2-1	Howells, Hodgson	6094	1		3	4	5	6	7		9	10	8				2			11			
20	24	Newcastle United	1-1	Marriott	26221	1		3	4	5	6	7		9	10	8				2			11			
21	30	WALSALL	2-0	Brownsword (p), McPherson(og)	7074	1		3	4	5	6	7		9	10	8				2			11			
22	Dec 8	Norwich City	3-3	Kaye 2, Howells	13387	1		3	4	5	6	7		9	10	8				2			11			
23	15	Southampton	1-1	Hodgson	11159	1		3	4	5	6	7		9	10	8				2			11			
24	21	GRIMSBY TOWN	1-1	Gibson	12542	1		3	4	5	6	7		9	10	8				2			11			
25	Feb 23	Plymouth Argyle	3-2	McGuigan, Howells, Brownsword (p)	11696	1		3	4	5	6		8	9	10	11		7		2						
26	Mar 9	Portsmouth	2-1	Hodgson, Wilson	8464	1		3	4	5	6	11	8	9				7	10	2						
27	15	CARDIFF CITY	2-2	Kaye, Brownsword (p)	7844	1		3	4	5	6		8	9		11		7	10	2						
28	23	Huddersfield Town	0-2		10929	1			4	5	6		8	9	10	7	3			2			11			
29	26	PRESTON NORTH END	4-1	McGuigan 2, Wilson, Hodgson	7002	1		3	4		6			9	10	8		7		2			11	5		
30	29	MIDDLESBROUGH	1-1	Gibson	7249	1		3	4		6			9	10	8		7		2			11	5		
31	Apr 3	Leeds United	0-1		15783	1		3	4					9	10	8		7		2	6		11	5		
32	6	Derby County	2-6	Hodgson 2	8933	1		3	4		6			9	10	8		7		2			11	5		
33	12	LUTON TOWN	2-0	McGuigan, Gibson	7528	1		3	4		6			9	10	8		7		2			11	5		
34	15	Luton Town	0-1		9043	1	6		4					9	10		3	7	8	2			11	5		
35	20	Walsall	1-1	Wilson	6839	1	6		4	5				9	10		3	7	8	2			11			
36	23	LEEDS UNITED	0-2		7794	1	6	3	4	5			8	9	10			7		2			11			
37	26	NORWICH CITY	3-1	Kaye 2, Wilson	5797		6	3	4					9	10	11		7		2				8	5	1
38	30	SUNDERLAND	1-1	Ashurst (og)	8853		6	3	4					9	10	11		7		2				8	5	1
39	May 4	Stoke City	3-2	McGuigan, Kaye, Hodgson	25590		6	3	4					9	10	11		7		2				8	5	1
40	7	CHARLTON ATHLETIC	2-0	Crawford, Tocknell(og)	6572		6	3	4					9	10	11		7		2				8	5	1
41	10	BURY	1-0	Kaye	6427		6	3						9	10	11		7	4	2				8	5	1
42	17	Rotherham United	0-1		7367		6	3	4				8	9	10			7		2				11	5	1
				Apps		36	11	38	40	30	28	11	17	39	40	36	6	26	16	38	6	2	9	15	12	6
				Goals				5	3		3	1	1	13	7	12		5	1					1	1	

Four own goals

F.A. Cup

Rd	Date	Opponent	Score	Scorers	Att	Jones K		Brownsword NJ	Gibson A	Neale P	Howells R	Marriott IL	Godfrey BC	Kaye J	McGuigan JJ	Hodgson K		Wilson A		Horstead JB				Crawford I		
R3	Jan 26	Portsmouth	1-1	Godfrey	15500	1		3	4		6	11	8	9	10			7		2				5		
rep	Mar 7	PORTSMOUTH	1-2	McGuigan	9765	1		3	4	5	6		8	9	10	11		7		2						

F.L. Cup

Rd	Date	Opponent	Score	Scorers	Att	Jones K		Brownsword NJ	Gibson A	Neale P			Godfrey BC		McGuigan JJ	Hodgson K		Wilson A	Lindsey B	Horstead JB	Anderson AA		Thorpe AW			
R2	Sep 24	Southampton	1-1	McGuigan	5905	1		3	4	5			7		10	9		11	8	2	6					
rep	Oct 2	SOUTHAMPTON	2-2	Gibson, Godfrey	6506	1		3	4	5			7		10	9		11	8	2	6					
rep2	9	Southampton	3-0	Godfrey, McGuigan, Wimhurst (og)	4984	1		3	4	5			7	9	10				8	2	6		11			
R3	17	Sunderland	0-2		18154	1		3	4	5			7	9	10				8	2	6		11			

R2 replay a.e.t. R2 replay 2 at Peterborough.

		P	W	D	L	F	A	W	D	L	F	A	Pts
1	Stoke City	42	15	3	3	49	20	5	10	6	24	30	53
2	Chelsea	42	15	3	3	54	16	9	1	11	27	26	52
3	Sunderland	42	14	5	2	46	13	6	7	8	38	42	52
4	Middlesbrough	42	12	4	5	48	35	8	5	8	38	50	49
5	Leeds United	42	15	2	4	55	19	4	8	9	24	34	48
6	Huddersfield Town	42	11	6	4	34	21	6	8	7	29	29	48
7	Newcastle United	42	11	8	2	48	23	7	3	11	31	36	47
8	Bury	42	11	6	4	28	20	7	5	9	23	27	47
9	SCUNTHORPE UNITED	42	12	7	2	35	18	4	5	12	22	41	44
10	Cardiff City	42	12	5	4	50	29	6	2	13	33	44	43
11	Southampton	42	15	3	3	52	23	2	5	14	20	44	42
12	Plymouth Argyle	42	13	4	4	48	24	2	8	11	28	49	42
13	Norwich City	42	11	6	4	53	33	6	2	13	27	46	42
14	Rotherham United	42	11	3	7	34	30	6	3	12	33	44	40
15	Swansea Town	42	13	5	3	33	17	2	4	15	18	55	39
16	Portsmouth	42	9	5	7	33	27	4	6	11	30	52	37
17	Preston North End	42	11	6	4	43	30	2	5	14	16	44	37
18	Derby County	42	10	5	6	40	29	2	7	12	21	43	36
19	Grimsby Town	42	8	6	7	34	26	3	7	11	21	40	35
20	Charlton Athletic	42	8	4	9	33	38	5	1	15	29	56	31
21	Walsall	42	7	7	7	33	37	4	2	15	20	52	31
22	Luton Town	42	10	4	7	45	40	1	3	17	16	44	29

SEASON 1962-63
Back: Horstead, Needham, Hodgson, McDowall, Jones, Reeves, Anderson, McGuigan, Hemstead
Standing: Barker (Trainer), Strong (Masseur), Marriott, Howells, Godfrey, Kaye, Passmoor,
Gannon, Bakes, Meecham, Holland, Duckworth (Manager)
Seated: Bramley, Wilson, B.Lindsey, Neale, Gibson, Thorpe, Brownsword, K.Lindsey

SEASON 1963-64
Back: Mahy, Reeves, Gannon
Standing: Duckworth (Manager), Hutton, unknown offical, Rogan, Hodgson, Horstead, Passmoor, Lawther,
Anderson, Brown, Strong (Masseur), Barker (Trainer)
Seated: Conde, Jones, Wilson, Gibson, Godfrey, Grawford, Neale, Brownsword, Smillie
Front: Gaughan, Harper, Lindsey, Marriott, Needham

1963/64   22nd in Division 2: Relegated

#	Date	Opponent	Score	Scorers	Att	Reeves TB	Horstead JB	Brownsword NJ	Lindsey B	Neale P	Gannon MJ	Wilson A	Hodgson K	Lawther WJ	Smillie AT	Crawford I	Jones K	Hutton J	Gibson A	Passmoor T	Hemstead DW	Harper IT	Mathy B	Godfrey BC	Marriott IL	Conde JP	Needham A	Kirkman AJ	Sloan D	Mason CE	Ellis KD
1	Aug 24	Swindon Town	0-3		18447	1	2	3	4	5	6	7	8	9	10	11															
2	27	NORTHAMPTON T	1-2	Lawther	8496		2	3	4	5	6		8	9	10	11	1	7													
3	30	CARDIFF CITY	1-2	Lawther	8123		2	3		6		7	8	9	10	11	1		4		5										
4	Sep 3	Northampton Town	0-2		15899		2	3		6		7	8	9	10	11	1		4		5										
5	7	Norwich City	1-2	Lawther	16099		2	3		6		7	8	9	10	11	1		4		5										
6	9	SUNDERLAND	1-1	Smillie	10261			3		5		7		9	10	11	1		4			2	6	8							
7	12	SWANSEA TOWN	2-2	Evans (og), Brownsword (p)	8297			3		5		7	8	9	10	11	1		4			2	6								
8	18	Sunderland	0-1		36128		6	3		5		7	8	9		11	1		4			2			10						
9	21	PORTSMOUTH	1-1	Hodgson	6673		6	3		5		7	8	9		11	1		4			2			10						
10	28	Rotherham United	1-2	Crawford	8655			3	8	5	6	7		9	10	11	1		4			2									
11	Oct 1	LEYTON ORIENT	0-0		6293			3	6	5		11	9		10	8	1		4			2			7						
12	5	LEEDS UNITED	0-1		10793		4	3	6	5		11	9		10	8	1					2			7						
13	19	MIDDLESBROUGH	1-0	Wilson	7126		6	3	8	9		7	10			11	1		4		5	2									
14	26	Preston North End	0-1		15622		6	3	8	9		7	10			11	1		4		5	2									
15	Nov 2	HUDDERSFIELD T	1-0	Neale	5840		6	3	8	9		10	11				1		4		5	2			7						
16	16	PLYMOUTH ARGYLE	1-0	Neale	5513		6	3	8	9		11	10				1		4		5	2			7						
17	23	Charlton Athletic	1-0	Hodgson	19648		6	3				11	8	10			1		4		5	2			7	9					
18	30	GRIMSBY TOWN	2-2	Conde, Lawther	8156		6	3				11	8	10			1		4		5				7	9	2				
19	Dec 7	Newcastle United	1-3	Hodgson	24717		6	3				11	8	10			1		4		5				7	9	2				
20	14	SWINDON TOWN	3-0	Hodgson, Lawther, Woodruff (og)	4986		6	3		5		11	8	10			1		4			2		9		9	7				
21	26	Manchester City	1-8	Lawther	26134		5	3			6	11	8	10		7	1		4			2					9				
22	28	MANCHESTER CITY	2-4	Brownsword (p), Kirkman	9088		5	3			6	11	8	10		7	1		4			2						9			
23	Jan 11	NORWICH CITY	2-2	Kirkman, Hodgson	5021			3	4	5		11	8	10		7	1					2					6	9			
24	16	Swansea Town	1-4	Sloan	7187		6	3	4	5		11		10		7	1					2						9	8		
25	25	Derby County	2-2	Hodgson, Sloan	8964		6	3	4	5		7	11	9			1					2						10	8		
26	29	Southampton	2-7	Sloan, Hodgson	13999		6	3	4	5		7	11	9			1				2							10	8		
27	Feb 1	Portsmouth	4-3	Hodgson 3, Smillie	11724		2	3	4	5		7	11	6	10		1								9				8		
28	8	ROTHERHAM UNITED	4-3	Lindsey, Wilson, Sloan, Madden (og)	7415		2		4	5		11	9	6	10		1										3	7	8		
29	15	Leeds United	0-1		28868		2		4	5		11	9	6			1	7							10		3		8		
30	22	SOUTHAMPTON	1-2	Brownsword	5591		2	3	4	5		11	9	6			1	7							10				8		
31	29	Plymouth Argyle	1-3	Hodgson	10162		6	3	4	5		11	9	10			1	7											8	2	
32	Mar 7	PRESTON NORTH END	1-0	Lindsey	6271		6	3	8	5		11	7	10			1				2									4	9
33	14	Leyton Orient	2-2	Wilson, Mason	4376		6	3	8	5		11	7	10			1				2									4	9
34	20	DERBY COUNTY	3-2	Wilson, Ellis, Brownsword (p)	6846		6	3		5		11	7	10			1				2								8	4	9
35	26	BURY	0-0		7406		6	3		5		11	7	10			1				2								8	4	9
36	28	Middlesbrough	0-2		8630		6	3	8	5		11		10			1				2								7	4	9
37	31	Bury	2-3	Lindsey, Wilson	6369		6	3	10	5		11		9			1	7			2								8	4	
38	Apr 4	CHARLTON ATHLETIC	1-1	Ellis	5138			3	6	5		11		10			1	7			2								8	4	9
39	8	Cardiff City	1-3	Lawther	9409			3	6	5		7	11	10			1										8		2	4	9
40	11	Grimsby Town	0-2		10406			3	6	5		7	11	10			1										8		2	4	9
41	18	NEWCASTLE UNITED	2-0	Lawther, Ellis	6434			3	6	5		7		10		11	1										8		2	4	9
42	25	Huddersfield Town	2-3	Ellis 2	5024			3	6	5		7		10		11	1										8		2	4	9
			Apps			1	33	39	28	37	4	40	33	38	12	20	41	6	19	10	25	2	4	2	8	4	10	12	12	12	10
			Goals					4	2	2		5	11	9	2	1										1		2	4	1	5

3 own goals

F.A. Cup

Round	Date	Opponent	Score	Scorers	Att	Horstead	Brownsword	Lindsey	Neale	Wilson	Hodgson	Lawther	Jones	Gibson	Harper	Godfrey	Conde
R3	Jan 4	BARNSLEY	2-2	Wilson, Lawther	11160	6	3	8	5	11	7	10	1	4	2	9	
rep	7	Barnsley	2-3	Brownsword 2 (2p)	21337	6	3	4	5	11	8	10	1		2		9

Replay a.e.t.

F.L. Cup

Round	Date	Opponent	Score	Scorers	Att	Horstead	Brownsword	Lindsey	Neale	Gannon	Wilson	Lawther	Smillie	Crawford	Jones	Gibson	Hemstead	Harper
R2	Sep 25	STOKE CITY	2-2	Smillie, Wilson	6945		3	8	5	6	7		9	10	11	1	4		2
rep	Oct 16	Stoke City	3-3	Horstead, Crawford, Neale	11062	6	3	8	9		7			10	11	1	4	5	2
rep2	22	Stoke City	0-1		4297	6	3	8	9		7			10	11	1	4	5	2

Replay a.e.t. Replay 2 at Hillsborough.

		P	W	D	L	F	A	W	D	L	F	A	Pts
1	Leeds United	42	12	9	0	35	16	12	6	3	36	18	63
2	Sunderland	42	16	3	2	47	13	9	8	4	34	24	61
3	Preston North End	42	13	7	1	37	14	10	3	8	42	40	56
4	Charlton Athletic	42	11	4	6	44	30	8	6	7	32	40	48
5	Southampton	42	13	3	5	69	32	6	6	9	31	41	47
6	Manchester City	42	12	4	5	50	27	6	6	9	34	39	46
7	Rotherham United	42	14	3	4	52	26	5	4	12	38	52	45
8	Newcastle United	42	14	2	5	49	26	6	3	12	25	43	45
9	Portsmouth	42	9	7	5	46	34	7	4	10	33	36	43
10	Middlesbrough	42	14	4	3	47	16	1	7	13	20	36	41
11	Northampton Town	42	10	2	9	35	31	6	7	8	23	29	41
12	Huddersfield Town	42	11	4	6	31	25	4	6	11	26	39	40
13	Derby County	42	10	6	5	34	27	4	5	12	22	40	39
14	Swindon Town	42	11	5	5	39	24	3	5	13	18	45	38
15	Cardiff City	42	10	7	4	31	27	4	3	14	25	54	38
16	Leyton Orient	42	8	6	7	32	32	5	4	12	22	40	36
17	Norwich City	42	9	7	5	43	30	2	6	13	21	50	35
18	Bury	42	8	5	8	35	36	5	4	12	22	37	35
19	Swansea Town	42	11	4	6	44	36	1	5	15	24	48	33
20	Plymouth Argyle	42	6	8	7	26	32	2	8	11	19	35	32
21	Grimsby Town	42	6	7	8	28	34	3	7	11	19	41	32
22	SCUNTHORPE UNITED	42	8	8	5	30	25	2	2	17	22	57	30

1964/65 18th in Division 3

#		Date	Opponent	Score	Scorers	Att	Reeves TB	Betts JB	Horstead JB	Lindsey B	Neale P	Bannister J	Hutton J	Kirkman AJ	Lawther WI	Sloan D	Ratcliffe JB	Brownsword NJ	Needham A	Wilson A	Smillie AT	Hemstead DW	Mahy B	Brown MR	Scott RSA	Bramley JS	Thomas BEB	Harper IT	Sidebottom G	Barton F	Smith RW
1	Aug	22	BRISTOL CITY	5-2	Lawther 2, Sloan 2, Kirkman	5562	1	2	3	4	5	6	7	8	9	10	11														
2		26	Gillingham	0-0		14067	1		2	4	5	6	7	8	9	10	11	3													
3		28	Queen's Park Rangers	1-2	Kirkman	6550	1		2	4	5	6	7	8	9	10	11	3													
4	Sep	4	SHREWSBURY TOWN	3-2	Lawther, Sloan, Ratcliffe	6694	1		2	4	5	6	7	8	9	10	11		3												
5		9	Hull City	2-1	Lawther 2	8012	1		2	4	5	6		8	9	10	11		3	7											
6		12	Reading	0-2		6726	1		2		5	6		8	9	10	11		3	7	4										
7		15	HULL CITY	1-1	Ratcliffe	7297	1		4		5	6		8	9	10	11		3	7		2									
8		18	SOUTHEND UNITED	2-1	Sloan, Lawther	5953	1	3	2	4	5	6		8	9	10	11			7											
9		25	Barnsley	0-2		6061	1	2	5			6		8	9	10			3	11			4	7							
10		29	WORKINGTON	1-1	Scott	4993	1				5			8	9	10		3	6	11				7	4						
11	Oct	3	Mansfield Town	2-3	Lawther 2	7803	1	2	6		5		7	8	9	10			3	11					4						
12		6	Workington	0-2		3842	1	2	6		5		7		9	10			3	11				8	4						
13		10	PETERBOROUGH UTD.	2-3	Scott, Sloan	5133	1	2	6	4	5		7		9	10			3	11					8						
14		13	Walsall	4-0	Lawther 2 (1p), Scott, Hutton	4007	1		6	4	5		7		9	8			3	11			2		10						
15		17	Bournemouth	1-2	Horstead	8264	1		6	4	5		7		9	8			3	11			2		10						
16		20	Walsall	2-1	Scott, Lawther	5391	1		6	4	5		7		9				3	11			2		10	8					
17		24	EXETER CITY	0-0		4086	1		6	4	5		7		9				3	11			2		10	8					
18		28	Luton Town	1-1	Scott	3876	1		6	4	5				9	7			3	11			2		10	8					
19		31	Oldham Athletic	1-2	Lawther	9258	1		6	4	5				9	7			3	11			2		10	8					
20	Nov	3	GILLINGHAM	2-3	Scott (p), Lawther	4290	1		5	4					9	10	11		3	7			2		6	8					
21		7	BRISTOL ROVERS	1-1	Lindsey	4213	1		5	4					9	10	11		3	7			2		6	8					
22		20	COLCHESTER UNITED	0-0		7610	1		4	8	5					10	11		3				2		6	7	9				
23		28	Port Vale	1-0	Ratcliffe	4620	1		4	8	5					10	11		3				2		6	7	9				
24	Dec	12	Bristol City	2-2	Thomas 2	8387	1		6	4	5		7	10						11			3		8	9	2				
25		18	QUEEN'S PARK RANGERS	2-1	Ratcliffe, Neale	5344	1				5		7	10			11		3				2		6	8	9	4			
26		26	GRIMSBY TOWN	2-1	Ratcliffe, Kirkman	10867	1			4	5		7	10			11						3		6	8	9	2			
27	Jan	2	Shrewsbury Town	2-3	Hutton, Scott	4707	1			4	5		7	10								3	11		6	8	9	2			
28		8	Exeter City	3-1	Thomas 2, Hutton	6092	1			4	5		7	10			11						3		6	8	9	2			
29		15	READING	1-1	Thomas	5992	1			4	5		7	10			11						3		6	8	9	2			
30		23	Southend United	1-0	Thomas	7630			3	4	5		7	10			11								6	8	9	2	1		
31		29	CARLISLE UNITED	0-1		6710			3	4	5		7	10			11								6	8	9	2	1		
32	Feb	5	BARNSLEY	2-3	Hutton, Thomas	6516			6	4	5		7							11			3		8	10	2		1	9	
33		12	MANSFIELD TOWN	0-1		6115			6	4	5		7							11			3		8	10	2		1	9	
34		26	BOURNEMOUTH	3-1	Ratcliffe, Bramley, Brown	5110				6	5		7				11						3	9	4	8	10	2	1		
35	Mar	6	Carlisle United	1-3	Thomas	9418				6	5		7			8				11			3	9		10	2	1		4	
36		8	Peterborough United	2-2	Brown 2	9661	1		3	8	5		7				11							9	6		10	2			4
37		12	OLDHAM ATHLETIC	1-1	Brown	5795			3	8	5		7				11							9	6		10	2			4
38		20	Bristol Rovers	0-2		6650			3	6	5		7											9	11	8	10	2			4
39		26	BRENTFORD	2-0	Ratcliffe, Scott	5081			3	8	5		7				11							9	6		10	2			4
40	Apr	3	Colchester United	1-2	Lindsey	3212			3	8	5		7				11							9	6			2	1	10	4
41		6	Grimsby Town	0-3		6756			3	8	5		7	10			11							9	6			2	1		4
42		9	PORT VALE	0-0		3894	1		3	8	5		7				11							9	6		10	2			4
43		16	Watford	0-5		7140			2	10	5		7				11						3		6	8	9		1		4
44		20	WATFORD	0-2		3597			2	6	5						11			7		3	10			8	9		1		4
45		24	LUTON TOWN	8-1	Thomas 5, Wilson, Mahy, Bramley	2755			2	6	5						11			3		10			8	7	9	1		4
46		27	Brentford	0-4		6164			2	6	5						11			3		10			8	7	9	1		4
						Apps	31	7	38	39	43	9	31	20	22	21	26	3	20	25	1	25	6	11	32	24	23	19	15	3	12
						Goals			1	2	1		4	3	13	5	7			1			1	4	8	2	13				

F.A. Cup

| R1 | Nov | 14 | DARLINGTON | 1-2 | Greener (og) | 5121 | 1 | | 6 | 4 | 5 | | 7 | | 9 | 8 | | | 3 | 11 | | | 2 | | 10 | | | | | | |

F.L. Cup

| R1 | Sep | 23 | WORKINGTON | 0-1 | | 3910 | 1 | 2 | | 5 | | | 6 | | 8 | 9 | 10 | 11 | | 3 | | 7 | | | 4 | | | | | | |

		P	W	D	L	F	A	W	D	L	F	A	Pts
1	Carlisle United	46	14	5	4	46	24	11	5	7	30	29	60
2	Bristol City	46	14	6	3	53	18	10	5	8	39	37	59
3	Mansfield Town	46	17	4	2	61	23	7	7	9	34	38	59
4	Hull City	46	14	6	3	51	25	9	6	8	40	32	58
5	Brentford	46	18	4	1	55	18	6	5	12	28	37	57
6	Bristol Rovers	46	14	7	2	52	21	6	8	9	30	37	55
7	Gillingham	46	16	5	2	45	13	7	4	12	25	37	55
8	Peterborough Utd.	46	16	3	4	61	33	6	4	13	24	41	51
9	Watford	46	13	8	2	45	21	4	8	11	26	43	50
10	Grimsby Town	46	11	10	2	37	21	5	7	11	31	46	49
11	Bournemouth	46	12	4	7	40	24	6	7	10	32	39	47
12	Southend United	46	14	4	5	48	24	5	4	14	30	47	46
13	Reading	46	12	8	3	45	26	4	6	13	25	44	46
14	Queen's Park Rgs.	46	15	5	3	48	23	2	7	14	24	57	46
15	Workington	46	11	7	5	30	22	6	5	12	28	47	46
16	Shrewsbury Town	46	10	6	7	42	38	5	6	12	34	46	42
17	Exeter City	46	8	7	8	33	27	4	10	9	18	25	41
18	SCUNTHORPE UNITED	46	9	8	6	42	27	5	4	14	23	45	40
19	Walsall	46	9	4	10	34	36	6	3	14	21	44	37
20	Oldham Athletic	46	10	3	10	40	39	3	7	13	21	44	36
21	Luton Town	46	6	8	9	32	36	5	3	15	19	58	33
22	Port Vale	46	7	6	10	27	33	2	8	13	14	43	32
23	Colchester United	46	7	6	10	30	34	3	4	16	20	55	30
24	Barnsley	46	8	5	10	33	31	1	6	16	21	59	29

1965/66 4th in Division 3

#	Date		Opponent	Score	Scorers	Att	Sidebottom G	Lindsey K	Hemstead DW	Scott RSA	Horstead IB	Burkinshaw KH	Hutton J	Barton F	Brown MR	Lindsey B	Colquhoun J	Smith RW	Sloan D	Mahy B	Bedford NB	Goodwin F	Thomas BEB	Bramley JS	Neale P	Ash M	Burrows F	Clemence RN	Taylor SR	Barker J
1	Aug	21	Hull City	2-3	Brown, Hutton	18829	1	2	3	4	5	6	7	8	9	10	11													
2		25	MANSFIELD TOWN	0-1		6894	1	2	3	4	5	6	7		9	10	11	8												
3		28	READING	2-0	Brown, Smith	4335	1	2	3	4	5	6			9	10	11	8	7	12										
4	Sep	4	Exeter City	0-4		5818	1		3	4	5	6	7		9	8	11	2			10									
5		11	PETERBOROUGH UTD.	1-1	Bedford	4828	1			3	6				9	4		2	11		10	5	7	8						
6		14	QUEEN'S PARK RANGERS	1-2	Bedford	5362	1			3	6				9	4		2	11		10	5	7	8						
7		18	Millwall	2-2	Snowdon(og), Hutton	11525	1	2		3	6	7			9	4	11	8			10				5					
8		25	GILLINGHAM	0-1		4325	1	2	3		6	7			9	4	11	8			10				5					
9	Oct	2	Oldham Athletic	3-1	Barton, Bedford, Colquhoun	6363	1	2	3		6	12	9		4	11	8				10				5	7				
10		4	Queen's Park Rangers	0-1		6726	1	2	3		6	7	9		4	11	8	12			10				5					
11		9	Brentford	1-0	Smith	7729	1		3	4	6	7	9		2	11	8				10	12			5					
12		16	BRISTOL ROVERS	3-0	Goodwin, Barton, Bedford	4219	1	2	3	4	6	7	9			11	8	12			10	5								
13		30	OXFORD UNITED	1-2	Smith (p)	4030	1	2	3	4	6	7	9			11	8				10	5								
14	Nov	6	Swansea Town	4-3	Ash, Thomas, Bedford, B.Lindsey	8853	1	2	3						6	11	4	7			10	5	9			8				
15		19	Workington	2-1	Thomas, Bedford	2934	1		3	6	5				2	11	4	7			10		9			8				
16		27	BOURNEMOUTH	3-0	Bedford 2, Smith	2766	1		3	6	5				2	11	4	7			10		9			8				
17	Dec	4	York City	3-1	Sloan, Bedford, Ash	4175	1		3	6	5		9		2	11	4	7			10					8				
18		11	SWINDON TOWN	2-1	Bedford 2	4483	1		3	6	5		9		2	11	4	7			10					8				
19		27	Shrewsbury Town	4-1	Bedford 3, Hutton	7520	1		3	6	5		9		2	11	4	7			10					8				
20		28	SHREWSBURY TOWN	1-4	Bedford	6249	1		3	6	5		9		2	11	4	7			10					8				
21	Jan	1	BRENTFORD	3-2	Sloan, Ash, Thomas	5738	1		3	6	5				2	11	4	7			10		9			8				
22		8	Walsall	0-3		7059	1		3	6	5	12			2	11	4	7			10		9			8				
23		15	YORK CITY	4-1	Burkinshaw, Sloan 2, Bedford	3680	1		3		5	6	9		2	11	4	7			10					12	8			
24		29	HULL CITY	2-4	Colquhoun, Ash	15570	1		3			6	9		2	11	4	7			10					8	5			
25	Feb	5	Reading	0-2		7102	1		3			6	9		2	11	4	7			10					8	5			
26		12	Brighton & Hove Albion	1-0	Bedford	12659	1		3		5	6		8	2	11	4	9			10					12	7			
27		19	EXETER CITY	2-1	Barton, Smith (p)	4576	1		3		5	6		8		11	4	9			10					2	7			
28		26	Peterborough United	1-3	Sloan	6696	1		3		5	6		8		11	4	9			10					12	7			
29	Mar	5	BRIGHTON & HOVE ALB	2-2	Sloan, Barton	4657	1		3		2			8		12	11	4	7		10				9	5		6		
30		7	Mansfield Town	2-2	Bedford, Smith (p)	6678	1	3	2					8		10	11	4	7		9					5		6		
31		12	MILLWALL	4-4	Snowdon(og),Smith,Colquhoun,Barto	5800	1	2	3			6		8		10	11	4	7		9					5				
32		19	Gillingham	1-0	Sloan	6110	1	2	3			6		8		10	11	4	7		9					12		5		
33		26	OLDHAM ATHLETIC	1-1	Bedford	5211	1	2	3			6		8		10	11	4	7		9							5		
34		29	Bristol Rovers	0-2		7376	1	2	3			6				10	11	4	7	8	9							5		
35	Apr	2	SWANSEA TOWN	1-1	Thomas	2914	1		2			6		8		11	4	7			9					12	5	1	3	
36		8	Grimsby Town	3-1	Sloan 3	10960	1		2			6		8		11	4	7			9					10	5		3	
37		12	GRIMSBY TOWN	2-2	Bedford, Colquhoun	7783	1				2	6			12	11	4	7		8	9					10	5		3	
38		16	WORKINGTON	4-1	Thomas 3, Sloan	4088	1		2			6		8		11	4	7			9	·				10	5		3	
39		23	Bournemouth	2-1	Burrows, Thomas	6161	1					6		8		11	4	7			9					10	5		2	3
40		26	Watford	1-2	Barton	4072	1		2			6		8		11	4	7			9					10	5		3	
41		30	SOUTHEND UNITED	0-0		4399	1		2		·	6		8		11	4	7			9					10	5		3	
42	May	7	Swindon Town	0-0		9251	1		2		·	6				11	4	7			9					10	5		3	
43		13	Southend United	1-0	Sloan	7326	1		3			6		8		2	11	4	7		9					10	5		1	
44		17	WATFORD	1-1	Colquhoun	3913	1		3			6				11	4	7	2	9	8					10	5		1	
45		21	WALSALL	4-2	Sloan 2, Thomas, Bedford	3429	1		3			6				11	4	7	2	9	8					10	5		1	
46		28	Oxford United	3-0	Thomas, Bedford, Mahy	4505	1		3			6				11	4	7	2	9	8					10	5			
			Apps				42	15	41	15	21	36	17	21	8	34	44	45	38	5	35	6	19	3	13	28	19	4	8	1
			Goals									1	3	6	2	1	5	7	14	1	22	1	10			4	1			

2 own goals

F.A. Cup

	Date		Opponent	Score		Att	Sidebottom G	Lindsey K	Hemstead DW	Scott RSA	Horstead IB	Burkinshaw KH	Hutton J	Barton F	Brown MR	Lindsey B	Colquhoun J	Smith RW	Sloan D	Mahy B	Bedford NB	Goodwin F	Thomas BEB	Bramley JS	Neale P	Ash M	Burrows F	Clemence RN	Taylor SR	Barker J
R1	Nov	13	Crewe Alexandra	0-3		5148	1	2	3						6	11	4	7			10	5	9			8				

F.L. Cup

	Date		Opponent	Score		Att	Sidebottom G	Lindsey K	Hemstead DW	Scott RSA	Horstead IB	Burkinshaw KH	Hutton J	Barton F	Brown MR	Lindsey B	Colquhoun J	Smith RW	Sloan D	Mahy B	Bedford NB	Goodwin F	Thomas BEB	Bramley JS	Neale P	Ash M	Burrows F	Clemence RN	Taylor SR	Barker J
R1	Sep	1	DARLINGTON	0-2		2856	1	2	3	7	4	6			9		11	8	10						5					

		P	W	D	L	F	A	W	D	L	F	A
1	Hull City	46	19	2	2	64	24	12	5	6	45	38
2	Millwall	46	19	4	0	47	13	8	7	8	29	30
3	Queen's Park Rgs.	46	16	3	4	62	29	8	6	9	33	36
4	SCUNTHORPE UNITED	46	9	8	6	44	34	12	3	8	36	33
5	Workington	46	13	6	4	38	18	6	8	9	29	39
6	Gillingham	46	14	4	5	33	19	8	4	11	29	35
7	Swindon Town	46	11	8	4	43	18	8	5	10	31	30
8	Reading	46	13	5	5	36	19	6	8	9	34	44
9	Walsall	46	13	7	3	48	21	7	3	13	29	43
10	Shrewsbury Town	46	13	7	3	48	22	6	4	13	25	42
11	Grimsby Town	46	15	6	2	47	25	2	7	14	21	37
12	Watford	46	12	4	7	33	19	5	9	9	22	32
13	Peterborough Utd.	46	13	6	4	50	26	4	6	13	30	40
14	Oxford United	46	11	3	9	38	33	8	5	10	32	41
15	Brighton & Hove A.	46	13	4	6	48	28	3	7	13	19	37
16	Bristol Rovers	46	11	10	2	38	15	3	4	16	26	49
17	Swansea Town	46	14	4	5	61	37	1	7	15	20	59
18	Bournemouth	46	9	8	6	24	19	4	4	15	14	37
19	Mansfield Town	46	10	5	8	31	36	5	3	15	28	53
20	Oldham Athletic	46	8	7	8	34	33	4	6	13	21	48
21	Southend United	46	15	1	7	43	28	1	3	19	11	55
22	Exeter City	46	9	6	8	36	28	3	5	15	17	51
23	Brentford	46	9	4	10	34	30	1	8	14	14	39
24	York City	46	5	7	11	30	44	4	2	17	23	62

234

SEASON 1964-65

Back: Horstead, Gaughan, Needham, Reeves, Conde, Wilson, Bannister. 2nd row: Strong (Masseur), Lawther, Sloan, Harper, Hutton, Hemstead, McCamley, Rogan, Ellis, Jeff Barker (Trainer), Duckworth (Manager).
3rd row:Ratcliffe,Brownsword,B.Lindsey,Neale, Kirkman, Mahy, Wilson, Bramley, Smillie. Seated:K.Lindsey,Barton,John Barker

SEASON 1965-66

Back: B.Lindsey, Sloan, Colquhoun, Brown, Mahy, Bramley
2nd row: Bushby (Coach), Strong (Masseur), Sidebottom, Wilson, Horstead,
Burrows, Burkinshaw, Storey (Asst. Secretary), Jeff Barker (Scout)
Seated: Vicary (Secretary), Scott, K.Lindsey, Goodwin (Manager), Smith, Hemstead, Neale, Thomas
Front: Naylor, Batton, Codd, John Barker, Verity, Barton

1966/67 18th in Division 3

Player columns (left→right):
1 Sidebottom G · 2 Mahy B · 3 Hemstead DW · 4 Smith RW · 5 Burrows F · 6 Burkinshaw KH · 7 Sloan D · 8 Barton F · 9 Thomas BEB · 10 Ash M · 11 Colquhoun J · 12 Bramley JS · 13 Horstead JB · 14 Clemence RN · 15 Barker J · 16 Taylor SR · 17 Welbourne D · 18 Bedford NB · 19 Neale P · 20 Lindsey B · 21 Rusling G · 22 Coatsworth FW · 23 Webster AJ · 24 Foxon DN

#	Date	Opponent	Res	Scorers	Att	Sb	My	He	Sm	Bu	Bk	Sl	Ba	Th	As	Co	Br	Ho	Cl	Bk	Ta	We	Be	Ne	Li	Ru	Coa	Web	Fox
1	Aug 20	GILLINGHAM	1-2	Thomas	5050	1	2	3	4	5	6	7	8	9	10	11													
2	27	Orient	1-3	Ash	5475	1	2	3	4	5	6	7	9		10	11	8	12											
3	Sep 3	BOURNEMOUTH	0-1		4173				4				7		10	11		5	1	2	3	6	8	9					
4	7	Grimsby Town	1-7	Bedford	8044				4					9	10	11	7	5	1	2	3	6	8						
5	10	Swansea Town	1-0	Lindsey	6165			2	4		6		8		10		7	5	1		3				9	11			
6	17	MIDDLESBROUGH	3-2	Bramley, Barton, Lindsey	3948			2	4		6		8		10	9	7	5	1		3				12	11			
7	24	Shrewsbury Town	3-4	Ash, Barton, Smith	4300			2	4	5	6		8		10	9	7		1		3					11			
8	27	GRIMSBY TOWN	0-0		11105			2	4	5	6		8	12	10	9	7		1		3				11				
9	30	COLCHESTER UNITED	3-1	Loughton(og), Thomas, Smith	5222			2	4	5	6		8	9	10	11	7		1		3								
10	Oct 8	Walsall	0-2		9326			2	4	5	6		8	9	10	11	7		1		3								
11	14	PETERBOROUGH UTD.	1-0	Smith (p)	5723			2	4	5	6	7	8	9	10	11			1		3								
12	18	Oldham Athletic	0-2		13975			2	4	5	6	7	8	9	10	11			1		3								
13	22	Torquay United	1-1	Colquhoun	5418			2	4	5	6	7	8	9	10	11			1		3								
14	24	Bristol Rovers	1-1	Thomas	11015			2	4	5	6	7	8	9	10	11			1		3								
15	28	BRIGHTON & HOVE ALB	0-1		5512			2	4	5	6	7	8	9	10	11			1		3								
16	Nov 5	Darlington	1-2	Smith	6650			2	4	5	6	7	8	9	10	11			1		3								
17	12	QUEEN'S PARK RANGERS	0-2		4912			2	4	5	6	7	8		10	11	9		1		3								
18	15	OLDHAM ATHLETIC	1-1	Colquhoun	3580		7	2	4		6	9	8		10	11		5	1		3								
19	19	Watford	1-0	Barton	7084		7	2	4		6	9	8		10	11		5	1		3								
20	Dec 3	Reading	0-4		5080		10	2	4		6	9	8	7		11		5	1		3								
21	9	DONCASTER ROVERS	2-1	Smith, Burkinshaw	6300		7	2	4		6	9	8		10	11		5	1		3								
22	17	Gillingham	1-0	Ash	5468		7	2	4		6	9	8		10	11		5	1		3								
23	23	MANSFIELD TOWN	2-1	Sloan, Barton	6263			2	4	9	6	7	8			11		5	1		3				10				
24	27	Mansfield Town	1-3	Lindsey	10292			2	4	9	6	7	8			11		5	1		3				10				
25	30	ORIENT	2-2	Sloan, Barton	5343			2	4	9	6	7	8			11		5	1		3				10				
26	Jan 14	SWANSEA TOWN	4-3	Hemstead, Rusling, Lindsey, Sloan	4461			2	4	9	6	7				11		5	1		3				10	8			
27	21	Middlesbrough	1-2	Burrows	19007			2	4	9	6	7				11		5	1		3				10	8			
28	28	Bournemouth	0-0		3941			2		9	6	7	10			11		5	1		3				4	8			
29	Feb 4	SHREWSBURY TOWN	2-0	Rusling 2	4447			2		9	6	7	10			11		5	1		3				4	8			
30	11	Colchester United	1-0	Sloan	3965			2		9	6	7	10			11		5	1		3				4	8			
31	18	Oxford United	1-2	Burkinshaw	7013			2		5	6	7	8			11			1		3				4	9	10		
32	24	WALSALL	2-0	Colquhoun, Barton	4839			2		5	6	7	8			11			1		3				4	9	10		
33	Mar 4	Peterborough United	0-1		5485			2		5	6	7	8			11			1	12	3				4	9	10		
34	10	OXFORD UNITED	2-2	Barton (p), Sloan	4616			2		5	6	7	8			11			1		3				4	9	10		
35	17	TORQUAY UNITED	3-1	Coatsworth, Smith(og), Sloan	4353			2		5	6	7	8			10			1		3				4	9	11		
36	25	Brighton & Hove Albion	2-2	Colquhoun, Hemstead	11624			2		5	6	7	8			10			1		3				4	9	11		
37	27	WORKINGTON	4-1	Colquhoun, Barton 2 (1 p), Sloan	5486			2		5	6	7	8			10			1		3				4	9	11		
38	28	Workington	0-1		2079			2		5	6	7	8			10			1	4	3					9	11		
39	31	DARLINGTON	2-0	Sloan, Rusling	4621			2		5	6	7	8			10			1	4	3					9	11		
40	Apr 8	Queen's Park Rangers	1-5	Rusling	13113			2		5	6	7	8			10			1		3				4	9	11		
41	14	WATFORD	1-0	Colquhoun	4927			2		5	6	7	8			10			1		3				4	9	11		
42	22	Swindon Town	1-2	Sloan	12786			2		5	6	7	8			10			1		3					9	11	4	
43	24	BRISTOL ROVERS	3-1	Barton 2, Coatsworth	4080			2		5	6		8			10		4	1		3					9	11		7
44	28	READING	0-2		4984			2			6	7	8			10		5	1		3				4	9	11		
45	May 5	Doncaster Rovers	0-3		3948			2		5	6	7	8			10			1		3				4	9	11		
46	12	SWINDON TOWN	1-2	Colquhoun	3544			2		5	6	7	8			10	12	11	1		3				4	9			
		Apps				2	7	44	25	41	44	35	44	10	21	45	8	25	44	21	27	2	2	3	23	20	14	1	2
		Goals						2	5	1	2	9	11	3	3	7	1						1		4	5	2		

2 own goals

F.A. Cup

Round	Date	Opponent	Res	Scorers	Att	Sb	My	He	Sm	Bu	Bk	Sl	Ba	Th	As	Co	Br	Ho	Cl	Bk	Ta	We	Be	Ne	Li	Ru	Coa	Web	Fox
R1	Nov 26	Lincoln City	4-3	Smith, Burrows, Barton, Mahy	6223		7	2	4		6	9	8		10	11		5	1		3								
R2	Jan 7	Mansfield Town	1-2	Foxon	9446			2	4	9	6		8			11		5	1		3				10				7

F.L. Cup

Round	Date	Opponent	Res	Scorers	Att	Sb	My	He	Sm	Bu	Bk	Sl	Ba	Th	As	Co
R1	Aug 24	Chesterfield	1-2	Barton	5418	1	2	3	4	5	6	7	8	9	10	11

		P	W	D	L	F	A	W	D	L	F	A
1	Queen's Park Rgs.	46	18	4	1	66	15	8	11	4	37	23
2	Middlesbrough	46	16	3	4	51	20	7	6	10	36	44
3	Watford	46	15	5	3	39	17	5	9	9	22	29
4	Reading	46	13	7	3	45	20	9	2	12	31	37
5	Bristol Rovers	46	13	8	2	47	28	7	5	11	29	39
6	Shrewsbury Town	46	15	5	3	48	24	5	7	11	29	38
7	Torquay United	46	17	3	3	57	20	4	6	13	16	34
8	Swindon Town	46	14	5	4	53	21	6	5	12	28	38
9	Mansfield Town	46	12	4	7	48	37	8	5	10	36	42
10	Oldham Athletic	46	15	4	4	51	16	4	6	13	29	47
11	Gillingham	46	11	9	3	36	18	4	7	12	22	44
12	Walsall	46	12	8	3	37	16	6	2	15	28	56
13	Colchester United	46	14	3	6	52	30	3	7	13	24	43
14	Orient	46	10	9	4	36	27	3	9	11	22	41
15	Peterborough Utd.	46	12	4	7	40	31	2	11	10	26	40
16	Oxford United	46	10	8	5	41	29	5	5	13	20	37
17	Grimsby Town	46	13	5	5	46	23	4	4	15	15	45
18	SCUNTHORPE UNITED	46	13	4	6	39	26	3	4	16	15	47
19	Brighton & Hove A.	46	10	8	5	37	27	3	7	13	24	44
20	Bournemouth	46	8	10	5	24	24	4	7	12	15	33
21	Swansea Town	46	9	9	5	50	30	3	6	14	35	59
22	Darlington	46	8	7	8	26	28	5	4	14	21	53
23	Doncaster Rovers	46	11	6	6	40	40	1	4	16	20	77
24	Workington	46	9	3	11	35	35	3	4	16	20	54

SEASON 1966-67
Back: Brownsword, Bushby, Neale, Horstead, Barker, Bramley, Burkingshaw, Hutton, Taylor, Hemstead,
Sidebottom, Clemence, unknown, Goodwin
Front: Thomas, Bedford, Naylor, unknown, Coatsworth, Ash, Sloan, Smith, Colquhoun, Lindsey

SEASON 1967-68   (Players only - three officials in darker shirts)
Standing: Lavery, Hemstead, Foxton, Holt, Deere, Drake, Kerr, Burrows
Kneeling: Harvey, Colquhoun, Heath, Barker, Punton

1967/68 24th in Division 3: Relegated

#	Date		Opponent	Score	Scorers	Att	Arblaster BM	Hemstead DW	Barker J	Lindsey B	Burrows F	Burkinshaw KH	Sloan D	Barton F	Harney D	Colquhoun J	Foley P	Taylor SR	Foxon DN	Horstead JB	Webster AJ	Drake S	Verity DA	Naylor G	Deere SH	Rusling G	Blyth MR	Lavery J	Welbourne D	Foxton DG	Punton WH	Kerr GAM	Heath RT
1	Aug	19	Peterborough United	1-1	Barton	6984	1	2	3	4	5	6	7	8	9	10	11																
2		25	MANSFIELD TOWN	3-3	Sloan, Barton (p), Burrows	6372	1	2	3	4	5	6	7	8	9	10	11	12															
3	Sep	2	Watford	0-4		6675	1	2	3	4	5	6	7	8	9	10	11	11															
4		4	Bournemouth	0-1		6302	1	2	3	4	5	6	7	8	9	10		12	11														
5		9	SOUTHPORT	1-0	Sloan	4655	1	2	3	4	5	6	7	8	9	10			11														
6		16	Grimsby Town	1-2	Barton	7825	1	2		4	5	6	9	8	12	10	7	3	11														
7		23	Oldham Athletic	4-3	Barton, Sloan 2, Horstead	5263	1	2		4	5	6	7	8	9	10		3	11	12													
8		26	BOURNEMOUTH	1-1	Barton	4936	1	2		4	5	6	7	8	9	10		3	11		12												
9		30	BRISTOL ROVERS	1-1	Sloan	3848	1	2			5	6	7	8	9	10		3	11		4												
10	Oct	3	Bury	3-4	Harney, Colquhoun 2	5932	1	2			5	6	7	4	9	8		3	11	12													
11		7	WALSALL	2-5	Barton 2 (1 p)	4170		2			5	6	7	8	9	9		3	11			4	1	12									
12		14	Northampton Town	0-1		10099		2			5	6	7	8	9	10		3	11			4	1										
13		21	Orient	1-1	Foxon	3431		2			5	6	7	8	9	10		3	11	4			1										
14		24	BURY	3-1	Sloan, Horstead, Barton	3847		2			5	6	7	8	9	10		3	11	4			1										
15		27	Tranmere Rovers	0-2		6977		2			5	6	7	8	9	10		3	11	4			1	12									
16	Nov	3	STOCKPORT COUNTY	0-2		4338		2			5	6	7	8	9	10		3	11	4			1	12									
17		11	Brighton & Hove Albion	1-3	Deere	11251		2			5	6	7	8	11	10		3	12				1	4	9								
18		14	WATFORD	1-1	Rusling	3445		2			5		7	8		9		3	11				1	4	6	10							
19		17	SHREWSBURY TOWN	0-0		3104		2			5		7	8		9		3	11				1	4	10	6							
20		25	Swindon Town	0-2		11944		2			5		7	8		9		3	11				1	4	10	6							
21	Dec	1	READING	1-1	Colquhoun	3541		2			5		7	8		9		3	11				1	4	10	6	12						
22		15	PETERBOROUGH UTD.	2-1	Deere, Barton	3519		2			5	6	7	8		11			3				1	4	9	10							
23		23	Mansfield Town	0-3		4907		2	3		5	6	7	8		11							1	4	9	10							
24		26	OXFORD UNITED	1-1	Sloan	3839		2	3		5	6	7	8		11		12					1	4	9	10							
25		30	Oxford United	3-2	Deere 2, Sloan	6392		2	3		5	6	7	8					11					4	9	10		1	10				
26	Jan	20	GRIMSBY TOWN	0-3		6886		2	3		5	6	7			8		11							9	10	1	4	12				
27		26	GILLINGHAM	2-1	Blyth 2	3484		2	3	4	5	6	8			9	7								10		1				11		
28	Feb	3	OLDHAM ATHLETIC	2-0	Sloan, Foley	3697		2	3	4	5	6	8			9	7								10		1				11		
29		10	Bristol Rovers	0-4		5666		2	3	4	5	6	8			9	7								10		1				11		
30		17	BARROW	2-4	Lindsey, Sloan	3229		2		4	5	6	8			9	7	3							10		1				11		
31		24	Walsall	0-0		8987		2		8	5	6				11		3		4					9		1					7	
32		26	Colchester United	0-1		3979		2			5	6				11		3		4	8				9		1	12				7	
33	Mar	2	NORTHAMPTON T	1-1	Kerr	2475	2	3	4	5						8							7		6	1	10				11	9	
34		9	COLCHESTER UNITED	5-1	Colquhoun 2, Punton, Heath, Deere	3098	2	3	4	5						7									9	6	1				11	8	10
35		16	Orient	1-2	Heath	5067	2	3	4	5						7									9	6	1				11	8	10
36		22	TRANMERE ROVERS	1-1	Colquhoun	3986	2	3	4	5						7									9	6	1				11	8	10
37		29	Stockport County	1-4	Heath	6779	2	3	4	5						7		12							9	6	1				11	8	10
38	Apr	6	BRIGHTON & HOVE ALB	1-3	Burrows (p)	2845	2	3	4	5						8					7				9	6	1				11		10
39		13	Shrewsbury Town	0-4		5578	3		4	5						7									9	6	1		2		11	8	10
40		15	Gillingham	1-3	Kerr	5031	3		4	5						7		12	1				9	6					2		11	8	10
41		19	SWINDON TOWN	3-1	Heath, Kerr 2	2725	3		4	5						7			1				9	6					2		11	8	10
42		25	Torquay United	1-2	Heath	10362	3		4	5						7			1				9	6					2		11	8	10
43		27	Reading	1-2	Colquhoun	3879	3		4	5						7			1	10			9	6					2		11	8	
44	May	3	TORQUAY UNITED	2-0	Rusling, Blyth	2700	3		4	5						7	12		1				9	6					2		11	8	10
45		6	Southport	1-1	Colquhoun	3238	2		4	5						11	7		1	12			9	6					3			8	10
46		11	Barrow	1-2	Kerr	3782	3		4	5		7	11	9					1					6					2			8	10
			Apps				10	46	18	27	46	28	30	25	18	45	13	24	20	9	5	21	4	10	19	8	27	15	4	9	16	15	12
			Goals							1	2		10	9	1	8	1			1	2				5	2	3				1	5	5

F.A. Cup

	Date		Opponent	Score	Scorers	Att	Hem	Bar	Bur	Brk	Slo	Brt	Col	Tay	Ver	Nay	Dee	Fxt	Pun
R1	Dec	9	SKELMERSDALE UNITED	2-0	Colquhoun, Barton (p)	3847	2		5	6	7	8	11	3	1	4	10		9
R2	Jan	6	Halifax Town	0-1		7804	2	3	5	6	7	8	11			4	9	1	10

F.L. Cup

	Date		Opponent	Score	Scorers	Att	Arb	Hem	Bar	Lin	Bur	Brk	Slo	Brt	Har	Col	Fol	Tay	Fox
R1	Aug	23	Doncaster Rovers	2-1	Barton, Foley	8666	1	2	3	4	5	6	7	8	9	10	11		
R2	Sep	13	NOTTM. FOREST	0-1		13523	1	2	3	4	5	6	9	8	11	10	7	12	

		P	W	D	L	F	A	W	D	L	F	A	Pts
1	Oxford United	46	18	3	2	49	20	4	10	9	20	27	57
2	Bury	46	19	3	1	64	24	5	5	13	27	42	56
3	Shrewsbury Town	46	14	6	3	42	17	6	9	8	19	32	55
4	Torquay United	46	15	6	2	40	17	6	5	12	20	39	53
5	Reading	46	15	5	3	43	17	6	4	13	27	43	51
6	Watford	46	15	3	5	59	20	6	5	12	15	30	50
7	Walsall	46	12	7	4	47	22	7	5	11	27	39	50
8	Barrow	46	14	6	3	43	13	7	2	14	22	41	50
9	Peterborough Utd.	46	14	4	5	46	23	6	6	11	33	44	50
10	Swindon Town	46	13	8	2	51	16	3	9	11	23	35	49
11	Brighton & Hove A.	46	11	8	4	31	14	5	8	10	26	41	48
12	Gillingham	46	13	6	4	35	19	5	6	12	24	44	48
13	Bournemouth	46	13	7	3	39	17	3	8	12	17	34	47
14	Stockport County	46	16	5	2	49	22	3	4	16	21	53	47
15	Southport	46	13	6	4	35	22	4	6	13	30	43	46
16	Bristol Rovers	46	14	3	6	42	25	3	6	14	30	53	43
17	Oldham Athletic	46	11	3	9	37	32	7	4	12	23	33	43
18	Northampton Town	46	10	8	5	40	25	4	5	14	18	47	41
19	Orient	46	10	6	7	27	24	2	11	10	19	38	41
20	Tranmere Rovers	46	10	7	6	39	28	4	5	14	23	46	40
21	Mansfield Town	46	8	7	8	32	26	4	6	13	19	36	37
22	Grimsby Town	46	10	7	6	33	21	4	2	17	19	48	37
23	Colchester United	46	6	8	9	29	40	3	7	13	21	47	33
24	SCUNTHORPE UNITE	46	8	9	6	36	34	2	3	18	20	53	32

238

1968/69 16th in Division 4

		Opponent	Score	Scorers	Att	Barnard G	FoxtonDG	Hemstead DW	Lindsey B	Holt R	Welbourne D	Colquhoun J	Kerr GAM	Harney D	Heath RT	Punton WH	Deere SH	Barker I	Foley P	Davidson I	Keegan IK	Wilson AP	Taylor SR	Cassidy N	Jackson NA	Rusling G	Currie JT
1	Aug 10	Rochdale	2-3	Kerr, Deere	3253	1	2	3	4	5	6	7	8	9	10	11	12										
2	17	BRENTFORD	1-1	Deere	3685	1	2	3	4	5	6	7	8		10	11	9										
3	23	Doncaster Rovers	3-4	Heath 2, Kerr	10474	1	2	3	4	5	6	7	8		10	11	9	12									
4	26	Colchester United	4-0	Kerr 2, Heath, Deere	3771	1		2	4	5	6	7	8		10	11	9	3									
5	30	CHESTER	2-2	Kerr, Colquhoun	4983	1		2	4	5	6	7	8		10	11	9	3									
6	Sep 6	BRADFORD CITY	1-0	Deere	5997	1	12	2	4	5	6	7	8		10	11	9	3									
7	14	York City	1-2	Colquhoun	5071	1		2	4	5	6	11	8		10		9	3	7	12							
8	16	Peterborough United	2-3	Foley, Heath	5401	1		2	4	5		11		12	10		9	3	8	6	7						
9	21	EXETER CITY	2-1	Deere, Foley (p)	3534	1		2	4	5	6	11			10		9	3	8	12	7						
10	28	Port Vale	1-4	Heath	3823	1		2		5	6	11			10		9	3	8	4	12	7					
11	Oct 4	HALIFAX TOWN	0-1		3942	1	2	3		5	6			8	10	11	9		4		7						
12	8	COLCHESTER UNITED	2-3	Kerr, Heath	2849	1	2	3		5	6		8		10	11	9		4		7						
13	12	Workington	1-1	Welbourne	2287	1	2	3		5	6		8		10	11	9		4		7						
14	18	NEWPORT COUNTY	1-0	Heath (p)	3360	1	2	3		5	6	11	8	12	10		9		4		7						
15	26	Aldershot	2-3	Heath, Rafferty (og)	4991	1		2	12	5	6	11	8		10		9	3	4		7						
16	Nov 1	SWANSEA TOWN	3-1	Kerr, Wilson 2	3451	1		2		5	6	11	8		10		9	3	4	12	7						
17	6	GRIMSBY TOWN	1-2	Colquhoun	5368	1		2		5	6	11	8		10		9	3	4	12	7						
18	9	Wrexham	1-0	Kerr	5848	1		2		5	6	4	8	11	10		9	3			7						
19	23	Darlington	1-0	Heath	4903	1		2		5	6		9		10	11		3		4	8	7					
20	30	LINCOLN CITY	0-0		5855	1		2		5			9		10	11	12	6		4	8	7	3				
21	Dec 6	BRADFORD PARK AVE.	1-0	Deere	3158	1		2		5	6		9			11	10	3		4	8	7					
22	26	Halifax Town	0-2		7092	1		2			5		8			11		6		4	10	7	3	9			
23	Jan 4	NOTTS COUNTY	2-1	Kerr, Cassidy	3410	1		2			5		8			11	10	6		4	12	7	3	9			
24	11	Swansea Town	0-2		4888	1				5	6		8	12		11	10	2		4	7			9			
25	25	Grimsby Town	1-0	Cassidy	5983	1		2	10	5	6		8			11				4	7			9			
26	28	WORKINGTON	0-1		4425	1		2	10	5			8			11	12	6		4	7			9	3		
27	Feb 1	Bradford Park Avenue	2-2	Kerr, Keegan	3050	1		2	10	5	6		8			11	12	3		4	7			9			
28	15	Lincoln City	2-1	Kerr, Cassidy	8186	1		2	10	5	6		8			11	12			4	7			9	3		
29	24	Newport County	1-1	Lindsey	1504	1		2	10	5			8			11	6			4	7			9	3		
30	Mar 1	ROCHDALE	0-0		3102	1		2	10	5			8			11	6			4	7		3	9			
31	5	Notts County	0-1		3311	1		2			6		8	12		11	5	3		4	10	7		9			
32	8	Brentford	1-2	Heath (p)	5456	1		2			6		8	10	11	5	3		4	7				9			
33	14	DONCASTER ROVERS	0-2		6650	1		2			6		8		10	5	3		4	11	7		9			12	
34	17	Southend United	3-0	Heath, Haydock(og), Cassidy	10131	1		2			6		8		10	5	3		4	7	11			9			
35	22	Chester	2-0	Wilson, Cassidy	5483	1		2			6		8		10	5	3		4	11	7		9				
36	25	WREXHAM	1-0	Wilson	2876	1		2			6		8		10	5			4	7	11	3	9				
37	29	Bradford City	0-3		6584	1		2			6		8		10	5			4	7	11	3	9				
38	Apr 5	PORT VALE	0-1		2966	1		2			6		8		10	11	5		4	7		3	9				
39	7	PETERBOROUGH UTD.	1-2	Punton	2822	1		2			6		8		10	11	5			7			9	3	4		
40	8	Chesterfield	2-1	Heath, Kerr	3793	1		2		5			8		4	11	6			10	7		9	3			
41	12	Exeter City	1-3	Heath (p)	4566	1		2		5			8		4	11	6			10	7		9	3			
42	15	CHESTERFIELD	0-1		2398	1		2		5			8		4	11	6		12	10	7		9	3			
43	18	YORK CITY	2-1	Kerr, Heath (p)	2300	1		3		5	6		12		10	11	4			4	8		9	2			
44	29	ALDERSHOT	4-1	Rusling, Cassidy, Keegan, Heath	2220	1		2		5			7			11	6	3		4	8		9			10	
45	May 2	DARLINGTON	0-0		2500	1		2		5			7			11	6	3		4	8		9			10	
46	12	SOUTHEND UNITED	4-1	Cassidy 2, Rusling 2	1850	1		2		5	6		7			11	3			8			9			10	4

Players substituted in games 1 and 23 unknown.

Apps	46	8	45	16	35	36	15	42	7	33	29	43	30	4	35	33	23	8	25	8	5	1
Goals				1		1	3	13		15	1	6		2		2	4		8		3	

2 own goals

F.A. Cup

| R1 | Nov 16 | Workington | 0-2 | | 3325 | 1 | | 2 | | 5 | 6 | | 8 | | 9 | 10 | | 4 | 11 | 7 | 3 | | | | |

F.L. Cup

R1	Aug 13	ROTHERHAM UNITED	2-1	Deere 2	4643	1	2	3	4	5	6	7	8		10	11	9								
R2	Sep 3	LINCOLN CITY	2-1	Kerr 2	11098	1		2	4	5	6	7	8		10	11	9	3							
R3	25	ARSENAL	1-6	Simpson (og)	17230	1		2		5	6	11			10		9	3	8	4	7			12	

1969/70 12th in Division 4

No	Date	Opponent	Res	Scorers	Att	Barnard G	Foxton DG	Barker J	Deere SH	Holt R	Welbourne D	Kerr GAM	Keegan JK	Cassidy N	Heath RT	Rusling G	Davidson AG	Jackson NA	Currie JT	Lindsey B	Atkin JM	Drake S
1	Aug 9	CHESTER	2-3	Rusling, Deere	3361	1	2	3	4	5	6	7	8	9	10	11						
2	15	Southend United	0-3		8808	1	2	3	4	5	6	7	8	9	10	11	12					
3	23	PETERBOROUGH UTD.	2-1	Heath, Deere	2582	1	2	3	4	5	6		8	9	10	11	7	12				
4	26	BRADFORD PARK AVE.	2-0	Rusling, Keegan	3191	1	2	3	4	5	6		8	9	10	11	7					
5	30	Oldham Athletic	3-1	Deere, Davidson, Cassidy	5426	1	2	3	4	5	6		8	9	10	11	7					
6	Sep 6	EXETER CITY	0-0		4073	1	2	3	4	5	6		8	9	10	11	7					
7	13	Grimsby Town	1-1	Heath (p)	7335	1	2	3	4	5	6		8	9	10	11	7					
8	15	Wrexham	1-2	Heath	9575	1	2	3	4	5	6	12	8	9	10	11	7					
9	20	ALDERSHOT	0-0		3596	1	2		4	5	6	3	8	9	10	11	7	12				
10	27	York City	2-3	Keegan 2	4610	1	2		4	5	6	11	8	9		7	3					
11	29	Colchester United	2-0	Deere, Heath	6328	1	2		4	5	6	11	8	9	10	7	3					
12	Oct 4	CHESTERFIELD	1-2	Cassidy	3889	1	2		4	5	6	11	8	9	10	7	3	12				
13	7	SOUTHEND UNITED	2-0	Rusling, Cassidy	2964	1	2		4	5	6		8	9	10	11	7	3	12			
14	11	Brentford	0-3		7490	1	2		4	5	6		8	9	10	11	7	3		12		
15	18	Lincoln City	2-1	Cassidy 2	8172	1	2				6	7	8	10	9	11		3		4	5	
16	25	HARTLEPOOL	3-1	Cassidy, Keegan, Rusling	3583	1	2				6	7	8	10	9	11		3		4	5	
17	Nov 1	Crewe Alexandra	2-0	Heath 2	3190	1	2				6	7	8	10	9	11		3		4	5	
18	8	DARLINGTON	2-0	Cassidy, Rusling	3488	1	2				6	7	8	10	9	11		3		4	5	
19	22	PORT VALE	2-1	Heath (p), Sproson (og)	5516	1	2	3			6	7	8	10	9	11				4	5	
20	25	WORKINGTON	1-0	Davidson	3256	1		3			6	7	8	10	9	11		2		4	5	
21	29	Notts County	1-3	Ball (og)	3497	1		3			6	7	8	10	9	11		2		4	5	
22	Dec 13	GRIMSBY TOWN	1-1	Cassidy	7154	1	2	3			6	9	7	8	10					4	5	
23	20	Exeter City	1-4	Cassidy	3534	1	2	3			6	9	7	8	10					4	5	
24	26	Peterborough United	2-2	Barker, Kerr	7796		2	3	5		6	8	7	10	9		11			4		1
25	27	OLDHAM ATHLETIC	2-1	Davidson, Cassidy	4949		2	3	5		6	9	7	10			11			4		1
26	Jan 10	Aldershot	1-3	Davidson	5520	1	2	3	4	5	6	9	7	8	10		11					
27	17	YORK CITY	1-1	Davidson	4740	1	2		4		6	9	7	8	10		11	3				
28	27	COLCHESTER UNITED	1-1	Cassidy	6276	1	2		4		6	9	7	8	10		11	3	12			
29	31	Chesterfield	1-2	Cassidy	11921	1	2	3	10		6	9	7	8			11	12	4			
30	Feb 10	BRENTFORD	1-1	Heath	5109	1	2	3	5		6	9	7	8	10		11		4			
31	14	Chester	1-1	Heath	3968	1	2	3	5		6	9	7	8	10		11		4			
32	18	Northampton Town	1-2	Heath (p)	3735	1	2	3	4		6	9	7	10	8		11	12			5	
33	20	Hartlepool	2-1	Heath, Kerr	1480	1	2	3	5		6	9	7	8	10		11		4			
34	28	LINCOLN CITY	2-1	Cassidy 2	6857	1	2	3	5		6	9	7	8	10		11		4			
35	Mar 3	SWANSEA TOWN	1-2	Keegan	4988	1	2	3	5		6	9	7	8	10		11		4			
36	9	Newport County	0-3		1917	1	2	3	5		6	9	7	8	10		11	12	4			
37	14	NOTTS COUNTY	2-3	Kerr, Cassidy	4166	1	2	3	5		6	9	7	8			10	11	12	4		
38	17	NORTHAMPTON T	1-0	Davidson	2984	1	2	3	5		6	9	7	8			10	11	3	4		
39	21	Swansea Town	1-2	Barker	10228	1	2	4	5		6	9	7	8			11	3				
40	23	Port Vale	2-1	Cassidy 2	6394	1	2	4	5			9	7	8			11	3			6	
41	28	NEWPORT COUNTY	4-0	Kerr, Cassidy 2, Davidson	3805	1	2		4		9		7	8	10		11	3			5	
42	30	Darlington	0-2		1717	1	2		6		9		7	8	10		11	3			5	
43	31	CREWE ALEXANDRA	0-1		3665	1	2		4		6		7	8	10	9	11	3	12		5	
44	Apr 4	Bradford Park Avenue	5-0	Kerr 2, Heath, Cassidy, Davidson	2563	1	2		5		6	9	7	8	10		11	3		4		
45	8	Workington	2-2	Heath, Cassidy	2475	1	2		5		6	9	7	8	10		11	3		4		
46	14	WREXHAM	1-3	Davidson	4107	1	2		5		6	9	7	8	10		11	3		4		
		Apps				44	44	27	46	15	36	31	46	44	44	26	45	25	5	22	17	2
		Goals						2	4			6	6	21	13	5	8					

2 own goals

F.A. Cup

Rd	Date	Opponent	Res	Scorers	Att	Barnard G	Foxton DG	Barker J	Deere SH	Holt R	Welbourne D	Kerr GAM	Keegan JK	Cassidy N	Heath RT	Rusling G	Davidson AG	Jackson NA	Currie JT	Lindsey B	Atkin JM	Drake S
R1	Nov 15	Macclesfield Town	1-1	Heath	5476	1	2	3			6		7	8	10	9	11			4	5	
rep	18	MACCLESFIELD TOWN	4-2	Keegan 2, Rusling, Cassidy	5131	1	2	3			6	12	7	8	10	9	11			4	5	
R2	Dec 6	Stockport County	0-0		4200	1	2	3			6		7	8	10	9	11			4	5	
rep	9	STOCKPORT COUNTY	4-0	Cassidy, Kerr 2, Keegan	5646	1	2	3			6	9	7	8	10		11			4	5	
R3	Jan 3	MILLWALL	2-1	Deere, Heath	7675	1	2	3			6	5	9	7	8	10	*11			4	12	
R4	24	Sheffield Wednesday	2-1	Barker, Cassidy	38047	1	2	3	4		6	9	7	8	10	12	11				5	
R5	Feb 7	Swindon Town	1-3	Cassidy	24612	1	2	3	4		6	9	7	8	10		11				5	

F.L. Cup

Rd	Date	Opponent	Res	Att	Barnard G	Foxton DG	Barker J	Deere SH	Holt R	Welbourne D	Kerr GAM	Keegan JK	Cassidy N	Heath RT	Rusling G	Davidson AG
R1	Aug 12	HARTLEPOOL	0-2	2800	1	2	3	4	5	6	7	8	9	10	11	12

		P	W	D	L	F	A	W	D	L	F	A	Pts
1	Chesterfield	46	19	1	3	55	12	8	9	6	22	20	64
2	Wrexham	46	17	6	0	56	16	9	3	11	28	33	61
3	Swansea Town	46	14	8	1	43	14	7	10	6	23	31	60
4	Port Vale	46	13	9	1	39	10	7	10	6	22	23	59
5	Brentford	46	14	8	1	36	11	6	8	9	22	28	56
6	Aldershot	46	16	5	2	52	22	4	8	11	26	43	53
7	Notts County	46	14	4	5	44	21	8	4	11	29	41	52
8	Lincoln City	46	11	8	4	38	20	6	8	9	28	32	50
9	Peterborough Utd.	46	13	8	2	51	21	4	6	13	26	48	48
10	Colchester United	46	14	5	4	38	22	3	9	11	26	41	48
11	Chester	46	14	3	6	39	23	7	3	13	19	43	48
12	SCUNTHORPE UNITED	46	11	6	6	34	23	7	4	12	33	42	46
13	York City	46	14	7	2	38	16	2	7	14	17	46	46
14	Northampton Town	46	11	7	5	41	19	5	5	13	23	36	44
15	Crewe Alexandra	46	12	6	5	37	18	4	6	13	14	33	44
16	Grimsby Town	46	9	9	5	33	24	5	6	12	21	34	43
17	Southend United	46	12	8	3	40	28	3	2	18	19	57	40
18	Exeter City	46	13	5	5	48	20	1	6	16	9	39	39
19	Oldham Athletic	46	11	4	8	45	28	2	9	12	15	37	39
20	Workington	46	9	9	5	31	21	3	5	15	15	43	38
21	Newport County	46	12	3	8	39	24	1	8	14	14	50	37
22	Darlington	46	7	8	8	31	27	5	3	15	22	46	36
23	Hartlepool	46	7	7	9	31	30	3	3	17	11	52	30
24	Bradford Park Ave.	46	6	5	12	23	32	0	6	17	18	64	23

SEASON 1968-69
Back: Kerr, Punton, Taylor, Foley, Barnard, Lavery, Drake
Middle: unknown, Jackson, Lindsey, Welbourne, Foxton, Harvey, Holt
Front: Keegan, Heath, Colquhoun, unknown, Hemstead, Deere

SEASON 1969-70
Barnard, Holt, Atkin, Jackson, Davidson, Keegan, Lindey, Rusling, Heath, Cassidy, Welbourne, Foxton, Deere, Kerr

League — Division 4

No		Date	Opponent	Score	Scorers	Att	Barnard G	Foxton DG	Jackson NA	Barker I	Deere SH	Welbourne D	Keegan JK	Cassidy N	Kerr GAM	Heath RT	Davidson AG	Lindsey B	McDonald CB	Atkin IM	Rusling G	Muldoon T	Kisby CN	Woolmer AJ	Kirk HJ	O'Riley P	Williams MJ
1	Aug	15	Exeter City	1-1	Keegan	5456	1	2	3	4	5	6	7	8	9	10	11	12									
2		22	SOUTHEND UNITED	3-0	Kerr, Foxton, Heath	3930	1	2	3	4	5	6	7	8	9	10	12		11								
3		28	Stockport County	0-2		4164	1	2	3	4	5	6	7	8	9	10	11	12									
4	Sep	1	OLDHAM ATHLETIC	2-3	Lindsey, Heath	4217	1	2		3		6	7	8	9	10			4	11	5						
5		5	CAMBRIDGE UNITED	0-0		3995	1	2		3		6	7	8	9	10	12		4	11	5						
6		11	Aldershot	1-0	Rusling	5959	1	2		3	5		7		9	10	11		4		6	8					
7		19	YORK CITY	0-1		3723	1	2		3	6		7	8	9	10	11		4		5	12					
8		22	BARROW	1-1	Keegan (p)	3030	1	2		3	6	12	10	8	9		11		4				7	5			
9		26	Workington	0-0		2242	1	2		3	5	6	10	8	9		11		4				7	12			
10		30	Bournemouth	2-0	Deere, Davidson	8219	1	2		3	5	6	10	8	9	11	7		4					12			
11	Oct	3	GRIMSBY TOWN	1-2	Keegan (p)	6945	1	2		3	5	6	10	8	9	11	7							4			
12		6	Oldham Athletic	1-1	Davidson	8341	1	2		3	5	6	10	8	9	11	7							4			
13		10	Newport County	3-2	Cassidy 2, Davidson	3539	1	2		3	5	6	10	8	9	11	7							4			
14		17	EXETER CITY	3-0	Keegan, Cassidy 2	3684	1	2		3	5	6	10	8	9	11	7							4			
15		20	PETERBOROUGH UTD.	5-2	Keegan, Heath 2, Cassidy, Barker	3801	1	2	12	3	5	6	10	8	9	11	7							4			
16		24	Crewe Alexandra	1-3	Davidson	2385	1	2		3	5	6	10	8	9	11	7							4			
17		31	NOTTS COUNTY	0-1		5559	1	2	3		5	6	10	8		11	7				4		9				
18	Nov	7	Lincoln City	1-4	Cassidy	7469	1	2	3	12	5	6	10	8		11	7				4		9				
19		9	Darlington	0-3		3651	1	2	3	12	5	6	10	8		11	7				4		9				
20		14	CHESTER	0-2		3099	1	2	3		5	6	10	8		11	7				4		9				
21		28	NORTHAMPTON T	2-2	Barker, Woolmer	3265	1	2	3		5	6	10				7				4		9	8	11		
22	Dec	4	Southport	1-5	Keegan	2444	1	2	12	3	5	6	10				7				4		9	8	11		
23		18	Southend United	2-2	Davidson, Kirk	4606	1	2		3	5	6				4	7		10					9	8		
24		26	BRENTFORD	1-1	Heath	4736	1	2		3	5					4	7		6	9					8		
25	Jan	9	BOURNEMOUTH	1-1	Heath	4140	1	2		3	5	6	10			4	7		8					9			
26		16	Peterborough United	2-1	Davidson, Kirk	4500	1	2		3	5	6	10			4	7		8					9			
27		23	HARTLEPOOL	2-1	McDonald, Kirk	3657	1		3		5	6	10			4	2		8	12			7	9	11		
28		30	Northampton Town	0-1		4607	1		3		5	6	10			4	2		8				7	9	11		
29	Feb	6	SOUTHPORT	2-0	Deere, Keegan	3228	1		3		5	6	10			4	2		8				7	9	11		
30		13	Hartlepool	1-1	Rusling	1261	1		3		5	6	10			4	2		8				7	9	11		
31		20	DARLINGTON	0-0		3505	1		3		5	6	10			4	2		8				7	9	11		
32		27	Notts County	0-3		10750	1		3		5	6	10			4	2		8	12			7	9	11		
33	Mar	6	CREWE ALEXANDRA	1-1	Woolmer	2633	1		3		5	6	10			4	2		8	11			7	9			
34		8	Barrow	2-1	Davidson, Heath	1604	1		3		5	6	10			4	2		8	11			7	9			
35		13	Chester	0-2		3738	1		3		5	6	10			4	2		8	11	12		7		9		
36		16	COLCHESTER UNITED	2-0	Woolmer, O'Riley	3715	1		3		5	6	10			4	2		8				7	11	9		
37		20	LINCOLN CITY	3-1	O'Riley 2, McDonald	5607	1		3		5	6	10			4	2		8				7	11	9		
38		22	Colchester United	0-2		5592			3		5	6	10			4	2		8				7	11	9	1	
39		27	Cambridge United	1-1	Keegan	3627	1		3		5	6	10			4	2		8	12			7	11	9		
40	Apr	3	STOCKPORT COUNTY	1-2	Keegan	2666	1	2	3				10			4	7				5		6	8	11	9	
41		9	Grimsby Town	0-1		7639	1	2	3	6			10			4	8				5			7	11	9	
42		10	Brentford	1-0	Heath	7560	1	2	6	3			10			4	7				5	12		8	11	9	
43		13	ALDERSHOT	2-1	O'Riley, Heath	3031	1	2	6	3			10			4	8				5	11		7		9	
44		17	NEWPORT COUNTY	0-1		2880	1	2	3				10			4	8		12		5	11		6	7	9	
45		24	York City	0-2		4823	1	2	6	3			10			4	7		8	5				9	11	9	
46	May	1	WORKINGTON	4-0	Jackson, Heath 2, Kirk	2568	1	2	4	3			6	10		8	7				5				11	9	
			Apps				45	33	28	30	38	36	45	19	16	43	44	9	22	25	22	1	9	26	21	11	1
			Goals					1	1	2	2		9	6	2	10	7	1	2		2			3	4	4	

F.A. Cup

		Date	Opponent	Score	Scorers	Att	Barnard G	Foxton DG	Jackson NA	Barker I	Deere SH	Welbourne D	Keegan JK	Cassidy N	Kerr GAM	Heath RT	Davidson AG	Lindsey B	McDonald CB	Atkin IM	Rusling G	Muldoon T	Kisby CN	Woolmer AJ	Kirk HJ	O'Riley P	Williams MJ
R1	Nov	21	Tranmere Rovers	1-1	Woolmer	3757	1	2		3	5	6	10			11	7							4	9	8		
rep		24	TRANMERE ROVERS	0-0		5431	1	2	12	3	5	6	10			11	7							4	9	8		
rep2		30	Tranmere Rovers	1-0	Rusling	7235	1	2	12	3	5	6	10			11	7							4	9	8		
R2	Dec	12	MANSFIELD TOWN	3-0	Rusling 2, Kirk	7656	1	2		3	5	6	10			4	7							9	8	11		
R3	Jan	2	West Bromwich Alb.	0-0		21960	1	2		3	5	6	10			4	7							9	8	11		
rep		11	WEST BROM ALB.	1-3	Deere	15926	1	2		3	5	6	10			4	7		8					9	12	11		

R1 replay and replay 2 a.e.t. Replay 2 at Goodison Park. R3 replay a.e.t.

F.L. Cup

		Date	Opponent	Score	Scorers	Att	Barnard G	Foxton DG	Jackson NA	Barker I	Deere SH	Welbourne D	Keegan JK	Cassidy N	Kerr GAM	Heath RT	Davidson AG	Lindsey B
R1	Aug	18	NORTHAMPTON TOWN	2-3	Keegan (p), Jackson	4470	1	2	3	4	5	6	7	8	9	10	11	12

Division 4 Final Table

		P	W	D	L	F	A	W	D	L	F	A	Pts
1	Notts County	46	19	4	0	59	12	11	5	7	30	24	69
2	Bournemouth	46	16	5	2	51	15	8	7	8	30	31	60
3	Oldham Athletic	46	14	6	3	57	29	10	5	8	31	34	59
4	York City	46	16	6	1	45	14	7	4	12	33	40	56
5	Chester	46	17	2	4	42	18	7	5	11	27	37	55
6	Colchester United	46	14	6	3	44	19	7	6	10	26	35	54
7	Northampton Town	46	15	4	4	39	24	4	9	10	24	35	51
8	Southport	46	15	2	6	42	24	6	4	13	21	33	48
9	Exeter City	46	12	7	4	40	23	5	7	11	27	45	48
10	Workington	46	13	7	3	28	13	5	5	13	20	36	48
11	Stockport County	46	12	8	3	28	17	4	6	13	21	48	46
12	Darlington	46	15	3	5	42	22	2	8	13	16	35	45
13	Aldershot	46	8	10	5	32	23	6	7	10	34	48	45
14	Brentford	46	13	3	7	45	27	5	5	13	21	35	44
15	Crewe Alexandra	46	13	1	9	49	35	5	7	11	26	41	44
16	Peterborough Utd.	46	14	3	6	46	23	4	4	15	24	48	43
17	SCUNTHORPE UNITED	46	9	7	7	36	23	6	6	11	20	38	43
18	Southend United	46	8	11	4	32	24	6	4	13	21	42	43
19	Grimsby Town	46	13	4	6	37	26	5	3	15	20	45	43
20	Cambridge United	46	9	9	5	31	27	6	4	13	20	39	43
21	Lincoln City	46	11	4	8	45	33	2	9	12	25	38	39
22	Newport County	46	8	3	12	32	36	5	2	16	23	49	28
23	Hartlepool	46	6	10	7	28	27	2	2	19	6	47	28
24	Barrow	46	5	5	13	25	38	2	3	18	26	52	22

SEASON 1970-71
Back: Davidson, Keegan, Rusling, Welbourne, Barnard, Barker, Atkin, Woolmer, Kirk
Seated: Jackson, Foxton, Lindsey, Deere, Heath, McDonald, Kisby

SEASON 1971-72
Back: Kisby, Barry, Hutchinson, William, Barnard, Foxton, Jackson, Davidson
2nd row: Strong (Masseur), Cowling (Secretary), Woolmer, Deere, John Barker, Atkin, Brownsword (Coach), Jeff Barker (Scout), Ashman (Manager)
3rd row: Fletcher, McDonald, Kerr, Archer (Director), Johnson (Director) Kirk, Heath, Welbourne
Seated: Sargent, Markham, Bawden, Mullen, Crellin, Sowden

#	Date	Opponent	Score	Scorers	Att	Barnard G	Foxton DG	Barker J	Jackson NA	Deere SH	Welbourne D	McDonald CB	Fletcher JR	Woolmer AJ	Heath RT	Kirk HJ	Davidson AG	Kisby CN	Hutchinson DN	Kerr GAM	Atkin JM	Markham P
1	Aug 14	Grimsby Town	1-4	Fletcher	7497	1	2	3	4	5	6	7	8	9	10	11	12					
2	21	LINCOLN CITY	2-1	Heath, Jackson	4868	1	2	3	4	5	6		7		8	11	9	10				
3	28	Crewe Alexandra	2-0	Jackson (p), Davidson	2800	1	2	3	6	4	5		9		8	11	10	7				
4	30	Southend United	3-2	Davidson 2, Fletcher	6704	1	2	3	4	5	6	7	9		10	11	8					
5	Sep 4	DONCASTER ROVERS	0-0		5047	1	2	3	8	4	5	6	9		7	11	10					
6	11	Peterborough United	1-0	Heath	6387	1	2	3	6	4	5		9		8	11	10	7				
7	17	NORTHAMPTON T	0-0		5253	1	2	3	4	5	6	12	8		10	11	9	7				
8	25	Aldershot	1-1	Heath	4675	1	2	3	4	5	6		9		8	11	10	7	12			
9	28	COLCHESTER UNITED	2-0	Fletcher, Davidson	5111	1	2	3		5	6	4	8		10	11	9	7				
10	Oct 2	DARLINGTON	3-1	Kisby, Davidson, Heath	5321	1	2	3	6	4	5		9		7	11	10	8				
11	9	Bury	1-3	Davidson	2733	1	2	3	6	5	4		9		8	11	10	7	12			
12	16	GRIMSBY TOWN	1-2	Deere	11510	1	2	3	6	4	5	12	9		7	11	10	8				
13	23	Barrow	1-0	3556	2190	1	2	3	8	5	6		9		7	11	4		10			
14	30	BRENTFORD	0-0		5859	1	2	3	8	5	6		9			11	4		10	7		
15	Nov 6	Exeter City	0-1		3556	1	2	3		5	6		8			11	7	4	9	10	12	
16	13	WORKINGTON	2-0	Kisby, McDonald	4535	1	2	3		5		7	9			11	10	4		8	6	
17	27	READING	1-1	Fletcher	4321	1	2	3		5	6		9		7	11	10	4				
18	Dec 4	Gillingham	1-0	Fletcher	6988	1		3	2	5		12	9		7	11	8			10	4	
19	11	CHESTER	2-0	McDonald, Fletcher	3776	1		3	2	5	6	8	9			11	7		12	10	4	
20	18	Doncaster Rovers	2-0	Fletcher, Kerr	5534	1		3	2	5		4	9		8	11	7			10	6	
21	27	HARTLEPOOL	2-2	McDonald, Kerr	6940	1	12	3	2	5		7	8		10	11	4			9	6	
22	Jan 1	Northampton Town	2-0	Jackson, Kerr	3929	1	2	3	8	4		7	9			11	6			10	5	
23	8	CREWE ALEXANDRA	2-0	Kerr 2	4323	1	2	3	4	5		7	9			11	8			10	6	
24	15	Southport	1-1	McDonald	3602	1	2	3	4	5		7	9			11	8			10	6	
25	21	Colchester United	1-1	Fletcher	4867	1	2	3	10	5		7	8			11	4			9	6	
26	29	NEWPORT COUNTY	1-0	Davidson	4580	1	2	3	6	5		8	9			11	7			10	4	
27	Feb 5	Stockport County	0-0		2452	1	2	3	8	5		7	9			11	4			10	6	
28	12	BARROW	2-1	Fletcher 2	5127	1	2	3	8	5		7	9	12		11	4			10	6	
29	19	Brentford	3-0	McDonald, Fletcher 2	11910	1	2	3	8	5		7	10			11	4			9	6	
30	26	EXETER CITY	3-0	Giles (og), Jackson, Fletcher	6250	1	2	3	7	5	6	10	9			11	8				4	
31	Mar 4	Workington	1-2	Fletcher	1977	1	2	3	10	5		4	9			11	7			8	6	
32	11	BURY	3-0	Saile (og), Fletcher 2	5082	1	2	3	8	5		4	9			11	7		12	9	6	
33	14	SOUTHPORT	1-0	Dunleavy (og)	6800	1	2	3	10	5		7	8			11	4			9	6	
34	18	Lincoln City	0-1		16498	1	2	3	10	6		7	8			11	4			9	5	
35	25	PETERBOROUGH UTD.	0-0		5555	1	2	3	10	4	6	7	8			11				9	5	
36	31	Darlington	1-0	Fletcher	2960	1	2	3	10	5		7	8	12		11	4			9	6	
37	Apr 1	Hartlepool	0-1		6192	1	2	3	10	5		7	8	9		11	4		12		6	
38	4	ALDERSHOT	1-0	Kirk	6929	1		3	10	5		7	8			11	4			9	6	2
39	8	STOCKPORT COUNTY	0-2		7183	1		3		5		10	8	12		11	7	4		9	6	2
40	11	CAMBRIDGE UNITED	2-1	Fletcher 2	5916	1		3		5		7	8	10		11	4			9	6	2
41	15	Reading	0-2		4163	1		3	2	5		7	8	10		11	4		12	9	6	
42	19	Chester	0-0		2347	1		3	10	5		8	7			11	4			9	6	2
43	22	GILLINGHAM	3-3	Kirk, Kerr, McDonald	5504	1	2	3	10	5		4	8			11	7			9	6	
44	25	SOUTHEND UNITED	1-1	Kirk	8540	1		3	10	5		7	8			11	4			9	6	2
45	29	Cambridge United	0-2		3927	1		3	10	5	12		8	9		11	4			7	6	2
46	May 1	Newport County	0-1		3686	1		3	10	5		8	7			11	4		12	9	6	2
		Apps				46	35	44	42	46	19	33	46	14	17	46	45	16	9	29	31	7
		Goals							4	1		6	19		4	4	7	2		6		

Player substituted in game 45 not known

3 own goals

F.A. Cup

#	Date	Opponent	Score	Scorers	Att	Barnard G	Foxton DG	Barker J	Jackson NA	Deere SH	Welbourne D	McDonald CB	Fletcher JR	Woolmer AJ	Heath RT	Kirk HJ	Davidson AG	Kisby CN	Hutchinson DN	Kerr GAM	Atkin JM	Markham P
R1	Nov 20	South Shields	3-3	Deere, Kerr 2	4000	1	2	3		5			9		7	11	8	4		10	6	
rep	29	SOUTH SHIELDS	2-3	Fletcher, Kirk	5272	1	2	3		5	6	12	8		7	11	9	4		10		

F.L. Cup

#	Date	Opponent	Score	Scorers	Att	Barnard G	Foxton DG	Barker J	Jackson NA	Deere SH	Welbourne D	McDonald CB	Fletcher JR	Woolmer AJ	Heath RT	Kirk HJ	Davidson AG	Kisby CN	Hutchinson DN	Kerr GAM	Atkin JM	Markham P
R1	Aug 18	LINCOLN CITY	0-1		5864	1	2	3	4	5	6		8	9	10	11	7					

		P	W	D	L	F	A	W	D	L	F	A	Pts
1	Grimsby Town	46	18	3	2	61	26	10	4	9	27	30	63
2	Southend United	46	18	2	3	56	26	6	10	7	25	29	60
3	Brentford	46	16	5	2	52	21	8	9	6	24	23	59
4	SCUNTHORPE UNITED	46	13	8	2	34	15	9	5	9	22	22	57
5	Lincoln City	46	17	5	1	46	15	4	9	10	31	44	56
6	Workington	46	12	9	2	34	7	4	10	9	16	27	51
7	Southport	46	15	5	3	48	21	3	9	11	18	29	50
8	Peterborough Utd.	46	14	6	3	51	24	3	10	10	31	40	50
9	Bury	46	16	4	3	55	22	3	8	12	18	37	50
10	Cambridge United	46	11	8	4	38	22	6	6	11	24	38	48
11	Colchester United	46	13	6	4	38	23	6	4	13	32	46	48
12	Doncaster Rovers	46	11	6	6	35	24	5	6	12	21	39	46
13	Gillingham	46	11	5	7	33	24	5	8	10	28	43	45
14	Newport County	46	13	5	5	34	20	5	3	15	26	52	44
15	Exeter City	46	11	5	7	40	30	5	6	12	21	38	43
16	Reading	46	14	3	6	37	26	3	5	15	19	50	42
17	Aldershot	46	5	13	5	27	20	4	9	10	21	34	40
18	Hartlepool	46	14	2	7	39	25	3	4	16	19	44	40
19	Darlington	46	9	5	9	37	24	5	2	16	27	58	39
20	Chester	46	10	11	2	34	16	0	7	16	13	40	38
21	Northampton Town	46	9	6	8	43	27	4	4	15	23	52	37
22	Barrow	46	8	8	7	23	26	5	3	15	17	45	37
23	Stockport County	46	7	10	6	33	32	2	4	17	22	55	32
24	Crewe Alexandra	46	9	4	10	27	25	1	5	17	16	44	29

1972/73 24th in Division 3: Relegated

#	Date		Opponent	Score	Scorers	Att	Barnard G	Foxton DG	Barker J	Davidson AG	Deere SH	Welbourne D	Kerr GAM	Fletcher JR	Collier GR	Heath RT	Kirk HJ	Jackson NA	McDonald CB	Sargent GS	Atkin JM	Sowden M	Kisby CN	Williams MJ	Markham P	Warnock N	Charnley DL	Krzywicki RL	Keeley NB
1	Aug	12	SWANSEA CITY	1-0	Davidson	5655	1	2	3	4	5	6	7	8	9	10	11												
2		18	Tranmere Rovers	1-2	Kirk (p)	3537	1	2	3		5	6	7	8	9	10	11	4	12										
3		26	WREXHAM	1-1	Deere	4135	1	2	3	7	5	6	12	8	9	10	11	4											
4		29	WALSALL	2-1	Fletcher, Kirk	4159	1	2	3	7	5	6	9	8		10	11	4											
5	Sep	2	Bournemouth	1-1	Fletcher	10034	1	2	3	4	5	6	10	9		7	11	8											
6		8	HALIFAX TOWN	0-3		4848	1	2	3	7	5	6	9	8		10	11	4											
7		16	Charlton Athletic	0-2		4970	1	2	3	7	5	6	9	8		10	11	4		12									
8		19	ROCHDALE	1-2	McDonald	3530	1	2	3	8	5	6	12	9		10	11	4	7										
9		23	GRIMSBY TOWN	1-2	Deere	10540	1		3		5	6	10	9	8	7	11	2	4										
10		25	Southend United	0-1		6411	1	2	3		5	6		8		10	11	4	7	9									
11		30	Blackburn Rovers	0-3		5764	1	2	3		5	6		9		7	11	4	8	10									
12	Oct	7	BRENTFORD	1-0	Welbourne	3143	1	2			5	6		8			11	3	7	9	4	10							
13		10	PLYMOUTH ARGYLE	1-1	Kirk	3650	1	2			5	6		8	12		11	3	7	9	4	10							
14		14	Bolton Wanderers	0-0		7175	1	2		8	5	6		9			11	3	7	10	4								
15		21	YORK CITY	1-0	Sargent	3538	1	2		7	5	6		8	12		11	3	10	9	4								
16		24	Oldham Athletic	0-3		5269	1		3	10	5	6		8			11	2	7	9	4		12						
17		28	Rotherham United	1-2	McDonald	4317			3	10	5	6		8	9		11		7		4		12	1	2				
18	Nov	4	SOUTHEND UNITED	0-0		3157			3	7	5	6		8	9		11		10		4			1	2				
19		11	Rochdale	2-0	Heath, Kirk	2551			3		5	6		8	9		11		10		4			1	2	7			
20		25	SHREWSBURY TOWN	1-0	Fletcher	2596		2	3		5		8	9		10	11		6		4			1		7			
21	Dec	2	Bristol Rovers	1-5	Fletcher	5715		2			5		7	9	12	8	10		6		4			1	3			11	
22		16	Port Vale	0-2		3833	1	2	3		5	6	8	9			11		10		4					7			
23		23	NOTTS COUNTY	1-0	Davidson	3820	1	2	3	10	5	6		8	9		11				4					7			
24		26	Grimsby Town	0-1		16580	1	2	3	10	5	6		8	9		11				4				12	7			
25		30	TRANMERE ROVERS	1-5	Fletcher	3374	1	2	3	10	5	4	8	12	9		11		11				6			7			
26	Jan	6	Wrexham	2-1	Heath, Fletcher	2595	1		3		5	4	10	8	9		11						6		2	7			
27		20	BOURNEMOUTH	1-1	Kirk (p)	3458	1			7	5	4	10	8	9		11					3	6		2				
28		27	Halifax Town	0-1		1769	1		3	7	5	4	10	8	9		11						6		2				
29	Feb	3	Swansea City	1-2	McDonald	1607	1		3	7	5	6	10	8	9		11		12			4			2				
30		6	Plymouth Argyle	0-3		10008			3	4	5	6	10	8	9		11		7					1	2		12		
31		10	CHARLTON ATHLETIC	0-2		2818			3	7	5	4	10	8			11		12				6	1	2		9		
32		24	PORT VALE	0-1		2580			3	2	5	4		9		8	11						6	1	12	7		10	
33	Mar	3	Brentford	0-1		7760			3	2	5			9	4		11					8	6	1		7		10	
34		6	Watford	1-5	Fletcher	4578			3	2	5	6		10			11			9	12		4	1		7			
35		10	BOLTON WANDERERS	1-1	Fletcher	4424			3	2	5	6	8	9			11		12	10				1		7			
36		13	OLDHAM ATHLETIC	0-0		2779			3		5	6	8	10			11		4	9	2			1		7			
37		17	York City	1-3	Kirk	2848			3		5	6	12	8	10		11		4	9	2			1		7			
38		20	CHESTERFIELD	0-1		2048			3		5	6	12	8	10		11		4	9	2			1		7			
39		24	ROTHERHAM UNITED	2-1	Kirk (p), Fletcher	2199		12	3		5	4		8	10		11		6	9	2			1		7			
40		30	Shrewsbury Town	2-4	Kirk (p), Collier	2277		2	3		5	6		8	10		11		4	9	12			1		7			
41	Apr	7	BRISTOL ROVERS	0-2		1784		2	3	10	5	4		8	9		11		6					1	12	7			
42		14	Chesterfield	1-2	Warnock	3678			3	4	5	6	9		10		11		8					1	2	7			
43		21	WATFORD	1-0	Fletcher	1544			3	4	5	6	12	9	10		11		8					1	2	7			
44		23	Notts County	0-2		15697		12	3	2	5	6	4	9	10		11		8					1		7			
45		24	BLACKBURN ROVERS	1-1	Garbett (og)	2546		12	3	2	5		4	9	10		11		8				6	1		7			
46		28	Walsall	1-1	Collier	3402	1		3	2	5		4		9	10	11		8					1		7			9
			Apps				24	25	40	30	46	41	24	45	21	27	45	15	31	15	27	3	14	22	9	23	1	2	1
			Goals							2	2	1		10	2	2	8		3	1						1			

One own goal

F.A. Cup

	Date		Opponent	Score	Scorers	Att	Barnard	Foxton	Barker	Davidson	Deere	Welbourne	Kerr	Fletcher	Collier	Heath	Kirk	Jackson	McDonald	Sargent	Atkin	Sowden	Kisby	Williams	Markham	Warnock
R1	Nov	18	Hartlepool United	0-0		4568			3	7	5	6		9		10	11		8		4			1	2	
rep		21	HARTLEPOOL UNITED	0-0		4478			3		5	6	8	12	9	11	10			4	7			1	2	
rep2		27	Hartlepool United	2-1	Dawes (og), Deere	7917		2			5		7	8	9		11		10	4		6	1		3	
R2	Dec	9	Halifax Town	3-2	Heath, Fletcher, Barker	4037	1	2	3		5	6		9		10	11		8		4					7
R3	Jan	13	CARDIFF CITY	2-3	Welbourne, Kirk	6379	1		3	12	5	6	10	8		9	11			4					2	7

R1 replay 2 at Roker Park. R1 replay and replay 2 a.e.t.

F.L. Cup

	Date		Opponent	Score	Att	Barnard	Foxton	Barker	Deere	Welbourne	Kerr	Fletcher	Collier	Heath	Kirk	Jackson
R1	Aug	15	CHESTERFIELD	0-0	5619	1	2	3	5	6	7	8	9	10	11	4
rep		23	Chesterfield	0-5	8288	1	2	3	5	6	7	8	9	10	11	4

		P	W	D	L	F	A	W	D	L	F	A	Pts
1	Bolton Wanderers	46	18	4	1	44	9	7	7	9	29	30	61
2	Notts County	46	17	4	2	40	12	6	7	10	27	35	57
3	Blackburn Rovers	46	12	8	3	34	16	8	7	8	23	31	55
4	Oldham Athletic	46	12	7	4	40	18	7	9	7	32	36	54
5	Bristol Rovers	46	17	4	2	55	20	3	9	11	22	36	53
6	Port Vale	46	15	6	2	41	21	6	5	12	15	48	53
7	Bournemouth	46	14	6	3	44	16	3	10	10	22	28	50
8	Plymouth Argyle	46	14	3	6	43	26	6	7	10	31	40	50
9	Grimsby Town	46	16	2	5	45	18	4	6	13	22	43	48
10	Tranmere Rovers	46	12	8	3	38	17	3	8	12	18	35	46
11	Charlton Athletic	46	12	7	4	46	24	5	4	14	23	43	45
12	Wrexham	46	11	9	3	39	23	3	8	12	16	31	45
13	Rochdale	46	8	8	7	22	26	6	9	8	26	28	45
14	Southend United	46	13	6	4	40	14	4	4	15	21	40	44
15	Shrewsbury Town	46	10	10	3	31	21	5	4	14	15	33	44
16	Chesterfield	46	13	4	6	37	22	4	5	14	20	39	43
17	Walsall	46	14	3	6	37	26	4	4	15	19	40	43
18	York City	46	8	10	5	24	14	5	5	13	18	32	41
19	Watford	46	11	8	4	32	23	1	9	13	11	25	41
20	Halifax Town	46	9	8	6	29	23	4	7	12	14	30	41
21	Rotherham United	46	12	4	7	34	27	5	3	15	17	38	41
22	Brentford	46	12	5	6	33	18	2	3	18	18	51	37
23	Swansea City	46	11	5	7	37	29	3	4	16	14	44	37
24	SCUNTHORPE UNITED	46	8	7	8	18	25	2	3	18	15	47	30

1973/74 18th in Division 4

#		Date	Opponent	Score	Scorers	Att
1	Aug	25	Lincoln City	0-1		6327
2	Sep	1	BARNSLEY	3-0	Houghton, Barker, Keeley	3441
3		8	Peterborough United	0-1		6399
4		12	Gillingham	2-7	Houghton, Welbourne	4610
5		14	CREWE ALEXANDRA	0-0		3476
6		18	BRADFORD CITY	2-1	Pilling, Fletcher	3155
7		21	Northampton Town	0-2		5049
8		29	HARTLEPOOL	1-1	Houghton	2466
9	Oct	3	Bradford City	1-2	Podd(og)	2445
10		6	Swansea City	2-1	Collier, Money	1743
11		13	NEWPORT COUNTY	0-0		2607
12		19	Colchester United	0-2		4862
13		23	GILLINGHAM	1-1	Simpkin	2402
14		27	BRENTFORD	4-1	Woods 2, Simpkin, Keeley	2376
15	Nov	2	Stockport County	1-3	Welbourne	2419
16		10	CHESTER	2-1	Keeley, Collier	2164
17		13	READING	1-0	Davidson	2526
18		17	Torquay United	1-1	Davidson	3155
19	Dec	8	MANSFIELD TOWN	5-3	Houghton 2(1 p), Horsfall 2, Davidso	2420
20		22	Hartlepool	0-3		832
21		26	DONCASTER ROVERS	2-1	Pilling, Barker	5582
22		29	PETERBOROUGH UTD.	2-1	Collier, Keeley	5004
23	Jan	1	Barnsley	0-5		5940
24		12	Crewe Alexandra	0-1		1591
25		19	LINCOLN CITY	1-1	Keeley	5379
26	Feb	3	Darlington	0-3		3006
27		10	NORTHAMPTON T	1-2	Collier	3421
28		17	Newport County	1-2	Warnock	3051
29		23	SWANSEA CITY	0-0		2238
30	Mar	2	Doncaster Rovers	0-1		1587
31		9	Brentford	1-2	Roberts	4050
32		16	COLCHESTER UNITED	1-0	Keeley	2134
33		19	DARLINGTON	1-0	Roberts	1715
34		23	Chester	0-2		2038
35		26	Bury	0-0		5190
36		30	STOCKPORT COUNTY	2-1	Davidson, Collier	1739
37	Apr	6	Reading	0-0		3562
38		10	Workington	2-1	Davidson, Keeley	1326
39		13	TORQUAY UNITED	0-0		2370
40		15	Rotherham United	1-1	Keeley	2341
41		16	ROTHERHAM UNITED	3-0	Warnock 2, Roberts	2610
42		20	Mansfield Town	2-2	Roberts, Andrews	2342
43		22	Exeter City	0-4		2226
44		27	WORKINGTON	0-1		1890
45		30	BURY	1-2	Keeley	2014

Home game with Exeter City not played.
Scunthorpe awarded two points.

Appearances / Goals

	Williams MJ	Lynch BJ	Collard JB	Welbourne D	Barker J	Davidson AG	Houghton K	Pilling S	Fletcher JR	Keeley NB	Warnock N	Barnard G	Collier GR	Money R	Goodwin SA	Simpkin CJ	Woods E	Charnley DL	Bennett R	Horsfall TW	Atkin IM	Roberts DE	Andrews LL	Markham P	Norris M
Apps	5	42	22	37	39	37	33	43	7	43	29	37	24	29	2	34	4	2	3	5	12	16	9	3	3
Goals			2	2	5	5	2	1		9	3		5	1		2	2			2		4	1		

One own goal

F.A. Cup

		Date	Opponent	Score	Scorers	Att
R1	Nov	24	DARLINGTON	1-0	Houghton	3191
R2	Dec	15	Mansfield Town	1-1	Houghton	4511
rep		18	MANSFIELD TOWN	1-0	Warnock	2679
R3	Jan	5	Millwall	1-1	Collier	7275
rep		8	MILLWALL	1-0	Pilling	4789
R4		26	Newcastle United	1-1	Keeley	37870
rep		30	NEWCASTLE UNITED	0-3		19028

F.L. Cup

		Date	Opponent	Score	Scorers	Att
R1	Aug	29	Peterborough United	2-2	Pilling, Keeley	6339
rep	Sep	4	PETERBOROUGH UNITED	2-1	Keeley 2	4472
R2	Oct	9	BRISTOL CITY	0-0		4418
rep		16	Bristol City	1-2	Welbourne	7837

Division 4 final table

		P	W	D	L	F	A	W	D	L	F	A	Pts
1	Peterborough Utd.	46	19	4	0	49	10	8	7	8	26	28	65
2	Gillingham	46	16	5	2	51	16	9	7	7	39	33	62
3	Colchester United	46	16	5	2	46	14	8	7	8	27	22	60
4	Bury	46	18	3	2	51	14	6	8	9	30	35	59
5	Northampton Town	46	14	7	2	39	14	6	6	11	24	34	53
6	Reading	46	11	9	3	37	13	5	10	8	21	24	51
7	Chester	46	13	6	4	31	19	4	9	10	23	36	49
8	Bradford City	46	14	7	2	45	20	3	7	13	13	32	48
9	Newport County	46	13	6	4	39	23	3	8	12	17	42	45
10	Exeter City	45	12	5	6	37	20	6	3	13	21	35	44
11	Hartlepool	46	11	4	8	29	16	5	8	10	19	31	44
12	Lincoln City	46	10	8	5	40	30	6	4	13	23	37	44
13	Barnsley	46	15	5	3	42	16	2	5	16	16	48	44
14	Swansea City	46	11	6	6	28	15	5	5	13	17	31	43
15	Rotherham United	46	10	9	4	33	22	5	4	14	23	36	43
16	Torquay United	46	11	7	5	37	23	2	10	11	15	34	43
17	Mansfield Town	46	13	8	2	47	24	0	9	14	15	45	43
18	SCUNTHORPE UNITED	45	12	7	3	33	17	2	5	16	14	47	42
19	Brentford	46	9	7	7	31	20	3	9	11	17	30	40
20	Darlington	46	9	8	6	29	24	4	5	14	11	38	39
21	Crewe Alexandra	46	11	5	7	28	30	3	5	15	15	41	38
22	Doncaster Rovers	46	10	7	6	32	22	2	4	17	15	58	35
23	Workington	46	10	8	5	33	26	1	5	17	10	48	35
24	Stockport County	46	4	12	7	22	25	3	8	12	22	44	34

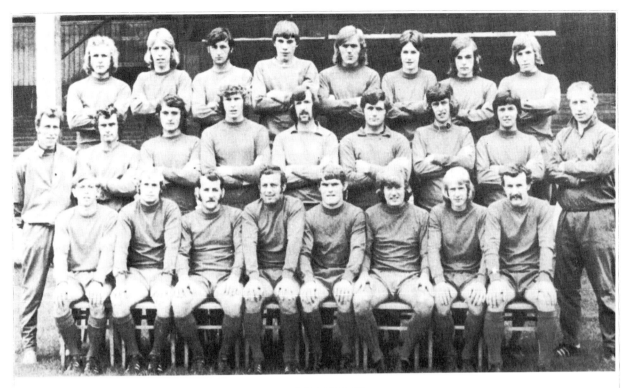

SEASON 1972-73
Back: Kisby, Sargent, Bawden, Norris, Atkin, Crellin, Sowden, Mullen
Middle: Brownsword (Trainer), Jackson, Barker, Deere, Williams, Barnard, Collier, Welbourne, Ashman (Manager)
Front: Markham, Foxton, Heath, Kerr, Fletcher, Kirk, McDonald, Davidson

SEASON 1973-74
Back: Houghton, Atkin, Keeley, Barker, Mullen, Charnley, Money
Middle: Jackson, Collier, Collard, Williams, Norris, Barnard, Welbourne, Fletcher, Storey (Sec.), Barker (Asst. Man.)
Front: Lynch, Pilling, Markham, Bradley (Manager), Warnock, Kirk, Davidson

#		Date	Opponent	Score	Scorers	Att	Barnard G	Markham P	Atkin JM	Simpkin CJ	Peacock JC	Keeley NB	Money R	Collier GR	Sproates A	Roberts DE	Davidson AG	Warnock N	Lavery J	Taylor EK	Welbourne D	Earl S	Barker J	Charnley DL	Anderson TK	Lynch BJ	Marshall B	Mountford RW	Pilling S	Oates RA	Norris M
1	Aug	17	Workington	1-1	Davidson	1656	1	2	3	4	5	6	7	8	9	10	11														
2		24	MANSFIELD TOWN	0-1		2794	1	2	3	4	5	12	6	7	8	10	11	9													
3		31	Bradford City	0-3		3255	1	2	3	4	5	6	7	8	9	10	11														
4	Sep	3	Barnsley	2-2	Collier, Roberts	5428		2		4	3	5	8	7	6	10	9		1	11											
5		7	READING	0-1		1693		2			5	3	9	4	7	10	6	8	1	11											
6		14	Darlington	1-3	Davidson	1863	1	2			5	11	7	8		9				10	4	6									
7		17	Doncaster Rovers	1-1	Roberts	3116		2		4	5	11	12	7	9	6			1	8	3	10									
8		21	HARTLEPOOL	1-1	Roberts	1663		2			5	12	11	7	9	6			1	8	3	10									
9		24	TORQUAY UNITED	0-2		1654		2	4				12	7	9	6			1	8	3	10	5	11							
10		28	Shrewsbury Town	0-5		3381		2	5			12	4	7	9	6			1	8	10	3		11							
11	Oct	1	BARNSLEY	1-0	Warnock	2157		2				11	4	7	10	6	9	9	1		3	5	8	12							
12		5	Chester	0-1		2857		2				11	4	7	10	9	12		1		6	5	3	8							
13		12	CAMBRIDGE UNITED	2-0	Warnock, Keeley	1774		2		5	3	11	6	12	9	7	1		4				10		8							
14		15	SOUTHPORT	3-3	Markham, Roberts, Keeley	1869		2		4	5	11	6		10	9	1				3		8		7	12						
15		19	Stockport County	2-3	Welbourne, Keeley	1500				10	5	11	4		9	7	1				3		6	2	8	12						
16		26	ROTHERHAM UNITED	0-3		2838	1				5	3	6	4	10	7	9						8	2		11	12					
17	Nov	2	CREWE ALEXANDRA	1-1	Roberts	1501	1	2				6	11	4		9		7			5		3		10				8		
18		9	Exeter City	0-0		3058	1	2			4	11	7		10	12	9				3		5		6				8		
19		16	ROCHDALE	2-2	Pilling 2	1621	1	2			6	11	7		10	12	9				3		5	4					8		
20		30	SWANSEA CITY	1-2	Roberts	1037	1	2	6	4			8	7	12	11		10			3		5						9		
21	Dec	7	Newport County	0-2		3139	1	2				11	4	6	7		10	9			3		5						8		
22		21	Brentford	0-2		4360	1	2				11	6	4	7		10	9			5		3						8		
23		26	DARLINGTON	1-1	Davidson (p), Collier	2122	1	2				10	4	7	6		11	9			5				3				8		
24		28	Lincoln City	0-1		7883	1	2				10	4	7	6	12	11	9			5				3				8		
25	Jan	4	DONCASTER ROVERS	0-0		2326	1	2				10	6	7	4	9	11				5				3				8		
26		11	NEWPORT COUNTY	4-1	Roberts 3, Collier	1529	1	2				12	6	7	4	10	11	9			5				3				8		
27		18	Swansea City	0-1		1428	1	2				9	4	7	6	10	11				5				3				8		
28	Feb	1	EXETER CITY	2-1	Collier, Roberts	1846	1	2				4	7	6	10	11	9				5				3				8		
29		8	Crewe Alexandra	1-1	Davidson	1986	1	2				12	4	7	6	10	11	9			5				3				8		
30		11	Northampton Town	0-3		3079	1	2				4	7	6	10	11	9				5				3				8		
31		15	NORTHAMPTON T	2-1	Roberts, Pilling	1833	1	2				9	6	7	4	10	11				5				3				8		
32		22	Rochdale	2-4	Collier, Roberts	1430	1	2				9	4	7		10					5		11		3				8	6	
33	Mar	1	BRADFORD CITY	1-2	Charnley	1959	1	2				9	4	7	6	10					5		11		3				8		
34		8	Torquay United	1-1	Warnock	1822		2		6		9	4	7				11			5				3				8	10	1
35		15	SHREWSBURY TOWN	1-0	Davidson	1663		2		5		10	7	9		11					6				3				8	4	1
36		18	WORKINGTON	2-1	Davidson (p), Collier	1913		2		4		9	7	10		12	11				5				3				8	6	1
37		22	Reading	1-1	Davidson	4475		2		6		10	11	7			9				5				3				8	4	1
38		28	Hartlepool	0-1		2471		2		4		9	7	10		12	11				5				3				8	6	1
39	Apr	1	LINCOLN CITY	1-1	Davidson	5463		2		4			7	12	10	11					5		3						8	6	1
40		5	Rotherham United	2-3	Keeley, Roberts	6469		2		5	6	9		7	12	10	11				3								8	4	1
41		8	Southport	0-1		924		2		4			5	7	12	10	11						3	9					8	6	1
42		12	CHESTER	1-3	Earl	1877		12		5	3		6	7		9	10					11						2	8	4	1
43		15	BRENTFORD	1-2	Pilling	1439		2			3		4	7	6	10						9	11						8	5	1
44		19	Cambridge United	0-2		3278		2	5		3		6	7	4	11						9							8	10	1
45		21	Mansfield Town	0-7		11020			5	4	3		6	7		10						9		2					11	8	1
46		26	STOCKPORT COUNTY	0-0		1438	1		6	5	2		8	7	11	10						9							3	4	

| | | | | | | Apps | 14 | 42 | 10 | 27 | 19 | 34 | 43 | 40 | 24 | 39 | 34 | 20 | 11 | 7 | 33 | 7 | 13 | 8 | 10 | 22 | 3 | 3 | 31 | 14 | 12 |
| | | | | | | Goals | | 1 | | | | 4 | 5 | 13 | 8 | 3 | | | | | 1 | 1 | | 1 | | | | | 4 | | |

F.A. Cup

		Date	Opponent	Score	Scorers	Att																								
R1	Nov	23	ALTRINCHAM	1-1	Keeley	2627	1	2		4		11	7	6		10	9	12			3		5						8		
rep		25	Altrincham	1-3	Collier	3500	1	2		4		11	7	6		10	9	12			3		5						8		

F.L. Cup

		Date	Opponent	Score	Scorers	Att																								
R1	Aug	20	SHEFFIELD WEDNESDAY	1-0	Davidson (p)	5214	1	2	3	4	5	9	6	7	8	10	11	12													
R2	Sep	10	Manchester City	0-6		14790		2	4	3	5	10	7	8		11	6		1	9					12						

		P	W	D	L	F	A	W	D	L	F	A	Pts
1	Mansfield Town	46	17	6	0	55	15	11	6	6	35	25	68
2	Shrewsbury Town	46	16	3	4	46	18	10	7	6	34	25	62
3	Rotherham United	46	13	7	3	40	19	9	8	6	31	22	59
4	Chester	46	17	5	1	48	9	6	6	11	16	29	57
5	Lincoln City	46	14	8	1	47	14	7	7	9	32	34	57
6	Cambridge United	46	15	5	3	43	16	5	9	9	19	28	54
7	Reading	46	13	6	4	38	20	8	4	11	25	27	52
8	Brentford	46	15	6	2	38	14	3	7	13	15	31	49
9	Exeter City	46	14	3	6	33	24	5	8	10	27	39	49
10	Bradford City	46	10	5	8	32	21	7	8	8	24	30	47
11	Southport	46	13	7	3	36	19	2	10	11	20	37	47
12	Newport County	46	13	5	5	43	30	6	4	13	25	45	47
13	Hartlepool	46	13	6	4	40	24	3	5	15	12	38	43
14	Torquay United	46	10	7	6	30	25	4	7	12	16	38	42
15	Barnsley	46	10	7	6	34	24	5	4	14	28	41	41
16	Northampton Town	46	12	6	5	43	22	3	5	15	24	51	41
17	Doncaster Rovers	46	10	9	4	41	29	4	3	16	24	50	40
18	Crewe Alexandra	46	9	9	5	22	16	2	9	12	31	40	40
19	Rochdale	46	9	9	5	35	22	4	4	15	24	53	39
20	Stockport County	46	10	8	5	26	27	2	6	15	17	43	38
21	Darlington	46	11	4	8	38	27	2	6	15	16	40	36
22	Swansea City	46	9	4	10	25	21	2	10	11	21	42	36
23	Workington	46	7	5	11	23	29	3	6	14	13	37	31
24	SCUNTHORPE UNITED	46	7	8	8	27	29	0	7	16	14	49	29

SEASON 1974-75
Back: Davidson, Oates, Unknown, Barnard, Norris, Money, Roberts
Middle: Collier, Sproates, Keeley, Pilling, Simpson, Warnock   Front: Atkin, Unkonwn, Peacock, Markham, Charnley

SEASON 1975-76
Back: O'Connor, Wigginton, Money, Norris, Pilling, Peacock, Markham
Front: Charnley, Keeley, Roberts, Collier, Woodward, Irvine, Davidson

1975/76 19th in Division 4

#		Date	Opponent	Result	Scorers	Att	Norris M	Markham P	Peacock JC	Irvine A	Wiggington CA	Money R	Charnley DL	Robinson A	Keeley NB	Pilling S	Davidson AG	Oates RA	Collier GR	Roberts DE	O'Connor D	Hemmerman IL	Woodward J	Welbourne D	Green R	O'Meara AM	Farrell KM	Bond LA	Ferguson RC	Dale AG
1	Aug	16	Darlington	0-2		1920	1	2	3	4	5	6	7	8	9	10	11	12												
2		23	EXETER CITY	0-1		1660	1	2	3	6	5	4	11		8	9			7	10											
3		30	Newport County	0-0		2735	1	2	3		5	4	11		10	8	9	6	7											
4	Sep	6	HUDDERSFIELD T	0-1		1992	1	2	3		6	5	10		11	8	9	4	7		12									
5		13	Hartlepool	2-1	Hemmerman, Collier	1970	1	2		4	6	5			9	3	8		7			10	11							
6		20	TORQUAY UNITED	3-1	Collier, Woodward 2	1989	1	2		6	5	4	12		11	3	9		8			10	7							
7		22	Tranmere Rovers	1-2	Money	2308	1	2		6	5	4	9		8		3		7			10	11	12						
8		27	Swansea City	0-2		3098	1	2		12	6	3			8		4		7			10	11	5	9					
9	Oct	4	READING	2-1	Keeley, Collier	2177	1	2	3	4	6	5			10		11	8	7						9					
10		11	ROCHDALE	1-3	Green	2508	1	2	3	4	6	5			10		11	8	7		12				9					
11		18	Crewe Alexandra	0-1		1939		2		4	5	6			11		3		7			9	10	8	1					
12		21	Watford	0-1		3581		2		6	5	3	12		8		9		7			11	4	10	1					
13		25	NORTHAMPTON T	0-2		1965		2		6	5	3			12		8		7	9		11	4	10	1					
14	Nov	1	Brentford	2-5	Charnley, Green	4220		2		6	5	3	9			8			7	11			4	10	1					
15		4	CAMBRIDGE UNITED	0-1		1526		2		6		5	8		10		3		7	9	12		4	11	1					
16		8	WORKINGTON	3-0	Keeley, Green 2	1503		2	3		5	10			7		9		6		11		4	8	1	12				
17		15	Bournemouth	0-1		4333		2	3		5	7			10	12	8		6		11		4	9	1					
18		28	Lincoln City	0-3		8494		2	3		5	10	12		8		6		7		9		4	11	1					
19	Dec	6	SOUTHPORT	1-2	Collier	1817		2	3		5	4	11		8		6		7			10		9			1			
20		13	Reading	0-1		5575		2	3		5	6			8		4	12	7			9		11			1	10		
21		20	STOCKPORT COUNTY	0-0		1570		2			5	4	3		8		6	12	7			9		11			1	10		
22		26	Bradford City	0-0		3465		2				5	4		8	3	9	6	7					10			1	11		
23		27	DONCASTER ROVERS	2-1	Davidson, Woodward	5801					5	4	2		10	3	7	8	6			9		11			1			
24	Jan	3	Barnsley	0-1		2823					5	4	2		10	3	7	8	6			9		11			1			
25		10	NEWPORT COUNTY	1-2	Money	1739					5	4	2		10	3	7	8	6		12	9		11			1			
26		17	Torquay United	0-1		2776					5	4			10	3	7		6		11			9		12	1			
27	Feb	7	Cambridge United	2-2	Keeley, Davidson	1777		2	3	6	5	4	12		8		9		7		11			10	1					
28		10	WATFORD	0-1		2200		2	3	6	5	4	12		8		9		7		11			10	1					
29		14	Workington	3-2	Green 2, Davidson	1273		2	3	7	5	4			8		9		6		11			10	1					
30		21	BOURNEMOUTH	2-0	Money, Charnley	2068		2	3	6	5	4	12		8		9		7		11			10	1					
31		24	TRANMERE ROVERS	2-2	Wiggington (p), O'Connor	3049		2	3	6	5	4	12		8		9		7		11			10	1					
32		27	Northampton Town	1-2	O'Connor	6804		2	3	6	5	4			8		9		7		11			10	1					
33	Mar	2	HARTLEPOOL	5-1	Collier 2, Green 2, Oates	2966		2	3		5	4			8		9	6	7		11		12	10	1					
34		6	Brentford	2-1	Green, O'Connor	3225		2	3		5	4			8		9	6	7		11			10	1					
35		12	Rochdale	1-1	Green	1430		2	3			4	5		8		9	7	6		11		12	10	1					
36		16	CREWE ALEXANDRA	1-0	Green	3126		2	3			5	6		8		9	4	7		11			10	1					
37		20	LINCOLN CITY	0-2		10329		2	3		5	4	12		8		9	7	6		11			10	1					
38		26	Southport	1-1	Collier	1805		2	3		5	4			8		9	7	6					10	1					
39		29	Stockport County	0-0		2078		2	3		5	6			8		9	4	7				11	10	1					
40	Apr	3	DARLINGTON	2-1	Irvine, Davidson	2492		2	3	11	5	6			8		9	4	7					10	1					
41		6	SWANSEA CITY	1-1	Green	3015		2	3	11	5	6			8		9	4	7					10	1					
42		10	Huddersfield Town	1-1	Davidson	6502		2	3	11	5	6	12		8		9	4	7					10	1					
43		17	BRADFORD CITY	2-0	Green, O'Connor	3254			3		5	6	2		8		9	4	7		11			10	1					
44		19	Doncaster Rovers	1-0	Green	4097		2	3		5	6			8		9	4	7		11			10	1					
45		20	BARNSLEY	1-0	O'Connor	4770		2	3		5			6	8		9	4	7		11		12	10	1					
46		23	Exeter City	4-5	Green, Woodward 2, Wiggington	1863		2	3		5	6	8				4	7					9	10	1					11
			Apps				10	42	31	23	42	45	27	1	43	12	45	25	45	4	21	5	19	10	39	28	2	8	3	1
			Goals							1	2	3	2		3		5	1	7	·	5	1	5		15					

F.A. Cup

			Opponent	Result	Scorers	Att	Markham P	Peacock JC	Wiggington CA	Money R	Keeley NB	Davidson AG	Collier GR	O'Connor D	Green R
R1	Nov	22	Preston North End	1-2	Green	8119	2	3	6	8	10	7	4	11	5 9 1

F.L. Cup

			Opponent	Result	Att	Norris M	Markham P	Peacock JC	Irvine A	Wiggington CA	Money R	Charnley DL	Keeley NB	Pilling S	Davidson AG	Oates RA	Collier GR
R1/1	Aug	20	Mansfield Town	0-4	4810	1	2	3	6	5	4	10	9	7	11	12	8
R1/2		26	MANSFIELD TOWN	0-2	1412	1	2	3		5	4		11	8	9	6	7 10

		P	W	D	L	F		W	D	L	F	A	Pts
1	Lincoln City	46	21	2	0	71	15	11	8	4	40	24	74
2	Northampton Town	46	18	5	0	62	20	11	5	7	25	20	68
3	Reading	46	19	3	1	42	9	5	9	9	28	42	60
4	Tranmere Rovers	46	18	3	2	61	16	6	7	10	28	39	58
5	Huddersfield Town	46	11	6	6	28	17	10	8	5	28	24	56
6	Bournemouth	46	15	5	3	39	16	5	7	11	18	32	52
7	Exeter City	46	13	7	3	37	17	5	7	11	19	30	50
8	Watford	46	16	4	3	38	18	6	2	15	24	44	50
9	Torquay United	46	12	6	5	31	24	6	8	9	24	39	50
10	Doncaster Rovers	46	10	6	7	42	31	9	5	9	33	38	49
11	Swansea City	46	14	8	1	51	21	2	7	14	15	36	47
12	Barnsley	46	12	8	3	34	16	2	8	13	18	32	44
13	Cambridge United	46	7	10	6	36	28	7	5	11	22	34	43
14	Hartlepool	46	10	6	7	37	29	6	4	13	25	49	42
15	Rochdale	46	7	11	5	27	23	5	7	11	13	31	42
16	Crewe Alexandra	46	10	7	6	36	21	3	8	12	22	36	41
17	Bradford City	46	9	7	7	35	26	3	10	10	28	39	41
18	Brentford	46	12	7	4	37	18	2	6	15	19	42	41
19	SCUNTHORPE UNITED	46	11	3	9	31	24	3	7	13	19	35	38
20	Darlington	46	11	7	5	30	14	3	3	17	18	43	38
21	Stockport County	46	8	7	8	23	23	5	5	13	20	53	38
22	Newport County	46	7	8	8	35	33	5	2	16	22	57	35
23	Southport	46	6	6	11	27	31	2	4	17	14	46	26
24	Workington	46	5	4	14	19	43	2	3	18	11	44	21

#	Date	Opponent	Score	Scorers	Att	Letheran G	Czuczman M	Peacock JC	Oates RA	Wiggington CA	Money R	Wadsworth M	Collier GR	Keeley NB	Green R	Pilling S	Davidson AG	O'Connor D	Markham P	O'Meara AM	Bridges B	Dale AG	Lee R	Kilmore K	Lumby JA	Walton II	Barnard G
1	Aug 21	ROCHDALE	0-1		3391	1	2	3	4	5	6	7	8	9	10	11	12										
2	28	Watford	1-2	Wadsworth	5950	1	4	3	6	5		8	7	10	9		2	11									
3	Sep 3	CREWE ALEXANDRA	4-0	Wiggington 2(1p), Keeley, O'Connor	3286	1	6	3	4	5			7	9	10		8	11	2								
4	11	Bournemouth	2-2	Green 2	4297	1	2	3	4	5	6	7	8	10	9		12	11									
5	18	WORKINGTON	3-1	Wiggington (p), Keeley, Peacock	3466	1		3	4	5	6		7	8	10		9	11	2								
6	24	Southend United	1-1	Keeley	5288	1		3	6	4	5		7	8	10		9	11	2								
7	29	Exeter City	0-2		2934	1		3	4	5	6		8	9	10	12	7	11	2								
8	Oct 2	HARTLEPOOL	2-0	Keeley, Davidson	3287	1		3	4	5	6		7	10	11		8	9	2								
9	9	Halifax Town	1-0	Wiggington	1854	1		3	4	5	6	12	7	10	11		8	9	2								
10	15	Cambridge United	0-1		3412	1		3	4	5	6	12	8	9	10	11	7		2								
11	23	COLCHESTER UNITED	2-0	Keeley, Pilling	3157	1		3	4	5	6	12	7	11	10	8	9		2								
12	30	DARLINGTON	3-0	Davidson, Green, Wadsworth	3905	1		3	4	5	6	12	7	10		11	8	9	2								
13	Nov 2	SOUTHPORT	1-1	Davidson	4768	1		3	4	5	6	12	8	9	10	11	7		2								
14	6	Barnsley	1-5	Pilling	4440	1		3		5	6	7	4	10		8	9		2								
15	13	ALDERSHOT	1-3	Keeley	3586	1		3	4	5	6	7	8	10		11	9		2								
16	27	Torquay United	3-1	O'Connor 3	2098	1		3	4	5	6		7	10	9		8	11	2								
17	Dec 11	Swansea City	0-2		2392	1	12	3	4	5	6		7	10	9		8	11	2								
18	17	Stockport County	0-1		2827	1	7	3	4	5	6			8	9	10	12	11	2								
19	27	DONCASTER ROVERS	1-1	Green	7003	1	7	3	4	5	6	12	8	9	10		11		2								
20	28	Huddersfield Town	0-1		7028	1	7	3	4	5	6	11	8	9	10		12		2								
21	Jan 8	BRADFORD CITY	2-1	Wiggington, Keeley	4218	1	4	3	12	5	6	11	7	8	9		10		2								
22	22	Rochdale	0-5		1640	1	6	3	12	5	4	11	7	10	9		8		2								
23	25	BRENTFORD	2-1	Wadsworth, Keeley	2726		2		4	5			11	8	9	10	3	7			1	6	12				
24	28	Newport County	0-0		1601		2		4	5	6		11	8	9	10	3	7			1						
25	Feb 5	WATFORD	0-0		3201	1	6	2	4	5			11	7	10	9	3	8					12				
26	8	BARNSLEY	1-2	Pilling	4557	1	6	2	4	5			11	8	9	10	3	7					12				
27	12	Crewe Alexandra	1-2	Keeley	2189	1	6	2	4	5			11	12	9	10	3	7					8				
28	19	BOURNEMOUTH	0-0		2715	1	6	2	4	5			11	7	10		3	9					8	12			
29	26	Workington	0-1		1200	1	6	2	4	5		7	12		10		3	9					8	11			
30	Mar 5	SOUTHEND UNITED	1-0	Lumby	2752	1	7	2	4	5	6				11		3						8	9	10		
31	7	Darlington	2-5	Kilmore, Keeley	2134		6	2	4	5		7		9			3				1		12	11	8	10	
32	12	Hartlepool	0-3		1673		7	2	4	5	6		8	9			3	11			1				10		
33	15	EXETER CITY	4-1	Lumby 2, Czuczman, Hore(og)	2147		7	2	4	5	6			9			3				1		11	8	10		
34	19	HALIFAX TOWN	2-1	Lumby, Keeley	2902		7	2	4	5	6			9			3				1		11	8	10		
35	26	CAMBRIDGE UNITED	0-2		3611		7	2	4	5	6			9			3	12			1		11	8	10		
36	Apr 2	Colchester United	1-1	Lumby	3799		7	2	4	5	6			9			3	12			1		8		10		
37	9	HUDDERSFIELD T	0-4		4207		4	2		5	6			9			3	7			1		11	8	10		
38	11	Doncaster Rovers	0-3		4676		2		4	5	6	12		9			3	7			1		11	8	10		
39	12	Southport	1-2	Lumby	941		7	2	4	5	6			9			3	8					12	10	11		
40	16	SWANSEA CITY	0-3		2079		2		4	5	6	8	7	9			3	11					12	10			
41	19	NEWPORT COUNTY	1-0	Keeley	1883		2		4	5	6	7		9			3	11					8	10			1
42	23	Aldershot	1-1	Kilmore	2392		2	12	4	5	6		9	8			3	7					11	10			1
43	30	TORQUAY UNITED	0-0		2105		2		4	5	6	9		11			3	7					8	10			1
44	May 4	Bradford City	0-4		5982		2		4	5	6		12	9			3	7					11	8	10		1
45	7	Brentford	2-4	Kilmore, Lumby	5300		2		4	5	6		12	9			3	7					11	8	10		1
46	14	STOCKPORT COUNTY	2-2	Lumby, Oates	2135		2		4	5	6			9			3	7					11	8	10		1
		Apps				27	31	41	44	46	38	28	31	46	27	33	41	10	19	13	1	2	16	19	16	1	6
		Goals					1	1	1	5		3		12	4	3	3	4						3	8		

One own goal

F.A. Cup

	Date	Opponent	Score	Scorers	Att	Peacock	Oates	Wiggington	Money	Collier	Keeley	Green	Davidson	O'Connor	Markham	O'Meara
R1	Nov 20	CHESTERFIELD	1-2	Keeley	5404	3	4	5	6	7	10	9	8	11	2	1

F.L. Cup

	Date	Opponent	Score	Scorers	Att	Letheran	Czuczman	Peacock	Oates	Wiggington	Money	Wadsworth	Collier	Keeley	Green	Pilling	Davidson	O'Connor
R1/1	Aug 14	Mansfield Town	0-2		5224	1	2	3	4	5	6		8	9	10	11	7	
R1/2	17	MANSFIELD TOWN	2-0	Keeley, Wiggington	3164	1	2	3	4	5	6	7	8	9	10	11		
rep	24	MANSFIELD TOWN	2-1	O'Connor, Wadsworth	4319	1	2	3	4	5	6	7	8	9	10		12	11
R2	31	NOTTS COUNTY	0-2		6208	1	6	3	4	5		7	8	9	10		2	11

		P	W	D	L	F	A	W	D	L	F	A	Pts
1	Cambridge United	46	16	5	2	57	18	10	8	5	30	22	65
2	Exeter City	46	17	5	1	40	13	8	7	8	30	33	62
3	Colchester United	46	19	2	2	51	14	6	7	10	26	29	59
4	Bradford City	46	16	7	0	51	18	7	6	10	27	33	59
5	Swansea City	46	18	3	2	60	30	7	5	11	32	38	58
6	Barnsley	46	16	5	2	45	18	7	4	12	17	21	55
7	Watford	46	15	7	1	46	13	3	8	12	21	37	51
8	Doncaster Rovers	46	16	2	5	47	25	5	7	11	24	40	51
9	Huddersfield Town	46	15	5	3	36	15	4	7	12	24	34	50
10	Southend United	46	11	9	3	35	19	4	10	9	17	26	49
11	Darlington	46	13	5	5	37	25	5	8	10	22	39	49
12	Crewe Alexandra	46	16	6	1	36	15	3	5	15	11	45	49
13	Bournemouth	46	13	8	2	39	13	2	10	11	15	31	48
14	Stockport County	46	10	10	3	29	19	3	9	11	24	38	45
15	Brentford	46	14	3	6	48	27	4	4	15	29	49	43
16	Torquay United	46	12	5	6	33	22	5	4	14	26	45	43
17	Aldershot	46	10	8	5	29	19	6	3	14	20	40	43
18	Rochdale	46	8	7	8	32	25	5	5	13	18	34	38
19	Newport County	46	11	6	6	33	21	3	4	16	9	37	38
20	SCUNTHORPE UNITED	46	11	6	6	32	24	2	5	16	17	49	37
21	Halifax Town	46	11	6	6	36	18	0	8	15	11	40	36
22	Hartlepool	46	8	9	6	30	20	2	3	18	17	53	32
23	Southport	46	3	12	8	17	28	0	7	16	16	49	25
24	Workington	46	3	7	13	23	42	1	4	18	18	60	19

1977/78 14th in Division 4

			Result	Scorers	Att	Crawford PG	Czuczman M	Peacock JC	Pilling S	Money R	Bridges B	Oates RA	Kilmore K	Keeley NB	Lumby JA	Heron B	Kavanagh EA	Farrell KM	Wigg RG	Cooper T	Davy SJ	Lee R	O'Donnell JD	Grimes V	Holyoak P	Deere SH	Couch GR
1	Aug 20	Southport	1-1	Lumby (p)	2068	1	2	3	4	5	6	7	8	9	10	11											
2	23	CREWE ALEXANDRA	3-0	Keeley, Kilmore, Lumby	3283	1	2	3	4	5	6	7	8	9	10	11											
3	26	BOURNEMOUTH	0-0		4110	1	2	3	4	5	6	7	8	9	10	11											
4	Sep 3	Hartlepool United	0-1		1946	1	2	3	4	5	6	7	8	9	10	11	12										
5	10	SOUTHEND UNITED	1-2	Lumby	2768	1	2	3	4	5	6	7	8	9	10	11											
6	13	Barnsley	0-3		5725	1	2	3	4	5	6	7	8	9	11	12											
7	17	WIMBLEDON	3-0	Lumby, Oates 2	2618	1	2	3	12	5	6	7	10	9	8	11	4										
8	24	Brentford	0-2		6120	1	2	3	12	5	6	7	8	9	10	11	4										
9	27	SWANSEA CITY	1-0	Kilmore	2654	1	2	3		5	6	7	8	9	10	11	4										
10	Oct 1	NORTHAMPTON T	2-2	Heron, Lumby (p)	2580	1	2	3	12	5	6	7	8	9	10	11	4										
11	4	Newport County	1-3	Farrell	3191	1	2	3	8	5	6	7		9	10	11	4	12									
12	8	Grimsby Town	0-0		5249	1	2	3	8	5		6		9	10	11	4	7									
13	15	READING	0-1		2569	1	2	3	7	5		6	12	9	10	11	4	8									
14	22	Torquay United	2-4	Lumby (p), Green (og)	2529	1	2		3	5	6	7	8	9	10		4		11								
15	29	HALIFAX TOWN	2-0	Lumby (p), Keeley	2420	1	2	3		5	6	7	8	9	10		4		11								
16	Nov 5	HUDDERSFIELD T	1-1	Lumby	3068	1	2	3		5	6	7	8	9	10	11	4										
17	12	Watford	1-4	Lumby	10565	1	2	3	12	5		7	8	9	10	11	4		6								
18	19	ROCHDALE	1-0	Kilmore	2078	1	2	3	12	5		7	8	9		11	4		10	6							
19	Dec 3	Aldershot	0-4		3070	1	6	3	8			5		9	10	12			11	4	2	7					
20	10	DARLINGTON	3-0	Lumby, Keeley, Oates	1803	1	5	3				4	8	9	10	12			11	6	2	7					
21	26	Doncaster Rovers	1-1	Wigg	5097	1	5	3			12	6	8	9	10				11		2	7	4				
22	27	YORK CITY	2-1	Lumby 2	3242	1	5	3				6	4	9	10	7			11		2		8				
23	31	Huddersfield Town	1-4	Lumby (p)	4000	1	5	3				6	4	12	9	10	7		11		2		8				
24	Jan 2	STOCKPORT COUNTY	3-0	Oates, Lumby 2	3237	1	5	3				6	4		9	10		7	11		2		8				
25	7	Crewe Alexandra	1-1	Lumby	1926	1	5	3				6	4	12	9	10		7	11		2		8				
26	14	SOUTHPORT	0-2		2574	1	5	3	12			6	4		9	10		7	11		2		8				
27	21	Bournemouth	1-1	Keeley	2869	1	5	3				6	4	8	9	10	7	12	11		2						
28	Feb 3	Southend United	0-2		6879	1	5	3				6	4		9	10	7		11		12		2	8			
29	11	Wimbledon	0-0		1603	1	5		3			4		9	10		11		12		2		8	7	6		
30	25	Northampton Town	2-1	Lumby, Deere	2972	1	5		3			4		9	10				11		2		8	7		6	
31	Mar 3	GRIMSBY TOWN	2-1	Lumby 2 (1p)	7612	1	6	3				4		9	10				11		2		8	7		5	
32	7	BARNSLEY	1-0	Keeley	4828	1	6	3				4		9	10				11		2		8	7		5	
33	11	Reading	0-1		3410	1	6	3	12			4		9	10				11		2		8	7		5	
34	14	BRENTFORD	1-1	Wigg	2925	1	6	3				4	12	9	10				11		2		8	7		5	
35	18	TORQUAY UNITED	0-1		2169	1	6		3			4		9	10	12			11		2		8	7		5	
36	24	York City	2-0	Grimes, Kilmore	2408	1	6		3			4	8	9	10				11		2			7		5	
37	27	DONCASTER ROVERS	0-0		3592	1	6		3			4	8	9	10				11		2			7		5	
38	28	Halifax Town	2-2	Lumby (p), Grimes	2215	1	6		3			4	8	9	10				11				2	7		5	
39	31	Stockport County	1-1	Keeley	2774	1	5					4	8	9	10				11		2		3	7		6	
40	Apr 4	NEWPORT COUNTY	2-0	Kilmore 2	2457	1	6					4	8	9	10				11		2		3	7		5	
41	8	WATFORD	0-1		5202	1	6		3			4	8	9			12		11				2	7		5	10
42	15	Rochdale	1-1	Oates	1005	1	6		3			4		9		8			11		12		2	7		5	10
43	18	HARTLEPOOL UNITED	2-0	Kilmore 2	2181	1	6		3			4	8	9					11				2	7		5	10
44	22	ALDERSHOT	1-1	Oates	2555	1	6		3			4	8	9					11				2	7		5	10
45	25	Swansea City	1-3	Oates	13228	1	6		3			4	8	9					11		12		2	7		5	10
46	29	Darlington	1-1	Wigg	1302	1	6		3			4	8	9			12		11		2			7		5	10
			Apps			46	46	31	30	18	22	46	32	46	39	25	15	7	32	4	24	3	23	18	1	17	6
			Goals									7	8	6	20	1		1	3					2		1	

One own goal

F.A. Cup

| R1 | Nov 26 | Stockport County | 0-3 | | 4512 | 1 | 6 | 3 | | | | 5 | 8 | 9 | 10 | | | 4 | 12 | 11 | | 2 | 7 | | | | |

F.L. Cup

R1/1	Aug 13	Darlington	0-0		2800	1	2	3		5	6	7	8	9	10	11							4				
R1/2	16	DARLINGTON	3-1	Lumby, Kilmore, Oates	2971	1	2	3	12	5	6	7	8	9	10	11							4				
R2	30	Peterborough United	1-1	Pilling	3697	1	2	3	4	5	6	7	8	9	10	11	12										
rep	Sep 6	PETERBOROUGH UTD.	0-1		4564	1	2	3	4		6	7	8	9	10	11	5										

		P	W	D	L	F	A	W	D	L	F	A	Pts
1	Watford	46	18	4	1	44	14	12	7	4	41	24	71
2	Southend United	46	15	5	3	46	18	10	5	8	20	21	60
3	Swansea City	46	16	5	2	54	17	7	5	11	33	30	56
4	Brentford	46	15	6	2	50	17	6	8	9	36	37	56
5	Aldershot	46	15	8	0	45	16	4	8	11	22	31	54
6	Grimsby Town	46	14	6	3	30	15	7	5	11	27	36	53
7	Barnsley	46	15	4	4	44	20	3	10	10	17	29	50
8	Reading	46	12	7	4	33	23	6	7	10	22	29	50
9	Torquay United	46	12	6	5	43	25	4	9	10	14	31	47
10	Northampton Town	46	9	8	6	32	30	8	5	10	31	38	47
11	Huddersfield Town	46	13	5	5	41	21	2	10	11	22	34	45
12	Doncaster Rovers	46	11	8	4	37	26	3	9	11	15	39	45
13	Wimbledon	46	8	11	4	39	26	6	5	12	27	41	44
14	SCUNTHORPE UNITED	46	12	6	5	31	14	2	10	11	19	41	44
15	Crewe Alexandra	46	11	8	4	34	25	4	6	13	16	44	44
16	Newport County	46	14	6	3	43	22	2	5	16	22	51	43
17	Bournemouth	46	12	6	5	28	20	2	9	12	13	31	43
18	Stockport County	46	14	4	5	41	19	2	6	15	15	37	42
19	Darlington	46	10	8	5	31	22	4	5	14	21	37	41
20	Halifax Town	46	7	10	6	28	23	3	11	9	24	39	41
21	Hartlepool United	46	12	4	7	34	29	3	3	17	17	55	37
22	York City	46	8	7	8	27	31	4	5	14	23	38	36
23	Southport	46	5	13	5	30	32	1	6	16	22	44	31
24	Rochdale	46	8	6	9	29	28	0	2	21	14	57	24

SEASON 1976-77
Back: Lee, Charnley, Walton, Czuczman, Wigginton, Pilling, Davidson
2nd row: Strong, Markham, Keeley, O'Meara, Oates, Bridges, Wadsworth, Barker
3rd row: O'Connor, Collier, Archer (Director), Ashman, Johnson (Director), Peacock, Money, Green
Front: Dale, Hirscher, Arrowsmith

SEASON 1977-78
Back: Kilmore, Keeley, Oates, O'Meara, Crawford, Dawson, Czuczman, Bridges, Farrell
Front: Dale, Pilling, Peacock, Lumby, Money, O'Donnell, Heron, Lee

#	Date		Opponent	Score	Scorers	Att	Crawford PG	Davy SJ	Peacock JC	Oates RA	Deere SH	Czuczman M	Grimes V	Wigg RG	Keeley NB	Pilling S	Kilmore K	Bloomer BMc	O'Donnell JD	Gibson D	Kavanagh EA	Couch GR	Armstrong KT	Earl S	Hall DA
1	Aug	19	Port Vale	2-2	Wigg, Pilling	3025	1	2	3	4	5	6	7	8	9	10	11	12							
2		22	BOURNEMOUTH	1-0	Pilling	2433	1		3	4	5	6	7	9		10	11	8	12	2					
3		25	HUDDERSFIELD T	3-1	Pilling, Grimes, Kilmore	3029	1		3		5	6	7	9		10	11	8		2	4				
4	Sep	1	Doncaster Rovers	0-0		4667	1		3	4	5	6	7	9		10	11	8	12	2					
5		9	BARNSLEY	0-1		7612	1		3	4	5	6	7	9			11	8	12	2	10				
6		12	Portsmouth	0-0		10965	1		3	4	5	6	7	9			11	8		2	10	12			
7		15	Northampton Town	0-1		3858	1		3	4	5	6	7	9			11	8		2	10	12			
8		23	STOCKPORT COUNTY	1-0	Wigg	2691	1		3	4	5	6	7	9			12	8		2	10	11			
9		26	ALDERSHOT	2-0	Kilmore 2	2566	1		3	4	5	6	7	9			11	8		2		10			
10		30	Wigan Athletic	0-1		4459	1		3	4	5	6	7	9			11	8		2	12	10			
11	Oct	7	NEWPORT COUNTY	2-3	Deere, Oates	2453	1		3	4	5	6		9			8		10	2	7	11			
12		14	Wimbledon	1-3	Wigg	3808	1		3	4	5	6	7	9		10	8			2		11			
13		17	Hartlepool United	1-1	Kilmore	2981	1	2		4	5	6	7	9			3	8				10	11	12	
14		21	BRADFORD CITY	3-2	Couch, Kilmore 2 (1 p)	2778	1	2		4	5	6	7		9		3	8				10	11		
15		28	York City	0-1		1970	1	2		4	5		7	6	9		3	8				10	11		
16	Nov	4	READING	0-3		2424	1	2		4	5	6	7	11	9		3	8				10	12		
17		11	DONCASTER ROVERS	0-0		3250	1	2		4		6	7	9		11	3	8	5			10			
18		18	Huddersfield Town	2-3	Oates, Keeley	3375	1	2		4	5	6	7	9	11		3	8	10				12		
19	Dec	2	Torquay United	1-0	Kilmore (p)	2794	1			4	5	6	7		10		3	8	2			11			9
20		16	HEREFORD UNITED	4-2	Kilmore 2, Pilling, Earl	1683	1			4	5	6	7		10		3	8	2			11			9
21		23	Darlington	2-2	Kilmore 2	1512	1			4	5	6	7		10		3	8	2			11			9
22		26	GRIMSBY TOWN	2-1	Kilmore (p), Grimes	8008	1			4	5	6	7		11		3	8	2			10			9
23		30	ROCHDALE	0-4		2620	1			4	5	6	7	12	10		3	8	2			11			9
24	Feb	3	Aldershot	0-2		3669	1			4	5	6	7		11		3	8	2	12	10				9
25		26	Stockport County	2-0	Kavanagh, Earl	2676	1			4	5	6	7		11		3	8	2	12	10				9
26	Mar	3	Bradford City	1-1	Pilling	4988	1		12	4	5	6	7		11		3	8	2		10				9
27		10	YORK CITY	2-3	Kilmore 2 (2p)	2261	1			4	5	6	7		11		3	8	2		10				9
28		13	Barnsley	1-4	Grimes	9308	1			4	5	6	7		11		3	8	2	9	10				
29		16	Reading	1-0	Keeley	5144	1			4	5	6	7		11		3	12	2	8	10				9
30		20	NORTHAMPTON T	0-3		1763	1			4	5	6	7		11		3	12	2	8	10				9
31		24	Bournemouth	0-0		3028	1		3	4	5	6	7		11			8	2		10				9
32		27	PORT VALE	2-0	Grimes, Earl	1472	1		3	4	5	6	7		11			8	2		10				9
33		31	CREWE ALEXANDRA	0-1		1868	1			4	5		7					8	2		10	11		9	6
34	Apr	3	PORTSMOUTH	2-2	Couch, Bloomer	1535	1	12	3	4	5		7					8	9	2	10	11			6
35		7	Hereford United	1-3	Kilmore (p)	2859	1	12	3	4	5	6	7					8	9	2	10		11		
36		10	DARLINGTON	1-0	Craig (og)	1372	1		12	4	5	2	7				9	8	3		10	11			6
37		14	Grimsby Town	1-1	Kavanagh	10197	1		3	4	5	2	7					8		2	12	10	11		9
38		16	HALIFAX TOWN	1-0	Earl	1624	1		3	4	5	2	7					8			11	10	12	9	6
39		18	Newport County	0-2		2572	1		3	4	5	2	7					8			11	10		9	6
40		21	Rochdale	0-1		1224	1	2	3	4	5		7					8			11	10	12	9	6
41		24	HARTLEPOOL UNITED	3-1	Oates, Earl 2	1226	1	2		4	5	3	7					8				10	9	11	6
42		28	TORQUAY UNITED	2-2	Kilmore (p), Earl	1426	1			2	4	5	3	7				8				10	9	11	6
43	May	1	WIGAN ATHLETIC	0-1		1582	1		3	4	5	2	7					8			11	10	9	6	12
44		5	Crewe Alexandra	2-0	Couch 2	1121	1	2	3	4	5		7		11			8				10	9	6	
45		8	WIMBLEDON	2-0	Kilmore (p), Earl	1777	1	2	3	4	5		7		6			8				10	9	11	
46		18	Halifax Town	3-2	Couch, Grimes, Gibson	1037	1	2	3	4	5		7					8			11	10	9		6
			Apps				46	14	28	45	45	39	45	18	25	30	46	7	32	18	39	18	1	23	11
			Goals							3	1		5	3	2	5	17	1		1		2	5		8

One own goal

Rnd	Date		Opponent	Score	Scorers	Att	Crawford PG	Oates RA	Deere SH	Czuczman M	Grimes V	Wigg RG	Keeley NB	Kilmore K	Bloomer BMc	Gibson D	Couch GR
R1	Nov	25	SHEFFIELD WEDNESDAY	1-1	Pilling	8697	1	4	5	6	7	9	11	3	8	2	10
rep		28	Sheffield Wednesday	0-1		9760	1	4	5	6	7	9	11	3	8	2*	10

Rnd	Date		Opponent	Score	Scorers	Att	Crawford PG	Peacock JC	Oates RA	Deere SH	Czuczman M	Grimes V	Wigg RG	Keeley NB	Pilling S	Kilmore K	Gibson D	Bloomer BMc
R1/1	Aug	12	NOTTS COUNTY	0-1		2389	1	3	4	5	6	7	9	10	11	12	2	8
R1/2		15	Notts County	0-3		5064	1	3	4	5	6	7	9	10	11	12	2	8

		P	W	D	L	F	A	W	D	L	F	A	Pts
1	Reading	46	19	3	1	49	8	7	10	6	27	27	65
2	Grimsby Town	46	15	5	3	51	23	11	4	8	31	26	61
3	Wimbledon	46	18	3	2	50	20	7	8	8	28	26	61
4	Barnsley	46	15	5	3	47	23	9	8	6	26	19	61
5	Aldershot	46	16	5	2	38	14	4	12	7	25	33	57
6	Wigan Athletic	46	14	5	4	40	24	7	8	8	23	24	55
7	Portsmouth	46	13	7	3	35	12	7	5	11	27	36	52
8	Newport County	46	12	5	6	39	28	9	5	9	27	27	52
9	Huddersfield Town	46	13	8	2	32	15	5	3	15	25	38	47
10	York City	46	11	6	6	33	24	7	5	11	18	31	47
11	Torquay United	46	14	4	5	38	24	5	4	14	20	41	46
12	SCUNTHORPE UNITED	46	12	3	8	33	30	5	8	10	21	30	45
13	Hartlepool United	46	7	12	4	35	28	6	6	11	22	38	44
14	Hereford United	46	12	8	3	35	18	3	5	15	18	35	43
15	Bradford City	46	11	5	7	38	26	6	4	13	24	42	43
16	Port Vale	46	8	10	5	29	28	6	4	13	28	42	42
17	Stockport County	46	11	5	7	33	21	3	7	13	25	39	40
18	Bournemouth	46	11	6	6	34	19	3	5	15	13	29	39
19	Northampton Town	46	12	4	7	40	30	3	5	15	24	46	39
20	Rochdale	46	11	4	8	25	26	4	5	14	22	38	39
21	Darlington	46	8	8	7	25	21	3	7	13	24	45	37
22	Doncaster Rovers	46	8	8	7	25	22	5	3	15	25	51	37
23	Halifax Town	46	7	5	11	24	32	2	3	18	15	40	26
24	Crewe Alexandra	46	3	7	13	24	41	3	7	13	19	49	26

SEASON 1978-79
Back: Nobble, Jeffery, Meadows, Ridley, Cook
Middle: Hall, Grimes, Crawford, Czuczman, O'Meara, Wigg, Wilkinson, Strong (Masseur)
Seated: Ashman (Manager), Kilmore, Peacock, Davy, Oates, Keeley, Kavanagh, Gibson, Pilling, O'Donnell, Kaye (Coach), Nigel Martinson (Mascot)

SEASON 1979-80
Back: Gibson, McDonald, Hall, Kilmore, Meadows, Pendleton, O'Berg
Middle: Strong (Masseur), Pilling, Kavanagh, Gordon, Crawford, Johnson, Partridge, Cowling, Jackson (Y.T Coach)
Front: Ashman (Manager), O'Donnell, Peacock, Earl, Grimes, Keeley, Oates, Davy, Kaye (Coach)

1979/80 14th in Division 4

#		Date	Opponent	Score	Scorers	Att	Crawford PG	Davy SJ	Peacock JC	Kavanagh EA	Deere SH	Oates RA	O'Berg PJ	Kilmore K	Earl S	Partridge M	Keeley NB	Pilling S	Green R	Cammack SR	Gibson D	Couch GR	Cowling C	Gordon JS	Grimes V	Dall DG	Hall DA	Stewart CD	Pugh IG	Skipper PD	Botham IT	O'Donnell ID	Neenan JP
1	Aug	18	Torquay United	0-3		3063	1	2	3	4	5	6	7	8	9	10	11	12															
2		21	HARTLEPOOL UNITED	1-3	Kavanagh	1710	1	2	3	4	5	6	7	8	9	10	11																
3		25	Portsmouth	1-6	Pilling	12234	1	2	3	4	5	6	7	8	9		5	11	10														
4	Sep	1	BOURNEMOUTH	2-1	Green, Earl	1471	1			2	4	5	6		8	9	7	11	3	10													
5		8	Aldershot	0-2		2709	1			2	4	5	6	12	8	9	7	11	3	10													
6		14	HUDDERSFIELD T	1-1	Green	2546	1	2	3	4	5	6	7			10	11		9	8	12												
7		18	YORK CITY	6-1	Green 2, Partridge 3(1p), Cammack	2365	1	2	3	4	5	6	7			10	11		9	8													
8		22	Bradford City	0-2		6248	1	2	3				7			10	11		9	8													
9		28	DONCASTER ROVERS	0-0		4465	1	2	3		5	6			7	10	11		9		4	8	12										
10	Oct	2	York City	0-2		2397	1	2	3	4	5	6	7			10	11		9				8	12									
11		6	WALSALL	2-2	Green, O'Berg	2492	1	2	3		5	6	7			10	11	4	9	8													
12		9	Hartlepool United	2-3	Partridge (p), Green	2810	1	2	3		5	6	7	12		10	11	4	9	8													
13		13	Lincoln City	0-4		4933		2	3		5	6	7	12		10		11	9	8						1	4						
14		20	NEWPORT COUNTY	1-3	Keeley	1875		2	3			4	6	7		10	11	12	9	8						1		5					
15		23	DARLINGTON	3-0	O'Berg, Cammack, Green	1559		2	3			4	6	7		10	11	12	9	8						1		5					
16		26	Tranmere Rovers	2-1	Green, Pilling	1876		2	3			4	6			10	11	7	9	8			12	1				5					
17	Nov	3	TORQUAY UNITED	1-1	Cammack	1868		2	3			4	6	7		10	11	12	9	8				1				5					
18		6	Darlington	1-3	Cammack	1306		2	3			4	6	7			11	10	9	8				1				5					
19		10	STOCKPORT COUNTY	1-1	Cammack	1853		2	3			4	6				11	10	9	8	12		7	1				5					
20		17	Wigan Athletic	1-4	Partridge	4618				4			6			10	11	3	9	8			7	1				5					
21		30	ROCHDALE	2-0	Oates 2	1771		2	3	12	6	4				10	9			8			7	1				5		11			
22	Dec	8	Northampton Town	0-0		2120		2	3		4	6				10		9		8			7	1				5		11			
23		15	Newport County	1-2	Stewart	4158		2	3	12	6	4				10		9		8			7	1				5		11			
24		21	HALIFAX TOWN	1-0	Cammack	1473		2	3		5	6				10		9	7	8			12	1				4		11			
25		26	Port Vale	0-1		3432		2	3		4	6				10		9	7	8			12	1				11		11			
26		29	HEREFORD UNITED	1-0	Green	1764		2	3		4	6				10		9	7	8				1				5		11			
27	Jan	5	Peterborough United	1-3	Davy	3014		2	3	12	4	6				10	7	9		8				1				5		11			
28		26	PORTSMOUTH	1-0	Partridge	2609		2	3		6	4				10		9	8				12	1				5		11	7		
29	Feb	9	BRADFORD CITY	3-3	Pilling, Partridge 2	2819		2	3		6	4				10		9	8					1				5		11	7		
30		16	Doncaster Rovers	0-5		3304		2			6	4	9			10		3	8					1				5		11	7	12	
31		23	LINCOLN CITY	1-0	Pilling	3672		2	3		4	5	11			10		6	9	8				1						7			
32	Mar	4	CREWE ALEXANDRA	1-1	O'Berg	1903		2	3		4	5				10		6	9	8			12	1						7			
33		8	TRANMERE ROVERS	2-2	Pilling, Cammack	1779		2	3	6	4	7	11			10		9		8				1				5	12				
34		15	Walsall	1-1	Partridge	5078		2	3	12	4	6	11			10		9		8				1				5	7				
35		21	Stockport County	2-1	Stewart, Partridge	2215		2	3		4	6				10		9		8				1				5	11	7			
36		25	Bournemouth	3-3	Pilling 2, Stewart	2675		2	3	4		6				10		9		8				1				5	11	7			
37		29	WIGAN ATHLETIC	1-3	Cammack	2140		2	3	4	5	6				10		9		8			7	1				11		12			
38	Apr	5	PORT VALE	1-0	Pilling	1855			3	4	5	6				10		9		8				1				11	7			2	
39		7	Crewe Alexandra	1-1	Cammack	2596			2	10	4	6				9		3		8				1				5	11	7			
40		8	Halifax Town	2-2	Oates, Cammack	1660			3		4	6				10		9		8			12	1				6	11	7		2	
41		12	PETERBOROUGH UTD.	1-0	Stewart	1908			3		4	6				10		9	12	8				1				5	11	7		2	
42		15	Huddersfield Town	1-2	Partridge	10900				4	6	9				10		3	12	8				1				5	11	7		2	
43		18	Rochdale	1-0	Partridge	1018					6	4				10		3	12	8				1				5	9	11	7	2	
44		22	Aldershot	1-1	Partridge	1562		2			6	4				10		9		8				1				5	11	7			
45		25	NORTHAMPTON T	3-0	Stewart, Cammack 2	1676		2			6	4				10		9		8								5	3	11	7		1
46	May	3	Hereford United	1-1	Pilling	2099			2		6	4				10		9		8				12				5	3	11	7		1
			Apps				12	37	40	23	43	44	18	5	9	44	21	39	26	38	3	2	15	32	1	27	6	23	17	1	2	5	2
			Goals					1		1		3	3		1	13	1	9	9	12								5					

F.A. Cup

R		Date	Opponent	Score	Scorers	Att	Crawford PG	Davy SJ	Peacock JC	Kavanagh EA	Deere SH	Oates RA	O'Berg PJ	Kilmore K	Earl S	Partridge M	Keeley NB	Pilling S	Green R	Cammack SR	Gibson D	Couch GR	Cowling C	Gordon JS	Grimes V	Dall DG
R1	Nov	24	Rochdale	1-2	Pilling	1985		2	3	4	5	6				10	9	11	12	8			7	1		

F.L. Cup

R		Date	Opponent	Score	Scorers	Att	Crawford PG	Davy SJ	Peacock JC	Kavanagh EA	Deere SH	Oates RA	O'Berg PJ	Kilmore K	Earl S	Partridge M	Keeley NB	Pilling S	Green R	Cammack SR	Gibson D	Couch GR	Cowling C
R1/1	Aug	11	Grimsby Town	0-2		5083	1	2	3	4	5	6	7	8	9	10	11						12
R1/2		14	GRIMSBY TOWN	0-0		3908	1	2	3	4	5	6	7	8	9	10	11						12

		P	W	D	L	F	A	W	D	L	F	A	Pts
1	Huddersfield Town	46	16	5	2	61	18	11	7	5	40	30	66
2	Walsall	46	12	9	2	43	23	11	9	3	32	24	64
3	Newport County	46	16	5	2	47	22	11	2	10	36	28	61
4	Portsmouth	46	15	5	3	62	23	9	7	7	29	26	60
5	Bradford City	46	14	6	3	44	14	10	6	7	33	36	60
6	Wigan Athletic	46	13	5	5	42	26	8	8	7	34	35	55
7	Lincoln City	46	14	8	1	43	12	4	9	10	21	30	53
8	Peterborough Utd.	46	14	3	6	39	22	7	7	9	19	25	52
9	Torquay United	46	13	7	3	47	25	2	10	11	23	44	47
10	Aldershot	46	10	7	6	35	23	6	6	11	27	30	45
11	Bournemouth	46	8	9	6	32	25	5	9	9	20	26	44
12	Doncaster Rovers	46	11	6	6	37	27	4	8	11	25	36	44
13	Northampton Town	46	14	5	4	33	16	2	7	14	18	50	44
14	SCUNTHORPE UNITED	46	11	9	3	37	23	3	6	14	21	52	43
15	Tranmere Rovers	46	10	4	9	32	24	4	9	10	18	32	41
16	Stockport County	46	9	7	7	30	31	5	5	13	18	41	40
17	York City	46	9	6	8	35	34	5	5	13	30	48	39
18	Halifax Town	46	11	9	3	29	20	2	4	17	17	52	39
19	Hartlepool United	46	10	7	6	36	28	4	3	16	23	36	38
20	Port Vale	46	8	6	9	34	24	4	6	13	22	46	36
21	Hereford United	46	8	7	8	22	21	3	7	13	16	31	36
22	Darlington	46	7	11	5	33	26	2	6	15	17	48	35
23	Crewe Alexandra	46	10	6	7	25	27	1	7	15	10	41	35
24	Rochdale	46	6	7	10	20	28	1	6	16	13	51	27

1980/81 16th in Division 4

#		Date	Opponent	Score	Scorers	Att	Neenan JP	Davy SJ	Jarvis NC	Grimes V	Dall DG	Oates RA	Pugh JG	Cammack SR	Lambert AJ	Partridge M	O'Berg PJ	Ashworth PA	Pilling S	Boxall AR	Stewart CD	Gordon JS	Cowling C	Wood HS	Green R	Duffy VG
1	Aug	16	ALDERSHOT	2-2	Grimes, Cammack	1325	1	2	3	4	5	6	7	8	9	10	11									
2		19	Rochdale	0-4		2427	1	2	3	4	5	6	7	8	9	10	11	12								
3		23	Bradford City	0-0		3177	1	2		4		6	7	8	9	10		3	5	11						
4		30	Wimbledon	1-2	O'Berg	1624		2		4		6	7	8	9	10	12	3	5	11			1			
5	Sep	6	CREWE ALEXANDRA	1-1	Partridge	1516		2		4	5	6		8	9	10	12	3		11			1	7		
6		13	Halifax Town	0-1		1226	1	2		4	5	6		8	9	10	12	3	7	11						
7		16	Darlington	1-0	Cammack	2633	1	2		4	5	6	7	8	9		12	11	10	3						
8		19	STOCKPORT COUNTY	2-0	Cammack, O'Berg	1985	1			4	5	6	7	8	9		11		10	3						
9		27	Lincoln City	2-2	Ashworth, Thompson (og)	4209	1	2		4	5	6	7	8	9		12	11	10	3						
10		30	DARLINGTON	3-0	Cammack 2, Partridge (p)	2106	1			4	5	6	7	8	9	2	11		10	3	12					
11	Oct	4	Bournemouth	2-2	Lambert, O'Berg	3079	1			4	5	6	7	8	9	2	11		10	3	12					
12		7	HARTLEPOOL UNITED	3-3	Cammack, Ashworth 2	2900	1			4	5	6	7	8	9	2	11		10	3	12					
13		11	NORTHAMPTON T	0-2		2650	1			4	5	6	7	8	9	2	11		10	3						
14		17	Southend United	0-2		5271	1		3	4	5	6	7	8		2	11	10			9				12	
15		22	Peterborough United	2-0	Lambert, Partridge	4262	1		3	4	5	6	7	8	9	2	11								10	
16		25	TORQUAY UNITED	0-2		2254	1		3	4	5	6	7	8	9	2	11	12							10	
17		28	DONCASTER ROVERS	1-1	Cammack	4053	1		3	4	5	6	7	8	9	2	11	12							10	
18	Nov	1	York City	0-1		1959	1		3	4	5	6	7	8	9	2	11	12							10	
19		4	Hartlepool United	0-2		4357	1		3	4	5	6	7	8	9	2	11	10							12	
20		8	HEREFORD UNITED	3-1	Stewart 2, Cammack	1539	1	2	3	4		6		8	12	7	11			5	9				10	
21		11	ROCHDALE	1-1	Stewart	2019	1	2	3	4		6		8		7	11			5	9				10	
22		15	Aldershot	0-0		2512	1	2	3	4		6		8		7	11			5	9				10	
23	Dec	6	Wigan Athletic	1-1	Partridge (p)	3672	1	2	3	4		6	12	8		7	11			5	9				10	
24		20	TRANMERE ROVERS	2-0	Lambert, Stewart	1664	1	2	3	4		6	10	8	7	9				5	12				11	
25		26	Mansfield Town	0-1		4261	1	2	3	4		6	10	8	7	9		12		5	11					
26		27	BURY	2-2	Boxall, Cammack	2960	1	2	3	4		6	10	8	7	9	12			5	11					
27	Jan	10	PETERBOROUGH UTD.	1-1	Green	2064	1	2	3	4		6	10	8		7				5	11				9	
28		19	Wimbledon	2-2	Green, O'Berg	2112	1	2	3	4	5	6	10	8		12	7				11				9	
29		31	BRADFORD CITY	1-0	Cammack	2558	1	2	3			6	10	8		4	7			5	11				9	
30	Feb	4	Torquay United	1-2	Green	1760	1	2	3	4	5	6	10	8		11	7				12				9	
31		7	HALIFAX TOWN	2-2	Stewart, Grimes	2073	1	2	3	4		6	10	8			7			5	11				9	
32		14	Crewe Alexandra	0-1		2231	1	2		4		6	10	8			7	3	5		11				9	
33		21	LINCOLN CITY	2-2	O'Berg, Pilling	4848	1			4		6	10	8		2	7	12	3	5	11				9	
34		24	PORT VALE	1-1	Cammack (p)	1946	1			4		6	10	8		2	7		3	5	11				9	12
35		27	Stockport County	0-2		1675	1	2		4		6	10	8		9	7	12	3	5	11					
36	Mar	3	Port Vale	2-2	Partridge (p), Cammack	2277	1	2		4		6	10	8		9	7	12	3	5	11					
37		6	BOURNEMOUTH	1-1	Partridge (p)	2392	1	2		4		6		8		9	7	10	3	5	11				12	
38		13	Northampton Town	3-3	Grimes, O'Berg, Green	2046	1	2		4		6		8			10	7	3	5	11				9	
39		22	SOUTHEND UNITED	2-1	Pilling, Green	3605	1	2		4		6		8			9	7	3	5	11				10	
40		27	Doncaster Rovers	0-1		8001	1	2		4		6		8			9	7	3	5	11				10	
41	Apr	4	YORK CITY	3-2	Green 2, Stewart	1694	1	2		4				8		6	9	7	3	5	11				10	
42		11	Hereford United	1-2	Price (og)	2009	1	2		4	6			9	8			7	3	5	11				10	
43		18	Bury	1-6	Stewart	2357	1	2		4	6			9	8			7	12	3	5	11			10	
44		20	MANSFIELD TOWN	2-0	O'Berg, Cammack	1850	1	2	3	4				10	8	12	5	7	6	11					9	
45		24	Tranmere Rovers	2-1	Pilling, Stewart	1063	1	2		4				10	8		5	7	6	3	11				9	
46	May	2	WIGAN ATHLETIC	4-4	O'Berg 2, Cammack 2	1704	1	2		4				8	10	5	7	6	3		11	9				
			Apps				44	31	21	45	22	40	38	46	24	40	43	23	26	24	34	2	2	1	27	1
			Goals							3				15	3	6	9	3	3	1	8				7	

Two own goals

F.A. Cup

		Date	Opponent	Score	Scorers	Att	Neenan	Davy	Jarvis	Grimes	Oates	Cammack	Partridge	O'Berg	Boxall	Stewart	Green
R1	Nov	22	HARTLEPOOL UNITED	3-1	Grimes, Green, Partridge (p)	5165	1	2	3	4	6	8	7	11	5	9	10
R2	Dec	13	ALTRINCHAM	0-0		3672	1	2	3	4	6	8	7	11	5	9	10
rep		15	Altrincham	0-1		5176	1	2	3	4	6	8	7	11	5	9	10

F.L. Cup

		Date	Opponent	Score	Scorers	Att	Neenan	Davy	Jarvis	Grimes	Dall	Oates	Pugh	Cammack	Lambert	Partridge	O'Berg	Boxall
R1/1	Aug	9	BARNSLEY	0-1		4550	1	2	3	4	5	6	7	8	9	10	12	11
R1/2		12	Barnsley	1-2	Cammack	8430	1	2	3	4	5	6	7	8	9	10	12	11

		Pl.		Home						Away					F.	A.	Pts
			W	D	L	F	A	W	D	L	F	A					
1	Southend United	46	19	4	0	47	6	11	3	9	32	25			79	31	67
2	Lincoln City	46	15	7	1	44	11	10	8	5	22	14			66	25	65
3	Doncaster Rovers	46	15	4	4	36	20	7	8	8	23	29			59	49	56
4	Wimbledon	46	15	4	4	42	17	8	5	10	22	29			64	46	55
5	Peterborough U.	46	11	8	4	37	21	6	10	7	31	33			68	54	52
6	Aldershot	46	12	9	2	28	11	6	5	12	15	30			43	41	50
7	Mansfield Town	46	13	5	5	36	15	7	4	12	22	29			58	44	49
8	Darlington	46	13	6	4	43	23	6	5	12	22	36			65	59	49
9	Hartlepool United	46	14	3	6	42	22	6	6	11	22	39			64	61	49
10	Northampton T.	46	11	7	5	42	26	7	6	10	23	41			65	67	49
11	Wigan Athletic	46	13	4	6	29	16	5	7	11	22	39			51	55	47
12	Bury	46	10	8	5	38	21	7	3	13	32	41			70	62	45
13	Bournemouth	46	9	8	6	30	21	7	5	11	17	27			47	48	45
14	Bradford City	46	9	9	5	30	24	5	7	11	23	36			53	60	44
15	Rochdale	46	11	6	6	33	25	3	9	11	27	45			60	70	43
16	SCUNTHORPE U.	46	8	12	3	40	31	3	8	12	20	38			60	69	42
17	Torquay United	46	13	2	8	38	26	5	3	15	17	37			55	63	41
18	Crewe Alexandra	46	10	7	6	28	20	3	7	13	20	41			48	61	40
19	Port Vale	46	10	8	5	40	23	2	7	14	17	47			57	70	39
20	Stockport County	46	10	5	8	29	25	4	6	13	15	32			44	57	39
21	Tranmere Rovers	46	12	5	6	41	24	1	5	17	18	49			59	73	36
22	Hereford United	46	8	6	9	27	29	3	5	15	9	42			38	62	35
23	Halifax Town	46	9	3	11	28	32	2	9	12	16	39			44	71	34
24	York City	46	10	2	11	31	23	2	7	14	16	43			47	66	33

1981/82 23rd in Division 4

#	Date		Opponent	Score	Scorers	Att.	Neenan IP	Davy SJ	Partridge M	Keeley AJ	Dall DG	Oates RA	Grimes V	Hughes DT	Green R	O'Berg PJ	Stewart CD	Pilling S	Duffy VG	Lambert AJ	Cowling C	Moss PM	DeVries RS	Arins AF	Telfer GA	Pointon NG	Johnson P	Duncan JP	Botham IT	Boyd G	Thompson WA	Hamill SP	Goodlass R	Cammack SR
1	Au	29	Northampton Town	1-1	Green	2064	1	2	3	4	5	6	7	8	9	10	11	12																
2	Se	5	BLACKPOOL	1-1	Oates	2200	1	2	12	4	5	6	7	8	9		11	3	10															
3		12	Torquay United	0-1		2033	1	2	8	4	5	6	7		9		11		10	3	12													
4		19	TRANMERE ROVERS	2-1	Cowling, Moss	1592	1	2		4	5	6	7	3	9		11				8	10												
5		22	HARTLEPOOL UNITED	2-1	Oates, Moss	1992	1	2		4	5	6	7	3	9	12	11				8	10												
6		26	Sheffield United	0-1		11687	1	2		4	5	6	7	3	9		11			12	8	10												
7		29	Bury	0-4		2684	1	2	12	4	5	6	7	3	9		11				8	10												
8	Oct	3	BRADFORD CITY	1-3	Grimes	3229	1	2	12	4	5	6	7	3s	9		11				8	10												
9		10	Crewe Alexandra	0-3		1586	1	8	2	4	5	6	7		9		11				12	10	3											
10		17	HEREFORD UNITED	2-2	Grimes, Moss	1499	1		2	4		6	7		9	8	11				5	10	3											
11		20	HULL CITY	4-4	Stewart, Partridge 2(2p), Green	3575	1	12	2	4		6	7		9	8	11				5	10	3											
12		24	Wigan Athletic	1-2	DeVries	4553	1	2	8	4		6	7		9		11			12		10	3											
13		31	PETERBOROUGH UTD	0-1		2004	1		8	4		6	7	2	9		11				5	12												
14	No	3	Bournemouth	0-2		5032	1		8	4		6	7	2	9		11	10	12		5		3											
15		7	YORK CITY	0-3		1622	1	3	8	4		6	7	5			11				2	10												
16		13	Colchester United	1-2	Stewart	3838	1		6	4		5	7		9	8	11	3		12	2	10												
17		28	Halifax Town	2-1	Cowling, Moss	1396	1	2		4		6	7			8	11	3			9	10	5											
18	De	5	PORT VALE	0-0		1902	1	2		4		6				8	11	3		7	9	10	5	12										
19	Jan	9	Blackpool	0-2		4136	1	2		4							11	3	8		9	10			7									
20		23	NORTHAMPTON T	2-1	Stewart, Telfer	1439	1			4	5	6	8	2			11	3			9	10			7									
21		30	Tranmere Rovers	1-0	Green	1520	1	12		4	5	6		2	9		11	3		8		10			7									
22	Fe	2	Mansfield Town	1-0	Dall	2099	1			4	5	6		2	9		11	3				10			7									
23		6	TORQUAY UNITED	0-2		1802	1			4	5	6		12	9		11					10		2	8	3								
24		10	Hartlepool United	3-3	Telfer, Stewart, Moss (p)	2001	1			4	5	6	9		12		11	3				10		2	8									
25		14	Bradford City	0-0		5103	1	2		4	5	6	9				11	3				10			8		1							
26		17	Darlington	1-4	Stewart	1663	1	2		4		6	9	12			11	3			5	10		7	8		1							
27		20	SHEFFIELD UNITED	2-1	Moss, Telfer	8105	1	2			5	6	9	7			11	3				10		7	8									
28		28	CREWE ALEXANDRA	0-1		2591	1	2		4	5	6	9				11	3				10		7	8				12					
29	Ma	6	Hereford United	1-2	Dall	2159	1			4	5	6	9				11	3		2		10		7	8									
30		9	Hull City	0-2		6121	1			4	5	6					11	3	12	9		10		7	8									
31		12	WIGAN ATHLETIC	2-7	Telfer 2	2511	1	12		4	5	6						3		2		10		7	8	11		9						
32		16	BOURNEMOUTH	0-2		1441	1	3		4	5	6					11			2		10		7	8			9						
33		20	Peterborough United	1-2	Stewart	4785	1	2		4	5	6	11				12					10		7	8			9						
34		23	ALDERSHOT	1-1	Telfer	1658	1	2		4	5		3				11					10		7	8			9	4					
35		26	York City	1-3	Arins	2189	1			3	5	9										10		2	8					4	6	7	11	
36		30	STOCKPORT COUNTY	0-0		1815	1			3		6										10		2	8					4	5	7	11	9
37	Apr	2	COLCHESTER UNITED	2-1	Moss, Telfer	1762	1			3		6	2									10		7	8					4	5		11	9
38		10	Rochdale	1-0	Keeley (p)	1742	1			3	5		2				7				12	10			8					4	6		11	9
39		13	Mansfield Town	1-1	Cowling	2202	1			3	5		2				7				9	10		4	8					6		11	12
40		17	Port Vale	1-2	Cammack	2507	1				5		2				3					10		4	8				12	6	7	11	9
41		20	Rochdale	1-1	Telfer	1129	1			6			2				3					10		4	8					5	7	11	9
42		24	HALIFAX TOWN	0-0		1643	1			6			2				3					10		4	8				12	4	5	11	9
43	Ma	1	Aldershot	0-4		1304	1	2		6			7				9					10		8					12	4	5	11	
44		4	BURY	2-2	Telfer, Cammack	1106	1	2		6			7			12	11				5	10		8	3					4			9
45		8	DARLINGTON	1-1	Cammack	1274	1	2		6			7			12	11				2	10		8	3					4	5		9
46		14	Stockport County	1-1	Cowling	1945	1	2		6			7				12				5	10	11	8	3					4	6		9
						Apps	44	28	13	42	28	37	34	20	18	10	40	18	7	15	26	42	6	20	29	5	2	3	4	11	11	4	9	10
						Goals			2	1	2	2	2		3		6				4	7	1	1	9									3

F.A. Cup

	Date		Opponent	Score	Scorers	Att.	Neenan	Davy	Partridge	Keeley	Dall	Oates	Grimes	Hughes	Green	O'Berg	Stewart	Pilling	Duffy	Lambert	Cowling	Moss	Telfer
R1	No	21	BRADFORD CITY	1-0	Cowling	3339	1	2		4	5	6	7			8	11	3		12	9	10	
R2	Jan	2	Crewe Alexandra	3-1	Cowling, Telfer, Dall	2729	1	2		4	5	6				8	11	3		12	9	10	7
R3		6	HEREFORD UNITED	1-1	Stewart	3781	1	2		4	5	6				8	11	3			9	10	7
rep		20	Hereford United	1-4	Grimes	4025	1			4	5	6	3	2		8	11	12			9	10	7

Milk Cup (F.L. Cup)

	Date		Opponent	Score	Att.	Neenan	Davy	Partridge	Keeley	Dall	Oates	Grimes	Hughes	Green	Stewart	Pilling	Duffy	Cowling
R1/1	Se	1	MANSFIELD TOWN	0-0	2249	1	2	12	4	5	6	7	8	9	11	3		10
R1/2		14	Mansfield Town	0-2	2258	1	2	12	4	5	6	7		9	11	3	10	8

League Table

		Pl.	Home W	D	L	F	A	Away W	D	L	F	A	F.	A.	Pts
1	Sheffield United	46	15	8	0	53	15	12	7	4	41	26	94	41	96
2	Bradford City	46	14	7	2	52	23	12	6	5	36	22	88	45	91
3	Wigan Athletic	46	17	5	1	47	18	9	8	6	33	28	80	46	91
4	Bournemouth	46	12	10	1	37	15	11	9	3	25	15	62	30	88
5	Peterborough U.	46	16	3	4	46	22	8	7	8	25	35	71	57	82
6	Colchester United	46	12	6	5	47	23	8	6	5	34	34	82	57	72
7	Port Vale	46	9	12	2	26	17	9	9	4	10	30	56	49	70
8	Hull City	46	14	3	6	36	23	5	9	9	34	38	70	61	69
9	Bury	46	13	7	3	53	26	4	10	9	27	33	80	59	68
10	Hereford United	46	10	9	4	36	25	6	10	7	28	33	64	58	67
11	Tranmere Rovers	46	7	9	7	27	25	7	9	7	24	31	51	56	60
12	Blackpool	46	11	5	7	40	26	4	11	8	26	34	66	60	58
13	Darlington	46	10	5	8	36	28	5	8	10	25	34	61	62	58
14	Hartlepool United	46	8	9	6	39	34	4	8	11	34	50	73	84	55
15	Torquay United	46	9	8	6	30	25	5	13	5	17	34	47	59	55
16	Aldershot	46	9	8	6	34	29	5	8	10	23	39	57	68	54
17	York City	46	9	5	9	45	37	5	9	15	24	54	69	91	50
18	Stockport County	46	10	5	8	34	28	4	13	14	39	48	67	49	49
19	Halifax Town	46	6	11	6	28	30	3	11	9	23	42	51	72	49
20	Mansfield Town	46	6	9	8	39	39	5	4	14	24	42	63	81	47
21	Rochdale	46	7	9	7	26	22	3	7	13	24	40	50	62	46
22	Northampton T.	46	9	9	5	32	27	2	4	15	17	57	49	84	42
23	SCUNTHORPE U.	46	7	9	7	26	35	2	4	15	17	44	43	79	42
24	Crewe Alexandra	46	3	6	14	19	32	3	3	17	10	52	29	84	27

SEASON 1980-81
Back: Burnside, Davy, Ashworth, Cowling, Lambert, Gaffney, Kearsley, Hindson
Middle: Strong(Masseur), Cammack, Green, Dall, Gordon, Neenan, Johnson, Boxall, Partridge, Jackson(Youth Team Coach)
Front: Ashman (Manager), O'Berg, Jarvis, Pilling, Grimes, Oates, Pugh, Stewart, Kaye (Coach)

SEASON 1981-82
Back: Stewart, Duffy, Pilling, Davy, Hughes, Keeley
2nd row: Lambert, Cowling, Neenan, Dall, Johnson, Partridge, Green
3rd row: Strong (Physio), Oates, Grimes, Duncan (Play/Man), O'Berg, McLoughlin (Youth Coach), Ashman (Gen.Man)
Front: Pointon, Hindson, Wooffindin, Brown

1982/83 4th in Division 4: Promoted

Player columns (left → right): Neenan JP, Keeley AJ, Pointon NG, Fowler M, Boxall AR, Hunter L, Cammack SR, Parkinson ND, Cowling C, Telfer GA, Leman D, O'Berg PI, Oates RA, Duncan JP, Baines SJ, Gilbert DJ, Angus MA, Cartwright P, Mann IA, Reid AJ, Graham T, Lester MJ, Webster IA, Snow SG, Johnson P, Tutty D

#	Date	Opponent	Score	Scorers	Att	Nee	Kee	Poi	Fow	Box	Hun	Cam	Par	Cow	Tel	Lem	OB	Oat	Dun	Bai	Gil	Ang	Car	Man	Rei	Gra	Les	Web	Sno	Joh	Tut
1	Aug 28	Hartlepool United	0-0		1009	1	2	3	4	5	6	7	8	9	10	11	12														
2	Sep 4	ALDERSHOT	1-1	Hunter	1309	1	2	11	4	5	6	7	8	9	10		12	3													
3	7	STOCKPORT COUNTY	3-0	Telfer 2, Cowling	1335	1		3	4	5	6		8	9	10	11	7	2	12												
4	11	Wimbledon	2-2	O'Berg 2	1611	1	2	3	4	5	6		8		10	11	7			9	12										
5	19	YORK CITY	0-0		2436	1	2	3	4	5	6		8		10	11	9			12		7									
6	25	Bristol City	2-0	O'Berg, Parkinson	3890	1	2	3	4	5	6	12		10	11		9			8		7									
7	28	Darlington	1-0	Hunter	1574	1	2	3	4	5	6	7	10	9		11				12		8									
8	Oct 2	COLCHESTER UNITED	2-1	O'Berg, Angus	2616	1	2	3	4	5	6	8		9		11	7					10									
9	9	Peterborough United	1-0	Angus	3075	1	2	3	4		6	8		9		11	7			5		10									
10	15	HULL CITY	0-1		7483	1	2	3		12	6	8	4	9		11	7			5		10									
11	18	Mansfield Town	2-0	Hunter, Cowling	2647	1	2	3			6		4	9		11	7			8	5	10									
12	23	TRANMERE ROVERS	2-1	Baines, Cowling	3052	1	2	3			6	8	4	9		11	7			5		10									
13	30	Torquay United	1-1	Cammack	3005	1	2	3	12		6	8	4	9		11	7			5		10									
14	Nov 2	PORT VALE	1-0	Cammack	3766	1	2	3			6	8	4	9		11	7			5		10									
15	6	NORTHAMPTON T	5-1	O'Berg 2, Cammack 3	3412	1	2	3			6	8	4	9		11	7			5		10									
16	12	Crewe Alexandra	1-0	O'Berg	2195	1	2	3			6	8	4	9		11	7			5		10									
17	27	BURY	0-1		6335	1	2	3	12		6	8	4	9		11	7			5		10									
18	Dec 4	Hereford United	2-0	Cammack, Cartwright	2103	1	2	3			6	8		9		11	7			5		10	4								
19	18	Blackpool	1-3	Cammack	2860	1	2	3			6	8		9		11	7	12		5		10	4								
20	27	ROCHDALE	1-1	Cammack	4845	1	2	3	4		6	8	11	9			7			5		10	12								
21	28	Halifax Town	1-3	Parkinson (p)	2270	1		3	4		6	8	11	9		7	10			5		2									
22	Jan 1	CHESTER	2-0	Cammack 2	3639	1		3	4		6	8	11	9		7	2			5		10	12								
23	3	Swindon Town	2-2	Parkinson, Cammack	6728	1		3	4		6	8	11	9		7	2			5		10									
24	16	HARTLEPOOL UNITED	3-0	Hunter, Cowling, Parkinson	4261	1		3	4	5	6	8	11	9	12	7	2					10									
25	23	York City	1-2	Cowling	7097	1		3		12	6	9	11	8		10		2		5		4		7							
26	29	WIMBLEDON	0-0		3846	1		3		5	6	8	10	9		11	7	2		4											
27	Feb 5	BRISTOL CITY	1-1	Parkinson	3624	1		3		4	6	8	10			11	7	2		5				9							
28	12	Stockport County	1-1	Cammack	2328	1		3	4	12	6	8	10			11	7	2		5											
29	26	Hull City	1-1	Leman	14252	1	2	3			6	8	10	9		11	7			5					4						
30	Mar 1	MANSFIELD TOWN	2-2	Cammack 2	3562	1	2	3		12	6	8	10	9		11		7		5					4						
31	5	Tranmere Rovers	4-0	Leman, Cammack 2, Parkinson	1652	1	2	3			6	8	10	9		11	7			5					4						
32	12	TORQUAY UNITED	2-0	Hunter 2	3342	1	2	3			6	8	10	9		11	7			5					4	12					
33	15	Aldershot	1-1	O'Berg	1422	1	2	3			6	8	10	9		11	7			5					4						
34	20	Northampton Town	1-2	Cowling	2634	1	2	3			6	8	10	9		11	7	12		5					4						
35	26	CREWE ALEXANDRA	2-0	Hunter 2	2938	1	2	3			6	8	10	9		11				5						7	4				
36	Apr 1	HALIFAX TOWN	2-0	Lester, Cammack	3775	1	2	3	4		6	8		9		11		12		5						7	10				
37	4	Rochdale	1-0	Graham	2056	1	2	3	4		6	8		9		11				5						7	10				
38	8	HEREFORD UNITED	1-2	Cammack (p)	3785	1	2	3	4		6	8		9		11				5						7	10				
39	15	Colchester United	1-5	Cammack	3155	1	2	3	4		6	8		9		11				5						7	10				
40	23	BLACKPOOL	4-3	Cowling 2, Cammack 2 (1p)	2791	1	2	3	4		6	8		9		11		12		5						7	10				
41	26	PETERBOROUGH UTD.	3-0	Lester, Cammack, Pointon	3211	1	2	3	4		6	8		9		11				5						7	10				
42	30	Bury	0-1		4739	1	12	3	4		6	8		9		11		2		5						7	10				
43	May 2	SWINDON TOWN	2-0	Cammack, Lester	3546	1		3	4		6	8		9			11	2		5						7	10				
44	7	DARLINGTON	2-2	Cammack 2	3305	1		3	4		6	8		9			11	2		5						7	10				
45	9	Port Vale	1-0	Cowling	6212	1	12	3	4		6	8		9			11	2		5						7	10				
46	14	Chester	2-1	Graham 2	2560	1	11	3										2		5						7				10	12
Apps						46	35	46	18	26	46	41	31	42	7	36	34	20	6	38	1	20	4	2	6	13	11	1	1	0	0
Goals							1				8	25	6	9	2	2	8			1		2	1			3	3				

F.A. Cup

Rd	Date	Opponent	Score	Scorers	Att	Nee	Kee	Poi	Fow	Box	Hun	Cam	Par	Cow	Tel	Lem	OB	Oat	Dun	Bai	Ang
R1	Nov 20	Darlington	1-0	Cammack	2540	1	2	3	12		6	8	4	9		11	7			5	10
R2	Dec 11	NORTHWICH VICTORIA	2-1	Cowling, O'Berg	5457	1	2	3	4		6	8		9		11	7			5	10
R3	Jan 8	GRIMSBY TOWN	0-0		11010	1		3	4		6	8	11	9		7	2			5	10
rep	11	Grimsby Town	0-2		9509	1		3	4		6	8	11	9	12	7	2			5	10

Milk Cup (F.L. Cup)

Rd	Date	Opponent	Score	Scorers	Att	Nee	Kee	Poi	Fow	Box	Hun	Cam	Par	Cow	Tel	Lem	OB	Oat	Dun
R1/1	Aug 31	GRIMSBY TOWN	1-2	Cowling	2620	1	2		4	5	6	7	8	9	10	11	12	3	
R1/2	Sep 14	Grimsby Town	0-0		3347	1	2	3	4	5	6		8		10	11	9		12

F.L. Trophy

Gp	Date	Opponent	Score	Scorers	Att	Nee	Kee	Poi	Fow	Box	Hun	Cam	Par	Cow	Tel	Lem	OB	Oat	Dun	Bai	Others
Gp	Aug 14	LINCOLN CITY	1-1	Hunter	1022	1	2	3	4	5	6	7	8	12	10	11	9				13
Gp	17	SHEFFIELD UNITED	0-0		1874		2	3	4	5	6		8	9	10	11	7	12		14	1
Gp	21	Grimsby Town	0-2		2334	1	12	3	4	5	6		8	9		11	7	10		14	2

Division 4 Final Table

		Pl	Home W	D	L	F	A	Away W	D	L	F	A	F	A	Pts
1	Wimbledon	46	17	4	2	57	23	12	7	4	39	22	96	45	98
2	Hull City	46	14	8	1	48	14	11	7	5	27	20	75	34	90
3	Port Vale	46	15	4	4	37	16	11	6	6	30	18	67	34	88
4	SCUNTHORPE U.	46	13	7	3	41	17	10	7	6	30	25	71	42	83
5	Bury	46	15	4	4	43	20	8	8	7	31	26	74	46	81
6	Colchester United	46	17	5	1	51	19	7	4	12	24	36	75	55	81
7	York City	46	18	4	1	59	19	4	9	10	29	39	88	58	79
8	Swindon Town	46	14	3	6	45	27	5	8	10	16	27	61	54	68
9	Peterborough U.	46	13	6	4	38	23	4	7	12	20	29	58	52	64
10	Mansfield Town	46	11	6	6	32	26	5	7	11	29	44	61	70	61
11	Halifax Town	46	9	8	6	31	23	7	4	12	28	43	59	66	60
12	Torquay United	46	12	3	8	38	30	5	4	14	18	35	56	65	58
13	Chester	46	8	6	9	28	24	7	5	11	27	36	55	60	56
14	Bristol City	46	10	8	5	32	25	3	9	11	27	45	59	70	56
15	Northampton T.	46	10	8	5	43	29	4	4	15	22	46	65	75	54
16	Stockport County	46	11	8	4	41	31	3	4	16	19	48	60	79	54
17	Darlington	46	8	5	10	27	30	5	8	10	34	41	61	71	52
18	Aldershot	46	11	5	7	40	35	1	10	12	21	47	61	82	51
19	Tranmere Rovers	46	8	8	7	30	29	5	3	15	19	42	49	71	50
20	Rochdale	46	11	8	4	38	25	0	8	15	17	48	55	73	49
21	Blackpool	46	10	8	5	32	23	3	4	16	23	51	55	74	49
22	Hartlepool United	46	11	5	7	30	24	2	4	17	16	52	46	76	48
23	Crewe Alexandra	46	9	5	9	35	32	2	3	18	18	39	53	71	41
24	Hereford United	46	8	6	9	19	23	3	2	18	23	56	42	79	41

SEASON 1982-83
Back: Boxall, Fowler, Johnson, Neenan, Hunter, Cowling
Middle: Keeley, Snow, Pointon, Telfer, Grimes, Cammack
Front: Leman, Baines (Player Coach), Duncan (Player Manager), McLoughlin (Y.T. Coach), Parkinson, O'Berg

SEASON 1983-84
Back: Snow, Green, Cowling, Hunter, Boxall, Webster, Pointon, Cammack
Middle: Leman, Pointon, Graham, Neenan, Johnson, Parkinson, O'Berg
Front: Shaw, Barlow (Coach), Broddle, Clarke (Manager), Lester, Dey, McLoughlin (Physio), Hill

1983/84 23rd in Division 3: Relegated

#	Date	Opponent	Score	Scorers	Att	Neenan JP	Longden DP	Pointon NG	Brolly MJ	Boxall AR	Hunter L	Graham T	Cammack SR	Cowling C	Dey G	Broddle JR	Webster IA	Green JR	Lester MJ	Holden R	O'Berg PJ	Richardson R	Snow SG	Hill DM	Wilson DJ	Leman D	Botham IT	Matthews M	Whitehead A	Bell DM	Pratley RG	Parkinson ND	Steele SP
1	Aug 27	Port Vale	0-0		4565	1	2	3	4	5	6	7	8	9	10	11	12																
2	Sep 3	EXETER CITY	3-1	Lester, Cammack, Graham	2768	1	2	3	4		6	7	8	9		11		5	10														
3	7	OXFORD UNITED	0-0		3516	1	2	3	4		6	7	8	9		11		5	10														
4	9	Orient	0-1		2702	1	2	3	4		6	7	8	9		11	12	5	10														
5	16	BOLTON WANDERERS	1-0	Cowling	4406	1	2	3	4	7	6		8	9		11		5	10	12													
6	24	Newport County	1-1	Green	2679	1	2	3	4	7	6			9		11		5	10	8	12												
7	27	Plymouth Argyle	0-4		3821	1	2	3	4	7	6			9		11		5	10	8	12												
8	30	SOUTHEND UNITED	1-6	Holden (p)	3335	1	2	3	4		6							5	10	8	7	2		9	11								
9	Oct 8	Bradford City	2-2	Leman, Lester	2476	1	2	3	7		6			9				5	10	8	12				4	11							
10	15	ROTHERHAM UNITED	1-2	Lester	3139	1	2	3	7		6	12		9				5	10	8					4	11							
11	18	WIGAN ATHLETIC	0-0		2345	1	2	3	7		6			9				5	10	8	11				4								
12	22	Bristol Rovers	1-4	Pointon	5324	1	2	3	7		6			9				5	10	8	11				4								
13	29	WIMBLEDON	5-1	Peters(og),Wilson 2(1p),Cammack 2	2347	1	2	3	7				8	6				5	10		11				4								
14	Nov 1	Sheffield United	3-5	Dey, Broddle, Wilson	10502	1	2	3			6	7	8	9	10	11		5							4								
15	5	WALSALL	0-0		2932	1	2	3	7		6		8	9				5	10		11				4								
16	12	Lincoln City	1-2	O'Berg	4657	1	2	3	7		6		8	9				5	10		11				4								
17	26	Millwall	1-2	Cammack	3776	1	2	3	7		6		8	9				5	10		11				4								
18	Dec 3	BOURNEMOUTH	1-2	Cammack	2344	1	2	3	7		6		8	9				5	10		11				4		12						
19	17	GILLINGHAM	2-0	Cammack (p), Cowling	2127	1	2	3	4		6		8	7				5	10		11							9					
20	26	Hull City	0-1		18461	1	2	3	4				8	7				5	10		11							9	6				
21	27	PRESTON NORTH END	1-5	Cammack	3986	1	2	3	12			4	8	7				5	10		11							9	6				
22	31	Burnley	0-5		7632	1	2	3	7		6	9	8					5	10		11							4					
23	Jan 2	BRENTFORD	4-4	Graham, Cammack 2, O'Berg	2239	1		3	7		6	9	8					5	10		11	2						4					
24	21	Bolton Wanderers	0-0		5379	1	2	3	7			9	8					5	10		11							4	6				
25	Feb 3	Southend United	0-0		1976	1	2	3	7			9	8	10	12	6		5										4	11				
26	10	NEWPORT COUNTY	3-3	Brolly 2, Cammack	2879	1	2	3	7				8			11	6	5	10									4	9				
27	18	Wimbledon	1-1	Cammack (p)	3117	1	2	3	7				8		11		6	5	10									4	9				
28	25	BRISTOL ROVERS	2-2	Cammack (p), O'Berg	2737	1	2	3	7				8				6	5	10		11							4	9				
29	Mar 3	Wigan Athletic	0-2		3092	1	2	3	7			11	8					5	10									4	9			6	
30	6	Walsall	1-1	Bell	4735	1	2	3	7			11	8					5	10									4	9	6			
31	10	LINCOLN CITY	0-0		3889	1	2	3	7			11	8					5	10									4	9	6			
32	17	BRADFORD CITY	2-1	Cammack, Matthews	3274	1	2	3	7			11	8					5	10									4	9	6			
33	27	SHEFFIELD UNITED	1-1	Bell	6750	1	2	3	7				8					5										4	10	9	6	11	
34	31	Oxford United	0-1		6747	1	2	3	7			12	8					5										4	10	9	6	11	
35	Apr 7	PLYMOUTH ARGYLE	3-0	Bell. Brolly, Cammack	2780	1	2	3	7			11	8					5										4	10	9	6		
36	11	Exeter City	1-1	Brolly	2003	1	2	3	7			11	8					5										4	10	9	6		
37	14	Bournemouth	1-1	Cammack	3501	1	2	3	7			11	8			3	2	5	4										10	9	6	12	
38	17	PORT VALE	1-1	Bell	2952	1	2	3	7			11	8					5	4										10	9	6		
39	21	HULL CITY	2-0	Bell (p), Cammack	8286	1	2	3	7			11	8					5										4	10	9		6	
40	24	Preston North End	0-1		3403	1	2	3	7			11	8					5										4	10	9		6	
41	27	MILLWALL	0-1		2867	1	2	3	7			11	8					5										4	10	9		6	
42	Ma 1	ORIENT	3-1	Graham 2, Parkinson	2284		2	3				11	8					5		7								4	10	9		6	1
43	5	Brentford	0-3		4561		2	3				11	8	12				5		7								4	10	9		6	1
44	7	BURNLEY	4-0	Cammack 2(1p),Cowling,Green	2620		2	3				11	8	9				5		7								4	10			6	1
45	12	Gillingham	1-1	Cowling	3513		2	3				8	9					5	11	7								4	10			6	1
46	15	Rotherham United	0-3		4298		2	3	6			11	8	9	12			5		7								4	10				1

| | | | | Apps | | 41 | 43 | 45 | 41 | 4 | 15 | 27 | 39 | 22 | 12 | 13 | 9 | 45 | 33 | 7 | 25 | 2 | 1 | 2 | 6 | 2 | 3 | 25 | 15 | 19 | 10 | 10 | 5 |
| | | | | Goals | | | 1 | 4 | | | 4 | 18 | 4 | 1 | 1 | | | 2 | 3 | 1 | 3 | | | | 3 | 1 | | 1 | | 5 | | 1 | |

One own goal

F.A. Cup

#	Date	Opponent	Score	Scorers	Att	Neenan JP	Longden DP	Pointon NG	Brolly MJ	Boxall AR	Hunter L	Graham T	Cammack SR	Cowling C	Dey G	Broddle JR	Webster IA	Green JR	Lester MJ	Holden R	O'Berg PJ	Richardson R	Snow SG	Hill DM	Wilson DJ	Leman D	Botham IT	Matthews M	Whitehead A	Bell DM	Pratley RG	Parkinson ND	Steele SP
R1	Nov 19	PRESTON NORTH END	1-0	Cammack (p)	3484	1	2	3	7			12	8	6	4	9		5	10		11												
R2	Dec 10	BURY	2-0	Pashley(og), Cammack	3246	1	2	3	4				8	7	6			5	10		11								9				
R3	Jan 7	Leeds United	1-1	Cammack	17130	1		3	7			9	8	4			6	5	10		11	2											
rep	10	LEEDS UNITED	1-1	Dey	13129	1	2	3	7			9	8	4			6	5	10		11												
rep2	16	LEEDS UNITED	4-2	Brolly, Cammack, Lester, Graha	13312	1	2	3	7			9	8	4			6	5	10		11												
R4	Feb 1	West Bromwich Albion	0-1		18235	1	2	3	7			9	8	10			6	5			11							4					

R3 replay a.e.t.

Milk Cup (F.L. Cup)

#	Date	Opponent	Score	Scorers	Att	Neenan JP	Longden DP	Pointon NG	Brolly MJ	Boxall AR	Hunter L	Graham T	Cammack SR	Cowling C	Dey G	Broddle JR	Webster IA	Green JR	Lester MJ
1/1	Aug 30	DONCASTER ROVERS	1-1	Cammack	4295	1	2	3	4	5	6	7	8	9		11			10
1/2	Sep 13	Doncaster Rovers	0-3		4377	1	2	3	4		6	7	8	9	11	5			10	12

Associate Members Cup

#	Date	Opponent	Score	Scorers	Att	Neenan JP	Longden DP	Pointon NG	Brolly MJ	Cammack SR	Green JR	Lester MJ	O'Berg PJ	Richardson R	Matthews M	Whitehead A	Bell DM	Parkinson ND	Steele SP
R1	Feb 21	CHESTERFIELD	2-1	Cammack, Brolly	2507	1	2	3	7	8	5	10	11	6	4	9			
R2	Mar 13	CREWE ALEXANDRA	4-4	Bell 3 (1 pen), Matthews	1524	1	2	3	7	8	5		11	10	4	9		6	12
R3	20	SHEFFIELD UNITED	2-3	Matthews, Cammack	2720	1	2		7	8	5	10	11	3	4	9	6		

R2 won on penalties, a.e.t. R3 a.e.t.

262

FINAL LEAGUE TABLES: 1983/84 - 1990/91

Final League Table 1983/84 Division 3

		Pl.	Home					Away					F.	A.	Pts
			W	D	L	F	A	W	D	L	F	A			
1	Oxford United	46	17	5	1	58	22	11	6	6	33	28	91	50	95
2	Wimbledon	46	15	5	3	58	35	11	4	8	39	41	97	76	87
3	Sheffield United	46	14	7	2	56	18	10	4	9	30	35	86	53	83
4	Hull City	46	16	5	2	42	11	7	9	7	29	27	71	38	83
5	Bristol Rovers	46	16	5	2	47	21	6	8	9	21	33	68	54	79
6	Walsall	46	14	4	5	44	22	8	5	10	24	39	68	61	75
7	Bradford City	46	11	9	3	46	30	9	2	12	27	35	73	65	71
8	Gillingham	46	13	4	6	50	29	7	6	10	24	40	74	69	70
9	Millwall	46	16	4	3	42	18	2	9	12	29	47	71	65	67
10	Bolton Wanderers	46	13	4	6	36	17	5	6	12	20	43	56	60	64
11	Orient	46	13	5	5	40	27	5	4	14	31	54	71	81	63
12	Burnley	46	12	5	6	52	25	4	9	10	24	36	76	61	62
13	Newport County	46	11	9	3	35	27	5	5	13	23	48	58	75	62
14	Lincoln City	46	11	4	8	42	29	6	6	11	17	33	59	62	61
15	Wigan Athletic	46	11	5	7	26	18	5	8	10	20	38	46	56	61
16	Preston North End	46	12	5	6	42	27	3	6	14	24	39	66	66	56
17	Bournemouth	46	11	5	7	38	27	5	2	16	25	46	63	73	55
18	Rotherham United	46	10	5	8	29	17	5	4	14	28	47	57	64	54
19	Plymouth Argyle	46	11	8	4	38	17	2	4	17	18	45	56	62	51
20	Brentford	46	8	9	6	41	30	3	7	13	28	49	69	79	49
21	**SCUNTHORPE U**	**46**	**9**	**9**	**5**	**40**	**31**	**0**	**10**	**13**	**14**	**42**	**54**	**73**	**46**
22	Southend United	46	8	9	6	34	24	2	5	16	21	52	55	76	44
23	Port Vale	46	10	4	9	33	29	1	6	16	18	54	51	83	43
24	Exeter City	46	4	8	11	27	39	2	7	14	23	45	50	84	33

Final League Table 1984/85 Division 4

		Pl.	Home					Away					F.	A.	Pts
			W	D	L	F	A	W	D	L	F	A			
1	Chesterfield	46	16	6	1	40	13	10	7	6	24	22	64	35	91
2	Blackpool	46	15	7	1	42	15	9	7	7	31	24	73	39	86
3	Darlington	46	16	4	3	41	22	8	9	6	25	27	66	49	85
4	Bury	46	15	6	2	46	20	9	6	8	30	30	76	50	84
5	Hereford United	46	16	2	5	38	21	6	9	8	27	26	65	47	77
6	Tranmere Rovers	46	17	1	5	50	21	7	2	14	33	45	83	66	75
7	Colchester United	46	13	7	3	49	29	7	7	9	38	36	87	65	74
8	Swindon Town	46	16	4	3	42	21	5	5	13	20	37	62	58	72
9	**SCUNTHORPE U**	**46**	**14**	**6**	**3**	**61**	**33**	**5**	**8**	**10**	**22**	**29**	**83**	**62**	**71**
10	Crewe Alexandra	46	10	7	6	32	28	8	5	10	33	41	65	69	66
11	Peterborough Utd.	46	11	7	5	29	21	5	7	11	25	32	54	53	62
12	Port Vale	46	11	8	4	39	24	3	10	10	22	35	61	59	60
13	Aldershot	46	11	6	6	33	20	6	2	15	23	43	56	63	59
14	Mansfield Town	46	10	8	5	25	15	3	10	10	16	23	41	38	57
15	Wrexham	46	10	6	7	39	27	5	3	15	28	43	67	70	54
16	Chester City	46	11	3	9	35	30	4	6	13	25	42	60	72	54
17	Rochdale	46	8	7	8	33	30	5	7	11	22	39	55	69	53
18	Exeter City	46	9	7	7	30	27	4	7	12	27	52	57	79	53
19	Hartlepool United	46	10	6	7	34	29	4	4	15	20	38	54	67	52
20	Southend United	46	8	8	7	30	34	5	3	15	28	49	58	83	50
21	Halifax Town	46	9	3	11	26	32	6	2	15	16	37	42	69	50
22	Stockport County	46	11	5	7	40	26	2	3	18	18	53	58	79	47
23	Northampton Town	46	10	1	12	32	32	4	4	15	21	42	53	74	47
24	Torquay United	46	5	11	7	18	24	4	3	16	20	39	38	63	41

Final League Table 1985/86 Division 4

		Pl.	Home					Away					F.	A.	Pts
			W	D	L	F	A	W	D	L	F	A			
1	Swindon Town	46	20	2	1	52	19	12	4	7	30	24	82	43	102
2	Chester City	46	15	5	3	44	16	8	10	5	39	34	83	50	84
3	Mansfield Town	46	13	8	2	43	17	10	4	9	31	30	74	47	81
4	Port Vale	46	13	9	1	42	11	8	7	8	25	26	67	37	79
5	Orient	46	11	6	6	39	21	9	6	8	40	43	79	64	72
6	Colchester United	46	12	6	5	51	22	7	7	9	37	41	88	63	70
7	Hartlepool United	46	15	6	2	41	20	5	4	14	27	47	68	67	70
8	Northampton Town	46	9	7	7	44	29	9	3	11	35	29	79	58	64
9	Southend United	46	13	4	6	43	27	5	6	12	26	40	69	67	64
10	Hereford United	46	15	6	2	55	30	3	4	16	19	43	74	73	64
11	Stockport County	46	9	9	5	35	28	8	4	11	28	43	63	71	64
12	Crewe Alexandra	46	10	6	7	35	26	8	3	12	19	35	54	61	63
13	Wrexham	46	11	5	7	34	24	6	4	13	34	56	68	80	60
14	Burnley	46	11	3	9	35	30	5	8	10	25	35	60	65	59
15	**SCUNTHORPE U**	**46**	**11**	**7**	**5**	**33**	**23**	**4**	**7**	**12**	**17**	**32**	**50**	**55**	**59**
16	Aldershot	46	12	5	6	45	25	5	2	16	21	49	66	74	58
17	Peterborough Utd.	46	9	11	3	31	19	4	6	13	21	45	52	64	56
18	Rochdale	46	12	7	4	41	29	2	6	15	16	48	57	77	55
19	Tranmere Rovers	46	9	1	13	46	41	6	8	9	28	32	74	73	54
20	Halifax Town	46	10	8	5	35	27	4	4	15	25	44	60	71	54
21	Exeter City	46	10	4	9	26	25	3	11	9	21	34	47	59	54
22	Cambridge United	46	12	2	9	45	38	3	7	13	20	42	65	80	54
23	Preston North End	46	7	4	12	32	41	4	6	13	22	48	54	89	43
24	Torquay United	46	8	5	10	29	32	1	5	17	14	56	43	88	37

Final League Table 1986/87 Division 4

		Pl.	Home					Away					F.	A.	Pts
			W	D	L	F	A	W	D	L	F	A			
1	Northampton Town	46	20	2	1	56	20	10	7	6	47	33	103	53	99
2	Preston North End	46	16	4	3	36	18	10	8	5	36	29	72	47	90
3	Southend United	46	14	4	5	43	27	11	1	11	25	28	68	55	80
4	Wolverhampton W.	46	12	3	8	36	24	12	4	7	33	26	69	50	79
5	Colchester United	46	15	3	5	41	20	6	4	13	23	36	64	56	70
6	Aldershot	46	13	5	5	40	22	7	5	11	24	35	64	57	70
7	Orient	46	15	2	6	40	25	5	7	11	24	36	64	61	69
8	**SCUNTHORPE U**	**46**	**15**	**3**	**5**	**52**	**27**	**3**	**9**	**11**	**21**	**30**	**73**	**57**	**66**
9	Wrexham	46	8	13	2	38	24	7	7	9	32	27	70	51	65
10	Peterborough Utd.	46	10	7	6	29	21	7	7	9	28	29	57	50	65
11	Cambridge United	46	12	6	5	37	23	5	5	13	23	39	60	62	62
12	Swansea City	46	13	3	7	31	21	4	8	11	25	40	56	61	62
13	Cardiff City	46	6	12	5	24	18	9	4	10	24	32	48	50	61
14	Exeter City	46	11	10	2	37	17	0	13	10	16	32	53	49	56
15	Halifax Town	46	10	5	8	32	32	5	5	13	27	42	59	74	55
16	Hereford United	46	10	6	7	33	23	4	5	14	27	38	60	61	53
17	Crewe Alexandra	46	8	9	6	38	35	5	5	13	32	37	70	72	53
18	Hartlepool United	46	6	11	6	24	30	5	7	11	20	35	44	65	51
19	Stockport County	46	9	6	8	25	27	4	6	13	15	42	40	69	51
20	Tranmere Rovers	46	6	10	7	32	37	5	7	11	22	35	54	72	50
21	Rochdale	46	8	8	7	31	30	3	9	11	23	43	54	73	50
22	Burnley	46	9	7	7	31	35	3	6	14	22	39	53	74	49
23	Torquay United	46	8	8	7	28	29	2	10	11	28	43	56	72	48
24	Lincoln City	46	8	7	8	30	27	4	5	14	15	38	45	65	48

Final League Table 1987/88 Division 4

		Pl.	Home					Away					F.	A.	Pts
			W	D	L	F	A	W	D	L	F	A			
1	Wolverhampton W.	46	15	3	5	47	19	12	6	5	35	24	82	43	90
2	Cardiff City	46	15	6	2	39	14	9	7	7	27	27	66	41	85
3	Bolton Wanderers	46	15	6	2	42	12	7	6	10	24	30	66	42	78
4	**SCUNTHORPE U**	**46**	**14**	**5**	**4**	**42**	**20**	**6**	**12**	**5**	**34**	**31**	**76**	**51**	**77**
5	Torquay United	46	10	7	6	34	16	11	7	5	32	25	66	41	77
6	Swansea City	46	9	7	7	35	28	11	3	9	27	28	62	56	70
7	Peterborough Utd.	46	10	5	8	28	26	10	5	8	24	27	52	53	70
8	Leyton Orient	46	13	4	6	55	27	6	8	9	30	36	85	63	69
9	Colchester United	46	10	5	8	23	22	9	5	9	24	29	47	51	67
10	Burnley	46	12	5	6	31	22	8	2	13	26	40	57	62	67
11	Wrexham	46	13	3	7	46	26	7	3	13	23	32	69	58	66
12	Scarborough	46	12	8	3	38	19	5	6	12	18	29	56	48	65
13	Darlington	46	13	6	4	39	25	5	5	13	32	44	71	69	65
14	Tranmere Rovers	46	14	2	7	43	20	5	7	11	18	33	61	53	64
15	Cambridge United	46	10	6	7	32	24	6	7	10	18	28	50	52	61
16	Hartlepool United	46	9	7	7	25	25	6	7	10	25	32	50	57	59
17	Crewe Alexandra	46	7	11	5	25	19	6	8	9	32	34	57	53	58
18	Halifax Town	46	11	7	5	37	25	3	7	13	17	34	54	59	55
19	Hereford United	46	8	7	8	25	27	6	5	12	16	32	41	59	54
20	Stockport County	46	7	7	9	26	26	5	8	10	18	32	44	58	51
21	Rochdale	46	5	9	9	28	34	6	6	11	19	42	47	76	48
22	Exeter City	46	8	6	9	33	29	3	7	13	20	39	53	68	46
23	Carlisle United	46	9	5	9	38	33	3	3	17	19	53	57	86	44
24	Newport County	46	4	5	14	19	36	2	2	19	16	69	35	105	25

Final League Table 1988/89 Division 4

		Pl.	Home					Away					F.	A.	Pts
			W	D	L	F	A	W	D	L	F	A			
1	Rotherham United	46	13	6	4	44	18	9	10	4	32	17	76	35	82
2	Tranmere Rovers	46	15	6	2	34	13	6	11	6	28	30	62	43	80
3	Crewe Alexandra	46	13	7	3	42	24	8	8	7	25	24	67	48	78
4	**SCUNTHORPE U**	**46**	**11**	**9**	**3**	**40**	**22**	**10**	**5**	**8**	**37**	**35**	**77**	**57**	**77**
5	Scarborough	46	12	7	4	33	23	9	7	7	34	29	67	52	77
6	Leyton Orient	46	16	2	5	61	19	5	10	8	25	31	86	50	75
7	Wrexham	46	12	7	4	44	28	7	7	9	33	35	77	63	71
8	Cambridge United	46	13	7	3	45	25	5	7	11	26	37	71	62	68
9	Grimsby Town	46	11	9	3	33	18	6	6	11	32	41	65	59	66
10	Lincoln City	46	12	6	5	39	26	6	4	13	25	34	64	60	64
11	York City	46	10	8	5	43	27	7	5	11	19	36	62	63	64
12	Carlisle United	46	9	6	8	26	25	6	9	8	27	27	53	52	60
13	Exeter City	46	14	4	5	46	23	4	2	17	19	45	65	68	60
14	Torquay United	46	15	2	6	32	23	2	6	15	13	37	45	60	59
15	Hereford United	46	11	8	4	40	27	3	8	12	26	45	66	72	58
16	Burnley	46	12	6	5	35	20	2	7	14	17	41	52	61	55
17	Peterborough Utd.	46	10	3	10	29	32	4	9	10	23	42	52	74	54
18	Rochdale	46	10	10	3	32	26	3	4	16	24	56	56	82	53
19	Hartlepool United	46	10	6	7	33	33	4	4	15	17	45	50	78	52
20	Stockport County	46	8	10	5	31	20	2	11	10	23	32	54	52	51
21	Halifax Town	46	10	7	6	42	27	3	4	16	27	48	69	75	50
22	Colchester United	46	8	7	8	35	30	4	7	12	25	48	60	78	50
23	Doncaster Rovers	46	9	6	8	32	32	4	4	15	17	46	49	78	49
24	Darlington	46	3	12	8	28	38	5	6	12	25	38	53	76	42

Final League Table 1989/90 Division 4

		Pl.	Home					Away					F.	A.	Pts
			W	D	L	F	A	W	D	L	F	A			
1	Exeter City	46	20	3	0	50	14	8	2	13	33	34	83	48	89
2	Grimsby Town	46	14	4	5	41	20	8	9	6	29	27	70	47	79
3	Southend United	46	15	3	5	35	14	7	6	10	26	34	61	48	75
4	Stockport County	46	13	6	4	45	27	8	5	10	23	35	68	62	74
5	Maidstone United	46	14	4	5	49	21	8	3	12	28	40	77	61	73
6	Cambridge United	46	14	3	6	45	30	7	7	9	31	36	76	66	73
7	Chesterfield	46	12	9	2	41	19	7	5	11	22	31	63	50	71
8	Carlisle United	46	15	4	4	38	20	6	4	13	23	40	61	60	71
9	Peterborough Utd.	46	10	8	5	35	23	7	9	7	24	23	59	46	68
10	Lincoln City	46	11	6	6	30	27	7	8	8	18	21	48	48	68
11	**SCUNTHORPE U**	**46**	**9**	**9**	**5**	**42**	**25**	**8**	**6**	**9**	**27**	**29**	**69**	**54**	**66**
12	Rochdale	46	11	4	8	28	23	9	2	12	24	32	52	55	66
13	York City	46	10	5	8	29	24	6	11	6	26	29	55	53	64
14	Gillingham	46	9	8	6	28	21	8	3	12	18	27	46	48	62
15	Torquay United	46	12	2	9	33	29	3	10	10	20	37	53	66	57
16	Burnley	46	6	10	7	19	18	8	4	11	26	37	45	55	56
17	Hereford United	46	7	4	12	31	32	8	6	9	25	30	56	62	55
18	Scarborough	46	10	5	8	35	28	5	5	13	25	45	60	73	55
19	Hartlepool United	46	12	4	7	45	33	3	6	14	21	55	66	88	55
20	Doncaster Rovers	46	7	7	9	29	29	7	2	14	24	31	53	60	51
21	Wrexham	46	8	8	7	28	28	5	4	14	23	39	51	67	51
22	Aldershot	46	8	7	8	28	26	4	7	12	21	43	49	69	50
23	Halifax Town	46	5	9	9	31	29	7	4	12	26	36	57	65	49
24	Colchester United	46	9	3	11	26	25	2	7	14	22	50	48	75	43

Final League Table 1990/91 Division 4

		Pl.	Home					Away					F.	A.	Pts
			W	D	L	F	A	W	D	L	F	A			
1	Darlington	46	13	8	2	36	14	9	9	5	32	24	68	38	83
2	Stockport County	46	16	6	1	54	19	7	7	9	30	28	84	47	82
3	Hartlepool United	46	15	5	3	35	15	9	5	9	32	33	67	48	82
4	Peterborough Utd.	46	13	9	1	38	15	8	8	7	29	30	67	45	80
5	Blackpool	46	17	3	3	55	17	6	7	10	23	30	78	47	79
6	Burnley	46	17	5	1	46	16	6	5	12	24	35	70	51	79
7	Torquay United	46	14	7	2	37	13	4	11	8	27	34	64	47	72
8	**SCUNTHORPE U**	**46**	**17**	**4**	**2**	**51**	**20**	**3**	**7**	**13**	**20**	**42**	**71**	**62**	**71**
9	Scarborough	46	13	5	5	36	21	6	7	10	23	35	59	56	69
10	Northampton Town	46	14	5	4	34	21	4	8	11	23	37	57	58	67
11	Doncaster Rovers	46	12	5	6	36	22	5	9	9	20	24	56	46	65
12	Rochdale	46	10	9	4	29	22	5	8	10	21	31	50	53	62
13	Cardiff City	46	10	6	7	26	23	5	9	9	17	31	43	54	60
14	Lincoln City	46	10	7	6	32	27	4	10	9	18	34	50	61	59
15	Gillingham	46	9	9	5	35	27	3	9	11	22	33	57	60	54
16	Walsall	46	7	12	4	25	17	5	5	13	23	34	48	51	53
17	Hereford United	46	9	10	4	32	19	4	4	15	21	39	53	58	53
18	Chesterfield	46	8	12	3	33	26	5	2	16	14	36	47	62	53
19	Maidstone United	46	9	5	9	42	34	4	7	12	24	37	66	71	51
20	Carlisle United	46	12	3	8	30	30	1	6	16	17	59	47	89	48
21	York City	46	8	6	9	21	23	3	7	13	24	34	45	57	46
22	Halifax Town	46	9	6	8	34	29	3	4	16	25	50	59	79	46
23	Aldershot	46	8	7	8	38	43	2	4	17	23	58	61	101	41
24	Wrexham	46	8	7	8	33	34	2	3	18	15	40	48	74	40

1984/85 9th in Division 4

Player column key (left to right): Neenan IP, Longden DP, Pointon NG, Matthews M, Green JR, Whitehead A, Brolly MJ, Dey G, Bell DM, Lester MJ, Cowling C, Webster IA, Cammack SR, Broddle JR, Hill DM, Graham T, Lees T, Gregory PG, Botham IT, Shutt SJ, O'Berg PJ, Finney SB, Ferry W, Atkins MN, Stobart SA, Stanley P

#	Date	Opponent	Score	Att	Neenan IP	Longden DP	Pointon NG	Matthews M	Green JR	Whitehead A	Brolly MJ	Dey G	Bell DM	Lester MJ	Cowling C	Webster IA	Cammack SR	Broddle JR	Hill DM	Graham T	Lees T	Gregory PG	Botham IT	Shutt SJ	O'Berg PJ	Finney SB	Ferry W	Atkins MN	Stobart SA	Stanley P
1	Aug 25	Chester City	1-1 Whitehead	2050	1	2	3	4	5	6	7	8	9	10	11	12														
2	31	COLCHESTER UNITED	2-2 Cammack, Cowling	1818	1	2	3	4	5	6		7		10	11		8	9												
3	Sep 8	Exeter City	1-2 Lester	2658	1	2	3	4	5	6	7	8		10	11			9												
4	15	CHESTERFIELD	2-4 Broddle, Cowling	2853	1	2	3	4	6	5	7		8	10	11			9												
5	18	CREWE ALEXANDRA	2-3 Scott(og), Cowling	1619	1	2	3	4	6	5	7		8	10	11			9												
6	22	Darlington	1-2 Bell	1762	1		3	4	2	5			8	10	11	6		9		7										
7	28	HALIFAX TOWN	4-0 Broddle, Cowling, Brolly, Matthews	1929	1	2	3	4	6		7			10	11	5		9		8		12								
8	Oct 3	Peterborough United	1-3 Brolly	3620	1	2	3	4	6	5	7			10	11			9		8										
9	6	Northampton Town	2-0 Matthews, Cowling	1873	1		3	4	6	5	7			10	11			9		8	2									
10	13	BLACKPOOL	1-1 Bell (pen)	2366	1		3	4		5	7		9	10	11			12		8	2									
11	19	Southend United	1-1 Cowling	2204			3	4	6	5	7			10	11		9	12		8	2	1								
12	23	TORQUAY UNITED	2-0 Broddle 2	2046			3	4	6	5				10	11		9	7		8	2	1								
13	27	Bury	1-0 Lester	3324			3	4	6	5				10	11		8	7		9	2	1								
14	Nov 3	ALDERSHOT	2-1 Cowling, Cammack	2253			3	4	6	5				10	11		8	7		9	2	1								
15	6	Swindon Town	0-0	2867			3	4	6	5				10	11		8	7		9	2	1								
16	9	HEREFORD UNITED	1-1 Graham	2902			3	4	6	5				10	11		8	7		9	2									
17	24	Hartlepool United	2-3 Cowling 2	3292	1		3	4	6	5				10	11		8	7		9	2									
18	30	WREXHAM	5-2 Cammack 3(1 p), Matthews, Whitehead	2180	1		3	4	6	5				10	11		8	7		9	2									
19	Dec 22	Port Vale	1-1 Graham	2521			3	4	6	5			12		11		8	7	10	9	2	1								
20	26	STOCKPORT COUNTY	1-0 Cammack	2881		2	3	4	6	5					11		8	7	9	10		1								
21	Jan 1	Tranmere Rovers	0-2	1943	1		3	4	6	5				10			8	7	11	9	2		12							
22	26	Chesterfield	0-1	3698			3		6	5	7			10	11		8	12	4	9	2	1								
23	Feb 1	Halifax Town	2-1 Whitehead, Broddle	1317			3	4	6	5				10	11		7	8		9	2	1								
24	8	DARLINGTON	0-1	1762			3		6	5		4		10	11		7	8		9	2	1								
25	12	PETERBOROUGH UTD.	2-1 Broddle, Brolly	1212			3		6	5	7			10			8	11	4	9	2	1		12						
26	16	Crewe Alexandra	1-1 Shutt	1782			3		6	5	11			10				7	4	9	2	1		8						
27	23	Aldershot	2-1 Graham, Broddle	1926			3		6	5	11			10			8	7	4	9	2	1								
28	26	ROCHDALE	4-2 Cammack 2, Brolly 2	1694			3		6	5	11			10			8	7	4	9	2	1								
29	Mar 2	BURY	2-2 Graham, Cammack	2710			3		6	5	7			10			8	11	4	9	2	1								
30	5	Torquay United	0-0	1158			3		6	5	7			10			8	11	4	9	2	1								
31	8	SOUTHEND UNITED	2-1 Cammack, Graham	1912		2	3		6	5	7			10			8	11	4	9		1								
32	12	CHESTER CITY	2-1 Cammack 2 (1p)	1875		2	3		6	5	7			10			8	11	4	9		1								
33	16	Blackpool	0-1	3937			3		6	5	7			10	12		8	11	4	9	2	1								
34	19	EXETER CITY	7-1 *See below	1566			3		6	5	7			10	12		8	11	4	9	2	1								
35	22	NORTHAMPTON T	2-1 Hill, Broddle	2042			3		6	5	7			10			8	11	4	9	2	1				12				
36	29	SWINDON TOWN	6-2 Cammack, Broddle, Brolly, Hill, Graham, Gree	2042			3		6	5	7			10			8	11	4	9	2	1								
37	Apr 2	Colchester United	1-1 Broddle	2409			3		6	5	7			10	12		8	11	4	9	2	1								
38	6	Stockport County	0-2	1285			3		6	5	7			10	12		8	11	4	9	2	1								
39	9	TRANMERE ROVERS	5-2 Brolly 2, Cammack 2, Broddle	2260			3		6	5	7			10			8	11	4	9	2	1				12				
40	13	Hereford United	0-1	3412			3		6	5	7			10			8	11	4	9	2	1								
41	19	HARTLEPOOL UNITED	2-0 Broddle, Lester	2037		2	3		6	5	7			10			8	11	4			1			9			12		
42	24	Mansfield Town	1-0 Cammack	1963		2	3		6	5	7			10			8	11	4			1			9			12		
43	27	Wrexham	1-2 Cammack	1352		2	3		6	5	7			10			8	11	4	9			12							
44	May 4	MANSFIELD TOWN	2-2 Cammack 2	1705			3		6	5	7			10			8	11	4	9	2									
45	6	Rochdale	3-3 Cammack 2 (2p), Stobart	1482		2	3		6	5	7			10			8	11	4	9		1							12	
46	8	PORT VALE	3-3 Graham, Broddle, Cammack	1867	1		3		6	5	7			10			8	11	4	9	2								12	
		Apps			14	14	46	22	46	45	34	5	3	44	27	3	34	45	29	38	31	32	2	2	2	2	1	2	2	0
		Goals						3	1	4	9		2	3	9		24	14	2	9				1					1	

Scorers in game 34: Broddle, Whitehead, Cammack 2 (1p), Graham 2, Brolly

One own goal

F.A. Cup

#	Date	Opponent	Score	Att	Neenan IP	Longden DP	Pointon NG	Matthews M	Green JR	Whitehead A	Brolly MJ	Dey G	Bell DM	Lester MJ	Cowling C	Webster IA	Cammack SR	Broddle JR	Hill DM	Graham T	Lees T	Gregory PG	Botham IT	Shutt SJ	O'Berg PJ	Finney SB	Ferry W	Atkins MN	Stobart SA	Stanley P
R1	Nov 17	Nuneaton Borough	1-1 Dixey (og)	4287	1		3	4	6	5				10	11		8	7			2									9
rep	20	NUNEATON BOROUGH	2-1 Lester, Cammack	3334	1		3	4	6	5	12			10	11		8	7			2									9
R2	Dec 7	Port Vale	1-4 Ridley (og)	4268	1	12	3	4	6	5	10				11		8	7	9		2									

R1 replay a.e.t. (90 mins. 1-1)

Milk Cup (F.L. Cup)

#	Date	Opponent	Score	Att	Neenan IP	Longden DP	Pointon NG	Matthews M	Green JR	Whitehead A	Brolly MJ	Dey G	Bell DM	Lester MJ	Cowling C	Webster IA	Cammack SR	Broddle JR	Hill DM	Graham T	Lees T	Gregory PG	Botham IT	Shutt SJ	O'Berg PJ	Finney SB	Ferry W	Atkins MN	Stobart SA	Stanley P
1/1	Aug 28	MANSFIELD TOWN	0-1	2106	1	2	3	4	5	6	7		9	10	11		8	12												
1/2	Sep 5	Mansfield Town	2-1 Brolly, Cowling	3107	1	2	3	4	5	6	7	8		10	11	12		9												
2/1	24	ASTON VILLA	2-3 Lester, Whitehead	6212	1	2	3	4	5	6	7		12	10	11			9		8										
2/2	Oct 10	Aston Villa	1-3 Pointon	11421	1		3	4	6	5	7			10	11			9		8	2									

R1 won on away goals rule

Freight Rover Trophy (Associate Members Cup)

#	Date	Opponent	Score	Att	Neenan IP	Longden DP	Pointon NG	Matthews M	Green JR	Whitehead A	Brolly MJ	Dey G	Bell DM	Lester MJ	Cowling C	Webster IA	Cammack SR	Broddle JR	Hill DM	Graham T	Lees T	Gregory PG	Botham IT	Shutt SJ	O'Berg PJ	Finney SB	Ferry W	Atkins MN	Stobart SA	Stanley P
1/1	Jan 22	BRADFORD CITY	1-4 Graham	1380			3	4	6	5	7			10	11		8		12	9	2	1					14			
1/2	Feb 6	Bradford City	1-2 Brolly	2388		2	3	4	6	5	7					12	11	8		9		1	10				14			

SEASON 1984-85
Back: Shaw, Stobart, Passmoor, Hill, Meadows, Dey
Middle: Broddle, Cowling, Whitehead, Neenan, Green, Webster, Pointon
Front: Brolly, Cammack, Matthews, McLoughlin (Physio), Barlow (Manager), Bell, Lester, Longden

SEASON 1985-86
Back: Huxford, Passmoor, Stobart, Atkins, Ferry, Nicol, Stevenson, Frizelle, Dulston
Middle: Coombs, Broddle, Lister, Green, Whitehead, Gregory, Webster, Hawley, Pointon, Hill, Finney
Front: Brolly, Matthews, Bell, Barlow (Manager), Cammack, Lester, Longden

1985/86 15th in Division 4

#	Date	Opponent	Score	Scorers	Att	Gregory PG	Russell WM	Pointon NG	Lister SH	Whitehead A	Green JR	Brolly MJ	Cammack SR	Broddle JR	Graham T	Hill DM	Lester MJ	Hawley JE	Matthews M	Smith MC	Longden DP	Money R	Ferry W	Matthews N	Barnes DO	Dixon KL	Webster IA	Stevenson AJ	Travis DA	Johnson P	Hunter L	Houchen KM
1	Aug 17	TORQUAY UNITED	4-0	Graham, Broddle, Cammack, Green	1929	1	2	3	4	5	6	7	8	9	10	11																
2	23	Halifax Town	1-2	Cammack (p)	1094	1	2	3	4	5	6	7	8	9	10	11																
3	26	WREXHAM	1-1	Broddle	2097	1	2	3	4	5	6	7	8	9	10	11																
4	31	Peterborough United	0-1		2928	1	2	3					8	9	10	11	7	12														
5	Sep 6	TRANMERE ROVERS	0-1		2058	1	2	3	4	5	6	7	8	9		11	10	12														
6	14	Southend United	1-2	Cammack (p)	2974	1	2	3	4	5	6	7	8	9		11	10	12														
7	18	Exeter City	0-2		1723	1	2	3	4	5	6		8	12	7	11	10	9														
8	21	MANSFIELD TOWN	0-3		1780	1	2	3	4	5	6	7	8			11	10	9	12													
9	28	Aldershot	1-2	Graham	1056	1	2	3	4	5			8	9	7	11	10			6	12											
10	Oct 1	CREWE ALEXANDRA	3-1	Graham, Holland (og), Hill	1443	1		3		5	6	7	8	9	4	11	10					2										
11	5	Orient	0-3		2847	1	12	3	6	5		7	8	9	4	11	10					2										
12	11	CAMBRIDGE UNITED	0-0		1496	1		3	6	5		7	8		4	11	10	9				2										
13	18	Colchester United	1-1	Broddle	3462	1	2	3	4	5		7	8	9		11	10					6										
14	22	PORT VALE	0-0		1888	1	2	3	4	5		7	8	9		11	10					6										
15	25	HEREFORD UNITED	2-1	Whitehead, Cammack	1564	1	2	3	4	5		7	8	9	12	11	10					6										
16	Nov 2	Northampton Town	2-2	Brolly, Lister	2343	1	2	3	4	5		7	8	9		11	10					6										
17	5	Preston North End	1-0	Cammack	2007	1	2	3	4	5		7	8	9			10					6	11									
18	9	SWINDON TOWN	0-2		1920	1	2		4	5		7	8	12	3		10					6	11	9								
19	23	Rochdale	0-1		1430	1	2		4	5		7	8	9	12	11	10				3	6										
20	30	BURNLEY	1-1	Hawley	2001	1	2		4	5			9		10	11		8			3	6			7							
21	Dec 14	Chester City	1-1	Hawley	2657	1	2			5			9			11	10	8	4		3	6			7							
22	22	HALIFAX TOWN	3-3	Hawley 3 (1 p)	2285	1	2		12	5			9			11	10	8	4		3	6			7							
23	26	HARTLEPOOL UNITED	1-0	Matthews M	2495	1	2		11	5			9		10			8	4		3	6			7							
24	Jan 1	Stockport County	0-0		3504	1	2		10	5			9			11		8	4		3	6			7							
25	11	PETERBOROUGH UTD.	2-0	Broddle, Whitehead	1832	1	2		4	5			9		10	11		8	12		3	6			7							
26	18	Torquay United	0-1		1064	1	2			5			9		10	11		8	4		3	6				7						
27	24	SOUTHEND UNITED	2-0	Hill, Broddle	1463	1	2			5			9		10	11		8			3	6				7	12					
28	31	Tranmere Rovers	1-2	Hawley	1417	1	2		4	5			9		10	11		8			3	6				7						
29	Feb 3	Port Vale	1-3	Graham	2977	1	2		4	5			9		10	11		8			3	6				7		12				
30	Mar 1	ALDERSHOT	1-0	Hawley	1270	1	2		4	5			9		10	11		8	7		3					6						
31	4	Crewe Alexandra	0-4		1072	1	2		4	5			9		10	11		8	7		3					6						
32	8	ORIENT	2-2	Whitehead, Cammack	1478	1	2		4	5		12	9			11		8			3	6				7			10			
33	15	Cambridge United	1-0	Cammack	1785	1	2		4	5			10	12		11		8			3					6						9
34	18	NORTHAMPTON T	1-0	Broddle	1355	1	2			5			9	12	4	11		8			3					7			10			
35	22	Hereford United	1-1	Graham	2367		2			5			8	9	4	11					3					7			10	1	6	
36	25	Mansfield Town	1-1	Travis	3919		2			5			9	8	4	11					3					7			10	1	6	
37	28	STOCKPORT COUNTY	2-3	Dixon, Cammack	2025		2		4	5			9	8	12	11					3					7			10	1	6	
38	Apr 1	Hartlepool United	1-0	Cammack	2781		2			5			8		4	11					2	3				7			10	1	6	9
39	4	PRESTON NORTH END	1-3	Cammack	2261		2		12	5			8		4	11					2	3				7			10	1	6	9
40	12	Swindon Town	1-1	Hunter	6783		2		4	5			8			11					3					7			10	1	6	9
41	15	COLCHESTER UNITED	1-1	Dixon	1238		2		4	5			8		12	11					3					7			10	1	6	9
42	18	ROCHDALE	3-1	Broddle, Houchen, Lister	1406		2		4			7	8		12	11					3	5							10	1	6	9
43	22	EXETER CITY	1-0	Cammack	1343		2					7	8		4	10	11				3	5								1	6	9
44	26	Burnley	2-1	Houchen, Overson (og)	2542		2					12	8		4	11	7				3	5								1	6	9
45	29	Wrexham	0-1		1042		2		4	5		7	8		10	11					3	5						12		1	6	9
46	May 3	CHESTER CITY	2-0	Brolly, Cammack	2256		2		4			7	8		10	11					3	5								1	6	9
		Apps				34	42	17	37	41	9	20	33	41	31	42	18	21	11	1	31	25	2	1	6	14	5	2	12	12	12	9
		Goals							2	3	1	2	12	7	5	2		7	1							2			1		1	2

Two own goals

F.A. Cup

Rd	Date	Opponent	Score	Scorers	Att	Gregory PG	Russell WM	Pointon NG	Lister SH	Whitehead A	Green JR	Brolly MJ	Cammack SR	Broddle JR	Graham T	Hill DM	Lester MJ	Hawley JE	Matthews M	Smith MC	Longden DP	Money R
R1	Nov 16	Halifax Town	3-1	Hill, Broddle, Lister	1501	1	2		4	5		7	8	9	12	11	10				3	6
R2	Dec 7	ROCHDALE	2-2	Graham, Hill	2868	1	2		7	5			9	10		11		8	4		3	6
rep	10	Rochdale	1-2	Broddle	5066	1	2		4	5			9	7		11	10	8			3	6

Milk Cup (F.L. Cup)

Rd	Date	Opponent	Score	Scorers	Att	Gregory PG	Russell WM	Pointon NG	Lister SH	Whitehead A	Green JR	Brolly MJ	Cammack SR	Broddle JR	Graham T	Hill DM	Lester MJ
R1/1	Aug 20	Darlington	2-3	Lister, Cammack	2159	1	2	3	4	5	6	7	8	9	10	11	12
R1/2	Sep 10	DARLINGTON	0-0		1504	1	2	3	4	5	6	7	8	9		11	10

(R1/2 also: Hawley 12)

Freight Rover Trophy (Associate Members Cup)

Rd	Date	Opponent	Score	Scorers	Att	Gregory PG	Russell WM	Lister SH	Whitehead A	Green JR	Cammack SR	Graham T	Hill DM	Hawley JE	Matthews M	Longden DP	Money R	Webster IA	Stevenson AJ	Travis DA
R1	Jan 15	Lincoln City	3-1	Money, Hawley (p), Whitehead	1235	1	2		5		9	10	11	8	4	3	6		7	
R1	21	HALIFAX TOWN	3-2	Matthews M, Hawley 2	1244	1	2	4	5		9	10	11	8	7	3	6	12	14	
QF	Mar 10	PORT VALE	1-1	Hawley	1415	1	2	4	5	9	8	12	11	8	7	3	6			10

QF lost on penalties (4-3) a.e.t.

1986/87 8th in Division 4

No	Date	Opponent	Score	Scorers	Att	Green RR	Russell WM	Longden DP	Money R	Lister SH	Hunter L	Birch A	Cammack SR	Johnson SA	McLean DJ	Stevenson AJ	Hill DM	Broddle JR	Whitehead A	Travis DA	Atkins MN	Nicol PJ	Ferry W	Richardson IP	Harle D	Gregory PG	Reeves D	De Mange KJP	North MV	Smith B	Flounders AJ
1	Aug 23	NORTHAMPTON T	2-2	Cammack, Hunter	2302	1	2	3	4	5	6	7	8	9	10	11															
2	30	Burnley	0-1		2958	1	2	3	4	5	6	7	8	9	10		11	12													
3	Sep 7	CREWE ALEXANDRA	2-1	Johnson, Hunter	2098	1	2	3	4	5	6	7	8	9			11	10	12												
4	13	Orient	1-3	Birch	1857	1	2	3	4		6	7	8	9		5	11	10	12												
5	16	Aldershot	1-2	McLean	1696	1	2	3	4	5	7			9	8		11	10			6										
6	19	PRESTON NORTH END	4-0	Lister 2, Broddle, Russell	2689	1	2	3	4	5	7			9	8		11	10			6										
7	30	CAMBRIDGE UNITED	1-1	Broddle	1694	1	2	3	4	5	7			9	8	12	11	10			6										
8	Oct 5	WOLVERHAMPTON W.	0-2		3296	1	2	3	4	5	7			9			11	10			6	8		12							
9	11	Swansea City	2-1	Whitehead, Broddle	5412	1		3	2	5	7			8			11	10			6	9	4	12							
10	17	TORQUAY UNITED	2-0	McLean, Johnson	1703	1		3	2	5	7			9	8		11	10			6	4									
11	21	Tranmere Rovers	0-1		1469	1	12	3	2	5	7			9	8		11	10			6		4								
12	25	Cardiff City	1-1	Johnson	2145	1		3	2	5	6	7		9	8		11	10			4			12							
13	Nov 1	WREXHAM	3-3	Richardson, Johnson, Broddle	1948	1		3	4	5	6			9	8		11	10			2			7							
14	4	Southend United	1-3	Johnson	2789	1	12	3	4	5	6			9	8		11	10			2			7							
15	9	HALIFAX TOWN	2-1	Johnson, Lister	2059	1	12	3	4	5	6			9	8		11	10			2			7							
16	21	COLCHESTER UNITED	5-2	Lister, Broddle, Johnson 2, McLean(p)	1725	1	7	3	4	5	6			9	8		11	10			2										
17	29	Hereford United	2-2	Rodgerson (og), Hill	2003	1	7	3		5	6			9	8		11	10			2	12			4						
18	Dec 13	Rochdale	1-1	Lister	1244	1	8	3		5	6			9			11	10			2	12		7	4	1					
19	19	EXETER CITY	3-1	Reeves 2, Hill	1545	1		3	2	5	6						11	10						8	4	1	9				
20	26	Peterborough United	1-1	Russell	4267	1	7	3		5	6						11	10			2			8	4		9				
21	27	LINCOLN CITY	2-1	Harle, Lister	4299	1	7	3	2	5	6			9			11	10						8	4						
22	Jan 1	HARTLEPOOL UNITED	1-2	Richardson	2726	1	7	3	2	5	6			9			11	10						8	4			12			
23	3	Colchester United	0-1		2100	1	7	3	2	5	6			9			11	10			12							8	4		
24	24	Crewe Alexandra	2-2	De Mange, Broddle	1430	1	4	3	11		6			8				10			2	5						7	9		
25	31	TRANMERE ROVERS	6-0	*See below	1611	1	4		2	5	6			9			11	10			3							7	8		
26	Feb 7	ALDERSHOT	2-0	North 2	1991	1	4	3	2		6			9			11	10			7				5				8		
27	10	ORIENT	0-2		2087	1	4	3	2		6			9			11	10			7	12		5					8		
28	14	Preston North End	1-2	Birch	7968		4	3	2		6	7		9	12		11	10			5			8	1						
29	21	STOCKPORT COUNTY	1-2	Hunter	1752	1		3	2	5	6			9	8		11	10			7			4					12		
30	28	Cambridge United	0-1		2136	1	7	3	2	5	6	12		9	8		11				10			4							
31	Mar 3	Wrexham	1-1	Lister	1360	1	2	3		5	6	7		9	8		11				10			4							
32	7	CARDIFF CITY	1-3	Smith	1936	1	2	3	11		6	7		9	8									4						5	10
33	11	Northampton Town	0-1		5352	1	2	3	8	11	5	7		9										4						6	10
34	14	Torquay United	2-2	Johnson, Flounders	1393	1	2	3	7	8	5			9					11					4						6	10
35	21	SWANSEA CITY	3-2	Johnson, Flounders, Lister	1590	1	2	3		8	5			9					11	12		7		4						6	10
36	28	Wolverhampton Wan.	0-1		7348	1	2	3		8	5			9					11	12		7		4						6	10
37	Apr 3	Halifax Town	1-1	Lister (p)	1232	1	2		7	8	5			9					11			3		4						6	10
38	11	SOUTHEND UNITED	3-0	Broddle, Johnson 2	1602	1	2	3	4	8				9					11	7				6	5						10
39	13	Stockport County	0-1		1773	1	2	3	4	8	5			9					11	7			6		12						10
40	17	Hartlepool United	2-0	Harle, Flounders	1713	1	2	3	4	8	5			9					11	7					6						10
41	20	PETERBOROUGH UTD.	2-0	Hill, Gage (og)	2470	1	2	3	4	8	5			9					11	7					6						10
42	25	Exeter City	0-0		1525	1	2	3	4	8	5		12	9					11	7					6						10
43	28	BURNLEY	2-1	Johnson 2	1770	1	2	3	4	5	7			9		8	11								6						10
44	Ma 1	HEREFORD UNITED	3-1	Johnson, Broddle, Russell	1660	1	2	3	4	8	5	7		9			11	12							6						10
45	4	Lincoln City	2-1	Flounders 2	2567	1	2	3	4	8	5	7					12	11	9						6						10
46	9	ROCHDALE	2-0	Lister, Flounders	2347	1	2	3	4	8	5						7	11	9		12				6						10

Scorers in game 25: Hunter, Lister, De Mange, Johnson, Broddle 2

| | | | Apps | | | 43 | 41 | 42 | 42 | 40 | 37 | 21 | 4 | 40 | 20 | 7 | 41 | 38 | 7 | 1 | 26 | 9 | 2 | 8 | 26 | 3 | 4 | 3 | 5 | 6 | 15 |
| | | | Goals | | | | 3 | | | 11 | 4 | 2 | 1 | 16 | 3 | | 3 | 10 | 1 | | | | | 2 | 2 | | | 2 | 2 | 1 | 6 |

Two own goals

F.A. Cup

No	Date	Opponent	Score	Scorers	Att	Green RR	Russell WM	Longden DP	Money R	Lister SH	Hunter L	Birch A	Cammack SR	Johnson SA	McLean DJ	Stevenson AJ	Hill DM	Broddle JR	Whitehead A	Travis DA	Atkins MN	Nicol PJ	Ferry W	Richardson IP	Harle D	Gregory PG	Reeves D	De Mange KJP	North MV	Smith B	Flounders AJ
R1	Nov 15	SOUTHPORT	2-0	Hill, Broddle	2601	1	14	3	4	5	6			9	8		11	10			2			7			12				
R2	Dec 6	RUNCORN	1-0	Broddle	3006	1	7	3		5	6			9			11	10	12		2	4		8							
R3	Jan 10	Tottenham Hotspur	2-3	Johnson S, De Mange	19339	1	7	3	2	5	12			9	8		11	10			6							4			

Littlewoods Challenge Cup (F.L. Cup)

No	Date	Opponent	Score	Scorers	Att	Green RR	Russell WM	Longden DP	Money R	Lister SH	Hunter L	Birch A	Cammack SR	Johnson SA	McLean DJ	Stevenson AJ	Hill DM	Broddle JR	Whitehead A	Travis DA	Atkins MN	Nicol PJ	Ferry W	Richardson IP	Harle D	Gregory PG	Reeves D	De Mange KJP	North MV	Smith B	Flounders AJ
1/1	Aug 26	DARLINGTON	2-0	Lister, Hill	1350	1	2	3	4	5	6	7	8	9	10		11					12									
1/2	Sep 2	Darlington	2-1	Lister 2	1469	1	2	3	4	5	6	7	8	9			11	10													
2/1	23	IPSWICH TOWN	1-2	Broddle	3919	1	2	3	4	5	7			9	8		11	10			6			12							
2/2	Oct 7	Ipswich Town	0-2		6587	1	2	3	9	5	7						11	10			6	8		4			12				

Freight Rover Trophy (Associate Members Cup)

No	Date	Opponent	Score	Scorers	Att	Green RR	Russell WM	Longden DP	Money R	Lister SH	Hunter L	Birch A	Cammack SR	Johnson SA	McLean DJ	Stevenson AJ	Hill DM	Broddle JR	Whitehead A	Travis DA	Atkins MN	Nicol PJ	Ferry W	Richardson IP	Harle D	Gregory PG	Reeves D	De Mange KJP	North MV	Smith B	Flounders AJ
PR	Nov 25	Lincoln City	0-1		1003	1	7	3		5	6			9	8		11	10			2	4									
PR	Dec 2	HARTLEPOOL UNITED	1-0	Broddle	952		7	3		5	6			9			11	10			2	8		4	1							
R1	Jan 27	WREXHAM	1-2	Hunter	1227	1	4	3	5		6	12		8				10			2	14		11				7	9		

#	Date	Opponent	Result	Att	Green RR	Russell WM	Longden DP	McLean DJ	Brown AJ	Nicol PJ	Dixon KL	Harle D	Daws A	Flounders AJ	Hill DM	Atkins MN	Johnson SA	Broddle JR	Stevenson AJ	Lister SH	Heyes D	Money R	Birch A	Taylor K	Reeves D	Cowling DR	Taylor MJ	Shearer DJ	Richardson IP	Johnson P
1	Aug 15	TRANMERE ROVERS	3-0 Russell, Flounders 2	2277	1	2	3	4	5	6	7	8	9	10	11															
2	22	Carlisle United	1-3 Johnson	2074	1	2	3	4		6	7	8		10	11	5	9	12												
3	29	COLCHESTER UNITED	2-2 Johnson, Flounders	2003	1	2	3	4	5	6	7	8		10	11		9	12												
4	31	Wolverhampton Wan.	1-4 Flounders	6672	1	2	3	4	5	6	7	8		10			9	11	12											
5	Sep 5	ROCHDALE	1-0 Dixon	1969	1	2	3		5		7	8		10	11	6	9	4												
6	12	Cambridge United	3-3 Flounders 2, Harle	1830	1	2	3		5		7	8		10		6	9	11		4										
7	15	BOLTON WANDERERS	1-1 Russell (p)	2501		2	3		5		7	8		10		6	9	11		4	1									
8	19	NEWPORT COUNTY	3-1 Flounders 2, Atkins	2004		2	3		5		7	8		10		6	9	11		4	1									
9	26	Darlington	4-1 Russell, Dixon, Lister, Flounders	1638	1	2	3		5		7	8		10		6	9	11		4										
10	29	STOCKPORT COUNTY	0-0	2181	1	2	3		5		7	8		10		6	9			4		11	12							
11	Oct 3	Peterborough United	1-1 Dixon	3594	1	2	3		5		7	8		10		6	9			4		11	12							
12	10	HALIFAX TOWN	1-0 Johnson	2105	1	2					7	8		10	11	3	9			5		6		4						
13	17	Hereford United	3-2 Reeves 3	2092	1	2	11				7	8		10		3				5		6		4	9					
14	20	Burnley	1-1 Flounders	6323	1	2	11				7	8		10		3			12	5		6		4	9					
15	24	CARDIFF CITY	2-1 Ford(og), Taylor	2872	1	2	11				7	8		10		3			12	5		6		4	9					
16	31	Hartlepool United	0-1	2763	1	2	11			6	7	8		10		3			12	5				4	9					
17	Nov 3	WREXHAM	3-1 Reeves, Flounders 2	2348	1	2	11		5		7	8		10		3						6		4	9					
18	7	SCARBOROUGH	0-1	4506	1	2	3				7	8		10		14	12			5		6		4	9	11				
19	21	Crewe Alexandra	2-2 Atkins, Flounders	2045	1	2	3				7	8		10		11	9			5		6		4						
20	28	SWANSEA CITY	1-2 Flounders	2309	1	2	3				7	8	12	10		11	9			5		6		4						
21	Dec 12	Exeter City	1-1 Johnson	1831		2	3				7	8	12	10		11	9		14	5	1	6								
22	18	TORQUAY UNITED	2-3 Impey(og), Russell	2261	7	3					12	8	11	10		2	9		14	5		6					1			
23	26	DARLINGTON	1-0 Flounders	3140		2	3			6	7	8	11	10			9			5				4			1			
24	28	Leyton Orient	1-1 Harle	5542		2	3				7	8	9	10	11					5		6		4			1			
25	Jan 1	Colchester United	3-0 Daws 2, Lister	2287		2	3				7	8	9	10	11					5				4			1			
26	2	CAMBRIDGE UNITED	3-2 Hill, Taylor K, Daws	3252		2	3	12	6		7	8	9	10	11					5				4			1			
27	16	Newport County	1-1 Taylor K	1760			3		6		7		9	10	11			12		8		5		2			1			
28	30	WOLVERHAMPTON W.	0-1	5476		2	3		6		7	8		10	11		9			5							1			
29	Feb 6	Rochdale	1-2 Flounders	1455		2	3		6		7	8		10	11	12				5				4			1			
30	13	LEYTON ORIENT	3-2 Harle 2, Shearer	2951	1	2	3			6		8		10	11	12				5		7		4				9		
31	20	Tranmere Rovers	3-1 Flounders 2, Lister	2803	1	2	3			6		8		10	11	12				5		7		4				9		
32	27	PETERBOROUGH UTD.	5-0 Shearer, Flounders 3, Gunn(og)	3378	1	2	3			6		8		10	11	12				5		7		4				9		
33	Mar 1	Stockport County	1-1 Shearer	1834	1	2	3			6	14	8		10	11	12				5		7		4				9		
34	5	HEREFORD UNITED	3-0 Hill, Taylor, Lister	3413	1	2	3			6	12	8		10	11					5		7		4				9		
35	12	Halifax Town	2-2 Harle (p), Lister	1807	1		3	12		6	7	8		10			9			5		2		4						
36	19	HARTLEPOOL UNITED	3-0 Flounders, Dixon, Hill	3783	1		3			6	7	8		10	11		12			5		2		4				9		
37	26	Cardiff City	1-0 Shearer	4527	1		3	12	6		7	8		10	11	2	14			5				4				9		
38	Apr 2	Scarborough	0-0	4677	1		3			6	7	8		10	11					5		2		4				9		
39	4	CREWE ALEXANDRA	2-1 Flounders, Taylor K	4091	1		3			6	7	8		10	11	12				5		2		4				9		
40	9	Wrexham	1-2 Shearer	2589	1		3	12	6		7	8			11		10		14	5		2		4				9		
41	12	CARLISLE UNITED	1-0 Shearer	3514	1		3			6	7	8		10	11					5		2		4				9		
42	19	Bolton Wanderers	0-0	6669	1					6	7	8		10	11	3				5		2		4				9		
43	23	BURNLEY	1-1 Harle (p)	5347	1		3		5	6	7	8		10	11	2	12							4				9		
44	30	Swansea City	1-1 Lister	3482	1	7	3	12		6		8	14	10	11					5		2		4				9		
45	May 2	EXETER CITY	1-1 Shearer	6736	1		3			6	7	8		10	11		12			5		2		4				9		
46	7	Torquay United	2-1 Flounders, Richardson	4989	1		3			6		8	9	10	11		12		14	5		2		4					7	

| | | | | Apps | 35 | 34 | 44 | 4 | 22 | 25 | 41 | 45 | 10 | 45 | 26 | 22 | 32 | 7 | 8 | 39 | 3 | 32 | 2 | 35 | 6 | 1 | 8 | 15 | 1 | 0 |
| | | | | Goals | | 4 | | | | | 4 | 6 | 3 | 24 | 3 | 2 | 4 | | | 6 | | | | 5 | 4 | | | 7 | 1 | |

Three own goals

Play Offs

	Date	Opponent	Result	Att	Green RR		Longden DP	McLean DJ		Nicol PJ	Dixon KL	Harle D	Daws A	Flounders AJ	Hill DM	Atkins MN				Lister SH		Money R		Taylor K				Shearer DJ	Richardson IP	
SF1	May 15	Torquay United	1-2 Flounders	4602	1		3	8		6			9	10	11	2				5				4				12	7	
SF2	18	TORQUAY UNITED	1-1 Lister (p)	6482	1		3	6			12		9	10	11	14				5		2		4				8	7	

F.A. Cup

	Date	Opponent	Result	Att	Green RR	Russell WM	Longden DP	McLean DJ		Nicol PJ	Dixon KL	Harle D	Daws A	Flounders AJ	Hill DM	Atkins MN	Johnson SA			Lister SH		Money R		Taylor K						Johnson P
R1	Nov 14	BURY	3-1 Russell 3 (1 p)	3151	1	2	3				7	8		10		11	9			5		6		4						
R2	Dec 5	SUNDERLAND	2-1 Taylor, Harle	7178	1	2	3				7	8		10		11	9			5		6		4						
R3	Jan 9	BLACKPOOL	0-0	6217		2	3			6	7	8	9	10	11					5				4						1
rep	12	Blackpool	0-1	6127		2	3			6	7	8	9	10	11		14			5		12								1

Littlewoods Challenge Cup (F.L. Cup)

	Date	Opponent	Result	Att	Green RR	Russell WM	Longden DP	McLean DJ	Brown AJ	Nicol PJ	Dixon KL	Harle D		Flounders AJ	Hill DM	Atkins MN	Johnson SA			Lister SH	Heyes D	Money R	Birch A							
R1/1	Aug 18	HARTLEPOOL UNITED	3-1 Hill, Nicol, Russell (p)	1613	1	2	3	4	5	6	7	8		10	11		9													
R1/2	26	Hartlepool United	1-0 Johnson	872	1	2	3	4	5	6	7	8		10	11		9													
R2/1	Sep 23	Leicester City	1-2 Flounders	7718		2	3				5	7		10		6	9			4	1	11	12							
R2/2	Oct 6	LEICESTER CITY	1-2 Johnson	4031	1	2	12		5		7	8		10		6	9			4		3	11							

Freight Rover Trophy (Associate Members Cup)

	Date	Opponent	Result	Att	Green RR	Russell WM	Longden DP	McLean DJ	Brown AJ	Nicol PJ	Dixon KL	Harle D	Daws A	Flounders AJ	Hill DM	Atkins MN	Johnson SA		Stevenson AJ	Lister SH	Heyes D	Money R		Taylor K						Johnson P
PR	Oct 13	GRIMSBY TOWN	2-0 Dixon, Stevenson	1710		2	11				7	8		10		3	9		12	5	1	6		4						
PR	Nov 24	Halifax Town	0-3	686		2	3			6	4	8	9	10		11	12			5	1									
Po	Dec 15	Grimsby Town	2-1 Harle, Flounders	970			3			5	7	8	11	10			9		2		1	6		4						
R2	Jan 19	Mansfield Town	0-1	3637			3				7	8	9	10	12	6	14			11	5			2		4				1

SEASON 1986-87
Back: Johnson, Lister, Whitehead, Ferry, Nicol, Hawley
Middle: Birch, Travis, Atkins, Money, Gregory, Hunter, Stevenson, Broddle, Longden
Front: Russell, Cammack, Green (Asst. Manager), Barlow (Manager), McLoughlin (Physio), McLean, Hill

SEASON 1987-88
Back: Birch, Richardson, Harle, Russell, Flounders, McLean, Broddle, Longden, Daws
Middle: Green (Asst. Manager), Talbot, Mountain, Huxford, Stevenson, Nicol,
Atkins, Shaw, Dunnill, Young, McLoughlin (Physio)
Front: Money, Hayes, Johnson, Brown, Lister, Green, Hill

1988/89 4th in Division 4

#		Date	Opponent	Res	Scorers	Att	Musselwhite PS	Longden DP	Rumble P	Taylor K	Lister SH	Brown AJ	Hodkinson AJ	Winter J	Shearer DJ	Flounders AJ	Cowling DR	Daws A	Stevenson AJ	Richardson IP	Money R	Smalley PT	Harle D	Hamilton IR	Brown DJ	Nicol PJ	Cork D	Cotton P	Alexander G
1	Aug	27	HEREFORD UNITED	3-1	Cowling, Daws, Taylor	3663	1	2	3	4	5	6	7	8	9	10	11	12											
2	Sep	3	Crewe Alexandra	2-3	Flounders, Lister (p)	1514	1	2		4	5	6	7	8		10	11	9	3	12									
3		10	GRIMSBY TOWN	1-1	Lister	6037	1	2	3	4	5	6	7	8		10	11	9											
4		17	York City	2-1	Daws 2	2735	1	2	3	4	5		7	8		10	11	9	6										
5		20	CARLISLE UNITED	1-1	Flounders	3113	1	2	3	4	5	6	7			10	11	9	8	12	14								
6		24	Exeter City	2-2	Daws, Rumble	1876	1	2	3	4	5	6	7			10	11	9	8	12									
7	Oct	1	SCARBOROUGH	0-3		4167	1	3		4	5	6	7			10		9		11		2	8						
8		5	Lincoln City	0-1		5443	1	3		4	5	12	7			10		9	6	11		2	8						
9		8	Colchester United	2-1	Flounders, Richardson	1299	1	12	3	4	5	11	7			10		9	6	14		2	8						
10		15	CAMBRIDGE UNITED	1-0	Taylor	3514	1	3		4	5	11	7			10		9	6			2	8						
11		22	Rochdale	0-1		2250	1	3		4	5	6	7			10	11	9				2	8						
12		25	WREXHAM	3-1	Daws, Hodkinson, Flounders	2999	1	3		4	5		7			10	11	9	6			2	8						
13		29	Peterborough United	2-1	Hodkinson, Harle (p)	3532	1	3			5		7			10	11	9	6		4	2	8						
14	Nov	5	BURNLEY	2-1	Flounders, Lister	6358	1	3			5		7			10	11	9	6		4	2	8						
15		8	Rotherham United	3-3	Flounders, Lister, Hodkinson	5923	1	3			5		7			10	11	9	6		4	2	8						
16		12	LEYTON ORIENT	2-2	Daws 2	4239	1	3		12	5		7			10	11	9	6	14	4	2	8						
17		26	TORQUAY UNITED	1-0	Daws	3359	1	3		4	5	12	7			10	11	9	6			2	8						
18	Dec	3	Darlington	3-3	Smalley, Daws, Lister	1745	1	3		4	5	11	7			10		9	6			2	8						
19		17	Doncaster Rovers	2-2	Hodkinson, Flounders	3381	1	3		4	5	6	7			10	11	9		12		2	8						
20		26	HARTLEPOOL UNITED	1-1	Harle (p)	4595	1	3		4	5	6	7			10	11	9	12			2	8	14					
21		31	TRANMERE ROVERS	0-1		4154	1	3		4	5	6	7			10	11	9	14			2	8	12					
22	Jan	2	Halifax Town	1-5	Hamilton	2650	1	3		4	5	6	7			12		9	11			2	8	10					
23		7	Stockport County	2-1	Flounders, Daws	2656		3		4	5		7			10	14	9	6			2	8	11	1	12			
24		14	CREWE ALEXANDRA	2-2	Daws 2	4032		12		4	5	14	7			10	3	9	6			2	8	11	1				
25		21	Hereford United	2-1	Hodkinson, Daws	2024		3		4		6	7			10	8	9				2		11	1	5			
26		28	YORK CITY	4-2	Smith(og), Brown A, Daws 2	4196		3		4		6	7			10	8	9				2		11	1	5			
27	Feb	4	Carlisle United	3-0	Lister, Taylor (p), Flounders	2627		3		4	7	6				10	8	9				2		11	1	5			
28		11	EXETER CITY	2-0	Lister, Cowling	4102	1			4	7	6				10	8	9	3			2		11		5			
29		18	COLCHESTER UNITED	2-3	Lister, Nicol	4286	1			4	7	6	12			10	8	9	3			2		11		5	14		
30		25	Cambridge United	3-0	Taylor, Flounders, Daws	2563	1			4	7	6	3			10	8	9				2		11		5			
31		28	Wrexham	0-2		2609	1			4	7	6	5			10	8	9				2		11		12			
32	Mar	4	ROCHDALE	4-0	Daws 2, Brown A, Hodkinson	4098	1	3		4	7	6	5			10	8	9				2		11		14	12		
33		11	Burnley	1-0	Lister	6813	1	3			7	6				10	8	9				2		11		5	4		
34		14	PETERBOROUGH UTD.	3-0	Flounders 3	3983	1	3			7	6				10	8	9				2		11		5	4		
35		18	Grimsby Town	1-1	Flounders	9796	1	3		12	7	6				10	8	9				2		11		5	4		
36		25	HALIFAX TOWN	0-0		4591	1	3		4	7	6	12			10	8	9				2		11		5			
37		27	Hartlepool United	2-0	Flounders, Daws	1923	1	3		4		6	7			10	8	9				2		11		5	12		
38	Apr	1	DONCASTER ROVERS	2-1	Taylor (p), Hodkinson	5334	1	3		4		6	7			10	8	9				2		11		5	12		
39		4	STOCKPORT COUNTY	1-1	Taylor (p)	3958	1	3		4			7			10	8	9	6			2		11		5	14		
40		7	Tranmere Rovers	1-2	Daws	10465	1	3		4		12				10	8	9	6		7	2		11		5	14		
41		15	Scarborough	0-1		4456	1	3		4		6	7			10	8	9				2		11		5	12		
42		22	LINCOLN CITY	0-0		5729	1	3		4			7			10	8	9				2		11		5	6		
43		28	Torquay United	2-0	Daws, Hodkinson	2544	1	3		4			7			10	8	9	12			2		11		5	6		
44	May	1	ROTHERHAM UNITED	0-0		8775	1	3		4			7			10		9	8	12		2		11		5	6		
45		6	DARLINGTON	5-1	Daws 3, Taylor, Flounders	5296	1	3		4			7			10	8	9				2		11		5	6		
46		13	Leyton Orient	1-4	Taylor	6366	1	3		4			7			10	8	9				2		11		5	6		
					Apps		41	41	8	41	34	32	41	4	1	46	39	46	26	9	6	39	18	27	5	23	15	1	0
					Goals				1	8	9	2	8			16	2	24		1		1	2	1		1			

One own goal

Play Offs

		Date	Opponent	Res	Scorers	Att	Mus	Lon		Tay			Hod			Flo	Cow	DaA	Ste	Ric		Sma		Ham		Nic	Cor	Cot	
SF1	May	21	Wrexham	1-3	Cowling	5449	1	3		4			7			10	8	9				2		11		5	6	12	
SF2		24	WREXHAM	0-2		5516	1	3		4			7			10	8	9	14	12		2		11		5	6		

F.A. Cup

		Date	Opponent	Res	Scorers	Att	Mus	Lon		Tay	Lis	BrA	Hod			Flo	Cow	DaA	Ste	Ric		Sma	Har						
R1	Nov	19	Blackpool	1-2	Harle (p)	3976	1	3		4	5	14	7			10	11	9	6	12		2	8						

Littlewoods Challenge Cup (F.L. Cup)

		Date	Opponent	Res	Scorers	Att	Mus	Lon		Tay	Lis	BrA	Hod			Flo	Cow	DaA	Ste	Ric	Mon	Sma	Har						
R1/1	Aug	30	HUDDERSFIELD TOWN	3-2	Flounders, Lister, Hodkinson	3820	1	2		4	5	6	7			10	11	9	3	12			8						
R1/2	Sep	6	Huddersfield Town	2-2	Flounders 2	4237	1	2		4	5	6	7			10	11	9	3				8						
R2/1		27	CHELSEA	4-1	Daws 2, Stevenson, Taylor	5061	1	3		4	5	6	7			10		9	2	11			8						
R2/2	Oct	12	Chelsea	2-2	Harle (p), Flounders	5814	1	3		4	5	11	7			10		9	6	12		2	8						
R3	Nov	2	Bradford City	1-1	Daws	8011	1	3			5		7			10	11	9	6		4	2	8						
rep		22	BRADFORD CITY	0-1		5793	1	3		4	5	12	7			10	11	9	6			2	8						

R1/2 a.e.t.

Sherpa Van Trophy (Associate Members Cup)

		Date	Opponent	Res	Scorers	Att	Mus	Lon		Tay	Lis	BrA	Hod	Win		Flo		DaA	Ste		Mon	Sma	Har						Ale
PR	Dec	6	HALIFAX TOWN	1-2	Harle (p)	1547	1	3		4	5	11	7			10		9	6			2	8						12
PR		13	Huddersfield Town	0-1		2216	1	3			5	4	7	12		10		9	6		11	2	8						

SEASON 1988-89

Back: Money (Youth Dev. Off.) , Buxton (Manager), Mountain, Stevenson, Thompson, Musselwhite, Nicol, Lister, Brown, Shearer, Green (Asst. Man), McLouchlin (Physio)
Front: Flounders, Cowling, Longden, Daws, Harle, Richardson, Taylor

SEASON 1989-90

Back: Brookes, Sykes, Barbrook, Smalley, Stevenson, Litchfield,
Musselwhite, Thatcher, Nicol, Hall, Cotton, Flounders, Cox
Middle: Alexander, McGlinchey, Longden, Cowling, Tucker, Lister, Marshall, Taylor, Hodkinson, Daws, Creaton
Front: McCormick, Godfrey, Evans, Gibbs, Lelliott, Spooner

1989/90 11th in Division 4

#	Date	Opponent	Score	Scorers	Att	Litchfield P	Smalley PT	Longden DP	Taylor K	Knight II	Tucker G	Hodkinson AJ	Cowling DR	Cotton P	Flounders AJ	Marshall G	Nicol PJ	Money R	Butler MC	Daws A	Hamilton IR	Musselwhite PS	Stevenson AJ	Lillis MA	Lister SH	Ward PT	Hall RA	Bramhall J	Alexander G	Cox NJ
1	Aug 19	Lincoln City	0-1		4504	1	2	3	4	5	6	7	8	9	10	11	12													
2	26	ROCHDALE	0-1		2808	1	2	12	4	3	6		8		10	11	5	7	9											
3	Sep 2	Gillingham	3-0	Taylor (p), Flounders 2	3467		2	3	4		6	7	8		10	11	5					1	9	12						
4	9	SCARBOROUGH	0-1		3330		2	3	4		6	7			10	11	5					1	9	8						
5	16	Peterborough United	1-1	Taylor	4350		2	3	4		6	7			10	11	5		9			1	8	12						
6	23	EXETER CITY	5-4	Lillis 2, Hamilton 2, Taylor	2935		2	3	4		6	7	12		10	11	5				8	1		9						
7	26	TORQUAY UNITED	2-0	Flounders, Lillis (p)	3242		2	3	4		6	7			10	11	5				8	1		9						
8	30	Aldershot	2-4	Lillis, Tucker	1892		2	3	4		6	7	14		10	11	5			12	8	1		9						
9	Oct 7	Hartlepool United	2-3	Lillis, Daws	1823	1	2	3	4		6	7	12		14	11	5			10	8			9						
10	14	MAIDSTONE UNITED	1-0	Lister (p)	3165	1	2	3	4				7			12	11			10	8		6	9	5					
11	17	Carlisle United	1-0	Lillis	4793	1	2	3	4		12		7			14	11			10	8		6	9	5					
12	21	COLCHESTER UNITED	4-0	Stevenson, Daws, Hamilton, Taylor	3254	1	2	3	4				7			11				10	8		6	9	5					
13	28	Cambridge United	3-5	Marshall, Daws, Hamilton	2395	1	2	3	4				7			14	11			10	8		6	9	5	12				
14	31	YORK CITY	1-1	Flounders	3800	1	2	3				5	7			10	11			9	8		6			4				
15	Nov 4	Doncaster Rovers	2-1	Daws, Flounders	3374	1		3					2			10	11			9	8		6	7		4				
16	11	BURNLEY	3-0	Marshall, Ward (p), Hamilton	4745	1		3				9	2			10	11				8		6	7		4				
17	25	Stockport County	2-4	Ward, Flounders	3259	1	12	3				9	2			10	11				8		6	7		4				
18	Dec 2	SOUTHEND UNITED	1-1	Ward	3714	1	2	3	8			9			14	10	11	5					6	7	12	4				
19	16	Hereford United	2-1	Nicol, Lillis	1924	1	2	3	8			4			14	12	11	5		9	10			7	5					
20	26	GRIMSBY TOWN	2-2	Daws, Marshall	8384	1	2	3	8			4				12	11	6		9	10			7				5		
21	30	CHESTERFIELD	0-1		5006		2	3	8			4				9	11	5		12	10	1		6	7					
22	Jan 1	Wrexham	0-0		1887		2	3	4			7	11			10		6		9	8	1		5						
23	6	HALIFAX TOWN	1-1	Taylor	3051		2	3	4				11	6		10	7			12	8	1		5	9					
24	13	Rochdale	0-3		1781		2	3	4				8	6		10	7			9	11	1		5						
25	20	LINCOLN CITY	1-1	Lillis	3830		2	3	14				8	6		10	7			9	11	1		12		4		5		
26	27	Scarborough	0-0		2329		2	3	6				8			7				9	11	1		10		4		5		
27	Feb 10	PETERBOROUGH UTD.	0-0		3188		2	3	6				8		12	7				9	11	1		10		4		5		
28	13	GILLINGHAM	0-0		2226		2	3	6				8		9	7				12	11	1		10		4		5		
29	16	Southend United	0-0		3154		2	3	6				8		10					9	11	1	12	7		4		5		
30	24	STOCKPORT COUNTY	5-0	Lillis 2, Daws 2, Ward	3280		2	3	6				8		10					9	11	1	12	7		4		5		
31	Mar 3	Halifax Town	1-0	Daws	1793		2	3					7	8						9	11	1		6		4		5		
32	6	ALDERSHOT	3-2	Lillis, Hamilton, Flounders	3202		2	3				8			10	12				9	11	1		6	7	4		5		
33	10	Torquay United	3-0	Daws, Flounders, Lillis	1935		2	3				6		8	10					9	11	1	12	7		4		5		
34	17	HARTLEPOOL UNITED	0-1		3868		2	3	14			6		8	10	12	5			9	11	1		7		4				
35	21	Maidstone United	1-1	Flounders	1299		2	3	6				8		10	7				9	11	1				4		5		
36	24	CARLISLE UNITED	2-3	Flounders, Lillis (p)	3406		2	3	6				8	9	10	7					11	1		12		4		5		
37	28	Exeter City	0-1		5805		2	3	6				8	9	10						11	1		7		4		5		
38	31	Colchester United	0-1		2920		2	3	6				8	9	10	14				12	11	1		7		4		5		
39	Apr 7	CAMBRIDGE UNITED	1-1	Taylor	2486		2	3	6					12	10					9	11	1	8	7		4		5		
40	10	York City	1-0	Taylor	2232		2	3	6						9	10					11	1	8			4		5		
41	14	WREXHAM	3-1	Flounders 2 (1 p), Taylor	2820		2	3	6						9	10	4				11	1	8					5		
42	17	Grimsby Town	1-2	Flounders	11894		2	3	6						9	10	4				11	1	8					5		
43	21	HEREFORD UNITED	3-3	Flounders 2 (1 p), Pejic (og)	2247		2	3	6				7	4	9	10				8	11	1	12					5		
44	28	Burnley	1-0	Cotton	3902	1	2	3	6				7	9	10					8	11					4				
45	May 1	Chesterfield	1-1	Daws	3469	1	2	3	6	7				9	10					8	11					4		5		
46	5	DONCASTER ROVERS	4-1	Flounders 3, Daws	3020	1	2	3	6	7				9	10					8	11					4		5		
			Apps			17	44	46	39	2	15	21	32	17	44	34	18	1	2	33	43	29	24	29	6	25	1	21	0	0
			Goals						8		1		1	1	18	3	1			11	6		1	13	1	4				

One own goal

F.A. Cup

	Date	Opponent	Score	Scorers	Att	Litchfield P	Smalley PT	Longden DP	Taylor K	Knight II	Tucker G	Hodkinson AJ	Cowling DR	Cotton P	Flounders AJ	Marshall G	Nicol PJ	Money R	Butler MC	Daws A	Hamilton IR	Musselwhite PS	Stevenson AJ	Lillis MA	Lister SH	Ward PT	Hall RA	Bramhall J	Alexander G	Cox NJ
R1	Nov 18	MATLOCK TOWN	4-1	Lillis 3, Hodkinson	4307	1	12	3				9	2		10	11	5				8			6	7		4				
R2	Dec 9	BURNLEY	2-2	Taylor 2	5698	1	12	3	8			9	2		10	11								6	7	5	4				
rep	12	Burnley	1-1	Daws	7682	1	2	3	10			12			14	11				9	8		6	7	5	4				
rep2	18	Burnley	0-5		7429	1	2	3	8			4			12	14	11	6		9	10			7	5					

R2 replay a.e.t.

Littlewoods Challenge Cup (F.L. Cup)

	Date	Opponent	Score	Scorers	Att	Litchfield P	Smalley PT	Longden DP	Taylor K	Knight II	Tucker G	Hodkinson AJ	Cowling DR	Cotton P	Flounders AJ	Marshall G	Nicol PJ	Money R	Butler MC	Daws A	Hamilton IR	Musselwhite PS	Stevenson AJ	Lillis MA	Lister SH	Ward PT	Hall RA	Bramhall J	Alexander G	Cox NJ
R1/1	Aug 23	Scarborough	0-2		2259	1	2	3	4		6		8	9	10	11	5	7						12						
R1/2	29	SCARBOROUGH	1-1	Flounders	1853		2	3	4		6	7	8		10	11	5		9			1								

Leyland DAF Trophy (Associate Members Cup)

	Date	Opponent	Score	Scorers	Att	Litchfield P	Smalley PT	Longden DP	Taylor K	Knight II	Tucker G	Hodkinson AJ	Cowling DR	Cotton P	Flounders AJ	Marshall G	Nicol PJ	Money R	Butler MC	Daws A	Hamilton IR	Musselwhite PS	Stevenson AJ	Lillis MA	Lister SH	Ward PT	Hall RA	Bramhall J	Alexander G	Cox NJ
PR	Nov 7	SCARBOROUGH	1-0	Flounders	1496	1		3				9	2		10	11	5				8			6	7		4				
PR	Dec 22	Carlisle United	1-1	Taylor	1942		2	3	8				7	10						9	11	1	6				5		4	12	
R1	Jan 9	Tranmere Rovers	1-2	Cotton	2766		2	3	4			14	11	6	10	7	12			9	8	1	5								

272

1990/91 — 8th in Division 4

#	Date		Opponent	Score	Scorers	Att	Litchfield P	Longden DP	Cowling DR	Ward PT	Hicks SJ	Hall RA	Taylor K	Hamilton IR	Lillis MA	Flounders AJ	Marshall G	Miller I	Daws A	Smalley PT	Cotton P	Musselwhite PS	Cox NJ	Bramhall J	Powell G	Stevenson AJ	Joyce JP	Humphries G	Hill DM	Hine M	Lister SH	Alexander G	Tucker G
1	Aug	25	BLACKPOOL	2-0	Flounders, Hamilton	3024	1	2	3	4	5	6	7	8	9	10	11																
2	Sep	1	Aldershot	2-3	Flounders (p), Daws	2001	1	2	3	4	5	6	7	12		10	11	8	9	14													
3		8	PETERBOROUGH UTD.	1-1	Flounders	3028	1	2	3	4	5			8	9	10	11	7			6												
4		15	Maidstone United	1-6	Lillis	1778	1	2	3	4	5		11	8	9	10		7			6												
5		18	Torquay United	1-1	Lillis	2811	1	2	3	4	5	6	12	8	9	10	11	7		14													
6		22	LINCOLN CITY	2-1	Hicks, Hall	2844	1	2	3	4	5	6	12	8	9	10	11	7															
7		29	CARDIFF CITY	0-2		2573	1	2	3	4	5	6	12	8	9	10	11	7	14														
8	Oct	2	Walsall	0-3		3676	1	2	3	4	5	6		8		10	11	7	9														
9		6	Halifax Town	0-0		1468		2	3	4	5	6	8	12	9	10						1	7	11									
10		13	GILLINGHAM	1-0	Hall	2357		2		4	5	6	8	3		10			9			1	7	11									
11		20	SCARBOROUGH	3-0	Daws 2, Taylor	2786		2		4	5	6	8	3		10			9			1	7	11									
12		23	Chesterfield	0-1		3371		2		4	5	6	8	3		10		14	9		12	1	7	11									
13		27	Darlington	0-1		3852		2		4	5	6	8	3		10			9			1	7	11									
14	Nov	3	STOCKPORT COUNTY	3-0	Lillis, Flounders (p), Daws	2826		2		4	5	6	8	3		10			9			1	7	11									
15		10	ROCHDALE	2-1	Flounders, Cotton	3070		2			5	6	8	3		10		12	9		4	1	7	11									
16		24	Wrexham	0-1		1333		2			5	6	8	3		10					4	1	7	11	9	12							
17	Dec	1	York City	2-2	Hall, Powell	2495		2		10	5	6	8	3		12			14		4	1	7	11	9								
18		15	DONCASTER ROVERS	1-1	Flounders	3963		2	11	4	5	6	14	3		10		9			8	1	7		12								
19		22	Hereford United	0-2		2218		2	11		5	6	4	12	3	10					8	1	7		9								
20		29	CARLISLE UNITED	2-0	Flounders (p), Lillis	2971		2	11		5		4	9	3	10					8	1	7	6									
21	Jan	1	Burnley	1-1	Lillis	8557		2	11	12	5		4	9	3	10		14			8	1	7	6									
22		12	ALDERSHOT	6-2	Cowling, Flounders 3(1p), Hamilton, Lillis	2727		2	11	8	5	6	4	9	3	10					12	1	7										
23		19	Blackpool	1-3	Cowling	2494		2	11	8	5	6	4	9		10			12		3	1	7										
24		26	MAIDSTONE UNITED	2-2	Ward, Daws	2703		2	11	3	5	6	4	9		10			8			1	7										
25	Feb	2	TORQUAY UNITED	3-0	Cowling, Cox, Flounders	2502		2	11	3	5	6		8		10			9		4	1	7				12						
26		23	Rochdale	1-2	Daws	1832		2	11	4	5			8	3	10			9			1					6	7					
27		26	HARTLEPOOL UNITED	2-1	Taylor, Lillis	2220		2		4	5		11	8	3	10			9			1					6	7					
28	Mar	2	YORK CITY	2-1	Ward, Daws	2860		2		4	5		11	8	3	10			9			1					6	7					
29		5	NORTHAMPTON T	3-0	Daws, Chard(og), Lillis	2852		2		4	5		11	8	3	10			9			1					6	7					
30		8	Doncaster Rovers	3-2	Flounders 2, Daws	4015		2		4	5		11	8	3	10			9			1					7	6					
31		12	WALSALL	1-0	Daws	3352		2		4	5		11	8	3	10			9			1					7	6					
32		16	Cardiff City	0-1		2873		2		4	5		11	8	3	10			9			1					7	6					
33		19	Gillingham	1-1	Flounders	2324		2		4	5		11	8	3	10			9			1					7	6					
34		23	HALIFAX TOWN	4-4	Flounders (p), Taylor, Humphries, Lillis	3134		2			4		11	8	3	10			9		12	1					7	6					
35		30	Northampton Town	1-2	Taylor	3728		2			5		11	8	12	10			9			1					7	6	3	4			
36	Apr	1	HEREFORD UNITED	3-0	Flounders 2, Daws	3001		2			5		11	8	12	10			9			1					7	6	3	4			
37		6	Carlisle United	3-0	Hill, Hine, Dalziel(og)	1909		2			5		11	8		10			9			1					7	6	3	4			
38		9	Hartlepool United	0-2		2840		2			5		11	8	12	10			9			1					7	6	3	4			
39		13	BURNLEY	1-3	Hine	4449		2			5		11	8	12	10			9	14		1					7	6	3	4			
40		17	Lincoln City	2-1	Flounders 2 (1p)	3212		2			5		11		8	10			9			1					12	7	3	4	6		
41		20	Scarborough	1-3	Flounders (p)	2026		2			5		11	12	8	10			9			1					14	7	3	4	6		
42		23	Peterborough United	0-0		5774		2			5		11	8		10			9			1					7		3	4	6		
43		27	CHESTERFIELD	3-0	Daws, Flounders 2	3046		2			5		11	8	3	10			9			1					7			4	6	12	
44	May	4	DARLINGTON	2-1	Flounders, Daws	5769		2			5		11	8	3	10			9			1					7			4	6		
45		7	WREXHAM	2-0	Daws, Lillis	3572		2			5		11	8	3	10			9			1					7			4	6		
46		11	Stockport County	0-5		6212		2			5		11	8	3	10			9			1					12	7		14	4	6	
			Apps				8	46	18	30	46	21	42	34	39	46	7	12	34	3	15	38	17	11	4	9	21	10	9	12	7	1	0
			Goals						3	2	1	3	4	2	10	23			14		1		1		1			1	1	2			

Two own goals

Play Offs

	Date		Opponent	Score	Scorers	Att																										
SF1	May	19	BLACKPOOL	1-1	Lillis	6536		2			5		11	12	3	10			9			1					7		8	4	6		
SF2		22	Blackpool	1-2	Hill	7596		2			5		11	4	3	10			9			1				6	7		8	12			

F.A. Cup

	Date		Opponent	Score	Scorers	Att																										
R1	Nov	17	Rochdale	1-1	Hicks	3259		2			5	6	8	3		10		9			4	1	7	11									12
rep		20	ROCHDALE	2-1	Flounders, Lillis	3761		2			5	6	8	3		10		9			4	1	7	11	12								
R2	Dec	8	TRANMERE ROVERS	3-2	Ward, Lillis, Flounders	3576		2	11	4	5	6		12	3	10		9			8	1	7										
R3	Jan	5	Brighton & Hove Albion	2-3	Flounders (p), Bramhall	7785		2	11	12	5		4	9	3	10		14			8	1	7	6									

R1 replay a.e.t.

Rumbelows Cup (F.L. Cup)

	Date		Opponent	Score	Scorers	Att																										
1/1	Aug	28	Carlisle United	0-1		2531	1	2	3	4	5	6	7	8		10	11		9														
1/2	Sep	4	CARLISLE UNITED	1-1	Lillis	2130	1	2	3	4	5	6		8	9	10	11	7	12														

Leyland DAF Trophy (Associate Members Cup)

	Date		Opponent	Score	Scorers	Att																										
PR	Nov	27	Doncaster Rovers	0-1		1394		2		12	5	6	8			3	10				4	1	7				9	11					
PR	Dec	18	CHESTERFIELD	3-1	Lillis 2, Taylor	859		2	11		5	6	4		3	10		9			8	1	7				12						
R1	Jan	15	Doncaster Rovers	0-0		1635		2	11	8	5	6	4	9		10		12			3	1	7										
R2		29	PRESTON NORTH END	1-4	Flounders	2155		2	11	3	5		4	9		10		8			12	1	7										6

R1 won on penalties (4-3) a.e.t.

273

1991/92   5th in Division 4

#	Date	Opponent	Score	Scorers	Att	Musselwhite PS	Batch N	Joyce JP	Longden DP	Hine M	Hicks SJ	Humphries G	Alexander G	Hamilton IR	Daws A	Buckley IW	Helliwell I	Martin DS	Lister SH	Hyde GS	Hill DM	White IG	Stevenson AJ	Whitehead PM	Marples C	Samways M	Elliott MS
1	Aug 17	Gillingham	0-4		3480		1	2	3	4	5	6	7	8	9	10	11	12									
2	24	DONCASTER ROVERS	3-2	Helliwell, Alexander, Daws	3505	1		2	3	4	5	6	7	8	9	10	11										
3	31	Blackpool	1-2	Buckley	3273	1		2	3		5	6	7	8	9	10	11	4	12	14							
4	Sep 3	SCARBOROUGH	1-1	Joyce	3185	1		2	3	4	5	6	7	8	9	10	11										
5	7	MAIDSTONE UNITED	2-0	Hill, Daws	2738	1		2	3	4	5	6	7	8	9		11		12	14	10						
6	14	Chesterfield	1-0	Humphries	3338	1		2	3		5	6	7	8	9		11	4		12	10						
7	17	Barnet	2-3	Humphries, White	3094	1		2	3			6	7	8	9		11	4	5		10	12					
8	21	CREWE ALEXANDRA	1-0	Hamilton	3021	1		2	3			6	7	8	9			4	5	12	10	11					
9	28	Wrexham	0-4		1635	1		2	3	14		6	7	8	9	12	11	4	5		10						
10	Oct 5	HEREFORD UNITED	1-1	Daws (p)	2384	1		2	3	8		6	14		9	7	11	4	5		10		12				
11	12	Carlisle United	0-0		1988	1		2	3			6	12	8	9	7	11	4	5		10						
12	19	Northampton Town	1-0	Helliwell	2575	1		2	3			6		8	9	7	11	4	5		10						
13	26	MANSFIELD TOWN	1-4	Daws	3610	1		2	3		5			8	9	7	11	4			10		6				
14	Nov 2	Cardiff City	2-2	Hill, Own goal (Pike)	2356	1		2	3		5		7	8	9	12	11	4		6	10						
15	5	ROCHDALE	6-2	*see below	2331	1		2	3		5		7	8	9		11	4		6	10						
16	9	ROTHERHAM UNITED	1-0	Daws	4175	1		2	3		5		7	8	9		11	4		6	10						
17	23	Lincoln City	2-4	Martin, Alexander	3078	1			3		5		2	8	9	7	11	4		6	10		1				
18	30	YORK CITY	1-0	Hamilton	2887			2	3		5		7	8	9		11	4		6	10		1				
19	Dec 14	Burnley	1-1	Own goal (Pender)	8419			2	3		5		7	8	9		11	4		6	10	12	1				
20	20	Doncaster Rovers	2-1	Humphries, Alexander	1825			2	3		5	6	7	8	9		11	4		12	10	14	1				
21	26	GILLINGHAM	2-0	White, Martin	3883			2	3		5	6	7	8	9			4			10	11	1				
22	28	BLACKPOOL	2-1	White 2	4271			2	3		5	6	7	8	9			4		12	10	11	1				
23	Jan 1	Scarborough	1-4	White	2237			2	3		5	6	7	8	9	12		4	14		10	11	1				
24	18	Halifax Town	4-1	White 3, Hamilton	1232			2			5	6	7	8	9		11	4		3	10		1				
25	25	WALSALL	1-1	White	3165			2	3		5	6	7	8			11	4			10	9	1				
26	Feb 8	Mansfield Town	3-1	Alexander, Hamilton (p), White	3496	1		2	3			6	7	8		5	11	4			10	9					
27	11	York City	0-3		2255	1		2	3	14	5		7	8		6	11	4	12		10	9					
28	15	BURNLEY	2-2	Helliwell, White	5303	1		2	3	12	5		7	8	14	6	11	4			10	9		1			
29	Mar 3	HALIFAX TOWN	1-0	Buckley	2448	1		2	3		5		7	8	12	10	11	4	6		9						
30	7	Walsall	1-2	Buckley	2722	1		2	3		5		7	8	12	10	11	4	6	14	9						
31	10	Rochdale	0-2		2036	1		2	3	7				8	9	10	11	4	6		5	12					
32	14	CARDIFF CITY	1-0	Buckley	2766	1		2	3	7			12	8	9	10	11	4	6		5	14					
33	21	Rotherham United	0-5		4528	1		2	3		5		14	8	9	10	11	4	6		7	12					
34	28	LINCOLN CITY	0-2		3297	1		2	14		5	6	7	8	9	10	11	4			3	12					
35	31	CHESTERFIELD	2-0	Helliwell, Hamilton (p)	2224			2				6	7	8		10	11				3	9			1		5
36	Apr 4	Maidstone United	1-0	Hamilton	1237			2	3			6	7	8		10	11				4	9			1		5
37	11	BARNET	1-1	Hamilton (p)	3361			2	3			6	7	8	12	10	11				4	9			1		5
38	14	NORTHAMPTON T	3-0	Hill, Buckley, Daws	2286			2	3			6	12	8	9	10	11	7			4				1		5
39	18	Crewe Alexandra	1-1	Helliwell	3313			2	3			6		8	9	10	11	7			4				1		5
40	20	WREXHAM	3-1	Joyce, Hamilton (p), Buckley	2900			2	3			6		8		10	11	7			4	9			1		5
41	25	Hereford United	2-1	Helliwell 2	1587			2	3			6	12	8	9	10	11	7			4				1		5
42	May 2	CARLISLE UNITED	4-0	Elliott, Daws, Hill, Helliwell	3851			2	3			6		8	9	10	11	7			4				1		5

Scorers in game 15: Hamilton, A Brown (og), Lister, Helliwell, Alexander, Hill

	Mus	Bat	Joy	Lon	Hin	Hic	Hum	Ale	Ham	Daw	Buc	Hel	Mar	Lis	Hyd	Hil	Whi	Ste	Wht	MarC	Sam	Eli
Apps	24	1	40	41	10	21	32	36	41	36	28	39	37	19	8	37	22	2	8	1	8	8
Goals			2				3	5	9	7	6	9	2	1		5	11					1

Three own goals

Play Offs

	Date	Opponent	Score	Scorers	Att	Joy	Lon	Hum	Ale	Ham	Daw	Buc	Hel	Mar	Hil	Whi	Sam	Eli
SF1	May 10	Crewe Alexandra	2-2	Helliwell 2	6083	2	3	6	12	8	9	10	11	7	4		1	5
SF2	13	CREWE ALEXANDRA	2-0	Martin, Hamilton	7938	2	3	6		8	9	10	11	7	4		1	5
F	23	BLACKPOOL	##	Daws	22741	2	3	6	14	8	9	10	11	7	4	12	1	5

Final lost on penalties (4-3) a.e.t.

F.A. Cup

	Date	Opponent	Score	Scorers	Att	Mus	Lon	Hic	Ale	Ham	Daw	Buc	Hel	Mar	Lis	Hil	Whi	Ste
R1	Nov 16	ROTHERHAM UNITED	1-1	Helliwell	4511	1	3	5	2	8	9	7	11	4	6	12	10	14
rep	26	Rotherham United	3-3	Helliwell, Daws, White	4829	1	3	5	2	8	9	7	11	4	6	12	10	14

Lost on penalties (7-6) a.e.t.

Rumbelows Cup (F.L. Cup)

	Date	Opponent	Score	Scorers	Att	Mus	Joy	Lon	Hin	Hic	Hum	Ale	Ham	Daw	Buc	Hel	Mar	Lis	Hyd	Hil	Ste
R1/1	Aug 20	Wrexham	0-1		1621	1	2	3	4	5	6	7	8	9	10	11			12		
R1/2	27	WREXHAM	3-0	Humphries, Alexander, Helliwell	2125	1	2	3	4	5	6	7	8	9	10	11		12			
R2/1	Sep 24	LEEDS UNITED	0-0		8392	1	2	3			6	7	8	9		11	4	5		10	
R2/2	Oct 8	Leeds United	0-3		14558	1	2	3	14			12	8	9	7	11	4	5		10	6

Autoglass Trophy (Associate Members Cup)

	Date	Opponent	Score	Scorers	Att	Mus	Joy	Lon	Hic	Hum	Ale	Ham	Daw	Buc	Hel	Mar	Lis	Hil	Whi	Ste	Wht
PR	Oct 22	BURY	1-3	Hamilton	1122	1	2	3		6	14	8	9	7	11	4	5	12	10		
PR	Jan 7	Halifax Town	2-0	White, Alexander	646		2	3	5		7	8	9			4	6	10		11	1
R1	21	Hartlepool United	1-2	Hamilton	1351		2		5	6	7	8		12	11	4		9	3	10	1

274

SEASON 1990-91

Back: Buxton (Manager), Green (Asst. Man), Alexander, Cotton, Marshall, Lillis, Lister, Musselwhite, Bramhall, Litchfield, Hall, Hicks, Stevenson, Cox, Ward, Moore (Youth Dev. Off.), McLoughlin (Physio)
Middle: Taylor, Tucker, Hamilton, Daws, Flounders, Cowling, Smalley, Longden
Front: Evans, Spooner, Godfrey, Gibbs, Thatcher, Bell, Lelliott, McCullagh, Creaton

SEASON 1991-92

Back: McLoughlin (Physio), Martin, Alexander, Stevenson, Hyde, Lillis, Musselwhite, Lister, Hick, Humphries, Hamilton, Joyce, Cowling (Youth Team Coach)
Front: Daws, Hine, Goodacre, Moore (Asst. Man), Green (Manager), Buckley, Godfrey, Longden

FINAL LEAGUE TABLES: 1991/92 - 1998/99

Final League Table 1991/92 Division 4

		Pl.	Home W	D	L	F	A	Away W	D	L	F	A	F.	A.	Pts
1	Burnley	42	14	4	3	42	16	11	4	6	37	27	79	43	83
2	Rotherham United	42	12	6	3	38	16	10	5	6	32	21	70	37	77
3	Mansfield Town	42	13	4	4	43	26	10	4	7	32	27	75	53	77
4	Blackpool	42	17	3	1	48	13	5	7	9	23	32	71	45	76
5	SCUNTHORPE U	42	14	5	2	39	18	7	4	10	25	41	64	59	72
6	Crewe Alexandra	42	12	6	3	33	20	8	4	9	33	31	66	51	70
7	Barnet	42	16	1	4	48	23	5	5	11	33	38	81	61	69
8	Rochdale	42	12	6	3	34	22	6	7	8	23	31	57	53	67
9	Cardiff City	42	13	3	5	42	26	4	12	5	24	27	66	53	66
10	Lincoln City	42	9	5	7	21	24	8	6	7	29	20	50	44	62
11	Gillingham	42	12	5	4	41	19	3	7	11	22	34	63	53	57
12	Scarborough	42	12	5	4	39	28	3	7	11	25	40	64	68	57
13	Chesterfield	42	6	7	8	26	28	8	4	9	23	33	49	61	53
14	Wrexham	42	11	4	6	31	26	3	5	13	21	47	52	73	51
15	Walsall	42	5	10	6	28	26	7	3	11	20	32	48	58	49
16	Northampton Town	42	5	9	7	25	23	6	4	11	21	34	46	57	46
17	Hereford United	42	9	4	8	31	24	3	4	14	13	33	44	57	44
18	Maidstone United	42	6	9	6	24	22	2	9	10	21	34	45	56	42
19	York City	42	6	9	6	26	23	2	7	12	16	35	42	58	40
20	Halifax Town	42	7	5	9	23	35	3	3	15	11	40	34	75	38
21	Doncaster Rovers	42	6	2	13	21	35	3	6	12	19	30	40	65	35
22	Carlisle United	42	5	9	7	24	27	2	4	15	17	40	41	67	34

Final League Table 1992/93 Division 3 (Formerly Division 4)

		Pl.	Home W	D	L	F	A	Away W	D	L	F	A	F.	A.	Pts
1	Cardiff City	42	13	7	1	42	20	12	1	8	35	27	77	47	83
2	Wrexham	42	14	3	4	48	26	9	8	4	27	26	75	52	80
3	Barnet	42	16	4	1	45	19	7	6	8	21	29	66	48	79
4	York City	42	13	6	2	41	15	8	6	7	31	30	72	45	75
5	Walsall	42	11	6	4	42	31	11	1	9	34	30	76	61	73
6	Crewe Alexandra	42	13	3	5	47	23	8	4	9	28	33	75	56	70
7	Bury	42	10	7	4	36	19	8	2	11	27	36	63	55	63
8	Lincoln City	42	10	6	5	31	20	8	3	10	26	33	57	53	63
9	Shrewsbury Town	42	11	3	7	36	30	6	8	7	21	22	57	52	62
10	Colchester United	42	13	3	5	38	26	5	2	14	29	50	67	76	59
11	Rochdale	42	10	3	8	38	29	6	7	8	32	41	70	70	58
12	Chesterfield	42	11	3	7	32	28	4	8	9	27	35	59	63	56
13	Scarborough	42	7	7	7	32	30	8	2	11	34	41	66	71	54
14	SCUNTHORPE U	42	8	7	6	38	25	6	5	10	19	29	57	54	54
15	Darlington	42	5	6	10	23	31	7	8	6	25	22	48	53	50
16	Doncaster Rovers	42	6	5	10	22	28	5	9	7	20	29	42	57	47
17	Hereford United	42	7	9	5	31	27	3	6	12	16	33	47	60	45
18	Carlisle United	42	7	5	9	29	27	4	6	11	22	38	51	65	44
19	Torquay United	42	6	4	11	18	26	6	3	12	27	41	45	67	43
20	Northampton Town	42	6	5	10	19	28	5	3	13	29	46	48	74	41
21	Gillingham	42	9	4	8	32	28	0	9	12	16	36	48	64	40
22	Halifax Town	42	3	5	13	20	35	6	4	11	25	33	45	68	36

Final League Table 1993/94 Division 3

		Pl.	Home W	D	L	F	A	Away W	D	L	F	A	F.	A.	Pts
1	Shrewsbury Town	42	10	8	3	28	17	12	5	4	35	22	63	39	79
2	Chester City	42	13	5	3	35	18	8	6	7	34	28	69	46	74
3	Crewe Alexandra	42	12	4	5	45	30	9	6	6	35	31	80	61	73
4	Wycombe Wands.	42	11	6	4	34	21	8	7	6	33	32	67	53	70
5	Preston North End	42	13	5	3	46	23	5	8	8	33	37	79	60	67
6	Torquay United	42	8	10	3	30	24	9	6	6	34	32	64	56	67
7	Carlisle United	42	10	4	7	35	23	8	6	7	22	19	57	42	64
8	Chesterfield	42	8	8	5	32	22	8	6	7	23	26	55	48	62
9	Rochdale	42	10	5	6	38	22	6	7	8	25	29	63	51	60
10	Walsall	42	7	5	9	28	26	10	4	7	20	27	48	53	60
11	SCUNTHORPE U	42	9	7	5	40	26	6	7	8	24	30	64	56	59
12	Mansfield Town	42	9	3	9	28	30	6	7	8	25	32	53	62	55
13	Bury	42	9	6	6	33	22	5	5	11	22	34	55	56	53
14	Scarborough	42	8	4	9	29	28	7	4	10	26	33	55	61	53
15	Doncaster Rovers	42	8	6	7	24	26	6	4	11	20	31	44	57	52
16	Gillingham	42	8	8	5	27	23	4	7	10	17	28	44	51	51
17	Colchester United	42	8	4	9	31	33	5	6	10	25	38	56	71	49
18	Lincoln City	42	7	4	10	26	29	5	7	9	26	34	52	63	47
19	Wigan Athletic	42	6	7	8	33	33	5	5	11	18	37	51	70	45
20	Hereford United	42	6	4	11	34	33	6	2	13	26	46	60	79	42
21	Darlington	42	7	5	9	24	28	3	6	12	18	36	42	64	41
22	Northampton Town	42	6	7	8	25	23	3	4	14	19	43	44	66	38

Final League Table 1994/95 Division 3

		Pl.	Home W	D	L	F	A	Away W	D	L	F	A	F.	A.	Pts
1	Carlisle United	42	14	5	2	34	14	13	5	3	33	17	67	31	91
2	Walsall	42	15	3	3	42	18	9	8	4	33	22	75	40	83
3	Chesterfield	42	11	7	3	26	10	12	5	4	36	27	62	37	81
4	Bury	42	13	7	1	39	13	10	4	7	34	23	73	36	80
5	Preston North End	42	13	3	5	37	17	6	7	8	21	24	58	41	67
6	Mansfield Town	42	10	5	6	45	27	8	6	7	39	32	84	59	65
7	SCUNTHORPE U	42	12	2	7	40	30	6	6	9	28	33	68	63	62
8	Fulham	42	11	5	5	39	22	5	9	7	21	32	60	54	62
9	Doncaster Rovers	42	9	5	7	28	20	8	5	8	30	23	58	43	61
10	Colchester United	42	8	5	8	29	30	8	5	8	27	34	56	64	58
11	Barnet	42	8	7	6	37	27	7	4	10	19	36	56	63	56
12	Lincoln City	42	10	7	4	34	22	5	4	12	20	33	54	55	56
13	Torquay United	42	10	8	3	35	25	4	5	12	19	32	54	57	55
14	Wigan Athletic	42	7	6	8	28	30	7	4	10	25	30	53	60	52
15	Rochdale	42	8	6	7	25	23	4	8	9	19	44	44	67	50
16	Hereford United	42	9	6	6	22	19	3	7	11	23	43	45	62	49
17	Northampton Town	42	8	5	8	25	29	2	9	10	20	38	45	67	44
18	Hartlepool United	42	9	5	7	33	32	2	5	14	10	37	43	69	43
19	Gillingham	42	8	7	6	31	25	2	4	15	15	39	46	64	41
20	Darlington	42	7	5	9	25	24	4	3	14	18	33	43	57	41
21	Scarborough	42	4	7	10	26	31	4	3	14	23	39	49	70	34
22	Exeter City	42	5	5	11	25	36	3	5	13	11	34	36	70	34

Final League Table 1995/96 Division 3

		Pl.	Home W	D	L	F	A	Away W	D	L	F	A	F.	A.	Pts
1	Preston North End	46	11	8	4	44	22	12	9	2	34	16	78	38	86
2	Gillingham	46	16	6	1	33	6	6	11	6	16	14	49	20	83
3	Bury	46	11	6	6	33	21	11	7	5	33	27	66	48	79
4	Plymouth Argyle	46	14	5	4	41	20	8	7	8	27	29	68	49	78
5	Darlington	46	10	6	7	30	21	10	12	1	30	21	60	42	78
6	Hereford United	46	13	5	5	40	22	7	9	7	25	25	65	47	74
7	Colchester United	46	13	7	3	37	22	5	11	7	24	29	61	51	72
8	Chester City	46	11	9	3	45	22	7	7	9	27	31	72	53	70
9	Barnet	46	13	6	4	40	19	5	10	8	25	26	65	45	70
10	Wigan Athletic	46	15	3	5	36	21	5	7	11	26	35	62	56	70
11	Northampton T.	46	9	10	4	32	22	9	3	11	19	22	51	44	67
12	SCUNTHORPE U	46	8	8	7	36	30	7	7	9	31	31	67	61	60
13	Doncaster Rovers	46	11	6	6	25	19	5	5	13	24	41	49	60	59
14	Exeter City	46	9	9	5	25	22	4	9	10	21	31	46	53	57
15	Rochdale	46	7	8	8	32	33	7	5	11	25	28	57	61	55
16	Cambridge United	46	8	8	7	34	30	6	4	13	27	41	61	71	54
17	Fulham	46	10	9	4	39	26	2	8	13	18	37	57	63	53
18	Lincoln City	46	8	7	8	32	26	5	7	11	25	47	57	73	53
19	Mansfield Town	46	6	10	7	25	29	5	10	8	29	35	54	64	53
20	Hartlepool United	46	8	9	6	30	24	4	4	15	17	43	47	67	49
21	Leyton Orient	46	11	4	8	29	22	1	7	15	15	41	44	63	47
22	Cardiff City	46	8	6	9	24	22	3	6	14	17	42	41	64	45
23	Scarborough	46	5	11	7	22	28	3	5	15	17	41	39	69	40
24	Torquay United	46	4	9	10	17	36	1	5	17	13	48	30	84	29

Final League Table 1996/97 Division 3

		Pl.	Home W	D	L	F	A	Away W	D	L	F	A	F.	A.	Pts
1	Wigan Athletic	46	17	3	3	53	21	9	6	8	31	30	84	51	87
2	Fulham	46	13	5	5	41	20	12	7	4	31	18	72	38	87
3	Carlisle United	46	16	3	4	41	21	8	9	6	26	23	67	44	84
4	Northampton T.	46	14	4	5	43	17	6	8	9	24	27	67	44	72
5	Swansea City	46	13	5	5	37	20	8	3	12	25	38	62	58	71
6	Chester City	46	11	8	4	30	16	7	8	8	25	27	55	43	70
7	Cardiff City	46	11	4	8	30	23	9	5	9	26	31	56	54	69
8	Colchester United	46	11	9	3	36	23	6	8	9	26	28	62	51	68
9	Lincoln City	46	10	8	5	35	25	8	4	11	35	44	70	69	66
10	Cambridge United	46	11	5	7	30	27	7	6	10	23	32	53	59	65
11	Mansfield Town	46	9	8	6	21	17	7	8	8	26	28	47	45	64
12	Scarborough	46	9	9	5	36	31	7	6	10	29	37	65	68	63
13	SCUNTHORPE U	46	11	3	9	36	33	7	6	10	23	29	59	62	63
14	Rochdale	46	10	6	7	34	24	4	10	9	24	34	58	58	58
15	Barnet	46	9	9	5	32	23	5	7	11	14	28	46	51	58
16	Leyton Orient	46	11	6	6	28	20	4	6	13	22	38	50	58	57
17	Hull City	46	9	8	6	29	26	4	10	9	15	24	44	50	57
18	Darlington	46	11	5	7	37	28	3	5	15	27	50	64	78	52
19	Doncaster Rovers	46	9	7	7	29	23	5	3	15	23	43	52	66	52
20	Hartlepool United	46	8	6	9	33	32	6	3	14	20	34	53	66	51
21	Torquay United	46	9	4	10	24	24	4	7	12	22	38	46	62	50
22	Exeter City	46	6	9	8	25	30	6	3	14	23	43	48	73	48
23	Brighton & Hove A.	46	12	6	5	41	27	1	4	18	12	43	53	70	47
24	Hereford United	46	6	8	9	26	25	5	6	12	24	40	50	65	47

Final League Table 1997/98 Division 3

		Pl.	Home W	D	L	F	A	Away W	D	L	F	A	F.	A.	Pts
1	Notts County	46	14	7	2	41	20	15	5	3	41	23	82	43	99
2	Macclesfield Town	46	19	4	0	40	11	4	9	10	23	33	63	44	82
3	Lincoln City	46	11	7	5	32	24	9	8	6	28	27	60	51	75
4	Colchester United	46	14	5	4	41	24	7	6	10	31	36	72	60	74
5	Torquay United	46	14	4	5	39	22	7	7	9	29	37	68	59	74
6	Scarborough	46	14	6	3	44	23	5	9	9	23	35	67	58	72
7	Barnet	46	10	8	5	35	22	9	5	9	26	29	61	51	70
8	SCUNTHORPE U	46	11	7	5	30	24	8	5	10	26	28	56	52	69
9	Rotherham United	46	10	9	4	41	30	6	10	7	26	31	67	61	67
10	Peterborough Utd.	46	13	6	4	37	16	5	7	11	26	35	63	51	67
11	Leyton Orient	46	14	5	4	40	20	5	7	11	22	27	62	47	66*
12	Mansfield Town	46	11	9	3	42	26	5	8	10	22	29	64	55	65
13	Shrewsbury Town	46	12	3	8	35	28	4	10	9	26	34	61	62	61
14	Chester City	46	12	7	4	34	15	5	3	15	26	46	60	61	61
15	Exeter City	46	10	8	5	39	25	5	7	11	29	38	68	63	60
16	Cambridge United	46	11	8	4	39	27	3	10	10	24	30	63	57	60
17	Hartlepool United	46	10	12	1	40	22	2	11	10	21	31	61	53	59
18	Rochdale	46	15	3	5	43	15	2	4	17	13	40	56	55	58
19	Darlington	46	13	6	4	43	28	1	6	16	13	44	56	72	54
20	Swansea City	46	8	8	7	24	16	5	3	15	25	46	49	62	50
21	Cardiff City	46	5	13	5	27	22	4	10	9	21	30	48	52	50
22	Hull City	46	10	6	7	36	32	1	2	20	20	51	56	83	41
23	Brighton & Hove A.	46	3	10	10	21	34	3	7	13	17	32	38	66	35
24	Doncaster Rovers	46	3	3	17	14	48	1	5	17	16	65	30	113	20

* 3 points deducted

Final League Table 1998/99 Division 3

		Pl.	Home W	D	L	F	A	Away W	D	L	F	A	F.	A.	Pts
1	Brentford	46	16	5	2	45	18	10	2	11	34	38	79	56	85
2	Cambridge United	46	13	6	4	41	21	10	6	7	37	27	78	48	81
3	Cardiff City	46	13	7	3	35	17	9	7	7	25	22	60	57	80
4	SCUNTHORPE U	46	14	3	6	42	28	8	5	10	27	30	69	58	74
5	Rotherham U.	46	11	8	4	41	26	9	5	9	38	35	79	61	73
6	Leyton Orient	46	12	6	5	40	30	7	9	7	28	29	68	59	72
7	Swansea City	46	11	9	3	33	19	8	5	10	23	29	56	48	71
8	Mansfield Town	46	15	2	6	38	18	4	8	11	22	40	60	58	67
9	Peterborough U.	46	11	4	8	41	29	7	8	8	31	27	72	60	66
10	Halifax Town	46	10	8	5	33	25	7	7	9	25	31	58	56	66
11	Dalington	46	10	6	7	41	24	8	5	10	28	34	69	58	65
12	Exeter City	46	13	5	5	32	18	4	7	12	15	32	47	50	63
13	Plymough Argyle	46	11	6	6	32	19	6	4	13	26	35	58	54	61
14	Chester City	46	6	12	5	28	30	7	6	10	29	36	57	66	57
15	Shrewsbury Town	46	11	6	6	36	29	3	8	12	16	34	52	63	56
16	Barnet	46	10	5	8	30	31	4	8	11	24	40	54	71	55
17	Brighton & H.A.	46	8	3	12	25	35	8	4	11	24	31	49	66	55
18	Southend United	46	8	6	9	24	21	6	6	11	28	37	52	58	54
19	Rochdale	46	9	8	6	22	21	4	7	12	20	34	42	55	54
20	Torquay United	46	9	9	5	29	20	3	8	12	18	38	47	58	53
21	Hull City	46	8	5	10	25	28	6	6	11	19	34	44	62	53
22	Hartlepool United	46	8	7	8	33	27	5	5	13	19	38	52	65	51
23	Carlisle United	46	8	7	8	25	21	3	8	12	18	32	43	53	49
24	Scarborough	46	8	3	12	30	39	6	3	14	20	38	50	77	48

1992/93   14th in Division 3

Re-classification of Divisions;
Division 4 became Division 3.

#		Date	Opponent	Score	Scorers	Att	Samways M	Stevenson AJ	Longden DP	Hill DM	Elliott MS	Humphries G	Martin DS	Alexander G	Daws A	Buckley JW	Helliwell I	White IG	Whitehead PM	Goodacre SD	Greaves SR	Broddle JR	McCullagh PA	Joyce JP	Charles S	Farrell D	Duffy DG	Constable S	Crisp RI	Platnauer NR	Foy DL	Thompstone IP	Wilmott R	Maxwell J
1	Aug	22	Halifax Town	0-0		1793	1	2	3	4	5	6	7	8	9		10	11	12															
2		29	SHREWSBURY TOWN	1-1	Alexander	3438	1	2	3	4	5	6	7	8	9		10	11																
3	Sep	1	WALSALL	2-0	Elliott, Helliwell	2828	1	2	3	4	5	6	7	8	9		11	10																
4		5	Lincoln City	0-1		3764		2	3	4	5	6	7	8	9		11	10	1															
5		12	Northampton Town	0-1		1835		2	3	4	5	6	7	8	9		11	10	1	12	14													
6		19	CREWE ALEXANDRA	3-3	Goodacre, Humphries, Daws (p)	2995		2	3		5	6	7	8	9		11	12	1	10	14	4												
7		26	Carlisle United	2-0	Helliwell 2	4772		2	3		5		7	8			11	9	1	10		4	6											
8	Oct	3	Chesterfield	2-1	Goodacre, White	3552		2	3		5			8	12		11	9	1	10	7	4	6											
9		10	YORK CITY	1-2	White	4114		2	3		5			8	12	14	11	9	1	10	7	4	6											
10		17	Barnet	0-3		2924		2	3		5		7	8	12	14	11	9	1		10	4												
11		24	COLCHESTER UNITED	3-1	Daws, Martin, Helliwell	2473		6	3		5		4	8	7		10	11	9	1					2									
12		31	Cardiff City	0-3		6027	1	6	3		5		4	8	7	10	11	9		14	12				2									
13	Nov	3	Wrexham	2-0	Stevenson, Buckley	2930	1	6	3		5		4	8	9	10	11			7					2									
14		7	DONCASTER ROVERS	0-1		4451	1	6	3		5		4	8	9	10	11	12		14	7				2									
15		21	Torquay United	1-0	Helliwell	1860	1		3		5	6		4	9		11	10			7		2			8								
16		28	SCARBOROUGH	1-2	McCullagh	2807	1		3		5	6	8	4	9	10	11	12				2			7								
17	Dec	12	HEREFORD UNITED	3-1	Alexander, Elliott 2	1970	1		3		5		6	4	9		11			10	7				2	8								
18		19	Darlington	2-2	White 2	1801	1	6	3		5		7	4	9		11	10							2	8								
19		26	Rochdale	0-2		3043	1	6	3		5	8	7	4	9		11	10							2									
20		28	GILLINGHAM	2-2	Daws 2 (1 p)	2835	1	6	3		5	12	7	4	9	10	11	8							2								
21	Jan	16	CARLISLE UNITED	0-0		2570	1	3			5	6	4	10	11	7	9	8					12		2								
22		26	Shrewsbury Town	1-2	Helliwell	2190	1	3			5	6	4	10	8	7	9	14					12		2		11						
23		30	HALIFAX TOWN	4-1	Helliwell 2, Martin, Buckley	2460	1	3			5	6	4	10	8	7	9	14					12		2		11						
24	Feb	13	LINCOLN CITY	1-1	Stevenson	3748	1	3				6	4	10		7	9	8							2		11	5	12				
25		20	Walsall	2-3	Stevenson, Helliwell	2935	1	3				6	4	10		7	9	8							2		11	5	12				
26		27	York City	1-5	Farrell	2990	1	3				5	6	4	7		9	8		14					2		12	10	11				
27	Mar	6	CHESTERFIELD	0-1		2725	1	3				5	6	4	7	11	9	8		12					2					10			
28		9	BURY	2-0	Alexander, Platnauer	2589	1			11	5	6	4	7			9	8		12					2					10	3		
29		13	Doncaster Rovers	1-0	Elliott	2760	1			11	5	6	4	7	9			8		12					2					10	3		
30		20	WREXHAM	0-0		3282	1			11	5	6	4				9	8							2					10	3	7	
31		23	Scarborough	2-1	White, Alexander	2007	1			11	5	6	4	7			9	8							2					10	3		
32		27	TORQUAY UNITED	2-2	Alexander, Elliott	2568	1	3		11	5	6	4	7			9	8		14					2					10		12	
33		30	NORTHAMPTON T	5-0	Elliott,Goodacre2,Helliwell,Thompstone	2307				11	5	6	4	7			9			8					2					12	3	10	1
34	Apr	3	Bury	0-0		2509				11	5	6	4	7			9			8					2					12	3	10	1
35		6	Hereford United	2-2	Helliwell, Goodacre	1740				11	5	6		7			9	12		8					2			4	14		3	10	1
36		10	ROCHDALE	5-1	Helliwell, Goodacre 2, Platnauer, Martin	2926	1			11	5	6	4	7			9	12		8					2				14		3	10	
37		12	Gillingham	1-1	Thompstone	3859	1			11	5	6	4	7			9	12		8					2						3	10	
38		17	DARLINGTON	1-3	Goodacre	2774	1			11	5	6	4	7			9	12		8					2					3	14	10	
39		20	Crewe Alexandra	0-1		3006	1			11	5	6	4	7			12	9		8					2					3		10	
40		24	BARNET	2-0	Goodacre, Helliwell	2810	1			11		6		4	7		9	6		8	5				2				12		3	10	
41	Ma	1	Colchester United	0-1		3421	1				5		4	7			9	8			6				2				11		3	12	10	14
42		8	CARDIFF CITY	0-3		7407	1			11	5	6	4	7			9	8							2						3	10	12

Played in game 10: TJ Ryan (at 6).

	Samways M	Stevenson AJ	Longden DP	Hill DM	Elliott MS	Humphries G	Martin DS	Alexander G	Daws A	Buckley JW	Helliwell I	White IG	Whitehead PM	Goodacre SD	Greaves SR	Broddle JR	McCullagh PA	Joyce JP	Charles S	Farrell D	Duffy DG	Constable S	Crisp RI	Platnauer NR	Foy DL	Thompstone IP	Wilmott R	Maxwell J
Apps	31	25	20	19	39	30	38	41	24	15	41	37	8	21	15	5	5		30	4	5	4	7	8	14	3	11	3	2
Goals		3			6	1	3	5	4	2	13	5		9			1			1				2		2		

F.A. Cup

| R1 | Nov | 14 | HUDDERSFIELD TOWN | 0-0 | | 4312 | 1 | 6 | 3 | | 5 | 12 | | 4 | 9 | 10 | 11 | 8 | | | 7 | | 2 | | | | | | | | | | | |
| rep | | 25 | Huddersfield Town | 1-2 | Buckley | 4841 | 1 | | 3 | | 5 | 6 | 8 | 4 | 9 | 12 | 11 | 10 | | | 7 | | 2 | | | | | | | | | | | |

Replay a.e.t.

Coca Cola Cup (F.L. Cup)

R1/1	Aug	18	Darlington	1-1	Helliwell	1489	1		3	4	5	6	7	8	9	10	11						2											
R1/2		25	DARLINGTON	2-0	Daws, Alexander	2299	1	2	3	4	5	6	7	8	9	10	11																	
R2/1	Sep	22	Leeds United	1-4	Helliwell	10113		2	3		5		7	8	9		11		1	10		4	6											
R2/2	Oct	27	LEEDS UNITED	2-2	Helliwell 2	7419		6	3		5			8	7	10	11	9	1	12	4				2									

Autoglass Trophy (Associate Members Cup)

R1	Dec	8	Rotherham United	1-3	Goodacre	1634	1		3		5		6	4	9		11	12		10	7		2			8								
R1		14	LINCOLN CITY	2-2	Clarke (og), Alexander	1263	1	12	3		5		6	4	9		11	10			7		2	8										
R2	Feb	2	Rochdale	2-1	Daws 2	1312	1	3			5	6	4	10	8	7	9						2		11									
QF		9	Wigan Athletic	1-2	Humphries (p)	1512	1	3			5	6	4	10	7	9	8				12		14	2		11								

1993/94 11th in Division 3

#		Date	Opponent	Score	Scorers	Att	Samways M	Thompstone IP	Mudd PA	Carmichael M	Elliott MS	Bradley R	Alexander G	Martin DS	Trebble ND	Thornber SJ	Smith MC	Hope CJ	Goodacre SD	Juryeff IM	Toman IA	Watson JI	White JG	Knill AR	Henderson DR	Sansam C	Bullimore WA	Danzey MJ	Ryan TJ	Heath M	Jobling KA
1	Aug	14	Wigan Athletic	2-0	Mudd, Smith	2353	1	2	3	4	5	6	7	8	9	10	11	12	14												
2		21	BURY	1-1	Thompstone	3375	1	7	3	2	5		14	4	12		11	6	8	9	10										
3		28	Mansfield Town	1-0	Toman	2751	1	7	3	8	5		2	4			11	6	12	9	10										
4		31	Walsall	0-0		2519	1	7	3	4	5		2	8	12	11		6		9	10										
5	Sep	4	HEREFORD UNITED	1-2	Thompstone	3091	1	7	3	8	5		2	4	14	12	11	6		9	10										
6		11	Chester City	2-0	Toman, Juryeff	2195	1	7	3	11	5	6	2	4	12			4		9	10										
7		18	CARLISLE UNITED	2-1	Carmichael 2	3361	1	7	3	11	5	6	2	8				12	4	9	10	14									
8		25	Gillingham	0-1		2872	1	2	3	11	5	6	7	8	14	10	12	4					9								
9	Oct	2	SCARBOROUGH	1-1	Thompstone	2910	1	7	3	4	5	6	2	8	11			12					9								
10		9	Colchester United	1-2	Carmichael	3405	1	7	3	4	5	6	2	8	14		9	10				11	12								
11		16	NORTHAMPTON T	7-0	Carmichael 3, Thompstone, Smith, Elliott, Toman	2814	1	7	3	9	5	6	2	8			11	4			14	10	12								
12		23	Torquay United	1-1	Toman	3241	1	7	3	9	5	6	2	8	11			4			10	12	14								
13		30	DARLINGTON	3-0	Carmichael (p), Alexander, Trebble	3025	1	7	3	9	5	6	2		11	8		4			10	12									
14	Nov	1	Doncaster Rovers	1-3	Trebble	4439	1	7	3	9	5	6	2		11	8		4			10	14	12								
15		6	WYCOMBE WANDERERS	0-0		3604	1	7	3	9		6	2			8		14	4			10	11	12	5						
16		20	Shrewsbury Town	0-0		2436	1	7	3	9		6	2	8			11	4		12				5	10						
17		27	ROCHDALE	2-1	Toman, Thompstone	3106	1	7	3	9		6	2	8			11	4		12	10		14	5							
18	Dec	11	Bury	0-1		2389	1	7	3	9		6	2	8			11	4						5	10						
19		18	WIGAN ATHLETIC	1-0	Carmichael	2873	1		3	9		6	2	8			11	4	12	14				5	10	7					
20		27	Lincoln City	0-2		6030	1		3	9		6	2	8		10	7	4		11				5	12						
21		28	CHESTERFIELD	2-2	Carmichael (p), Mudd	3266	1		3	9		6	2	8				4		12				5	11	7	10				
22	Jan	1	Preston North End	2-2	Knill, Carmichael	7669	1		3	9		6	2	8	3			4		11				5	10	7	14				
23		3	WALSALL	5-0	Martin, Smith, Bullimore, Carmichael, Henderson	3417	1	12		9		6		8	7		11	4			3			5	10	14	2				
24		22	COLCHESTER UNITED	1-1	Carmichael	2854	1	7	3	9		6	2				11	4						5	8	12	10				
25		29	Darlington	1-2	Carmichael	2142	1	7	3	9		6	2	8				4						5	11		10				
26	Feb	5	TORQUAY UNITED	2-3		2755	1		3	9		6	2	8				4						5	7	12	10	11			
27		12	Crewe Alexandra	3-3	Martin, Carmichael, Danzey	3507	1		3	9		6	2	8		12	11	4						5	7			10			
28		19	MANSFIELD TOWN	2-3	Carmichael 2	3089	1	12	3	9		6	2	8		14	11	4						5	7			10			
29	Mar	5	CHESTER CITY	1-1	Mudd	2669	1	7	3	9		6	2	8	11	10	12	4	14					5							
30		8	Northampton Town	0-4		3192	1	2	10	6			7	8		3		4						5	9	11					
31		12	Carlisle United	1-3	Goodacre	4076	1		3	6			2				10	11	4	7	9			5	14	12	8				
32		15	CREWE ALEXANDRA	2-1	Alexander, Thornber	2122	1		3	6			2			8	11	4	7	9				5	14	12	10				
33		19	GILLINGHAM	1-1	Juryeff	2386	1		3	6			2			8	11	4	7	9				5	14	12	10				
34		26	Scarborough	1-0	Smith	1571	1	3		6	5		2			10	11	4	7	9							8				
35		29	Hereford United	2-1	Carmichael, Juryeff	1767	1	3		6	5		2			10	11	4	7	9							8	12			
36	Apr	2	LINCOLN CITY	2-0	Alexander, Goodacre	3571	1	3		6	5		2			10	11	4	7	9							8				
37		4	Chesterfield	1-1	Alexander	3629	1	3		6	5		2			10		4	7	9			11		14		8	12			
38		9	PRESTON NORTH END	3-1	Smith, Bradley, Bullimore	3790	1	3		6	5		2			8	11		9						4	7	10				
39		16	DONCASTER ROVERS	1-3	Goodacre	4151	1	3		6	5		2			10	11	12	9						4	7	8				
40		23	Wycombe Wanderers	2-2	Smith, Bullimore (p)	5755			6		5		2			10	11	3	12	9					4	7	8		1		
41		30	SHREWSBURY TOWN	1-4	Juryeff	4587	1			6	5		2			10	11	3	12	9					4	7	8				
42	May	7	Rochdale	3-2	Thornber, Juryeff, Lancaster (og)	3118	1	3		6	5		2			10	11	12	7	9					4		8				
			Apps				41	30	33	42	14	34	41	26	14	24	30	41	18	23	15	5	9	25	20	10	18	3	1	2	0
			Goals					5	3	18	1	1	4	2	2	2	6		3	5	5		1		1		3	1			

One own goal

F.A. Cup

	Date	Opponent	Score	Scorers	Att	Samways M	Thompstone IP	Mudd PA	Carmichael M	Elliott MS	Bradley R	Alexander G	Martin DS	Trebble ND	Thornber SJ	Smith MC	Hope CJ	Goodacre SD	Juryeff IM	Toman IA	Watson JI	White JG	Knill AR	Henderson DR	Sansam C	Bullimore WA
R1	Nov 14	Accrington Stanley	3-2	Toman, Goodacre 2	5816	1	7	3	6			2	8			11	4	12		10		9	5			
R2	Dec 4	Walsall	1-1	Carmichael	4962	1	7	3	9		6	2	8			11	4			10		12	5			
rep	14	WALSALL	0-0		3300	1	7	3	9		6	2	8		14	12	4		10	11			5			
R3	Jan 8	Wimbledon	0-3		4944	1		3	9		6	2	8	7		11	4			12			5	10		

R2 replay won on penalties (7-6) a.e.t.

Coca Cola Cup (F.L. Cup)

	Date	Opponent	Score	Scorers	Att	Samways M	Thompstone IP	Mudd PA	Carmichael M	Elliott MS	Bradley R	Alexander G	Martin DS	Trebble ND	Thornber SJ	Smith MC	Hope CJ	Goodacre SD	Juryeff IM	Toman IA	Watson JI	White JG
/1	Aug 17	Shrewsbury Town	0-1		1939	1	2	3	4	5		7	8		10		6	12			14	9
/2	24	SHREWSBURY TOWN	1-1	Martin	2320	1	7	3		5		2	4	12		11	6	8		10		9

Autoglass Trophy (Associate Members Cup)

	Date	Opponent	Score	Scorers	Att	Samways M	Thompstone IP	Mudd PA	Carmichael M	Elliott MS	Bradley R	Alexander G	Martin DS	Trebble ND	Thornber SJ	Smith MC	Hope CJ	Goodacre SD	Juryeff IM	Toman IA	Watson JI	White JG	Knill AR	Henderson DR	Sansam C	Bullimore WA	Jobling KA
R1	Sep 27	Scarborough	2-2	Carmichael 2 (1 p)	412	1		3	7	5	6	2	8	10			11	4	9							12	
R1	Oct 19	HULL CITY	1-1	Carmichael	2366	1		3	9	5	6	2	8				11	4	7		10	12	14				
R2	Dec 1	Scarborough	2-0	Carmichael 2	679	1	7	3	9		6	2	8			10	11	4								12	5
QF	Jan 11	Stockport County	0-2		4404	1		3	9		6	2			12		11	4	7				5				10	8

SEASON 1992-93
Back: McCullagh, Hill, Samways, Martin, Alexander
Middle: McLoughlin (Physio), White, Elliott, Green (Manager), Moore (Asst. Man),
Helliwell, Hicks,Cowling (Youth Team Coach)
Front: Stevenson, Daws, Longden, Joyce, Buckley, Goodacre, Humphries

SEASON 1993-94
Back: McNiel, Ryan, White, Hope, Ellander, Thompstone, Smith, Nixon, Thornber
Middle: Whyte (Youth Dev. Off.), Foy, Carmichael, Wilmot, Trebble, Helliwell, Elliott, Samways, Bradley, Brown, Moore (Physio)
Front: Watson, Mudd, Money (Manager), Martin, Morris (Chief Coach), Alexander, Goodacre

1994/95 7th in Division 3

No		Date	Opponent	Result	Scorers	Att	Samways M	Ford T	Mudd PA	Thornber SJ	Knill AR	Bradley R	Alexander G	Bullimore WA	Juryeff IM	Henderson DR	Smith MC	Carmichael M	Goodacre SD	Hope CI	Martin DS	Thompstone IP	Sansam C	Nicholson M	Eyre JR	Young SR	Eli R	Turnbull LM	Gregory NR	Kiwomya AD	Housham SJ	Walsh MS
1	Aug	13	Barnet	2-1	Henderson, Juryeff	2208	1	2	3	4	5	6	7	8	9	10	11															
2		20	FULHAM	1-2	Juryeff	3165	1	2	3	4	5	6	7	8	9	10	11	12		14												
3		27	NORTHAMPTON T	1-1	Bradley	2499	1	2	3	4		6	7	8	9	10	11	12		5	14											
4		30	GILLINGHAM	3-0	Thornber, Henderson, Smith	2098	1	2	3	4	5	6	7	8		10	11			9	12											
5	Sep	3	CARLISLE UNITED	2-3	Juryeff, Thornber	3217	1	2	3	4	5	6	7	8	9	10	11			12	14											
6		10	Bury	0-2		2540	1	4	3		5	6	7	8	9	10	11	2														
7		13	Darlington	3-1	Bullimore, Ford, Alexander	2181	1	4	3		5	6	7	8	9	10	11	2			12											
8		17	BARNET	1-0	Juryeff	2481	1	2	3	4	5	6	7	8	9	10	11															
9		24	WIGAN ATHLETIC	3-1	Thornber, Alexander, Bullimore (p)	2602	1	2	3	4	5	6	7	8	9	10	11															
10	Oct	1	Hereford United	1-2	Bradley	2267	1	2	3	4	5	6	7	8	9	10	11			14	12											
11		8	Preston North End	1-0	Alexander	6895	1	2	3	4	5	6	7	8	9	10	11					11										
12		15	WALSALL	0-1		3609	1	2	3	4	5	6	7	8	9	10		12		11		14										
13		22	Exeter City	2-2	Henderson, Juryeff	2511	1	2	3	4	5	6	7			9	10	11	14	8		12										
14		29	HARTLEPOOL UNITED	0-0		2624	1	2	3	4	5	6	7			9	10	11	12	14	8											
15	Nov	5	Torquay United	1-1	Juryeff	3036	1	2	3	4	5	6	7			9	10	11	12	8												
16		19	MANSFIELD TOWN	3-4	Bullimore, Nicholson, Juryeff	2975	1	4	3		5	6	7	8	9			2						10	11							
17		26	Colchester United	2-4	Thornber, Knill	2904	1	2	3	4	5		7	8	9			6				12		14	10	11						
18	Dec	10	Fulham	0-1		3358	1	2	3	4	5	6	7	8	9	10	11	12				14										
19		16	Northampton Town	1-0	Knill	3845	1	2	3	4	5	6	7	8	9		11	14				12				10						
20		26	LINCOLN CITY	2-0	Juryeff, Eyre	4785	1	2	3	4	5	6	7	8	9		11	14				12				10						
21		27	Doncaster Rovers	1-1	Carmichael	3852	1	2	3	4	5	6	7	8	9		11	14				12				10						
22		31	ROCHDALE	4-1	Mudd, Bullimore (p), Eyre, Thompstone	2653	1	2	3	4		6	7	8				11	5			12			10	9						
23	Jan	7	EXETER CITY	3-0	Eyre 2, Alexander	2463	1	2	3	4		6	7	8				11	5						10	9						
24		14	Chesterfield	1-3	Bullimore (p)	3245	1	2	3	4	5	6	7	8				11	14			12			9	10						
25		21	TORQUAY UNITED	3-2	Smith, Eyre, Carmichael	2229	1	2	3	4	5	6	7	8				11	12						10	9						
26		28	Hartlepool United	4-1	Knill, Young, Thornber, Eyre	1660	1	2	3	4	5		7	8				11	6			12		14	10	9						
27	Feb	4	COLCHESTER UNITED	3-4	Bullimore, Eyre 2	2748	1	2	3	4	5		7	8				12	6					14	11	10	9					
28		18	CHESTERFIELD	0-1		3566	1	2			4	5		7		10			6		3	8			11		9	12				
29		21	Mansfield Town	0-1		3079	1	2			4	5		7				12	6		3	8	10		11		9	14				
30		25	HEREFORD UNITED	1-0	Nicholson	2193	1	2	3		4	5		7	8				12			6		10	11		9					
31		28	Scarborough	0-3		1179	1	2	3		4	5		7	11			14	12			6		9	10		8					
32	Mar	11	BURY	3-2	Gregory 2, Hughes (og)	2767	1	2	3	4	5							12				6		7	11	9			8	10		
33		18	Gillingham	2-2	Young, Turnbull	2459	1	2	3	4	5		7	14				12				6		11		9		8		10		
34		25	Carlisle United	1-2	Kiwomya	6704	1	2	3	4	5		7	9								6						8		10	11	
35	Apr	1	DARLINGTON	2-1	Gregory 2	2449	1	2	3	4	5		7	9				12				6						8		10	11	
36		4	Wigan Athletic	0-0		1307	1		3	4	5		7	9								6	2					8		10	11	
37		8	Rochdale	2-1	Turnbull, Kiwomya	1720	1		3	4	5		7					12				6	2		9			14	8	10	11	
38		15	DONCASTER ROVERS	0-5		4366	1			4	5	12	7	9				3				6	2					14	8	10	11	
39		17	Lincoln City	3-3	Turnbull, Gregory, Nicholson	3330	1				5		7	4				3				6			9			8	10	11	2	
40		22	SCARBOROUGH	3-1	Kiwomya, Nicholson	2079	1				5		8					12				6			9			8	10	11	2	3
41		29	Walsall	1-2	Gregory	4539	1	7			5		12	8								6		14	9			4	10	11	2	3
42	May	6	PRESTON NORTH END	2-1	Ford, Knill	3691	1	7		12	5		14	8								6			10	9		4		11	2	3

	Samways M	Ford T	Mudd PA	Thornber SJ	Knill AR	Bradley R	Alexander G	Bullimore WA	Juryeff IM	Henderson DR	Smith MC	Carmichael M	Goodacre SD	Hope CI	Martin DS	Thompstone IP	Sansam C	Nicholson M	Eyre JR	Young SR	Eli R	Turnbull LM	Gregory NR	Kiwomya AD	Housham SJ	Walsh MS
Apps	42	38	35	37	39	25	40	35	21	17	32	20	5	24	5	19	6	15	9	14	2	10	10	9	4	3
Goals		2	1	5	4	2	4	6	8	3	2	2			1		4	8	2			3	7	3		

One own goal

F.A. Cup

		Date	Opponent	Result	Scorers	Att	Samways M	Ford T	Mudd PA	Thornber SJ	Knill AR	Bradley R	Alexander G	Bullimore WA	Juryeff IM	Henderson DR	Smith MC	Carmichael M	Goodacre SD	Hope CI	Martin DS	Thompstone IP	Sansam C	Nicholson M	Eyre JR	Young SR
R1	Nov	12	Bradford City	1-1	Hope	5481	1	8	3		5	6	7	4	9		11			2		10				
rep		22	BRADFORD CITY	3-2	Carmichael, Alexander, Thompstone	4514	1	4	3	11	5	6	7	8	9			12		2		14	10			
R2	Dec	2	Birmingham City	0-0		13832	1	2	3	4	5	6	7	8	9	10	11	12		14						
rep		14	BIRMINGHAM CITY	1-2	Bullimore	6280	1	2	3	4	5	6	7	8	9		11	12		10	14					

R1 replay a.e.t.

Coca Cola Cup (F.L. Cup)

		Date	Opponent	Result	Scorers	Att	Samways M	Ford T	Mudd PA	Thornber SJ	Knill AR	Bradley R	Alexander G	Bullimore WA	Juryeff IM	Henderson DR	Smith MC	Carmichael M	Goodacre SD	Hope CI
R1/1	Aug	16	HUDDERSFIELD TOWN	2-1	Henderson, Bullimore	2841	1	2	3	4	5	6	7	8	9	10	11			
R1/2		23	Huddersfield Town	0-3		6455	1	2	3		5	6	7	8	9	10	11	12	14	4

Auto Windscreen Trophy (Associate Members Cup)

		Date	Opponent	Result	Scorers	Att	Samways M	Ford T	Mudd PA	Thornber SJ	Knill AR	Bradley R	Alexander G	Bullimore WA	Juryeff IM	Henderson DR	Smith MC	Carmichael M	Goodacre SD	Hope CI	Martin DS	Thompstone IP	Sansam C									Walsh MS
R1	Sep	27	ROTHERHAM UNITED	1-3	Alexander	1404	1	2	3	4	5	6	7	8		10	11		9		12		14									
R1	Nov	8	Chesterfield	1-1	Bullimore (pen)	1424	1			6	5	3	7	8			11	9	10	2		4	14									12

SEASON 1994-95
Back: Juryeff, Henderson, Sansam, Ryan, Bullimore, Housham
Middle: Whyte (Youth Dev. Off.), Hope, Bradley, Samways, Knill, Heath, Thompstone, Carmichael
Front: Martin, Mudd, Alexander, Moore (Manager), Ford, Thornber, Smith, Goodacre

SEASON 1995-96
Back: Wake, Hope, Ziccardi, Knill, Samways, Bradley, Murfin
2nd row: Whyte (Youth Dev. Off.), Field, Sansam, Walsh, Housham, Turnbull, Bullimore, Thornber, Exley
3rd row: Young, Ford, Moore (Manager), Eyre, Nicholson   Front: Vickers, Heath, Wilson, Spark

1995/96   12th in Division 3

No	Date	Opponent	Res	Scorers	Att	Samways M	Walsh MS	Wilson PA	Thornber SJ	Knill AR	Bradley R	Ford T	Turnbull LM	McFarlane AA	Eyre JR	Nicholson M	Hope CJ	Bullimore WA	Young SR	Housham SJ	Graham DWT	Sansam C	Murfin AJ	Varadi I	Paterson JR	Clarkson PI	D'Auria DA	Jones RA	Butler LS	Germaine GP	O'Halloran KJ
1	Aug 12	CAMBRIDGE UNITED	1-2	Eyre	2561	1	2	3	4	5	6	7	8	9	10	11															
2	19	Wigan Athletic	1-2	Turnbull	3153	1	2	3	4		6	7	8	9	10	11	5	12	14	13											
3	26	BARNET	2-0	Thomas (og), McFarlane	1970	1		3	4	7	6			9	10	11	5	8		2											
4	28	Lincoln City	2-2	Graham, Eyre	2674	1		3	4	7	6			9	10	11	5	8		2	12										
5	Sep 2	Exeter City	0-1		2893	1		3						9	10		6	8	12	2	7		11								
6	9	GILLINGHAM	1-1	Hope	2423	1		3	4	5	6	12		9	10	11	7	8	13	2											
7	12	CHESTER CITY	0-2		1875	1		3	4	5	6	12		9	10	11	7	8	14	2	13										
8	16	Preston North End	2-2	Bullimore (p), Sansam	7391	1	2	3		5	14	4		12	10	11	6	8	9	7		13									
9	23	Mansfield Town	1-1	McFarlane	2478	1	2	3		5	14	4		12	10	11	6	8	9	7		13									
10	30	COLCHESTER UNITED	1-0	Eyre	2051	1		3	8	5	6	4		14	10	13	2	9		7					11	12					
11	Oct 7	NORTHAMPTON T	0-0		2455	1		3	8	5	6	4		13	10	12	2	9		7					11	14					
12	14	Hartlepool United	0-2		2608	1		3	8	5	6	4		13	10			9		7		14			11						
13	21	LEYTON ORIENT	2-0	Paterson, Hope	2315	1		3	8	5		4		9	10	13	2	8	12	7					11						
14	28	Torquay United	8-1	McFarlane 4, Eyre 2, Knill, Ford	2137	1	12	3	7	5		4		9	10	14	6	8	13	2					11						
15	31	Cardiff City	1-0	McFarlane	2024	1	12	3	7	5	6	4		9	10	13				2					11	8					
16	Nov 4	ROCHDALE	1-3	Ford	3003	1		3	7	5	6	4		9	10				12	2					11	8					
17	18	Darlington	0-0		2078	1		3	12	5	6	4		9	10				8						11	7					
18	25	SCARBOROUGH	3-3	Ford, Clarkson, Bullimore (p)	2231	1	2	3		5	6	4		9	10	13	12	8							11	7					
19	Dec 9	MANSFIELD TOWN	1-1	McFarlane	2552	1	2	3			6	4	12	9	10	7	5			13					11	8					
20	16	Colchester United	1-2	Young	2138	1	2	3			6	4	7	9			12	5	10						11	8					
21	19	Hereford	0-3		2516	1	2	3	13		6	4	7	9			12	5	10						11	8					
22	Jan 13	WIGAN ATHLETIC	3-1	Jones, D'Auria, McFarlane	2288	1	2	3			6	4	13	9	10		12	5							11		8	7			
23	20	Cambridge United	2-1	McFarlane, Wilson (p)	2413	1	2	3			6	4	13	9	10		12	5							11		8	7			
24	23	Plymouth Argyle	3-1	Hope, Turnbull, McFarlane	4712	1	2	3			6	4	10	9			11	5		12							8	7			
25	30	Fulham	3-1	D'Auria, Jones, Paterson	2176	1	2	3		5		4	10	9			12	6		13					11		8	7			
26	Feb 3	Barnet	0-1		1674	1	2	3			6	4	10	9	12	8	5			13					11			7			
27	10	PLYMOUTH ARGYLE	1-1	McFarlane	2789		2	3		5	6	12		9	10										11	4	8	7	1		
28	17	Chester City	0-3		2401		2	3			6	4		9	10					12					11		8	7	1		
29	24	PRESTON NORTH END	1-2	Jones	3638	1	2			5	6	4		9	13	14	3			12					11	7	8				
30	27	Gillingham	0-0		5557	1				5	6	4		9	10		2			3					11	7	8				
31	Mar 2	Bury	0-3		3035	1	13			5	6	4	14	9	10	12	2			3					11	8	7				
32	5	LINCOLN CITY	2-3	Eyre, Clarkson	2411	1	2	3		5	6	4	13	9	10	12									11	8	7				
33	9	HEREFORD UNITED	0-1		1903		2	3		5	6	4	13	9	10	12	14								11	8	7			1	
34	16	Doncaster Rovers	0-2		1920		2	3		5	6	4	12	9	10	11	7								13	8				1	
35	23	FULHAM	3-1	Knill, Ford, D'Auria	1919			3		5	6	4	7	9	10		2					12			11	8				1	
36	26	EXETER CITY	4-0	Eyre 2, Ford, McFarlane	1615	1		3		5	6	4	7	9	10		2								12	8					11
37	30	Northampton Town	2-1	Clarkson, McFarlane	4290			3		5	6	4	7	9	10		2								11	8				1	7
38	Apr 2	HARTLEPOOL UNITED	2-1	Ford, Bradley	2100			3		5	6	4	7	9	10		2								11	8				1	7
39	6	TORQUAY UNITED	1-0	Ford	2247			3		5		4		9	10	13	2			6					12	11	8			1	
40	8	Leyton Orient	0-0		2814			3		5			7	9	10	12	2			6					4	11	8			1	
41	13	CARDIFF CITY	1-1	Knill	2044			3		5	6	4	7	9	10	13	2								12	11	8			1	6
42	16	Bury	1-2	Nicholson	2132			3		5	6	4	7	9		13	2								11	12	8			1	10
43	20	Rochdale	1-1	Clarkson	1654			3		5	6		7	9			12			2					13	10	11	8		1	
44	23	DONCASTER ROVERS	2-2	Turnbull, Clarkson	2614	1				5	6		7	9	10	12	2								3	11	8				13
45	27	Scarborough	4-1	McFarlane, Clarkson, D'Auria 2 (1p	1738			3		5	6		7	9	12	10	2								4	11	8			1	
46	May 4	DARLINGTON	3-3	Eyre 2, McFarlane	4847			3		5	6			9	10	12	2								4	11	8			1	
				Apps		33	25	40	16	38	38	38	23	46	39	36	40	14	14	28	3	5	1	2	26	24	27	11	2	11	7
				Goals				1		3	1	7	3	16	10	1	3	2	1			1	1		2	6	5	3			

One own goal

F.A. Cup

	Date	Opponent	Res	Scorers	Att	Samways M	Walsh MS	Wilson PA	Thornber SJ	Knill AR	Bradley R	Ford T	Turnbull LM	McFarlane AA	Eyre JR	Nicholson M	Hope CJ	Bullimore WA	Young SR	Housham SJ	Graham DWT	Sansam C			Paterson JR
R1	Nov 11	Northwich Victoria	3-1	Ford, McFarlane 2	2685	1		3	7	5	6	4		9	10	12			8		2				11
R2	Dec 2	SHREWSBURY TOWN	1-1	Eyre	2718	1	2	3			6	4	7	9	10	8	5								11
rep	12	Shrewsbury Town	1-2	Paterson	3313	1	2	3			6	4	7		10	12	5	8	9						11

Coca Cola Cup (F.L. Cup)

	Date	Opponent	Res	Scorers	Att	Samways M	Walsh MS	Wilson PA	Thornber SJ	Knill AR	Bradley R	Ford T	Turnbull LM	McFarlane AA	Eyre JR	Nicholson M	Hope CJ	Bullimore WA	Young SR
R1/1	Aug 15	ROTHERHAM UNITED	4-1	Eyre 2, McFarlane, Ford	2110	1	2	3	4	5	6	7	8	9	10	11	12	13	14
R1/2	22	Rotherham United	0-5		2206	1	2	3	4		6	7	8	9	10	11	5	13	12

R1/2 a.e.t.

Auto Windscreens Shield (Associate Members Cup)

	Date	Opponent	Res	Scorers	Att	Samways M		Wilson PA	Thornber SJ	Knill AR	Bradley R	Ford T		McFarlane AA	Eyre JR	Nicholson M	Hope CJ	Bullimore WA	Young SR	Housham SJ	Graham DWT	Sansam C			Paterson JR
R1	Sep 26	Wigan Athletic	1-1	Housham	1064	1		3	8	5	6	4		9		12	2		10	7					11
R1	Oct 17	BURY	4-0	McFarlane 2, Matthewson (og), Eyr	877	1		3		5	6	4		9	10	12	2	8	13	7		14			11
R2	Nov 28	YORK CITY	0-3		1734	1	2	3			6	4	7	9	10	12	5	8	13						11

282

1996/97 13th in Division 3

League — Division 3

No	Date	Opponent	Score	Scorers	Att	Samways M	Hope C	Wilson P A	Serton M	Knill A	Bradley R	O'Auria D	Moss D	McFarlane A	Eyre J	Clarkson P	Francis J	Walsh M	Paterson J	Gavin M	Housham S	Borland J	Dunn I	Jackson K	Baker P	Calvo-Garcia A	Turnbull L	Lucas D	Laws B	Clarke T	Jones G	Forrester J	McAuley S	Walker J	Wilson P D
1	Aug 17	Leyton Orient	1-0	Clarkson	4430	1	2	3	4	5	6	7	8	9	10	11	12																		
2	24	TORQUAY U.	1-0	Clarkson	2236	1	2	3	4	5	6	7	8	9	10	11	12	13																	
3	27	SCARBOROUGH	0-2		2512	1	2	3	4	5	6	7	8	9	10	11			13																
4	31	Brighton & H.A.	1-1	Eyre	4365	1	2	3	4	5	6	7	8	9	10	11	12																		
5	Sep 7	Wigan Ath.	0-3		3321	1	2	3	4	5	6	7			10	11	9				8	12													
6	10	CAMBRIDGE U.	3-2	McFarlane, Clarkson, Wilson	1643	1	2	3	4		6			9	10	11				5	8	7													
7	14	CARDIFF C.	0-1		2121	1	2	3	4					9	10	11		5			12	8	7	13											
8	21	Chester C.	0-1		1901	1	2	3	4	5	6				10	11					12	8	7	13											
9	28	BARNET	1-2	Clarkson	1942	1	2	3	4		6	5			10	11					12	8	7	9											
10	Oct 1	Hereford U.	2-3	Bradley, Jackson	1785	1	2	3	4		6	10		12		11		5	13		8	7		9	14										
11	5	Hull C.	2-0	Clarkson, Baker	5414	1	2	3	4		6	10				11		5	12		8	7		14	9	13									
12	12	LINCOLN C.	2-0	Housham, D'Auria	3274	1	2	3	4		6	8		12	10	11		5			7				9										
13	15	NORTHAMPTON T.	2-1	D'Auria, Hope	2079	1	2	3	4		6	8		12	10	11		5	13		7				9										
14	19	Swansea C.	1-1	Eyre	2373	1	2	3	4		6	8			10	11		5	12		7				9										
15	26	ROCHDALE	2-2	Baker, Eyre(p)	2628	1	2	3	4		6	8		12	10	11		5	13		7				9	14									
16	29	Fulham	1-2	Hope	4566	1	2	3	4	5	6	8			10	11		13	12		7				9										
17	Nov 2	Mansfield T.	0-2		2210	1	2	3	4		6	8		12	10	11			13		7				9										
18	9	DONCASTER R.	1-2	Clarkson	3270	1	2	3	4	5		8			10	11		12	6		7				9	13									
19	19	Colchester U.	1-1	Clarkson	1842	1	5	3	4			8		12	10	11		2	6		7				9										
20	23	DARLINGTON	3-2	Clarkson, Baker(2)	2366	1	5	3	4			8				11		2	6		7		12		9	10									
21	30	Rochdale	2-1	Baker, Eyre	1969	1	5	3	4		6	8			10	11		2							9	7	12								
22	Dec 3	HARTLEPOOL U.	2-1	Baker, Clarkson	1778	1	5	3	4		6	8			10	11		2							9	7									
23	14	EXETER C.	4-1	Calvo-Garcia, Sertori, Clarkson(2)	2000	1	5	3	4		6	8			10	11		2					12		9	7									
24	21	Carlisle U.	2-3	Clarkson, McFarlane	5646	1	5	3	4	6		8		12	10	11		2	13			7			9	14									
25	28	WIGAN ATH.	2-3	Eyre(p), McFarlane	2833		5	3				8		9	10	11	6	7				2				12	4	1							
26	Jan 18	HEREFORD U.	5-1	Housham, Clarkson, Eyre(p), Baker(2)	1986		6	3		5		8			10	11						2			9		4	1							
27	25	FULHAM	1-4	Turnbull	3259		6	3		5		8			10	11		2	13	12		7			9		4	1							
28	Feb 1	Doncaster R.	1-1	Baker	3022		6	3		5					10	11		2	7		8				9				1	4					
29	8	MANSFIELD T.	0-2		2600		6	3	4	5					10			2	12		11	7			9				1	8					
30	15	Darlington	0-2		2245		6	3	4	5		8			10			2			11	7			9	12			1						
31	18	CHESTER C.	0-2		1524	1	6	3	4	5		8						2	12		11	7			9	10									
32	22	COLCHESTER U.	2-1	D'Auria, Jones	2738		6	3	4	5		8				12		2				7			9	11					1	10			
33	25	Cambridge U.	2-0	Eyre, Housham	2033		6	3	4	5		8			9			2				7				11					1	10			
34	Mar 1	Hartlepool U.	1-0	Eyre	1300		6	3	4	5		8			9			2				7				11	12				1	10			
35	8	CARLISLE U.	0-0		3470		6	3	4	5		8			9			2				7				11					1	10			
36	15	Exeter C.	1-0	Jones	3378		6	3	4	5		8			9			2	7					12		11					1	10			
37	22	Torquay U.	2-1	Forrester, Jones	1761		6	3	4	5		8			9				7							11					1	10	2		
38	29	LEYTON ORIENT	1-2	Forrester	3365		6		4	5		8			9				7							11					1	10	2	3	12
39	31	Scarborough	2-3	Jones, Forrester	3212		6		4	5		8			9											11					1	10	7	3	2
40	Apr 5	BRIGHTON & H.A.	1-0	Hope	2925		6		4	5		8			9			12								11					1	10	7	3	2
41	8	Barnet	1-1	Jones	1393		5		4	6		8			9			2	12							11				1	13	10	3	7	
42	12	HULL C.	2-2	Forrester(2)	4257		5		4	6		8			9			2	11											1	12	10	3	7	
43	15	Cardiff C.	0-0		4490		5		4	6		8			9			2	11											1		10	3	7	12
44	19	Lincoln C.	0-2		4755		5		4	6		8			9			2	11										12	1		10	3	7	
45	26	SWANSEA C.	1-0	Forrester	3130		5		4			8			9			2	12							6			11			10	3	7	
46	Ma 3	Northampton T.	0-1		6828		5		4			8			9			2	12					14		6	13		11	1		10	3	7	
		Apps.				25	46	37	42	29	22	39	4	14	42	28	5	36	29	11	34	2	3	4	21	13	14	6	4	15	11	10	9	9	1
		Goals					3	1	1		1	3		3	8	13					3			1	9	1	1				5	6			

F.A. Cup

No	Date	Opponent	Score	Scorers	Att	Samways M	Hope C	Wilson P A	Serton M	Knill A	Bradley R	O'Auria D	Moss D	McFarlane A	Eyre J	Clarkson P	Francis J	Walsh M	Paterson J	Gavin M	Housham S	Borland J	Dunn I	Jackson K	Baker P	Calvo-Garcia A
R1	Nov 16	Rotherham U.	4-1	Baker(2), D'Auria, Clarkson	3896	1		3	4	5		8			10	11		2	6		7				9	
R2	Dec 7	Wrexham	2-2	Baker(2)	3780	1	5	3	4		6	8		12	10	11		2							9	7
rep	17	WREXHAM	2-3	Baker, Clarkson	3976	1	5	3	4			8		12	10	11		2	14		6				9	7

Coca-Cola Cup (F.L. Cup)

No	Date	Opponent	Score	Scorers	Att	Samways M	Hope C	Wilson P A	Serton M	Knill A	Bradley R	O'Auria D	Moss D	McFarlane A	Eyre J	Clarkson P	Francis J	Housham S	Borland J
R1/1	Aug 30	BLACKPOOL	2-1	Moss, Clarkson	1880	1	2	3	4	5	6	7	8	9	10	11			
R1/2	Sep 3	Blackpool	0-2		2560	1	2	3	4	5	6	7		9	10	11	12	8	14

Auto Windscreens Shield (Ass. Members Cup)

No	Date	Opponent	Score	Scorers	Att	Hope C	Wilson P A	Serton M	Knill A	Moss D	Clarkson P	Walsh M	Paterson J	Housham S	Baker P	Calvo-Garcia A	Turnbull L	Clarke T	Jones G
R1	Jan 28	NOTTS COUNTY	1-1	Hope	1076	6	3	12	5	8	11	7	15	2	14	9	10	1	4
R2	Feb 11	Shrewsbury T.	1-2	Hope	1728	6	3	4	5	12	10	2	11	7		9		1	8

Rd 1 won 4-2 on penalties
Rd 2 lost on 'sudden death' (first goal in extra time)

1997/98   8th in Division 3

No	Date	Opponent	Score	Scorers	Att	Clarke T	Walsh M	Neil J	Sertori M	Wilcox R	Hope C	Walker J	D'Auria D	Regis D	Forrester J	Calvo-Garcia A	Eyre J	Housham S	AcAuley S	Shakespeare C	Ormondroyd I	Laws B	Harsley P	Marshall L	Stamp D	Murphy M	Phillips M	Woods N	Evans T	Pemberton M	Graves W	Stanton N	Featherstone J	Nottingham S	Sheldon G
1	Aug 9	Peterborough U.	1-0	Forrester	5761	1	2	3	4	5	6	7	8	9	10	11																			
2	16	LEYTON ORIENT	1-0	Forrester	3068	1	2	3	4	5	6	7	8	9	10	11	12	13																	
3	23	Swansea	0-2		4865	1	2	3	4	5	6	7	8	9	10	11	12		13	14															
4	30	MANSFIELD T.	1-0	Calvo-Garcia	3414	1	2	12	4		6	7	8	5	10	11	9	13			3														
5	Sep 2	CHESTER C.	2-1	Eyre(2,1p)	2633	1	2		4		6	7	8	9	10	11	12	5		3															
6	7	Notts Co.	1-2	Strodder (og)	5009	1		3	4		6	7	8		10	11	12	5	2			9	13												
7	13	DONCASTER R.	1-1	Eyre	3378	1	12		4		6	7	8		10	11	5	2	3			9	13												
8	20	Barnet	1-0	Eyre (p)	1951	1			4		6	7			10	11	9	2	3	8		5	12												
9	27	HULL C.	2-0	Forrester, Calvo-Garcia	4905	1			4		6	7	5		10	11	9	2	3	8				12	13										
10	Oct 4	Rochdale	0-2		2087	1	5		4		6	7			10	11	9	2	3	8	13	12		14											
11	18	LINCOLN C.	0-1		4152	1			4		6	7	12		10	11	9		3		8	5		2	13										
12	21	SHREWSBURY T.	1-1	Forrester	2362	1	2		4		6	7	12		10	11	9	13	3			5		8											
13	25	Exeter C.	3-2	Walsh, Hope, D'Auria	4552	1	2		4		6	7	8		10		9					5		11											
14	31	Colchester U.	3-3	Hope, D'Auria(2)	3134	1	2		4		6	7	8		10	12	9					5		11											
15	Nov 4	CAMBRIDGE U.	3-3	Forrester, Eyre, D'Auria	2417	1	2		4		6	7	8		10	11	9	12	3			5													
16	8	HARTLEPOOL U.	1-1	Hope	3272	1	2		4	5	6	7	8		10	11	9		3																
17	11	Cardiff C.	0-0		2340	1	2		4	5	6	7	8		10	11	9		3				12												
18	18	Rotherham U.	3-1	Eyre(2), Forrester	3355	1	2		4	5	6	7	8		10	11	9		3	12															
19	22	Torquay U.	4-2	Calvo-Garcia(2), D'Auria, Wilcox	2152	1	2		4	5	6				10	11	9		3					7											
20	29	BRIGHTON & H.A.	0-2		3187	1	2		4	5	6				10	11	9				13	12		7											
21	Dec 13	SCARBOROUGH	1-3	D'Auria	2535	1	2		4	5	6	7	8		10	11		13		3						9									
22	20	Darlington	0-1		2267	1	2		4	5	6	7	8		10	11	9	12	3		13						14								
23	26	NOTTS CO.	1-2	Hendon (og)	4781	1	2	5	4	12	6	7	8		10	13	9	11	3		14														
24	28	Chester C.	0-1		2263	1		2	4	5	6	7	8		10	12	9	11	13		3								14						
25	Jan 10	PETERBOROUGH U.	1-3	Forrester	3584	1	2		4	5	6	7	8		10	11	9		3		12								13						
26	17	Mansfield T.	1-1		2375	1	2		4		6	7			10	11	9		3			8		13	12		5								
27	20	Macclesfield T.	0-2		1450	1	2		4	5	6	7	12		10	11	13		3		14									8	9				
28	24	SWANSEA C.	1-0	D'Auria	2123		2		4	5	6	7	8		10	11	12		3					9					1						
29	30	Doncaster R.	2-1	D'Auria, Housham	2086	1	2		4	5	6	7	8		10	11	12	13						3					9						
30	Feb 7	BARNET	1-1	Walker	2313	1	2		4	5	6	7	8	10		11	9		3		13				12										
31	14	ROCHDALE	2-0	Regis, Eyre	2284	1	12		4	5	6	7	8	10	2	11	9		3		14		13												
32	21	Hull C.	1-2	Regis	4904	1			4	5	6	7	8	10	2	11	9		3		12		13												
33	24	Lincoln C.	1-1	Forrester	3407	1			4	5	6	7	8	10	11			13			12	9	2	3											
34	28	CARDIFF C.	3-3	Eyre(p), Forrester, Calvo-Garcia	2135	1	5		4		6	7	8	10		13				14		9	2	3											
35	Mar 3	Hartlepool U.	1-0	Wilcox	1588	1	2		4	5	6	7	12	13	11		9					8	10												
36	7	COLCHESTER U.	1-0	McAuley	2143	1	2		4	5	6	7			12	11	9				13	8	10												
37	14	Cambridge U.	2-2	Forrester, Stamp	2423	1	2			5	6	7			4	11	9				10	8	12	13											
38	21	ROTHERHAM U.	1-1	Eyre	4011	1	2			5	6	7	8		4	11	9					12		10											
39	21	TORQUAY U.	2-0	Hope, Calvo-Garcia	3264	1	2			5	6	7	8		4	11	9							10						12					
40	Apr 4	Brighton & H.A.	1-2	Hope	2141	1	2		12	5	6		8		4	11	9				13		7	10						14					
41	11	MACCLESFIELD T.	1-0	D'Auria	2949	1	2		4	5	6		8		10	11					3		7	12	13					9	14				
42	13	Scarborough	0-0		3427		2		4	5	6				10	11					3		7	12					1	9		13			
43	18	Darlington	1-0	Sertori	2267		2		4	5	6		8		10	11	12				3		7	13					1	9					
44	21	Leyton Orient	0-1		2735		2		4	5	6	12	8		10	11	9				3		7	13					1	14					
45	25	EXETER C.	2-1	D'Auria, Harsley	2024		2			5	6	12	8		10	11	9				3		7	4					1					13	14
46	Ma 2	Shrewsbury T.	2-0	Marshall, Forrester	2704	1	2				6	7	8		10	12	9				3		11	4										5	14
				Apps.		41	39	7	41	31	46	40	41	9	45	45	42	24	35	4	20	14	15	21	10	3	3	2	5	6	3	1	1	1	1
				Goals			1		1	2	5	1	10	2	11	6	10	1	1				1	1	1										

Two own goals

F.A. Cup

Round	Date	Opponent	Score	Scorers	Att	Clarke T	Walsh M	Neil J	Sertori M	Wilcox R	Hope C	Walker J	D'Auria D	Regis D	Forrester J	Calvo-Garcia A	Eyre J	Housham S	AcAuley S	Shakespeare C	Ormondroyd I	Laws B	Harsley P	Marshall L
R1	Nov 15	SCARBOROUGH	2-1	Wilcox, Calvo-Garcia	3039	1	2		4	5	6	7	8		10	11			9	3		14	12	
R2	Dec 6	ILKESTON	1-1	Forrester	4187	1	2		4	5	6		8		10	11	9			3	14	12		7
rep	17	Ilkeston	2-1		2109	1	2		4	5	6	7	8		10	11	5	2	12	3				
R3	Jan 3	Crystal Palace	0-2		11624	1	2		4	5	6	7	8		10	11	9	2	3		14	12		

Coco-Cola Cup (F.L. Cup)

Round	Date	Opponent	Score	Scorers	Att	Clarke T	Walsh M	Neil J	Sertori M	Wilcox R	Hope C	Walker J	D'Auria D	Regis D	Forrester J	Calvo-Garcia A	Eyre J	Housham S	AcAuley S	Shakespeare C	Ormondroyd I	Laws B	Stamp D
R1/1	Aug 12	Scarborough	2-0	Calvo-Garcia(2)	1907	1	2	3	4	5	6	7	8		10	11		9					12
R1/2	26	SCARBOROUGH	2-1	Calvo-Garcia(2)	2149	1	2		4	5	6	7	8		10	11	9			3	12		
R2/1	Sep 16	EVERTON	0-1		7145	1			4		6	7	8		10	11	5	2	3			9	
R2/2	Oct 1	Everton	0-5		11562				4	15	6	7	8		10	11	9	2	3	8		12	14

Auto Windscreens (Associate Members Cup)

Round	Date	Opponent	Score	Scorers	Att	Clarke T	Walsh M	Neil J	Sertori M	Wilcox R	Hope C	Walker J	D'Auria D	Regis D	Forrester J	Calvo-Garcia A	Eyre J	Housham S	AcAuley S	Shakespeare C	Ormondroyd I	Harsley P	Phillips M
R1	Dec 9	CHESTER C.	2-1	Eyre(2p)	813	1	2		4	5	6	7	8		10		9		3	11	12		
R2	Jan 6	Hartlepool U.	2-1	Calvo-Garcia, Housham	1491	1	2		4	5	6		8		10	11	9	3			12		7
QF	27	GRIMSBY T.	0-2		4596	1	2		4	5	6	7	8		10	11	12			13		3	9

284

SEASON 1996-97
Back: Wilson, Jackson, Samways, Turnbull, Ziccardi, Bradley, Hope
Middle: Wilson (Youth Dev. Off.), Sertori, McFarlane, Knill, Moss, Walsh, Adkins (Physio)
Front: Paterson, D'Auria, Clarkson, Buxton (Manager), Rowing (Chief Executive), Eyre, Housham, Murfin

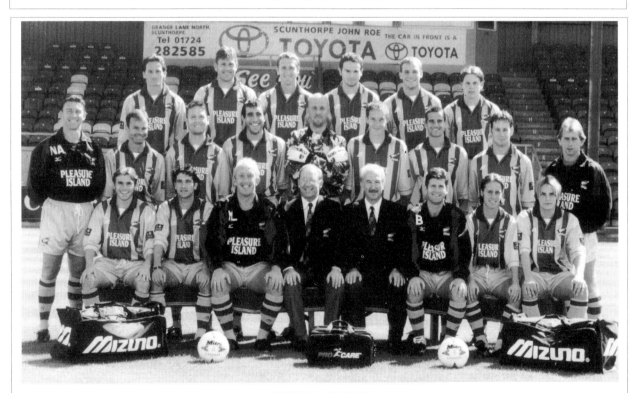

SEASON 1997-98
Back: D'Auria, Shakespear, McAuley, Eyre, Housham, Harsley
Middle: Adkins (Physio), Gavin, Wilcox, Setori, Clarke, Stamp, Hope, Walsh, Wilson (Youth Dev. Off.)
Front: Forrester, Calvo-Garcia, Lillis (Asst. Manager), Rowing (Chief Exe.),
Wagstaff (Chairman), Laws (Manager), Marshall, Walker

1998/99 4th in Division 3

#	Date	Opponent	Score	Scorers	Att	Clarke T	Marshall L	McAuley S	Harsley P	Hope C	Fickling A	Walker J	Calvo-Garcia A	Eyre J	Gayle J	Forrester J	Stamp D	Bull G	Wilcox R	Logan R	Housham S	Stanton N	Atkinson G	Dawson A	Evans T	Sheldon G	Witter A
1	Aug 8	Shrewsbury	1-2	Forrester	3600	1	2	3	4	5	6	7	8	9	10	11											
2	15	CARLISLE U.	3-1	Hope, Eyre, Gayle	2810	1		3	4	6	2	7	11	9	10	8	12	13	5	14							
3	22	Hartlepool U.	2-1	Calvo-Garcia, Logan	2697	1		3	4	6	2	7	11	9	10	8	12	13	5	14							
4	29	PLYMOUTH A.	0-2		2868	1		3	4	6	2	7	11	9	10	8	12	13	5	14							
5	31	Swansea C.	2-1	Eyre(p), Forrester	4024	1	13	3		6	2	7	11	9	10	8	12		5	4							
6	Sep 5	TORQUAY U.	2-0	Hope, Gayle	2421	1	13	3		6	2	7	11	9	10	8		14	5	4							
7	8	CAMBRIDGE U.	3-2	Forrester(2), Logan	2431	1	13	3		6	2	7	11	9	10	8			5	4							
8	12	Rochdale	2-2	Forrester, Stamp	1929	1	13	3		6	2	7	11	9	10	8	12	14	5	4							
9	19	MANSFIELD T.	3-2	Forrester, Eyre(2)	3554	1		3		6	2	7	11	9	10	8	12		5	4							
10	26	Brighton & H.A.	3-1	Stamp(2), Eyre	2623	1		3		6	2	7	11	9		8	10	14	5	4							
11	Oct 3	HALIFAX T.	0-4		4989	1	13	3		6	2	7	11	9	10	8	12	14	5	4							
12	10	SOUTHEND U.	1-1	Calvo-Garcia	3747	1				6	2	7	11	9	10	8	12		5	4	3						
13	17	Exeter C.	2-2	Forrester, Hope	2885	1	13			6	2	7	11	9	10	8	12		5	4	3						
14	20	Brentford	1-2	Forrester	4700	1			13	6	2	7	11	9	10	8			5	4	3						
15	24	ROTHERHAM U.	4-3	Wilcox, Eyre(p), Knill (og), Logan	4783	1	13			6	2	7	11	9	10	8			5	4	3						
16	31	Leyton Orient	0-1		3919	1	13			6	2	7	11		10	8			9	5	4						
17	Nov 7	CHESTER C.	2-1	Forrester, Logan	3160	1		3		6	2	7	11	9		8	10		5	4							
18	10	Barnet	0-1		1314	1	13	3	14	6		7	11		10	8	12		9	5	4	2					
19	21	HULL C.	3-2	Gayle, Forrester, Marshall	5633	1	13	3	7				11	9	10	8	12		5	4		2					
20	28	Peterborough U.	1-2	Calvo-Garcia	5160	1	13	3	7	6		14	11	9	10	8			5	4		2					
21	Dec 12	CARDIFF C.	0-2		3200	1	4	3	10	6	2	7			9		8		12	5		11	14	13			
22	19	Darlington	1-3	Brumwell (og)	2456	1	13	3		6	2	7	14	9	10	8			5	4				11			
23	26	HARTLEPOOL U.	1-0	Forrester	3621		13	5		6	2	7	11	9	10	8				4				3	1		
24	28	Scarborough	4-1	Hope, Calvo-Garcia, Forrester(2)	2300			5		6	2	7	11	9	10	8	12			4				3	1		
25	Jan 9	SHREWSBURY	3-0	Forrester, Eyre, Gayle	2860			5		6	2	7	11	9	10	8				4				3	1		
26	16	Carlisle U.	1-0	Eyre	3044		13	5		6	2	7	11	9	10	8				4				3	1		
27	30	SCARBOROUGH	5-1	Logan, Calvo-Garcia(2), Eyre, Hope	3779			5		6		7	11	9		8			10	4		2		3	1	12	
28	Feb 6	Torquay United	0-1		2071			5		6	4	7	11	9		8	12	10		14		2		3	1		
29	13	Cambridge United	0-0		5596			5		6	2	7		9		8	12	10		11				3	1		4
30	20	ROCHDALE	0-1		3749		11	5		6	2	7		9	8	10	12	14		13				3	1		4
31	27	Mansfield Town	1-2	Forrester	3208				10	6	2	7	11	9		8			5	14	4			3	1		
32	Mar 6	BRIGHTON & H.A.	3-1	Eyre(3)	4148			5		6		7	11	9	10	8	14	12		4				3	1		2
33	13	Chester City	2-0	Calvo-Garcia, Forrester	2215			5		6		7	11		10	8	14			4				3	1	9	2
34	20	LEYTON ORIENT	2-0	Calvo-Garcia, Forrester	4163			5		6		7	11	9	10	8			2	4	13			3	1		2
35	23	SWANSEA CITY	1-2	Walker	3631			5		6		7	11	9	10	8	14	12	2	4	13			3	1		2
36	27	Rotherham U.	0-0		4939			5		6		7	11	9	10	8				4				3	1	14	2
37	30	Plymouth A.	0-5		3589		13	5		6		7	11	9	10	8	12	14		4				3	1		2
38	Apr 3	EXETER CITY	2-0	Eyre, Logan	3419		7	5		6			11	9	10	8	12			4				3	1		2
39	5	Southend U.	1-0	Sheldon	4814		7	5		6			11		10	8			12	4				3	1	9	2
40	10	BRENTFORD	0-0		5604			5		6			11		10	8	13	14		4	7			3	1	9	2
41	13	PETERBOROUGH U.	1-1	Forrester	3296			5		6			11	9	10	8	13			4				3	1	7	2
42	17	Hull City	3-2	Forrester, Stamp, Eyre	9835			5		6		7	11	9		8	10	12		4				3	1	13	2
43	24	BARNET	3-1	Calvo-Garcia, Eyre, Forrester	3930			5		6	3	7	11	9	10	8				4					1	13	2
44	Ma 27	Halifax Town	0-1		3486			5		6		7	11	9	10	8				14	4			3	1	13	2
45	1	Cardiff City	0-0		12455			5		6		7	11	9	12	8		13	14	4				3	1	10	2
46	8	DARLINGTON	0-1		4238			5		6	13	7	11	9	10	8	12		2	4				3	1	14	
		Apps				22	19	17	34	46	29	41	43	41	37	46	25	22	27	41	16	4	1	24	24	11	14
		Goals					1			5		1	9	15	4	20	4		1	6						1	

Two own goals

Play-offs

	Date	Opponent	Score	Scorers	Att	Clarke T	Marshall L	McAuley S	Harsley P	Hope C	Fickling A	Walker J	Calvo-Garcia A	Eyre J	Gayle J	Forrester J	Stamp D	Bull G	Wilcox R	Logan R	Housham S	Stanton N	Atkinson G	Dawson A	Evans T	Sheldon G	Witter A
SF1	Ma 15	Swansea City	0-1		7822	1				6	4	7	11	9	10	8				5		2		3			
SF2	18	SWANSEA CITY	3-1	Dawson, Sheldon(2)	7089	1			2	6		7	11	9	10	8				5	4	12		3		13	
F	29	Leyton Orient	1-0	Calvo-Garcia	36985				2	6		7	11		10	8	13	14	5	4	12			3	1	9	

* a.e.t. Full time 1-0

F.A.Cup

	Date	Opponent	Score	Scorers	Att	Clarke T	Marshall L	McAuley S	Harsley P	Hope C	Fickling A	Walker J	Calvo-Garcia A	Eyre J	Gayle J	Forrester J	Stamp D	Bull G	Wilcox R	Logan R	Housham S	Stanton N	Atkinson G	Dawson A	Evans T	Sheldon G	Witter A
R1	Nov 14	Woking	1-0	Forrester	3399	1	9	3	14	6		7	11			8		10	5	4	2						
R2	Dec 5	BEDLINGTON	2-0	Eyre(p), Forrester	4719	1	15	3	7	6	2		11	9		8	10	12	5	4							
R3	Jan 2	Wrexham	3-4	Housham, Eyre, Harsley	4429		14	3	5	6	2	7	11	9	10	8				4	15				1		

Worthington Cup (F.L.Cup)

	Date	Opponent	Score	Scorers	Att	Clarke T	Marshall L	McAuley S	Harsley P	Hope C	Fickling A	Walker J	Calvo-Garcia A	Eyre J	Gayle J	Forrester J	Stamp D	Bull G	Wilcox R	Logan R	Housham S	Stanton N	Atkinson G	Dawson A	Evans T	Sheldon G	Witter A
R1/1	Aug 11	Blackpool	0-1		1813	1		3	4	5	6	7	8	9	10	11	14	12	2								
R1/2	18	BLACKPOOL	1-1	Forrester	2211	1	16	3	4	6	2	7	11	9	10	8			5								

Auto Windscreen Shield (Ass. Members Cup)

	Date	Opponent	Score	Scorers	Att	Clarke T	Marshall L	McAuley S	Harsley P	Hope C	Fickling A	Walker J	Calvo-Garcia A	Eyre J	Gayle J	Forrester J	Stamp D	Bull G	Wilcox R	Logan R	Housham S	Stanton N	Atkinson G	Dawson A	Evans T	Sheldon G	Witter A
R2	Jan 19	Carlisle U.	1-1	Walker	1507				5	6	2	7	11	9	10	8		12		4	14			3	1	13	

Lost 4-3 on penalties a.e.t.

~ ADVANCED SUBSCRIBERS ~

Club Officials:
Chairman - Mr. K. Wagstaff
Vice Chairman - Mr. R. Garton
Director - Mr. J.B. Borrill
Director - Mr. B. Collen
Director - Mr. J.S. Wharton
Director - Mr. J.A.C. Godfrey CBE
Director - Mr. D.Comerford
Chief Exec. - Mr. A.D. Rowing
Team Manager - Mr. B. Laws
Asst. Manager - Mr. R. Wilcox
Youth Dev. Off. - Mr. P. Wilson
Physiotherapist - Mr. N. Adkins
Physiotherapist - Miss B. Daly
Football in Comm. - Mr. L. Turnbull
Club Staff
Mrs. J.A. Short
Mrs. J. Turtle
Mrs. S. Draper
Miss A. Harrison
Mrs. J. Litherland
Mr. T. Chapman
Mr. P. Longden
Mr. G. Colby
Mr. K. Cumming
Mr. F. New
Miss T. Smith
Mr. S. Hawksley
Mrs. D. Space
Mrs. M. Tayleure
Mrs. P. Oakley
Mr. A. Collingwood
Mrs. L. Richardson

Andrew Guest
Robert Guest
Kris Small, Scotton, Lincs.
Philip Brown - Brigg
Shaun Donnelly, Hampshire, England
Robert Garton - Nottingham
Tony Burns, Scunthorpe
Jack Cameron James, Scunthorpe
Glyn Welch, Hemingrough, Yorkshire
Mr. B.O. Pike, Scunthorpe
Mr. D.E. Pike, Scunthorpe
Steve Clarke, Gainsborough
Andy Skeels, Kingston, Surrey
Mick Potter, Scunthorpe
Bob Batchelor, Glasgow, Scotland
Phil Walters, Brigg
Howard Paynter, Newbury
Mark Elliott/Irish Iron
Russell Taylor, Scunthorpe
Graham Stevens, Aberdeen
Raymond Ogg, Flixborough
Dave & Ingrid Stevens, Ilford
John Greensides, Bridgwater, Somerset
Paul Rockall, Burton Stather
Paul Robson A.K.A. Pop
Hugh M. Deary

C. Morgan
Tony Douglas, Scunthorpe
Jake Stockdale, Scunthorpe
Helen Smith, Barton
Robin Moss, Peel, I.O.M.
Alan Sharp, Bingley
Stuart Simpson, Pathfinder, Scotland
Geoff Chapman, Sheffield
Earl Priestley - Owston Ferry
Peter Osborn, Scunthorpe
Stuart Holland
Neil Holland
David & Thomas Simpson, Manchester
Steve Ogg, Bottesford, Scunthorpe
Sly on Tour
Ben Drage, Scunthorpe
Ian Snowden, Scunthorpe
Becky Torn, Ashby, Scunthorpe
Martin Redfern, Ashby, Scunthorpe
David Johnson, Scunthorpe
Peter Fenwick, Scunthorpe
Bruce Andrew Charlton, Penzance
Tracey Jane Bailey
Malcolm Barnard, Scunthorpe
John Collingwood (Brigg)
Jezz Altoft/Martin Altoft
Mandy Grimshaw, Chorleywood, Herts.
N.R. Hallam
Stephen Rodwell, Coventry
R. Brackley, Oundle, Peterborough
Dave Seddon, Goole
Philip Bulmer, Scunthorpe
Mark Baggley - Beverley, Yorks.
Andy & Lindsey Brown
Mick Johnson - Gainsborough
Malcolm Hall, Scunthorpe
Michael Stocks, Scunthorpe
Denis Laycock, Parwich Ashbourne
Mike Barwick, Barton-on-Humber
Alan Jones, West Butterwick
Alan Thompson, Groby, Leics.
Jamie Smith, H.M.S. Splendid
Ken Wood, Kirton Lindsey
Brian Clarvis, Holme Moor
Richard Matthews, Appleby
Steve Parrott, Bottesford, Scunthorpe
Chris Todd
Adam Wall
Paul Richardson, Keadby
Mark Wilson, Goole
Graeme King, Irish Iron
Ray Matthews, Appleby
Fred William Widdowson, Epworth
Jason Jarvill, Winterton
John Jeffery
Mall Scholey
Andy & Sarah Marr (Epworth)
John Key, Scunthorpe
David Boothby, Ashby, Scunthorpe
James Philip Moody, Scunthorpe

David Paul Owen, Scunthorpe
Simon Walshe
Adrian Hill (Fletcher Close)
Rob Fox, Louth
Stephen Hendrie, St. Clements, Jersey
Toby Hendrie, Calgary, Canada
Russell Bean, Ashby
Richard Guest
Stephen Douglas Farr, Nottingham
Adrian Irving, Worthing, Sussex
Richard Avery, Twickenham
William Earl
Stephen David Crompton, Halifax
Keith Hornsby Crosby/Brumby
Rachel Ling, Bottesford
Fred & Sheila Wilkinson, Scunthorpe
Howard Johnson/South Cave
Paul Donnelly, Scunthorpe
David Steele
Trevor Veail, Brentwood, Essex
Richard Guy Johnson, Wrawby
Chris Jacklin, Singapore
Clare & Craig Ruxton, Cardiff
The Wright Family, Barton
Peter Hodgson, Horsforth
Simon Wilkinson, Wapping, London
Andrew Thorpe, Baldock, Herts.
Nige Austin from Broughton
Graeme Norris, Scunthorpe
Jim Martin, Sheffield
Mr. & Mrs. Trippett, Cheltenham
Nick Ashton, Scunthorpe
Tony Pollard, Gateman
Martin Guest, Old Brumby
Dr. Damon M. Berridge (Lancaster)
Michael Coupland, Scunthorpe
Cara Richards, Wolverhampton
Les Arnott, Sheffield
Terry & Luke Martin, Ashby
Kevin John Crompton, Scunthorpe
Dave Hunter, Grimsby
Steven Seaton, Scunthorpe, Ashby
Lee Collinson, Colton, Leeds
Tracey Jane White, Scunthorpe
A. Theaker R.A.F. Brize Norton
Darren Michael White, Scunthorpe
Steve Maddern, Scunthorpe
Mr. Glyn Wyld, Scunthorpe
Gerald Frear, Scunthorpe, Lincs
The Herron Family, Leeds
Roger Simpson of Ashby
Darron Scott, Stockton
Damon, Bradey, Claire, Campion
Chris Jarman, Belton, N. Lincs.
Anthony Hay, Brigg
Keith Dixon (Scunthorpe)
Matthew Burrell, Crowle
Graham Haller, Scunthorpe
Leon Thackeray - Scunthorpe
Brian, Katie, Daniel, Empson

~ ADVANCED SUBSCRIBERS (Continued) ~

M. & B.M. Robinson, Croydon
Elizabeth Wall, Gunness
Daniel Grieve, East Yorkshire
Jim Billinger North Vancouver
Harrison Family, North Yorkshire
Lynsay Brighton - Benton House
Paul Spry, Scunthorpe
Kerris George
Bernard Griffin, Irish Iron
Ted Flanagan, Scunthorpe
Michael Hirst, Leeds
Jeremy Ronald Smith, Northcotes
Stephan Hope, Scunthorpe, N. Lincs.
Stephen Stocks, Scunthorpe
J. Whitehead, Measham
Tim & Viv Baker, Glossop
Steven Askew, Scunthorpe
Graham Askew, Barton
Glenn, Richard, Robert Devine
David Baillie, Bodenham Moor
Martin Baillie, Ealing, London
Tim Baillie, I.O.W.
Ian & Allan Starr, Scunthorpe
Peter & Owen Broadhurst, Scunthorpe
Kevin Pullin, Scunthorpe
Dave Willey, Scunthorpe
John Kelsey, Ealand.
John & Andrew Brodie, Sutton Bonnington
Chris Bennett, Scotton
Paul Bennett, Scotton
Andrew Richardson, Scunthorpe
Steve Nicholson, Scunthorpe
Gemma Nicholson, Scunthorpe
Alan Brook, Messingham, Scunthorpe
John Michael Staff, Hibaldstow
Robert James Staff, Hibaldstow
Bruce & James Warr, Scunthorpe
Lesley Langton, Winterton

Mike Clark, Scunthorpe
Richard Owen, Portsmouth (Club Historian)
Steve Emms
L.A. Zammit, Fareham
Peter Cogle, Aberdeen
David Keats, Thornton Heath
John Treleven
Richard Wells
Mark Tyler, Billericay Town FC
Plymouth Argyle. The "Pilgrims"
Graham Spackman
Moira & Frederick Furness
Geoff Allman
Derek Hyde
Chas Sumner, Kelsall, Cheshire
Philip H. Whitehead
Gordon Macey (Q.P.R. Historian)
W.D. Phillips
J. Ringrose
Chris Marsh, Chesterfield
Steve Rayner, Scotter, 1999
Geoffrey Wright
Frank Grande
Jonny Stokkeland, Kvinesdal, Norway
Dave Windross, York City
Raymond Shaw
Ian Nannestad
Robert Michael Smith
Martin Simons
George Mason
Paul Johnson - Birmingham City
Raymond Koerhuis, Netherlands
Richard Stocken, Cheshire
Willy Østby - Proud Potter
Richard Shore
Alan Davies
Allan Grieve, Tillicoultry
Vaughan, Adam, Darren, Foster

B.H. Standish
A.N. Other
Stephen Kieran Byrne
Michael Grayson
Dave Parine
Michael Campbell
A. & J.A. Waterman
Bob Lilliman
Vic Duke
Colin Cameron
Richard Lane, Norwell, Notts.
John & James Davies
S. Metcalfe
Christer Svensson, Ödeshög, Sweden
Keith & Kieron Coburn
Andrew and Patrick Mullen
Gareth A. Evans
Martyn Girdham, Winterton,
Lincolnshire
Roger Wash, Newmarket
Phil Hollow,Plymouth Argyle
Peter Frankland, Manchester
David Jowett, Keighley
John Rawnsley
Ray Bickel
Trond Isaksen, Norway
Gilbert Upton
Gordon Small
Mick McConkey, Luton
Brian Tabner
David & Matthew Fleckney
Terry Frost, Football Historian
Peter Baxter
Reg. White
David Woods
David J.Godfrey
Arran Matthews
Nicholas Matthews

Yore Publications (est. 1991)

We specialise in books, normally of an historic nature, especially fully detailed and well illustrated Football League club histories (over 20 to date). Also books with a diverse appeal are included in our range, e.g. the *Rejected F.C.* series (compendium histories of the former Football League and Scottish League clubs), *'The Code War'* (the history of 'football' in respect of its split into the three 'codes' during the late 19th century), *'Theatre of Dreams - The History of Old Trafford'*, *'The History of Oxford University Association Football Club'*, *'Forgotten Caps'* (English Internationals of two World Wars), various clubs' *'Who's Who'* books, etc.

Unusual titles included, *Fifty Years of Flicking Football'* (the history of table football, and in particular 'Subbuteo') and *'The Little Red Book of Chinese Football* (a concise history of football in this area, and the Author's experiences travelling to the Grounds). Non-League football is covered principally with the twice yearly series *'Gone But Not Forgotten'* (concise histories of former clubs and grounds).

We publish a free Newsletter three times per year, which give full details of all our titles.
For your first copy please send a S.A.E. to:

YORE PUBLICATIONS, 12 The Furrows, Harefield, Middlesex, UB9 6AT.